A. A. Vasiliev

HISTORY OF THE

BYZANTINE EMPIRE

324-1453

Volume I

MADISON—1958

THE UNIVERSITY OF WISCONSIN PRESS

Published by

THE UNIVERSITY OF WISCONSIN PRESS

430 Sterling Court

Madison 6, Wisconsin

Copyright © 1952 by

The Regents of the University of Wisconsin

Copyright, Canada, 1952

Distributed in Canada by

Burns & MacEachern, Toronto

First English edition (in two volumes), 1928

Second English edition (in one volume), 1952

Second printing (in two volumes), 1958

Printed in U.S.A.

Library of Congress Catalog Card Number 58—9277

To
The University of Wisconsin

PREFACE

M Y "History of the Byzantine Empire," which now comes out in a new English edition, has a rather long history. Its original text had been published in Russia, in Russian. The first volume was in press during the last months of imperial Russia and in the early days of the first revolution, and appeared in 1917, without footnotes, under the title "Lectures in the History of Byzantium" (down to the Crusades). The second volume, in three separate parts, "Byzantium and the Crusades," "The Latin Sway in the Levant," and "The Fall of Byzantium," was printed in 1923–1925, and was supplied with references to the original and secondary sources. The Russian edition is now entirely out of date.

The first English edition came out twenty-three years ago (1928–1929) in two volumes, in the University of Wisconsin Studies. Basing the text of this edition on the Russian original, I thoroughly revised, supplemented, and brought it up to date. This edition has long been out of print.

In 1932, I revised and enlarged considerably the text for the French edition which appeared in Paris in the same year, and which is now out of print also. Later, I made just a few changes for the Spanish edition, which was published in Barcelona in 1948. The Turkish edition of the first volume of this work, which came out at Ankara in 1943, is the translation from the French edition. Surprisingly enough, this edition is entirely out of print, so that even I myself, the author, have no copy of my own, and saw a copy from the Library of Congress.

This second English edition is based on the French. But since 1932 when the French edition appeared, nineteen years have passed, and during this period many works of great value have been published and are to be incorporated in the new edition. In 1945, in accordance with the wish of the University of Wisconsin, I revised the text again for a new edition, and even added a special section on Byzantine feudalism. However, this revision was made in 1945, and during the period from 1945 to 1951 other more important publications have appeared. I have tried to do my best to make a list of necessary additions and changes; but this has been made sporadically, not systematically, and I am afraid that several essential lacunae may be discovered in the most recent period.

During the last two years, my former student and now the distinguished professor at Rutgers University, Peter Charanis, was of great help to me, particularly in the preparation of bibliography, and it is my duty and pleasure to express to him my deep gratitude. As I said in the preface to the first English edition, however, it is not my intention to give a complete bibliography of the subject, so that in the text as well as in the bibliography, I give only the most important or most recent publications.

Though fully aware that the chronological scheme of my work sometimes presents serious inconveniences, I have not changed it in this new edition; to do so I should have had to write an entirely new book.

I express my cordial thanks to Mr. Robert L. Reynolds, Professor of History at the University of Wisconsin, and the University of Wisconsin Geography Department who have been very kind and cooperative in assisting the editors of this book with the preparation of maps. I also tender my warmest thanks to Mrs. Ednah Shepard Thomas who, with remarkable conscientiousness, has revised my manuscript and corrected the inadequacies of my English. Finally, I should like to thank Mr. Kimon T. Giocarinis for the difficult task of compiling an index for this book.

A. A. Vasiliev

Dumbarton Oaks,
Harvard University
Washington, D.C.

POSTSCRIPT

Now, six years after Professor Vasiliev wrote the foregoing, tracing the lengthy and varied publication history of his book, we are pleased to undertake this new printing. In two volumes and a paper cover, the text and all reference matter remain unchanged from the 1952 edition, except for the correction of a few typographical errors.

The Publisher

February, 1958

TABLE OF CONTENTS

LIST OF MAPS

HISTORY OF THE BYZANTINE EMPIRE
324-1453

CHAPTER I: THE STUDY OF BYZANTINE HISTORY

THE period of the Italian Renaissance was primarily concerned with the classical literature of Greece and Rome. Byzantine literature was almost unknown in Italy, and there seemed to be no marked desire to become acquainted with it. This neglectful attitude toward medieval Greek literature gradually changed as a result of frequent visits to the East in search of Greek manuscripts and the thorough study of the Greek language, but during the fourteenth and fifteenth centuries interest in Byzantine literature was only casual and was completely overshadowed by interest in the classical world.

During the sixteenth century, however, interest in Byzantine history and literature became more pronounced. In this century numerous works of Byzantine writers, though unequal in importance and chosen at random, were published in various parts of Europe: in Germany by Hieronymus Wolf, in Holland by Meursius, in Italy by two Greeks—Alemannus and Allatius.

The part played by France

The truly scientific study of the Byzantine period was begun in France during the seventeenth century. It was during the brilliant period of Louis XIV that Byzantine scholarship found a place of honor in France—the era when French literature became a model for all Europe, when kings, ministers, bishops, and private individuals vied with each other in founding libraries and collecting manuscripts, when every kind of favor and attention was showered upon learned men.

In the early part of the seventeenth century Louis XIII translated from the original Greek into French the instructions of Deacon Agapetus to Justinian. Cardinal Mazarin, a lover of books and a tireless collector of manuscripts, founded a rich library which included numerous Greek writings. After his death this collection passed into the possession of the Paris Royal Library (now the National Library), which had been founded in the sixteenth century by Francis I. The famous minister of Louis XIV, Colbert, who was also director of the royal library, strove constantly to add to its literary treasures and to obtain manuscripts from abroad. In the eighteenth century the king

3

acquired for the royal library the rich private collection of Colbert, which contained a large number of Greek manuscripts. Cardinal Richelieu founded the royal press in Paris (the Louvre Press) for the purpose of publishing in a satisfactory style the works of outstanding writers. The type face used by this press, known as Royal Greek, was remarkable for its beauty. In 1648, under the patronage of Louis XIV and Colbert, the royal printing house published one volume of the first collection of the works of Byzantine historians. By the year 1711 thirty-four folio volumes of this collection had been published. The edition was a great achievement for its time, and has not been supplanted entirely to this day. At the time the first volume of this collection appeared the French editor and scholar Labbé (Labbaeus) issued an appeal (Protrepticon) to all lovers of Byzantine history in which he stressed the importance of the history of the Eastern Greek Empire, "so astonishing in the number of events, so alluring in its diversity, so remarkable in the length of its duration." He urged European scholars to search out and publish documents buried in the dust of libraries, promising to all collaborators eternal fame "more enduring than marble and brass."[1]

Du Cange.—The leading French scholar of the seventeenth century was the famous Du Cange (1610–88), whose numerous and varied writings have retained their vitality and importance. Historian and philologist, archeologist and numismatist, artistic editor, Du Cange was a highly skilled worker in all these capacities, a tireless and accurate scholar. He was born at Amiens in 1610, and was sent by his father to the Jesuit college. After some years at Orléans and Paris as a lawyer, he returned to his native city. He married and was the father of ten children. In 1668, forced by the plague to leave Amiens, he settled in Paris, where he lived until his death on October 23, 1688. It is surprising that at forty-five years of age he had published nothing and his name was little known outside Amiens. He accomplished his gigantic work in the last thirty-three years of his life. The number of his literary works would be incredible if the originals, all in his own writing, were not still extant. His biographer writes: "Un savant du XVIIIe siècle s'est écrié dans un bizarre accès d'enthousiasme: 'Comment peut-on avoir tant lu, tant pensé, tant écrit et avoir été cinquante ans marié et père d'une nombreuse famille?' "[2] The outstanding works of Du Cange on Byzantine history are: *The History of the Empire of Constantinople under the French Emperors* (*Histoire de l'empire de Constantinople sous les empereurs français*), revised by Du Cange toward the end of his life but not published in this revision until the nineteenth century; *On Byzantine Families* (*De familiis byzantinis*), containing

[1] Ph. Labbé, *De byzantinae historiae scriptoribus ad omnes per orbem eruditos* προτρεπτικόν, 5–6.

[2] L. Feugère, *Étude sur la vie et les ouvrages de Ducange,* 9.

rich genealogical material; and *The Christian Constantinople* (*Constanti-nopolis Christiana*), full of detailed accurate information about the topography of Constantinople up to 1453 A.D. The last two works are known under one common title, *Historia Byzantina duplici commentario illustrata*. Three months before his death Du Cange published the two volumes (in folio) of his *Dictionary of Medieval Greek* (*Glossarium ad scriptores mediae et infimae graecitatis*), which, according to the Russian Byzantine scholar, V. G. Vasilievsky, "is an unparalleled work, the compilation of which might well have employed an academy of scholars."[3] Even today this glossary is indispensable to all students of Byzantine, as well as of general, medieval history. Besides all these original works Du Cange produced many standard editions of the writings of distinguished Byzantine historians. These editions are particularly valuable because of their learned notes. Of very great importance to Byzantine scholars is another enormous work by Du Cange, *The Dictionary of Medieval Latin* (*Glossarium ad scriptores mediae et infimae latinitatis*). After a lifetime of excellent health, Du Cange suddenly fell ill in June, 1688, and died in October, at the age of seventy-eight, surrounded by his family and friends. He was buried at the Church of Saint-Gervais. No trace remains of his grave. A narrow and remote Paris street is still called "Rue Du Cange."[4]

Other French writers.—Du Cange was not the only worker in this field. During the same period Mabillon (1632–1707) wrote his immortal *Diplomatics* (*De re diplomatica*), which created an entirely new science of documents and charters. The early part of the eighteenth century saw the publication of a most important work by Montfaucon (1655–1741), *Greek Paleography,* which continues to be valuable. At this time appeared also the voluminous work of the Benedictine monk from Ragusa, Banduri (1670–1743), who lived and wrote in Paris. His *Eastern Empire* (*Imperium Orientale*), published in 1711, contains a wealth of material on the historical geography, historical topography, and the archeology of the Byzantine period. Almost contemporary with this work is the extensive study of the Dominican monk Le Quien (1661–1733), *The Christian Orient* (*Oriens christianus*), which is a rich collection of historical information with special emphasis on the church of the Christian Orient.[5] Thus until the middle of the eighteenth

[3] V. Vasilievsky, *A Survey of Works on Byzantine History,* 139. See the letters of the publisher, Jean Amission, to Du Cange in H. Omont, "Le Glossaire grec du Du Cange. Lettres d'Amisson à Du Cange relatifs à l'impression du Glossaire (1682–88)," *Revue des études grecque,* V (1892), 212–49.

[4] See Feugère, *Étude sur Ducange,* 67–71. A very interesting letter on his illness and

death written by a contemporary scholar, Étienne Baluze, appears in the Bonn edition of the *Chronicon Paschale,* II, 67–71. There is no satisfactory biography of Du Cange.

[5] See J. U. Bergkamp, *Dom Jean Mabillon and the Benedictine Historical School of Saint-Maur;* rich bibliography, 116–19. S. Salaville, "Le second centenaire de Michel le Quien (1733–1933)," *Échos d'Orient,* XXXII (1933),

century France was undoubtedly the leading center of Byzantine research, and many French works of that period are still of great value.

The eighteenth century and the Napoleonic era

In this same century conditions in France changed. The Age of Reason, characterized by denial of the past, by skepticism toward religion, by strong criticism of clerical power and despotic monarchy, could no longer find anything of interest in the Byzantine Empire. Medieval history was thought of as the history of a "Gothic, barbarian" period, as a source of darkness and ignorance. Without any study of that period some of the best minds of the eighteenth century advanced severe criticisms of medieval Greek history. Voltaire, criticizing the imperial epoch of Roman history, adds, "There exists another history, more absurd [*ridicule*] than the history of Rome since the time of Tacitus: it is the history of Byzantium. This worthless collection [*recueil*] contains nothing but declamations and miracles. It is a disgrace to the human mind."[6] Montesquieu, a serious historian, wrote that, beginning with the early part of the seventh century, "the history of the Greek Empire is nothing but a tissue of revolts, seditions, and perfidies."[7] The writings of the English historian Gibbon also were greatly influenced by the ideology of the eighteenth century. This negative and derogatory attitude toward Byzantine history which had developed during the latter half of the eighteenth century survived the period of the French Revolution and persisted through the early part of the nineteenth century. The well-known German philosopher, Hegel (1770–1831), for example, wrote in his *Lectures on the Philosophy of History:* "The Byzantine Empire was distracted by passions of all kinds *within,* and pressed by the barbarians—to whom the emperors could offer but feeble resistance—*without.* The realm was in a condition of perpetual insecurity. Its general aspect presents a disgusting picture of imbecility; wretched, nay insane, passions stifle the growth of all that is noble in thoughts, deeds, and persons. Rebellion on the part of the generals, depositions of the emperors by their means or through the intrigues of the courtiers, assassination or poisoning of the emperors by their own wives and sons, women surrendering themselves to lusts and abominations of all kinds—such are the scenes which history here brings before us; till at last about the middle of the fifteenth century (A.D. 1453) the rotten edifice of the Eastern Empire crumbled in pieces before the might of the vigorous Turks."[8] Statesmen cited Byzantium as an unworthy example. Thus, Napoleon I, during the time of the Hundred

257–66. James Westfall Thompson, "The Age of Mabillon and Montfaucon," *American Historical Review,* XLVII (1942), 225–44.

[6] *Le pyrrhonisme de l'histoire,* chap. XV.

[7] *Considérations sur les causes de la gran-*

deur des Romains et de leur décadence, trans. J. Baker, chap. XXI, 437.

[8] *Vorlesungen über die Philosophie der Geschichte,* III, part 3, "Kapitel." See *Lectures on the Philosophy of History,* trans. J. Sibree, 353.

Days, in his speech to the Houses in June, 1815, said, "Help me save our country. . . . Let us not follow the example of the Byzantine Empire [n'imitons pas l'example du Bas-Empire], which, being pressed from all sides by the barbarians, became the laughing-stock of posterity because it was preoccupied with petty quarrels while the battering-ram was breaking through the city gates."[9]

It was not until the middle of the nineteenth century that the attitude toward medievalism changed in scholarly circles. After the storms of the revolutionary period and the Napoleonic Wars, Europeans regarded the Middle Ages differently. There was an awakening of interest in the study of this "Gothic, barbarian" period. Byzantine history once more became a field for serious scholarly investigation.

Montesquieu.—It was in the first half of the eighteenth century that the famous representative of the Age of Reason, Montesquieu (1689–1755), wrote his *Reflections on the Causes of the Greatness and Fall of the Romans* (*Considérations sur les causes de la grandeur des Romains et de leur décadence*), published in 1734. The first part of this book gives a brief, very interesting, and brilliant account of the development of the Roman Empire beginning with the founding of Rome, while the last four chapters are devoted to the Byzantine period, ending with the capture of Constantinople by the Turks in 1453 A.D. This work, naturally written under the influence of the ideas of the eighteenth century, makes it very apparent that Montesquieu held the correct view in regard to the history of this period; he considered Byzantine history as a continuation of Roman history. As he says, he begins calling the Roman Empire the "Greek Empire" only from the second half of the sixth century. His attitude toward the history of this Empire was very harsh. He contended that the Byzantine Empire had so many organic defects in its social structure, in its religious life, in its methods of warfare, that it is hard to understand how a polity so corrupt could have lasted until the middle of the fifteenth century. This question seemed of much importance to him and he devoted the last chapter to an explanation of the factors that accounted for the prolonged existence of the Empire. He pointed out the strife among the victorious Arabs, the invention of "Greek fire," the prosperous trade of Constantinople, the settlement of the barbarians in the Danube regions, who thus protected the Empire against new invasions, as the chief causes of the long life of the Eastern Empire. "It was thus," he wrote, "that, while the Empire was weakening because of poor government, it was being aided by unusual outside causes." The Empire under the last Palaeologi, threatened by the Turks, reminded Montesquieu of the Rhine, "which resembles a little stream when it becomes lost in the ocean."

[9] *Moniteur*, 13 Juin, 1815. See H. Houssaye, *1815*, I, 622–23.

Though Montesquieu's chief interest lay outside Byzantine history, and though he shared fully the disdain of his time for medievalism, he did leave thought-provoking pages which even today may be read with great interest. One of the modern students of Montesquieu, the French scholar A. Sorel, calls his chapters on the Byzantine Empire "a masterly account and a model interpretation."[10]

Gibbon.—The eighteenth century produced also the English historian Edward Gibbon (1737–94), author of the famous *History of the Decline and Fall of the Roman Empire.* Gibbon was born on April 27, 1737. He received his early education partly at Westminster and partly under the care of tutors, and in 1752 he matriculated at Magdalen College, Oxford. After a short stay there he went to Lausanne, Switzerland, where he was placed under the guidance of a Calvinist. Here he remained for five years, spending most of his time studying the French language and reading classical literature and important historical and philosophical works. This long stay left a strong and lasting impression on the mind of the young Gibbon, and Switzerland became his second home. As he wrote later, "I had ceased to be an Englishman. At the flexible period of youth, from the age of sixteen to twenty-one, my opinions, habits, and sentiments were cast in a foreign mold; the faint and distant remembrance of England was almost obliterated; my native language was grown less familiar; and I should have cheerfully accepted the offer of a moderate independent fortune on the terms of perpetual exile." At Lausanne, Gibbon "has the satisfaction of seeing the most extraordinary man of the age —a poet, a historian, a philosopher," Voltaire.[11]

Upon his return to London, Gibbon published in 1761 his first work, written in French, *An Essay on the Study of Literature (Essai sur l'étude de la littérature),* which was received warmly in France and Holland but with indifference in England. The next two and a half years Gibbon spent with the Hampshire militia, organized during the Seven Years' War between France and England, and in 1763 he returned by way of Paris to his beloved Lausanne. During that year he traveled through Italy, visiting Florence, Rome, Naples, Venice, and other Italian cities. The stay in Rome was of special importance to Gibbon's subsequent career, for it suggested to him the idea of writing a history of the Eternal City. "It was in Rome," he wrote, "on the fifteenth of October, 1764, as I sat musing amidst the ruins of the Capitol, while the barefooted fryars were singing Vespers in the temple of Jupiter, that the idea of writing the decline and fall of the City first started to my mind."[12] Gibbon's original plan was to write only about the city of Rome; it was later that the project developed into a history of the entire

---

[10] *Montesquieu* (2nd ed., 1889), 64.
[11] *The Autobiographies of Edward Gib-* *bon,* ed. J. Murray, 148, 152.
[12] *Ibid.,* 302.

Roman Empire, both western and eastern, down to the fall of Constantinople in 1453.

Upon his second return to London, Gibbon began a very active search for materials for this prospective work. The first volume of the history, which begins at the time of Augustus, appeared in 1776. Its success was instantaneous. Within a few days the first edition was sold out. According to Gibbon, his "book was on every table, and almost on every toilette."[13] The subsequent volumes, in which it was clear that his own religious views were quite in harmony with the spirit of the eighteenth century, caused a storm of protest, especially among the Italian Catholics.

Gibbon had one abiding desire: he wanted Lausanne, the school of his youth, to shelter the declining years of his life. Finally, twenty years after his second visit to Lausanne, Gibbon had acquired sufficient means for an independent existence. He returned to his favorite city and there completed his history. He himself described the moment of finishing his work of many years:

It was on the day, or rather the night, of the twenty-seventh of June, 1787, between the hours of eleven and twelve, that I wrote the last lines of the last page in a summer-house in my garden. After laying down my pen I took several turns in a *berceau,* or a covered walk of acacias, which commands a prospect of the country, the lake, and the mountains. The air was temperate, the sky was serene, the silver orb of the moon was reflected from the waters, and all Nature was silent. I will not dissemble the first emotions of joy on the recovery of my freedom, and perhaps the establishment of my fame. But my pride was soon humbled, and a sober melancholy was spread over my mind by the idea that I had taken everlasting leave of an old and agreeable companion, and that, whatsoever might be the future date of my history, the life of the historian must be short and precarious.[14]

The sweeping events of the French Revolution forced Gibbon to return to England, where he died in January, 1794.

Gibbon is one of the few writers who has a prominent place in literature as well as in history. The distinction of his style prompted a contemporary historian to compare him with Thucydides and Tacitus. Gibbon left an excellent autobiography, of which the English editor Birkbeck Hill says, "It is so brief that it can be read by the light of two candles; it is so interesting in its contents and so attractive in turn of thought and in style that it can be read a second and third time with as much enjoyment as it is read the first time."

Reflecting the thought of his age, Gibbon maintained in his history this idea: "I have described the triumph of barbarism and religion." In other words, Gibbon considered that the historical development of human society from

---

[13] *Ibid.,* 311.   [14] *Ibid.,* 333–34.

the second century A.D. was a retrogressing movement. Today, of course, Gibbon's chapters on Christianity are of little more than historical interest.

Several factors affect modern judgments of Gibbon. Since his time historical materials are more abundant, the problems of history have changed, the examination of sources has become more critical, the problem of interrelationship of sources is more clearly defined, and new sciences, such as numismatics, epigraphy, sigillography (the science of seals), and papyrology have been admitted to full citizenship in the domain of history. Moreover, Gibbon was not proficient in Greek. He was indebted for his materials on the period until 518 A.D., that is up to the death of Emperor Anastasius I, to his excellent predecessor, the French scholar Tillemont, author of a work well known in its own time, *The History of the Emperors* (*Histoire des Empereurs*), published in Brussels beginning in 1692. Gibbon's discussion of this period is therefore more detailed and accurate than his history of other periods.

In his treatment of the subsequent period, that is the history of the Eastern Roman or Byzantine Empire, Gibbon was not very successful. This was due in part to the fact that he did not have access to some of the original sources and in part to the strong influence of the ideas of his age, so unfavorable to Byzantine history. As the English historian Freeman wrote:

> Now, with all Gibbon's wonderful power of grouping and condensation, which is nowhere more strongly shown than in his Byzantine chapters, with all his vivid description and his still more effective art of insinuation, his is certainly not the style of writing to excite respect for the persons or period of which he is treating, or to draw many to a more minute study of them. His matchless faculty of sarcasm and depreciation is too constantly kept at work; he is too fond of anecdotes showing the weak and ludicrous side of any age or person; he is incapable of enthusiastic admiration for any thing or person. Almost any history treated in this manner would leave the contemptible side uppermost in the reader's imagination. Perhaps no history could pass unscathed through such an ordeal; the Byzantine history, of all others, was the least capable of enduring such a mode of treatment.[15]

Byzantine history thus treated is presented in the wrong light. The personal histories and domestic affairs of all the emperors, from the son of Heraclius to Isaac Angelus, are compressed into one chapter. "This mode of dealing with the subject," remarked J. B. Bury, "is in harmony with the author's contemptuous attitude toward the 'Byzantine' or 'Lower' Empire."[16] Gibbon's interpretation of the internal history of the Empire after Heraclius not only is superficial but also gives an entirely false impression of the facts. Gibbon was limited, however, by the fact that in his time entire periods of

[15] *Historical Essays* (3rd series, 1879), 234–35.
[16] Edward Gibbon, *The History of the De-* cline and Fall of the Roman Empire, ed. J. B. Bury, I, liii.

history, such as the Iconoclastic epoch or the social history of the tenth and eleventh centuries, remained unexplored and unexplained. In spite of these defects and gaps, or rather with full recognition of them, Gibbon's work is both interesting and worthwhile today.

The first edition of *The History of the Decline and Fall of the Roman Empire* was published in six volumes in London during the years 1776-88. Since that time it has appeared in many editions. At the end of the nineteenth century the English Byzantine scholar J. B. Bury published a new edition of the work, supplementing it with extremely valuable comments, many interesting and refreshing additions on numerous questions, and an excellent index. Bury's additions include the results of historical investigation since the time of Gibbon. Gibbon's work has been translated into practically all European languages. Before the appearance of Bury's edition, the French translation of the well-known historian and politician, Guizot (13 volumes), published in Paris in 1828, was very valuable because of its critical and historical notes. A Russian translation by Nevedomsky was published in Moscow during the years 1883 to 1886.[17]

Lebeau.—The slighting attitude toward Byzantium on the part of French writers of the eighteenth century did not prevent the Frenchman Charles Lebeau from recording the events of Byzantine history in great detail.[18] He knew little Greek and therefore had to rely on Latin translations of original sources, which he used without critical discrimination. He entitled his compilation, *Histoire du Bas-Empire en commençant à Constantin le Grand,* and for a long time this title served as a symbol of the prevalent attitude of disdain toward the Byzantine Empire.[19] Although twenty-one volumes were published between 1757 and 1786, it was unfinished. It was later completed by six more volumes, but the finished work is of little importance today. It was revised and enlarged in the nineteenth century by two orientalists, M. de Saint-Martin, a specialist in Armenian history, and M. Brosset, a specialist in Georgian history. Saint-Martin wrote: "This is not only a new edition of Lebeau's work which we announce, but a matter of a new work whose importance is not to be contested by anyone interested in the progress of historical studies."[20] This new edition (Paris, 1824-36), under the title *His-*

---

[17] See William Chamberlain, "On Rereading Gibbon," *The Atlantic Monthly,* CLXXIV (October, 1944), 65-70, for the reaction of a modern reader.

[18] Among several biographies of Lebeau see "Eloge de Lebeau par Dupuy," in *Works,* ed. M. de Saint Martin and M. Brosset, I, xiii-xxvii.

[19] In French the adjective *bas* has a double

meaning: "low" in position, and "late" in time. Lebeau had in mind the latter.

[20] *Histoire du Bas-Empire,* I, xi. In 1847 a five-volume abridgement of Lebeau's work was published, edited by F. Delarue, *Abrégé de l'histoire de Bas-Empire de Lebeau.* The first 22 volumes of the first edition were translated into German by J. A. Hiller. See E. Gerland, *Das Studium der byzantinischen*

toire du Bas-Empire, may have some value even at present because of the abundant additions from oriental, chiefly Armenian, sources.

Nougaret.—In 1799 a French writer, P. J. B. Nougaret, published a five-volume work under a very long title, the abridgement of which is: *Anecdotes of Constantinople, or of the Bas-Empire, from the reign of Constantine, its founder, to the capture of Constantinople by Mahomet II, and down to our days . . . with most striking examples of the vicissitudes of fortune and most extraordinary revolutions.* This work is merely a compilation of extracts from various writings, particularly from the *Histoire du Bas-Empire* by Lebeau, and has no historical value. In the preface Nougaret reflected the political apprehensions of his time; he anticipated "a catastrophe which seems to be preparing before our eyes and which may make the second Rome fall into the power of the Tartars who are now called Russians. . . . Constantinople is now often spoken of, since a monstrous alliance has united the Turks and Russians against France."[21]

In 1811 Nougaret abridged this five-volume work into a single volume which he published under the title *Beauties of the History of the Bas-Empire containing most curious and interesting accounts from Constantine the Great down to the capture of Constantinople by Mahomet II.* He dedicated it to the instruction of youth: "These disastrous and bloody scenes," the author wrote, "these events so worthy of memory, will inspire in our young readers the most useful reflexions; they will feel how precious is virtue, seeing that vice and crime very often cause evil to peoples; they will bless heaven for living at an epoch when revolutions are known only through history; and they will be able to appreciate the happiness of a nation which is governed by a magnanimous prince and benefactor of his subjects."[22]

Royou.—During the Napoleonic period J. C. Royou, a journalist who became an attorney during the Directory and a play-censor in the period of the Restoration, wrote his nine-volume *History of the Late Empire from the Time of Constantine to the Capture of Constantinople in 1453 (Histoire du Bas-Empire depuis Constantin jusqu'à prise de Constantinople en 1453).* Most of the existing histories written in French needed revision, said Royou, especially those of the "Bas-Empire," and Lebeau, "while possessing some good qualities, is hardly readable." In Royou's opinion, Lebeau forgot that "history must not be an account of all that has happened in the world, but rather a record of only those events which are of an interesting nature; what gives no instruction or pleasure must be sacrificed without any hesitation."

Geschichte vom Humanismus bis zur Jeztseit, 9. According to N. Iorga, Lebeau's work was also translated into Italian. See *Revue historique du sud-est européen,* IX (1932), 428, n. 3.

[21] *Anecdotes* (2nd ed., 1814), I, xiv–xv.
[22] *Ibid.,* 6.

He believed that "by studying the causes of the fall of empires, means can be found to prevent, or at least to retard, their fall in the future. . . . Finally, in Constantinople we can observe with pleasure, to some extent, the shadow of the Roman Empire. The spectacle is fascinating until the last moment of its existence."[23] The often anecdotal history of Royou is not based on original sources nor is it supplemented by any references. The quotations above are a fair indication of the value of the work.

Shortly after Royou's work there appeared *The History of the Bas-Empire* by an amazingly prolific French writer, M. le Comte de Ségur. His study of the whole period of Byzantine history is without historical value, but it enjoyed vast popularity among French readers and passed through several editions.[24]

Mid-nineteenth century to the present

Not until the middle of the nineteenth century did serious general works on the history of the Byzantine Empire begin to appear.

Finlay.—Byzantine historical study was greatly advanced by the work of the English historian George Finlay, *A History of Greece from the Conquest by the Romans to the Present Time* (B.C. 146—A.D. 1864). Like Gibbon, Finlay left an autobiography which throws much light on the factors in his interesting life which influenced his work. He was born in England in 1799, and received his elementary education there. Later, having chosen the bar as his future career, he went to the German city of Göttingen to complete his studies in Roman law. As the young Finlay was taking leave of his uncle, the latter said to him, "Well, George, I hope you will study hard at Roman law, but I suppose you will visit the Greeks before I see you again."[25] These words proved to be prophetic.

The Greek Revolution which broke out at this time attracted the attention of all Europe. Instead of diligently studying Roman law, Finlay read widely on the history of Greece, studied the Greek language, and in 1823 decided to visit Greece to become acquainted with the life of its people. He also wished to decide for himself what promise the Greek revolt had for success. During his stay in Greece in 1823 and 1824 he frequently met Lord Byron, who had come to Greece to participate in the work of national liberation and who died there prematurely. In 1827, after a short visit to England, Finlay returned to Greece and took part in the work of the expedition formed by General Gordon to raise the siege of Athens. According to Finlay, the arrival of Count Capodistria as president of Greece and the protection of the three great

[23] *Histoire du Bas-Empire,* preface.
[24] *Ibid.* See bibliography for various editions. I have used the 7th edition.

[25] See the autobiography of Finlay in the first volume of his *History of Greece,* ed. H. F. Tozer, I, xxxix–xlvi.

European powers, promised the Greeks a period of peaceful progress. A philhellenist by conviction, believing implicitly in the future of the new state, Finlay was seized by such a passion for Greece that he decided to make the soil of Hellas his home forever. He bought a landed estate, and on the purchase and improvement of it he spent all his money. It was at this time that he began to think of writing a history of the Greek Revolution; in preparation for this he began a study of the country's past. Gradually from his pen came a series of works on Greek history. His *Greece Under the Romans,* covering the events from 146 B.C. to 717 A.D. was published in 1844. Ten years later the *History of the Byzantine and Greek Empires from 716 to 1453* appeared. These were followed by two works on modern and contemporary Greek history. Later he examined all his works carefully and decided to prepare them for a new edition, but before he finished this undertaking he died in Athens in January, 1875. The general work, *A History of Greece from Its Conquest by the Romans to the Present Time (B.C. 146—A.D. 1864)* was published in 1877 in a seven-volume edition by H. F. Tozer, who inserted the autobiography of Finlay at the beginning of the first volume. This last edition is the one which should be used today.

In Finlay's opinion the history of Greece during twenty centuries of foreign domination records the degradation and calamities of the nation that attained the highest level of civilization in the ancient world. Yet its national character had not been obliterated nor its national ambition extinguished. Historians ought not to ignore the history of a people that after these vicissitudes still had the energy to form an independent state. The condition of Greece during its long period of servitude, Finlay observed, was not one of uniform degeneracy. Under the Romans, and subsequently under the Ottomans, the Greeks formed only an insignificant portion of a vast empire. Their unwarlike character rendered them of little political importance, and many of the great changes and revolutions which occurred in the dominions of the emperors and of the sultans exerted no direct influence on Greece. Consequently, neither the general history of the Roman nor that of the Ottoman Empire forms a portion of Greek history. Under the Byzantine emperors the case was different for then the Greeks became identified with the imperial administration. The difference in the political position of the nation during these periods requires a different treatment from the historian to explain its characteristics.[26]

Finlay divided the history of the Greeks as a dependent nation into six periods: (1) The era of Roman domination, which did not end until the first half of the eighth century with the accession of Leo the Isaurian, who gave the administration of Constantinople a new character. (2) The second period

[26] *Ibid.,* I, xv–xvii.

embraces the history of the Eastern Roman Empire in its new form, under its conventional title of the Byzantine Empire. The records of this despotism, modified, renovated, and invigorated by the Iconoclast emperors, constitute one of the most remarkable and instructive lessons in the history of monarchical institutions. During this period the history of the Greeks is closely interwoven with the annals of the imperial government, so that the history of the Byzantine Empire forms a portion of the history of the Greek nation. Byzantine history extends from the accession of Leo the Isaurian in 716, to the conquest of Constantinople by the Crusaders in 1204. (3) After the destruction of the Eastern Roman Empire, Greek history diverges into many channels. The exiled Roman-Greeks of Constantinople fled to Asia and established their capital at Nicaea; they prolonged the imperial administration in some provinces on the old model and with the old names. In less than sixty years they recovered possession of Constantinople; but though the government they established retained the proud title of Roman Empire, it was only a very poor replica of even the Byzantine state. This third period Finlay called the Greek Empire of Constantinople. Its feeble existence was terminated by the Ottoman Turks when they took Constantinople in 1453. (4) When the Crusaders conquered the greater part of the Byzantine Empire, they divided their conquest with the Venetians and founded the Latin Empire of Romania with feudal principalities in Greece. The domination of the Latins marked the decline of Greek influence in the East and caused a rapid diminution in the wealth and numbers of the Greek nation. This period extends from the conquest of Constantinople in 1204 until the conquest of Naxos by the Ottoman Turks in 1566. (5) The conquest of Constantinople in 1204 caused the foundation of a new Greek state in the eastern provinces of the Byzantine Empire, called the Empire of Trebizond. It represents a curious episode in Greek history. Its government bore a strong resemblance to the Georgian and Armenian monarchies, indicating the influence of Asiatic rather than European manners. For two and a half centuries it exercised considerable influence, based, however, on its commercial position and resources rather than on its political strength or Greek civilization. It had little influence on the fate of Greece, and its conquest in 1461 excited little sympathy. (6) The sixth and last period of the history of Greece under foreign domination extends from 1453 to 1821, and embraces both the Ottoman rule and the temporary occupation of the Peloponnesus by the Venetian Republic, from 1685 to 1715.[27]

Finlay made a great contribution to the study of Byzantine history. Though his division of Greek history into periods is, like any schematic division, a debatable procedure, still his is the unquestionable distinction of having

[27] *Ibid.*, I, xvii–xix.

been the first to turn his attention to the internal history of the Byzantine state in its juridical, social, and economic phases. This was not, of course, a series of profound original investigations; such investigations are still wanting on many subjects. Most of Finlay's accounts of the internal history were based upon general considerations and on analogies with recent historical events. His signal service was to raise many interesting questions concerning the internal history of the Byzantine Empire. Finlay's work is interesting even today, in spite of the fact that he studied Byzantine history only as a preparation for writing a history of modern Greece.

The English historian Freeman evaluated Finlay's work in 1855. For deep and original research, he said, for a comprehensive grasp of his subject, and above all for a bold and independent spirit of inquiry, Finlay may take his place among great historical writers of his age. In the light of its vast scope and the difficulties of its execution, his work may be regarded as the greatest historical literature produced in Britain since the days of Gibbon. Finlay passed his life in the land and among the people of whom he wrote. Perhaps no great historical work ever owed its origin so directly to the events of the contemporary world. A man with a keen and observant mind, a student of law and political economy rather than a professional scholar, Finlay reflected deeply on the state of the land in which he lived and traced the causes of what he saw to their origin two thousand years before. His works have both gained and lost by the peculiar circumstances under which they were written. No work produced by either an ordinary scholar or an ordinary politician, Freeman concluded, could ever come near to the native strength and originality of the work of this solitary thinker, studying, using, and recording the events of two thousand years in order to solve the problems which he saw at his own door.[28] Freeman showed a real understanding of Finlay's distinction, the attempt to explain by means of ancient survivals in the present time, analogous phenomena in the past.[29]

Paparrigopoulo.—About the middle of the nineteenth century the attention of men interested in Byzantine history turned to the works of K. Paparrigopoulo, a serious Greek scholar and professor at the University of Athens who devoted his life to the study of the past of Greece. As early as the third and fourth decade of the nineteenth century he published some brief and interesting historical works, for example *On the Settlement of Some*

[28] Freeman, *Historical Essays* (1st ed., 1871), III, 241–43.

[29] On Finlay, see W. Miller, "The Finlay Library," *Annual of the British School at Athens,* XXVI (1923–25), 46–66; W. Miller, "The Finlay Papers, George Finlay as a Journalist and The Journals of Finlay and Jarvis,"

English Historical Review, XXXIX (1924), 386–98, 552–67; XLI (1926), 514–25. Finlay's death is incorrectly dated (1876 instead of the correct date, 1875) in his autobiography published by Tozer. Cf. *English National Biography.*

Slav Tribes in the Peloponnesus (Περὶ τῆς ἐποικήσεως Σλαβικῶν τινων φύλων εἰς τὴν Πελοπόννησον), published in Athens in 1843. But these were only preparatory steps toward his more extensive work. The main enterprise of his life was the history of his people. The result of his thirty years of effort was a five-volume *History of the Greek People from the Most Ancient Times to Recent Years* (Ἱστορία τοῦ Ἑλληνικοῦ ἔθνους ἀπὸ τῶν ἀρχαιοτάτων χρόνων μέχρι τῶν νεωτέρων), published in Athens between 1860 and 1877. Several editions were published, the most recent edited by Karolides, published in Athens in 1925. This work gives the history of the Greek people until 1832. Written in modern Greek, this rather bulky work was not widely accessible, and Paparrigopoulo later decided to summarize his most important results in one volume, written in French and entitled *A History of Hellenic Civilization* (*Histoire de la civilisation hellénique*), published in Paris in 1878. Toward the end of his life he undertook to publish a similar volume in Greek, but he died before he finished this book. After his death the work was published under the title *The Most Instructive Results of the History of the Greek People* (Athens, 1899). It represents an abstract or an outline, with some revisions, of the material which was given in great detail in the five-volume history. The last four volumes of this work are concerned with Byzantine history.

In spite of its strongly biased character, the work of Paparrigopoulo deserves much attention. The author looked upon history from the purely nationalistic point of view of an ardent Greek patriot. In all important phenomena he saw Greek origin; he considered Roman influence only casual and superficial. He devoted special attention to his favorite period, the epoch of the Iconoclast emperors. Not limiting himself to the religious aspects of the period, Paparrigopoulo saw in this movement an attempt to effect real social reform coming out of the innermost depths of the Hellenic spirit. Enthusiastically he contended that, "leaving aside the fundamental religious dogmas, the Hellenic reforms of the eighth century were, from the standpoint of social changes, much broader and more systematic than more recent Western European reforms, advocating principles and dogmas which, to our great astonishment, are found in the eighth century."[30] But these reforms were too bold and radical for Byzantine society; hence the Iconoclast epoch was followed by a reactionary period. This explains why the Macedonian dynasty followed a conservative policy. Hellenism retained its importance during the entire medieval period. There were no inner causes for the fall of Constantinople in 1204; the capital of the empire yielded only to the crude physical force of the crusaders. And if the sad event of 1204 dealt a heavy blow to "Byzantine Hellenism" a dominating influence was soon exercised by "mod-

[30] *Histoire de la civilisation hellénique*, 194.

ern Hellenism," from which the modern Greeks of the nineteenth century descend directly. Thus, in the opinion of Paparrigopoulo, Hellenism in one form or another continued a healthy existence during the entire Byzantine period. Although the work of this Greek scholar naturally reflects the enthusiasm of a Greek patriot, his large *History of the Greek People* and the French *History of Hellenic Civilization* are very valuable books. Paparrigopoulo's chief service was to point out the great importance and complexity of the Iconoclast movement. His work cannot be used readily because it lacks index and references; the verification of facts and conclusions is very difficult and inconvenient.

Hopf.—To the body of serious and tireless scholars in the field of Byzantine history in the nineteenth century belongs the German professor Carl Hopf (1832–73). A native of Westphalia, Hopf was the son of a secondary school teacher. At a very early age he showed evidence of a striking memory and a capacity for foreign languages. After completing his studies at the University of Bonn he remained there as an assistant and devoted himself passionately to the solution of his chief scientific problem, the study of Greek history under Frankish domination, the period after 1204 A.D. In 1853 and 1854 Hopf made his first journey; he went by way of Vienna to northern Italy, which at that time was still in the hands of Austria. There he worked intensively, devoting most of his time to some private family archives. His labors resulted in the publication of archive documents and monographs devoted to the history of separate Frankish kingdoms in Greece and of the islands of the Aegean Sea. While he was a professor at Greifswald and later chief librarian and professor at Königsberg, Hopf continued his study of the Middle Ages. He made a second journey (1861–63) to Genoa, Naples, Palermo, Malta, Corfù, Zante, Syra, Naxos, and Greece, and collected an enormous amount of manuscript material. Upon his return home Hopf began his work of organizing these materials, but his health broke down and he died at Wiesbaden in 1873, at the prime of his life and at the height of his creative scholarly career. He published a considerable number of monographs and articles, as well as numerous collections of sources relating to the Frankish epoch.

Hopf's most important and valuable work is his *History of Greece from the Beginning of the Middle Ages to the Most Recent Times (Geschichte Griechenlands vom Beginne des Mittelalters bis auf die neuere Zeit (1867–68).* This work, especially the portions based on manuscripts collected by Hopf himself, shows the author's wide acquaintance with original sources. He devoted most of his book to the period of Frankish domination in the East; basing his narrative on a mass of archive material, he was the first to give a detailed account of the external history of this domination, not only in the important centers, but also in the small islands of the Aegean Sea. Not all the manuscripts collected by Hopf have been published; therefore certain portions of his book based upon them may be considered a genuine primary source. Hopf's history analyzes in detail the question of the Slavs in Greece. He advanced facts and arguments against the famous Fallmerayer theory, which maintained that the blood of the modern Greeks contains not a drop of the ancient Hellenic blood, and that the Greeks of today are descendants of the Slavs and Albanians who invaded Greece in the Middle Ages.[31] Unfortunately, Hopf's valuable work was published in the old *General Encyclopedia of Arts and Sciences* (Ersch-Gruber, *Allgemeine Encyklopädie der Wissenschaften und Künste,* vols. LXXXV and LXXXVI), which has a very limited circulation. This unsatisfactory edition lacks such indispensable tools as an index and a table of contents. Moreover, the book was not entirely finished by the author, the material is arranged without any plan, and the style is dry and heavy. But its enormous amount of fresh, unpublished material opens up entirely new pages of Greek medieval history during the period of Frankish domination. At present Hopf's manuscript treasures can be found at the Berlin National Library. They constitute a very rich source of information for historians.

In later years several German scholars made use of Hopf's work in writing more readable surveys of medieval Greek or Byzantine history. Of such historians at least two should be mentioned: Hertzberg and Gregorovius.

Hertzberg.—G. F. Hertzberg was for some time a student of ancient Greek and Roman history. He later became interested in the Middle Ages, and wrote two works of a general nature: *The History of Greece from the End of the Classical Period to the Present Time* (*Geschichte Griechenlands seit dem Absterben des antiken Lebens bis zum Gegenwart*), four volumes published at Gotha, 1876–79; and *History of the Byzantines and of the Ottoman Empire until the End of the Sixteenth Century* (*Geschichte der Byzantiner und des Osmanischen Reiches bis gegen Ende des sechzehnten Jahrhunderts*), published in Berlin in 1883. While not truly original, these two books have introduced many of the results of Hopf's work to a wider circle of readers, particularly because of their fine easy style. The second book was published in a Russian translation by P. V. Bezobrazov (Moscow, 1896). This translation, as compared with the German original, is particularly valuable because Bezobrazov not only indicated the available literature on the subject, but also added several appendices which present the main results of studies made by Russian scholars in the field of Byzantine internal history. These additions concern phases neglected by Hertzberg, such as the great palace and the court ceremonial, handicrafts and trades corporations, peasants, the peasant com-

---

[31] This question is discussed at length on pp. 176–79.

munity and the rural code, the measures for protecting peasant landowner-ship and the serfdom of the peasants, the position of the serfs, the peasant lots, the tax roll, the system of taxation, and the abuses of tax collectors. This book is very valuable for an elementary acquaintance with Byzantine history.

Gregorovius.—Another scholar who used Hopf's investigations as a foundation for his own work was F. Gregorovius, famous for his large work on the history of Rome in the Middle Ages. This work suggested to the author the idea of studying the medieval history of another center of ancient civilization, Athens. The results of this study was his two-volume *History of the City of Athens in the Middle Ages* (*Geschichte der Stadt Athen im Mittelalter*), published in Stuttgart in 1889. This work is founded upon the works of Hopf, which, according to Gregorovius, form a firm foundation for all investigations made since Hopf, as well as for any which might be undertaken in the future.[32] But Gregorovius drew also upon the cultural life of the country, a phase Hopf neglected. He handled his problem brilliantly. By adding material discovered since the time of Hopf, he gave an excellent account of the history of medieval Athens, with the general history of Byzantium as a background. He brought his account down to the time of the formation of the Greek Kingdom in the nineteenth century. The interest and value of his work continues.

Bury.—J. B. Bury (1861–1927) was a professor at Cambridge University. He wrote, besides other books in the field of Byzantine studies, three volumes on the general history of the Byzantine Empire, including events from 395 to 867. The first two volumes were published in 1889 under the title *A History of the Later Roman Empire from Arcadius to Irene*. These two volumes discuss events up to 800 A.D., that is, until the coronation of Charlemagne by Pope Leo III in Rome. N. H. Baynes has said, "No one could have been prepared for the revelation of the width and depth of Bury's Byzantine studies made in 1889 when there appeared the two volumes of his *History of the Later Empire*. This was an amazing piece of pioneer work, and by it Bury established his position as a historian."[33] The third volume was published twenty-three years later, entitled *A History of the Eastern Roman Empire from the Fall of Irene to the Accession of Basil I* (London, 1912). This volume deals with the period from 802 to 867. In 1923 the second edition of the first two volumes was published. It covered events only up to the end of the reign of Justinian the Great (565 A.D.). This is more than a revised and enlarged

---

[32] *Geschichte der Stadt Athen im Mittelalter von der Zeit Justinian's bis zur türkischen Eroberung,* I, xviii–xix.

[33] N. H. Baynes, ed., *A Bibliography of the Works of J. B. Bury,* 5–6. This is an excellent work. A biography of Bury appears on pp. 1–124; obituary notice, 124; complete bibliography of Bury's work, 125–75.

edition; it is almost a new work on the early history of the Byzantine Empire. The first of these two volumes, in the words of the author, might be entitled "The German Conquest of Western Europe," and the second "The Age of Justinian."[34] The history of the period from 565 to 800 has not yet been·edited for the second time. Bury evidently intended to write a Byzantine history on the grand scale, but unfortunately he died in Rome on June 1, 1927 without having carried out this project.

In his work Bury supported the one right idea concerning the Roman Empire: its continuous existence from the first to the fifteenth centuries. There is no period of history, said Bury in the preface to the first edition, which has been so much obscured by incorrect and misleading titles as the period of the later Roman Empire. It is due more to improper nomenclature than one might at first suppose, that the import of the period is so constantly misunderstood and its character so often misrepresented. The first step toward grasping the history of those centuries through which the ancient evolved into the modern world is comprehension of the fact that the old Roman Empire did not cease to exist until the year 1453. The line of Roman emperors continued in an unbroken succession from Octavius Augustus to Constantine Palaeologus, the last of the Byzantine emperors. This essential fact is now obscured by applying the name "Byzantine" or the name "Greek" to the Empire in its later stages. Historians who use the phrase "Byzantine Empire" generally disagree as to the date at which the "Roman Empire" ends and the "Byzantine Empire" begins. Sometimes the line is drawn at the foundation of Constantinople by Constantine the Great, sometimes at the death of Theodosius the Great, sometimes at the reign of Justinian, sometimes (as by Finlay) at the accession of Leo the Isaurian; and the historian who adopts one line of division cannot assert that the historian who adopts a different line is wrong, for all such divisions are purely arbitrary. The Roman Empire did not come to an end until 1453, and such expressions as "Byzantine," "Greek," "Romanic," or "Greco-Roman Empire" serve only to obscure an important fact and perpetuate a serious error. Bury asserted in 1923, however, that quite a new period of history, which is conventionally called Byzantine history, began with the period of Constantine the Great. Bury began the first volume of his *History of the Later Roman Empire* with this statement: "The continuity of history, which means the control of the present and future by the past, has become a commonplace, and chronological limits, which used to be considered important, are now recognized to have little significance except as convenient landmarks in historical survey. Yet there are what we may call culminating epochs, in which the accumulating tendencies of the past, reaching a certain point, suddenly effect a visible transformation which seems

---

[34] Bury, *Later Roman Empire*, preface, vii.

to turn the world in a new direction. Such a culminating epoch occurred in the history of the Roman Empire at the beginning of the fourth century. The reign of Constantine the Great inaugurated a new age in a much fuller sense than the reign of Augustus, the founder of the Empire."[35]

For these reasons, Bury entitled the first edition of his two volumes, concerned with the period preceding 800 A.D., *A History of the Later Roman Empire*. In 800 Charlemagne was proclaimed emperor in Rome. Hence from this moment it is quite correct to distinguish between the two rival empires by prefixing the adjectives western and eastern. But unhappily the phrase "Eastern Roman Empire" is not confined to this legitimate use. We hear of an Eastern and a Western Roman Empire in the fifth century; references are made to the fall of a Western Empire in 476. Such language, though it has the sanction of high names, is incorrect in itself and leads to a further confusion. It is incorrect because the Roman Empire was one and undivided in the fifth century, and though there were generally more emperors than one, there were never two empires. To speak of two empires in the fifth century is to misrepresent in the grossest manner the theory of the imperial constitution. No one talks about two Roman empires in the days of Constantius and Constans (successors of Constantine the Great); yet the relations between Arcadius and Honorius, between Theodosius II and Valentinian III, between Leo I and Anthemius were exactly the same as the political relations which existed between the sons of Constantine. However independent, or even hostile, the rulers may have been from time to time, theoretically the empire which they ruled was unaffected. No empire fell in 476; that year marks only a stage, and not even the most important stage, in the process of disintegration which was going on during the whole century. The resignation of Romulus Augustulus did not even shake the Roman Empire; far less did it cause an empire to fall. It is unfortunate, therefore, that Gibbon spoke of the "fall of the Western Empire," and that many modern writers have given their sanction to the phrase.

Thus the Roman Empire existed from the first century B.C. to the fifteenth century A.D. Only from the year 800 forward it may be distinguished as the Eastern Roman Empire because of the foundation of another Roman Empire in the West.[36] Bury therefore entitled his third volume, published in 1912 and narrating events from 802 forward, *A History of the Eastern Roman Empire* in order to distinguish it from the first two volumes.

Bury pointed out the superficial manner in which Byzantine history has

[35] *Ibid.*, I, 1. See G. Ostrogorsky, "Die Perioden der byzantinischen Geschichte," *Historische Zeitschrift*, CLXIII (1941), 235, n. 1.

[36] Bury, *Later Roman Empire*, I, v–vii. This introduction has been omitted in the 2nd ed., but it still bears upon our historical survey. See F. Dölger, "Review: Bury," *Byzantinische Zeitschrift*, XXVI, 1–2 (1926), 97.

been treated by the philosophers and writers of the eighteenth century and noted that these eminent men had entirely ignored one of the most important and essential factors in the development of western European civilization, that is, the influence of the later Roman Empire and New Rome.[37] Of course, Bury's point of view was not new. The idea of a continuous Roman Empire was recognized before his time by such men as Montesquieu, in his *Considérations sur les causes de la grandeur des Romains et de leur décadence.* But Bury advanced this thesis with unusual force and made it convincing.

His history deserves close attention. While relating the history of the eastern part of the empire, he follows, until 800, the events in the western part. This, of course, is in keeping with his idea of the unity of the Roman Empire. Bury does not limit himself to political history; entire chapters of his book are devoted to questions of administration, literature, social life, geography, and art. The first two chapters of the second edition, devoted to the constitution of the monarchy and the administrative machinery, are considered by a very well-known specialist in the history of the Roman Empire to be the best short description of the general conditions which prevailed in the late Roman Empire.[38] Bury knew Russian as well as other Slavonic languages; hence he used and evaluated all the Russian and Bulgarian literature bearing on the history of Byzantium.

Lampros.—Spiridon Lampros (Λάμπρος), a Greek scholar and professor at the University of Athens, was an active editor of manuscripts and historical texts, and the author of a catalogue of Greek manuscripts from Athos. His chief contribution was a six volume work begun in 1886 and completed in 1908, nine years before his death: *Illustrated History of Greece from the Earliest Times to the Capture of Constantinople* ('Ιστορία τῆς 'Ελλάδος μετ' εἰκόνων ἀπὸ τῶν ἀρχαιοτάτων χρόνων μέχρι τῆς ἁλώσεως τῆς Κωνσταντινουπόλεως). This work, intended for a wide, rather than a scholarly, circle of readers, narrates clearly and comprehensively the events of Byzantine history until the end of the existence of the Empire. The author did not indicate his sources. His text is illustrated by numerous drawings.[39]

Gelzer.—A professor of the University of Jena, the late H. Gelzer, wrote for the second edition of Krumbacher's *History of Byzantine Literature* an *Outline of Byzantine Imperial History* (*Abriss der byzantinischen Kaisergeschichte,* Munich, 1897). Parts of this outline, concerned primarily with

[37] *Ibid.*

[38] M. Rostovtzeff, *The Social and Economic History of the Roman Empire,* 628.

[39] See the memorial volume dedicated to Lampros in modern Greek, Σπυρίδων II. Λάμπρος, *1851-1919,* edited by A. N. Skias, 5-29; bibliography of Lampros' works, 35-85;

unpublished manuscripts found after his death, 86-138. See also E. Stephanu, "Spyridon Lambros (1851-1919); Xénophon Sidéridès (1851-1929)," *Échos d'Orient,* XXIX (1930), 73-79. Lampros' work in the Byzantine field has not been adequately estimated.

external history, are directly dependent upon the works of Hertzberg. As a political partisan, Gelzer sometimes permitted his sympathy and antipathy to dictate his evaluation of historical events of the Byzantine period. His outline may be valuable for elementary reference.

It is interesting to read from the pen of this German scholar this statement in the conclusion of his outline:

The Russian Tsar married a princess from the house of the Palaeologi; the crown of Constantine Monomachus was bestowed in the Kremlin upon the autocrat of All Russia. The Russian state represents a direct continuation of the Byzantine Empire. And if St. Sophia is ever returned to true faith, if Asia Minor is ever torn out of the hideous hands of the Turks, it will be done only by the Russian Tsar. English interference goes against nature and history and will surely, though perhaps slowly, be broken. Only the protector of the orthodox Greek religion, the Russian Tsar, can become Emperor of Constantinople, in so far as he earnestly realizes the great duties connected with this task.[40]

Hesseling.—In 1902 D. C. Hesseling, professor at Leiden University, Holland, published his *The Byzantine Empire: Studies Concerning our Civilization from the Time of the Foundation of Constantinople (Byzantium: Studien over onze beschaving na de stichting van Konstantinopel,* Haarlem, 1902). Since Dutch is not a widely read language, this book was inaccessible to many until 1907 when a French translation of it appeared entitled *Essai sur la civilisation byzantine par D. C. Hesseling.* The translation was made by a well-known French Byzantine scholar and member of the Academy, G. Schlumberger, who hinted somewhat obscurely that the "translation is adapted for the taste of the French reading public."

Hesseling's brief yet compact book describes Byzantine civilization in broad terms and considers all sides of the multiform life of the Eastern Empire. Among political events the author chooses only those which throw some light on Byzantine civilization, and among individual names and single facts only those appear which bear upon general ideas. Hesseling devoted much attention to literature and art. This *Essay on Byzantine Civilization,* though somewhat elementary for the specialist, is of value to those who seek acquaintance with the general significance of the Byzantine period through a readable account that is at the same time well grounded.

Bussell.—The two-volume English work of F. W. Bussell, *The Roman Empire: Essays on the Constitutional History from the Accession of Domitian (81 A.D.) to the Retirement of Nicephorus III (1081 A.D.),* was published in London in 1910. Though this work is not lacking in interesting ideas and analogies, it suffers from vague narration, repetition, and lack of clarity in plan, so that the valuable ideas are at times obscured. The chronological frame-

[40] *Abriss der byzantinischen Kaiserschichte,* 1067.

work of this investigation is chosen at random, although the author tried to give it some foundation (see vol. I, pp. 1–2, 13–17). In the second volume the reader is surprised to find an outline of the history of the relations between Armenia and the Byzantine Empire from 520 to 1120. Bussell's book is difficult to read. It has no references. The author's main conception is that republican forms of the Roman imperial constitution, quite in evidence during the earlier epoch, continued to exist in one phase or another up to the period of the Comneni, that is, until 1081, at which time they were definitely replaced by the Byzantine form of autocracy, tyranny.

The Cambridge Medieval History.—A complete history of the Byzantine Empire, supplied with an excellent bibliography, is to be found in the *Cambridge Medieval History.* Volume I contains chapters on the history from Constantine the Great to the death of Anastasius in 518; in volume II are chapters on the period from the accession of Justinian I in 518 to the time of the Iconoclasts; the entire volume IV is devoted to the history of the Byzantine Empire from 717 to 1453 in connection with the history of the ancient Slavs, Armenia, the Mongols, and the Balkan states. There is no special chapter on the period of the Palaeologi. This general history of the Middle Ages was edited under the guidance of the late J. B. Bury and represents the joint work of well-known European scholars.

Romein.—In 1928, Jan Romein published in Dutch a very fine survey of Byzantine history entitled *Byzantium. A Historical Review of the State and Civilization in the Eastern Roman Empire (Byzantium. Geschiedkundig Overzicht van Staat en Beschaving in het Oost-Romeinsche Rijk).* This is a very reliable book, and although references are not given, it is based on original sources. It deals not only with political history but also with social, economic, and cultural development of the empire. There are thirty-five excellent illustrations.

Vasiliev.—The *History of the Byzantine Empire* by A. A. Vasiliev was published in Madison, Wisconsin in 1928 and 1929. This work covers the whole history of the Empire from the fourth century down to its fall in 1453. In 1932 this book was published in French as an enlarged and revised edition with illustrations and rather unsatisfactory maps. This French edition was introduced by a generous preface written by the famous French Byzantine scholar, the late Charles Diehl.[41]

Runciman.—Steven Runciman's valuable *Byzantine Civilization* appeared in 1933. Runciman began his book with a discussion of the foundation of

[41] A. A. Vasiliev, *Histoire de l'Empire Byzantine,* trans. from Russian by P. Brodin and A. Bourguina; edited by A. Picard, with preface by Charles Diehl. The statement on the title page that the book was translated from the Russian is inexact; it was translated from the English edition, but the translators might have used also the obsolete Russian edition. See Bibliography for the various editions.

Constantinople; in succeeding chapters he gave a very brief but clear outline of political history, the imperial constitution, administration, religion and the Church, the army and navy, the diplomatic service, commerce, urban and rural life, education and learning, literature and art, and, finally, a discussion of "Byzantium and the Neighboring World." This is an interesting and very well-written book.[42]

Iorga.—In 1934 the late Roumanian historian, N. Iorga, published in French his *History of the Byzantine Life. Empire and Civilization* (*Histoire de la vie byzantine. Empire et civilisation*). The author divides the history of the Byzantine Empire into three periods: (1) from Justinian down to the death of Heraclius, "the ecumenical empire" (l'empire oecuménique); (2) from the time of Heraclius to the time of the Comneni, "the middle empire of Hellenic civilization" (l'empire moyen de civilisation hellénique); (3) the period of the Comneni and Palaeologi, "the empire of Latin penetration" (l'empire de pénétration latine). The book contains a vast amount of information on all aspects of Byzantine history and many acute observations and original, sometimes debatable, ideas. It is supplied with a very rich and extensive bibliography.

Diehl and Marçais.—*Le Monde oriental de 365 à 1081,* by Charles Diehl and Georges Marçais, was published in Paris in 1936 as a volume in the series of *Histoire générale,* published under the direction of Gustave Glotz. For the first time in the course of Byzantine studies, the history of the Moslem world, whose destinies are indissolubly connected with the Oriental Empire, was included in a book dealing with Byzantium. Two such eminent scholars assured a fine piece of work. Diehl, of course, depended entirely upon his previous works. Conforming with the plan of the series, Diehl began the book with the year 395, so that the whole fourth century, which is so important for Byzantine studies, was not covered. Diehl carried the history of Byzantium down to 1081, down to the epoch of the crusades, when a wholly new period in the history of the Near East begins. The book gives a fine presentation not only of the political history of the Empire, but also of its internal life, social and economic structure, legislation, and finally its manifold and picturesque civilization. The book contains an excellent bibliography of primary sources as well as modern works.[43]

---

[42] See Charles Diehl's review of Runciman, *Byzantine Civilization* in *Byzantinische Zeitschrift,* XXXIV (1934), 127-30. Diehl indicates some mistakes but concludes by pronouncing the work excellent.

[43] In a review E. Stein remarked that "all serious critics agree in regretting profoundly that the *History of Byzantium* by Ch. Diehl

has appeared in Glotz's Collection." *Revue belge de philologie et d'histoire,* XVII (1938), 1024-44. This statement is not only unjust but also inexact. See Henri Grégoire's energetic protest in *Byzantion,* XIII, 2 (1938), 749-57, referring to a laudatory review of Diehl's book by G. Ostrogorsky written in Serbo-Croatian and translated by Grégoire.

The second volume of *Le Monde oriental* was written by Charles Diehl, Rodolphe Guilland, Lysimaque Oeconomos, and René Grousset under the title *L'Europe Orientale de 1081 à 1453*. This was published in 1945. Diehl, with the collaboration of Oeconomos, described the period from 1081 to 1204; Guilland presented the history of Byzantium from 1204 to 1453; Grousset dealt with the history of the Latin Orient. The book includes sketches in the history of neighboring peoples, such as the Bulgars, Serbs, Ottoman Turks, the civilization of Venice and Genoa, the Empire of Trebizond, the Kingdom of Cyprus, the Kingdom of Cilician Armenia, and Latin possessions in the seas of Greece. This is a very useful and important contribution.[44]

Heichelheim.—In 1938 Fritz Heichelheim published in German two bulky volumes on *Economic History of Antiquity from the Paleolithic Era down to the Migration of the Germans, Slavs and Arabs* (*Wirtschaftsgeschichte des Altertums von Paläolitickum bis zur Völkerwanderung der Germanen, Slaven und Arabes*). Two chapters particularly interesting today are the eighth, "The Time from Augustus to Diocletian," and the ninth, "The Late *Antike* from Diocletian to Heraclius as Guardian of the Treasure of Ancient Civilization for the Future." The book contains much varied information on social and economic conditions of the Empire in the fourth, fifth, sixth, and seventh centuries; this is presented in confused form, however, so that it is difficult to use as a reference work. The book is written in a heavy German style, but the Byzantine section is worthy of study and would merit a detailed critical report by a Byzantine scholar.

Amantos.—A Greek scholar, Constantine Amantos (Ἄμαντος), published in 1939 the first volume of his *History of the Byzantine Empire* (Ἱστορία τοῦ Βυζαντινοῦ Κράτους). The volume covers the time from 395 to 867, that is, up to the accession of the Macedonian dynasty. At the beginning of his book, Amantos gives a fine picture of conditions in the Empire in the fourth century, laying stress upon the triumph of Christianity, the foundation of Constantinople, and Germanic invasions. This is a very reliable piece of work with many important observations. It shows that Greeks of the present day are seriously interested not only in classical studies and modern politics, but also in the middle ages of the Near East, which are of great significance for the history of Greece. Amantos' second volume which covers the time 867–1204 came out in 1947.

Ostrogorsky.—In 1940 a Russian scholar now living in Belgrade, Georg Ostrogorsky, published in German the *History of the Byzantine State*

See also A. A. Vasiliev's review, *Byzantinisch-Neugriechische Jahrbücher*, XIII, 1 (1937), 114-19.

[44] Charles Diehl died in Paris November 4, 1944. On Diehl's works and their importance

see V. Laurent, "Charles Diehl, historien de Byzance," and G. Brătianu, "Charles Diehl et la Roumanie," *Revue historique du sud-est européen*, XXII (1945), 5-36.

(*Geschichte des byzantinischen Staates*).[45] This is a work of the first rank. It covers the whole period of Byzantine history down to the fall of the Empire. Ostrogorsky includes an excellent picture of the development of Byzantine historical studies beginning with the sixteenth century. The earlier period of the Empire, 324–610, is sketched only briefly, according to the plan of *Handbook* in which it appeared. The text, supplied with extremely useful and well-chosen notes and references, gives a very reliable picture of the history of the Eastern Empire. As the title indicates, the chief aim of the author was to show the development of the Byzantine State as it was influenced by internal and external political changes. Therefore, political history prevails in the book, although social, economic, and cultural phenomenon are taken into account. As a supplement to this volume, Ostrogorsky's excellent chapter on "Agrarian Conditions in the Byzantine Empire in the Middle Ages," published in the first volume of *The Cambridge Economic History of Europe from the Decline of the Roman Empire,* can be warmly recommended. Ostrogorsky's book is an excellent piece of scholarship and is absolutely indispensable for the student of Byzantine history.[46] In 1947–50 the three volumes of the work of the distinguished French Byzantinist, Louis Bréhier, who died in October, 1950, came out under the title *Le Monde Byzantin: I. Vie et mort de Byzance;* II. *Les Institutions de l'Empire Byzantin;* III. *La Civilisation Byzantine.*

General Brief Sketches.—Among other historical works several surveys of Byzantine history are intended for the general reading public. Most of them have little or no serious scientific value, yet these popular accounts, rarely original in nature, are of value in awakening in some readers a desire for further study of the history of the Byzantine empire. Most of them are written in English.

C. W. Oman's *Byzantine Empire* (3rd ed., London, 1892) is vivid and well illustrated. F. Harrison, in his sketch (63 pages) on *Byzantine History in the Early Middle Ages* (London, 1900), attempts, on the basis of Finlay's and Bury's investigations, to determine the importance of the Byzantine Empire from the point of view of western European civilization.[47] The Frenchman Pierre Grenier, never a serious student of Byzantine history, made a curious attempt to paint a picture of the social and political evolution of the

[45] Ostrogorsky's book is the first part of the second volume of *Byzantinisches Handbuch im Rahmen des Handbuchs der Altertumswissenschaft,* ed. Walter Otto. Neither the first volume nor the second part of the second volume has yet appeared.

[46] See H. Grégoire's very fine review of Ostrogorsky's book, *Byzantion,* XVI, 2 (1944),

545–55. See also the very interesting remarks on this book by Germaine Rouillard, "A propos d'un ouvrage récent sur l'histoire de l'État byzantin," *Revue de philologie,* 3rd ser. XIV (1942), 169–80.

[47] Later reprinted in F. Harrison, *Among My Books: Centenaries, Reviews, Memoirs,* 180–231.

Byzantine Empire. His book was published in two volumes entitled *The Byzantine Empire: Its Social and Political Evolution* (*L'Empire byzantin: Son évolution sociale et politique,* Paris, 1904). Grenier's general treatment is not always satisfactory and he makes both major and minor mistakes, pardonable in one who is not a specialist, but his work is interesting because it gives a large amount of varied information. A brief but compact history of Constantinople related to the general history of the Empire is W. N. Hutton's *Constantinople: The Story of the Old Capital of the Empire,* published in London in 1904.

K. Roth gave a very brief and dry survey of Byzantine history in his *History of the Byzantine Empire* (*Geschichte des Byzantinischen Reiches,* Leipzig, 1904). He also published in 1917 a brief *Social and Cultural History of the Byzantine Empire* (*Sozial und Kulturgeschichte des Byzantinischen Reiches*). Professor R. von Scala wrote for inclusion in Helmholt's *Universal History* a very compact outline of Byzantine history based on a wide knowledge of original sources and literature on the subject. He entitled this section "Hellenism Since the Time of Alexander the Great" ("Das Griechentum seit Alexander dem Grossen"). In this outline Scala centered his attention on analyzing and determining the significance of Byzantine civilization. There exists another English book, brief but serious and well done, by the Roumanian historian N. Iorga, entitled *The Byzantine Empire,* published in London in 1907. E. Foord's well-illustrated and vividly written book, *The Byzantine Empire—the Rearguard of European Civilization,* appeared in 1911. It is regrettable that this book gives only a very brief and superficial account of the history of the Byzantine Empire during the epoch of its fall, the period after 1204.

Another brief survey of Byzantine history is included in the *General History from the Fourth Century to Our Time* (*Histoire générale du IVe siècle à nos jours*) by E. Lavisse and A. Rambaud. The Italian work of N. Turchi, *La civiltà bizantina* (Turin, 1915), is a valuable outline of Byzantine culture.

In 1919 Charles Diehl published his *History of the Byzantine Empire* (*Histoire de l'Empire Byzantin*). In this book Diehl attempted more than a survey of the political history of the Byzantine Empire; he gave an account of the more important inner processes and an explanation of the significance of Byzantine civilization. This book contains a brief bibliography as well as many maps and illustrations. It has gone through several editions in France. An English translation was published in America in 1925 (*History of the Byzantine Empire*), translated from the French by G. Ives.

In *Byzance: Grandeur et Decadence* (Paris, 1919), Charles Diehl painted a brilliant picture of Byzantine internal life. He discussed the causes for the greatness and for the fall of the Empire, the influence of Byzantine civilization upon neighboring nations, and the Byzantine heritage in Turkey, Russia, and the Balkan states.[48] August Heisenberg gave serious and well-written accounts of life and civilization in his *Staat und Gesellschaft des Byzantinischen Reiches* which forms a part of *Die Kultur der Gegenwart,* edited by P. Hinneberg. Norman H. Baynes gave a similar picture in his *Byzantine Empire* (London, 1926), which covers the period from the fourth century to the capture of Constantinople by the Crusaders in 1204. The history of the Byzantine Empire to the end of the eleventh century was treated briefly in L. Halphen's *Les Barbares: des grandes invasions aux conquêtes turques du XIe siècle* (Paris, 1926); some bibliography is given. A recent book of a general nature is Robert Byron's *The Byzantine Achievement. An Historical Perspective. A.D. 330–1453* (London, 1929). A little French book by Auguste Bailly, *Byzance* (Paris, 1939), embracing in popular form the whole history of the Empire, is not only useful but also is pleasant reading. *Imperial Byzantium,* the English edition of an original German work by Bertha Diener, appeared in 1938.[49] Depending upon modern Byzantinologists for her facts, she related the history of the Empire in a somewhat picturesque style, as the chapter titles suggest. Chapter III is entitled "Angels and Eunuchs," and the last chapter, which contains a general survey of the situation of the Empire after the Fourth Crusade, is appropriately called "Midsummer Night's Dream." A brief but very fine *History of Byzantium* (*Histoire du Byzance*) by Paul Lemerle was published in Paris in 1943.[50] Compact and meritorious general accounts of Byzantine history were given by E. Gerland in the *Catholic Encyclopedia* and by J. B. Bury in the eleventh edition of the *Encyclopaedia Britannica.*

An excellent introduction to the history of Byzantium is the monumental work by O. Seeck, *History of the Downfall of the Ancient World* (*Geschichte des Untergangs der antiken Welt*), published between 1895 and 1920, which brings events down to the year 476. Two other very useful introductions to Byzantine history are: E. Stein, *Geschichte des spätrömischen Reiches;* and F. Lot, *La Fin du monde antique et le debut du moyen âge* (Paris, 1927), which includes the epoch of Justinian the Great. Stein's second volume, in French, *Histoire du Bas-Empire,* which covers the period 476–565, came out in 1949.

Byzantine literature.—An indispensable reference work on Byzantine liter-

---

[48] The substance of this book served as a basis for Diehl's work in the *Cambridge Medieval History,* IV, chaps. xxiii and xxiv. This appears in more concise form in *Les grands problèmes de l'histoire byzantine,* 178.

[49] The original German edition in 1937 was entitled *Byzanz. Von Kaisern, Engeln und*

Eunuchen, and appeared under the pseudonym "Sir Galahad." A French edition was published the same year.

[50] See a very favorable review of this book by V. Grumel, *Études byzantines,* II (1945), 275.

ature is the second edition of the excellent *History of Byzantine Literature from Justinian to the End of the Eastern Roman Empire* (*Geschichte der byzantinischen Litteratur von Justinian bis zum Ende des oströmischen Reiches,* Munich, 1897), published by Karl Krumbacher, late professor in the University of Munich. The theological literature in this edition was collected by Professor A. Ehrhard. The same edition contains H. Gelzer's *Survey of Byzantine Political History.* Krumbacher's work is the most important existing reference book for the study of Byzantine literature. It contains a vast amount of material and does credit to the profound scholarship and unusual industry of the author. Since Krumbacher was well acquainted with Russian and other Slavic languages, he used sources in these languages. His book is, of course, intended for specialists only and not for the general reader. However, he made available for a wider circle of readers a history of Byzantine literature in a more accessible booklet of fifty pages, *Greek Literature of the Middle Ages* (*Die Griechische Literatur des Mittelalters*), in the collection, *Die Kultur der Gegenwart,* edited by P. Hinneberg. K. Dieterich's book, *History of Byzantine and Modern Greek Literature* (*Geschichte der byzantinischen und neugriechischen Literatur,* Leipzig, 1902), is of some importance. Valuable material is included in the brief history of Byzantine literature written in Italian by G. Montelatici, *Storia della letteratura bizantina* (*324–1453*), published in the *Manuali Hoepli, serie scientifica,* Milan, 1916. This book is not a repetition of Krumbacher's work; it was published nineteen years later and includes a great quantity of new information. S. Mercati wrote a detailed review, which lists many errors (*Roma e l'Oriente,* VIII [1918], 171–83). The brief survey of Byzantine literature in Polish by Jan Saidak, *Litteratura Bizantynska* (Warsaw, 1933), is not reliable. For the earlier period of Byzantine literature, from the fourth century, A.D., W. Christ's *Geschichte der Griechischen Litteratur* (Vol. II, Munich, 1924), is very useful. Three other books are of value: F. A. Wright, *A History of Later Greek Literature from the Death of Alexander in 323 B.C. to the Death of Justinian in 565 A.D.* (New York, 1932); Otto Bardenhewer, *Patrologie* (3rd ed., Freiburg, 1910); and Bardenhewer's *Geschichte der altkirchlichen Literatur* (Freiburg, 1910, 5 vols.). In the last-named work, the concluding three volumes, covering the period from the fourth to the eighth centuries, are especially important. N. Iorga has analyzed the literature briefly in "La littérature byzantine, son sens, ses divisions, sa portée," *Revue historique du sud-est européen,* II (1925), 370–97.

BYZANTINE STUDIES IN RUSSIA

The nineteenth century

Russian scholars began to show an active interest in Byzantine history in the second half of the nineteenth century.

The German academicians.—During the first half of the nineteenth century some studies in the field were made by German scholars in Russia, who were elected members of the Russian Academy of Sciences and remained permanently in Petrograd. These German scholars were especially interested in determining the importance of Byzantium and Byzantine sources in Russian history. Of these academicians Ph. Krug (1764–1844) and A. Kunik (1814–99) deserve mention.

Westerners and Slavophiles.—Among eminent representatives of Russian thinkers in the first half of the nineteenth century, Byzantine history often served as material for supporting a particular social movement. For example, some Slavophiles[51] drew from the history of the Byzantine Empire facts supporting and justifying their theories. The Westerners took from the same sources facts which were supposed to show the unfavorable influence of Byzantine history and to point definitely to the great danger which would threaten if Russia should decide to follow the traditions of the fallen Empire. In one of his works, Herzen wrote:

> Ancient Greece had ceased to exist when Roman domination came in and saved her, just as the lava and ashes saved Pompeii and Herculaneum. The Byzantine period had opened the lid of the coffin, but the dead body remained dead; like any other grave it was taken over by the priests (popes) and monks and was fittingly handled by eunuchs, those true representatives of sterility. . . . The Byzantine Empire could live, but her function was ended; and history in general is interested in nations only while they are on the stage, i.e. while they are doing something.[52]

Another Westerner, P. Y. Tchaadayev, wrote in his first philosophic letter: "Complying with our evil fate, we turned to the woeful, deeply hated Byzantine Empire for a moral code, which was to be the basis of our education."[53] But these statements have no historical value whatever. Unquestionably gifted and highly educated as these thinkers were, they were not real students of Byzantine history.

[51] The Slavophiles admired the Russian Orthodox Church and the old Russian political and social institutions preceding the time of Peter the Great, whose reforms, they believed, had led Russia astray. The Westerners, on the contrary, held that the Russians should live in complete affiliation with the west of Europe and that Russia had become a civilized country only since the reforms of Peter the Great.
[52] *The Past and Thoughts. Venezia la Bella,* X, 53–54.
[53] *Works and Letters,* ed. Herschensohn, II, 118; French ed., I, 85. A still stronger expression is found in a different version of this letter, II, 13 (Herschensohn ed.).

A realization of the importance of Byzantine historical study was very apparent in the middle of the nineteenth century. A fervent Slavophile, A. S. Khomiakov, wrote in the 1850's: "In our opinion, to speak of the Byzantine Empire with disdain means to disclose one's own ignorance."[54] In 1850 the famous University of Moscow professor, T. N. Granovsky, wrote:

Do we need to speak of the importance of Byzantine history for us, Russians? We have taken over from Tsargrad[55] the best part of our national culture, namely, our religious beliefs and the beginnings of civilization. The Eastern Empire introduced Russia into the family of Christian nations. But besides these connections we are bound up with the fate of the Byzantine Empire by the mere fact that we are Slavs. This side of the question has not been, and could not be, fully appreciated by foreign scholars.[56]

The proper solution of the main problems of Byzantine history, in the opinion of Granovsky, could be reached in his time only by Russian or Slavic scholars: "It is our duty to study the phenomenon to which we are so much indebted."[57]

Vasilievsky.—The real founder of the scientific study of Byzantine history on a large scale was V. G. Vasilievsky (1838–99), professor at the University of Petrograd and a member of the Russian Academy of Sciences. He published a large number of distinguished works on special problems in Byzantine history, internal as well as external, and devoted much of his energy and fine analytical ability to the study of Russo-Byzantine relations. Some of Vasilievsky's works are of great importance in the field of general history. For instance, it is admitted by many distinguished European scholars that Vasilievsky's work on "Byzantium and the Patzinaks," is indispensable to any student of the First Crusade.[58] The late Professor N. P. Kondakov, who died in 1925, and the academician Th. I. Uspensky are also distinguished scholars, the former in the field of Byzantine art and the latter in the realm of Byzantine social history. No discussion or evaluation of the work of these three historians appears here, because Vasilievsky published works on special questions only and Kondakov's works deal mainly with Byzantine art;[59] this survey is intended to indicate general works on Byzantine history. Uspensky is somewhat of an exception; more will be said later about his two volumes

[54] "The Voice of a Greek in Defense of Byzantium," *Works* (4th ed., 1914), III, 366 in note.

[55] Russian name for Constantinople.

[56] "The Latin Empire: A Review of Medovikov's Work," *Complete Works of T. N. Granovsky* (4th ed., 1900), 378.

[57] *Ibid.,* 379.

[58] The centennial of Vasilievsky's birth was 1938. See A. A. Vasiliev, "My Reminiscences of V. G. Vasilievsky," and G. Ostrogorsky,

"V. G. Vasilievsky as Byzantinologist and Creator of Modern Russian Byzantology," both in *Annales de l'Institut Kondakov,* XI (1940), 207–14, 227–35. A very fine article appeared in Soviet Russia on Vasilievsky and the importance of his work, by N. S. Lebedev, *Istoričesky Journal,* 1944.

[59] See however Kondakov's posthumous work, *Sketches and Notes on the History of Mediaeval Art and Culture,* III, 455.

on the general history of the Empire, which appeared in 1914 and in 1927.

On the whole, the chief contribution of the Russian scholars down to the beginning of the twentieth century was their detailed investigations which shed much light on special, and at times extremely important, questions.[60]

Ertov.—In 1837 I. Ertov published in Russian his two-volume *History of the Eastern Roman or Constantinopolitan Empire, Selected from the General History.* The last words of the title indicated that this work was merely an extract from his fifteen-volume *General History and Continuation of the General History of the Migration of Nations and the Establishment of New States in Europe, Asia, and Africa, from the Time of the Formation of the Russian State until the Destruction of the Eastern Roman Empire,* published 1830–34. Ertov was the son of a merchant and was a self-taught man. In writing this history of the Byzantine Empire he was guided by the idea that "the Russian reader needs, above all, a narrative history." He stated that he used as sources, "besides many excerpts from numerous books and periodicals [in French], the history of Royou, Lebeau's abridged history of the Eastern Roman Empire, and Adam's abridged translation of Gibbon's history."[61] Naturally, Ertov's compilation embracing events until the fall of Constantinople has no scientific value, but it was an unexpected attempt for his time.

The twentieth century

Kulakovsky.—The first attempt to write a serious general history of the Byzantine Empire was made by the late J. A. Kulakovsky, professor at the University of Kiev. His special field was Roman literature, but he taught Roman history at the University and did much work in the field of Roman antiquities and the history of Roman institutions of the imperial epoch. During the period following 1890 he spent part of his time studying Christian archeology and Byzantine history. In the early part of the present century (1906–08) he translated the work of the well-known pagan Roman historian of the fourth century A.D., Ammianus Marcellinus, and this translation served as a kind of introduction to his later Byzantine studies. In 1910 he published the first volume of his *History of the Byzantine Empire,* covering the period from 395 to 518 A.D. The second volume appeared in 1912 and the third in 1915. These embrace the history of the Empire from 518 to 717, i.e., up to the Iconoclast period. A revised edition of the first volume appeared as early as 1913. With unusual industry and untiring energy the author studied Byzantine sources, Greek, Latin, and Oriental (in translation), and on the

---

[60] In 1926 an English historian, Norman H. Baynes, wrote: "All the literature on landholding and taxation is highly technical and most of the best work is in the Russian language," *The Byzantine Empire,* 248.

[61] *History of the Eastern Roman or Constantinopolitan Empire,* introduction.

basis of all these and a wide acquaintance with the literature of the period he wrote his detailed history of the Byzantine Empire up to 717. In his work Professor Kulakovsky deals with some phases of internal life, but they are at times lost in the mass of details concerning external political life. The third volume is of particularly great interest and value. According to his own statement in the preface to the first volume, Kulakovsky attempted, through a vivid and realistic account, to make it possible for the reader to sense the spirit of those ancient times. "Our Russian past," said Kulakovsky, "is bound up with the Byzantine Empire by unbreakable ties; and on the basis of this union our Russian national consciousness has defined itself." He bitterly regretted the abolition of the study of Greek in Russian secondary schools: "perhaps some day we Russians will understand, as they do in Western Europe, that not the last word of the Modern, but the first word of the Hellene, contains the creative beginnings of European culture." In the preface to the third volume the author once more defined the plan of his Byzantine history: "My aim was to present a consecutive, chronologically exact, and, as far as possible, complete picture of the life of the Empire, based on a direct study of sources and a modern investigation of materials as they appear in monographs referring to this period in numerous studies of individual questions given in various periodicals devoted to Byzantine problems." The work of Professor Kulakovsky is of great value for the facts of Byzantine history and for the contents of some of the original sources. It contains also the important conclusions and theories of modern historians on the main problems of Byzantine history, social as well as political. Kulakovsky's account of historical events is very detailed; this explains the fact that three volumes, comprising about 1,400 pages, cover the history of the Empire only until the beginning of the eighth century.

Th. I. Uspensky.—The first volume of the *History of the Byzantine Empire* by the Russian academician and former director of the Archeological Institute in Constantinople, Th. I Uspensky, appeared in 1914. This beautiful work, with numerous maps, plates, and pictures, gives an account of historical events from the fourth century until the beginning of the eighth century, i.e., until the Iconoclast period. This book represents the first attempt made by a specialist in this field to write a general history of the Byzantine Empire. The man who undertook it was one of the most distinguished scholars in the field of Byzantine history and culture. He devoted his long and industrious life almost exclusively to the study of different aspects and epochs of the complex history of the Empire. He died in Leningrad in 1928, at the age of eighty-three. Wishing to offer an accessible narrative history to a wide circle of readers, Uspensky did not supply his work with many references, either in footnotes or at the ends of chapters, but limited himself to mentioning his main sources and secondary works. The first part of the second volume, published in 1927, contains a discussion of the Iconoclast epoch and the problem of the Slavonic apostles, Cyril (Constantine) and Methodius.

Uspensky's first volume serves as a broad introduction to the history of the Empire at the time when the main elements of "Byzantinism" were being created and the complex Byzantine culture was being formed. The author cannot refrain from finding in certain past events of Byzantine history some "lessons" for modern life. When he spoke of the dominant importance of the Oriental Byzantine provinces and pointed out that it was precisely in Asia Minor, in the Empire of Nicaea, that the idea of restoring the Byzantine Empire in the thirteenth century had grown and ripened, he concluded that "the lesson of history must be strictly examined" and weighed by his contemporaries waiting for the division of the inheritance of the "dangerously ill patient on the Bosphorus."[62] He commented further:

> We should be greatly mistaken were we to insist that it is within our power to avoid taking an active part in the settlement of matters connected with the Byzantine heritage. Although it usually depends upon the heir to accept or refuse the heritage left to him, still Russia's part in the Eastern question was bequeathed by history and cannot be changed voluntarily unless some unforseen shock should give us the faculty to forget and stamp out the memory of the things which made us live, strive, and suffer.[63]

Throughout his work Uspensky attempted to explain the problem of Slavic-Byzantine relations, and at the close of his introduction, written in October, 1912, he referred the reader to the chapters on the history of the southern Slavs for the explanation of "today's sad events in the Balkan peninsula," i.e., the events of the Second Balkan War.[64] His goal, Uspensky explained, was to provide for the Russian reader serious material which would help him gain a clear understanding of a carefully weighed and well-thought-out system. In addition, he hoped that his readers would appreciate his conviction that a thorough study of Byzantine history and its relation to Russia's past is not only indispensable to Russian scholarship but is equally necessary for the formation and proper guidance of Russian political and national consciousness.

As an adherent of "Byzantinism," Uspensky took particular care to define this term. In his conception the essential features which gave rise to Byzantinism were the immigration of the barbarians into the Empire and the cultural and religious crisis of the third and fourth centuries.[65] "Byzantinism is a historical principle, the effect of which is revealed in the history of the people of Southern and Eastern Europe; this principle directs the develop-

[62] *History of the Byzantine Empire*, I, xii.
[63] *Ibid.*, 46–47.
[64] *Ibid.*, xiv.
[65] *Ibid.*, 47–48.

ment of many states even in our own times; it expresses itself in a particular set of beliefs and political institutions, and, one might say, in special forms of class organization and land relations."[66] By Byzantinism, which is the result of a fusion of Romanism with older cultures, such as Hebrew, Persian, and Hellenic, "is meant primarily the combination of all elements which influenced the gradual reformation of the Roman Empire from the fifth to the eighth centuries, before it was transformed into the Byzantine Empire."[67] "Many changes were caused by Germanic and Slavic immigration, bringing on reforms in the social and economic structure and in the military system of the Empire. The new elements exerted much influence upon the reformation of the Roman Empire in the East, causing it to acquire gradually the characteristics of Byzantinism."[68] Byzantinism manifests itself in the following phenomena: (1) "in a steady abolition of the prevailing Latin tongue and its gradual replacement by the Greek, or properly speaking, Byzantine, language; (2) in the struggle of nationalities for political supremacy; (3) in the new development of art, in the appearance of new motives which contributed to the creation of new monuments, as well as in peculiar works in the field of literature, where a new and original method is gradually developed under the influence of the patterns and traditions of Oriental culture."[69]

Uspensky's opinion that the Roman Empire in the East acquires the distinguishing traits of Byzantinism at about the eighth century agrees with that of the English Byzantine scholar, Finlay. Uspensky's general theses are not proved in the first volume; they can be judged properly only when his complete history of the Byzantine Empire, or at least a history up to the Latin conquest, is available.

These are the main problems raised in the first volume: (1) Slavic migration in the Balkan peninsula and its effect upon Byzantine life; (2) landownership in the Byzantine Empire; and (3) the system of themes, i.e., provincial administration of the Empire. Although these questions were not finally answered in Uspensky's book, the interpretations which he gave indicate the need for a further study of these complex questions.

This work by Uspensky was conceived more than twenty-five years before its publication, and it was written over a long period of time; various parts of it differ greatly in value. In contrast to new, vivid, and interesting chapters are other chapters based on obsolete materials, far below the level reached by modern scholars. Discussions of the Arabs and Muhammedans are examples of the latter. Uspensky devoted much space to the social life of the Empire, and this is one of the chief merits of the book. The volume makes

[66] *Ibid.*, 16.
[67] *Ibid.*, 39.
[68] *Ibid.*, 39-40.
[69] *Ibid.*, 40.

possible for the reader an acquaintance with the early period of Byzantine history; it provides a clear exposition by a specialist who devoted his scholarly life almost exclusively to the study of the Byzantine period. In 1948 the third volume of his *History,* which covers the period 1081–1453, came out. The second half of the second volume has not been published.

Shestakov.—In 1913 S. P. Shestakov published his *Lectures on the History of the Byzantine Empire.* The author was a professor at the University of Kazan. A second revised and enlarged edition of these lectures appeared in 1915. The volume deals with historical events beginning with the migrations of the barbarians within the boundaries of the Western and Eastern Roman Empire in the third, fourth, and fifth centuries and ending with the coronation of Charlemagne in 800. The author relates many facts about external political affairs and the social life of the Empire and gives some information about the historiography and literature of this branch of history. The information is not always exact and the narrative is very hasty.

C. N. Uspensky.—A very refreshing and vivid impression is left by the *Outlines in Byzantine History,* published in 1917 in Moscow, by the Russian scholar, C. N. Uspensky.[70] The volume, only 268 pages long, contains a very interesting general introduction and survey of the social and economic evolution of the Roman Empire. It brings the reader in contact with the important internal problems of the Byzantine period. The account ends with the late Iconoclast period and the restoration of image worship in 843, during the reign of Theodora. The distinguishing feature of the *Outlines* is the emphasis placed on questions of internal organization of the Empire and religious and social evolution; political events are brought in only at points where the author finds them valuable in the explanation of certain phenomena of social life. Uspensky carefully developed his main and wholly correct idea of the Hellenistic nature of the Roman and Byzantine Empires. He made an interesting attempt to investigate the feudalizing processes of Byzantine life in the field of laic as well as monastic landholding. Uspensky was particularly interested in the Iconoclast period, and the last chapters of his *Outlines* deserve particular attention. He analyzed the formation of the first barbarian kingdoms within the Empire, administrative reforms and financial management under Justinian, the organization of themes, the peasantry of the sixth, seventh, and eighth centuries, and the so-called "rural code," the problems of landholding and the *exkuseia* (Byzantine immunity). Small in size but rich in content, this book is of very great value.

Vasiliev.—A. A. Vasiliev's *History of the Byzantine Empire* was originally a Russian work published in Russia. The complete work is in two volumes and embraces the whole history of the Byzantine Empire. The first volume

[70] He died in Moscow in 1917.

was published in 1917 under the title *Lectures in Byzantine History,* vol. I, *The Period Until the Beginning of the Crusades (1081).* The second volume, covering the history from the Crusades until the fall of Constantinople, was published in three parts: (1) *Byzantium and the Crusaders* (Petrograd, 1923); (2) *Latin Domination in the East* (Petrograd, 1923); and (3) *The Fall of the Byzantine Empire* (Leningrad, 1925). Information on the translations, and the revised and enlarged editions of this work are included in the general bibliography of this volume.

Bezobrazov.—Sketches in Byzantine Culture, a posthumous study by P. V. Bezobrazov, who died in October, 1918, was published in Petrograd in 1919. This vividly written book is marked by the author's unsympathetic approach toward much of Byzantine life, which he described in rather dark colors. He discussed emperors and empresses, churchmen and government officials, landowners, artisans, literature, spectacles and amusements, and judicial matters. Bezobrazov was a very able scholar and his book is pleasant and profitable.

*Levchenko.—*The first attempt to sketch Byzantine history from the Marxist point of view appeared in Soviet Russia in 1940, the brief *History of Byzantium* by M. V. Levchenko (Moscow and Leningrad, 1940). Putting aside the author's commonplace attacks on "bourgeois byzantinists" which apparently are compulsory in Soviet Russia, the book reveals a good knowledge of material, gives an interesting though somewhat biased selection of excerpts from sources, and devotes much attention to internal history, especially socio-economic problems, which Levchenko connected with the interests of the masses. The author wrote: "Russia received Christianity from Byzantium. Along with Christianity the Slavs received writing and some elements of higher Byzantine culture. It is clear that the working masses of our country are right in becoming interested in the history of the Byzantine Empire, and the Soviet historian must satisfy this interest and give a scholarly history of Byzantium erected on the foundation of the Marxist-Lenin methodology." (p. 4)

PERIODICALS, GENERAL REFERENCES, AND PAPYROLOGY

The first periodical devoted to Byzantine studies, *Byzantinische Zeitschrift* (*Byzantine Journal*), appeared in Germany in 1892. In addition to numerous articles and book reviews, it contains a detailed bibliography of all the publications related to Byzantine history. Much space is devoted to all Russian and Slavic publications. Professor Karl Krumbacher was the founder and the first editor of this publication. Twenty-two volumes had appeared by 1914, and an excellent analytical index to the first twelve volumes was published in 1909. During the first World War *Byzantinische Zeitschrift* was discontinued, but it was resumed after the war. The journal is at present edited by Franz Dölger.

In 1894 the Russian Academy of Sciences began the publication of the *Vizantiysky Vremennik (Byzantine Annals)*, edited by V. G. Vasilievsky and V. E. Regel. This journal followed along the same lines as its German predecessor. In the bibliographical division much space is given to works connected with the history of Slavic peoples and Christian nations of the Near East. The journal is written in Russian, but occasionally it includes articles in French and modern Greek. Its publication also was suspended during the first World War. By 1917 twenty-two volumes had been published, but the twenty-third did not appear until 1923 and the twenty-fifth was published in 1928. The sixteenth volume contains an analytical index to the first fifteen volumes compiled by P. V. Bezobrazov. Th. I. Uspensky edited the *Vizantiysky Vremennik* until his death. After 1947, in Soviet Russia, a new series of *Vizantiysky Vremennik* was begun; in 1951 the fourth volume came out.

Another Byzantine periodical, *Byzantis* (Βυζαντίς), was started in 1909 by the Byzantine Society in Athens. Only two volumes have appeared. Since 1915 three volumes of a new Russian periodical, *Vyzantiyskoe Obozrenie (Byzantine Review)* have been published by the faculty of History and Philology of the Youryev (Dorpat) University under the general editorship of V. E. Regel. The third volume appeared in 1917.

N. A. Bees began in 1920 in Berlin the publication of the *Byzantinisch-neugriechische Jahrbücher,* whose general aims coincide with those of the *Byzantinische Zeitschrift*. Beginning with the fifth volume this journal has been published in Athens, Greece, where Bees is a university professor. Volume XVII appeared in 1944.

At the Fifth International Historical Congress gathered at Brussels in 1923, the section on Byzantine studies expressed a desire to create a new international Byzantine journal. At the First International Congress of Byzantine scholars at Bucharest in 1924 the final plans for the publication of such a periodical were completed, and in 1925 the first volume appeared. It was entitled *Byzantion, an International Review of Byzantine Studies (Byzantion. Revue Internationale des Etudes Byzantines)*, and was edited by Paul Graindor and Henri Grégoire. This volume was dedicated to the well-known Russian scholar, N. P. Kondakov, to commemorate his eightieth birthday, but on the very day of its appearance news came of Kondakov's death (February 16, 1925).

Between 1924 and 1950 twenty volumes of a new Greek publication, *Annual* of the Society of Byzantine Studies (Ἐπετηρὶς Ἑταιρείας Βυζαντινῶν Σπουδῶν), were published in Athens. Many articles printed in this *Annual* are interesting and important.

In addition to materials given in these special periodicals, much valuable information pertaining to the study of the Byzantine period may be found in journals not directly concerned with Byzantine scholarship. Particularly important for Byzantine studies are the Greek periodical Νέος Ἑλληνομνήμων, edited by S. Lampros from 1904 and continued after his death by several Greek scholars; *Echos d'Orient;* and *Revue de l'Orient Chrétien.*

The fundamental work on Byzantine law is *History of Greek-Roman Law* (*Geschichte des griechisch-römischen Rechts*) from the pen of the distinguished German student of law, Karl Eduard Zachariä von Lingenthal. The third edition appeared in Berlin in 1892. Among earlier works on law is Jacques Godefroy's edition of the *Codex Theodosianus.* Godefroy (Gothofredus, 1587–1652), jurist, was born in Geneva and was sent to France to study law and history. After thirty years of labor, he produced his edition of the *Codex Theodosianus* and enriched it with important notes and comments which still are extremely valuable for the early period of Byzantine law. His work was first printed thirteen years after his death. Other important works are Mortreuil's French *History of Byzantine Law* (*Histoire du droit Byzantin*), three volumes published in Paris, 1843–47; the German survey by E. Heimbach in the *Ersch und Gruber Encyclopedia* (LXXXVI, 191–471); the Russian study by August Engelman, *On the Scholarly Study of Greco-Roman Law, with a survey of its most recent literature,* an "attempt at an introduction into the study of Byzantine juridical history," published in 1857. This last study is now obsolete, but since it is very seldom mentioned and is rather inaccessible, an outline of its contents may interest students: importance of the history of Byzantium and of Greco-Roman law, survey of the history of the literature of Greco-Roman law, conception and size of Greco-Roman juridical history, the division of the law into periods and the characteristics of each period, principal objects of the study of Greco-Roman law at present, and survey of the literature of Greco-Roman law since 1824. Another Russian work is by Azarevitch, *A History of Byzantine Law* (2 parts, Jaroslavl, 1876–77). A very comprehensive outline, provided with valuable bibliographical notes, was published in 1906 by the Italian scholar, L. Siciliano, in *Italian Juridical Encyclopedia* (*Enciclopedia Giuridica Italiana,* vol. IV, part 5, fasc. 451 and 460). This was published separately in Milan in 1906. Also useful are Aldo Albertoni, *Per una esposizione del diritto bizantino con riguardo all' Italia* (Imola, 1927), together with some additions by Norman

Baynes in the *Byzantinische Zeitschrift* (XXVIII [1928], 474–76), and H. v. Wittken, *Die Entwicklung des Rechtes nach Justinian in Byzanz* (Halle, 1928).

The most important works on Byzantine art are: N. P. Kondakov, *The History of Byzantine Art and Iconography according to Miniatures of Greek Manuscripts* (Odessa, 1876; Atlas, 1877; revised French edition, Paris, 1886–91, in two volumes); Bayet, *Byzantine Art* ("L'Art byzantin" in the *French History of Art*, compiled by A. Michel, vols. I and III, Paris, 1905 and 1908); Charles Diehl, *A Manual of Byzantine Art* (*Manuel d'art byzantin*, Paris, 1910; revised and enlarged edition in two volumes, 1925–26); O. M. Dalton, *Byzantine Art and Archeology* (Oxford, 1911); O. M. Dalton, *East Christian Art: A Survey of the Monuments* (Oxford, 1925; this work by Dalton contains a section on architecture); L. Bréhier, *L'Art Byzantin* (Paris, 1924); H. Peirce and R. Tyler, *L'Art Byzantin*, two vols. (Paris, 1934).

Among works on Byzantine chronology those of great importance are: H. L. Clinton, *Fasti Romani* (English edition, 2 vols., Oxford, 1845–50), bringing historical events down to the death of the Emperor Heraclius in 641 A.D.; Muralt, *Essay in Byzantine Chronography* (*Essai de chronographie byzantine*, 2 vols., St. Petersburg and Basel, 1855 and 1873) which embraces all of Byzantine history until 1453, but should be used with great caution; Otto Seeck, *Regesten der Kaiser und Päpste für die Jahre 311 bis 476 N. Chr. Vorarbeit zu einer Prosopographie der christlichen Kaiserzeit* (Stuttgart, 1919), is very useful, as is Franz Dölger, *Regesten der Kaiserurkunden des oströmischen Reiches* (Munich and Berlin, 1924–1932), in the *Corpus der griechischen Urkunden des Mittelalters und der neueren Zeit* (Akademien der Wissenschaften in München und Wien); and see also V. Grumel, *Les Régestes des Actes du Patriarcat de Constantinople* (Istanbul, 1932 and 1936), covering the years 381–1043. A new scientific study of Byzantine chronology is one of the real problems of contemporary Byzantology.

Bibliographical information of a general nature on other branches of Byzantine studies, such as numismatics, sigillography, and papyrology, may be found in Krumbacher's *History of Byzantine Literature*, as well as in the bibliographical sections of the special Byzantine periodicals.

It is only in the last thirty or forty years that the great importance and real interest of the Byzantine Age has been generally recognized in the field of papyrology. The earlier generations of the papyrologists, said one of the best modern scholars in this field, H. I. Bell, looked upon the Byzantine age with a rather stepmotherly eye, devoting their attention mainly to the Ptolemaic and Roman periods.[71]

71 Bell, "The Decay of a Civilization," *Journal of Egyptian Archaeology*, X (1924).

CHAPTER II: THE EMPIRE FROM THE TIME OF CONSTANTINE THE GREAT TO JUSTINIAN

CONSTANTINE AND CHRISTIANITY

THE cultural and religious crisis through which the Roman Empire was passing in the fourth century is one of the most significant events in the history of the world. The old pagan culture came into collision with Christianity, which received official recognition during the reign of Constantine at the beginning of the fourth century and was declared the dominant state religion by Theodosius the Great at the end of that same century. It might have seemed at first that these two clashing elements, representing two diametrically opposed points of view, would never find a basis for mutual agreement. But Christianity and pagan Hellenism did intermix gradually to form a Christian-Greco-Eastern culture subsequently known as Byzantine. Its center was the new capital of the Roman Empire, Constantinople.

The person who was chiefly responsible for the many changes in the empire was Constantine the Great. During his reign Christianity stepped for the first time on the firm ground of official recognition. From this time forward the old pagan empire gradually changed into a Christian empire.

The conversion of nations or states to Christianity has usually taken place during the early stage of their historical existence when the past has created no firmly established traditions, but merely some crude and primitive customs and forms of government. In such cases the conversion has caused no great crisis in the life of the people. But this was not characteristic of the Roman Empire in the fourth century. It already possessed an old world culture and had developed forms of government perfect for that time. It had a great past and an extensive body of ideas which had been assimilated by the population. This empire, changing in the fourth century into a Christian state, entered upon an era during which its past was contradicted, at times completely denied; this was bound to lead to an extremely acute and difficult crisis. Apparently the old pagan world, at least in the domain of religion, no longer satisfied national wants. New needs and new desires appeared, which only Christianity could satisfy.

When a moment of unusual importance is associated with some historical

43

personage who happens to play a leading part in it, a whole literature about him is created which aims to evaluate his significance for the given period and attempts to penetrate into the innermost regions of his spiritual life. For the fourth century this important personage was Constantine the Great.

Constantine was born at the city of Naissus (Nish at present). On the side of his father, Constantius Chlorus, Constantine belonged probably to an Illyrian family. His mother, Helena, was a Christian who later became St. Helena. She made a pilgrimage to Palestine where, according to tradition, she found the true cross on which Christ was crucified.[1] In 305, after Diocletian and Maximian had renounced their imperial rank according to the established agreement and had retired into private life, Galerius became the Augustus in the East, and Constantius, father of Constantine, assumed the title of Augustus in the West. In the following year Constantius died in Britain, and his legions proclaimed his son Constantine Augustus. At this time a revolt broke out in Rome. The mutinous population and the army rejected Galerius and proclaimed as emperor Maxentius, the son of the Maximian who had resigned his imperial power. The aged Maximian joined his son and again assumed the imperial title. A period of civil war followed, during which both Maximian and Galerius died. Constantine then formed an alliance with one of the new Augusti, Licinius, and defeated Maxentius in a decisive battle near Rome in 312. Maxentius was drowned in the Tiber while trying to flee from the enemy (at Saxa Rubra near the Milvian bridge across the Tiber). The two victorious emperors, Constantine and Licinius, met at Milan where, according to historical tradition, they proclaimed the famous Edict of Milan. The peaceful relations between the two emperors did not last very long, however. A struggle soon broke out between them, which ended in a complete victory for Constantine. Licinius was killed in 324 A.D., and Constantine became the sole ruler of the Roman Empire.

The two main events of Constantine's reign which were of paramount significance for the subsequent course of history were the official recognition of Christianity and the transfer of the capital from the shores of the Tiber to the shores of the Bosphorus, from ancient Rome to Constantinople, the "New Rome." In studying the position of Christianity in Constantine's time scholars have considered two problems in particular: the "conversion" of Constantine and the Edict of Milan.[1a]

[1] See, e.g., H. Vincent and F. M. Abel, *Jérusalem. Recherches de topographie, d'archéologie et d'histoire*, II, 202–3.

[1a] For general information on what has been recently done on the problems connected with Constantine the Great, see the very useful article of A. Piganiol, "L'état actuel de la question constantinienne 1930/49," *Historia*, I (1950), 82–96.

The conversion of Constantine

Historians and theologians have been primarily interested in the causes of Constantine's "conversion." Why did Constantine favor Christianity? Should his attitude be viewed only as an indication of his political wisdom? Did he see in Christianity merely a means of gaining his political aims? Or did he adopt Christianity because of his own inner conviction? Or, finally, was this "conversion" influenced by both political motives and a spiritual leaning toward Christianity?

The main difficulty in solving this problem lies in the contradictory information found in the sources. Constantine as depicted by the Christian bishop Eusebius does not in the least resemble Constantine created by the pen of the pagan writer Zosimus. Historians have found ample opportunity for answering this entangled question according to their own preconceived opinions. The French historian Boissier wrote in his *Fall of Paganism:*

> Unfortunately, when we deal with great people who play a leading part in history and try to study their lives and account for their actions, we are seldom satisfied with the most natural explanations. Since these men have the reputation of unusual people, we never want to believe that they acted just like other ordinary people. We search for hidden reasons behind their simplest actions; we attribute to them subtle considerations, depth of thought and perfidies of which they never dreamed. All this is true in the case of Constantine. A preconceived conviction became current that this skilful politician wanted to fool us; the more fervently he devoted himself to religious affairs and declared himself a true believer, the more definite were our attempts to prove that he was indifferent to these matters, that he was a skeptic, who in reality was not concerned about any religion and preferred that religion which could benefit him most.[2]

For a long time historical opinion was influenced greatly by the skeptical judgment of the well-known German historian, Jacob Burckhardt, expressed in his brilliant work, *The Time of Constantine the Great.* He represents Constantine as a statesman of genius, seized by high ambitions and a strong desire for power, a man who sacrificed everything to the fulfillment of his worldly aims. "Attempts are often made," wrote Burckhardt, "to penetrate into the religious conscience of Constantine and then draw a picture of the changes which presumably took place in his religious beliefs. All this is done in vain. For in the case of this man of genius, whose ambitions and thirst for power troubled every hour of his life, there could be no question of Christianity and paganism, of a conscious religiousness or non-religiousness; such a man is essentially irreligious [*unreligiös*]. . . . If he had stopped even for a moment to consider his real religious consciousness it would have been fatal." This "deadly egotist," having recognized that Christianity was bound

[2] I, 24–25.

to become a world force, made use of it precisely from that point of view. In this recognition, according to Burckhardt, lies Constantine's great merit. Yet Constantine gave very definite privileges to paganism as well as to Christianity. To look for any system in the actions of this inconsistent man would be all in vain; there was only chance. Constantine, "an egotist in a purple mantle, does and permits all that will increase his personal power." Burckhardt used as his main source Eusebius' *Life of Constantine,* disregarding the fact that this work is not authentic.[3] The judgment of Burckhardt, given briefly here, makes no allowance for any genuine religious feeling on the part of the Emperor.

Basing his arguments on different grounds, the German theologian Adolph Harnack, in *The Expansion of Christianity in the First Three Centuries,*[4] arrived at similar conclusions. After a study of the status of Christianity in individual provinces of the empire he admitted the impossibility of determining the exact number of Christians and concluded that though toward the fourth century they were numerous and influential in the empire, they did not constitute the majority of the population. But he remarked further:

Numerical strength and real influence need not coincide in every case; a small circle may exercise very powerful influence if its members are largely drawn from the leading classes, whilst a large number may represent quite an inferior amount of influence if it is recruited from the lower classes, or in the main from country districts. Christianity was a religion of towns and cities; the larger the town or city, the larger (even relatively) was the number of Christians. This lent it an extraordinary advantage. But alongside of this, Christianity had already penetrated deep into the country districts, throughout a large number of provinces; as we know definitely with regard to the majority of provinces in Asia Minor, and no less so as regards Armenia, Syria, Egypt, Palestine, and Northern Africa (with its country towns).

Dividing all the provinces of the empire into four categories according to the wider or narrower spread of Christianity, Harnack analyzed the position of Christianity in each category and concluded that the headquarters of the Christian church at the opening of the fourth century lay in Asia Minor. It is well known that for a number of years previous to his famous "flight" to Gaul, Constantine stayed at the court of Diocletian in Nicomedia. His impressions of Asia became apparent in Gaul, in the form of political considerations which led him to make his decisive resolve: he could benefit by the support of the firm and powerful Church and episcopate. It is idle to ask whether the Church would have gained her victory even apart from Constantine. Some Constantine or other would have come upon the scene. In

---

[3] J. Burckhardt, *Die Zeit Constantin's des Grossen* (3rd ed., 1898), 326, 369-70, 387, 407.
[4] Trans. into English by J. Moffatt, 1904; 4th ed., enlarged and revised, in original German, 1925.

any event, the victory of Christianity all over Asia Minor was achieved before Constantine came on the scene at all, and it was assured in other provinces. It required no special illumination and no celestial army chaplain to bring about what was already in existence. All that was needed was an acute and forceful statesman who had a vital interest in the religious situation. Such a man was Constantine. He was gifted, inasmuch as he clearly recognized and firmly grasped what was inevitable.[5]

It is quite apparent that Harnack viewed Constantine as a gifted statesman only. Naturally, even an approximate statistical estimate of the number of Christians at that period is out of the question. It is admitted by many of the best modern scholars, however, that paganism was still the dominant element in the state and society, while the Christians were decidedly in the minority. According to the calculations of Professor V. Bolotov, which coincided with the estimates of several other scholars, "it is probable that toward the time of Constantine the Christians constituted one-tenth of the entire population; perhaps even this figure needs to be reduced. Any claim that the number of Christians exceeded one-tenth is precarious."[6] At present there seems to be uniform agreement that the Christians were in the minority during the time of Constantine. If that is true, then the purely political theory in regard to Constantine's attitude toward Christianity must be dropped. A great statesman would not have allowed his wide political schemes to depend upon one-tenth of the population which at that time was taking no part in political affairs.

Duruy, the author of the *History of Rome and of the Roman People,* wrote somewhat under the influence of Burckhardt in evaluating Constantine's activities; he referred to "honest and calm deism, which was shaping Constantine's religion." According to Duruy, Constantine "very early became aware of the fact that Christianity in its fundamental dogmas corresponds with his own belief in one God."[7] But in spite of this, Duruy continued, political considerations were of primary importance to Constantine:

As Bonaparte sought to conciliate the Church and the Revolution, so Constantine proposed to have the old and the new religions live peaceably side by side, at the same time favoring the latter. He understood which way the world was moving, and aided its movement without precipitating it. It is to the honor of this Emperor that he made good his claim to the title assumed by him on his triumphal arch, *quietis custos* (custodian of peace). . . . We have sought to penetrate the deepest recesses of Constantine's mind, and have found there a policy of government rather than a religious conviction.[8]

[5] A. Harnack, *Die Mission und Ausbreitung des Christentums in den ersten drei Jahrhunderten* (2nd ed., 1906), II, 276–85; trans. Moffatt, 452–66.

[6] *Lectures on the History of the Ancient Church,* III, 29.

[7] *Histoire des Romains,* VII, 102; trans. M. M. Ripley, VII, 517.

[8] *Ibid.,* 86, 88, 519–20.

Duruy remarked elsewhere, however, that "the Constantine pictured by Eusebius often saw between earth and heaven things which no one else ever noticed."[9]

Two of the large number of publications which appeared in 1913 in connection with the celebration of the sixteenth centennial of the so-called Edict of Milan were: *Kaiser Constantin und die christliche Kirche,* written by E. Schwartz, and *Collected Papers (Gesammelte Studien),* edited by F. Dölger. Schwartz stated that Constantine, "with the diabolical perspicacity of a world-master, realized the importance which the alliance with the church had for the universal monarchy which he was planning to build, and he had the courage and energy to accomplish this union against all traditions of Caesarism."[10] E. Krebs, in the *Papers* edited by Dölger, wrote that all the steps taken by Constantine toward Christianity were but secondary causes of the acceleration of the victory of the church; the main cause lay in the supernatural power of Christianity itself.[11]

Opinions of various scholars on this subject differ widely. P. Batiffol defended the sincerity of Constantine's conversion,[12] and more recently J. Maurice, a well-known scholar in the field of numismatics of Constantine's time, attempted to substantiate the miraculous element in his conversion.[13] Boissier noted that for Constantine the statesman to deliver himself into the hands of the Christians, who constituted a minority and were of no political importance, would have meant a risky experiment; therefore, since he did not change his faith for political reasons, it must be admitted he did it through conviction.[14] F. Lot was inclined to accept the sincerity of Constantine's conversion.[15] E. Stein maintained a political reason. The greatest significance of Constantine's religious policy, he said, is the introduction of the Christian Church into the organism of the State, and he presumed that Constantine was influenced to some extent by the example of the Zoroastrian state church in Persia.[16] H. Grégoire wrote that policy always takes precedence over religion, particularly external policy.[17] A. Piganiol said that Constantine was a Christian without knowing it.[18]

[9] *Ibid.,* VI, 602.

[10] *Kaiser Constantin und die Christliche Kirche,* 2.

[11] "Konstantin der Grosse und seine Zeit," *Gesammelte Studien,* ed. F. Dölger, 2.

[12] *La Paix Constantinienne et le Catholicisme,* 256–59 (in connection with the discussion of O. Seeck on the same subject).

[13] *Constantin le Grand. L'Origine de la civilisation chrétienne,* 30–36.

[14] G. Boissier, *La Fin du paganisme; étude sur les dernières luttes religieuses en Occident au quatrième siècle,* I, 28; and H. Le-

clercq, "Constantin," *Dictionnaire d'archéologie chrétienne et de liturgie,* III (2), col. 2669.

[15] *La Fin du monde antique,* 32–38.

[16] *Geschichte des spätrömischen Reiches,* I, 146–47. On the works of Lot and Stein see an interesting comment by N. Baynes, *Journal of Roman Studies,* XVIII (1928), 220.

[17] "La 'conversion' de Constantin," *Revue de l'Université de Bruxelles,* XXXVI (1930–31), 264.

[18] *L'Empereur Constantin,* 75.

However, the "conversion" of Constantine, generally connected with his victory over Maxentius in 312, should not be considered as his real conversion to Christianity; he actually adopted the religion in the year he died. During his entire reign he remained the *pontifex maximus;* he never called Sunday anything but "the day of the sun" (*dies solis*); and the "invincible sun" (*sol invictus*) at that period usually meant the Persian God, Mithras, whose worship was spread throughout the Empire, in the East as well as in the West. At times this cult of the sun was a serious rival to Christianity. It is certain that Constantine was a supporter of the cult of the sun; such devotion was hereditary in his own family. In all probability his *sol invictus* was Apollo. Maurice observed that this solar religion assured him an immense popularity in the Empire.[19]

Recently some historians made an interesting attempt to represent Constantine as merely the continuator and executor of a policy initiated by others, rather than as the sole champion of Christianity. According to Grégoire, Licinius, before Constantine, originated a policy of tolerance toward Christianity. Schoenebeck, the German historian, questioned Grégoire's opinion; he considered Maxentius a champion of Christianity in his section of the Empire and the one who provided a model for Constantine to follow.[20]

Granting Constantine's leanings toward Christianity, his political schemes were nevertheless bound to have a dominating influence upon his attitude toward Christianity, which could be helpful to him in many ways. He understood that in the future Christianity would be the main unifying element among the races of the Empire. "He wanted to strengthen the unity of the Empire through a unity of the Church."[21]

The conversion of Constantine is usually connected with the famous story of the appearance of a luminous cross in the sky during the struggle between Constantine and Maxentius; an element of miracle is thus introduced as one of the causes of the conversion. However, the sources related to this event arouse much disagreement among historians. The earliest account of a miracle belongs to a Christian contemporary of Constantine, Lactantius, who, in his work *On the Death of the Persecutors* (*De mortibus persecutorum*), spoke only of the warning Constantine received in a dream to inscribe on his shields the likeness of the divine sign of Christ (*coeleste signum Dei*).[22] Lactantius said nothing about the heavenly vision which Constantine was supposed to have seen.

[19] *Numismatique constantinienne,* II, viii, xii, xx–xlviii.

[20] Grégoire, "La 'conversion' de Constantin," *Revue de l'Université de Bruxelles,* XXXVI (1930–31), 231–32. Hans von Schoenebeck, *Beiträge zur Religionspolitik des Maxentius und Constantin,* 1–5, 14, 22, 27.

[21] E. Trubezkoy, *Religious and Social Ideals of Western Christianity in the Fifth Century,* I, 2.

[22] *De mortibus persecutorum,* 44.

Another contemporary of Constantine, Eusebius of Caesarea, wrote in two of his works about the victory over Maxentius. In his earlier work, *The Ecclesiastical History,* Eusebius remarked only that Constantine, starting out to save Rome, "invoked in prayer the God of Heaven and his Word, Jesus Christ, the Savior of all."[23] Apparently nothing was said here about the dream, or about signs on the shields. Another work, *The Life of Constantine,* was written about twenty-five years after the victory over Maxentius and is usually, though probably wrongly, attributed to Eusebius. This work relates that the emperor himself told and confirmed by oath the famous story of how during his march on Maxentius he saw above the setting sun a luminous cross, with the words "By This Conquer!" (τούτῳ νίκα). He and his legions were awe-struck at this vision. The following night Christ came to Constantine in a dream, bearing the same sign, and bade him make a likeness of the cross and with it march against his enemies. As soon as dawn broke the Emperor communicated to his friends the marvelous dream and then, calling together artificers, he described to them the outlines of the vision he had seen and ordered them to execute the standard,[24] which is known as the labarum.[25] The labarum was a long cross formed like a spear. From the transverse bar hung a silk cloth, embroidered in gold and adorned with precious stones, bearing the images of Constantine and his two sons; at the peak of the cross was a golden wreath surrounding the monogram of Christ.[26] From the time of Constantine the labarum became the banner of the Byzantine Empire. Reference to the divine apparition and to armies marching in heaven, which were sent by God to aid Constantine in his struggle, may be found in the works of other writers. The information on this point is so confusing and contradictory that it cannot be properly evaluated from a historic point of view. Some writers go so far as to say that the miracle took place, not during the march against Maxentius, but before Constantine's departure from Gaul.

The so-called Edict of Milan

During the reign of Constantine the Great, Christianity received official permission to exist and develop. The first decree favoring Christianity was issued in 311 by Galerius, who had been one of its most ferocious persecutors.

---

[23] *Historia ecclesiastica,* ix, 9, 2. See *A Select Library of Nicene and Post-Nicene Fathers of the Christian Church,* ed. P. Schaff, H. Wace, and others, 2nd ser., I, 363.

[24] Eusebius, *Vita Constantini,* I, 38–40.

[25] The riddle of the origin of this word has been solved at last by H. Grégoire, "L'Etymologie de 'Labarum,'" *Byzantion,* IV (1929), 477–82: this is the Latin word *lau-*reum in the sense of *signum* or *vexillum.* Also see *ibid.,* XI (1937) and XIII (1939), 583. Grégoire's etymology of *labarum* was advanced by Valesius (H. Valois) in the seventeenth century.

[26] The image of the labarum may be seen on the coins of the epoch of Constantine. See, e.g., Maurice, *Numismatique constantinienne,* I, 2, and plate IX.

This decree gave pardon to the Christians for their former stubborn resistance to government orders aimed at turning them back to paganism, and announced their legal right to exist. It declared: "Christians may exist again, and may establish their meetings, yet so that they do nothing contrary to good order. Wherefore, in accordance with this indulgence of ours, they will be bound to pray their God for our good estate, that of the commonwealth, and their own."[27]

Two years later, after his victory over Maxentius and agreement with Licinius, Constantine met Licinius in Milan, where they issued the very interesting document incorrectly called the Edict of Milan. The original text of this document has not been preserved, but a Latin rescript of Licinius sent to the prefect of Nicomedia has been preserved by Lactantius. A Greek translation of the Latin original is given by Eusebius in his *Ecclesiastical History*.

According to this document the Christians and people of other religions were given full freedom to follow whatever faith they chose. All measures directed against the Christians were declared null and void:

From now on every one of those who have a common wish to observe the Christian worship may freely and unconditionally endeavor to observe the same without any annoyance or disquiet. These things we thought good to signify in the fullest manner to your Carefulness [i.e., the *praeses* of Bithynia], that you might know that we have given freely and unreservedly to the said Christians authority to practice their worship. And when you perceive that we have made this grant to the said Christians, your Devotion understands that to others also freedom for their own worship and observance is likewise left open and freely granted, as befits the quiet of our times, that every man may have freedom in the practice of whatever worship he has chosen, for it is not our will that aught be diminished from the honor of any worship.[28]

The document also ordered that private buildings and churches previously confiscated from Christians be restored to them freely and unreservedly.

In 1891 the German scholar O. Seeck advanced the theory that no Edict of Milan was ever issued. The only edict which ever appeared, he stated, was the edict of tolerance issued by Galerius in 311.[29] For a long time most historians failed to accept this view. In 1913 the sixteen-hundredth anniversary of the Edict of Milan was solemnly celebrated in many countries and a vast literature on the subject was produced. In reality, however, the edict quoted above, promulgated at Nicomedia by Licinius in 313, was a confirmation of Galerius' edict of 311, which apparently had not been satisfactorily carried out. The document which was issued at Milan in March, 313 by Constantine

---

[27] Lactantius, *De mortibus persecutorum*, 34, 4–5; Eusebius, *Historia ecclesiastica*, viii, 17, 9–10.

[28] Lactantius, *De mortibus persecutorum*, 48, 4–8; Eusebius, *Historia ecclesiastica*, x, 5, 6–9.

[29] "Das sogenannte Edikt von Mailand," *Zeitschrift für Kirchengeschichte*, XII (1891), 381–86. See also his *Geschichte des Untergangs der antiken Welt* (2nd ed., 1897), 495.

and Licinius was not an edict but a letter to the governors of the provinces in Asia Minor and in the East in general, explaining and directing how they should treat the Christians.[30]

The conclusion, on the basis of this edict, is that Constantine and Licinius gave Christianity the same rights enjoyed by other faiths, including paganism. It is premature to speak of the triumph of Christianity in Constantine's time. To Constantine, Christianity seemed compatible with paganism. The great significance of his act is that he not only allowed Christianity to exist but actually placed it under the protection of the government. This was an extremely significant moment in the history of early Christianity. The Edict of Nicomedia, however, gave no basis for the claim made by some historians that during the reign of Constantine Christianity was placed above all other religions, that the others were only tolerated,[31] and that the "Edict of Milan" proclaimed, not a policy of toleration, but the predominance of Christianity.[32] When the question of the dominance or the equal rights of Christianity is raised, the decision must be in favor of equal rights. Nevertheless, the significance of the Edict of Nicomedia is great. As one historian has said, "In reality, without any unnecessary exaggeration, the importance of the 'Edict of Milan' remains unquestionably great, for it was an act which ended the illegal position of the Christians in the empire and declared at the same time complete religious freedom, thus reducing paganism *de jure* from its former position of the only state religion to the rank of all other religions."[33]

The attitude of Constantine toward the Church

Constantine did more than merely grant equal rights to Christianity as a definite religious doctrine. The Christian clergy (*clerici*) were given all the privileges granted to the pagan priests. They were exempted from state taxa-

[30] I shall give a few examples of scholars' comments. J. Knipfing, "Das Angebliche 'Mailänder Edikt' von J. 313 im Lichte der neueren Forschung," *Zeitschrift für Kirchengeschichte*, XL (1922), 218: "The existence of the pretended edict of Milan is to be denied." N. Baynes, *Journal of Roman Studies*, XVIII (1928), 228: "We now know that there was no 'Edict of Milan.'" E. Caspar, *Geschichte des Papsttum*, I, 105, n. 3: "An 'Edict of Milan' must be deleted from history." Grégoire, "La 'conversion' de Constantin," *Revue de l'Université de Bruxelles*, XXXVI (1930–31), 263: "The edict of tolerance of March 313, issued by Constantine in Milan, is not an edict but a rescript or a letter to the governors of the provinces of Asia and the Orient."

[31] A. Lebedev, *The Epoch of Christian Persecutions* (3rd ed., 1904), 300–1.

[32] N. Grossu, "The Edict of Milan," *Publications of the Spiritual Academy of Kiev*, 1913, 29–30.

[33] A. Brilliantov, *Emperor Constantine the Great and the Edict of Milan*, 157. Cf. M. A. Huttman, *The Establishment of Christianity and the Proscription of Paganism*, 123: "While we may regard Constantine as the first Christian emperor and the first to put Christianity quite on a par with paganism, he was not the first to make Christianity a legal religion, for Galerius had done that in 311." Striking evidence of the free coexistence of Christianity and the pagan cults is given by coins. See Maurice, *Numismatique constantinienne*, II, iv.

tion and duties as well as from the officeholding which might divert them from the performance of their religious obligations (the right of immunity). Any man could bequeath his property to the Church, which thereby acquired the right of inheritance. Thus, simultaneously with the declaration of religious freedom, the Christian communities were recognized as legal juridical entities; from a legal point of view, Christianity was placed in an entirely new position.

Very important privileges were given to episcopal courts. Any man had the right, if his opponent agreed, to carry a civil suit to the episcopal court, even after proceedings in that suit had already been started in the civil court. Toward the end of Constantine's reign the authority of the episcopal courts was enlarged still more: (1) The decision of a bishop had to be accepted as final in cases concerning people of any age; (2) any civil case could be transferred to the episcopal court at any stage of the proceedings, even if the opposing side did not agree; (3) the decisions of the episcopal courts had to be sanctioned by civil judges. All these judicial privileges increased the authority of the bishops in society but at the same time added a heavy burden to their responsibilities and created many complications. The losing side, in view of the illegality of appealing a bishop's decision, which could not always be correct, often remained dissatisfied and irritated. Moreover, these additional duties introduced too many worldly interests into the lives of the bishops.

The Church at the same time was growing in material wealth through gifts from state resources of landed property or money and grain. Christians could not be forced to participate in pagan festivals. At the same time Christian influence brought about some mitigation in the punishment of criminals.

In addition to all this, Constantine's name is connected with the erection of many churches in all parts of his immense empire. The basilica of St. Peter and the basilica of the Lateran in Rome are ascribed to him. He was particularly interested in Palestine, where his mother, Helena, supposedly found the true cross. In Jerusalem, in the place where Christ was buried, the Church of the Holy Sepulchre was erected; on the Mount of Olives Constantine built the Church of the Ascension and at Bethlehem the Church of the Nativity. The new capital, Constantinople, and its suburbs were also adorned with many churches, the most prominent the Church of the Apostles and the Church of St. Irene; it is possible that Constantine laid the foundations of St. Sophia, which was completed by his successor, Constantius. Many churches were being constructed in other places during Constantine's reign, at Antioch, Nicomedia, and North Africa.[34]

[34] See, for example, on Nicomedia, J. Sölch, "Historisch-geographische Studien über bithynische Siedlungen. Nikomedia, Nizäa, Prusa," *Byzantinisch-neugriechische Jahrbücher,* I (1920), 267–68; on Africa, D. Gsell, *Les Monuments antiques de l'Algérie,* II, 239.

After the reign of Constantine three important Christian centers developed: the early Christian Rome, in Italy, although pagan sympathy and tradition continued to exist there for some time; Christian Constantinople, which very soon became a second Rome in the eyes of the Christians of the East; and, finally, Christian Jerusalem. After the destruction of Jerusalem by the Emperor Titus in 70 A.D., and the formation in its place of the Roman colony, Aelia Capitolina, during the reign of the Emperor Hadrian in the second century A.D., old Jerusalem had lost its significance, although it was the mother church of Christendom and the center of the first apostolic preaching. Christian Jerusalem was called to new life in the period of Constantine. Politically, Caesarea, and not Aelia, was the capital of that province. The churches built during this period in the three centers stood as symbols of the triumph of the Christian church on earth. This church soon became the state church. The new idea of the kingdom on earth was in direct contrast with the original conception of Christianity as a kingdom "not of this world," and of the rapidly approaching end of the world.[35]

Arianism and the Council of Nicaea

Because of the new conditions created in the early part of the fourth century, the Christian church experienced a period of intense activity which manifested itself particularly in the field of dogma. In the fourth century problems of dogma preoccupied not only individual men, as was the case in the third century with Tertullian or Origen, but also entire parties, consisting of large, well-organized groups of individuals.

In the fourth century councils became a common occurrence and they were considered the only effective means for settling debatable problems. But in this movement a new element is present in the relations between church and state, highly significant for the subsequent history of relations between the spiritual and the temporal powers. Beginning with Constantine the Great, the state took part in the religious disputes and directed them as it saw fit. In many cases, obviously, the interests of the state did not coincide with those of the church.

For many centuries the cultural center of the East was the Egyptian city Alexandria, where intellectual activity rushed forth in a powerful stream. Quite naturally, the new dogmatical movements originated in Alexandria which, according to Professor A. Spassky, "became the center of theological development in the East and attained in the Christian world the particular fame of a philosophical church which never tired of studying higher problems of religion and science."[36] Although it was an Alexandrian presbyter,

[35] V. Barthold, in the *Transactions of the Oriental College*, I (1925), 463.
[36] *The History of the Dogmatic Movements During the Period of the Ecumenical Councils*, 137.

Arius, who gave his name to the most significant "heretical" teaching of Constantine's period, the doctrine had originated in the second half of the third century in Antioch, Syria, where Lucian, one of the most learned men of the time, had founded an exegetical-theological school. This school, as A. Harnack said, "is the nursery of the Arian doctrine, and Lucian, its head, is the Arius before Arius."[37]

Arius advanced the idea that the Son of God was a created being. This idea formed the basis of the Arian heresy. Beyond the boundaries of Egypt, Eusebius, bishop of Caesarea, and Eusebius, bishop of Nicomedia, sided with Arius. Feeling ran high. Arius, in spite of the efforts of his adherents, was refused communion by Alexander, bishop of Alexandria. Local efforts to pacify the disturbances in the church did not succeed.

Constantine, who had just defeated Licinius and had become sole Emperor, arrived in 324 at Nicomedia, where he received numerous complaints from both the opponents and the adherents of Arius. Desiring above all to maintain religious peace in the Empire and not realizing the full significance of the dogmatic dispute, the Emperor sent a letter to Bishop Alexander and Arius, urging them to come to an agreement. He pointed out as an example the philosophers, who had their disputes yet lived in peace. He also indicated in his letter that it should not be difficult for them to come to an agreement, since both of them believed in Divine Providence and Jesus Christ. "Restore me then my quiet days, and untroubled nights, that the joy of undimmed light, the delight of a tranquil life, may henceforth be my portion," Constantine wrote in his letter.[38]

This letter was delivered to Alexandria by Bishop Hosius (Osius) of Cordova (Spain), whom Constantine held in great esteem. He delivered the letter, investigated the matter thoroughly, and explained to the Emperor on his return the full significance of the Arian movement. It was only then that Constantine decided to call a council.

The First Ecumenical Council was called together by imperial edicts in the Bithynian city, Nicaea. The exact number of people who came to this council is not known; the number of Nicaean Fathers is often estimated at 318.[39] Most of them were eastern bishops. The aged bishop of Rome sent in his place two presbyters. Among the matters taken up by the council the most important was the Arian dispute. The Emperor presided at the council and sometimes even led the discussions.

[37] *Lehrbuch der Dogmengeschichte* (4th ed., 1919), II, 187.

[38] Eusebius, *Vita Constantini*, II, 72; ed. I. von Heikel, *Eusebius Werke*, 71; *Nicene and Post-Nicene Fathers*, I, 518.

[39] Different figures were given by Batiffol, *La Paix constantinienne* (3rd ed., 1914), 321– 22. See E. Honigmann, "La liste originale des Pères de Nicee," *Byzantion*, XIV (1939), 17– 76. Honigmann, "The Original Lists of the Members of the Council of Nicaea, the Robber-Synod and the Council of Chalcedon," *Byzantion*, XVI, 1 (1944), 20–80.

The acts of the Council of Nicaea have not been preserved. Some doubt that any written records of the proceedings were kept at all. Information about the council comes from the writings of those who participated in it as well as from the accounts of historians.[40] The most enthusiastic and skillful opponent of Arius was the archdeacon of the Alexandrian church, Athanasius. After heated discussions the council condemned the heresy of Arius, and after introducing some corrections and additions, it adopted the Creed in which, contrary to the teachings of Arius, Jesus Christ was recognized as the Son of God, unbegotten, and consubstantial (of one essence) with His Father. The Nicene Creed was signed by many of the Arian bishops. The more persistent of them, including Arius himself, were subjected to exile and confinement. One of the best authorities on Arianism wrote: "Arianism had started with a vigour promising a great career, and in a few years seemed no unequal claimant for the supremacy of the East. But its strength collapsed the moment the council met, withered by the universal reprobation of the Christian world. . . . Arianism seemed hopelessly crushed when the council closed."[41] The solemn proclamation of the council announced to all communities the new state of harmony and peace within the church. Constantine wrote: "The devil will no longer have any power against us, since all that which he had malignantly devised for our destruction has been entirely overthrown from the foundations. The Splendor of Truth has dissipated at the command of God those dissensions, schisms, tumults, and so to speak, deadly poisons of discord."[42]

Reality did not fulfill Constantine's hopes. The Council of Nicaea, by its condemnation of Arianism, not only failed to put an end to Arian disputes, but caused many new similar movements and complications. In the attitude of Constantine himself there came to be a marked change in favor of the Arians. A few years after the council, Arius and his most fervent followers were recalled from exile.[43] But Arius' restoration was prevented by his sudden death. Their place in exile was taken by the leaders who supported the Nicene Creed. And while the Nicene creed was never officially repealed and condemned, it was purposely forgotten and partly replaced by other formulas.

It is very difficult to explain the origin of the strong opposition to the Nicene Council and the cause of the change in Constantine's attitude. Perhaps among the many varied explanations, such as court influences, intimate family rela-

[40] S. A. Wilkenhauser, "Zur Frage der Existenz von Nizänischen Synodalprotocolen," in *Gesammelte Studien,* ed. F. Dölger, 122–42.

[41] H. Gwatkin, *Studies on Arianism* (2nd ed., 1900), 1–2.

[42] Socratis, *Historia ecclesiastica,* I, 9. See *Nicene and Post-Nicene Fathers,* 2nd ser., II, 13.

[43] See two very interesting articles by N. Baynes in the *Journal of Egyptian Archaeology,* "Athanasiana," XI (1925), 58–69, and "Alexandria and Constantinople: A Study in Ecclesiastical Diplomacy," XII (1926), 149.

tions, and the like, attention should be called to this view: When Constantine first attempted to solve the Arian problem he was not acquainted with the religious situation in the East, where the prevailing sentiment was in favor of Arianism; the Emperor was educated in the West and influenced by his western leaders, such as Hosius, bishop of Cordova, and so he decided in favor of the Nicene Creed. This was in harmony with his views at the time but was not suitable to conditions in the East. When later Constantine realized that the Nicene decisions were contrary to the spirit of the church majority and conflicted with the desires of the masses in the East he assumed a more favorable attitude toward Arianism. During the last years of Constantine's reign Arianism penetrated even to the court and became every year more firmly established in the eastern part of the Empire. Many of the partisans of the Nicene Creed were deprived of their sees and sent into exile. The history of Arian predominance during that period is still not sufficiently clear because of the unsatisfactory condition of the sources.[44]

Constantine remained a pagan until the last year of his life. Only on his death bed was he baptized by Eusebius, bishop of Nicomedia, an Arian; but A. Spassky remarked that he died while directing that Athanasius, the famous opponent of Arius, be recalled.[45] Constantine made his sons Christian.

The foundation of Constantinople

The second event of primary importance during Constantine's reign, next to the recognition of Christianity, was the foundation of a new capital on the European shore of the Bosphorus, at its entrance to the Propontis (Sea of Marmora), on the site of the former Megarian colony, Byzantium (Βυζάντιον).

Long before Constantine the ancients had been fully aware of the strategic and commercial advantages of Byzantium, situated as it was on the border of Asia and Europe, commanding the entrance to two seas, the Black and the Mediterranean. It was also close to the main sources of the glorious ancient cultures. Judging by the sources, in the first half of the seventh century B.C. the Megarians had founded a colony named Chalcedon, on the Asiatic shore of the southern end of the Bosphorus, opposite the site where Constantinople was built in later years. A few years after the founding of this colony another party of Megarians established a colony on the European shore of the south end of the Bosphorus, Byzantium, named for the chief of the Megarian expedition, Byzas (Βύζας). The advantages of Byzantium over Chalcedon were well understood by the ancients. The Greek historian of the fifth century,

---

[44] See, e.g., Gwatkin's attempt to explain Constantine's new attitude towards Arianism by a reference to the conservatism of Asia, in *Studies on Arianism* (2nd ed., 1900), 57, 96.
[45] *Dogmatic Movements,* 258.

B.C., Herodotus (iv, 144) wrote that the Persian general, Megabazus, upon arriving at Byzantium, called the inhabitants of Chalcedon blind people, because, having a choice of sites for their city, they had chosen the worse of the two, disregarding the better site, where Byzantium was founded within a few years. Later literary tradition, including Strabo (vii, 6, c. 320) and the Roman historian, Tacitus (*Ann.* xii, 63), ascribes this statement of Megabazus, in a slightly modified form, to the Pythian Apollo who, in answer to the Megarian's question as to where they should build the city, answered that they should settle opposite the land of the blind. Byzantium played an important part during the epoch of the Greco-Persian Wars and the time of Philip of Macedon. The Greek historian of the second century B.C., Polybius, analyzed thoroughly the political and economic position of Byzantium. Recognizing the importance of trade relations between Greece and the cities along the Black Sea, he wrote that without the consent of the inhabitants of Byzantium not a single commercial vessel could enter or leave the Black Sea and that the Byzantians thus controlled all the indispensable products of the Pontus.[46]

After Rome ceased to be a republic the emperors more than once wanted to transfer the capital from republican-minded Rome to the East. According to the Roman historian, Suetonius (I, 79), Julius Caesar intended to move from Rome to Alexandria or to Ilion (former Troy). In the first centuries of the Christian era the emperors often deserted Rome for long periods during their extensive military campaigns and journeys through the empire. At the end of the second century Byzantium received a heavy blow: Septimius Severus, upon defeating his rival, Pescennius Niger, who was supported by Byzantium, submitted the city to a terrible sack and almost complete destruction. Meanwhile the East continued to attract the emperors. Diocletian (284–305) preferred to live in Asia Minor in the Bithynian city, Nicomedia, which he beautified with many magnificent new edifices.

When Constantine decided to create a new capital, he did not choose Byzantium at once. For a while, at least, he considered Naissus (Nish) where he was born, Sardica (Sofia), and Thessalonica. His attention turned particularly to Troy, the city of Aeneas, who according to tradition, had come to Latium in Italy and laid the foundations for the Roman state. The Emperor set out personally to the famous place, where he himself defined the limits of the future city. The gates had already been constructed when, as Sozomen, the Christian writer of the fifth century, related, one night God visited Constantine in a dream and induced him to look for a different site for his capital. After this Constantine's choice fell definitely upon Byzantium. Even a century later travelers sailing near the shores of Troy could see the unfinished structures begun by Constantine.[47]

[46] Polybius, *Historia*, IV, 38, 44.　　　　　[47] Sozomenis, *Historia ecclesiastica*, II, 3.

Byzantium, which had not yet fully recovered from the severe destruction caused by Septimius Severus, was at that time a mere village and occupied only part of the cape extending to the Sea of Marmora. In 324 A.D. Constantine decided upon the foundation of the new capital and in 325 the construction of the main buildings was begun.[48] Christian legend tells that the Emperor, with spear in his hand, was outlining the boundaries of the city when his courtiers, astonished by the wide dimensions planned for the capital, asked him, "How long, our Lord, will you keep going?" He answered, "I shall keep on until he who walks ahead of me will stop."[49] This was meant to indicate that some divine power was leading him. Laborers and materials for the construction work were gathered from everywhere. Pagan monuments of Rome, Athens, Alexandria, Ephesus, and Antioch were used in beautifying the new capital. Forty thousand Goth soldiers, the so-called *"foederati,"* participated in the construction of the new buildings. Many commercial and financial privileges were proclaimed for the new capital in order to attract a larger population. Toward the spring of 330 A.D. the work had progressed to such an extent that Constantine found it possible to dedicate the new capital officially. The dedication took place on May 11, 330 and was followed by celebrations and festivities which lasted for forty days. In this year Christian Constantinople was superimposed upon pagan Byzantium.[50]

Although it is difficult to estimate the size of the city in the time of Constantine, it is certain that it exceeded by far the extent of the former Byzantium. There are no precise figures for the population of Constantinople in the fourth century; a mere assumption is that it might have been more than 200,000.[51] For protection against the enemy from the land, Constantine built a wall extending from the Golden Horn to the Sea of Marmora.

In later years ancient Byzantium became the capital of a world empire and it was called the "City of Constantine" or Constantinople. The capital adopted the municipal system of Rome and was subdivided into fourteen districts or regions, two of which were outside the city walls. Of the monuments of Constantine's time almost none have survived to the present day. However, the Church of St. Irene, which was rebuilt twice during the time of Justinian

---

[48] See J. Maurice, *Les Origines de Constantinople,* 289–92; L. Bréhier, "Constantin et la fondation de Constantinople," *Revue historique,* CXIX (1915), 248; D. Lathoud, "La consécration et la dédicace de Constantinople," *Échos d'Orient,* XXIII (1924), 289–94. C. Emereau, "Notes sur les origines et la fondation de Constantinople," *Revue archéologique,* XXI (1925), 1–25. E. Gerland, "Byzanzion und die Gründung der Stadt Konstantinopel," *Byzantinisch-Neugriechische Jahrbücher,* X (1933), 93–105. R. Janin, *Constantinople Byzantine* (Paris, 1950), 27–37.

[49] Philostorgii, *Historia ecclesiastica,* II, 9: ed. J. Bidez, 20–21, and other sources.

[50] N. Baynes, *The Byzantine Empire,* 18.

[51] Stein, *Geschichte des spätrömischen Reiches,* I, 196. Lot, *La Fin du monde antique,* 81. A. Andreades is inclined to admit from 700 to 800,000: "De la population de Constantinople sous les empereurs byzantins," *Metron,* I (1920), 80. See also J. B. Bury, *A History of the Later Roman Empire* (2nd ed., 1931), I, 88.

the Great and Leo III, dates back to Constantine's time and is still preserved. The famous small serpent column from Delphi (fifth century B.C.), erected in commemoration of the battle of Plataea, transferred by Constantine to the new capital, and placed by him in the Hippodrome, is still there today, although it is somewhat damaged.

Constantine, with the insight of genius, appraised all the advantages of the position of the city, political as well as economic and cultural. Politically, Constantinople, or, as it was often called, the "New Rome," had exceptional advantages for resisting external enemies. It was inaccessible from the sea; on land it was protected by walls. Economically, Constantinople controlled the entire trade of the Black Sea with the Aegean and the Mediterranean seas and was thus destined to become the commercial intermediary between Europe and Asia. Finally, in the matter of culture, Constantinople had the great advantage of being situated close to the most important centers of Hellenistic culture, which under Christian influence resulted in a new Christian-Greco-Roman, or "Byzantine," culture. Th. I. Uspensky wrote:

> The choice of a site for the new capital, the construction of Constantinople, and the creation of a universal historical city is one of the indefeasible achievements of the political and administrative genius of Constantine. Not in the edict of religious toleration lies Constantine's great service to the world: if not he, then his immediate successors would have been forced to grant to Christianity its victorious position, and the delay would have done no harm to Christianity. But by his timely transfer of the world-capital to Constantinople he saved the ancient culture and created a favorable setting for the spread of Christianity.[52]

Following the period of Constantine the Great, Constantinople became the political, religious, economic, and cultural center of the Empire.[53]

REFORMS OF DIOCLETIAN AND CONSTANTINE

The reforms of Constantine and Diocletian were characterized by establishment of a strict centralization of power, introduction of a vast bureaucracy, and definite separation of civil and military power. These reforms were not new and unexpected. The Roman Empire began its trend toward centralization of power as early as the time of Augustus. Parallel with Roman absorption

[52] *History of the Byzantine Empire*, I, 60–62.

[53] We sometimes notice a tendency to diminish the importance of the founding of Constantinople. See Seeck, *Geschichte des Untergangs der antiken Welt* (2nd ed., 1921), III, 426–28. Stein follows him, *Geschichte des spätrömischen Reiches*, I, 2–3, 193 n. 6; also in *Gnomon*, IV (1928), 411–12; but cf. E. Stein, "Ein Kapital vom persischen und vom byzantinischen Staate," *Byzantinisch-Neugriechische Jahrbücher*, I (1920), 86. Lot declares that from any point of view the founding of Constantinople is a very great historical event but calls it "an enigma," adding that the city was born from a despot's caprice due to intense religious exaltation; see *La Fin du monde antique*, 39–40, 43.

of the new regions of the Hellenistic East, which developed through long centuries higher culture and older forms of government, especially in the provinces of Ptolemaic Egypt, there was a gradual borrowing from the living customs and Hellenistic ideals of these newly acquired lands. The distinguishing characteristic of the states built on the ruins of the empire of Alexander the Great of Macedon, Pergamon of the Attalids, Syria of the Seleucids, and Egypt of the Ptolemies, was the unlimited, deified power of the monarchs, manifested in particularly firm and definite forms in Egypt. To the Egyptian population Augustus, the conqueror of this territory, and his successors continued to be the same unlimited deified monarchs as the Ptolemies had been before them. This was quite the opposite of the Roman conception of the power of the first princeps, which was an attempt to effect a compromise between the republican institutions of Rome and the newly developing forms of governmental power. The political influences of the Hellenistic east, however, gradually changed the original extent of the power of the Roman principes, who very soon showed their preference for the East and its conceptions of imperial power. Suetonius said of the emperor of the first century, Caligula, that he was ready to accept the imperial crown—the diadem;[54] according to the sources, the emperor of the first half of the third century, Elagabalus, already wore the diadem in private;[55] and it is well known that the emperor of the second half of the third century, Aurelian, was the first one to wear the diadem publicly, while the inscriptions and coins call him "God" and "Lord" (*Deus Aurelianus, Imperator Deus et Dominus Aurelianus Augustus*).[56] It was Aurelian who established the autocratic form of government in the Roman Empire.

The process of development of the imperial power, primarily on the basis of Ptolemaic Egypt and later under the influence of Sassanid Persia, was almost completed by the fourth century. Diocletian and Constantine desired to effect the definite organization of the monarchy and for this purpose they simply replaced the Roman institutions with the customs and practices which predominated in the Hellenistic East and were already known in Rome, especially after the time of Aurelian.

The times of trouble and military anarchy of the third century greatly disturbed and disintegrated the internal organization of the empire. For a while Aurelian re-established its unity and for this achievement contemporary documents and inscriptions bestow upon him the name of the "restorer of the Empire" (*Restitutor Orbis*). But after his death a period of unrest followed.

[54] *Caligula*, 22: *nec multum afuit quin statim diadema sumeret.*

[55] Lampridius, *Antonini Heliogabali Vita,* 23, 5: *quo (diademate gemmato) et usus est domi.*

[56] L. Homo, *Essai sur le règne de l'empereur Aurelien*, 191–93.

It was then that Diocletian set himself the goal of directing the entire state organism along a normal and orderly path. As a matter of fact, however, he simply accomplished a great administrative reform. Nevertheless, both Diocletian and Constantine introduced administrative changes of such extreme importance to the internal organization of the Empire that they may be considered to be the true founders of a new type of monarchy created under the strong influence of the East.

Diocletian, who spent much of his time in Nicomedia and was on the whole favorably inclined toward the East, adopted many characteristics of the eastern monarchies. He was a true autocrat, an emperor-god who wore the imperial diadem. Oriental luxury and the complex ceremonial were introduced at his court. His subjects, when granted an audience, had to fall on their knees before they dared to lift their eyes to view their sovereign. Everything concerning the Emperor was considered sacred—his words, his court, his treasury; he himself was a sacred person. His court, which Constantine later transferred to Constantinople, absorbed large sums of money and became the center of numerous plots and intrigues which caused very serious complications in the later periods of Byzantine life. Thus autocracy in a form closely related to Oriental despotism was definitely established by Diocletian and became one of the distinguishing marks of government structure in the Byzantine Empire.

In order to systematize the administration of the vast Empire, which included many races, Diocletian introduced the system of tetrarchy, "of the power of four persons." The administrative power was divided between two Augusti, who had equal plenipotence. One of them was to live in the eastern, and the other in the western, part of the Empire; but both had to work in the interests of *one* Roman state. The Empire remained undivided; the appointment of two Augusti, however, indicated that the government recognized even in those days that a difference existed between the Greek East and the Latin West, and that the administration of both could not be entrusted to the same person. Each Augustus was to be assisted by a Caesar, who, in case of the death or retirement of the Augustus, became the Augustus and selected a new Caesar. This created a sort of artificial dynastic system which was supposed to do away with the conflicts and conspiracies originating in the ambitions of various competitors. This system was also meant to deprive the legions of their decisive influence at the time of the election of a new emperor. The first two Augusti were Diocletian and Maximian, and their Caesars were Galerius and Constantius Chlorus, the father of Constantine the Great. Diocletian retained his Asiatic provinces and Egypt, with headquarters at Nicomedia; Maximian kept Italy, Africa, and Spain, with headquarters at Mediolanum (Milan); Galerius kept the Balkan peninsula and the adjoining

Danubian provinces, with a center at Sirmium on the River Save (near present Mitrovitz); and Constantius Chlorus kept Gaul and Britain, with centers at Augusta Trevirorum (Trier, Treves) and Eburacum (York). All four rulers were considered as rulers of a single empire, and all government decrees were issued in the name of all four. Although theoretically the two Augusti were equal in their power, Diocletian, as an emperor, had a decided advantage. The Caesars were subjects of the Augusti. After a certain period of time the Augusti had to lay down their titles and transfer them to the Caesars. In fact Diocletian and Maximian did lay down their titles in 305 and retired to private life. Galerius and Constantius Chlorus became the Augusti. But the troubles which followed put an end to the artificial system of tetrarchy, which had already ceased to exist at the beginning of the fourth century.

Great changes in the provincial government were introduced by Diocletian. During his reign the distinction between senatorial and imperial provinces disappeared; all provinces were dependent directly upon the emperor. Formerly, the provinces being comparatively few and territorially very large, their governors had enormous power in their hands. This condition had created many dangerous situations for the central government; revolts were frequent and the governors of these large provinces, supported by their legions, were often serious pretenders to the imperial throne. Diocletian, wishing to do away with the political menace of the large provinces, decided to divide them into smaller units. The fifty-seven provinces in existence at the time of his ascension were divided into ninety-six new ones, perhaps more. Moreover, these provinces were placed under governors whose powers were purely civil. The exact number of smaller provinces created by Diocletian is not known because of the unsatisfactory information given by the sources. The main source on the provincial structure of the Empire at this time is the so-called *Notitia dignitatum,* an official list of court, civil, and military offices, which contains also a list of provinces. According to scholarly investigations, this undated document refers to the first half of the fifth century and hence includes the changes in provincial government introduced by the successors of Diocletian. The *Notitia dignitatum* numbers 120 provinces. Other lists, also of doubtful but earlier dates, give a smaller number of provinces.[57] Under Diocletian also a certain number of small new neighboring provinces were grouped together in a unit called a diocese under the control of an official whose powers were likewise purely civil. There were thirteen dioceses. In their extent the dioceses resembled the old provinces. Finally, in the course of the fourth century the dioceses in turn were grouped into four (at times

---

[57] Between 426 and 437. See J. B. Bury, "The *Notitia Dignitatum*," *Journal of Roman Studies,* X (1920), 153; Bury, "The Provincial List of Verona," *Journal of Roman Studies,* XIII (1923), 127–51.

three) vast units (prefectures) under praetorian prefects, the most important officials of that time. Since Constantine had shorn them of their military functions, they stood at the head of the whole civil administration and controlled both the diocesan and the provincial governors. Toward the end of the fourth century the Empire, for purposes of civil government, was divided into four great sections (prefectures): (1) *Gaul,* including Britain, Gaul, Spain, and the northwestern corner of Africa; (2) *Italy,* including Africa, Italy, the provinces between the Alps and the Danube, and the northwestern portion of the Balkan peninsula; (3) *Illyricum,* the smallest of the prefectures, which embraced the provinces of Dacia, Macedonia, and Greece;[58] and (4) *the East,* comprising the Asiatic territory, as well as Thrace in Europe in the north and Egypt in the south.

Many details of Diocletian's reforms are not yet available because of the lack of adequate sources on the subject. It should be stressed, however, that in order to secure his power still more against possible provincial complications, Diocletian strictly separated military authority from civil authority; from his time onward the provincial governors had only judicial and administrative functions. The provincial reforms of Diocletian affected Italy in particular; from the leading district she was transformed into a mere province. The administrative reforms resulted in the creation of a large number of new officials and a complex bureaucratic system with strict subjection of the lower officials to the higher. Constantine the Great further developed and enlarged in some respects the reorganization of the Empire begun by Diocletian.

Thus the chief features of Diocletian's and Constantine's reforms were the definite establishment of absolute monarchical power and a strict separation of military and civil functions, which led to the creation of a large and complex bureaucracy. During the Byzantine period the first feature was preserved; the second experienced a great change because of a constant tendency to concentrate military and civil authority in the same hands. The numerous offices and titles were retained in the Byzantine Empire. This bureaucratic system survived to the last years of the Empire, but many changes took place in the nature of the functions and the names of the dignitaries. Most of the titles were changed from Latin to Greek; many offices degenerated into mere

---

[58] On the complicated history of *Illyricum* at the close of the fourth century when *Illyricum* was sometimes united with the *Praefectura praetoris Italiae et Africae,* see E. Stein, "Untersuchungen zur spätrömischen Verwaltungsgeschichte," *Rheinisches Museum für Philologie,* N.S. LXXIV (1925), 347–54. See also the map in Stein, *Geschichte des spä-* *trömischen Reiches,* I: "Imperium Romanum anno 390 P. Ch. N." (three prefectures). See J.-R. Palanque, *Essai sur la préfecture du prétoire du Bas-Empire;* E. Stein's lengthy criticism in *Byzantion,* IX (1934), 327–53. Palanque's reply: "Sur la liste des préfets du prétoire du IVe siècle. Réponse à M. Ernest Stein," *Byzantion,* IX (1934), 703–13.

titles or ranks; and a number of new offices and dignities were created during subsequent periods.

A very important factor in the history of the Empire in the fourth century was the gradual immigration of the barbarians, that is, the Germans (Goths). A detailed examination of this question appears after the discussion of general conditions in the fourth century.

Constantine the Great died in 337 A.D. He has met with rare and deep appreciation from many different points of view. The Roman senate, according to the historian of the fourth century, Eutropius, enrolled Constantine among the gods;[59] history has named him "the Great"; and the church has proclaimed him a saint and equal of the Apostles (*Isoapostolic*). Modern historians have likened him to Peter of Russia[60] and Napoleon.[61]

Eusebius of Caesarea wrote his "Panegyric of Constantine" to glorify the triumph of Christianity in putting an end to the creations of Satan, the false gods, and destroying the pagan states:

> One God was proclaimed to all mankind. At the same time one universal power, the Roman Empire, arose and flourished. At the selfsame period, by the express appointment of the same God, two roots of blessing, the Roman Empire and the doctrine of Christian piety, sprang up together for the benefit of men. . . . Two mighty powers starting from the same point, the Roman Empire swayed by a single sovereign and the Christian religion, subdued and reconciled all these contending elements.[62]

EMPERORS AND SOCIETY FROM CONSTANTINE THE GREAT TO THE EARLY SIXTH CENTURY

After the death of Constantine his three sons, Constantine, Constantius, and Constans, all assumed the title of Augustus and divided among themselves the rule of the Empire. A struggle soon broke out among the three rulers, during which two of the brothers were killed, Constantine in the year 340 and Constans ten years later. Constantius thus became the sole master of the Empire and ruled until the year 361. He was childless, and after the death of his brothers he was greatly troubled by the question of a successor to the throne. His policy of extinguishing all the members of his family spared only two cousins, Gallus and Julian, whom he kept away from the capital.

---

[59] *Breviarium historiae Romanae*, X, 8.

[60] *A Dictionary of Christian Biography*, "Constantine I," 644: "If we compared Constantine with any great man of modern times it would rather be with Peter of Russia than with Napoleon." Cf. Duruy, *Histoire des Romains*, VII, 88; trans. Ripley, VII, 2, 519.

[61] Grégoire, "La 'conversion' de Constantin," *Revue de l'Université de Bruxelles*, XXXVI (1930–31), 270: "By a comparison which is justified on account of his military genius, Constantine was the Napoleon of the great religious revolution of the fourth century."

[62] *De laudibus Constantini*, XVI, 3–5; ed. Heikel, I, 249; *Nicene and Post-Nicene Fathers*, 2nd ser., I, 606.

Anxious, however, to secure the throne for his dynasty, he made Gallus Caesar. But the latter incurred the Emperor's suspicions and was assassinated in the year 354.

Such was the state of affairs when the brother of Gallus, Julian, was called to the court of Constantius, where he was appointed to the position of Caesar (355) and married Helena, a sister of Constantius. The short reign (361–63) of Julian, whose death ended the dynasty of Constantine the Great, was followed by the equally short rule of his successor, the former commander of the court guards, Jovian (363–64), who was elected Augustus by the army. After his death the new choice fell on Valentinian I (364–75) who, immediately after his own election, was forced by the demands of his soldiers to appoint his brother, Valens, as Augustus and co-ruler (364–78). Valentinian ruled the western part of the Empire and entrusted the eastern half to Valens. Valentinian was succeeded in the west by his son Gratian (375–83), while at the same time the army proclaimed as Augustus Valentinian II (375–92), the four-year-old stepbrother of Gratian. Following the death of Valens (378), Gratian appointed Theodosius to the high position of Augustus and commissioned him to rule over the eastern half of the Empire and a large part of Illyricum. Theodosius, originally from the far West (Spain), was the first emperor of the dynasty which occupied the throne until the death of Theodosius the Younger in 450 A.D.

After the death of Theodosius his sons Arcadius and Honorius divided the rule of the Empire; Arcadius ruled in the east and Honorius in the west. As in previous instances in the fourth century under the joint rule of Valens and Valentinian I, or of Theodosius, Gratian, and Valentinian II, when the division of power did not destroy the unity of the Empire, so under Arcadius and Honorius that unity was maintained: there were two rulers of one state. Contemporaries viewed the situation precisely in this light. The historian of the fifth century, Orosius, the author of the *History Against the Pagans,* wrote: "Arcadius and Honorius began to keep the common empire, having only divided their seats."[63]

Among the emperors who reigned in the eastern part of the Empire during the period 395–518, the first were from the lineage of Theodosius the Great: his son Arcadius (395–408), who married Eudoxia, the daughter of a German (Frankish) chief; and the son of Arcadius, Theodosius the Younger (408–50), whose wife Athenais was the daughter of an Athenian philosopher and was named Eudocia when she was baptized. After the death of Theodosius II his sister Pulcheria married Marcian of Thrace, who became emperor (450–57). Thus in 450 A.D. ended the male line of the Spanish dynasty of Theodosius. Following Marcian's death Leo I (457–74), born in Thrace or "Dacia in Illyricum," i.e. in the prefecture of Illyricum, a military tribune, was chosen

[63] *Historiae adversum paganos,* VII, 36, I.

emperor. Ariadne, the daughter of Leo I, who was married to the Isaurian Zeno, had a son Leo, who, after the death of his grandfather, became emperor (474) at the age of six. He died a few months later, after he had succeeded in appointing as co-emperor his father, Zeno, of the wild tribe of Isaurians, dwellers of the Taurus Mountains in Asia Minor. This Leo is known in history as Leo II the Younger. His father, Zeno, reigned from 474 to 491. When Zeno died his wife, Ariadne, married a silentiary,[64] the aged Anastasius, originally from Dyrrachium (Durazzo) in Illyria (present-day Albania). He was proclaimed emperor in 491 and ruled as Anastasius I until 518.

This list of emperors indicates that from the death of Constantine the Great until 518 A.D. the throne at Constantinople was occupied first by the Dardanian dynasty of Constantine, or rather the dynasty of his father, who probably belonged to some Romanized barbarian tribe of the Balkan peninsula; then by a number of Romans—Jovian and the family of Valentinian I; then by three members of the Spanish dynasty of Theodosius, followed by occasional emperors belonging to various tribes: Thracians, one Isaurian, and an Illyrian (perhaps an Albanian). During this entire period the throne was never occupied by a Greek.

Constantius (337–61)

The sons of Constantine ruled the Empire jointly after the death of their father. The hostility among the three brothers who had divided the rule of the Empire was further complicated by the hard struggle with the Persians and Germans which the Empire had to face at that time. The brothers were kept asunder not only by political differences, but by religious ones as well. While Constantine and Constans were adherents of the Nicene Creed, Constantius, continuing the development of the religious policy of the last years of his father's life, openly sided with the Arians. During the ensuing civil strife Constantine, and a few years later Constans, were slain. Constantius became the sole ruler of the Empire.

As an ardent adherent of Arianism, Constantius carried out a persistent Arian policy against paganism. One of the decrees of Constantius proclaimed: "Let there be an end to all superstition, and let the insanity of sacrifices be rooted out."[65] But the pagan temples outside the city walls still remained inviolable for the time being. A few years later a decree ordered the temples closed, forbade entrance to them, and prohibited the offering of sacrifices in all localities and cities of the Empire under the threat of death and confiscation of property. Still another edict stated that the penalty of death would be incurred by anyone who offered sacrifices or worshiped the gods.[66] When Constantius, wishing to celebrate the twentieth anniversary of his reign,

---

[64] The *silentiarii* were ushers at the doors of the imperial palace.

[65] *Codex Theodosianus*, XVI, 10, 2.
[66] *Ibid.*, 10, 3–6.

arrived for the first time at Rome, he inspected the numerous monuments under the guidance of the senators, who were still pagans, and ordered that the Altar of Victory, personifying for paganism all the former greatness of Rome, be removed from the Senate. This act made a very deep impression on the pagans, for they sensed that the last days of their existence were approaching. Under Constantius the immunities of the clergy were broadened; bishops were exempted from civil trial.

In spite of the harsh measures directed against paganism, it not only continued to exist side by side with Christianity, but at times it even found some protection from the government. Thus Constantius did not disperse the vestals and priests in Rome, and in one of his edicts he even ordered the election of a priest (*sacerdos*) for Africa. Until the end of his life Constantius bore the title of Pontifex Maximus. On the whole, however, paganism experienced a number of setbacks during his reign, while Christianity in its Arian interpretation advanced.

The persistent Arian policy of Constantius led to serious friction between him and the Nicaeans. Particularly persistent was he in his struggle with the famous leader of the Nicaeans, Athanasius of Alexandria. Constantius died in 361, and neither the Nicaeans nor the pagans could sincerely mourn the death of their emperor. The pagans rejoiced because the throne was to be occupied by Julian, an open adherent of paganism. The feelings of the Christian party in the matter of Constantius' death was expressed in the words of St. Jerome: "Our Lord awakes, he commands the tempest; the beast dies and tranquillity is restored."[67] Constantius died during the Persian campaign in Cilicia, but his body was transported to Constantinople. His pompous funeral took place in the presence of the new Emperor Julian in the Church of the Apostles, supposedly erected by Constantine the Great.[67a] The Senate enrolled the deceased emperor among the gods.

Julian the Apostate (361–63)

The name of Julian, the successor of Constantius, is closely connected with the last attempt to restore paganism in the Empire. Julian was an extremely interesting personality, who for a long time has attracted the attention of scholars and writers. The literature about him is very extensive. The writings of Julian himself, which have been preserved, give abundant material for judging his philosophy and actions. The chief aim of investigators in this field has been to understand and interpret this enthusiastic "Hellen" so firmly

[67] Hieronymi, *Altercatio Luciferiani et Orthodoxi*, 19; ed. J. P. Migne, *Patrologia Latina*, XXIII, 181.

[67a] This church is ascribed by some sources to Constantine the Great, by others to Constantius. G. Downey, "The Builder of the Original Church of the Apostles at Constantinople," *Dumbarton Oaks Papers*, VI (1951), 51–80.

convinced of the righteousness and success of his undertaking, the man who in the second half of the fourth century set out to restore and revive paganism and make it the basis of the religious life of the Empire.

Julian lost his parents at a very early age: his mother died a few months after his birth, his father died when he was only six years old. He received a very good education. His most influential tutor and general guide was Mardonius, a scholar of Greek literature and philosophy, who had taught Homer and Hesiod to Julian's mother. While Mardonius acquainted Julian with the masterpieces of classical literature, a Christian clergyman, probably Eusebius, bishop of Nicomedia and later of Constantinople, a convinced Arian, introduced him to the study of the Holy Scriptures. Thus, according to one historian,[68] Julian received two different kinds of education which lodged in him side by side without affecting each other. Julian was baptized in his early youth. In later years he recalled this event as a nightmare which he must try to forget.

The early years of Julian's life were spent in great fear and anxiety. Constantius, regarding him as a possible rival and suspecting him of having designs on the throne, sometimes kept him in provinces far from the capital as a kind of exile and sometimes called him to the capital in order to keep him under observation. Conscious of all the facts about the massacre of many members of his family who had been slain by the order of Constantius, Julian feared death constantly. Constantius forced him to spend a few years in Cappadocia, where he continued the study of ancient writers under the guidance of Mardonius, who accompanied him, and where he also became well acquainted with the Bible and the Gospels. Later Constantius transferred Julian first to Constantinople and then to Nicomedia, where he continued his studies and first exhibited his serious leanings toward paganism.

The greatest rhetorician of that period, Libanius, was lecturing in Nicomedia at that time. He was the true leader of Hellenism, who refused to study Latin, regarding it with disdain. He despised Christianity and attributed the solution of all problems to Hellenism. His enthusiasm for paganism knew no bounds. His lectures were exceedingly popular at Nicomedia. When Constantius decided to send Julian there, he foresaw perhaps what ineffaceable impression the enthusiastic lectures of Libanius might make upon the mind of the young student, and he forbade Julian to attend the lectures of the famous rhetorician. Julian did not formally disobey this imperial command, but he studied the writings of Libanius, discussed the lectures of the inspiring teacher with people who had heard them, and adopted the style and mode of his writings to such an extent that he was afterwards spoken of as a pupil of Libanius. It was also at Nicomedia that Julian studied with enthusiasm the

---

[68] P. Allard, *Julien l'Apostat*, I, 269.

occult neo-Platonic teachings, which at that time aimed to penetrate the
future through calling out, by means of certain conjuring formulas, not only
ordinary dead people but even the gods (theurgy). The learned philosopher
Maximus of Ephesus greatly influenced Julian on this subject.

After surviving the dangerous period of the death of his brother Gallus,
slain by the orders of Constantius, Julian was called to the court at Milan for
acquittal and then exiled to Athens. This city, famous for its great past, was
no more than a quiet provincial town where the famous pagan school stood
as a reminder of the former glorious days. Julian's stay at Athens was full of
deep interest. In later life in one of his letters he "recalled with great pleasure
the Attic discourses . . . the gardens and suburbs of Athens and its myrtles,
and the humble home of Socrates."[69] Many historians claim that it was during
this stay in Athens that Julian was initiated by an Eleusinian hierophant into
the ancient mysteries of Eleusis. This, according to Boissier, was a sort of
baptism of a newly converted soul.[70] Some scholars, however, have expressed
doubt about the Eleusinian conversion of Julian.[71]

In 355 Constantius appointed Julian to the position of Caesar, married him
to his sister, Helena, and sent him as head of the army to Gaul to aid in the
long and arduous campaign against the advancing Germans, who were devastating the land, ravaging the cities, and slaying the population. Julian
handled the difficult task of saving Gaul very successfully and defeated the
Germans near Argentoratum (later Strassburg). Julian's main seat in Gaul
was in Lutetia (Lutetia Parisiorum, later Paris). At that time it was a small
city on an island of the Seine, which still bears the name La Cité (Latin *civi-
tas*), a city which was connected with both banks of the river by means of
wooden bridges. On the left side of the Seine, already occupied by many
houses and gardens, was the palace erected probably by Constantius Chlorus;
the remains of it may still be seen near the Cluny Museum in Paris. Julian
chose this palace as his residence. He was fond of Lutetia, and in one of his
later works he recalled wintering in his "beloved Lutetia."[72]

Julian was successful in driving the Germans across the Rhine. "Three
times, while I was still Caesar," he wrote, "I crossed the Rhine; twenty thousand persons who were held as captives on the farther side of the Rhine I
demanded and received back. . . . I have now with the help of the gods
recovered all the towns, and by that time I had already recovered almost
forty."[73] Among his soldiers Julian inspired great love and admiration.

[69] Julian, *Quae supersunt omnia*, ed. F. C.
Hertlein, I, 328, 335; *The Works of the Emperor Julian*, ed. W. C. Wright, II, 217.
[70] *La Fin du Paganisme*, I, 98. See J.
Geffcken, *Kaiser Julianus*, 21–22: the author
had no doubt of Julian's initiation. See G. Negri, *Julian the Apostate*, trans. Duchess Litta-
Visconti-Arese, I, 47.
[71] Allard, *Julien*, I, 330. On the early years
of Julian, see N. H. Baynes, "The Early Life
of Julian the Apostate," *Journal of Hellenic
Studies*, XLV (1925), 251–54.
[72] Julian, *Opera*, II, 438; ed. Wright, II, 429.
[73] *Ibid.*, I, 361; ed. Wright, II, 273.

Constantius regarded the success of Julian with suspicion and envy. While undertaking the Persian campaign he demanded that Julian send him a re-inforcement of legions from Gaul. The Gallic soldiers revolted against this demand and, lifting Julian upon a shield, they proclaimed him Augustus. The new Augustus demanded that Constantius recognize the *fait accompli,* but Constantius refused to do so. A civil war seemed to be unavoidable. But just at this time Constantius died. In the year 361 Julian was recognized as Em-peror throughout the Empire. The adherents and favorites of Constantius were condemned to harsh punishments and persecution instigated by the new Emperor.

Julian for a long time had been an enthusiastic adherent of paganism, but he was forced to hide his religious convictions until the death of Constantius. Upon becoming the full master of the Empire, he set out to realize his sacred dream of restoring his favorite religion. During the first weeks following his ascent to the throne, Julian issued an edict in connection with his cherished plan. The historian Ammianus Marcellinus described this period:

Although from his earliest childhood, Julian inclined to the worship of the gods, and gradually, as he grew up, became more attached to it, yet he was influenced by many apprehensions which made him act in things relating to that subject as secretly as he could. But when his fears were terminated, and he found himself at liberty to do what he pleased, he then showed his secret inclinations, and by plain and positive decree ordered the temples to be opened, and victims to be brought to the altars for the worship of the gods.[74]

This edict was not unexpected, for everyone knew of Julian's leaning toward paganism. The joy of the pagans knew no bounds; to them the restoration of paganism meant not only religious freedom but religious victory as well.

At the time of Julian's accession there was not a single pagan temple in Constantinople itself, and since it was impossible to erect temples in a short period of time, it is very likely that Julian performed his solemn offering of sacrifices in the main basilica, originally intended for promenades and con-ferences and decorated since the time of Constantine the Great by the statue of Fortuna. According to the church historian Sozomen, the following in-cident took place in the basilica: An aged blind man led by a child approached the Emperor and publicly called him an irreligious man, an atheist, and an apostate. Julian answered to this: "Thou art blind, and the Galilean, thy God, will not cure thee." The aged man answered, "I thank God for my blindness, since it prevents me from beholding thy impiety." Julian passed by this daring remark without any comment and continued the offering of sacrifices.[75]

In proposing to revive paganism Julian was fully aware that it was im-

[74] *Res Gestae,* XXII, 5, 1–2.   [75] Sozomenis, *Historia ecclesiastica,* V, 4; Socratis, *Historia ecclesiastica,* III, 2.

possible to restore it in its former purely material form; it was necessary to reform and improve paganism in many respects in order to create an organization capable of combating the Christian church. For this purpose the Emperor decided to borrow many elements from the Christian organization, with which he was well acquainted. He organized the pagan priesthood along the principles of the hierarchy of the Christian church; the interiors of pagan temples were arranged according to the examples set by Christian temples; the pagans were to conduct discourses and read about the mysteries of Hellenic wisdom (this compared with the Christian sermons); singing was introduced into pagan services; an irreproachable mode of living was demanded of priests; orders were threatened with excommunication and penance. In other words, in order to revive and adapt the restored paganism, Julian turned to a source which he despised deeply.

The number of beasts sacrificed on the altars of the gods was so great that it called forth doubt and a certain amount of jest even among the pagans. The Emperor himself took an active part in the offering of sacrifices and did not abhor even the lowest menial labor connected with these performances. According to Libanius, he ran around the altar, kindled the fire, handled the knife, slaughtered the birds, and knew all about their entrails.[76] In connection with the unusually large number of animals used for sacrifices, the epigram once directed toward another emperor, the philosopher Marcus Aurelius, became current again: "The white cattle to Marcus Caesar, greeting! If you conquer there is an end of us."[77]

This apparent triumph of paganism was bound to affect strongly the position of the Christians in the Empire. At first it seemed that no serious menace was threatening Christianity. Julian invited the dissenting leaders of various religious parties and their congregations to the palace and announced that now, civil strifes having been ended, every man could follow his chosen religion without any impediment or fear. Thus a proclamation of religious tolerance was one of the first acts of Julian's independent rule. Sometimes the Christians would begin their disputes in the presence of Julian, and then the Emperor would say, in the words of Marcus Aurelius, "Listen to me, to whom the Alemanni and Franks have listened."[78] Soon after Julian's accession an edict recalled from exile all the bishops banished during the reign of Constantius, no matter what their religious convictions, and returned to them their confiscated property.

Because these religious leaders recalled from exile belonged to different religious parties and were irreconcilable in their opinions, they could not

---

[76] *Oratio,* "Εἰς Ἰουλιανὸν αὐτοκράτορα ὕπατον," XII, 82; ed. R. Förster, II, 38.

[77] Ammianus Marcellinus, *Res Gestae,* XXV, 4, 17.

[78] *Ibid.,* XXII, 5, 3–4.

live peacefully side by side and soon became involved in very serious disputes. Apparently Julian had counted on just such a development. Although seemingly he granted religious freedom to all, Julian was well acquainted with the psychology of the Christians and felt certain that discord would follow immediately; a disunited Christian church could not be a serious menace to paganism. At the same time Julian offered great privileges to those who would consent to renounce Christianity. There were many cases of such apostasy. St. Jerome called this policy of Julian "a gentle persecution, which attracted rather than forced people to join in the offering of sacrifices."[79]

Meanwhile, Christians were being gradually removed from civil and military posts and their places were being taken by pagans. The famous labarum of Constantine, which served as the standard in the army, was abolished, and the shining crosses on the soldiers' shields were replaced with pagan emblems.

But the act which dealt Christianity the most painful blow was Julian's school reform. The first edict concerned the appointment of professors in the leading cities of the Empire. The candidates were to be elected by the cities, but each choice was to be submitted to the Emperor for approval. The latter could thus refuse to sanction the election of any professor he disliked. Formerly the appointment of professors had been within the jurisdiction of the city. Still more important was a second decree, preserved in the letters of Julian. It stated that "all who profess to teach anything whatever must be men of upright character and must not harbor in their souls opinions irreconcilable with the spirit of the state."[80] By "the spirit of the state" this decree meant the paganistic tendencies of the Emperor himself. In this order Julian declared it absurd that men who expounded the works of Homer, Hesiod, Demosthenes, Herodotus, and other classical writers should dishonor the gods whom these writers honored:

I give them this choice, either not to teach what they do not think admirable, or, if they wish to teach, let them first really persuade their pupils that neither Homer nor Hesiod nor any of these writers whom they expound and have declared to be guilty of impiety, folly, and error in regard to the gods, is such as they declare. For since they make a livelihood and receive pay from the works of these writers, they thereby confess that they are most shamefully greedy of gain, and that, for the sake of a few drachmae, they would put up with anything. It is true that, until now, there were many excused for not attending the temples, and the terror that threatened on all sides absolved men for concealing the truest beliefs about the gods. But since the gods have granted us liberty, it seems to me absurd that men should teach what they do not believe to be sound. But if they believe that those whose interpreters they are and for whom they sit, so to speak, in the seat of the prophets, were wise men, let them be the first to emulate their piety toward the gods. If, how-

---

[79] Hieronymi *Chronicon, ad olympiad,* 285; ed. Migne, *Patrologia Latina,* XXVII, 691–92. [80] Julian, *Opera,* II, 544 ff., *Epistola 42;* ed. Wright, III, 117–23.

ever, they think that those writers were in error with respect to the most honored gods, let them betake themselves to the churches of the Galilaeans to expound Matthew and Luke. . . . Such is the general ordinance for religious and secular teachers. . . . Though indeed it might be proper to cure these, even against their will, as one cures the insane, except that we concede indulgence to all for this sort of disease. For we ought, I think, to teach, but not punish, the demented.[81]

Ammianus Marcellinus, a friend of Julian and his companion in military campaigns, explained briefly this edict: "[Julian] forbade the Christian masters of rhetorical grammar to teach unless they came over to the worship of the gods,"[82] in other words, unless they became pagans. On the basis of references made by some of the Christian writers of that time, some people suppose that Julian issued a second decree forbidding Christians not only to teach but even to study in the public schools. St. Augustine wrote: "And did not Julian, who forbade the Christians to teach and study the liberal arts (*liberales litteras*), persecute the church?"[83] But the text of the second decree has not been preserved; it is possible that such a decree was never issued, especially since the first decree forbidding the Christians to teach indirectly involved the restriction upon study. After the publication of the teaching edict the Christians could send their children only to grammar and rhetorical schools with pagan teaching, and from that the majority of Christians abstained because they feared that within one or two generations of pagan instruction Christian youth might return to paganism. On the other hand, if Christians were not to receive a general education, they were bound to become the intellectual inferiors of the pagans. Thus Julian's decree, even if there was only one, was of extreme significance to the Christians, since it greatly endangered the future of Christianity. Gibbon quite justly remarked: "The Christians were *directly* forbidden to teach; they were also *indirectly* forbidden to study, since they could not [morally] attend pagan schools."[84]

An overwhelmingly large majority of the Christian rhetoricians and grammarians preferred to abandon their profession rather than turn back to paganism. Even among the pagans the attitude toward Julian's edict varied. The pagan writer Ammianus Marcellinus wrote concerning this: "But Julian's forbidding masters of rhetoric and grammar to instruct Christians was a cruel action, and one deserving to be buried in everlasting silence."[85]

It is interesting to note how the Christians reacted to this edict. Some of them naïvely rejoiced that the Emperor made it more difficult for the faithful ones to study the pagan writers. In order to replace the forbidden pagan literature, the Christian writers of that period, especially Apollinarius the

[81] *Ibid.*
[82] *Res Gestae*, XXV, 4, 20.
[83] *De civitate Dei*, XVIII, 52.
[84] *History of the Decline and Fall of the*

Roman Empire, ed. J. B. Bury, chap. 23. See Negri, *Julian*, II, 411–14.
[85] *Res Gestae*, XXII, 10, 7.

Elder and Apollinarius the Younger, father and son, proposed to create for use in the school, a new literature of their own. With this aim in view, they translated the Psalms into forms similar to the odes of Pindar; the Pentateuch of Moses they rendered into hexameter; the Gospels were rewritten in the style of Plato's dialogues. Of this sudden literature, which could not possess any genuine artistic qualities, nothing has survived. It disappeared immediately after Julian's death, when his decree lost its significance.

In the summer of 362 Julian undertook a journey through the eastern provinces and stopped at Antioch, where the population, according to Julian himself, "have chosen atheism,"[86] that is, Christianity. The predominance of Christians explains why in the triumphal official reception accorded the Emperor at Antioch there was felt, and at times manifested, a certain coldness and even hatred. Julian's stay at Antioch is very significant, because it convinced him of the difficulty, and even impossibility, of restoring paganism. The Syrian capital remained completely unmoved by the religious sympathies of the visiting Emperor. Julian told the story of his visit in his satirical work, *Misopogon, or Beardhater*.[87] During an important pagan holiday he expected to see at the temple of Apollo, in the Antioch suburb of Daphne, a large crowd of people, beasts for sacrifice, libations, incense, and other attributes of a pagan festival. Upon entering the temple, he found, to his great astonishment, only one priest with a single goose for sacrifice. In Julian's version:

In the tenth month, according to your reckoning—Loos, I think you call it—there is a festival founded by your forefathers in honor of this god [Helios, Sun God, Apollo], and it was your duty to be zealous in visiting Daphne. Accordingly, I hastened thither from the temple of Zeus Kasios, thinking that at Daphne, if anywhere, I should enjoy the sight of your wealth and public spirit. And I imagined in my own mind the sort of procession it would be, like a man seeing visions in a dream, beasts for sacrifice, libations, choruses in honor of the god, incense, and the youths of your city there surrounding the shrine, their souls adorned with all holiness and themselves attired in white and splendid raiment. But when I entered the shrine I found there no incense, not so much as a cake, not a single beast for sacrifice. For the moment I was amazed and thought that I was still outside the shrine and that you were waiting the signal from me, doing me that honor because I am supreme pontiff. But when I began to inquire what sacrifice the city intended to offer to celebrate the annual festival in honor of the god, the priest answered, "I have brought with me from my own house a goose as an offering to the god, but the city this time has made no preparations."[88]

Thus Antioch failed to respond to this festival occasion. Similar occurrences provoked Julian's hatred against the Christians. His irritation grew still

---

[86] Julian, *Opera*, II, 461; ed. Wright, II, 475.

[87] Julian had a long beard, which was rather unusual for an emperor, and the population often laughed at him. On the *Miso-*

pogon, see Negri, *Julian*, II, 430–70 (most of the *Misopogon* is translated there).

[88] Julian, *Opera*, II, 467; ed. Wright, II, 487–89.

stronger when a sudden fire broke out in the temple of Daphne. Naturally the Christians were suspected of setting the temple on fire. Greatly provoked by this calamity, Julian ordered that the Christians should be punished by the closing of the main church of Antioch, which was immediately robbed of its treasures and subjected to sacrilege. This example was followed by many other cities. Conditions were becoming very grave. The Christians in their turn destroyed images of the gods. Some of the Christian leaders suffered martyrdom. Complete anarchy menaced the Empire.

In the spring of 363 Julian left Antioch and started out on his Persian campaign, during which he was mortally wounded by a spear. He died shortly after being transported to his tent. No one knew exactly who struck the fatal blow, and later many versions of this incident became current. Among them, of course, was the version that the Emperor was killed by the Christians. Christian historians, however, relate the well-known legend "that the Emperor threw a handful of his own blood [from his wound] into the air and exclaimed, 'Thou hast conquered, Oh, Galilaean!' "[89]

His army generals and close friends gathered about the dying Emperor in his tent and Julian addressed to them his farewell message. This speech is preserved in the writings of Ammianus Marcellinus (xxv, 3, 15–20). While anticipating his death with philosophical calmness, the Emperor presented a defense of his life and actions, and, feeling that his strength was ebbing, he expressed the hope that a good sovereign might be found to take his place. However, he did not name any successor. Noticing that all around him were weeping, he reproved them with still undiminished authority, saying that it was humiliating to mourn for an emperor who was just united to heaven and the stars. He died at midnight, on June 26, in the year 363, at the age of thirty-two. The famous rhetorician Libanius compared the death of Julian to the death of Socrates.[90]

The army proclaimed as emperor the head of the court guards, Jovian, a Christian of the Nicene Creed. Forced by the king of Persia, Jovian had to sign a peace treaty according to which Persia obtained several provinces on the eastern bank of the Tigris. The death of Julian was greeted with joy by the Christians. Christian writers named the Emperor "dragon," "Nebuchadnezzar," "Herod," and "monster." But he was buried in the Church of the Holy Apostles in a porphyry sarcophagus.

Julian left a number of writings which afford an opportunity to become

---

[89] Theodoreti, *Historia ecclesiastica*, III, 7; ed. L. Parmentier, 204–5, and other sources.
[90] *Oratio,* "Ἐπιτάφιος ἐπὶ Ἰουλιανῷ," XVIII, 272; ed. Förster, II, 355. See N. Baynes,

"The Death of Julian the Apostate in a Christian Legend," *Journal of Roman Studies,* XXVII (1937), 22–29.

more closely acquainted with him. The center of Julian's religious convictions was the cult of the sun, which was created under the direct influence of the cult of the bright god, Mithras, and the ideas of a degenerated Platonism. From his very early childhood Julian loved nature, especially the sky. In his discourse on the "King Sun,"[91] the main source for his religious philosophy, he wrote that from early childhood an extraordinary longing for the rays of the divine planet penetrated deep into his soul. And not only did he desire to gaze intently at the sun in the daytime, but on clear nights he would abandon all else without exception and give himself up to the beauties of the heavens. Absorbed in his meditations he would not hear those who spoke to him and would at times be unconscious of what he himself was doing. According to Julian's own rather obscure account of his religious theories, his religious philosophy reduced itself to a belief in the existence of three worlds in the form of three suns. The first sun is the supreme sun, the idea of all being, the spiritual intelligible ($\nu o\eta\tau\acute{o}s$) whole; it is the embodiment of absolute truth, the kingdom of supreme principles and first causes. The visible world and the visible sun, i.e. the material world, is only a reflection of the first world, but not an immediate reflection. Between these two worlds, the intelligible and the material, there lies the intellectual ($\nu o\epsilon\rho\acute{o}s$) world with a sun of its own. Thus, a triad of suns is formed: the intelligible or spiritual, the intellectual, and the material. The intellectual world is a reflection of the intelligible or spiritual and in its turn serves as an example for the material world, which is thus only a reflection of a reflection, an inferior reproduction of the absolute model. The supreme sun is too inaccessible for man. The sun of the physical is too material for deification. Therefore Julian concentrated all his attention on the central intellectual sun. He called it the "King Sun" and adored it.

In spite of his enthusiasm, Julian understood that the restoration of paganism involved many great difficulties. In one of his letters he wrote: "I need many to help me to raise up again what has fallen on evil days."[92] But Julian did not understand that the fallen paganism could not rise again because it was dead. His undertaking was doomed to failure. "His schemes," Boissier said, "could afford to be wrecked; the world had nothing to lose by their failure."[93] "This enthusiastic philhellen," Geffcken wrote, "is half Oriental and 'Frühbyzantiner.'"[94] Another biographer said, "The Emperor Julian seems as a fugitive and luminous apparition on the horizon beneath which had already disappeared the star of that Greece which to him was the Holy

[91] Julian, *Opera*, I, 168–69, *Oratio IV;* ed. Wright, I, 353–55.

[92] Julian, *Opera*, II, 520, *Epistola 21;* ed.

Wright, III, 17.

[93] *La Fin du Paganisme*, I, 142.

[94] *Kaiser Julianus*, 126.

Land of civilization, the mother of all that was good and beautiful in the world, of that Greece which, with filial and enthusiastic devotion, he called his only true country."⁹⁵

The Church and the State at the end of the fourth century

Theodosius the Great and the triumph of Christianity.—During the reign of Julian's successor, Jovian (363–64), a devoted follower of the Nicene Creed, Christianity was restored to its former position. This did not involve new persecutions of the pagans, however, whose fears on this account at the time of Jovian's succession proved to be unfounded. Jovian intended to establish throughout the empire the order which had existed before Julian. He proclaimed complete religious toleration. He allowed the pagans to reopen their temples and continue the offering of sacrifices. In spite of his adherence to the Nicene doctrines, he undertook no compulsory legislation against the other ecclesiastical parties. Christian exiles of different sects returned from banishment. The labarum appeared again in the army. Jovian reigned only a few months, but his activity in the realm of ecclesiastical affairs made a strong impression on his contemporaries. The Christian historian of the fifth century, Philostorgius, an Arian, remarked: "The Emperor Jovian restored the churches to their original uses, and set them free from all the vexatious persecutions inflicted on them by the Apostate."⁹⁶

Jovian died suddenly in February, 364. He was succeeded by two brothers, Valentinian I (364–75) and Valens (364–78), who divided the rule of the Empire: Valentinian became the ruler of the western half of the Empire and Valens was authorized to govern the eastern half. The brothers differed greatly in their religious outlook. Valentinian followed the Nicene Creed; Valens was an Arian. But the Nicene allegiance of Valentinian did not make him intolerant of other creeds, and during his reign religious freedom was more secure and complete than before. At the beginning of his rule he issued a decree granting each man "the freedom of worshiping whatever his conscience dictated to him."⁹⁷ Paganism was freely tolerated. Yet Valentinian showed that he was a Christian emperor by a number of measures; one of them restored all the privileges granted the clergy by Constantine the Great. Valens followed an entirely different policy. Upon declaring himself a follower of Arianism, he became intolerant of all other Christian doctrines, and though his persecutions were neither severe nor systematic, people in the

⁹⁵ Negri, *Julian,* II, 632. On Julian's financial policy see an interesting study by E. Condurachi, "La politique financière de l'Empereur Julien," *Bulletin de la section historique de l'Académie roumaine,* XXII, 2 (1941), 1–59.
⁹⁶ *Historia ecclesiastica,* VIII, 5; ed. Bidez, 106–7.
⁹⁷ *Codex Theodosianus,* IX, 16, 9.

eastern part of the Empire did go through a period of great fear and anxiety during his reign.

In the matter of external affairs the brothers were forced to face a very severe struggle with the Germans. Valens died prematurely during his campaign with the Goths. Valentinian was succeeded in the West by his sons, Gratian (375–83) and the child Valentinian II (375–92). After the death of Valens (378), Gratian appointed Theodosius as Augustus of the East and Illyricum.

Disregarding the young and irresolute Valentinian II, an Arian adherent, who played no important role in the internal policies of the Empire, the government under Gratian and Theodosius quite definitely forsook the policy of religious toleration and manifested a decided inclination toward the Nicene Creed. Of particular significance in this respect was the policy of the eastern ruler, Theodosius, surnamed "The Great" (379–95), whose name is always associated with the triumph of Christianity. His decided preference for his chosen creed left no room for toleration of paganism.

The family of Theodosius came into the foreground in the second half of the century as a result of the efforts of the father of the Emperor, also named Theodosius, who was one of the brilliant army generals in the West during the reign of Valentinian I. Before his appointment to the high rank of Augustus, Theodosius was only slightly interested in Christian ideas; but in the year following his appointment he was baptized in Thessalonica by the bishop of the city, Ascholius, a Nicaean.

Theodosius has to face two difficult problems: (1) the establishment of unity within the Empire which was being torn asunder by the dissenting religious parties; and (2) the defense of the Empire against the steady advance of the German barbarians, the Goths, who at the time of Theodosius threatened the very existence of the Empire.

During the reign of Valens, Arianism played the dominant role. After the death of Valens, especially in the absence of a ruler during the short period preceding the election of Theodosius, religious disputes burst forth once more and at times assumed very crude forms. These disquieting movements were felt particularly in Constantinople. The disputes on dogma, passing beyond the limited circle of the clergy, were taken up by all classes of society and were discussed even by the crowds in the streets. The problem of the nature of the Son of God had aroused heated discussions everywhere since the middle of the fourth century: in the cathedrals and churches, in the imperial palace, in the huts of hermits, in the squares and markets. Gregory, Bishop of Nyssa, wrote, not without sarcasm, of the prevailing conditions in the second half of the fourth century: "Everything is full of those who are speaking of unintelligible things—streets, markets, squares, crossroads. I ask how many oboli I have to pay; in answer they are philosophizing on the born or unborn; I wish to know the price of bread; one answers: 'The Father is greater than the Son'; I inquire whether my bath is ready; one says, 'The Son has been made out of nothing.' "[98]

By the time of the succession of Theodosius conditions had changed. Upon arriving in Constantinople, he proposed to the Arian bishop that he renounce Arianism and join the creed of Nicaea. The bishop, however, refused and preferred to leave the capital and live outside the city gates, where he continued to hold Arian meetings. All the churches in Constantinople were turned over to the Nicaeans.

Theodosius was confronted with the questions of regulating his relations with the heretics and pagans. Even in Constantine's time the Catholic (i.e. universal) church (*ecclesia catholica*) had been contrasted with the heretics (*haeretici*). During the reign of Theodosius the distinction between a Catholic and a heretic was definitely established by law: a Catholic was an adherent of the Nicene Creed; followers of other religious tendencies were heretics. The pagans (*pagani*) were considered in a separate category.

After Theodosius had openly declared himself a follower of the Nicene Creed, he began his long and obstinate struggle with the pagans and heretics, inflicting upon them penalties which grew more harsh as time went on. By the decree of 380 A.D. only those who believed in the trinity of Father, Son, and Holy Ghost, as preached by the apostolic writings and the Gospels, were considered Catholic Christians; all others, "the mad and insane" people, who adhered to "the infamy of heretic doctrine," had no right to call their meeting places churches and were subject to severe punishment.[99] According to one historian, this decree shows clearly that Theodosius "was the first of the emperors to regulate for his own sake, and not for the sake of the church, the body of Christian doctrine obligatory on his subjects."[100] Theodosius issued several other decrees which definitely forbade the heretics to hold assemblies, either public or private; the right to assemble was reserved solely for the followers of the Nicene symbol, who were to take over all the churches in the capital and throughout the Empire. The civil rights of the heretics were greatly curtailed, especially those concerned with bequests and inheritance.

For all his partisanship, Theodosius was anxious to establish peace and harmony in the Christian church. For this purpose he convoked a council in the year 381 at Constantinople, in which only members of the eastern church participated. This council is known as the Second Ecumenical Council. Of no other ecumenical council is the information so inadequate. The proceedings

---

[98] *Oratio de Deitate Filii et Spiritus Sancti;* ed. Migne, *Patrologia Graeca,* XLVI, 557.

[99] *Codex Theodosianus,* XVI, 1, 2.

[100] N. Tcherniavsky, *The Emperor Theodosius and His Religious Policy,* 188–89.

(acts) of this one are unknown. For a while it was not even recognized as an ecumenical council; only in the year 451, at a later ecumenical council, was it officially sanctioned as such. The chief religious question discussed at the Second Ecumenical Council was the heresy of Macedonius, a semi-Arian who attempted to prove that the Holy Spirit was created. The council condemned the heresy of Macedonius, as well as a number of other heresies based upon Arianism; confirmed the declaration of the Nicene symbol about the Father and Son, adding to it the part about the procession of the Holy Spirit from the Father; and adopted the teaching that the Holy Spirit is of one essence with the Father and the Son. Because information about this council is so inadequate, some western European scholars are dubious as to the creed of Constantinople, which became not only the dominant creed, but the official symbol as well, for all Christian denominations, in spite of their divergence as to dogma. Some scholars have affirmed that this new creed was not and could not be the work of the second council, that it was apocryphal; others have tried to prove that this symbol was composed either before or after the second council. The majority of scholars, however, especially the Russian church historians, agree that the creed of Constantinople was actually framed by the Fathers of the second council, though it became widespread only after the victory of orthodoxy at the Council of Chalcedon.

The second council also established the rank of patriarch of Constantinople in relation to the bishop of Rome. The third canon of the council declares: "The bishop of Constantinople shall rank next to the bishop of Rome, because Constantinople is New Rome," because of the political pre-eminence of the city as the capital of the Empire. Patriarchs of older eastern sees objected to this exaltation of the patriarch of Constantinople.

The see of Constantinople was at that time occupied by Gregory of Nazianzus, the Theologian, who had played a very important role in the capital during the first years of the reign of Theodosius. He was unable to manage the numerous dissenting parties represented at the council and was later forced to withdraw from his see, leave the council, and depart from Constantinople. His place was taken by Nectarius, a man of the world, one of limited theological attainments, who knew how to keep on good terms with the Emperor. Nectarius became president of the council, which in the summer of the year 381 closed its sessions.

In his attitude toward the clergy at large, that is, the Catholic (Nicene) clergy, Theodosius was rather generous. He conserved and occasionally enlarged the privileges granted by some of his predecessors to the bishops and clergy, privileges regarding personal duties, court responsibilities, and the like. He took care, however, that all these privileges should not interfere with the interests of the government. Thus by one edict Theodosius imposed upon the church extraordinary government duties (*extraordinaria munera*).[101] The availability of the church as a refuge for criminals prosecuted by the government was greatly limited because of the frequent abuses of this privilege. In particular, people indebted to the government were forbidden to seek protection in the temples against debt collectors, and the clergy were prohibited from hiding them.[102]

Theodosius aimed to be the sole arbiter of the church affairs of the Empire, and on the whole he succeeded in this aim. In one instance, however, he came into serious conflict with one of the distinguished leaders of the western church, Ambrose, bishop of Mediolanum (Milan). Theodosius and Ambrose held diametrically opposed views on the relation between the church and the state: the former stood for the supremacy of the state over the church; the latter assumed that the church could not be subject to the temporal power.

The conflict centered about the massacres which took place in Thessalonica. In this rich and populous city a large number of Germanic troops were quartered, headed by a very tactless and inefficient commander who did nothing to prevent the violence of the soldiers. The city population, provoked by the German outrages, finally revolted and killed the commanding officers as well as many soldiers. The infuriated Theodosius, well disposed toward the Germans, who ranked high in his army, smote the citizens of Thessalonica with a bloody massacre, showing no mercy to sex or age; the Emperor's orders were executed by the Germans. The horrible deed was not allowed to pass unpunished. Ambrose excommunicated Theodosius, who, in spite of his power, was forced publicly to acknowledge his own guilt and then to observe humbly the penance imposed by Ambrose, who forbade him to wear the imperial regalia during the period of atonement.

During the merciless struggle with the heretics, Theodosius took decisive steps also against the pagans. Several decrees prohibited the offering of sacrifices, the divinations by the entrails of animals, and the visiting of the temples. In effect this amounted to the closing of many pagan temples, some of which were then used for government purposes, while others were almost completely destroyed, and all their rich treasures of art demolished by the fanatical mob. The destruction of the famous temple of the god Serapis, the Serapeum, which still remained the center of pagan worship in the city of Alexandria, is particularly significant. The last decree against the pagans was issued by Theodosius in the year 392. It prohibited completely the offering of sacrifices, burning of incense, hanging of garlands, libations, divinations, and so forth. It also declared all who disobeyed these orders guilty of offense against the Emperor and religion and liable therefore to severe penalties. This decree

[101] *Codex Theodosianus*, XI, 16, 18.   [102] *Ibid.*, IX, 45, 1.

referred to the old religion as "a pagan superstition" (*gentilicia superstitio*).[103]

One historian called this edict of 392 "the funeral song of paganism."[104] It was the last step taken by Theodosius in his war upon paganism in the East.

In the western part of the Empire a particularly well-known episode during the struggle of Gratian, Valentinian II, and Theodosius against paganism centered about the removal of the Altar of Victory from the Roman Senate. The altar had been removed during Constantine's reign, but had been restored by Julian the Apostate. The senators, who were still half pagan, viewed this forced removal of the altar as the final ruin of the former greatness of Rome. The famous pagan orator, Symmachus, was sent to the Emperor with a plea for the restoration of the statue to the Senate. Th. I. Uspensky spoke of this plea as "the last song of a dying paganism which timidly and mournfully begged mercy of the young Emperor (Valentinian II) for the faith to which his ancestors were indebted for their fame, and Rome for its greatness."[105] Symmachus did not succeed in his mission. The year 393 saw the last celebration of the Olympic games. Among other monuments of antiquity, the statue of Zeus, the work of Phidias, was transferred from Olympia to Constantinople.

The religious policy of Theodosius, therefore, differed greatly from that of his predecessors, who, while favoring some one Christian party or paganism (as did Julian), still followed to some extent a policy of toleration toward other religious groups; *de jure* parity of religious beliefs still persisted. But by designating the Nicene Creed as the only legal creed, Theodosius laid an absolute veto upon all other tendencies in the Christian fold, as well as upon paganism. Theodosius was one of those emperors who believed that their authority should encompass the church and the religious life of their subjects. The aim of his life was to create a single Nicene church; but in spite of his efforts he did not succeed. Religious disputes, far from ceasing, only multiplied and spread very rapidly, making religious life in the fifth century most stormy and passionate. Over paganism Theodosius attained a complete triumph. Deprived of opportunity to avow its faith openly, paganism ceased to exist as an organized whole. There were still pagans, of course; only as separate families or individuals did they cherish secretly the beloved past of their dying religion. The famous pagan school at Athens, however, was not affected by any of the decrees of Theodosius; it continued its work of spreading the knowledge of classical literature among its students.

---

[103] *Ibid.*, XVI, 10, 12.
[104] G. Rauschen, *Jahrbücher der christ-* *lichen Kirche unter dem Kaiser Theodosius dem Grossen,* 376.
[105] *Byzantine Empire,* I, 140.

The German (Gothic) problem in the fourth century.—The Gothic question was the most acute problem of the Empire at the end of the fourth century. For reasons still unknown the Goths, who at the opening of the Christian era had occupied the southern shore of the Baltic Sea, migrated, probably in the latter part of the second century, further south into the territory of present-day Southern Russia. They reached as far as the shores of the Black Sea and settled in the districts between the Don and lower Danube. The Dniester divided the Goths into two tribes: the eastern Goths, otherwise named Ostrogoths or Ostgoths, and the western Goths, or Visigoths. Like all other Germanic tribes of this period, the Goths were barbarians. In their new territory they found themselves under very favorable cultural conditions. The northern shore of the Black Sea for a long time before the Christian era, had been covered with numerous rich Greek colonies, whose cultural level was very high. Their influence, as proved by archeological data, reached out far into the north, and was felt even centuries later during the early Christian period. At the time of the Gothic migration to the shores of the Black Sea, the Crimea was occupied by the rich and civilized kingdom of the Bosporus. Through contact with these old Greek colonies and the kingdom of the Bosporus, the Goths became acquainted with the classical culture of antiquity, while by continuous proximity to the Roman Empire in the Balkan peninsula they came in touch with more recent developments of civilization. As a result of these influences, the Goths, when later they appeared in western Europe, were culturally superior to all the other Germanic tribes, who entered their historical life in the West in a state of complete barbarism.

During the third century, following their settlement in the south near the Black Sea, the Goths directed their activities along two distinct paths: on the one hand, they were attracted by the sea and the possibilities it offered for raiding the cities along its shores; on the other hand, in the southwest, the Goths reached the borders of the Roman Empire on the Danube and came in contact with the Empire.

The Goths first gained a hold on the north shore of the Black Sea, and then, in the third century A.D., they invaded the greater part of the Crimea and the kingdom of the Bosporus. In the second half of the third century they undertook a number of piratical raids, using Bosporian vessels. They repeatedly robbed the rich coastland of the Caucasus and Asia Minor. By following the western shore of the Black Sea they entered the Danube, and crossing the sea, they even made their way, by the Bosphorus, to the Propontis (Sea of Marmora), and through the Hellespont (the Dardanelles) into the Archipelago. On these raids they pillaged Byzantium, Chrysopolis (on the Asiatic side facing Byzantium; Scutari at present), Cyzicus, Nicomedia, and the islands of the Archipelago. The Gothic pirates went even farther than this: they attacked Ephesus and Thessalonica, and upon reaching the Greek shores they sacked Argos, Corinth, and probably even Athens. Fortunately, however, the invaluable monuments of classical art in Athens were spared. The islands of Crete, Rhodes, and even far-removed Cyprus suffered from several Gothic attacks. Still, in all these expeditions by sea, they contented themselves with pillage, after which the Gothic vessels would return to their homes on the northern shores of the Black Sea. Many of these bands of sea robbers were either exterminated on foreign shores or captured by Roman troops.

Far more serious were the relations of the Goths with the Empire on land. Taking advantage of the troubles and anarchy in the Empire in the third century, the Goths began to cross the Danube and to enter the territory of the Empire as early as the first half of that century. The Emperor Gordian was forced to pay the Goths an annual tribute. But even this did not suffice. A short while later the Goths again entered Roman territory and swarmed over Macedonia and Thrace. The Emperor Decius marched against them and fell in battle in the year 251. In 269 Claudius succeeded in defeating the Goths near Naissus (Nish). Of the large number of prisoners captured during this battle, some were placed in the army, while others were made to settle as *coloni* in the depopulated Roman provinces. For this victory over the Goths, Claudius was surnamed "the Gothic" (Gothicus). But Aurelian, who had temporarily restored the Empire (270–75), was forced to give up Dacia to the barbarians and transfer its population to Moesia. In the fourth century there are frequent references to Goths in the army. According to the historian Jordanes, a division of Goths served the Romans faithfully during the reign of Maximian.[106] It is well known that the Goths in the army of Constantine the Great helped him in his struggle with Licinius. In Constantine's time the Visigoths agreed to furnish the Emperor with 40,000 soldiers. There was also a Gothic regiment in the army of Julian.

In the third century Christianity began to spread among the Goths; it was most probably imported by Christian prisoners captured in Asia Minor during the numerous sea raids. The Gothic Christians were even represented at the First Ecumenical Council in Nicaea by their bishop, Theophilus, one of the signers of the Nicene symbol. The true enlightener of the Goths on the Danube during the fourth century was Ulfila (Vulfila), supposed by some to be of Greek extraction, but born on Gothic soil. He had spent a number of years in Constantinople, where he was later ordained bishop by an Arian bishop. When he returned to the Goths he preached Christianity according to the Arian doctrine for a number of years. In order to introduce the Gospels among his people he invented a Gothic alphabet, based in part on the Greek

---

[106] *Getica*, XXI, 110; ed. T. Mommsen, 86.

letters, and translated the Bible into the Gothic language. The spread of Arian Christianity among the Goths was of great significance for their subsequent historical life, for during the period of their settlement on the territory of the Roman Empire it was this difference in religious convictions which prevented them from blending with the natives, who were followers of the Nicene Creed. The Crimean Goths remained orthodox.

Peaceful relations between the Goths and the Empire ceased in the year 376 with the advance of the Huns from Asia. They were a savage people of Mongolian race.[107] In their onward march to the West they defeated the east Goths, or Ostrogoths, and with them advanced farther, reaching the territory occupied by the Visigoths. The latter, exposed as a border nation to the full force of the attack and unable to offer adequate resistance to the Huns, whose horrible massacres did not even spare the Gothic women and children, had to force their way across the border into the territory of the Roman Empire. The sources relate that the Goths stood on the northern bank of the Danube and with loud lamentations entreated the Roman authorities to permit them to cross the river. The barbarians offered to settle in Thrace and Moesia and till the soil, and promised to furnish soldiers for the army and to obey all commands of the Emperor just as his subjects did. A delegation was sent to the Emperor to state the case of the Goths. The majority of high Roman officials and generals were in favor of accepting the Goths, for they recognized all the advantages the government would gain by doing so. First, they thought it a good way of rehabilitating the farming districts and the army. Then, too, the new subjects would defend the Empire, while the old inhabitants of the provinces could be exempted from military service by the payment of a money tax, which would greatly increase the government income. The men in favor of admitting the Goths were victorious, and the barbarians received official permission to cross the Danube. "Thus," said Fustel de Coulanges, "four or five hundred thousand barbarians, half of whom could handle arms, were admitted to the territory of the Empire."[108] Even if the foregoing figure be considered an exaggeration, the fact still remains that the number of Goths who settled in Moesia was very large. At first these barbarians led a very peaceful life, but gradually they became dissatisfied and irritated because of the peculations of the generals and officials, who made a practice of concealing part of the funds assigned for the needs of

---

[107] There are three principal theories of the origin of the Hunnic races: Mongolian, Turkish, and Finnish. See K. Inostrantzev, *Hunnu and Huns* (2nd ed., 1926), 103-9. This is a very valuable study. The Russian historian Ilovaisky (died in 1920) throughout his scholarly career argued with incomprehensible obsti-

nacy the Slavic origin of the Huns. A Russian writer about a hundred years ago (Weltman, in 1858) even called Attila "the autocrat of all Russia"!

[108] *Histoire des institutions politiques de l'ancienne France* (2nd ed., 1904), 408.

the settlers. Not only did these high officials feed the Goths poorly, but they also mistreated the men, insulted their wives, and offended their children. Many of the Goths were shipped across the sea and settled in Asia Minor. The complaints of the Goths received no attention, and the barbarians finally revolted. They obtained the help of Alans and Huns, forced their way into Thrace, and headed for Constantinople. At that time the Emperor Valens was carrying on a campaign with Persia, but when the news of the Gothic revolt reached him he left Antioch and arrived at Constantinople promptly. A decisive battle took place near Hadrianople in the year 378, in which Valens was killed and the Roman army completely defeated.

The road to the capital apparently lay open before the Goths, who overran the Balkan peninsula as far as the walls of Constantinople, but they evidently had no general plan of attacking the Empire. The successor of Valens, Theodosius, aided by his own Gothic troops, was successful in defeating and stopping their raids within the Empire. Thus, while one group of the Goths struggled against the Empire, the others were willing to serve in the imperial army and fight against men of their own tribe. The pagan historian of the fifth century, Zosimus, related that after the victory of Theodosius, "peace was established in Thrace, for the barbarians who had been there had perished."[109] The victory of the Goths at Hadrianople did not aid them in becoming established in any one province of the Empire.

On the other hand, from this time forward the Germans began to influence the life of the Empire in a peaceful manner. Theodosius was fully aware that he could not master the barbarians within the Empire by force, and he decided to follow a policy of peaceful relations with the Goths, to introduce among them certain elements of Roman culture, and to draw them into the ranks of the Roman army. In the course of time the army, whose duty it was to defend the Empire, was gradually transformed in its greater part into a German army, whose members often had to defend the Empire against their own kinsmen. Gothic influence was felt in higher military circles as well as in the administration. Many very responsible posts were in German hands. Theodosius, in following his Germanophile policy, failed to realize that a free growth of Germanism might menace the Empire's existence. He showed particular lack of wisdom in placing the defense of the Empire in the hands of the Germans. In due time the Goths assimilated the Roman art of warfare, Roman tactics and methods of combat, and were rapidly growing into a powerful force which could at any moment challenge the Empire. The native Greco-Roman population, forced into the background, watched the growth of German power with restlessness. An anti-German movement grew up, which might have led to very grave crises in the life of the Empire.

[109] *Historia nova*, IV, 25, 4; ed. L. Mendelssohn, 181.

Theodosius died in the year 395 at Milan; his embalmed body was transferred to Constantinople and buried in the Temple of the Apostles. For his great service to Christianity in its struggle with paganism Theodosius was surnamed "the Great." His too young and weak sons, Arcadius and Honorius, were proclaimed the rulers of the Empire; Arcadius became the emperor of the eastern part, and Honorius ruled in the West.

Theodosius did not succeed in solving the main problems of his period. The Second Ecumenical Council, by proclaiming the Nicene Creed the dominant form of Christianity, failed to achieve church unity. Arianism in its various manifestations continued to exist and in its further development caused new religious movements, which in the fifth century involved not only the religious interests of the Empire, but also connected with them, the social life of that period. This was particularly true of the eastern provinces, Syria and Egypt, where the new religious developments caused extremely significant consequences. In fact, Theodosius was forced during the later years of his life to recede from his original firm Nicene position. He was compelled to make concessions to the Arian Germans, who at the time formed the overwhelming majority in the army. Thus, in the religious field as well as in administrative and military realms, the Goths exerted great influence. The main center of their power was the capital itself, the Balkan peninsula, and part of Asia Minor. The eastern provinces, Syria, Palestine, and Egypt, did not feel the Gothic power to any considerable extent. Thus on religious as on racial grounds, the dissatisfaction of the native population was growing very strong. In short, Theodosius failed to solve the two significant problems of his reign: the creation of a unique and uniform church and the establishment of harmonious relations with the barbarians. These two exceedingly complicated problems remained for his successors.

Nationality and religion in the fifth century.—This epoch is of particularly great importance for the ways in which the main national and religious problems were met. The national problem was concerned with the discord among the different nationalities within the Empire as well as the conflicts with the tribes attacking it from without.

Hellenism, it would seem, should have been the main force unifying the varied population of the eastern part of the Roman Empire, but in reality it was not. Hellenistic influence could be found in the East as far as the Euphrates and in Egypt as early as the time of Alexander of Macedon and his successors. Alexander himself considered colonization one of the best means for transplanting Hellenism; it is said that he alone founded more than seventy cities in the East. His successors continued this policy of colonization. The areas to which Hellenism had spread to some extent reached as far as Armenia in the north and the Red Sea in the south and as far as Persia and

Mesopotamia in the East. Beyond these provinces Hellenism did not reach. The main center of Hellenistic culture became the Egyptian city, Alexandria. All along the coast of the Mediterranean Sea, in Asia Minor, Syria, and Egypt, Hellenic culture predominated. Of these three sections, Asia Minor was perhaps the most Hellenized; its coast had been occupied for a long period of time by Greek colonies, and their influence gradually, though not easily, penetrated into the interior of the region.

Hellenization of Syria, where Hellenic culture reached only the higher educated class, was much weaker. The mass of the population, unacquainted with the Greek language, continued to speak their own native tongues, Syriac or Arabic. One learned orientalist wrote: "If even in such a world-city as Antioch the common man still spoke Aramaic, i.e., Syriac, then one may safely suppose that inside the province the Greek language was not the language of the educated class, but only the language of those who made a special study of it."[110] The *Syrian-Roman Lawbook* of the fifth century was striking proof of the fact that the native Syriac language was widely used in the East.[111] The oldest Syriac manuscript of this lawbook now in existence was written in the early part of the sixth century, before Justinian's time. This Syriac text, which was probably written in northeastern Syria, is a translation from the Greek. The Greek original has not yet been discovered, but on the basis of some existing data it must have been written some time during the seventies of the fifth century. In any case the Syriac translation appeared almost immediately after the publication of the Greek original. In addition to the Syriac text there exist also Arabic and Armenian versions of the lawbook, which indicate that the book was very probably of church origin, since it analyzes with much detail the items of marriage and inheritance laws and boldly advances the privileges of the clergy. The fact that it was very widely distributed and applied to the living problems in the East, in the territory between Armenia and Egypt, as evidenced by the numerous versions of the lawbook as well as by the borrowings from it found in many Syriac and Arabic works of the thirteenth and fourteenth centuries, shows the continuing predominance of the native tongues. Later, when Justinian's legislation became officially obligatory upon the whole Empire, his code proved to be too bulky and difficult of comprehension for the eastern provinces, so that in actual practice they continued to use the Syriac lawbook as a substitute for the codex. In the seventh century, following the Moslem conquest of the eastern provinces, the same Syriac lawbook was in wide use even under the Moslem

[110] Th. Nöldeke, "Ueber Mommsen's Darstellung der römischen Herrschaft und römischen Politik im Orient," *Zeitschrift der morgenländischen Gesellschaft,* XXXIX (1885), 334.

[111] K. G. Bruns and E. Sachau, *Syrisch-Römisches Rechtsbuch aus dem fünften Jahrhundert.*

domination. The fact that this lawbook was translated into Syriac as early as the second half of the fifth century indicates clearly that the mass of the people were still unacquainted with Greek or Latin and clung strongly to the native Syriac tongue.

In Egypt also, in spite of the proximity of Alexandria, the very center of world culture, Hellenism spread among the higher class only, among the people prominent in the social and religious life of the province. The mass of the people continued to speak their native Egyptian (Coptic) language.

The central government found it difficult to manage the affairs of the eastern provinces, not only because of the racially varied composition of the population, but also because the great majority of the population of Syria and Egypt and a certain part of eastern Asia Minor firmly held to Arianism with its subsequent ramifications. The complex racial problem became further complicated in the fifth century by important new developments in the religious life of these provinces.

In the western provinces of the Eastern Empire, that is in the Balkan peninsula, in the capital, and the western part of Asia Minor, the important problem of this period was that of Germanic power, which threatened the very existence of the Empire. After this problem was settled favorably for the government in the middle of the fifth century it seemed for a while that the savage Isaurians would occupy in the capital a commanding position similar to that of the Goths. In the East the struggle with the Persians continued, while in the northern part of the Balkan peninsula the Bulgarians, a people of Hunnic (Turkish) origin,[112] and the Slavs began their devastating attacks.

Arcadius (395–408)

Arcadius was only seventeen when he ascended the throne. He possessed neither the experience nor the force of will necessary for his high position, and he soon found himself completely overruled by his favorites, who directed the affairs of the Empire in a manner satisfactory to their own interests and the interests of their respective parties. The first influential favorite was Rufinus, appointed during Theodosius' lifetime as general guide of Arcadius. Rufinus was soon murdered and two years later the eunuch Eutropius exerted the greatest influence upon the Emperor. The rapid rise of this new favorite was due primarily to his success in arranging the marriage of Arcadius and Eudoxia, the daughter of a Frank who served as an officer in the Roman army. Honorius, the younger brother of Arcadius, had been placed by his father

---

[112] On the origin of the earlier Bulgarians see V. Zlatarsky, *A History of the State of Bulgaria*, I, 23 ff. L. Niederle, *Manuel de l'antiquité slave*, I, 100; J. Moravcsik, "Zur Geschichte der Onoguren," *Ungarische Jahrbücher*, X (1930), 68–69.

under the guidance of the gifted chief, Stilicho, a true example of a Romanized Germanic barbarian, who had rendered great service to the Empire during its struggle with his own people.

The settlement of the Gothic problem.—The central issue for the government in the time of Arcadius was the Germanic problem. The Visigoths, who had settled during an earlier period in the northern part of the Balkan peninsula, were now headed by a new and ambitious chief, Alaric Balta. At the beginning of the reign of Arcadius, Alaric set out with his people for Moesia, Thrace, and Macedonia, threatening even the capital. The diplomatic intervention of Rufinus brought about a change in Alaric's original plan for attacking Constantinople. The attention of the Goths was directed to Greece. Alaric crossed Thessaly and advanced into Middle Greece by way of Thermopylae.

The population of Greece at that period was almost purely Greek and, on the whole, almost the same as Pausanias and Plutarch had known it. According to Gregorovius, the old language, religion, customs, and laws of the forefathers remained almost unchanged in the towns and villages. And in spite of the fact that Christianity had been officially pronounced the dominant religion, and the worship of the gods, condemned and forbidden by the state, was doomed to die out, ancient Greece still bore the spiritual and artistic impress of paganism, mainly because of the preservation of the monuments of antiquity.[113]

In their march through Greece the Goths pillaged and devastated Boeotia and Attica. The Athenian harbor, Peiraeus, was in their hands; fortunately they spared Athens. The pagan historian of the fifth century, Zosimus, narrated the legend of how Alaric, upon surrounding the Athenian walls with his army, beheld the goddess Athena Promachos in armor and the Trojan hero Achilles standing before the wall. So greatly astonished was Alaric by this apparition that he abandoned the idea of attacking Athens.[114] The Peloponnesus suffered greatly from the Gothic invasion, for the Visigoths sacked Corinth, Argos, Sparta, and several other cities. Stilicho undertook to defend Greece and landed with his troops in the Gulf of Corinth on the Isthmus, thus cutting off Alaric's way back through Middle Greece. Alaric then pushed his way to the north into Epirus with great effort and against many difficulties. The Emperor Arcadius apparently was not ashamed to honor the man who had devastated the Greek provinces of the Empire with the military title of Master of Soldiers in Illyricum (*Magister militum per Illyricum*). After this Alaric ceased to threaten the eastern part of the Empire and directed his main attention to Italy.

[113] Gregorovius, *Geschichte der Stadt Athen*, I, 35.   [114] Zosimus, V, 6; ed. Mendelssohn, 222–23.

In addition to the menace of the Goths in the Balkan peninsula and in Greece, the prevailing Gothic influence since the time of Theodosius the Great was felt particularly in the capital, where the most responsible army posts and many of the important administrative positions were in Germanic hands.

When Arcadius ascended the throne the most influential party in the capital was the Germanic party, headed by one of the outstanding generals of the imperial army, the Goth Gaïnas. About him were gathered soldiers of Gothic origin and representatives of the local pro-Germanic movement. The weakness of this party lay in the fact that the majority of the Goths were Arians. Second in strength, during the first years of Arcadius' reign, was the party of the powerful eunuch, the favorite Eutropius. He was supported by various ambitious flatterers who were interested in him only because he was able to help them to promote their greedy personal interests. Gaïnas and Eutropius could not live side by side in peace, since they were competing for power. Besides these two political parties, historians speak of a third party, hostile to the Germans as well as to Eutropius; its membership included senators, ministers, and the majority of the clergy. This party represented the nationalist and religious ideology in opposition to the growing foreign and barbaric influence. This movement, naturally, refused to lend its support to the coarse and grasping Eutropius. The party's main leader was the city prefect, Aurelian.[115]

Many people of the time were aware of the menace of Germanic dominance, and ultimately the government itself became conscious of it. A remarkable document has been preserved which describes vividly the reaction of certain social groups to the Germanic question. This document is the address of Synesius on "The Emperor's Power," or, as it is sometimes translated, "Concerning the Office of King," which was presented, or perhaps even read, to Arcadius. Synesius, a native of the North African city of Cyrene, was an educated neo-Platonist who adopted Christianity. In the year 399 A.D. he set out for Constantinople to petition the Emperor for the remission of the taxes of his native city. Later, upon his return home, he was chosen bishop of the North African Ptolemaïs. During his three years' stay at Constantinople, Synesius came to see very clearly the German menace to the Empire, and he composed the address, which, according to one historian, may be called the anti-German manifesto of the national party of Aurelian.[116] Synesius cautioned the Emperor:

The least pretext will be used by the armed [barbarians] to assume power and become the rulers of the citizens. And then the unarmed will have to fight with men well exercised in military combats. First of all, they [the foreigners] should

[115] Bury, *Later Roman Empire*, I, 127.   [116] *Ibid.*, I, 129; (1889), 83.

be removed from commanding positions and deprived of senatorial rank; for what the Romans in ancient times considered of highest esteem has become dishonorable because of the influence of the foreigners. As in many other matters, so in this one, I am astonished at our folly. In every more or less prosperous home we find a Scythian [Goth] slave; they serve as cooks and cupbearers; also those who walk along the street with little chairs on their backs and offer them to people who wish to rest in the open, are Scythians. But is it not exceedingly surprising that the very same light-haired barbarians with Euboic headdress, who in private life perform the function of servants, are our rulers in political life? The Emperor should purify the troops just as we purify a measure of wheat by separating the chaff and all other matter, which, if allowed to germinate, harms the good seed. Your father, because of his excessive compassion, received them [the barbarians] kindly and condescendingly, gave them the rank of allies, conferred upon them political rights and honors, and endowed them with generous grants of land. But not as an act of kindness did these barbarians understand these noble deeds; they interpreted them as a sign of our weakness, which caused them to feel more haughty and conceited. By increasing the number of our native recruits and thus strengthening our own army and our courage, you must accomplish in the Empire the things which still need to be done. Persistence must be shown in dealing with these people. Either let these barbarians till the soil following the example of the ancient Messenians, who put down their arms and toiled as slaves for the Lacedaemonians, or let them go by the road they came, announcing to those who live on the other side of the river [Danube] that the Romans have no more kindness in them and that they are ruled by a noble youth! [117]

What Synesius advocated, then, in the face of the Germanic menace to the government, was the expulsion of the Goths from the army, the formation of an indigenous army, and the establishment of the Goths as tillers of the soil. Should the Goths be unwilling to accept this program, Synesius suggested that the Romans should clear their territory of Goths by driving them back across the Danube, the place from which they originally came.

The most influential general in the imperial army, the Goth Gaïnas, could not view calmly the exclusive influence of the favorite, Eutropius, and an opportunity to act soon arose. At this time the Goths of Phrygia, who had been settled in this province of Asia Minor by Theodosius the Great, had risen in rebellion and were devastating the country under the leadership of their chief, Tribigild. Gaïnas, sent out against this dangerous rebel, later proved to be his secret ally. Joining hands with Tribigild, he deliberately arranged the defeat of the imperial troops sent out to suppress the revolt, and the two Goths became masters of the situation. They then presented to the Emperor a demand that Eutropius be removed and delivered into their hands. Com-

---

[117] "Περὶ Βασιλείας," *Opera*, par. 14–15; ed. Migne, *Patrologia Graeca*, LXVII, 1092–97. See Bury, *Later Roman Empire*, I, 129–30. A. Fitzgerald, *The Letters of Synesius of Cyrene*, 23–24. Fitzgerald, *The Essays and Hymns of Synesius of Cyrene*, includes the address to the Emperor Arcadius and the political speeches. Trans. into English (1930), I, 134–39; notes on the address "On Kingship," 206–9.

plaints against Eutropius were coming from Eudoxia, the wife of Arcadius, and from the party of Aurelian. Arcadius, pressed by the success of the Germans, was forced to yield. He sent Eutropius into exile (399 A.D.). But this did not satisfy the victorious Goths. They compelled the Emperor to bring Eutropius back to the capital and to have him tried and executed. This accomplished, Gaïnas demanded that the Emperor allow the Arian Goths to use one of the temples of the capital city for Arian services. A strong protest against this request came from the bishop of Constantinople, John Chrysostom ("the Golden-Mouthed"). Knowing that not only the entire capital but also the majority of the population of the Empire sided with the bishop, Gaïnas did not insist on this demand.

After gaining a stronghold in the capital, the Goths became complete masters of the fate of the Empire. Arcadius and the natives of the capital were fully aware of the danger of the situation. But Gaïnas, in spite of all his success, proved himself incapable of keeping his dominant position in Constantinople. While he was away from the capital a sudden revolt broke out in which many Goths were killed and he was unable to return to the capital. Arcadius, encouraged by the new course of events, sent against Gaïnas his loyal pagan Goth, Fravitta, who defeated Gaïnas at the time when he tried to sail across to Asia Minor. Gaïnas tried to find refuge in Thrace, but there he fell into the hands of the king of the Huns, who cut off his head and sent it as a gift to Arcadius. Thus the Gothic menace was warded off through the efforts of a German, Fravitta, who was designated consul for this great service to the Empire. The Gothic problem at the beginning of the fifth century was finally settled in favor of the government. Later efforts of the Goths to restore their former influence were of no great importance.

John Chrysostom.—Against the background of Germanic complications appeared the significant figure of the patriarch of Constantinople, John Chrysostom.[118] He was born in Antioch and studied with the famous rhetorician, Libanius, intending to follow a worldly career. He later forsook this idea and after his baptism devoted himself completely to preaching in Antioch,

---

[118] In 1926 N. Baynes wrote: "It is indeed strange that there is no worthy biography of Chrysostom." See "Alexandria and Constantinople: A Study in Ecclesiastical Diplomacy," *Journal of Egyptian Archaeology*, XII (1926), 150. We now have a detailed and very accurately documented biography in two volumes by a Benedictine, P. Chrysostomus Baur, *Der heilige Johannes Chrysostomus und seine Zeit.* I have nowhere found mention of the very detailed biography of Chrysostom, with abundant references to sources, published in *Oeuvres complètes de saint Jean Chrysostome,* trans. by M. Jeannin. See also N. Turchi, *La civiltà bizantina,* 225–67. This article is not mentioned in the bibliography of Baur's book. L. Meyer, *S. Jean Chrysostome, maître de perfection chrétienne.* A Crillo de Albornoz, *Juan Crisostomo y su influencia social en el imperio bizantino,* 187. S. Attwater, *St. John Chrysostome,* 113. See *Histoire de l'église depuis les origines jusqu'à nos jours,* ed. A. Fliche and V. Martin, IV, 129–48.

where he remained for a number of years as a presbyter. After the death of the patriarch Nectarius, Eutropius chose this preacher of Antioch, whose fame was already widespread, as the new patriarch. He was transported to the capital secretly for fear that the population of Antioch, devoted to their preacher, might oppose his departure. In spite of the intrigues of Theophilus, bishop of Alexandria, John was consecrated bishop and given the see of the capital in the year 398. Thus the episcopal throne came into the hands of a man unusually accomplished in the art of oratory, an idealist whose actions were always in harmony with his theories, and an advocate of very severe moral principles. As a ruthless opponent of superfluous luxury and a firm defender of Nicene doctrines, John made many enemies among his flock. One of his most dangerous enemies was Empress Eudoxia, a lover of luxury and pleasure, whom John publicly denounced in his addresses. In his sermons he went so far as to compare her with Jezebel and Herodias.[119] His harsh policy toward the Arian Goths also earned him many enemies; it was he who strongly opposed the granting of one of the large churches of the capital to the Goths for their services. The Goths later became reconciled to the Emperor's refusal, however, and continued to use the church allotted to them outside the city gates. John was very considerate of the orthodox Goths. He gave them one of the city churches, visited it very often, and held frequent conferences with them through an interpreter.

John's earnest religious ideals, his unwillingness to compromise with anyone, and his harsh criticism of luxury gradually increased the number of his enemies. The Emperor himself soon fell under the influence of those who were opposed to the patriarch and openly expressed himself against John. This open opposition caused John to retire to Asia Minor, but the unrest among the masses in the capital which followed the departure of the beloved Patriarch forced the Emperor to recall him from exile. The new peace between the state and the Patriarch did not last very long, however. The inaugural ceremonies at the dedication of the statue to the Empress furnished a new occasion for a fiery speech in which John denounced the vices of the Empress. He was again deposed, and his followers, the Johannites, were severely persecuted. Finally, in the year 404, John was exiled to the Cappadocian city Cucusus, which he reached only after a long and strenuous journey, a city which he described as "the most deserted place in the universe."[120] Three years later he was sent to a new place of exile on the distant eastern shore of the Black Sea, and he died on the journey. Thus ended the life of one of

[119] The authenticity of some of these sermons is questioned. See Seeck, *Geschichte des Untergangs der antiken Welt*, V, 365, 583. Baur, *Der heilige Chrysostomus*, II, 144-45, 196, 237. Bury, *Later Roman Empire*, I, 155.

[120] John Chrysostom, *Epistola 234;* ed. Migne, *Patrologia Graeca*, LII, 739.

the most remarkable leaders of the eastern church in the early Middle Ages. The pope and the Emperor of the West, Honorius, had both interceded in an attempt to stop the persecutions of John and the Johannites, but without success.

John left a rich literary treasure, containing a vivid picture of the social and religious life of his period. Personally he was one of the very few men who did not fear to speak out openly against the Arian pretensions of the all-powerful Gaïnas and he defended with conviction and steadiness the ideals of the apostolic church. He has been called one of the most beautiful moral examples humanity has ever had. "He was merciless to sin and full of mercy for the sinner."[121]

Arcadius died in the year 408, when his wife, Eudoxia, was already dead and his son and successor, Theodosius, was only seven years old.

Theodosius II, the Younger (408–50)

According to some sources, Arcadius left a testament in which he appointed as guardian for his young successor the Persian king, Yezdegerd I, because he feared that the favorites at Constantinople might deprive Theodosius of the throne. The king of Persia devotedly fulfilled the office conferred upon him, and through one of his own loyal men he guarded Theodosius against the intrigues of the courtiers. Many scholars deny the authenticity of this story, but there is nothing intrinsically implausible about it; since similar instances occur in other periods of history, there seems to be no good reason for rejecting it.[122]

The harmonious relations between the two empires explain the unusually favorable position of Christianity in Persia during the reign of Yezdegerd I. The Persian tradition, which reflects the state of mind of the Magi and nobles, calls Yezdegerd "the Apostate," "the Wicked," the friend of Rome and the Christians, and the persecutor of the Magi. But Christian sources praise him for his goodness, mildness, and munificence and at times claim that he was even at the point of becoming converted to Christianity. In reality, however, Yezdegerd I, like Constantine the Great, appreciated how important the

---

[121] The authenticity is sometimes questioned of a fascinating contemporary source depicting the relations between Chrysostom and the Empress and giving a general picture of court life under Arcadius, the *Vita Porphyrii*, bishop of Gaza by Marcus the Deacon, his companion and friend. But without doubt the document has a very reliable historical foundation. See H. Grégoire and M. A. Kugener, "La vie de Porphyre, évêque de Gaza, est-elle authentique?" *Revue de l'Université de Bruxelles*, XXXV (1929–30), 53–60. See also a remarkable introduction to their edition and translation of the life of Porphyrius: *Marc le Diacre, Vie de Porphyre évêque de Gaza*, ix–cix. Lengthy extracts from the *Vita* in Bury, *Later Roman Empire*, I, 142–48. Baur considers the *Vita* a very reliable source (I, xvi; but cf. II, 157–60). The problem deserves further investigation.

[122] Bury, *Later Roman Empire*, II, 2 and n. 1.

Christian element in his empire was to his political plans. In 409 he formally granted permission to the Christians to worship openly and to restore their churches. Some historians call this decree the Edict of Milan for the Assyrian Christian church.[123]

In 410 a council met at Seleucia at which the Christian church in Persia was organized. The bishop of Seleucia (Ctesiphon) was elected head of the church. He was given the title of "Catholicos," and was to reside in the capital of the Persian Empire. The members of the council made the following declaration: "We all unanimously implore our Merciful God that He increase the days of the victorious and illustrious king Yezdegerd, King of Kings, and that his years be prolonged for generations of generations and for ages of ages."[124] The Christians did not enjoy complete freedom for long. Persecutions were renewed within the later years of Yezdegerd's reign.

Theodosius II was not a gifted statesman, nor was he particularly interested in matters of government. Throughout his long reign he kept aloof from the actual affairs of government and led a solitary monastic life. Devoting most of his time to calligraphy, he copied many old manuscripts in his very beautiful handwriting.[125] But around Theodosius were very able and energetic people who contributed much to crowning his period with such important events in the internal life of the Empire that historians no longer look upon Theodosius as a weak and ill-fated emperor. One of the most influential persons during the reign of Theodosius was his sister, Pulcheria. It was she who arranged the marriage of Theodosius and Athenais (later baptized Eudocia), the daughter of an Athenian philosopher and a woman of high cultural attainment and some literary genius. Eudocia wrote a number of works, treating chiefly of religious topics, but reflecting also some contemporary political events.

In external struggles the eastern half of the Empire was more fortunate than the western half during the period of Theodosius II. No strenuous campaign had to be organized in the East, but the West was going through a very severe crisis because of the German migrations. The most terrific shock to the Romans was the entrance into Rome, former capital of the pagan Roman Empire, of the commander of the Visigoths, Alaric. Shortly afterwards the barbarians formed their first kingdoms on Roman territory in western Europe and northern Africa. The eastern part of the Empire was for a time endangered by the Huns, who attacked Byzantine territory and raided almost

[123] See J. Labourt, *Le Christianisme dans l'Empire Perse sous la dynastie Sassanide* (2nd ed., 1904), 93; W. A. Wigram, *An Introduction to the History of the Assyrian Church*, 89.

[124] *Synodicon Orientale, ou Recueil de Synodes Nestoriens,* ed. J. B. Chabot, in *No-tices et extraits des Manuscrits de la Bibliothèque Nationale,* XXXVII (1902), 258.

[125] See L. Bréhier, "Les empereurs byzantins dans leur vie privée," *Revue historique,* CLXXXVIII (1940), 203-4.

as far as the walls of Constantinople. Before friendly relations were established, the Emperor was forced to pay them a large sum of money and cede the territory south of the Danube. Later, however, an embassy headed by Maximin was sent from Constantinople to Pannonia. His friend, Priscus, who accompanied him, wrote an extremely important and full account of the embassy, describing the court of Attila and many of the customs and manners of the Huns. This description is particularly valuable for the light it throws not only on the Huns but also on the Slavs of the Middle Danube whom the Huns had conquered.[126]

Theological disputes and the Third Ecumenical Council.—The first two ecumenical councils definitely settled the question that Jesus Christ is both God and man. But this decision fell short of satisfying the probing theological minds haunted by the problem of how the union of the divine substance of Jesus Christ with his human nature was to be conceived. In Antioch at the end of the fourth century originated the teaching that there was no complete union of the two natures in Christ. In its further developments this teaching attempted to prove the absolute independence of Christ's human nature both before and after its union with the divine nature. As long as this doctrine remained within the confines of a limited circle of men it did not cause any serious disturbance in the church. But with the passing of the patriarchal throne of Constantinople to the Antiochene presbyter Nestorius, an ardent follower of this new teaching, conditions changed considerably, for he imposed the teaching of Antioch upon the church. Famous for his eloquence, he addressed the Emperor immediately after his consecration: "Give me, my prince, the earth purged of heretics, and I will give you heaven as a recompense. Assist me in destroying heretics, and I will assist you in vanquishing the Persians."[127] By heretics Nestorius meant all those who did not share his views on the independence of the human nature in Jesus Christ. Nestorius' name for the Virgin Mary was not the "Mother of God" but the "Mother of Christ," the "Mother of a man."

Nestorius' persecutions of his opponents aroused a great storm in the church. Particularly strong was the protest by the Alexandrian patriarch, Cyril, and Pope Celestine, who condemned the new heretical teaching at a council gathered in Rome. Theodosius, wishing to put an end to these church disputes, convoked at Ephesus the Third Ecumenical Council, which condemned the Nestorian doctrine in the year 431. Nestorius was exiled to Egypt where he spent the remainder of his life.

---

[126] For a free English translation of Priscus' account, see Bury, *Later Roman Empire,* I, 279–88. See also W. Ennslin, "Maximinus und sein Begleiter, der Historiker Priskos," *Byzantinisch-Neugriechische Jahrbücher,* V (1926), 1–9.

[127] Socratis, *Historia ecclesiastica,* VII, 29; in *Nicene and Post-Nicene Fathers,* II, 169.

The condemnation of Nestorianism did not end it; there still remained numerous followers of this teaching in Syria and Mesopotamia and the Emperor ordered the administration of these provinces to take severe measures against them. The main center of Nestorianism was Edessa, the home of the famous school which spread the ideas of Antioch. In the year 489, during the reign of Zeno, this school was destroyed and the teachers and pupils were driven out of the city. They went to Persia and founded a new school at Nisibis. The king of Persia gladly admitted the Nestorians and offered them his protection, for, since he considered them enemies of the Empire, he counted on using them to his advantage when an opportunity arose. The Persian church of the Nestorian or Syro-Chaldean Christians, was headed by a bishop who bore the title of Catholicos. From Persia, Christianity in its Nestorian form spread widely into central Asia and was accepted by a considerable number of followers in India.

The Council of Ephesus was followed in the Byzantine church itself, and in Alexandria in particular, by the development of new movements in opposition to Nestorianism. The followers of Cyril of Alexandria, while they believed in the preponderance of the divine nature over the human in Jesus Christ, arrived at the conclusion that the human was completely absorbed by the divine substance; hence Jesus Christ possessed but one—divine—nature. This new teaching was called Monophysitism, or the Monophysitic doctrine, and its followers are known as the Monophysites (from the Greek μόνος, "one," and φύσις, "nature"). Monophysitism made great progress with the aid of two ardent Monophysites, the Alexandrian bishop Dioscorus, and Eutyches, the archimandrite of a monastery in Constantinople. The Emperor sided with Dioscorus, whom he considered an advocate of the ideas of Cyril of Alexandria. The new teaching was opposed by the patriarch of Constantinople and by Pope Leo I the Great. Dioscorus then urged the Emperor to call a council in the year 449 at Ephesus, which is known as the "Robber Council." The Alexandrian party of Monophysites headed by Dioscorus, who presided at the council, forced members of the council who did not agree with them to recognize the teaching of Eutyches (Monophysitism) as orthodox and to condemn the opponents of the new doctrine. The Emperor ratified the decisions of the council, officially recognizing it as an ecumenical council. Naturally the council failed to establish harmony in the church. A period of stormy disturbances followed, during which Theodosius died, leaving to his successors the solution of the problem of Monophysitism, highly important in Byzantine history.

Besides the stormy and significant religious events of the period of Theodosius there were a number of events in the internal life of the Empire which marked this epoch as historically important.

The higher school at Constantinople.—The organization of the higher school at Constantinople and the publication of the Theodosian Code, which took place during the reign of Theodosius, were both of great significance in the life of the Byzantine Empire.

Until the fifth century the city of Athens, the home of the famous philosophical school, was the main center of pagan teaching in the Roman Empire. Greek teachers of rhetoric and philosophy, better known as the sophists, came there from all parts of the Empire, some to display their knowledge and oratorical eloquence, others in hopes of obtaining good positions in the teaching profession. These teachers were supported partly from the imperial treasury, partly from the treasuries of the various cities. Tutoring and lecturing were also better paid in Athens than elsewhere. The triumph of Christianity at the end of the fourth century dealt the Athenian school a heavy blow, and intellectual life there was also greatly affected at the very close of the century by the devastating advances of the Visigoths into Greece. Even after the departure of Alaric and the Visigoths, the Athenian school did not rise to its former position; the number of philosophers was greatly decreased. Most severe of all was the blow dealt the Athenian pagan school by the organization of the higher school, or university, in Constantinople.

When Constantinople became the capital of the Empire, many rhetoricians and philosophers came to the new city, so that even before Theodosius II a kind of high school may have existed there. Teachers and scholars were invited to Constantinople from Africa, Syria, and other places. St. Hieronymus remarked in his *Chronicle* (360–62 A.D.): "Euanthius, the most learned grammarian, died at Constantinople, and in his place Charisius was brought from Africa."[128] Accordingly a recent student of the problems of the higher schools in Constantinople in the Middle Ages says that under Theodosius II the higher school was not founded but reorganized.[129] In the year 425 Theodosius II issued a decree dealing with the organization of a higher school.[130] There were to be thirty-one professors teaching grammar, rhetoric, jurisprudence, and philosophy. Three rhetors (*oratores*) and ten grammarians were to conduct their teaching in Latin, and five rhetors or sophists (*sofistae*) and ten grammarians were to teach in Greek. In addition to this the decree provided for one chair for philosophy and two chairs for jurisprudence. While Latin still remained the official language of the Empire, the foundation of Greek chairs at the University indicates that the Emperor was beginning to see that in the new capital Greek had undeniable rights as the language most spoken

[128] *Chronicon;* ed. Migne, *Patrologia Latina,* XXVII, 689–90. See H. Usener, "Vier Lateinische Grammatiker," *Rheinisches Museum für Philologie,* XXIII (1868), 492.

[129] See F. Fuchs, *Die Höheren Schulen von Konstantinopel im Mittelalter,* 2.
[130] *Codex Theodosianus,* XIV, 9, 3.

and understood in the eastern part of the Empire. The number of Greek rhetors exceeded the number of Latin rhetors by two. The new higher school was given a separate building with large lecture rooms and auditoriums. The professors were forbidden to tutor anyone privately in their homes; they were to devote all their time and effort to teaching at the school. They were provided with a definite salary from the imperial exchequer and could advance to very high rank. This educational center at Constantinople became a dangerous rival of the Athenian pagan school, which was steadily declining. In the subsequent history of the Byzantine Empire the higher school of Theodosius II long stood as the center about which were assembled the best cultural forces of the Empire.

Codex Theodosianus.—From the period of Theodosius II also dates the oldest collection of decrees of Roman emperors which has been preserved. For a long time such a collection had been needed because the numerous separate decrees were easily forgotten and lost, thus introducing much confusion into the juridical practices of the day and creating many difficult situations for the jurists. There were two earlier collections of decrees, the Gregorian and the Hermogenian codes (*Codex Gregorianus* and *Codex Hermogenianus*), named perhaps after their authors, Gregory and Hermogenes, about whom little is known. The first collection dates back to the epoch of Diocletian and probably contained decrees from the period of Hadrian to that of Diocletian. The second collection, compiled during the reign of the successors of Diocletian in the fourth century, contained decrees dating from the late third century to the sixth decade of the fourth century. Neither of the two collections has survived; both are known only through the small fragments which have been preserved.

Theodosius' idea was to issue a collection of laws modeled after the two earlier collections. It was to contain decrees issued by the Christian emperors from Constantine the Great to Theodosius II, inclusive. The commission appointed by the Emperor produced, after eight years' work, the so-called *Codex Theodosianus,* in Latin. It was published in the year 438 in the East and shortly afterwards it was introduced in the western part of the Empire. The code of Theodosius is divided into sixteen books, which in turn are subdivided into a definite number of titles (*tituli*). Each book treats of some phase of government, such as offices, military affairs, religious life. In each title the decrees are arranged in chronological order. The decrees which appeared after the publication of the code were called novels (*leges novellae*).[131]

The code of Theodosius is of very great historical importance. First, it is the most valuable source on the internal history of the fourth and fifth cen-

[131] O. Seeck, "Die Quellen des Codex Theodosianus," *Regesten der Kaiser und Päpste* *für die Jahre 311 bis 476 n. Chr.,* 1–18.

turies. Since it also embraces the period when Christianity became the state religion, this legal collection may be considered as a sort of summary of what the new religion accomplished in the field of law and what changes it brought about in juridical practices. Furthermore, this code, together with the earlier collections, formed a solid foundation for the subsequent juridical activities of Justinian. Finally, the code of Theodosius, introduced in the West during the period of Germanic migrations, together with the two earlier codes, later novels, and a few other juridical monuments of imperial Rome (the Institutions of Gaius, for example), exerted great influence, both direct and indirect, upon barbarian legislation. The famous "Roman Law of the Visigoths" (*Lex Romana Visigothorum*), intended for the Roman subjects of the Visigothic kingdom, is nothing more than an abridgment of the Theodosian code and the other sources mentioned. It is for this reason that the "Roman Law of the Visigoths" is also called the "Breviary of Alaric" (*Breviarium Alaricianum*), that is, an abridgment issued by the Visigoth king, Alaric II, in the early part of the sixth century. This is an instance of direct influence exerted by the code of Theodosius upon barbarian legislation. But still more frequent was its indirect influence through the Visigoth code. During the early Middle Ages, including the epoch of Charlemagne, western European legislation was influenced by the *Breviarium,* which became the chief source of Roman law in the West. This indicates clearly that Roman law at that period influenced western Europe but not through the code of Justinian, which spread in the West much later, sometime during the twelfth century. This fact is sometimes overlooked by scholars; and even such a distinguished historian as Fustel de Coulanges stated that "science has proved that Justinian's collections of laws maintained their force in Gaul late into the Middle Ages."[132] The influence of the code went still further, for the *Breviarium* of Alaric has apparently played some part in the history of Bulgaria. At least it is the opinion of the famous Croatian scholar, Bogišič, whose arguments were later developed and confirmed by the Bulgarian scholar, Bobtchev, that the *Breviarium Alaricianum* was sent by Pope Nicholas I to the Bulgarian king Boris, after he had petitioned the pope in the year 866 to send to Bulgaria "the mundane laws" (*leges mundanae*). In answer to this demand the pope, in his "Responses to the Consults of the Bulgarians" (*Responsa papae Nicolai ad consulta Bulgarorum*), announced that he was sending them the "venerable laws of the Romans" (*venerandae Romanorum leges*), which Bogišič and Bobtchev considered to be the breviary of Alaric.[133] Even if this be so, the value of this code in the life of the ancient Bulgarians should not be exag-

---

[132] *Histoire des institutions politiques* (2nd ed., 1904), 513.

[133] V. Bogišič, *Pisani Zakoni na slovenskom*

jugu. U Zagrebu, 11–13; S. Bobtchev, *History of the Ancient Bulgarian Law,* 117–20.

gerated, because only a few years later Boris broke away from the Roman curia and drew nearer to Constantinople. But the mere fact that the pope sent the *Breviarium* may indicate its significance in European life during the ninth century. All these instances show clearly the great and widespread influence of the *Codex Theodosianus*.[134]

The walls of Constantinople.—Among the important events of the time of Theodosius was the construction of the walls of Constantinople. Constantine the Great had surrounded the new capital with a wall. By the time of Theodosius II the city had far outgrown the limits of this wall. It became necessary to devise new means for the defense of the city against the attacks of enemies. The fate of Rome, taken by Alaric in the year 410, became a serious warning for Constantinople, since it too was menaced in the first half of the fifth century by the savage Huns.

The solution of this very difficult problem was undertaken by some of the gifted and energetic men of Theodosius' court. The walls were built in two shifts. In 413, during the early childhood of Theodosius, the praetorian prefect, Anthemius, who was at that time regent, erected a wall with numerous towers which extended from the Sea of Marmora to the Golden Horn, somewhat to the west of Constantine's wall. This new wall of Anthemius, which saved the capital from the attack of Attila, exists even today north of the Sea of Marmora as far as the ruins of the Byzantine palace known as the Tekfour Serai. After a violent earthquake which destroyed the wall, the praetorian prefect Constantine repaired it and also built around it another wall with many towers and surrounded with a deep ditch filled with water. Thus, on land, Constantinople had a threefold series of defenses, the two walls separated by a terrace and the deep ditch which surrounded the outer wall. Under the administration of Cyrus, prefect of the city, new walls were also constructed along the seashore. The two inscriptions on the walls dating back to this period, one Greek and the other Latin, speak of the building activities of Theodosius. They are still legible today. The name of Cyrus is also associated with the introduction of night illumination of the streets in the capital.[135]

---

[134] There is a complete English translation of the Code by Clyde Pharr, in collaboration with T. S. Davidson and M. B. Pharr. Princeton University Press, 1951. See also Adolph Berger and A. Arthur Schiller, *Bibliography of Anglo-American Studies in Roman, Greek, and Greco-Egyptian Law and Related Sciences*, 75–94. A very useful publication. Many items deal with Byzantine times.

[135] See *Chronicon Paschale*, I, 588. On the constructive activities of Cyrus and Constan- tine, see Bury, *Later Roman Empire*, I, 70, 72 and n. 2. Cf. A. Van Millingen, *Byzantine Constantinople, the Walls of the City and Adjoining Historical Sites*, 48; B. Meyer-Plath and A. M. Schneider, *Die Landmauer von Konstantinopel* (Berlin, 1943). Some new information on the biography of Cyrus which has not been used by Bury is given in "Life of St. Daniel the Stylite," ed. H. Delehaye, *Analecta Bollandiana*, XXXII (1913), 150. Delehaye, *Les Saints Stylites*, 30–31. See also

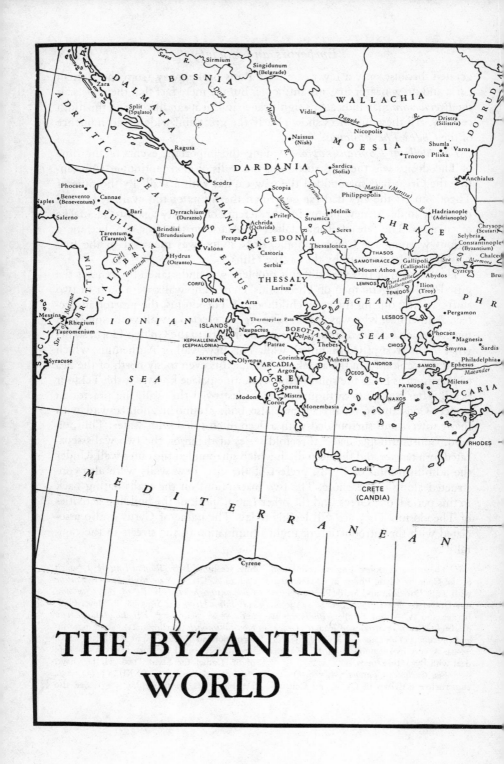

THE BYZANTINE
WORLD

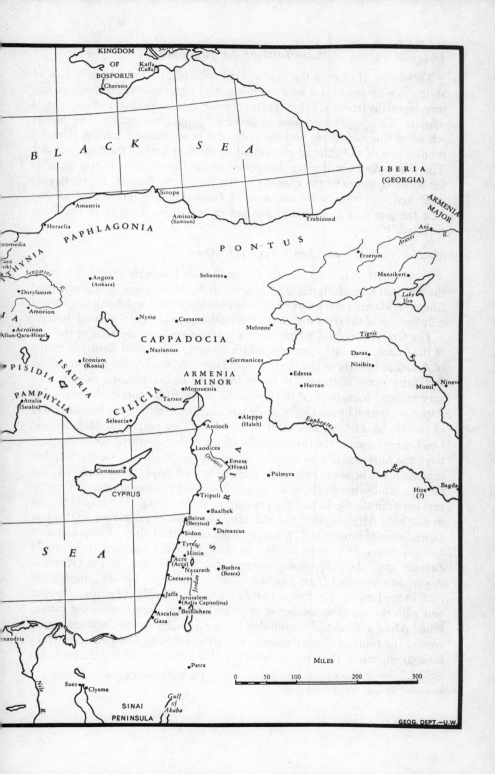

BLACK SEA

KINGDOM
OF
BOSPORUS
Kaffa
(Caffa)
Cherson

IBERIA
(GEORGIA)

ARMENIA
MAJOR

Amastris

Sinope

Amisus
(Samsun)

Trebizond

Ani
R.

Heraclia

PAPHLAGONIA

comedia

ea
nik)

Sangarios R.

Angora
(Ankara)

Sebastea

PONTUS

Araxes

Erzerum

Manzikert

Dorylaeum

Amorion

Nyssa

Caesarea

Lake
Van

Acroinon
Afiun-Qara-Hisar)

CAPPADOCIA

Nazianzus

Melitene

Tigris R.

Daras

Nisibis

Mosul

Nineve

Iconium
(Konia)

Germanicea

PISIDIA

ISAURIA

ARMENIA
MINOR

Edessa

Harran

PAMPHYLIA

Mopsuestia

Attalia
(Satalia)

CILICIA

Tarsus

Euphrates R.

Aleppo
(Haleb)

Seleucia

Antioch

Laodicea

Orontes R.

Emesa
(Hims)

Palmyra

Hira
(?)

Bagda

Constantia

CYPRUS

Tripoli

Baalbek

Damascus

Beirut
(Berytus)

Sidon

Tyre

Acre
(Acca)

Hittin

Nazareth

Bothra
(Bosra)

Caesarea

Jaffa

Jerusalem
(Aelia Capitolina)

Bethlehem

Ascalon

Gaza

S E A

xandria

Petra

MILES

0   50   100   200   300

Suez

Clysma

Gulf
of
Akaba

SINAI
PENINSULA

Nile R.

GEOG. DEPT.—U.W.

Theodosius II died in the year 450. In spite of his weakness and lack of ability as a statesman, his long reign was very significant for subsequent history, especially from the cultural point of view. By a lucky choice of responsible officials, Theodosius succeeded in accomplishing great results. The higher school of Constantinople and the code of Theodosius still remain splendid monuments of the cultural movement in the first half of the fifth century. The city walls built during this period made Constantinople impregnable for many centuries to the enemies of the Byzantine Empire. N. H. Baynes remarked: "In some sense the walls of Constantinople represented for the East the gun and gunpowder, for lack of which the Empire in the West perished."[136]

Marcian (450–57) and Leo I (457–74). Aspar

Thedosius died leaving no heir. His aged sister Pulcheria agreed to become the nominal wife of Marcian, a Thracian by birth, who was later proclaimed Emperor. Marcian was a very capable but modest soldier and rose to the throne only because of the entreaties of the influential general Aspar, of Alan descent.

The Gothic problem, which became a real menace to the state at the end of the fourth, and early part of the fifth century, was settled during the time of Arcadius in favor of the government. However, the Gothic element in the Byzantine army continued to be an influence in the Empire, though in a very reduced measure, and in the middle of the fifth century the barbarian Aspar, supported by the Goths, made a final effort to restore the former power of the Goths. He was successful for a while. Two emperors, Marcian and Leo I, were raised to the throne by the efforts of Aspar, whose Arian leanings were the only obstacle to his own accession to the throne. Once more the capital openly began to express its discontent with Aspar, his family, and the barbarian influence in the army in general. Two events aggravated the tension between the Goths and the population of the capital. The sea expedition to northern Africa against the Vandals, which Leo I undertook with great expenditure of money and effort, proved a complete failure. The population accused Aspar of treason because he had originally opposed it, naturally enough, since the purpose was to crush the Vandals, that is, the Germans. Aspar then obtained from Leo the rank of Caesar for his son, the highest rank in the Empire. The Emperor decided to free himself of Germanic power and with the aid of a number of warlike Isaurians quartered in the capital killed Aspar and part of his family, dealing a final blow to Germanic influence at the court of Constantinople. For these murders Leo I received from his contemporaries the name of *Makelles*, that is, "Butcher," but the historian

N. Baynes, "The Vita S. Danielis," *English Historical Review*, XL (1925), 397.

[136] *The Byzantine Empire*, 27.

Th. I Uspensky affirmed that this alone may justify the surname "Great" sometimes given Leo, since it was a significant step in the direction of nationalizing the army and weakening the dominance of barbarian troops.[137]

The Huns, who constituted so great a menace to the Empire, moved at the beginning of Marcian's reign from the middle Danube to the western provinces of the Empire, where they later fought the famous Catalaunian battle. Shortly afterwards Attila died. His enormous empire fell to ruin so that the Hunnic danger to the Byzantine Empire disappeared in the latter years of Marcian's reign.

The Fourth Ecumenical Council.—Marcian inherited from his predecessor a very complicated state of affairs in the church. The Monophysites were now triumphant. Marcian, favoring the stand taken by the first two ecumenical councils, could not become reconciled to this triumph, and in the year 451 he called the Fourth Ecumenical Council, at Chalcedon, which proved to be of great importance for all subsequent history. The number of delegates to this council was very large and included legates representing the pope.

The council condemned the acts of the Robber Council of Ephesus and deposed Dioscorus. Then it worked out a new religious formula completely rejecting the doctrine of the Monophysites and wholly according with the views of the Pope of Rome. The Council affirmed "one and the same Christ in two natures without confusion or change, division or separation." The dogmas approved by this Council of Chalcedon, triumphantly confirming the main doctrines of the first ecumenical councils, became the basis of the religious teachings of the orthodox church.

The decisions of the Council of Chalcedon were also of great political significance in Byzantine history. The Byzantine government, by openly opposing Monophysitism in the fifth century, alienated the eastern provinces, Syria and Egypt, where the majority of the population was Monophysitic. The Monophysites remained true to their religious doctrine even after the condemnations of the council of 451 and were unwilling to make any compromises. The Egyptian church abolished the use of Greek in its services and introduced the native Egyptian (Coptic) language. The religious disturbances in Jerusalem, Alexandria, and Antioch caused by the forced introduction of the decisions of the council assumed the character of serious national revolts and were suppressed by the civil and military authorities only after much bloodshed. The suppression of these revolts, however, did not settle the fundamental problems of the period. Against the background of the conflicting religious disputes, which became more and more acute, clearly defined racial contradictions, particularly in Syria and Egypt, began to appear. The

[137] *Byzantine Empire*, I, 330.

Egyptian and Syrian native populations were gradually becoming convinced of the desirability of seceding from the Byzantine Empire. The religious disturbances in the eastern provinces, aided by the composition of the population, created toward the seventh century conditions which facilitated the transfer of these rich and civilized districts into the hands of first the Persians and later the Arabs.

The twenty-eighth canon of the Council of Chalcedon, which called forth a correspondence between the Emperor and the pope, was also of great importance. Although not confirmed by the pope, this canon was generally accepted in the East. It raised the question of the rank of the patriarch of Constantinople in relation to the Pope of Rome, a question already decided by the third canon of the Second Ecumenical Council. Following this decision, the twenty-eighth canon of the Chalcedon council gave "equal privileges to the most holy throne of New Rome, rightly judging that the city which is honored with the Sovereignty and the Senate and enjoys equal privileges with the old Imperial Rome should in ecclesiastical matters also be magnified as she is, and rank next after her."[138] Furthermore, the same canon granted the archbishop of Constantinople the right to ordain bishops for the provinces of Pontus, Asia, and Thrace, inhabited by people of various tribes. "It is sufficient to recall," said Th. I. Uspensky, "that these three names embraced all the Christian missions in the East, in southern Russia, and in the Balkan peninsula, as well as all those acquisitions of the eastern clergy which could eventually be made in the indicated districts. At least, this is the opinion of later Greek canonists who defended the rights of the Constantinopolitan patriarch. Such, in brief, is the universal historical significance of the twenty-eighth canon."[139] Both Marcian and Leo I, then, were emperors of strict orthodox mind.

Zeno (474–91). Odovacar and Theodoric the Ostrogoth

After the death of Leo I (474) the throne passed to his six-year-old grandson, Leo, who died in the same year, after conferring the imperial rank upon his father, Zeno. Following the death of his son, Zeno became sole emperor (474–91). His accession to the throne marks the supplanting of the former Germanic influence at the court by a new barbarian influence, that of the Isaurians, a savage race of which he was a member. The Isaurians now occupied the best positions and most responsible posts in the capital. Very soon Zeno became aware that even among his own people men were plotting against him, and he showed much determination in quelling the revolt in mountainous Isauria, ordering the inhabitants to pull down the greater part

[138] J. D. Mansi, *Sacrorum conciliorum nova et amplissima collectio* (1762), VII, 445.   [139] *Byzantine Empire*, I, 276.

of their fortifications. The dominance of Isaurians in the Empire continued, however, throughout Zeno's lifetime.

During the period of Zeno's reign very significant events took place in Italy. In the second half of the fifth century the importance of the leaders of German troops increased very greatly until their will was almost decisive in making and deposing Roman emperors in the West. In the year 476 one of these barbarian chiefs, Odovacar, deposed the last western emperor, the young Romulus Augustulus, and himself became the ruler of Italy. In order to make his rule in Italy more secure, he sent ambassadors to Zeno from the Roman Senate with the assurance that Italy needed no separate emperor and that Zeno might be the ruler of the entire Empire. At the same time Odovacar asked Zeno to confer upon him the rank of Roman patrician and to entrust to him the administration of Italy. This request was granted and Odovacar became the legally appointed ruler of Italy. The year 476 formerly was considered the year of the fall of the Western Roman Empire, but this is not correct, because in the fifth century there was still no separate Western Roman Empire. There was, as before, one Roman Empire ruled by two emperors, one in the eastern, the other in the western, part. In the year 476 there was again only one emperor in the Empire, namely Zeno, the ruler of the eastern part.

Upon becoming the ruler of Italy, Odovacar assumed an attitude of marked independence. Zeno was fully aware of it; unable to struggle against Odovacar openly, he decided to act through the Ostrogoths. The latter, after the collapse of the power of Attila, remained in Pannonia and, under the leadership of their king, Theodoric, carried on devastating raids in the Balkan peninsula, menacing even the capital of the Empire. Zeno succeeded in directing the attention of Theodoric to the rich provinces of Italy, thus attaining a double aim: He got rid of his dangerous northern neighbors and settled his disagreements with the undesirable ruler of Italy through the efforts of an outside party. In any event, Theodoric in Italy was less of a menace to Zeno than he would have been had he remained in the Balkan peninsula.

Theodoric moved on to Italy, defeated Odovacar, seized his principal city, Ravenna, and after Zeno's death, founded his Ostrogothic kingdom on Italian territory with the capital at Ravenna. The Balkan peninsula was thus definitely freed from the Ostrogothic menace.

The Henoticon.—The main internal problem during the reign of Zeno was the religious problem, which continued to cause many disturbances. In Egypt and Syria and to some extent in Palestine and Asia Minor, the population held firmly to the doctrine of one nature. The firm orthodox policy of the two emperors who preceded Zeno was little applauded in the eastern provinces. The leaders of the church were fully aware of the seriousness of the situation. The Patriarch of Constantinople, Acacius, who at first favored the decisions of Chalcedon, and the Patriarch of Alexandria, Peter Mongus, were particularly anxious to find some way of reconciling the dissenting parties in the church. They proposed to Zeno that he attempt to reach some mutual agreement by means of compromises on both sides. Zeno accepted this proposal and issued in 482 the Act of Union, or the Henoticon (ἐνωτικόν), addressed to the churches subject to the Patriarch of Alexandria. In this act he tried above all to avoid any sign of disrespect toward either the orthodox or the Monophysitic teachings on the union in Jesus Christ of two natures, the divine and the human. The Henoticon recognized as entirely sufficient the religious foundations developed at the first and second ecumenical councils and ratified at the third council; it anathematized Nestorius and Eutyches, as well as all their followers, and stated that Jesus Christ was "of the same nature with the Father in the Godhead and also of the same nature with us in the manhood." Yet it obviously avoided the use of the phrases "one nature" or "two natures" and did not mention the statement of the Council of Chalcedon in regard to the union of two natures in Christ. The Council of Chalcedon is mentioned in the Henoticon only once, in this statement: "And here we anathematize all who have held, or hold now or at any time, whether in Chalcedon or in any other synod whatsoever, any different belief."[140]

At first the Henoticon seemed to improve conditions in Alexandria, but in the long run it failed to satisfy either the orthodox or the Monophysites. The former could not become reconciled to the concessions made to the Monophysites; the latter, in view of the lack of clarity in the statements of the Henoticon, considered the concessions insufficient, and new complications were thus introduced into the religious life of the Byzantine Empire. The number of religious parties increased. Part of the clergy favored the idea of reconciliation and supported the Act of Union, while the extremists in both the orthodox and the Monophysitic movements were unwilling to make any compromise. These firmly orthodox men were called the Akoimetoi, that is "the Sleepless," because the services in their monasteries were held continuously during the day and night, so that they had to divide their groups into three relays; the extreme Monophysites were called the Akephaloi, that is "the Headless," because they did not recognize the leadership of the Alexandrian Patriarch, who accepted the Henoticon. The Pope of Rome also protested against the Henoticon. He analyzed the complaints of the eastern clergy, dissatisfied with the decree, then studied the Act of Union itself and decided to excommunicate and anathematize the Patriarch of Constantinople, Acacius,

---

[140] Evagrii, *Historia Ecclesiastica*, III, 14; ed. J. Bidez and L. Parmentier, 113. *The Syriac Chronicle,* known as the *Chronicle of* *Zachariah of Mitylene,* V, 8; trans. F. J. Hamilton and E. W. Brooks, 123.

at a council gathered in Rome. In reply Acacius ceased to mention the pope in his prayers. This was in reality the first true breach between the eastern and western churches; it continued until the year 518, when Justin I ascended the throne.[141] Thus the political breach between the eastern and western parts of the Empire, in evidence since the founding in the fifth century of the barbarian German kingdoms in the West, became wider during the reign of Zeno because of the religious secession.

Anastasius I (491-518)

Settlement of the Isaurian problem. The Persian War. Bulgarian and Slavic attacks. The Long Wall. Relations with the West.—Following the death of Zeno, his widow, Ariadne, chose the aged Anastasius, a native of Dyrrachium, who held the rather minor court position of silentiary (*silentiarius*).[142] Anastasius was crowned as emperor only after he had signed a written promise not to introduce any ecclesiastical innovations, a promise extracted by the Patriarch of Constantinople, an ardent adherent of the Council of Chalcedon.

Anastasius' first problem was to settle with the Isaurians, who had acquired so much authority during the reign of Zeno. Their privileged position irritated the population of the capital and when it was also discovered that after the death of Zeno they were plotting against the new Emperor, Anastasius acted with dispatch. He removed them from the responsible posts, confiscated their property, and drove them out of the capital. A long and hard struggle followed this action, and only after six years of fighting were the Isaurians completely subjugated in their native Isauria. Many of them were transported to Thrace. The great service of Anastasius was this decisive settlement of the Isaurian problem.

Among external events, in addition to the exhausting and profitless war with Persia, the state of affairs on the Danube boundary was of great consequence to subsequent history. After the departure of the Ostrogoths to Italy, devastating raids against the northern boundary were undertaken by the Bulgarians, Getae, and Scythians during the reign of Anastasius I. The Bulgarians, who raided the borders of Byzantine territory during the fifth century, were a people of Hunnic (Turkish) origin. They are first mentioned in the Balkan peninsula during the reign of Zeno in connection with the Ostrogothic migrations north of the Byzantine Empire.

As to the rather vague names of Getae and Scythians, the chroniclers of that period were not well informed about the ethnographic composition of

---

[141] See S. Salaville, "L'Affaire de l'Hénotique ou le premier schisme byzantin au Vᵉ siècle," *Échos d'Orient*, XVIII (1916), 225–65, 389–97; XIX (1920), 49–68, 415–33. Anasta-

sius' reign is included in the discussion.

[142] The *silentiarii* were the ushers who kept guard at the doors during meetings of the imperial council and imperial audiences.

the northern peoples; hence it is very likely that these were collective names, and historians consider it probable that some Slavic tribes were included among them. Theophylact, the Byzantine writer of the early seventh century, directly identified the Getae with the Slavs.[143] Thus, during the reign of Anastasius, the Slavs, together with the Bulgarians, first began their irruptions into the Balkan peninsula. According to one source, "a Getic cavalry" devastated Macedonia, Thessaly, and Epirus, and reached as far as Thermopylae.[144] Some scholars have even advanced the theory that the Slavs entered the Balkan peninsula at an earlier period. The Russian scholar Drinov, for example, on the basis of his study of geographical and personal names in the peninsula, placed the beginning of Slavic settlement in the Balkan peninsula in the late second century A.D.[145]

The attacks of the Bulgarians and Slavs during the reign of Anastasius were not of very great consequence for that epoch, for these bands of barbarians, after robbing the Byzantine population, went back to the places from which they came. Yet these raids were the forerunners of the great Slavic irruptions into the Balkan peninsula in the sixth century during the reign of Justinian.

In order to protect the capital against the northern barbarians, Anastasius erected in Thrace, about forty miles west of Constantinople, the so-called "Long Wall" which extended from the Sea of Marmora to the Black Sea, "making the city," said one source, "practically an island instead of a peninsula."[146] This wall did not fulfill the purpose for which it was erected, however. Because of its hurried construction and the breaches made by earthquakes it did not serve as a real barrier to the enemy's approach to the city walls. The modern Turkish fortifications of the Chatalja lines erected in almost the same place pretty closely approximate the Anastasian wall, traces of which may still be seen today.

In western Europe further important changes were taking place in the time of Anastasius. Theodoric became the king of Italy; and in the far northwest Clovis founded a strong Frankish kingdom even before Anastasius ascended the throne. Both these kingdoms were established on territory which theoretically belonged to the Roman, in this case the Byzantine, emperor. Quite naturally, the distant Frankish kingdom could in no way be dependent upon Constantinople; yet in the eyes of the conquered natives the power of

[143] *Historiae*, III, 4, 7; ed. C. de Boor, 116; see Bury, *Later Roman Empire*, I, 434–36.

[144] Comitis Marcellini *Chronicon, ad annum 517;* ed. T. Mommsen, II, 100.

[145] *The Slavic Occupation of the Balkan Peninsula.* At present in Soviet Russia very great interest is exhibited in the early penetration of the Slavs in the Balkan peninsula.

Many articles have been published on the subject, and Drinov's theory is being favorably reconsidered. Drinov's book has been reprinted in a new edition of his works, edited by V. Zlatarsky, I, 139–364.

[146] Evagrii, *Historia ecclesiastica*, III, 38; ed. Bidez and Parmentier, 136.

the newcomers had real authority only after official approval from the shores of the Bosphorus. So it was that when the Goths proclaimed Theodoric king of Italy "without waiting," said a contemporary chronicler, "for directions from the new princeps [Anastasius],"[147] Theodoric nevertheless asked the latter to send him the insignia of imperial power previously returned to Zeno by Odovacar. After long negotiations and the sending of several envoys to Constantinople, Anastasius recognized Theodoric as the ruler of Italy, and the latter then became the legal sovereign in the eyes of the native population.[148] The Arian beliefs of the Goths stood in the way of a closer friendship between the Goths and the natives of Italy.

To Clovis, the king of the Franks, Anastasius sent a diploma conferring upon him the consulship, which Clovis accepted with gratitude.[149] This, of course, was only an honorary consulship, which did not involve the exercise of the duties of the position. Nevertheless it was of great importance to Clovis. The Roman population in Gaul looked upon the eastern emperor as the bearer of supreme authority, who alone could bestow all other power. The diploma of Anastasius conferring the consulship proved to the Gallic population the legality of Clovis' rule over them. It made him a sort of viceroy of the province, which theoretically still remained a part of the Roman Empire.

These relations of the Byzantine emperor with the Germanic kingdom show clearly that in the late fifth and early sixth centuries the idea of a single empire was still very strong.

The religious policy of Anastasius. The rebellion of Vitalian. Internal reforms.—In spite of the promise of the Patriarch of Constantinople not to introduce any ecclesiastical innovations, Anastasius in his religious policy favored Monophysitism; somewhat later, he openly sided with the Monophysites. This act was greeted with joy in Egypt and Syria, where Monophysitism was widespread. In the capital, however, the Monophysitic leanings of the Emperor aroused great confusion and when Anastasius, following the example of Antioch, ordered that the Trisagion ("Holy, Holy, Holy, Lord God of Hosts") be chanted with the addition of the words "who wast crucified for us," (that is, "Holy God, Holy Strong One, Holy Immortal One, crucified for us, be merciful to us"), great disturbances took place in Constantinople and almost brought about the deposition of the Emperor.

This religious policy of Anastasius led to the rebellion of Vitalian in Thrace. At the head of a large army composed of Huns, Bulgarians, and perhaps Slavs, and aided by a large fleet, Vitalian advanced toward the capital. His

[147] Anonymous Valesianus, par. 57; ed. V. Gardhausen, 295; ed. T. Mommsen, *Chronica Minora*, I, 322.

[148] See J. Sundwell, *Abhandlungen zur Geschichte des ausgehenden Römertums,* 190–229.

[149] Gregorii Turonensis Episcopi *Historia Francorum*, II, 38 (XXVIII); ed. H. Omont and G. Collon, 72.

aim was political; he wished to depose the Emperor. But to the world he announced that he rose to defend the oppressed orthodox church. After a long and strenuous struggle the rebellion was finally suppressed. This revolt was of no little importance in history. "By three times bringing his heterogeneous troops close to Constantinople and by obtaining from the government enormous sums of money," said Th. I. Uspensky, "Vitalian revealed to the barbarians the weakness of the Empire and the great riches of Constantinople, and taught them something about combined movement on land and sea."[150]

The internal policy of Anastasius, not yet sufficiently studied or evaluated in historical literature, was marked by intense activity and affected important economic and financial problems of the Empire.

One of his very important financial reforms was the abolition of the hated *chrysargyron,* a tax paid in gold and silver (in Latin it was called *lustralis collatio,* or sometimes by a fuller name, *lustralis auri argentive collatio*). This tax, from as far back as the early part of the fourth century, applied to all the handicrafts and professions in the Empire, even to servants, beggars, and prostitutes. It was levied, perhaps, even on the tools and livestock of the farmers, such as horses, mules, donkeys, and dogs. The poor classes suffered particularly from the burden of the *chrysargyron.* Officially, this tax was supposed to be collected only once in five years, but in reality the date for its collection was set by the administration arbitrarily and unexpectedly, and these frequent collections at times drove the population to despair.[151] In spite of the large income poured into the government treasury from this tax, Anastasius definitely abolished it and publicly burned all the documents connected with it. The population greeted the abolition of the tax with great joy; to describe this imperial favor, according to one historian of the sixth century, one "needs the eloquence of Thucydides or something still more lofty and graceful."[152] A Syriac source of the sixth century described the joy with which the edict of abolition was received in the city of Edessa:

The whole city rejoiced, and they all put on white garments, both small and great, and carried lighted tapers and censers full of burning incense, and went forth with psalms and hymns, giving thanks to God and praising the emperor, to the church of St. Sergius and St. Simeon, where they celebrated the eucharist. They then re-entered the city and kept a glad and merry festival during the whole week, and enacted that they should celebrate this festival every year. All the artisans were reclining and enjoying themselves, bathing and feasting in the court of the great Church and in all the porticos of the city.

[150] *Byzantine Empire,* I, 352.
[151] O. Seeck, "Collatio lustralis," *Real-Encyclopädie der Classischen Altertumswissenschaft,* ed. A. F. Pauly, G. Wissowa, and others, IV, 370–76.
[152] Evagrii, *Historia ecclesiastica,* III, 39;

ed. Bidez and Parmentier, 137. E. W. Brooks, *Cambridge Medieval History,* I, 484, calls the chrysargyron "a tax on all kinds of stock and plant in trade" and Bury, *Later Roman Empire,* I, 441, "the tax on receipts."

The amount raised by the *chrysargyron* at Edessa was 140 pounds of gold every four years.[153] The abolition of this tax gave special satisfaction to the church, because, by participating in the earnings of prostitutes, the tax implicitly gave legal sanction to vice.[154]

Of course the abolition of the *chrysargyron* deprived the exchequer of considerable revenue but this loss was very soon made good by the introduction of a new tax, the *chrysoteleia* (χρυσοτέλεια), a "gold tax," or "a tax in gold," or a tax in cash instead of kind. It was apparently a land tax, which Anastasius applied to the support of the army. This also weighed heavily on the poorer classes, so that the whole financial reform had in view a more regular distribution of tax burdens rather than a real diminution of them.[155] Perhaps the most important financial reform of Anastasius was the abolition, upon the advice of his trusted praetorian prefect, the Syrian Marinus, of the system under which the town corporations (*curiae*) were responsible for collecting the taxes of the municipalities; Anastasius assigned this task to officials named *vindices,* who probably were appointed by the praetorian prefect. Although this new system of collecting the taxes increased the revenue considerably, it was modified in following reigns. Under Anastasius the problem of sterile lands seems to have become more acute than ever. The burden of additional taxation fell on persons unable to pay, as well as on the unproductive land. The owners of productive land thus became responsible for the full payment of taxes to the government. This additional assessment, called in Greek "epibole" (ἐπιβολή), that is, "increase," "surcharge," was a very old institution going back to Ptolemaic Egypt. It was enacted with particular firmness during the reign of Justinian the Great.[156] Anastasius also decreed that a free peasant-tenant, who had lived in the same place for thirty years, became a *colonus,* a man attached to the soil, but he did not lose his personal freedom and right to own property.

The time of Anastasius I was marked also by the great currency reform. In the year 498 the large bronze *follis* with its smaller denominations was introduced. The new coinage was welcome, especially to the poorer citizens, for the copper money in circulation had become scarce, was bad in quality,

[153] *The Chronicle of Joshua the Stylite,* trans. W. Wright, chap. XXXI, 22.

[154] Bury, *Later Roman Empire,* I, 442 n.

[155] E. W. Brooks, "The Eastern Provinces from Arcadius to Anastasius," *Cambridge Medieval History,* I, 484; E. Stein, *Studien zur Geschichte des byzantinischen Reiches,* 146.

[156] On the *epibole,* in addition to the study of H. Monnier, "Études du droit byzantin," *Nouvelle Revue historique de droit,* XVI

(1892), 497–542, 637–72, see F. Dölger, *Beiträge zur Geschichte der byzantinischen Finanzverwaltung besonders des 10. und 11. Jahrhunderts,* 128–33; G. Ostrogorsky, "A Byzantine Treatise on Taxation," *Recueil d'études dédiées à N. P. Kondakov,* 114–15; Ostrogorsky, "Die ländliche Steuergemeinde des byzantinischen Reiches im X. Jahrhundert," *Vierteljahrschrift für sozial- und Wirtschaftsgeschichte,* XX (1927), 25–27. These three studies furnish a good bibliography.

and had no marks of value. The new coins were struck at the three mints which were in operation under Anastasius, at Constantinople, Nicomedia, and Antioch. The bronze coinage introduced by Anastasius remained the model of imperial currency until about the second half of the seventh century.[157]

To his list of humanitarian reforms Anastasius added a decree forbidding fights between men and beasts in the circus.

Although Anastasius often granted tax reductions to many provinces and cities, especially those in the East devastated by the Persian War, and although he carried out a building program including the Long Wall, aqueducts, the lighthouse of Alexandria, and other projects, the government toward the end of his reign still possessed a large reserve which the historian Procopius estimated, perhaps with some exaggeration, at 320 thousand pounds of gold, equivalent to about $65,000,000 or $70,000,000.[158] The economy of Anastasius was of great importance to the abundant activities of his second successor, Justinian the Great. The time of Anastasius was a splendid introduction to the Justinian epoch.

Summary

The main interest of the epoch beginning with Arcadius and ending with Anastasius (395–518) lies in the national and religious problems and in the political events, which were always closely connected with the religious movements. The Germanic, or, to be more exact, the Gothic, tyranny grew very strong in the capital and menaced the entire state in the late fourth century. This was further complicated by the Arian leanings of the Goths. This menace decreased at the beginning of the fifth century under Arcadius and was completely removed by Leo I at the time of its later and much weaker outburst in the middle of the fifth century. Then, at the end of the century, came the new Ostrogothic menace from the north, which was successfully diverted by Zeno into Italy. Thus the Germanic problem in the eastern part of the Empire was settled to the advantage of the government.

The eastern part of the Empire was also successful in achieving in the second half of the fifth century a favorable settlement of the less acute and significant

[157] See W. Wroth, *Catalogue of the Imperial Byzantine Coins in the British Museum*, I, xiii–xiv, lxxvii. Bury, *Later Roman Empire*, I, 446–47. The most recent study is by R. P. Blake, "The Monetary Reform of Anastasius I and Its Economic Implications," *Studies in the History of Culture*, 84–97. Blake wrote: "The inflational prices of the early fourth century have vanished and a reasonable stable level appears to have been attained; how much

Anastasius' reform actually helped in this matter must remain uncertain in the absence of further data" (p. 97).

[158] *Historia quae dicitur Arcana*, 19, 7–8; ed. J. Haury, 121. Delehaye, "Life of Daniel the Stylite," *Analecta Bollandiana*, XXXII (1913), 206; French ed., 86. See Baynes, "Vita S. Danielis," *English Historical Review*, XL (1925), 402.

national problem, that of the Isaurian predominance. The Bulgarians and Slavs were only beginning their attacks upon the borders of the Empire during this period and it was not yet possible to foretell the great role which these northern peoples were destined to play in the history of the Byzantine Empire. The period of Anastasius may be viewed as only an introduction to the Slavic epoch in the Balkan peninsula.

The religious problem of this epoch falls into two phases: the orthodox, up to the time of Zeno, and the Monophysitic, under Zeno and Anastasius. Zeno's favorable attitude towards the Monophysitic doctrine and the explicit Monophysitic sympathies of Anastasius were important not only from the dogmatical point of view but from the political point of view as well. By the end of the fifth century the western part of the Empire, in spite of a theoretically recognized unity, had practically detached itself from Constantinople. In Gaul, in Spain, and in northern Africa new barbaric kingdoms were formed; Italy was practically ruled by German chiefs, and at the end of the fifth century the Ostrogothic kingdom was founded on Italian territory. This state of affairs explains why the eastern provinces—Egypt, Palestine, and Syria— became of exceptionally great importance to the eastern half of the Empire. The great merit of both Zeno and Anastasius lies in the fact that they understood that the center of gravity had shifted and, appreciating the importance of the eastern provinces, they used every possible means to find a way of binding them to the capital. Since these provinces, especially Egypt and Syria, were in general devoted to the Monophysitic doctrine, there could be only one course for the Empire—to make peace with the Monophysites at any cost. This explains Zeno's evasive and purposely rather obscure Henoticon. It was one of the first steps toward the reconciliation with the Monophysites. When this attempt failed to bring results, Anastasius decided to follow a very definite Monophysitic policy. Both these emperors were politically perspicacious rulers as compared with the emperors of the subsequent period. In their Monophysitic policy both were confronted by the orthodox movement, widely supported in the capital, in the Balkan peninsula, in most of the provinces of Asia Minor, in the islands, and in some portions of Palestine. Orthodoxy was also defended by the pope, who broke off all relations with Constantinople because of the Henoticon. The inevitability of the collision between politics and religion explains the internal religious upheavals during the reign of Anastasius. He did not succeed in bringing about during his lifetime the desired peace and harmony within the Empire. His successors, moreover, led the Empire along an entirely different path, and alienation of the eastern provinces was already beginning to be felt at the end of this period.

On the whole this was a period of struggle on the part of the different nationalities, spurred by greatly differing aims and hopes: the Germans and the Isaurians wanted to attain political supremacy, while the Copts in Egypt and the Syrians were concerned primarily with the triumph of their religious doctrines.

LITERATURE, LEARNING, EDUCATION, AND ART

The developments in literature, learning, and education during the period from the fourth to the beginning of the sixth century are closely connected with the relations established between Christianity and the ancient pagan world with its great culture. The debates of the Christian apologists of the second and third centuries on the question of whether or not it was permissible for a Christian to use pagan materials brought no definite conclusion. While some of the apologists found merit in Greek culture and considered it reconcilable with Christianity, others denied that pagan antiquity was of any significance to the Christian and repudiated it. A different attitude prevailed in Alexandria, the old center of heated philosophic and religious disputes, where discussions on the compatibility of ancient paganism with Christianity tended to draw together these two seemingly irreconcilable elements. Clement of Alexandria, for example, the famous writer of the late second century, said: "Philosophy, serving as a guide, prepares those who are called by Christ to perfection."[159] Still, the problem of the relation between pagan culture and Christianity was by no means settled by the debates of the first three centuries of the Christian era.

But life did its work, and pagan society was gradually being converted to Christianity, which received a particularly great impetus in the fourth century. It was aided on the one hand by the protection of the government, and on the other by the numerous so-called "heresies," which awakened intellectual disputes, aroused passionate discussions, and created a series of new and important questions. Meanwhile Christianity was gradually absorbing many of the elements of pagan culture, so that, according to Krumbacher, "Christian topics were being unconsciously clothed in pagan garb."[160] Christian literature of the fourth and fifth centuries was enriched by the works of great writers in the field of prose as well as that of poetry. At the same time the pagan traditions were continued and developed by representatives of pagan thought.

In the wide realm of the Roman Empire, within the boundaries which existed until the Persian and Arabian conquests of the seventh century, the Christian Orient of the fourth and fifth centuries had several distinct, well-

---

[159] *Stromata,* I, 5; ed. Migne, *Patrologia Graeca,* VIII, 717–20.
[160] *Die griechische Literatur des Mittelal-* ters. *Die Kultur des Gegenwart: ihre Entwicklung und ihre Ziele* (3rd ed., 1912), 337.

known literary centers, whose representative writers exerted great influence far beyond the limits of their native cities and provinces. Cappadocia, in Asia Minor, had in the fourth century the three famous "Cappadocians," Basil the Great, his friend Gregory the Theologian, and Gregory of Nyssa, younger brother of Basil. Important cultural centers in Syria were the cities of Antioch and Berytus (Beirut) on the seacoast; the latter was particularly famous for studies in the field of law, and the time of its brilliance lasted from about 200 to 551 A.D.[161] In Palestine, Jerusalem had at this time not yet completely recovered from the destruction during the reign of Titus, and consequently it did not play a very significant part in the cultural life of the fourth and fifth centuries. But Caesarea, and toward the end of the fourth century, the southern Palestinian city of Gaza, with its flourishing school of famous rhetoricians and poets, contributed much to the treasures of thought and literature in this period. But above all these the Egyptian city of Alexandria still remained the center which exerted the widest and deepest influence upon the entire Asiatic Orient. The new city of Constantinople, destined to have a brilliant future in the time of Justinian, was only beginning to show signs of literary activity. Here the official protection of the Latin language, somewhat detached from actual life, was particularly pronounced. Of some importance to the general cultural and literary movements of this epoch were two other western centers of the eastern Empire, Thessalonica and Athens, the latter with its pagan academy, eclipsed in later years by its victorious rival, the University of Constantinople.

A comparison of the cultural developments in the eastern and the western provinces of the Byzantine Empire reveals an interesting phenomenon: in European Greece, with its old population, spiritual activity and creativeness were infinitely small in comparison with developments in the provinces of Asia and Africa, despite the fact that the greater part of these provinces, according to Krumbacher, were "discovered" and colonized only from the time of Alexander the Great. The same scholar, resorted to "our favorite modern language of numbers," and asserted that the European group of Byzantine provinces was responsible for only ten per cent of the general cultural productivity of this period.[162] In truth, the majority of writers of this epoch came from Asia and Africa, whereas after the founding of Constantinople almost all the historians were Greeks. Patristic literature had its brilliant period of development in the fourth, and the early part of the fifth, century.

The Cappadocians Basil the Great and Gregory of Nazianzus received an admirable education in the best rhetorical schools of Athens and Alexandria. Unfortunately, no definite information exists about the early education of

---

[161] See P. Collinet, *Histoire de l'École de droit de Beyrouth*, 305.

[162] *Die griechische Literatur des Mittelalters*, 330.

Basil's younger brother, Gregory of Nyssa, the most profound thinker of the three. They were all well acquainted with classical literature and represented the so-called "new Alexandrian" movement. This movement, while using the acquisitions of philosophical thinking, insisting upon a place for reason in the study of religious dogma, and refusing to adopt the extremes of the mystical-allegorical movement of the so-called "Alexandrian" school, still did not discard the church tradition. In addition to the wealth of literary works on purely theological subjects wherein they ardently defend orthodoxy in its struggle with Arianism, these three writers left also a large collection of orations and letters. This collection constitutes one of the richest sources of cultural material for the period and even yet it has not been fully exhausted from a historical point of view. Gregory of Nazianzus also left a number of poems, which are chiefly theological, dogmatical, and didactic but are also somewhat historical. His long poem *About His Own Life* should by reason of form and content take a high place in the field of literature in general. Brilliant as they were, these three writers were the only representatives of their city. "When these three noble geniuses had passed away, Cappadocia returned into the obscurity from which they had drawn it."[163]

Antioch, the Syrian center of culture, produced in opposition to the Alexandrian school its own movement, which defended the literal acceptance of the Holy Scriptures without allegorical interpretations. This movement was headed by such unusual men of action as the pupil of Libanius and favorite of Antioch, John Chrysostom. He combined thorough classical education with unusual stylistic and oratorical ability and his numerous works constitute one of the world's great literary treasures. Later generations fell under the spell of his genius and high moral qualities, and literary movements of subsequent periods borrowed ideas, images, and expressions from his works as from an unlimited source. So great was his reputation that in the course of time many works of unknown authors have been ascribed to him; but his authentic works, sermons, and orations and more than two hundred letters, written mainly during his exile, represent an extremely valuable source regarding the internal life of the Empire.[164] The attitude of posterity is well characterized by a Byzantine writer of the fourteenth century, Nicephorus Callistus, who wrote: "I have read more than a thousand sermons by him, which pour forth unspeakable sweetness. From my youth I have loved him and listened to his voice as if it were that of God. And what I know and what I am, I owe to him."[165]

[163] E. Fialon, *Étude historique et littéraire sur Saint Basile* (2nd ed., 1869), 284.

[164] See J. M. Vance, *Beiträge zur byzantinische Kulturgeschichte am Ausgange des IV. Jahrhunderts aus den Schriften des Johannes Chrysostomos.*

[165] *Historia ecclesiastica*, XIII, 2; ed. Migne, *Patrologia Graeca*, CXLVI, 933. With this beautiful passage P. Baur opens his biography of Chrysostom, I, vii.

From the Palestinian city of Caesarea came the "father of ecclesiastical history," Eusebius, who lived in the second half of the third century and the early part of the fourth century. He died about the year 340. He has been cited earlier as the chief authority on Constantine the Great. Eusebius lived on the threshold of two highly significant historical epochs: on one hand, he witnessed the severe persecutions of Diocletian and his successors and suffered much personally because of his Christian convictions; on the other hand, after the Edict of Galerius he lived through a period of gradual triumph of Christianity under Constantine and participated in the Arian disputes, inclining sometimes to the Arians. He later became one of the greatly trusted and intimate friends of the Emperor. Eusebius wrote many theological and historical works. *The Evangelic Preparation* (Εὐαγγελικὴ προπαρασκευή, *Praeparatio evangelica*), the large work in which he defends the Christians against the religious attacks of the pagans, *The Evangelic Demonstration* (Εὐαγγελικὴ ἀπόδειξις, *Demonstratio evangelica*), in which he discusses the merely temporal significance of the Mosaic law and the fulfillment of the prophecies of the Old Testament by Jesus Christ, his writings in the field of criticism and interpretation of the Holy Scriptures, as well as several other works entitle him to a high place of honor in the field of theological literature. These works also contain valuable extracts from older writings which were later lost.

For this study the historical writings of Eusebius are of greater importance. *The Chronicle,* written apparently before Diocletian's persecutions, contains a brief survey of the history of the Chaldeans, Assyrians, Hebrews, Egyptians, Greeks, and Romans and in its main portion gives chronological tables of the most important historical events. Unfortunately it has survived only through an Armenian translation and partly through a Latin adaptation of St. Jerome. Thus no accurate conception of the form and contents of the original exists today, especially since the translations which have survived were made not from the original Greek, but from an adaptation of *The Chronicle* which appeared soon after Eusebius' death.

His outstanding historical work is the *Ecclesiastical History,* ten books covering the period from the time of Christ to the victory of Constantine over Licinius. According to his own statement, he did not aim to tell of wars and the trophies of generals, but rather to "record in ineffaceable letters the most peaceful wars waged in behalf of the peace of the soul, and to tell of men doing brave deeds for truth rather than country, for piety rather than dearest friends."[166] Under the pen of Eusebius, church history became the history of martyrdom and persecutions, with all the accompanying terror and atrocities. Because of its abundance of documentary data, his history must be recognized as one of the very important sources for the first three centuries

---

[166] Eusebius, *Historia ecclesiastica,* intro. to book V, *Nicene and Post-Nicene Fathers,* I, 211.

of the Christian era. Besides, Eusebius was important also because he was the first to write a history of Christianity, embracing that subject from all possible aspects. His *Ecclesiastical History,* which brought him much fame, became the basis for the work of many later church historians and was often imitated. As early as the fourth century it became widely spread in the West through the Latin translation of Rufinus.[167]

The Life of Constantine, written by Eusebius at a later period—if it was written by him at all—has called forth many varied interpretations and evaluations in the scholarly world. It must be classed not so much among the purely historical types of writing as among the panegyrics. Constantine is represented as a God-chosen emperor endowed with the gift of prevision, a new Moses destined to lead God's people to freedom. In Eusebius' interpretation the three sons of Constantine personified the Holy Trinity, while Constantine himself was the true benefactor of the Christians, who now attained the high ideal of which they had only dreamed before. In order to keep the harmony of his work intact, Eusebius did not touch upon the darker sides of the epoch, did not reveal the sinister phenomena of his day, but rather gave full sway to the praise and glorification of his hero. Yet, by a skillful use of this work one may gain much valuable insight into the period of Constantine, especially because it contains many official documents which probably were inserted after the first version was written.[168] In spite of his mediocre literary ability, Eusebius must be considered one of the greatest Christian scholars of the early Middle Ages and a writer who greatly influenced medieval Christian literature.

A whole group of historians continued what Eusebius had begun. Socrates of Constantinople carried his *Ecclesiastical History* up to the year 439; Sozomen, a native of the district near the Palestinian city of Gaza, was the author of another *Ecclesiastical History,* also up to the year 439; Theodoret, bishop of Cyrus, a native of Antioch, wrote a similar history covering the period from the Council of Nicaea until the year 428; and, finally, the Arian Philostorgius, whose works have survived only in fragments, narrated events up to the year 425 from his own Arian point of view.

The most intense and varied intellectual life during this period was to be found in Egypt, especially in its progressive center, Alexandria.

An unusual and interesting figure in the literary life of the late fourth and early fifth centuries was Synesius of Cyrene. A descendant of a very old pagan family, educated in Alexandria and later introduced to the mysteries of the

---

[167] Among many other writings on Eusebius' *History,* see R. Laqeur, *Eusebius als Historiker seiner Zeit.* The author has shown the historical importance of Eusebius' last three books, VIII–X.

[168] In 1938 Grégoire convincingly proved, I believe, that Eusebius was not the author of the *Life of Constantine* in the form in which it has come down to us: *Byzantion,* XIII (1938), 568–83; XIV (1939), 318–19.

neo-Platonic philosophy, he shifted his allegiance from Plato to Christ, married a Christian girl, and became bishop of Ptolemaïs during the last years of his life. In spite of all this, Synesius probably always felt more of a pagan than a Christian. His mission to Constantinople and his address "on Kingship" show his interest in politics. He was not essentially a historian, yet he left extremely important historical materials in 156 letters which reflect his brilliant philosophic and rhetorical attainments and which set the standard of style for the Byzantine Middle Ages. His hymns, written in the meter and style of classical poetry, reveal a peculiar mixture of philosophical and Christian views. This bishop-philosopher felt that the classical culture so dear to him was gradually approaching its end.[169]

During the long and harsh struggle with Arianism appeared the brilliant figure of the ardent Nicaean, Athanasius, bishop of Alexandria, who left a number of writings devoted to theological disputes in the fourth century. He also wrote the *Life of St. Anthony,* one of the founders of eastern monasticism, painting in it an ideal picture of ascetic life. This work greatly influenced the spread of monasticism. To the fifth century belongs also the greatest historian of Egyptian monasticism, Palladius of Helenopolis, born in Asia Minor, but well acquainted with Egyptian monastic life because of a sojourn of about ten years in the Egyptian monastic world. Under the influence of Athanasius of Alexandria, Palladius once more presented the ideals of monastic life, introducing into his history an element of legend. The ruthless enemy of Nestorius, Cyril, bishop of Alexandria, also lived during this period. During his stormy and strenuous life he wrote a large number of letters and sermons which the Greek bishops of a later period sometimes learned by heart. He also left a number of dogmatic, polemical, and exegetic treatises which serve as one of the main sources on the ecclesiastical history of the fifth century. According to his own confession, his rhetorical education was insufficient and he could not pride himself upon the Attic purity of his style.

Another extremely interesting figure of this epoch is the woman philosopher, Hypatia, who was killed by the fanatical mob of Alexandria some time in the early part of the fifth century. She was a woman of exceptional beauty and unusual intellectual attainments. Through her father, a famous Alexandrian mathematician, she became acquainted with the mathematical sciences and classical philosophy. She gained wide fame through her remarkable activities as a teacher. Among her pupils were such great literary men as Synesius of Cyrene, who mentions the name of Hypatia in many of his letters.

[169] Fitzgerald, *Letters of Synesius,* 11–69. Fitzgerald, *Essays and Hymns of Synesius,* 1–102 (an ample introduction); 103–7 (excellent bibliography). Also C. H. Coster, "Synesius, a Curialis of the Time of the Emperor Arcadius," *Byzantion,* XV (1940–41), 10–38. Good documentation.

122 Constantine to Justinian

One source told how, "clothed in a mantle, she used to wander about the city and expound to willing listeners the works of Plato, Aristotle, or some other philosopher."[170]

Greek literature flourished in Egypt until the year 451, when the Council of Chalcedon condemned the Monophysitic doctrine. Since this doctrine was the official Egyptian religion, the action of the council was followed by the abolition of Greek from the church and the substitution of the Coptic language in its stead. The Coptic literature which developed after this is of some importance even to Greek literature, because certain original Greek works which have been lost are preserved at present only through their Coptic translations.

This period saw the development of the literature of religious hymns. The hymn writers gradually abandoned their original practice of imitating classical meters and developed forms of their own. These forms were quite original and for some time were considered merely as prose. It is only in comparatively recent times that these meters have been even partially explained. They are marked by various types of acrostics and rhymes. Unfortunately very little is known of the religious hymns of the fourth and fifth centuries and the history of their gradual development is therefore obscure. Yet it is quite apparent that this development was vigorous. While Gregory the Theologian followed the antique meters in most of his poetical hymns, Romanus the Melode ("Hymn-writer"), whose works appeared in the early sixth century under Anastasius I, used the new forms and made use of acrostics and rhyme.

Scholars have long disputed as to whether Romanus lived in the sixth or in the early eighth century. His brief *Life* alludes to his arrival at Constantinople during the reign of the Emperor Anastasius, but for a long time it was impossible to determine whether this was Anastasius I (491–518) or Anastasius II (713–16). The scholarly world, however, after a long study of the works of Romanus, has definitely agreed that he referred to Anastasius I.[171] Romanus the Melode is sometimes called the greatest poet of the Byzantine period. This "Pindar of rhythmical poetry,"[172] "the greatest religious genius,"

---

[170] Suidae, *Lexicon, s. v.* Ὑπατία. The very well-known novel of Charles Kingsley, *Hypatia, or New Foes with an Old Face,* may be read with great interest and profit.

[171] See A. A. Vasiliev, "The Lifetime of Romanus the Melode," *Vizantiysky Vremennik,* VIII (1901), 435–78. P. Maas, "Die Chronologie der Hymnen des Romanos," *Byzantinische Zeitschrift,* XV (1906), 1–44. More recent studies: M. Carpenter, "The Paper that

Romanos Swallowed," *Speculum,* VII (1932), 3–22; "Romanos and the Mystery Play of the East," *The University of Missouri Studies,* XI, 3 (1936); E. Mioni, *Romano il Melode. Saggio critico e dieci inni inediti,* VI, 230 (he does not know Vasiliev's study); G. Cammelli, *Romano il Melode.*

[172] K. Krumbacher, *Geschichte der byzantinischen Litteratur,* 663.

"the Dante of the neo-Hellenes,"[173] is the author of a large number of superb hymns among which is the famous Christian hymn, "Today the Virgin Brings Forth the Supersubstantial."[174] The poet was born in Syria, and it is very probable that the flowering of his genius occurred during the reign of Justinian, for according to his *Life* he was a young deacon when he came, during the rule of Anastasius, from Syria to Constantinople, where he miraculously acquired from heaven the gift of writing hymns. The finished work of Romanus in the sixth century seems to indicate that religious poetry in the fifth century had reached a high stage of development; unfortunately the data is inadequate on this point. It is certainly difficult to conceive the existence of this unusual poet in the sixth century without some previous development of church poetry. Unfortunately, also, he cannot be appreciated fully because most of his hymns are still unpublished.[175]

Lactantius, an eminent Christian writer from north Africa in the early part of the fourth century, wrote in Latin. He is particularly important as the author of *De mortibus persecutorum*. This work gives very interesting information on the time of Diocletian and Constantine down to the so-called rescript of Milan.[176]

The Christian literature of this period is represented by many remarkable authors, but pagan literature does not lag far behind. Among its representatives, too, were a number of gifted and interesting men, one of whom is Themistius of Paphlagonia, who lived in the second half of the fourth century. He was the philosophically educated director of the school of Constantinople, the court orator, and a senator highly esteemed by both pagans and Christians. He wrote a large collection of "Paraphrases of Aristotle," in which he sought to clarify the more complicated ideas of the Greek philosopher. He is the author also of about forty orations which give abundant information about the important events of the period as well as about his own personal life. The greatest of all the pagan teachers of the fourth century was Libanius of Antioch, who influenced his contemporaries more than any other man of

[173] H. Gelzer, *Die Genesis der byzantinischen Themenverfassung*, 76. Gelzer thought that Romanus lived in the eighth century. Cf. E. Stein in *Gnomon*, IV (1928), 413: "The church poet Romanus appears to me merely dull [*langweilig*]."

[174] See G. Cammelli, "L'inno per la natività de Romano il Melode," *Studi Bizantini* (1925), 45–48. Cammelli, *Romano il Melode*, 88.

[175] A critical edition of Romanus' works has been prepared by P. Maas. See *Byzantinische Zeitschrift*, XXIV (1924), 284.

[176] See M. Schanz, *Geschichte der römischen Litteratur* (3rd ed., 1922), III, 413–37; on the *De mortibus persecutorum*, 462–67; (3rd ed.), 427 ff. The best work on Lactantius is R. Pichon, *Lactance. Étude sur le movement philosophique et religieux sous le règne de Constantin*. The most recent bibliography on Lactantius is in K. Roller, *Die Kaisergeschichte in Laktanz De mortibus persecutorum*, 41. English trans. W. Fletcher, *Ante-Nicene Christian Library*, XXI–XXII.

the period. Among his pupils were John Chrysostom, Basil the Great, and Gregory of Nazianzus, and his lectures were studied enthusiastically by the young Julian before he ascended the throne. Libanius' sixty-five public addresses are of particular interest and provide abundant material about the internal life of the time. Of no lesser importance is the collection of his letters, which in richness of content and remarkable spirit may be compared with the letters of Synesius of Cyrene.

The Emperor Julian was an extremely brilliant figure in the intellectual life of the fourth century, and despite the brevity of his career he clearly demonstrated his talent in various departments of literature. His orations, reflecting his obscure philosophical and religious speculations, such as his appeal "To the King Sun"; his letters; his "Against the Christians," which is preserved in fragments only; his satirical *Misopogon* ("The Beardhater"),[177] written against the people of Antioch, important as a biographical source—all these reveal Julian as a gifted writer, historian, thinker, satirist, and moralist. The extent to which his writings were interwoven with the actual realities of the period should be emphasized. The early and sudden death of this young emperor prevented the full development of his unusual genius.

Pagan literature of the fourth and fifth centuries is represented also by several writers in the field of pure history. Among the most significant was the author of the very well-known collection of biographies of Roman emperors written in Latin in the fourth century and known under the title of *Scriptores Historiae Augustae*. The identity of its author, the time of its compilation, and its historical significance are all debatable and have produced an enormous literature.[178] But in 1923 an English historian wrote: "The time and labour spent upon the Augustan history . . . are overwhelming and their results, so far as any practical use for history goes, are precisely nil."[179] N. Baynes recently made a very interesting attempt to prove that this collection was written under Julian the Apostate with a definite object: propaganda for Julian, his whole administration and religious policy.[180] This point of view has not been accepted by scholars.[181]

Priscus of Thrace, a historian of the fifth century and a member of the embassy to the Huns, was another who made significant contributions. His

---

[177] The people of Antioch ridiculed Julian's beard.

[178] See for example, Schanz, *Geschichte der römischen Litteratur* (2nd ed., 1905), III, 83–90. A Gercke and E. Norden, *Einleitung in die Altertumswissenschaft* (2nd ed., 1914), III, 255–56. A. Rosenberg, *Einleitung und Quellenkunde zur römischen Geschichte*, 231–41.

[179] B. Henderson, *The Life and Principate of the Emperor Hadrian*, 275.

[180] *The Historia Augusta: Its Date and Purpose*, 57–58, a very good bibliography, 7–16. The author begins his book with the passage quoted from Henderson.

[181] N. Baynes, *"The Historia Augusta: its date and purpose.* A Reply to Criticism," *The Classical Quarterly*, XXII (1928), 166. The author himself remarks that his suggestion had, on the whole, "a bad press."

Byzantine History, which has survived in fragments, and his information on the life and customs of the Huns are both extremely interesting and valuable. In fact, Priscus was the main source on the history of Attila and the Huns for the Latin historians of the sixth century, Cassiodorus and Jordanes. Zosimus, who lived in the fifth century and early part of the sixth, wrote *The New History,* bringing his account down to Alaric's siege of Rome in the year 410. As an enthusiastic believer in the old gods he explained that the fall of the Roman Empire was caused by the anger of the gods at being forsaken by the Romans and he blamed Constantine the Great above all. His opinion of Julian was very high. According to a recent writer, Zosimus is not only a historian of the "decline of Rome" but he is also a theoretician of the republic which he defends and glorifies; he is the sole "republican" of the fifth century.[182]

Ammianus Marcellinus, a Syrian Greek born in Antioch, wrote at the end of the fourth century his *Res Gestae,* a history of the Roman Empire in Latin. He intended it to be a continuation of the history of Tacitus, bringing the account through the period from Nerva to the death of Valens (96–378). Only the last eighteen books of this history have survived, covering historical events during the period 353–378. The author profited from his harsh military experience in Julian's campaigns against the Persians and has given firsthand information about contemporary events. Although he remained a pagan to the end of his life, he showed great tolerance toward Christianity. His history is an important source for the period of Julian and Valens, as well as for Gothic and early Hunnic history. His literary genius has been very highly estimated by recent scholars. Stein called him the greatest literary genius in the world between Tacitus and Dante,[183] and N. Baynes called him the last great historian of Rome.[184]

Athens, the city of declining classical thought, was in the fifth century the home of the last distinguished representative of neo-Platonism, Proclus of Constantinople, who taught and wrote there for a long period of years. It was also the birthplace of the wife of Theodosius II, Eudocia Athenais, who possessed some literary ability and wrote several works.

Western European literature of this period, which was brilliantly represented by the remarkable works of St. Augustine and several other gifted writers of prose and poetry, is not discussed here.

After the transfer of the capital to Constantinople, Latin still remained the official language of the Empire during the fourth and fifth centuries. It was

[182] E. Condurachi, "Les Idées politiques de Zozime," *Revista Clasică,* XIII–XIV (1941–42), 125, 127.

[183] *Geschichte der spätrömischen Reiches,* I, 331.

[184] *Journal of Roman Studies,* XVIII, 2 (1928), 224.

used for all the imperial decrees collected in the Theodosian code as well as for the later decrees of the fifth and the beginning of the sixth centuries. But in the curriculum of the higher school at Constantinople in the time of Theodosius II there was a decline of the predominance of Latin and a definite preference for Greek, which was, after all, the most widely spoken language in the eastern part of the Empire. The Greek tradition was also upheld by the Athenian pagan school.

The time from the fourth to the sixth centuries is one when various elements were gradually blending into a new art which bears the name of Byzantine or East-Christian. As the science of history probes more deeply into the roots of this art, it becomes increasingly clear that the East and its traditions played the predominant part in the development of Byzantine art. By the end of the nineteenth century German scholars advanced the theory that the "art of the Roman Empire" (*Römische Reichskunst*), which had developed in the West during the first two centuries of the Empire, replaced the old Hellenistic culture of the East, which was in a state of decline, and, so to speak, laid the cornerstone for Christian art of the fourth and fifth centuries. At present this theory is repudiated. Since the appearance in 1900 of the famous work of D. V. Aïnalov, *Hellenistic Origin of Byzantine Art,* and the publication in 1901 of the remarkable work of the Austrian scholar J. Strzygowski, *Orient or Rome,* the problem of the origin of Byzantine art has assumed an entirely new form; it is taken for granted that the main role in the development of East-Christian art belongs to the East, and the problem is only that of determining what is to be understood by the term "East" and eastern influences. In a large number of very stimulating works the tireless Strzygowski argued the enormous influence exerted by the ancient Orient. At first he sought the center of this influence in Constantinople; later he turned to Egypt, Asia Minor, and Syria, and moving still farther to the east and north, he crossed the borders of Mesopotamia and sought the roots of the main influences in the plateau and mountains of Altaï-Iran and in Armenia. He contended, "What Hellas was to the art of antiquity, that Iran was to the art of the new Christian world."[185] He drew also upon India and Chinese Turkestan for further elucidation of the problem. While recognizing his great services in investigating the origin of Byzantine art, contemporary historical science is still very cautious with regard to his most recent hypotheses.[186]

The fourth century was an extremely important period in the history of Byzantine art. The new status of the Christian faith in the Roman Empire,

[185] *Ursprung der christlichen Kirchenkunst,* 18; English trans. O. Dalton and H. Braunholtz, *Origin of Christian Church Art,* 21; a list of Strzygowski's works, 253–59.

[186] See, for example, C. Diehl, *Manuel d'art byzantin* (2nd ed., 1925–26), I, 16–21; O. Dalton, *East Christian Art,* 10–23, and especially 366–76.

first as a legal religion and later as the state religion, furthered the rapid growth of Christianity. Three elements—Christianity, Hellenism, and the Orient—met in the fourth century, and out of their union grew what is known as East-Christian art.

Having been made the political center of the Empire, Constantinople gradually became also the intellectual and artistic center. This did not happen at once. "Constantinople had no established pre-existing culture to resist or to control the influx of exotic forces; she had first to balance and assimilate new influences, a task which required at least a hundred years."[187]

Syria and Antioch, Egypt guided by Alexandria, and Asia Minor, reflecting in their artistic life the influences of more ancient traditions, exerted a very strong and beneficial influence on the growth of East-Christian art. Syrian architecture flourished throughout the fourth, fifth, and sixth centuries. The magnificent churches of Jerusalem and Bethlehem, as well as some churches at Nazareth, were erected as early as the reign of Constantine the Great. Unusual splendor characterized the churches of Antioch and Syria. "Antioch, as the center of a brilliant civilization, naturally assumed the leadership of Christian art in Syria."[188] Unfortunately for a long time very little data was available on the art of Antioch, and it is only recently that its beauty and importance have become better known.[189] The "dead cities" of central Syria uncovered in 1860 and 1861 by M. de Vogue give some conception of what Christian architecture of the fourth, fifth, and sixth centuries was like. One of the most remarkable products of the end of the fifth century was the famous monastery of St. Simeon Stylites (Kalat Seman), located between Antioch and Aleppo, impressive even today in its majestic ruin.[190] The well-known frieze of Mschatta, east of the Jordan, now in the Kaiser Friedrich Museum of Berlin, is apparently also a work of the fourth, fifth, or sixth centuries.[191] To the beginning of the fifth century belongs a beautiful basilica in Egypt erected by the Emperor Arcadius over the grave of Menas, a renowned Egyptian saint. Its ruins have only recently been excavated and studied by C. M. Kaufmann.[192] In the field of mosaics, portraiture, textiles (figured silks of early Christian times), and so forth, several interesting products of the early part of the Byzantine period exist.

---

[187] O. Dalton, *Byzantine Art and Archaeology*, 10.

[188] Diehl, *Manuel d'art byzantin*, I, 26.

[189] See C. R. Morey, *The Mosaics of Antioch*, and three beautiful volumes, *Antioch-on-the-Orontes*.

[190] See the plan and pictures in Diehl, *Manuel d'art byzantin*, I, 36–37, 45–47. J. Mattern, "A travers les villes mortes de Haute-Syrie,"

Mélanges de l'Université Saint-Joseph, XVII, 1 (1933), 175; on the sanctuary of St. Simeon, 87–104; many illustrations. A new edition of this book, *Villes mortes de Haute-Syrie* (1944), 115–38.

[191] On the chronological discrepancy see Diehl, *Manuel d'art byzantin*, I, 53; Dalton, *East Christian Art*, 109, n. 1.

[192] *Die Menasstadt*, I.

The city walls which surrounded Constantinople in the fifth century have survived to the present day. The Golden Gate (Porta Aurea), through which the emperors made their official entry into Constantinople, was built at the end of the fourth century or the early part of the fifth; remarkable for its architectural splendor, it is still in existence.

With the name of Constantine is bound up the erection of the Church of St. Irene and the Church of the Apostles in Constantinople. St. Sophia, the construction of which might have begun in his time, was completed in the time of his son Constantius. These churches were reconstructed in the sixth century by Justinian. In the fifth century another church embellished the new capital, the Basilica of St. John of Studion, which is now the mosque Mir-Achor djami.

A number of monuments of early Byzantine art have been preserved in the western parts of the Empire. Among these are some churches at Thessalonica (Salonika); Diocletian's palace at Spalato, in Dalmatia (early fourth century); some paintings in S. Maria Antiqua at Rome, dating apparently from the end of the fifth century;[193] the mausoleum of Galla Placidia and the orthodox baptistery at Ravenna (fifth century); and some monuments in North Africa.

In the history of art the fourth and fifth centuries may be viewed as the preparatory period for the epoch of Justinian the Great, when "the capital had attained a full self-consciousness and had assumed to itself a directive power," the epoch which has been justly described as the First Golden Age of Byzantine Art.[194]

---

[193] Dalton, *East Christian Art,* 249. Cf. Diehl, *Manuel d'art byzantin,* I, 352.

[194] Dalton, *Byzantine Art and Archaeology,* 10.

CHAPTER III: JUSTINIAN THE GREAT AND HIS IMMEDIATE SUCCESSORS (518–610)

IN THEIR external as well as in their religious policy the successors of Zeno and Anastasius followed a path directly opposite to that of their two predecessors, for they turned their faces from the East to the West.

During the period from 518 to 578 the throne was occupied by the following persons: Justin the Elder (518–27), a chief of the Guard (Count of the Excubitors),[1] who by a mere accident was elected to the throne after the death of Anastasius; his famous nephew, Justinian the Great (527–65); and a nephew of the latter, Justin II, known as the Younger (565–78). The names of Justin and Justinian are closely connected with the problem of their Slavonic extraction, which was long regarded by many scholars as a historical fact. This theory was based upon a *Life* of the Emperor Justinian written by the abbot Theophilus, a teacher of Justinian, and published by the keeper of the Vatican Library, Nicholas Alemannus, in the early part of the seventeenth century. This *Life* introduces special names for Justinian and his relatives, names by which they were known in their native land and which, in the opinion of the high authorities in Slavonic studies, were Slavonic names, as, for example, Justinian's name Upravda, "the truth, justice." When the manuscript used by Alemannus was found and studied at the end of the nineteenth century (1883) by the English scholar Bryce, he proved that it was composed in the early part of the seventeenth century and was purely legendary, without historical value. The theory of Justinian's Slavonic origin must therefore be discarded at present.[2] Justin and Justinian were probably Illyrians or perhaps Albanians. Justinian was born in one of the villages of upper Macedonia, not far from present-day Uskub, on the Albanian border. Some scholars trace Justinian's family back to Roman colonists of Dardania, i.e., upper Macedonia.[3] The first three emperors of this epoch, then, were

---

[1] The Excubitors were a regiment of the Byzantine guard.

[2] J. Bryce, "Life of Justinian by Theophilus," *Archivio della Reale Società Romana di Storia Patria*, X (1887), 137–71; also in the *English Historical Review*, II (1887), 657–84.

[3] C. Jireček, *Geschichte der Serben*, I, 36.

J. B. Bury, *History of the Later Roman Empire*, II, 18, n. 3. On the origin of Justinian see A. A. Vasiliev, "The Problem of Justinian's Slavic Origin," *Vizantiysky Vremennik*, I (1894), 469–92. There are many recent articles on Justinian's origin.

Illyrians or Albanians, though of course they were Romanized; their native language was Latin.

The weak-minded and childless Justin II adopted the Thracian Tiberius, a commander in the army, whom he designated as Caesar. On this occasion he delivered a very interesting speech which made a deep impression on contemporaries for its tone of sincerity and repentance.[4] Since the speech was taken down in shorthand by scribes, it is preserved in its original form. After the death of Justin II, Tiberius reigned as Tiberius II (578–82). With his death ended the dynasty of Justinian, for he was succeeded by his daughter's husband, Maurice (582–602). Sources differ on the question of Maurice's origin; some claim that his home and that of his family was the distant Cappadocian city of Arabissus,[5] while others, though still calling him a Cappadocian, consider him the first Greek on the Byzantine throne.[6] There is really no contradiction in terms here, for it is possible that he really may have been born in Cappadocia of Greek descent.[7] Still another tradition claims that he was a Roman.[8] J. A. Kulakovsky considered it possible that he was of Armenian origin, the native population of Cappadocia being Armenian.[9] Maurice was dethroned by the Thracian tyrant, Phocas (602–10), the last emperor of this period.

JUSTIN I

Immediately after his accession, Justin I departed from the religious policy of his two predecessors by siding definitely with the followers of the Council of Chalcedon and by opening a period of severe persecutions against the Monophysites. Peaceful relations were established with Rome, and the disagreement between the eastern and western churches, dating back to the time of Zeno's Henoticon, came to an end. The religious policy of the emperors of this period was based upon orthodoxy. This once more alienated the eastern provinces, and a very interesting hint of mildness appeared in a letter written

[4] The text of the speech is reproduced in Theophylact Simocatta, *Historia*, III, 11; ed. C. de Boor, 132–33. Evagrius, *Historia ecclesiastica*, V, 13; ed. J. Bidez and L. Parmentier, 208–9. John of Ephesus, *Ecclesiastical History*, III, 5; trans. R. Payne-Smith, 172–76; trans. E. W. Brooks, 93–94. In an interesting article on this speech a Russian scholar, V. Valdenberg, suggests that the texts of these three writers are three different versions of the same speech: "An Oration of Justin II to Tiberius," *Bulletin de l'Académie des sciences de l'Union des Republiques socialistes sovi-*

etiques, No. 2 (1928), 129. English trans. Bury, *Later Roman Empire*, II, 77–78.

[5] Evagrii, *Historia ecclesiastica*, V, 19. John of Ephesus, *Ecclesiastical History*, V, 21; trans. Payne-Smith, 361.

[6] "Pauli Diaconti," *Historia Langobardorum*, III, 15.

[7] E. Stein, *Studien aus Geschichte des byzantinischen Reiches vornehmlich unter den Kaisern Justinus II und Tiberius Constantinus*, 100, n.°2.

[8] Evagrii, *Historia ecclesiastica*, V, 19.

[9] *History of Byzantium*, II, 419.

to Pope Hormisdas in 520 by Justin's nephew Justinian, whose influence was felt from the first year of his uncle's reign. He tactfully suggested gentleness toward the dissidents: "You will conciliate the people to our Lord, not by persecutions and bloodshed but by patience, lest, wishing to gain souls, we may lose the bodies of many people and souls as well. For it is appropriate to correct errors of long duration with mildness and clemency. That doctor is justly praised who eagerly endeavors to cure old sicknesses in such a way that new wounds may not originate from them."[10] It is all the more interesting to hear such advice from Justinian since in later years he himself did not often follow it.

At first sight some inconsistency appears in Justin's relations with the far-off Abyssinian kingdom of Axum. In his war against the King of Yemen, the protector of Judaism, the king of Abyssinia, with the effective backing of Justin and Justinian, gained a strong foothold in Yemen, located in southwestern Arabia across the Strait of Bab el Mandeb, and restored Christianity in this country. We are at first surprised that the orthodox Justin, who adhered to the Chalcedonian doctrine and took the offensive against Monophysites within his own empire, should support the Monophysite Abyssinian king. But outside the official boundaries of the Empire, the Byzantine Emperor protected Christianity in general, whether it was in accord with his religious dogmas or not. From the point of view of external policy, the Byzantine emperors regarded every gain for Christianity as an essential political, and perhaps economic, advantage.

This *rapprochement* between Justin and the Abyssinian king has had a rather unexpected reflection in later times. In Abyssinia in the fourteenth century was compiled one of the most important works of Abyssinian (Ethiopian) literature, the *Kebra Nagast* (The Glory of the Kings), containing a very interesting collection of legends. It proclaims that the Abyssinian reigning dynasty traces its lineage back to the time of Solomon and the Queen of Sheba; and indeed at the present day Abyssinia claims to be governed by the oldest dynasty in the world. The Ethiopians, according to the *Kebra Nagast,* are an elect people, a new Israel; their kingdom is higher than the Roman Empire. The two kings, Justinus, the king of Rome, and Kaleb, the king of Ethiopia, shall meet together in Jerusalem and divide the earth between them. This extremely interesting legend shows clearly the deep impress left upon Abyssinian historical tradition by the epoch of Justin I.[11]

---

[10] *Collectio Avellana,* no. 196, *Corpus Scriptorum Ecclesiasticorum Latinorum,* XXXV (1895), 655–56.

[11] See A. A. Vasiliev, "Justin I (518–27) and Abyssinia," *Byzantinische Zeitschrift,* XXXIII (1933), 67–77. Also *Justin the First,* 299–302, by the same author.

Justin's successor, his nephew Justinian (527-65), is the central figure of this entire period. His name is closely connected with the name of his royal wife, Theodora, one of the very interesting and gifted women of the Byzantine period. *The Secret History,* which is from the pen of Procopius, the historian of Justinian's epoch, paints in exaggerated colors the perverted life of Theodora in the days of her youth, when, as the daughter of the keeper of the bears in the amphitheater, she lived in the morally corrupt atmosphere of the stage of that period and became a woman who gave freely of her love to many men. Nature had endowed her with beauty, grace, intelligence, and wit. According to one historian (Diehl), "she amused, charmed, and scandalized Constantinople."[12] Procopius said that people who met Theodora in the street would shrink from getting close to her, fearing that a mere touch might sully their robes.[13] But all these dark details about the early years of the future empress must be viewed with some skepticism, for they all come from Procopius, whose chief aim in *The Secret History* was to defame Justinian and Theodora. After the very stormy period of her early life, Theodora disappeared from the capital and remained in Africa for a few years. When she returned to Constantinople she was no more the former flighty actress. She had left the stage and was leading a solitary life, devoting much of her time to spinning wool and developing a great interest in religious questions, when Justinian saw her for the first time. Her beauty impressed him greatly and he took her to court, bestowed upon her the rank of patrician, and soon married her. With his accession to the throne she became empress of the Byzantine Empire. Theodora proved herself to be adequate to her new and lofty position. She remained a faithful wife and showed much interest in government affairs, exhibiting very keen insight and exerting much influence upon Justinian in all his undertakings. In the revolt of 532, which will be discussed later, Theodora played one of the most significant parts. By her coolheaded actions and unusual energy she perhaps saved the Empire from further commotions. In her religious preferences she openly favored the Monophysites and was thus the direct opposite of her wavering husband. He adhered to orthodoxy throughout his long reign, though he made some concessions to Monophysitism. She showed a better understanding than he of the significance of the eastern Monophysitic provinces, which were in reality the vital parts of the Empire and she definitely aimed to bring about peaceful relations with them. Theodora died of cancer in the year 548, long before Justinian's death.[14]

[12] Charles Diehl, *Figures byzantines,* I, 56; English trans. H. Bell, *Byzantine Portraits,* 54.
[13] *Historia arcana,* 9, 25; ed. J. Haury, 60-61.
[14] Victoris Tonnennensis *Chronica, s. a. 549:* Theodora Augusta Chalcedonsis synodi inimica canceris plaga corpore toto perfusa vitam prodigiose finivit; in *Chronica Minora,* ed. T. Mommsen, II, 202.

In the famous mosaic in the Church of St. Vitale at Ravenna, dating back to the sixth century, Theodora is represented in imperial robes, surrounded by her court. Church historians contemporary with Theodora, as well as those of a later period, are very harsh with regard to her character. In spite of this, in the orthodox calendar under November 14 appears "The Assumption of the Orthodox King Justinian and the memory of the Queen Theodora."[15] She was buried in the Church of the Holy Apostles.

The external policy of Justinian and his ideology

The numerous wars of Justinian were partly offensive and partly defensive. The former were carried on against the barbarian Germanic states of western Europe; the latter were directed against Persia in the East and the Slavs in the north.

The main forces were directed to the west, where the military activities of the Byzantine army were crowned with triumphant success. The Vandals, the Ostrogoths, and to some extent the Visigoths were forced into subjection to the Byzantine emperor. The Mediterranean Sea was almost converted into a Byzantine lake. In his decrees Justinian called himself Caesar Flavius Justinian the Alamannicus, Gothicus, Francicus, Germanicus, Anticus, Alanicus, Vandalicus, Africanus. But this outer splendor had its reverse side. The success was attained at a price too dear for the Empire, for it involved the complete economic exhaustion of the Byzantine state. In view of the fact that the army was transferred to the west, the east and the north remained open to the attacks of the Persians, Slavs, and Huns.

The principal enemies of the Empire, in Justinian's opinion, were the Germans. Thus the German question reappeared in the Byzantine Empire during the sixth century, with this difference only: in the fifth century the Germans were attacking the Empire; in the sixth century it was the Empire that pressed upon the Germans.

Justinian mounted the throne with the ideals of an emperor both Roman and Christian. Considering himself a successor of the Roman Caesars, he deemed it his sacred duty to restore a single Empire extending to the same boundaries it had had in the first and second centuries. As a Christian ruler he could not allow the German Arians to oppress the orthodox population. The rulers of Constantinople, as lawful successors of the Caesars, had historical rights to western Europe, occupied at this time by barbarians. The Germanic kings were but vassals of the Byzantine Emperor, who had delegated them to rule in the West. The Frankish king, Clovis, had received his rank of consul from Anastasius; it was Anastasius also who had given official recognition to the Ostrogothic king, Theodoric. When he decided to wage war against the

[15] Arch. Sergius, *The Complete Liturgical Calendar (Menelogion) of the Orient* (2nd ed., 1901), II, 1, 354.

Goths, Justinian wrote, "The Goths, having seized by violence our Italy, have refused to give it back."[16] He remained, he felt, the natural suzerain of all the rulers within the boundaries of the Roman Empire. As a Christian emperor, Justinian had the mission of propagating the true faith among the infidels, whether they were heretics or pagans. This theory, expressed by Eusebius in the fourth century was still alive in the sixth century. It was the basis of Justinian's conviction of his duty to re-establish a united Roman Empire which, in the words of one Novel,[17] formerly reached the shores of two oceans, and which the Romans had lost because of their carelessness. From this old theory arose also Justinian's belief in his duty to introduce in the restored empire a sole Christian faith among the schismatics as well as among the pagans. Such was Justinian's ideology, which made this all-embracing statesman and crusader dream of conquering the entire known world.

But it must be remembered that the Emperor's broad claims to the old parts of the Roman Empire were not exclusively a matter of his personal views. They seemed quite natural to the population of the provinces occupied by the barbarians. The natives of the provinces which had fallen into the hands of Arians viewed Justinian as their sole protector. Conditions in northern Africa under the Vandals were particularly difficult, because these barbarians initiated severe persecutions against the native orthodox population and put many citizens and representatives of the clergy in jail, confiscating much of their property. Refugees and exiles from Africa, including many orthodox bishops, arrived at Constantinople and implored the Emperor to inaugurate a campaign against the Vandals, assuring him that a general revolt of the natives would follow.

A similar state of affairs prevailed in Italy, where the natives, in spite of a prolonged period of religious tolerance under Theodoric and his high regard for Roman civilization, continued to harbor hidden discontent and still turned their eyes to Constantinople, expecting aid from there in the cause of liberating their country from the newcomers and restoring the orthodox faith.

Still more interesting is the fact that the barbarian kings themselves supported the Emperor's ambitious plans. They persisted in expressing signs of deep respect for the Empire, in demonstrating in many ways their subservience to the Emperor, in striving to attain high Roman ranks by any means, in imprinting the image of the Emperor on their coins, etc. The French scholar Diehl[18] said that they would have willingly repeated the words of

[16] Procopius, *De bello gothico*, I, 5, 8; ed. J. Haury, II, 26.
[17] Justinian, *Novellae Constitutiones*, No. 30 (44), II; ed. K. E. Zachariä von Lingenthal, I, 276.
[18] *Justinien et la civilisation byzantine au VIᵉ siècle*, 137.

the Visigothic chief who said, "The emperor is undoubtedly God on earth and whoso raises a hand against him is guilty of his own blood."[19]

However, in spite of the fact that the state of affairs in Africa and Italy was favorable for Justinian, the campaigns waged against the Vandals and the Ostrogoths were extremely difficult and long drawn out.

Wars with the Vandals, Ostrogoths, and Visigoths. The results of these wars. Persia. The Slavs.—The expedition against the Vandals presented no easy problem. It involved the transfer of a vast army by sea to northern Africa, and this army would have to contend with a people who possessed a powerful fleet and who even in the middle of the fifth century had succeeded in raiding Rome. Besides, the transfer of the main military forces to the west was bound to have serious consequences in the east, where Persia, the most dangerous enemy of the Empire, waged continual war against Constantinople. Procopius gives an interesting account of the council at which the question of the African expedition was discussed for the first time.[20] The most loyal magistrates of the Emperor expressed doubt about the possible success of the undertaking and considered it precipitate. Justinian himself was beginning to waver; in the end he overcame this temporary weakness and insisted upon his original project. The expedition was definitely decided upon. Meanwhile a change took place in the Persian ruling house, and in the year 532 Justinian succeeded in concluding an "endless" peace with the new ruler on the humiliating condition that the Byzantine Empire should pay a very large annual tribute to the king of Persia. This treaty, however, made it possible for Justinian to act more freely in the east and south. At the head of the vast army and fleet he placed the gifted general Belisarius, who was the most valuable assistant of the Emperor in his military undertakings and who shortly before this appointment had succeeded in quelling the dangerous internal *Nika* revolt, of which we shall speak later.

At this time the Vandals and Ostrogoths were no longer the dangerous enemies they had been in former days. Unaccustomed to the enervating southern climate and influenced by Roman civilization, they had rapidly lost their former energy and force. The Arian beliefs of these Germans caused unfriendly relations with the native Roman population. The continual uprisings of the Berber tribes also contributed much to the weakening of the Vandals. Justinian had a keen insight into existing conditions, and by skillful diplomacy he increased the internal discord among the Vandals, meanwhile feeling quite certain that the Germanic kingdoms would never unite to oppose him jointly, because the Ostrogoths were on bad terms with the Vandals,

[19] Jordanis, *Getica,* XXVIII; ed. T. Mommsen, 95.
[20] *De bello vandalico,* I, 10; ed. Haury, I, 355–60; English trans. H. B. Dewing, II, 90–101.

the orthodox Franks were constantly struggling with the Ostrogoths, and the Visigoths in Spain were too far distant to take a serious part in a war. All this encouraged Justinian in his hope of defeating each enemy separately.

The Vandal war lasted, with some peaceful intervals, from 533 to 548.[21] Belisarius rapidly subjugated the entire Vandal kingdom by a number of brilliant victories so that Justinian could proclaim triumphantly: "God, in his mercy, gave over to us not only Africa and all her provinces, but also returned our imperial insignia which had been taken away by the Vandals when they took Rome."[22] Considering the war ended, the Emperor recalled Belisarius and the greater part of the army to Constantinople. Immediately the Moors (a native Berber tribe) rose in terrible rebellion, and the remaining troops were forced to engage in an overwhelming struggle. Belisarius' successor, Solomon, was utterly defeated and slain. The exhausting war lasted until the year 548, when the imperial power was definitely restored by a decisive victory on the part of John Troglita, a diplomatist as well as a talented general. The third hero of the imperial reoccupation of Africa, he secured complete tranquillity there for nearly fourteen years. His deeds were narrated by the contemporary African poet, Corippus, in his historical work *Iohannis*.[23]

These conquests did not entirely satisfy Justinian's hopes, for, with the exception of the powerful fortress of Septum, near the Pillars of Hercules (now the Spanish fortress Ceuta), the western portion of northern Africa, reaching to the Atlantic Ocean, was not reannexed. Yet the greater part of northern Africa, Corsica, Sardinia, and the Balearic Islands became part of the Empire, and Justinian spent much energy in his efforts to restore order in these conquered lands. Even today the majestic ruins of numerous Byzantine fortresses and fortifications bear witness to the strenuous efforts of the Emperor for the defense of his land.

Still more exhausting was the Ostrogothic campaign, which lasted, also with peaceful intervals, from 535 to 554. During the first thirteen years this was contemporaneous with the Vandal war. Justinian opened military action by intervening in the internal strife of the Ostrogoths. One army began the conquest of Dalmatia, which at this time formed a part of the Ostrogothic kingdom. Another, transported by sea and headed by Belisarius, occupied Sicily without much difficulty. Later, when transferred to Italy, this army conquered Naples and Rome. Soon after this, in 540, the Ostrogothic capital, Ravenna, opened its gates to Belisarius, who shortly afterward left Italy for Constantinople, taking with him the captive Ostrogothic king. Justinian

[21] On this war see Charles Diehl, *L'Afrique byzantine*, 3–33, 333–81. Diehl, *Justinien*, 173–80. W. Holmes, *The Age of Justinian and Theodora* (2nd ed., 1912), II, 489–526. Bury, *Later Roman Empire*, II, 124–48.

[22] *Codex Justinianus*, I, 27, 1, 7.

[23] See Bury, *Later Roman Empire*, II, 147.

added "Gothicus" to his title "Africanus and Vandalicus." Italy seemed definitely conquered by the Byzantine Empire.

However, at this time there appeared among the Goths an energetic and gifted king, Totila, the last defender of Ostrogothic independence. With speed and decision he reversed the state of affairs. His military successes were so great that Belisarius was recalled from Persia to cope with them and was sent to Italy to assume the supreme command. Belisarius, however, was unable to deal with the situation. In rapid succession the territories conquered by the Byzantine army in Italy and on the islands were reclaimed by the Ostrogoths. The unfortunate city of Rome, which several times passed back and forth from Romans to Ostrogoths, was transformed into a heap of ruins. After Belisarius' failures had led to his recall from Italy, his successor, Narses, another gifted Byzantine general, finally succeeded in conquering the Goths by a number of actions displaying great strategic skill. Totila's army was defeated in 552 in the battle of Busta Gallorum in Umbria. Totila himself fled, but in vain.[24] "His blood-stained garments and the cap adorned with gems which he had worn were taken to Narses who sent them to Constantinople, where they were laid at the feet of the emperor as a visible proof that the enemy who had so long defied his power was no more."[25] In the year 554, after twenty years of devastating warfare, Italy, Dalmatia, and Sicily were reunited with the Empire. The Pragmatic Sanction, published by Justinian in the same year, returned to the large landed aristocracy of Italy and to the church the land taken away from them by the Ostrogoths and restored all their former privileges; it also outlined a number of measures intended to lessen the burdens of the ruined population. But the Ostrogothic wars for a long time prevented the development of industry and commerce in Italy and, as a result of the lack of laborers, many Italian fields remained uncultivated. For a time Rome became a second-rate ruined city of no political importance. The pope, however, chose it as his refuge.

Justinian's last military undertaking was directed against the Visigoths in the Pyrenean peninsula. Taking advantage of civil war between different pretenders to the Visigothic throne, he sent a navy to Spain in 550. Although the armament must have been small, it achieved remarkable success. Many maritime cities and forts were captured, and finally Justinian succeeded in taking from the Visigoths the southeastern corner of the peninsula, with the cities of Carthage, Málaga, and Córduba, and then in extending the territory which eventually reached from Cape St. Vincent on the west to beyond Car-

---

[24] The most detailed record of this battle is in Bury, *Later Roman Empire*, II, 261–69, 288–91.

[25] *Chronicle of John Malalas*, 486. The-ophanes *Chronographia s. a. 6044;* ed. C. de Boor, 228. See Bury, *Later Roman Empire*, II, 268.

thage on the east.[26] With some modifications the imperial province thus established in Spain remained under the rule of Constantinople for about seventy years. It is not perfectly clear whether this province was independent or was subordinate to the governor of Africa.[27] Some churches and other architectural monuments of Byzantine art have recently been discovered in Spain, but as far as one may judge, they are not of great value.[28]

The result of all these offensive wars was to double the extent of Justinian's empire. Dalmatia, Italy, the eastern part of North Africa (part of present-day Algeria and Tunis), the southeast of Spain, Sicily, Sardinia, Corsica, and the Balearic Islands all became part of the Empire. The Mediterranean again became practically a Roman lake. The boundaries of the Empire extended from the Pillars of Hercules, or the Straits of Gades, to the Euphrates. But in spite of this enormous success, Justinian's achievements fell far short of his hopes. He did not succeed in reconquering the entire Western Roman Empire. The western part of North Africa, the Pyrenean peninsula, the northern portion of the Ostrogothic kingdom, north of the Alps (the former provinces of Rhaetia and Noricum) still remained outside of his power. The entire province of Gaul not only was completely independent of the Byzantine Empire but even to a certain extent was victorious over it, for Justinian was forced to cede Provence to the King of the Franks. It must also be remembered that the power of the Emperor was not equally firm throughout the vast newly conquered territory. The government had neither the authority nor the means to establish itself more solidly. And yet these territories could be retained by force only. That is why the brilliant outward success of Justinian's offensive wars brought with it the beginnings of serious future complications, both political and economic.

The defensive wars of Justinian were far less successful and at times were even humiliating. These wars were carried on with Persia in the east and with the Slavs and the Huns in the north.

The two great powers of the sixth century, the Byzantine Empire and Persia, had been engaged for centuries in bloody wars on the eastern border. After the "endless" peace with Persia, the Persian king, Chosroes Nushirvan, a gifted and skillful ruler, recognized the high ambitions of Justinian in the

[26] Diehl, *Justinien,* 204–6. Bury, *Later Roman Empire,* II, 287. Georgii Cyprii *Descriptio Orbis Romani,* ed. H. Gelzer, xxxii–xxxv. F. Görres, "Die byzantinischen Besitzungen an den Küsten des spanischwestgothischen Reiches (554–624)," *Byzantinische Zeitschrift,* XVI (1907), 516. E. Bouchier, *Spain under the Roman Empire,* 54–55. R. Altamira, *The Cambridge Medieval History,* II, 163–64. P.

Goubert, "Byzance et l'Espagne wisigothique (554–711)," *Études byzantines,* II (1945), 5–78.

[27] Bury, *Later Roman Empire,* II, 287. Goubert, "Byzance et l'Espagne," *Études byzantines,* II (1945), 76–77 (until 624).

[28] See J. Puigi i Cadafalch, "L'Architecture religieuse dans le domaine byzantin en Espagne," *Byzantion,* I (1924), 530.

West and took advantage of the situation.[29] Aware of his own important interests in the border provinces, he seized upon a plea for help from the Ostrogoths as an opportunity to break the "endless" peace and open hostilities against the Byzantine Empire.[30] A bloody war ensued, with apparent victory for the Persians. Belisarius was recalled from Italy but was unable to stop the advance of Chosroes, who forced his way into Syria and sacked and destroyed Antioch, "the city which was both ancient and of great importance and the first of all the cities which the Romans had throughout the East both in wealth and in size and in population and in beauty and in prosperity of every kind."[31] In his onward march Chosroes reached the coast of the Mediterranean Sea. In the north the Persians attempted to force their way to the Black Sea but encountered an obstacle in the Lazi of the Caucasian province of Lazica (now Lazistan), which at the time was dependent on the Byzantine Empire. It was only after great difficulty that Justinian finally succeeded in buying a truce for five years, and then he was forced to pay a large sum of money for it. But even Chosroes wearied of the endless collisions, and in the year 561 or 562 the Byzantine Empire and Persia reached an agreement establishing peace for fifty years. The historian Menander[32] contributed accurate and detailed information about the negotiations and the terms of this treaty. The Emperor undertook to pay Persia annually a very large sum of money, while the king of Persia promised to preserve religious toleration for Christians in Persia on the strict condition that they refrain from proselytizing. Roman and Persian merchants, whatever their wares, were to carry on their traffic solely at certain prescribed places where customhouses were stationed. In this treaty the most important point for the Byzantine Empire was the agreement of the Persians to leave Lazica, the province on the southeastern coast of the Black Sea, and to resign it to the Romans. In other words, the Persians did not succeed in gaining a stronghold on the shores of the Black Sea; it remained in complete possession of the Byzantine Empire, a fact of great political and economic importance.[33]

[29] E. Stein ranked Chosroes very high, and not only him but his father Kawadh (Kavad), a man of genius. He compared Kawadh with Philip of Macedon and Frederick William I of Prussia, men whose famous sons by their own success overshadowed the less brilliant but perhaps more arduous achievements of the fathers on whose work they built. Stein, "Ein Kapitel vom persichen und vom byzantinischen Staate," *Byzantinisch-Neugriechische Jahrbücher,* I (1920), 64.

[30] On the Persian war under Justinian, see Diehl, *Justinien,* 208-17. Holmes, *Justinian*

and Theodora, II, 365-419, 584-604. Bury, *Later Roman Empire,* II, 79-123. J. Kulakovsky, *History of Byzantium,* II, 188-208.

[31] Procopius, *De bello persico,* II, 8, 23; ed. Haury, I, 188; ed. Dewing, I, 330-31.

[32] Menandri *Excerpta;* ed. B. G. Niebuhr, *Corpus Scriptorum Historiae Byzantinae* (Bonn, 1829), 346 ff. This collection is referred to hereafter as Bonn ed. *Excerpta historica jussu imp. Constantini Porphyrogeniti confecta,* ed. C. de Boor, I, 175 ff.

[33] On the details of the treaty see K. Güterbock, *Byzanz und Persien in ihren diploma-*

Quite different was the nature of the defensive wars in the north, in the Balkan peninsula. The northern barbarians, the Bulgarians, and the Slavs had devastated the provinces of the peninsula even as far back as the reign of Anastasius. In the time of Justinian the Slavs appear for the first time under their own name, "Sclavenes," in Procopius. Large hordes of Slavs and Bulgarians, whom Procopius calls Huns, crossed the Danube almost every year and penetrated deep into the Byzantine provinces, destroying everything with fire and sword. On one side they reached the outskirts of the capital and penetrated to the Hellespont; on the other they went through Greece as far as the Isthmus of Corinth and the shores of the Adriatic Sea in the west. During Justinian's reign also the Slavs began to show a clearly defined movement toward the shores of the Aegean Sea. In their effort to reach this sea they menaced Thessalonica, one of the most important cities of the Empire, which, together with its environs, soon became one of the main Slavic centers in the Balkan peninsula. The imperial troops fought desperately against the Slavic invasions and often forced the Slavs to retreat beyond the Danube. But not all the Slavs went back. Justinian's troops, occupied in other important campaigns, could not put a decisive end to the yearly incursions of the Slavs in the Balkan peninsula, and some Slavs remained there. The beginning in this period of the Slavonic problem in the Balkan peninsula should be emphasized; the problem was to become one of very great significance for the Empire during the late sixth and early seventh centuries.

Besides the Slavs, the German Gepids and Kotrigurs, a branch of the Hunnic race, invaded the Balkan peninsula from the north. In the winter of 558–59 the Kotrigurs under their chieftain, Zabergan, entered Thrace. From there one band was sent to ravage Greece, another invaded the Thracian Chersonese, and the third, consisting of cavalry, rode under Zabergan himself to Constantinople. The country was devastated. Panic reigned in Constantinople. The churches of the invaded provinces sent their treasures to the capital or shipped them to the Asiatic side of the Bosphorus. Justinian appealed to Belisarius to save Constantinople in this crisis. The Kotrigurs eventually were defeated in all three points of attack, but Thrace, Macedonia, and Thessaly suffered a terrible economic blow from the invasion.[34]

The Hunnic danger was felt not only in the Balkan peninsula but also in the Crimea in the lonely Tauric peninsula, which was located in the Black Sea and which belonged in part to the Empire. Two cities there, Cherson

---

tisch-völkerrectlichen Beziehungen im Zeitalter Justinians, 57–105. Bury, *Later Roman Empire*, II, 120–23; the year of the treaty, 562.

Stein, *Justinus II und Tiberius*, 5–6; the year of the treaty, 561 (pp. 2 and 28 n. 3).

[34] See Bury, *Later Roman Empire*, II, 298–308.

and Bosporus, were famous for preserving Greek civilization for centuries in barbarous surroundings, and they also played an important part in the trade between the Empire and the territory of present-day Russia. Toward the close of the fifth century the Huns had occupied the plains of the peninsula and had begun to threaten the Byzantine possessions there, as well as a small Gothic settlement centered around Dory in the mountains under Byzantine protection. Under the pressure of the Hunnic danger, Justinian built and restored several forts and erected long walls whose traces are still visible,[35] a sort of *limes Tauricus,* which proved successful protection.[36]

Lastly, the missionary zeal of Justinian and Theodora did not overlook the African peoples who lived on the Upper Nile between Egypt and Abyssinia, above the First Cataract, the Blemyes, and the Nobadae (Nubians), their southern neighbors. Through the energy and artfulness of Theodora, the Nobadae with their king, Silko, were converted to Monophysite Christianity, and the convert king joined with a Byzantine general to force the Blemyes to adopt the same faith. In order to celebrate his victory, Silko set up in a temple of the Blemyes an inscription about which Bury remarked: "The boast of this petty potentate might be appropriate in the mouth of Attila or of Tamurlane."[37] The inscription was: "I, Silko, kinglet ($\beta\alpha\sigma\iota\lambda\acute{\iota}\sigma\kappa\sigma\varsigma$) of the Nobadae and of all the Ethiopians."[38]

Significance of Justinian's external policy.—To summarize Justinian's entire external policy we must say that his endless and exhausting wars, which failed to realize all his hopes and projects, had a fatal effect upon the Empire in general. First of all, these gigantic undertakings demanded enormous expenditures. Procopius in his *Secret History* estimated, perhaps with some exaggeration, that Anastasius left a reserve, enormous for that time, which amounted to 320,000 pounds of gold (about $65,000,000 or $70,000,000), and this Justinian is supposed to have spent in a short time, even during his uncle's reign.[39] According to another source of the sixth century, the Syrian John of Ephesus,[40] Anastasius' reserve was not completely exhausted until the reign of Justin II, after the death of Justinian; this statement, however, is incorrect. The fund left by Anastasius, admittedly smaller than Procopius would have us believe, must have been of great value to Justinian in his undertakings. Yet

[35] W. Tomaschek, *Die Goten in Taurica,* 15–16. A. A. Vasiliev, *The Goths in the Crimea,* 70–73. The remains of Justinian's walls should be studied *in situ.*

[36] Vasiliev, *Goths in the Crimea,* 75. J. Kulakovsky, *The Past of the Tauris* (2nd ed., 1914), 60–62. The Tauris is the ancient name of the Crimea. Bury, *Later Roman Empire,* II, 310–12.

[37] Bury, *ibid.,* 330.

[38] *Corpus Inscriptionum Graecarum,* III, 5072 (p. 486). G. Lefebvre, *Recueil des inscriptions grecques chrétiennes d'Egypte,* 628.

[39] Procopius, *Historia arcana,* 19, 7–8; ed. Haury, 121.

[40] *Ecclesiastical History,* V, 20; trans. Payne-Smith, 358; trans. Brooks, 205.

it alone could not suffice. The new taxes were greater than the exhausted population could pay. The Emperor's attempts to curtail the expenditures of the state by economizing on the upkeep of the army brought about a reduction in the number of soldiers, which naturally made the western conquered provinces very unsafe.

From Justinian's Roman point of view, his western campaigns are comprehensible and natural, but from the point of view of the welfare of the Empire they must be recognized as superfluous and pernicious. The gap between the East and the West in the sixth century was already so great that the mere idea of uniting the two was an anachronism. A real union was out of the question. The conquered provinces could be retained by force only, and for this the Empire had neither power nor means. Allured by his delusive dreams, Justinian failed to grasp the importance of the eastern border and the eastern provinces, which embodied the really vital interests of the Byzantine Empire. The western campaigns, displaying only the personal will of the Emperor, could not bring about lasting results, and the plan of restoring a united Roman Empire died with Justinian, though not forever. Meanwhile, his general external policy brought about an extremely severe internal economic crisis within the Empire.

The legislative work of Justinian and Tribonian

Justinian became universally famous because of his legislative work, remarkable for its sweeping character. It was his opinion that an emperor "must be not only glorified with arms, but also armed with laws, so that alike the time of war and the time of peace may be rightly guided; he must be the strong protector of law as well as the triumpher over vanquished enemies."[41] Furthermore, he believed, it was God who bestowed upon the emperors the right to create and interpret laws, and an emperor must be a lawgiver, with his rights sanctified from above. But, quite naturally, in addition to all these theoretical foundations, the Emperor was guided also by practical considerations, for he realized fully that Roman law of his time was in a very chaotic state.

Back in the days of the pagan Roman Empire, when the legislative power was entirely in the hands of the emperor, the sole form of legislation was the issuing of imperial constitutions, called laws or statute laws (*leges*). In contrast with these, all laws created by earlier legislation and developed by the jurists of the classical period were called *jus vetus* or *jus antiquum*. From the middle of the third century A.D., jurisprudence declined very rapidly. Juridical publications were limited to pure compilations, which aimed to assist judges unable to study the entire juridical literature by providing them with col-

[41] Justinian, *Institutiones,* introduction; trans. J. T. Abdy and B. Walker, xxi.

lections of extracts from imperial constitutions and the works of universally famous old jurists. But these collections were of a private nature and had no official sanction whatever, so that in real practice a judge had to look into all the imperial constitutions and into all of the classical literature, a task quite beyond the powers of any one man. There was no one central organ for the publication of the imperial constitutions. Increasing in quantity annually, scattered in various archives, they could not be used easily in practice, especially since new edicts very often repealed or changed old ones. All this explains the acute need for a single collection of imperial edicts accessible to those who had to use it. Much had been done in this direction before Justinian. In his own legislative work he was greatly aided by the earlier *Codex Gregorianus, Codex Hermogenianus,* and *Codex Theodosianus.* In order to facilitate the use of classical literature (the *jus vetus*), a decree was issued during the reign of Theodosius II and his western contemporary, Valentinian III, which granted paramount authority only to the works of the five most famous jurists. The remaining juridical writers could be disregarded. Of course, this was only a formal solution of the problem, especially since in the works of the five chosen jurists it was not at all easy to find suitable decisions for a given case, because the jurists often contradicted one another and also because the decisions of the classical jurists were often too much out of date to be practical for the changed living conditions. Official revision of the entire legal system and a summing up of its development through many centuries was greatly needed.

The earlier codes contained only the imperial constitutions issued during a certain period and did not touch upon juridical literature. Justinian undertook the enormous task of compiling a code of imperial constitutions up to his own time as well as revising the old juridical writings. His main assistant in this task and the soul of the entire undertaking was Tribonian.

The work progressed with astonishing rapidity. In February, 528, the Emperor gathered a commission of ten experts, including Tribonian, "the Emperor's right hand in his great legal enterprise, and perhaps partly their inspirer," and Theophilus, professor of law at Constantinople.[42] The problem of the commission was to revise the three older codes, to eliminate from them all the obsolete material, and to systematize the constitutions which had appeared since the publication of the Theodosian code. The results of all these labors were to be gathered in one collection. As early as April, 529, the Justinian code (*Codex Justinianus*) was published. It was divided into ten books, containing the constitutions from the reign of the Emperor Hadrian to the time of Justinian; it became the sole authoritative code of laws in the Empire, thus repealing the three older codes. Although the compilation of Justinian's

[42] Bury, *Later Roman Empire,* II, 396.

code was greatly aided by the older codes, the attempt to revise the *jus vetus* was an original undertaking of the Emperor. In the year 530 Tribonian was instructed to gather a commission which would revise the works of all the classical jurists, make excerpts from them, reject all obsolete materials, eliminate all contradictions, and, finally, arrange all the materials collected in some definite order. For the purpose of doing this the commission had to read and study about two thousand books, containing over three million lines. This enormous work, which in Justinian's own words, "before his command none ever expected or deemed to be at all possible for human endeavor"[43] and "which freed all *jus vetus* of superfluous redundance,"[44] was completed in three years. The new code, published in the year 533, was subdivided into fifty books and was called the "Digest" (*Digestum*), or the "Pandects" (*Pandectae*). It found immediate application in the legal practices of the Empire.[45]

Though this Digest of Justinian is of very great importance, the haste with which it was compiled necessarily caused the work to be defective in certain respects. It contained many repetitions, contradictions, and some quite obsolete decisions. In addition to this, the full power given to the commission in the matter of abbreviating texts, interpreting them, and combining several texts into one, produced a certain arbitrariness in the final results, which sometimes even mutilated the ancient texts. There was a decided lack of unity in this work. This fault is responsible for the fact that the learned jurists of the nineteenth century, who had high regard for Roman classical law, judged Justinian's Digest very harshly. Still, the Digest, in spite of all its shortcomings, was of great practical value. It also preserved for posterity a wealth of material extracted from the classical Roman juridical writings which have not been preserved.

During the time of the compiling of the Digest, Tribonian and his two learned coadjutors, Theophilus, professor in Constantinople, and Dorotheus, professor at Beirut (in Syria), were charged with the solution of another problem. According to Justinian, not all "were able to bear the burden of all this mass of knowledge," i.e., the Code and the Digest. The young men, for instance, "who, standing in the vestibules of law, are longing to enter the secrets thereof,"[46] could not attempt to master all the contents of the two large works, and it was necessary to make up a usable practical manual for them. Such a handbook of civil law, intended primarily for the use of students, was issued in the year 533. It was divided into four books and was called the "In-

---

[43] *Constitutio Tanta*, preface; ed. P. Krüger, 13; trans. C. H. Monro, I, xxv.

[44] *Codex Justiniani, de emendatione Codicis,* ed. Krüger, 4.

[45] See A. A. Vasiliev, "Justinian's Digest. In commemoration of the 1400th anniversary of

the publication of the Digest (A.D. 533–1933)," *Studi bizantini e neoellenici,* V (1939), 711–34.

[46] *Constitutio Tanta,* ii; ed. Krüger, 18; trans. Monro. xxx.

stitutions" (*Institutiones*), or the "Institutes." According to Justinian, these were supposed to conduct "all muddy sources of the *jus vetus* into one clear lake."[47] The imperial decree which sanctioned the Institutions was addressed to "youth eager to know the laws" (*cupidae legum juventuti*).[48]

During the time that the Digest and the Institutions were being compiled, current legislation did not come to a standstill. Many new decrees were issued and a number of matters needed revision. In short, the Code, in its edition of the year 529, seemed out of date in many parts, and a new revision was undertaken and completed in the year 534. In November the second edition of the revised and enlarged Code, arranged in twelve books, was published under the title *Codex repetitae praelectionis*. This edition nullified the earlier edition of 529 and contained the decrees of the period beginning with Hadrian and ending with the year 534. This work concluded the compilation of the Corpus. The first edition of the Code has not been preserved.

The decrees issued after the year 534 were called "Novels" (*Novellae leges*). While the Code, the Digest, and the Institutions were written in Latin, a great majority of the Novels were drawn up in Greek. This fact was an important concession to the demands of living reality from an emperor steeped in Roman tradition. In one Novel, Justinian wrote, "We have written this decree not in the native language, but in the spoken Greek, in order that it may become known to all through the ease of comprehension."[49] In spite of Justinian's intention to collect all the Novels in one body, he did not succeed, though some private compilations of Novels were made during his reign. The Novels are considered the last part of Justinian's legislative work and serve as one of the main sources on the internal history of his epoch.

Justinian felt that the four indicated parts, namely, the Code, the Digest, the Institutions, and the Novels, should form one Corpus of law, but during his reign they were not combined into such a collection. Only much later, in the Middle Ages, beginning with the twelfth century, during the revival of the study of Roman law in Europe, all of Justinian's legislative works became known as the *Corpus juris civilis*, i.e., the "Corpus of Civil Law." Today they are still known by this name.

The bulkiness of Justinian's legislative work and the fact that it was written in Latin, little understood by the majority of the population, were responsible for the immediate appearance of a number of Greek commentaries and summaries of certain parts of the Code as well as some more or less literal translations (paraphrases) of the Institutions and the Digest with explanatory notes. These small legal collections in Greek, called forth by the needs of the

---

[47] *Constitutio Omnem*, 2; ed. Krüger, 10; trans. Monro, xx.

[48] *Institutiones*, ed. Krüger, xix; trans. Abdy, xxi.

[49] *Novella* 7 (15) a; ed. K. E. Zachariä von Lingenthal, I, 80.

time and by practical considerations, contained numerous mistakes and oversights with regard to their original Latin text; even so they thrust the original into the background and almost completely supplanted it.[50]

In conformity with the new legislative works the teaching of legal studies was also reformed. New programs of study were introduced. The course was announced to be of five years' duration. The main subject for study during the first year was the Institutions; for the second, third, and fourth years, the Digest; and finally, in the fifth year, the Code. In connection with the new program Justinian wrote, "When all legal secrets are disclosed, nothing will be hidden from the students, and after reading through all the works put together for us by Tribonian and others, they will turn out distinguished pleaders and servants of justice, the ablest of men and successful in all times and places."[51] In addressing the professors Justinian wrote, "Begin now under the governance of God to deliver to the students legal learning and to open up the way found by us, so that they, following this way, may become excellent ministers of justice and of the state, and the greatest possible honor may attend you for all ages to come."[52] In his address to the students the Emperor wrote, "Receive with all diligence and with eager attention these laws of ours and show yourselves so well versed in them that the fair hope may animate you of being able, when the whole course of your legal study is completed, to govern our Empire in such regions as may be attributed to your care."[53] The teaching itself was reduced to a simple mastery of the materials taught and to the interpretations based on these materials. Verifying or reinterpreting the text by citing original works of the classical jurists was not permitted. The students were allowed only to make literal translations and to compose brief paraphrases and extracts.

In spite of all the natural shortcomings in the execution and the numerous defects in method, the stupendous legislative work of the sixth century has been of unceasing and universal importance. Justinian's code preserved the Roman law, which gave the basic principles for the laws regulating most of modern society. "The will of Justinian performed one of the most fruitful deeds for the progress of mankind," said Diehl.[54] In the twelfth century, when the study of Roman law, or, as this phenomenon is usually called, the reception of Roman law, began in western Europe, Justinian's code of civil

---

[50] See K. E. Zachariä von Lingenthal, *Geschichte des griechisch-römischen Rechts* (3rd ed., 1892), 5–7. Cf. P. Collinet, "Byzantine Legislation from Justinian (565) to 1453," *Cambridge Medieval History*, IV, 707. Collinet, *Histoire de l'école de droit de Beyrouth*, 186–88, 303.

[51] *Constitutio Omnem*, 6; ed. Krüger, 11; trans. Monro, xxiii.

[52] *Ibid.*, II; ed. Krüger, 12; trans. Monro, xxiv.

[53] *Constitutio Imperatoriam majestatem*, 7; ed. Krüger, xix; trans. Abdy, xxiv. This is a decree concerning the Institutions.

[54] *Justinien*, 248.

law became the real law for many places. "Roman law," said Professor I. A. Pokrovsky, "awoke to new life and for a second time united the world. All legal developments in western Europe, even those of the present day, continue under the influence of Roman law. . . . The most valuable contents of Roman legislation were introduced into paragraphs and chapters of contemporary codes and functioned under the name of these codes."[55]

An interesting shift of viewpoint in the study of the legislative work of Justinian has occurred recently. Up to now this work, with the exception of the Novels, has been considered primarily as an aid for a closer acquaintance with Roman law, that is, as of auxiliary, not primary, significance. The Code was not studied for itself and never served as a subject for "independent" investigation. From this viewpoint it was objected that Justinian, or rather Tribonian, distorted classical law by either abbreviating or enlarging the text of the original. At present, however, emphasis is placed on whether or not Justinian's work met the needs of his time and to what extent it did so. The changes in the classical text are properly ascribed not to the arbitrariness of the compiler but to a desire to adapt Roman law to living conditions in the Eastern Empire in the sixth century. The success of the Code in accomplishing this purpose must be studied with reference to the general social conditions of the time. Both Hellenism and Christianity must have influenced the work of the compilers, and the living customs of the East must have been reflected in the revisions of the ancient Roman law. Some scholars accordingly speak of the eastern character of the legislative work of Justinian. The problem of contemporary historical-juridical science, then, is to determine and evaluate Byzantine influences in Justinian's Code, Digest, and Institutions.[56] The Novels of Justinian, as products of current legislation, naturally reflected the conditions and needs of contemporary life.

In Justinian's time three law schools were flourishing, one in Constantinople, one in Rome, and one in Beirut. All other schools were suppressed lest they serve as bases for paganism. In 551 the city of Beirut (Berytus) was destroyed by a terrific earthquake followed by a tidal wave and fire. The school of Beirut was transferred to Sidon but had no further importance.

In Russia under the Tsar Fedor Alekseievich (1676–1682) a project was organized to translate Justinian's *Corpus Juris* into Russian. A German scholar published a contemporary report on the subject and called the project "a deed worthy of Hercules" (*hoc opus Hercule dignum*), but unfortunately it was not carried out.[57]

---

[55] *History of Roman Law* (2nd ed., 1915), 4.

[56] See P. Collinet, *Études historiques sur le droit de Justinien*, I, 7–44.

[57] See G. Ostrogorsky, "Das Projekt einer Rangtabelle aus der Zeit des Caren Fedor Alekseevič," *Jahrbuch für Kultur und Geschichte der Slaven*, IX (1933), 133 n. 131, with reference to L. Loewenson, *Zeitschrift für Osteuropäische Geschichte*, N.S. II, part 2, 234 ff.

The ecclesiastical policy of Justinian

As the successor of Roman Caesars, Justinian considered it his duty to restore the Roman Empire, and at the same time he wished to establish within the Empire one law and one faith. "One state, one law, and one church"— such was the brief formula of Justinian's entire political career. Basing his conceptions on the principle of absolute power, he assumed that in a well-ordered state everything is subject to the authority of the emperor. Fully aware of the fact that the church might serve as a powerful weapon in the hands of the government, he used every effort to bring it into subjection. Historians have tried to analyze the motives which guided Justinian's church policy; some have concluded that with him politics was foremost and religion only a servant of the state,[58] others that this "second Constantine the Great was ready to forget his direct administrative duties wherever church matters were concerned."[59] In his desire to be full master of the church, Justinian not only aimed to keep in his own hands the internal administration and the fate of the clergy, even those of highest rank, but he also considered it his right to determine a specific dogma for his subjects. Whatever religious tendency was followed by the Emperor had to be followed also by his subjects. The Byzantine Emperor had the right to regulate the life of the clergy, to fill the highest hierarchic posts according to his own judgment, to appear as mediator and judge in the affairs of the clergy. He showed his favorable attitude toward the church by protecting the clergy and by promoting the erection of new churches and monasteries, to which he granted special privileges. He also exerted much effort in attempting to establish a unity of faith among his subjects. He frequently participated in dogmatical disputes, passing final decisions on debatable questions of doctrine. This policy of temporal authority in religious and ecclesiastical affairs, penetrating even the deepest regions of inner religious convictions of individuals, is known in history as Caesaropapism, and Justinian may be considered one of the most characteristic representatives of the Caesaropapistic tendency.[60] In his conception the ruler of the state was to be both Caesar and pope; he was to combine in his person all temporal and spiritual power. The historians who emphasize the political side of Justinian's activities claim that the chief motive in his Caesaropapism was a desire to make secure his political power, to strengthen the government,

[58] See, e.g., A. Knecht, *Die Religions-Politik Kaiser Justinians*, 53, 147. J. Lebon, *Le monophysisme sévérien*, 73–83, Kulakovsky, *Byzantium*, II, 233–62. Bury, *Later Roman Empire*, II, 360–94.

[59] A. Lebedev, *The Ecumenical Councils of the Sixth, Seventh, and Eighth Centuries* (3rd ed., 1904), 16.

[60] On Caesaropapism in Byzantium see G. Ostrogorsky, "Relation between the Church and the State in Byzantium," *Annales de l'Institut Kondakov*, IV (1931), 121–23. See also Biondo Biondi, *Giustiniano Primo Principe e Legislatore Cattolico*, 11–13.

and to find religious support for the throne which he had procured by chance.

Justinian had received a good religious education. He knew the Scriptures very well, was fond of participating in religious discussions, and wrote a number of church hymns. Religious conflicts seemed dangerous to him, even from a political point of view, for they menaced the unity of the Empire.

Although two predecessors of Justin and Justinian, Zeno and Anastasius, had followed the path of peaceful relations with the eastern Monophysitic church, thereby breaking away from the Roman church, Justin and Justinian definitely favored the Roman church and renewed friendly relations with it. This state of affairs was bound to alienate the eastern provinces, a fact that did not harmonize with the projects of Justinian, who was exceedingly anxious to establish a uniform faith throughout his vast Empire. The achievement of a church unity between the East and the West, between Alexandria, Antioch, and Rome, was impossible. "Justinian's government," said one historian, "was in its church policy a double-faced Janus with one face turned to the west, asking for direction from Rome, while the other, looking east, sought the truth from the Syrian and Egyptian monks."[61]

The fundamental aim of Justinian's church policy from the very beginning of his reign was the establishment of closer relations with Rome; hence he had to appear as the defender of the Council of Chalcedon, the decisions of which were strongly opposed by the eastern provinces. During Justinian's reign the see of Rome enjoyed supreme church authority. In his letters to the bishop of Rome, Justinian addressed him as "Pope," "Pope of Rome," "Apostolic Father," "Pope and Patriarch," etc., and the title of pope was applied exclusively to the bishop of Rome. In one epistle the Emperor addressed the Pope as the "head of all holy churches" (*caput omnium sanctarum ecclesiarum*),[62] and in one of his Novels he definitely stated that "the most blessed see of the archbishop of Constantinople, the New Rome, ranks second after the most holy apostolic see of Old Rome."[63]

Justinian came into collision with the Jews, the pagans, and the heretics. The latter included the Manichaeans, the Nestorians, the Monophysites, the Arians, and representatives of other less significant religious doctrines. Arianism was widely spread in the West among the Germanic tribes. Survivals of paganism existed in various parts of the Empire, and the pagans still looked upon the Athenian school as their main center. The Jews and the followers of minor heretical movements were centered primarily in the eastern provinces. The widest following was, of course, the Monophysitic. The struggle with the Arians in the West assumed the form of military undertakings, which

---

[61] A. Dyakonov, *John of Ephesus and His Ecclesiastical-Historical Works*, 52–53.

[62] Knecht, *Die Religions-Politik Kaiser Justinians*, 62–65.

[63] *Novella 131 β*; ed. Zachariä von Lingenthal, II, 267.

ended in the complete or partial subjection of the Germanic kingdoms. In view of Justinian's conviction of the necessity of a unified faith in the Empire there could be no tolerance toward the leaders of other faiths and heretical teachings, who consequently were subjected during his reign to severe persecution carried out with the aid of military and civil authorities.

The closing of the Athenian school.—In order to eradicate completely the survivals of paganism, Justinian in the year 529 closed the famous philosophic school in Athens, the last rampart of effete paganism, the decline of which had been already precipitated by the organization of the University of Constantinople in the fifth century during the reign of Theodosius II. Many of the professors were exiled and the property of the school was confiscated. One historian writes, "The same year when St. Benedict destroyed the last pagan national sanctuary in Italy, the temple of Apollo in the sacred grove of Monte Cassino, saw also the destruction of the stronghold of classical paganism in Greece."[64] From this period onward Athens definitely lost its former importance as a cultural center and deteriorated into a quiet, second-rate city. Some of the philosophers of the closed school decided to migrate to Persia, where, they had heard, King Chosroes was interested in philosophy. They were received in Persia with great esteem, but life in a foreign country was unbearable to these Greeks, and Chosroes determined to let them go back to their land, first arranging a treaty with Justinian by which the latter promised not to persecute them or force them to embrace the Christian faith. Justinian kept this promise and the pagan philosophers spent the rest of their lives in the Byzantine Empire in complete peace and safety. Justinian failed to bring about the complete eradication of paganism; it continued to exist secretly in remote localities.

The Jews and their religious kinsmen, the Samaritans of Palestine, unable to be reconciled to the government persecutions, rose in rebellion but were soon quelled by cruel violence. Many synagogues were destroyed, while in those which remained intact it was forbidden to read the Old Testament from the Hebrew text, which had to be replaced by the Greek version of seventy translators (the so-called "Septuagint"). The civil rights of the population were curtailed. The Nestorians were also severely persecuted.

Religious problems and the Fifth Ecumenical Council.—Most important of all, of course, was Justinian's attitude toward the Monophysites. First of all, his relations with them were of great political importance and involved the extremely significant problem of the eastern provinces, Egypt, Syria, and Palestine. In the second place, the Monophysites were supported by Justinian's wife, Theodora, who had a powerful influence over him. One contemporary Monophysitic writer (John of Ephesus) called her a "Christ-loving woman

[64] Knecht, *Die Religions-Politik Kaiser Justinians,* 36.

filled with zeal" and "the most Christian empress, sent by God in difficult times to protect the persecuted."[65]

Following her advice, Justinian attempted at the beginning of his reign to establish peaceful relations with the Monophysites. He permitted the bishops who had been exiled during the reign of Justin and at the beginning of his own reign to return home. He invited many Monophysites to the capital to a conciliatory religious conference, at which, according to an eyewitness, he appealed to them to discuss all doubtful questions with their antagonists "with all mildness and patience as behooves orthodox and saintly people."[66] He gave quarters in one of the palaces in the capital to five hundred Monophysitic monks; they were likened to "a great and marvelous desert of solitaries."[67] In 535 Severus, the head and "true legislator of Monophysitism," arrived in Constantinople and remained there a year.[68] "The capital of the Empire, at the beginning of the year 535, was assuming somewhat the aspect which it had presented under the reign of Anastasius."[69] The see of Constantinople was entrusted to the bishop of Trapezus (Trebizond), Anthimus, famous for his conciliatory policy towards the Monophysites. The Monophysites seemed triumphant.

However, things changed very soon. Pope Agapetus and a party of the Akoimetoi (extreme orthodox), upon arriving at Constantinople, raised such an uproar against the religious pliancy of Anthimus that Justinian was forced regretfully to change his policy. Anthimus was deposed and his place was taken by the orthodox presbyter, Menas. One source relates the following conversation between the Emperor and the pope: "I shall either force you to agree with us, or else I shall send you into exile," said Justinian, to which Agapetus answered, "I wished to come to the most Christian of all emperors, Justinian, and I have found now a Diocletian; however, I fear not your threats."[70] It is very likely that the Emperor's concessions to the pope were caused partly by the fact that the Ostrogothic war began at this time in Italy and Justinian needed the support of the West.

In spite of this concession, Justinian did not forsake further attempts of reconciliation with the Monophysites. This time he raised the famous question of the Three Chapters. The matter concerned three church writers of the

[65] *Commentarii de Beatis Orientalibus,* ed. W. J. van Douwen and J. P. N. Land, 114, 247; ed. E. W. Brooks, *Patrologia Orientalis,* XVIII (1924), 634 (432), 677 (475), 679 (477). See A. Dyakonov, *John of Ephesus,* 63.

[66] J. D. Mansi, *Sacrorum Conciliorum nova et amplissima collectio* (1762), VIII, 817. Caesari Baronii, *Annales ecclesiastici,* ed. A. Theiner, IX, 32 (s. a. 532), 419.

[67] John of Ephesus, *Commentarii,* 155; ed.

Brooks, II, 677 (475). See Dyakonov, *John of Ephesus,* 58.

[68] J. Maspero, *Histoire des patriarches d'Alexandrie,* 3, 100, 110. Lebon, *Le Monophysisme sévérien,* 74-77.

[69] Maspero, *Patriarches d'Alexandrie,* 110.

[70] *Vita Agapeti papae,* ed. L. Duchesne, *Liber Pontificalis,* I, 287. Mansi, *Amplissima Collectio Conciliorum,* VIII, 843.

fifth century: Theodore of Mopsuestia, Theodoret of Cyrus, and Ibas of Edessa. The Monophysites accused the Council of Chalcedon because in spite of the Nestorian ideas of these three writers, it had failed to condemn them. The pope and the Akoimetoi advanced very strong opposition. Justinian, greatly provoked, declared that in this case the Monophysites were right and the orthodox must agree with them. He issued in the early forties a decree which anathematized the works of the three writers and threatened to do the same to all people who might attempt to defend or approve them.[71]

Justinian wished to make this edict obligatory on all churches and demanded that it be signed by all the patriarchs and bishops. But this was not easy to accomplish. The West was troubled by the fact that the willingness to sign this imperial edict might mean an encroachment upon the authority of the Council of Chalcedon. One learned deacon of Carthage wrote, "If the definitions of the Council of Chalcedon are being disputed, then is it not possible that also the Council of Nicaea might be subject to a similar menace?"[72] In addition to this the question was raised as to whether it was permissible to condemn dead men, since all three writers had died in the preceding century. Finally, some leaders of the West were of the opinion that by this edict the Emperor was violating the conscience of members of the church. This view was not held in the eastern church, where the intervention of the imperial power in deciding dogmatical disputes was approved by long practice. The eastern church also cited King Josiah in the Old Testament, who not only put down the living idolatrous priests, but also opened the sepulchers of those who died long before his reign and burned their bones upon the altar (II Kings 23:16). Thus the eastern church was willing to accept the decree and condemn the Three Chapters; the western church was not. In the end, Justinian's decree never received general church recognition.

In order to attract the western church to his support Justinian had to secure first the approval of the Pope of Rome. Consequently the pope of that period, Vigilius, was summoned to Constantinople, where he remained for more than seven years. Upon his arrival he declared openly that he was against the edict and excommunicated the Patriarch of Constantinople, Menas. But gradually he yielded to the influence of Justinian and Theodora, and in the year 548 he issued the condemnation of the Three Chapters, or the so-called "Judicatum," thus adding his voice to the votes of the four eastern patriarchs. This was the last triumph of Theodora, who was convinced of the inevitable final victory of Monophysitism. She died in the same year. Upon the invitation of Virgilius,

---

[71] The Edict of the Three Chapters was called this because it contained three chapters or paragraphs devoted to the three before-named writers, but the original meaning of this name was soon forgotten and the "Three

Chapters" later signified Theodore, Theodoret, and Ibas.

[72] Fulgentii Ferrandi *Epistola*, VI, 7; ed. J. P. Migne, *Patrologia Latina*, LXVII, 926.

the priests of western Europe had to put up incessant prayers for "the most clement princes, Justinian and Theodora."[73]

The western church, however, did not approve of the concession made by Vigilius. The African bishops, having summoned a council, went even so far as to excommunicate him. Stirred by these events, the pope wavered in his decision and revoked the Judicatum. Justinian decided to resort to the aid of an ecumenical council, which was convoked in Constantinople in the year 553.

The problem of this Fifth Ecumenical Council was much simpler than the problems of the earlier councils. It did not have to deal with any new heresy; it was faced only with the problem of regulating some questions connected with the decisions of the third and fourth councils, relative partly to Nestorianism, but concerning primarily the Monophysitic faith. The Emperor was very desirous that the pope, who was in Constantinople at the time, be present at the Council, but under various excuses Vigilius avoided attending it, and all the sessions of the Council took place without him. The Council looked into the works of the three disputed writers and agreed with the opinion of the Emperor. The resolution of the Council condemned and anathematized "the impious Theodoret who was bishop of Mopsuestia, together with his impious works, and all that Theodoret had written impiously, and the impious letter, attributed to Ibas, and those who have written or are writing to defend them (*ad defensionem eorum*)."[74] The decrees of this Council were declared obligatory, and Justinian instituted a policy of persecuting and exiling the bishops who did not agree with the condemnation of the Three Chapters. Pope Vigilius was exiled to one of the islands of the Sea of Marmora. In the end he consented to sign the condemnation and was then permitted to return to Rome, but he died on his way at Syracuse. The West did not accept the decisions of the Council of 553 until the end of the sixth century, and only when Gregory I the Great (590–604) proclaimed that "at the Synod, which was concerned with the Three Chapters, nothing was violated or in any way changed in the matter of religion,"[75] was the Council of 553 recognized throughout the West as an ecumenical council on a par with the first four councils.

The intense religious struggle which Justinian expected would reconcile the Monophysites with the orthodox, did not bring the results he hoped for. The Monophysites did not seem satisfied with the concessions made to them. In the last years of his life Justinian apparently favored the Monophysites. The

---

[73] *Monumenta Germaniae Historica, Epistolarum* III, 62 (no. 41).

[74] Mansi, *Amplissima Collectio Conciliorum*, IX, 376.

[75] *Epistolae Gregorii Magni*, II, 36; Mansi, *Amplissima Collectio Conciliorum*, IX, 1105. *Gregorii I papae Registrum epistolarum*, ed. L. M. Hartmann, II, 49, in *Monumenta Germaniae Historica, Epistolarum*, I, 151.

bishops who disagreed with him were exiled. Monophysitism might have become the state religion, obligatory on all, and this would have led to new and very serious complications. But at this time the aged Emperor died, and with his death came a change in the religious policy of the government.

In summarizing the religious and ecclesiastical policy of Justinian the question might be asked whether or not he succeeded in establishing a united church in the Empire. The answer must, of course, be in the negative. Orthodoxy and Monophysitism did not become reconciled; Nestorianism, Manichaeism, Judaism, and, to some extent, paganism, continued to exist. There was no religious unity, and Justinian's attempt to bring it about must be admitted a failure.

But in speaking of Justinian's religious policy we must not disregard his missionary activities. As a Christian emperor he considered it his duty to spread Christianity beyond the boundaries of his empire. The conversion of the Heruli on the Danube, and of some Caucasian tribes, as well as of the native tribes of Northern Africa and the Middle Nile occurred in Justinian's time.[76]

The internal policy of Justinian

The Nika revolt.—At the time of Justinian's accession to the throne the internal life of the Empire was in a state of disorder and disturbance. Poverty was widespread, especially in the provinces; taxes were not paid regularly. The factions of the circus, the large landowners, the relatives of Anastasius, robbed of their right to the throne, and finally, the dissenting religious groups increased the internal troubles and created an alarming situation.

When he mounted the throne, Justinian understood clearly that the internal life of the Empire was greatly in need of wide reforms, and he attacked this problem courageously. The main sources of information on this phase of Justinian's activity are his Novels, the treatise of John the Lydian, *On the Administration (Magistrates) of the Roman State,* and *The Secret History* of his contemporary, Procopius. In recent times much valuable material has been found also in the papyri.

At the very beginning of his reign Justinian witnessed a frightful rebellion in the capital which nearly deprived him of the throne. The central quarter in Constantinople was the circus or the Hippodrome, the favorite gathering place of the inhabitants of the capital, so fond of chariot races. A new emperor, after his coronation, usually appeared at this Hippodrome in the imperial box, the *Kathisma,* to receive the first greetings of the mob. The charioteers wore

---

[76] See Maspero, *Patriarches d'Alexandrie,* 135. Maspero gives a very fine history of the Monophysitic problem under Justinian, 102– 65. Also see Dyakonov, *John of Ephesus,* 51– 87.

robes of four colors: green, blue, white, and red. The chariot races had remained the favorite spectacle at the circus since the time when the early Christian church had prohibited gladiatorial combats. Well-organized factions were formed around the charioteers of each color. These groups had their own treasury for financing the charioteers, their horses and chariots, and always competed and struggled with the parties of other colors. They soon became known under the names of Green, Blue, White, and Red. The circus and the races, as well as the circus factions, came to the Byzantine Empire from the Roman Empire, and later literary tradition attributes their origin to the mythical times of Romulus and Remus. The original meaning of the names of the four parties is not very clear. The sources of the sixth century, Justinian's period, claim that these names corresponded to the four elements: the earth (green), water (blue), air (white), and fire (red). The circus festivities were distinguished by extreme splendor and the number of spectators sometimes reached 50,000.

The circus factions, designated in the Byzantine period as *demes,* gradually changed into political parties expressing various political, social, or religious tendencies. The voice of the mob in the circus became a sort of public opinion and voice of the nation. "In the absence of the printing press," said Th. I. Uspensky, "the Hippodrome became the only place for a free expression of public opinion, which at times imposed its will upon the government."[77] The emperor himself was sometimes obliged to appear in the circus to offer the people explanation of his actions.

In the sixth century the most influential factions were the Blues (Venetoi), who stood for orthodoxy, hence also called Chalcedonians, adherents of the Council of Chalcedon; and the Greens (Prasinoi), who stood for Monophysitism. In the time of Anastasius a rebellion had arisen against the Greens, whom the Monophysite emperor favored. After terrible raids and destruction the orthodox party proclaimed a new emperor and rushed to the Hippodrome, where the frightened Anastasius appeared without his diadem and ordered the heralds to announce to the people that he was ready to renounce his title. The mob, mollified at seeing the emperor in such a pitiful state, calmed down and the revolt subsided. But the episode illustrates the influence exerted by the Hippodrome and the mob of the capital upon the government and even the emperor himself. With the accession of Justin and Justinian orthodoxy prevailed, and the Blues triumphed. Theodora, however, favored the Greens, so that even on the imperial throne itself there was division.

It is almost certain that the demes represented not only political and religious tendencies, but also different class interests. The Blues may be regarded as the party of the upper classes, the Greens of the lower. If this is true, the

[77] Th. I. Uspensky, *History of the Byzantine Empire,* I, 506.

Byzantine factions acquire a new and very important significance as a social element.[78]

An interesting recurrence of pattern is to be found in the fact that early in the sixth century in Rome under Theodoric the Great two rival parties, the Greens and the Blues, continued to fight, the Blues representing the upper classes and the Greens the lower.[79]

An important new approach to this question has recently been emphasized and discussed. A Russian scholar, the late A. Dyakonov, pointed out "the error in method" of Rambaud, Manojlović, and others who fail to differentiate between the demes and the factions, which of course are not identical at all and must be dealt with separately. The object of Dyakonov's study was not to solve the problem, but to raise it again, so that this new approach may be considered in future more highly specialized works.[80]

The causes of the formidable rebellion of 532 in the capital were numerous and diverse. The opposition directed against Justinian was threefold: dynastic, public, and religious. The surviving nephews of Anastasius felt that they had been circumvented by Justin's, and later Justinian's, accession to the throne, and, supported by the Monophysitical-minded party of the Greens, they aimed to depose Justinian. The public opposition arose from general bitterness against the higher officials, especially against the famous jurist, Tribonian, and the praetorian prefect, John of Cappadocia, who aroused great

[78] See the extremely important monograph by M. Manojlović, originally published in Serbo-Croatian in 1904 and almost never referred to. H. Grégoire has translated it into French under the title "Le peuple de Constantinople," *Byzantion*, XI (1936), 617–716. Manojlović's thesis has not been universally accepted. F. Dolger accepts it (*Byzantinische Zeitschrift*, XXXVII [1937], 542); Ostrogorsky declines it (*Geschichte des byzantinischen Staates*, 41, n. 1). E. Stein declined it in 1920 (he had not himself read the original Serbo-Croatian text), but accepted it in 1930 (*Byzantinische Zeitschrift*, XXX [1930], 378). I myself believe that Manojlović has convincingly proved his thesis.

[79] See E. Condurachi, "Factions et jeux de cirque à Rome au début du VIe siècle," *Revue historique du sud-est européen*, XVIII (1941), 95–102, especially 96–98. The source for this important conclusion is the contemporary work of Cassiodorus, the *Variae*. Cf. Manojlović's casual remark, unsupported by any reference: "This 'crystallization' [of the classes]

originated in the circus of the elder Rome." *Byzantion*, XI (1936), 642, 711–12.

[80] "The Byzantine Demes and Factions [τὰ μέρη] in the Fifth to the Seventh Centuries," *Vizantiysky Sbornik*, 1945, ed. M. V. Levchenko, 144–227; introduction, 144–49. An excellent study which must serve as an indispensable foundation for further studies on this question. On the history of the demes and factions in later times, especially in the seventh century when the political importance of the factions was gradually waning, see G. Brătianu, "La Fin du regime des parties à Byzance et la crise antisemite du VIIe siècle, *Revue historique du sud-est européen*, XVIII (1941), 49–57. Dyakonov, "Byzantine Demes," *Vizantiysky Sbornik*, 1945, 226–27. Grégoire may be somewhat inexact in his statement: "It is a fact that after 641 one finds no further trace of the political role of the colors of the Circus [*des couleurs du Cirque*]," "Notules epigraphique," *Byzantion*, XIII (1938), 175. F. Dvornik, "The Circus Parties in Byzantium," *Byzantina Metabyzantina*, I (1946), 119–133.

dissatisfaction among the people by their violation of laws and their shameful extortions and cruelty. Finally, the religious opposition was that of the Monophysites, who had suffered great restrictions during the early years of Justinian's reign. All these causes together brought about a revolt of the people in the capital, and it is interesting to note that the Blues and the Greens, abandoning for a time their religious discrepancies, made common cause against the hated government. The Emperor negotiated with the people through the herald in the Hippodrome, but no settlement was reached.[81] The revolt spread rapidly through the city, and the finest buildings and monuments of art were subjected to destruction and fire. Fire was also set to the basilica of St. Sophia, the site of which was later chosen for the famous cathedral of St. Sophia. The rallying cry of the rioters, *Nika,* meaning "victory" or "vanquish," has given this uprising the name of the Nika revolt. Justinian's promise to dismiss Tribonian and John of Cappadocia from their posts and his personal appeal to the mob at the Hippodrome were of no effect. A nephew of Anastasius was proclaimed emperor. Sheltered in the palace, Justinian and his councilors were already contemplating flight when Theodora rose to the occasion. Her exact words appear in *The Secret History* of Procopius: "It is impossible for a man, when he has come into the world, not to die; but for one who has reigned, it is intolerable to be an exile. . . . If you wish, O Emperor, to save yourself, there is no difficulty: we have ample funds; yonder is the sea, and there are the ships. Yet reflect whether, when you have once escaped to a place of security, you will not prefer death to safety. I agree with an old saying that the purple is a fair winding sheet."[82] The Emperor rallied and entrusted to Belisarius the task of crushing the revolt, which had already lasted for six days. The general drove the rioters into the Hippodrome, enclosed them there, and killed from thirty to forty thousand. The revolt was quelled, the nephews of Anastasius were executed, and Justinian once more sat firmly on the throne.[83]

Taxation and financial problems.—One of the distinguishing features of Justinian's internal policy was his obstinate, still not fully explained, struggle with the large landowners. This strife is discussed in the Novels and the papyri, as well as in *The Secret History* of Procopius, who, in spite of defending the views of the nobility and in spite of crowding into this libel a number of

---

[81] See a curious conversation between the Emperor and the Greens through a herald or *mandator* in Theophanes, *Chronographia,* ed. de Boor, 181–84; also *Chronicon Paschale,* 620–21. Cf. P. Maas, "Metrische Akklamationen der Byzantiner," *Byzantinische Zeitschrift,* XXI (1912), 31–33, 46–51. Bury thinks that this may refer to some other period

of Justinian's reign; see *Later Roman Empire,* II, 40 and n. 3, 72. Bury gives an English translation of the conversation, 72–74.

[82] *De bello persico,* I, 24, 35–37; ed. Haury, I, 130; ed. Dewing, I, 230–33.

[83] On the *Nika* revolt see Dyakonov's remarks in "The Byzantine Demes," *Vizantiysky Sbornik,* 1945, 209–12.

absurd accusations against Justinian, in his eyes an upstart on the imperial throne, still paints an extremely interesting picture of the social struggle in the sixth century. The government felt that its most dangerous rivals and enemies were the large landowners, who conducted the affairs of their large estates with complete disregard for the central power. One of Justinian's Novels, blaming the desperate condition of state and private landownership in the provinces upon the unrestrained conduct of local magnates, directed to the Cappadocian proconsul the following significant lines: "News has come to us about such exceedingly great abuses in the provinces that their correction can hardly be accomplished by one person of high authority. And we are even ashamed to tell with how much impropriety the managers of landlords' estates promenade about, surrounded by body-guards, how they are followed by large mobs of people, and how shamelessly they rob everything. . . . State property has almost entirely gone over into private ownership, for it was robbed and plundered, including all the herds of horses, and not a single man spoke up against it, for all the mouths were stopped with gold."[84] It appears that the Cappadocian magnates had full authority in their provinces and that they even maintained troops of their own, armed men and body-guards, and seized private as well as state lands. It is interesting to note also that this Novel was issued four years after the Nika revolt. Similar information about Egypt in the time of Justinian is found in the papyri. A member of a famous Egyptian landowning family, the Apions, possessed in the sixth century vast landed property in various parts of Egypt. Entire villages were part of his possessions. His household was almost regal. He had his secretaries and stewards, his hosts of workmen, his own assessors and tax collectors, his treasurer, his police, even his own postal service. Such magnates had their own prisons and maintained their own troops.[85] Large estates were concentrated also in the hands of the churches and monasteries.

Against these large landowners Justinian waged a merciless struggle. By intervention in problems of heredity, forced and sometimes false donations to the Emperor, confiscation on the basis of false evidence, or the instigation of religious trials tending to deprive the church of its landed property, Justinian consciously and persistently aimed at the destruction of large landownership. Particularly numerous confiscations were made after the revolutionary attempt of the year 532. Justinian did not succeed, however, in com-

[84] *Novella, 30* (44), 5; ed. Zachariä von Lingenthal, I, 268.

[85] See H. Bell, "The Byzantine Servile State in Egypt," *Journal of Egyptian Archaeology,* IV (1917), 101-2. Bell, "An Epoch in the Agrarian History of Egypt," *Études égyp-* *tologiques dédiées à Jean-François Champollion,* 263. M. Gelzer, *Studien zur byzantinischen Verwaltung Aegyptens,* 32, 83-90. A. E. R. Boak, "Byzantine Imperialism in Egypt," *American Historical Review,* XXXIV (1928), 6.

pletely crushing large landownership, and it remained one of the unfailing features of the life of the Empire in later periods.

Justinian saw and understood the defects of the administration expressed in the venality, theft, and extortions which caused so much poverty and ruin, and which inevitably aroused internal troubles. He realized that such a state of things within the Empire had evil effects upon social security, city finance, and agricultural conditions, and that financial disorder introduced general confusion into the life of the Empire. He was truly anxious to remedy the existing situation. He conceived it to be the emperor's duty to introduce new and great reforms, which he viewed as an obligation of imperial service and an act of gratitude to God, who bestowed upon the emperor all his favors. But as a convinced representative of absolute imperial power, Justinian considered a centralized administration with an improved and completely obedient staff of bureaucrats the only means of ameliorating conditions in the Empire.

His attention turned first of all to the financial situation in the Empire, which very justly inspired extremely serious fears. The military undertakings demanded enormous means, yet taxes were coming into the treasury with constantly increasing difficulties. This fact alarmed the Emperor, and in one of his Novels he wrote that in view of the large war expenses his subjects "must pay the government taxes willingly and in full."[86] Thus, on the one hand, he was the champion of the inviolability of the rights of the treasury, while on the other hand he proclaimed himself the defender of the taxpayer against the extortions of officials.

Two great Novels of the year 535 are exceedingly important for the study of Justinian's reforms. They contain the principal foundations of the administrative reforms and the definitions of the new duties of government officials. One Novel orders the rulers "to treat with fatherly consideration all the loyal citizens, to protect the subjects against oppression, to refuse all bribes, to be just in sentences and administrative decisions, to persecute crime, protect the innocent, and punish the guilty according to law, and, on the whole, treat the subjects as a father would treat his own children."[87] But at the same time officials, "while keeping their hands clean [of bribes] everywhere," must vigilantly look after the government income, "increasing the state treasury and exerting all possible effort for its benefit."[88] Taking into consideration the conquest of Africa and the Vandals, as well as the newly contemplated campaigns, says the Novel, "it is imperative that the government taxes be paid in full and willingly at definite dates. Thus, if you will meet the rulers reasonably

---

[86] *Novella 8* (16), 10; ed. Zachariä von Lingenthal, I, 104.

[87] *Novella 8* (16), 8; ed. *ibid.*, I, 102.
[88] *Novella 28* (31), 5; ed. *ibid.*, I, 197.

and help them collect for us the taxes with ease and dispatch, then we will laud the officials for their zeal and you for your wisdom; and beautiful and peaceful harmony will reign everywhere between the rulers and the ruled."[89] The officials had to take a solemn oath to administer their duties honestly, but were at the same time made responsible for the complete payment of taxes in the provinces entrusted to them. The bishops were supposed to watch the behavior of the officials. Those who were found guilty of offense were subject to severe punishment, while those who carried out their duties honestly were promised promotion. Thus, the duty of government officials and government taxpayers is very simple in Justinian's conception: the former must be honest men; the latter must pay their taxes willingly, fully, and regularly. In subsequent decrees the Emperor often cited these basic principles of his administrative reforms.

Not all the provinces of the Empire were governed alike. There were some, especially those along the borders, populated by restless natives, which demanded firmer administration than others. The reforms of Diocletian and Constantine increased excessively the provincial division and established a vast staff of bureaucracy, separating very distinctly civil and military authority. In Justinian's time, in some instances, there was a break with this system and a return to the former pre-Diocletian system. Justinian introduced the practice of combining several small provinces, particularly in the East, into larger units; while in some provinces of Asia Minor, in view of frequent disagreements and conflicts between military and civil authorities, he ordered the combining of the two functions in the hands of one person, a governor, who was called *praetor*. The Emperor's particular attention was directed to Egypt, mainly to Alexandria, which supplied Constantinople with corn. According to one Novel, the organization of the trade in Egypt and the delivery of corn to the capital was in great disorder.[90] With the aim of re-establishing this highly important branch of government life, Justinian entrusted a civil official, the Augustalis (*vir spectabilis Augustalis*), with military authority over the two Egyptian provinces[91] as well as over Alexandria, that densely populated and restless city. But these attempts to centralize territories and power in the provinces were not systematic during his reign.

While carrying out the idea of combining authority in some of the eastern provinces, Justinian retained the former separation of civil and military power in the West, especially in the recently conquered prefectures of North Africa and Italy.

[89] *Novella 8* (16), 10; ed. *ibid.*, I, 106.
[90] *Edictum 13* (96), introduction; ed. *ibid.*, I, 529-30.
[91] Gelzer, *Studien zur byzantinischen Verwaltung Aegyptens*, 21-36. Bury, *Later Roman Empire*, II, 342-43. G. Rouillard, *L'Administration civile de l'Egypte byzantine* (2nd ed., 1928), 30.

The Emperor hoped that his numerous hasty decrees had corrected all internal shortcomings of the administration and "given the empire, through his brilliant undertakings, a new period of bloom."[92] He was mistaken. All his decrees could not change mankind. It is very evident from later novels that rebellions, extortion, and ruin continued. It became necessary to republish constantly imperial decrees to remind the population of their existence, and in some provinces it was occasionally necessary to proclaim martial law.

At times, when the need for money was very urgent, Justinian used the very measures which were prohibited in his decrees. He sold offices at high prices and, regardless of his promise to the contrary, introduced new taxes, though his Novels show clearly that he was fully aware of the incapacity of the population to meet them. Under the pressure of financial difficulties he resorted to the corruption of money and issued debased coin; but the attitude of the populace became so threatening that he was forced almost immediately to revoke his measure.[93] All possible means were used to fill the government treasury, the fisc, "which took the place of a stomach feeding all parts of the body," as Corippus, a poet of the sixth century, puts it.[94] The strict measures which accompanied the collection of taxes reached their extreme limits and had a disastrous effect upon the exhausted population. One contemporary says that "a foreign invasion seemed less formidable to the taxpayers than the arrival of the officials of the fisc."[95] Villages became impoverished and deserted because their inhabitants fled from government oppression. The productivity of the land was reduced to nothing. Revolts sprang up in various localities.

Realizing that the Empire was ruined and that economy was the only means of salvation, Justinian resorted to economy in the most dangerous directions. He reduced the army in numbers, and frequently kept back its pay. But the army, consisting mainly of mercenaries, often revolted against this practice and took vengeance on the unprotected people. The reduction of the army had other serious consequences: it left the borders unprotected and the barbarians crossed the Byzantine boundaries freely to carry on their devastating raids. The fortresses constructed by Justinian were not maintained. Unable to oppose the barbarians by force, Justinian had to resort to bribes, which involved very large new expenditures. According to the French scholar, Diehl, this formed a vicious circle. Lack of money forced a decrease of the army; the absence of soldiers necessitated more money to buy off enemies.[96]

---

[92] *Novella 33* (54), introduction; ed. Zachariä von Lingenthal, I, 360.

[93] *Chronicle of John Malalas*, 486. If I am not mistaken Bury does not mention this text.

[94] *De laudibus Justini*, II, vss. 249–50.

[95] Joannis Lydi *De Magistratibus*, III, 70; ed. I. Bekker, Bonn edition, 264; ed. R. Wuensch, *Bibliotheca scriptorum graecorum et romanorum Teubneriana*, 162.

[96] *Justinien*, 311.

When to all this was added the frequent famines, epidemics, and earthquakes which ruined the population and increased the demands for government aid, the state of the Empire at the end of Justinian's reign was truly lamentable. Among these calamities the devastating plague of 542 must be mentioned. It began near Pelusium, on the borders of Egypt. The suggested Ethiopian origin is vague; there was a sort of ancient and traditional suspicion that disease usually came out of Ethiopia. As Thucydides studied the plague at Athens at the beginning of the Peloponnesian war, so the historian Procopius, who witnessed its course at Constantinople, detailed the nature and effects of the bubonic disease. From Egypt the infection spread northward to Palestine and Syria; in the following year it reached Constantinople, then spread over Asia Minor and through Mesopotamia into Persia. Over the sea it invaded Italy and Sicily. In Constantinople the visitation lasted four months. The mortality was enormous; cities and villages were abandoned, agriculture stopped, and famine, panic, and the flight of large numbers of people away from the infected places threw the Empire into confusion. All court functions were discontinued. The Emperor himself was stricken by the plague, although the attack did not prove fatal.[97] This was only one contributing factor to the gloomy picture reflected in the first Novel of Justin II, where he speaks of "the government treasury overburdened with many debts and reduced to extreme poverty," and "of an army so desperately in need of all necessaries that the empire was easily and frequently attacked and raided by the barbarians."[98]

Justinian's attempts in the field of administrative reform were a complete failure. Financially the Empire stood on the verge of ruin. There was a close connection between the internal and external policies of the Emperor; his sweeping military undertakings in the West, which demanded colossal expenditure, ruined the East and left his successors a troublesome heritage. As evinced by the early Novels, Justinian sincerely intended to bring order into the Empire and to raise the moral standards of government institutions, but these noble intentions gave way to the militarism dictated by his conception of his duties as heir of the Roman Caesars.

Commerce during the reign of Justinian

The period of Justinian left distinct traces in the history of Byzantine commerce. In the Christian period, as in the days of the pagan Roman Empire, the main trade was carried on with the East. The rarest and most valuable

---

[97] The best and principal authority is Procopius, who was living in Constantinople during the visitation. *De bello persico*, II, 22–23. See Bury, *Later Roman Empire*, 62–66; Procopius' description is reproduced on 63–64. H. Zinsser, *Rats, Lice and History*, 144–49; translation from Procopius, 145–47.

[98] K. E. Zachariä von Lingenthal, *Jus graeco-romanum*, III, 3.

articles of trade arrived from the distant lands of China and India. Western Europe of the earlier Middle Ages, in the period of the formation of new Germanic states, some of which were conquered by Justinian's generals, lived under conditions extremely unfavorable for the development of its own economic life. The Eastern Roman Empire, with its advantageously situated capital became, by force of circumstances, the mediator between the West and the East, and kept this position until the period of the Crusades.

But the commercial relations of the Byzantine Empire with the peoples of the Far East were not direct; the mediating agent here was the Persian Empire of the Sassanids, which gained enormous profits on the commercial transactions of the Byzantine merchants. There were at this time two main trade routes: one by land, the other by sea. The overland caravan route led from the western borders of China through Sogdiana (now Bokhara or Bukhara) to the Persian border, where the wares were transferred by Chinese merchants to the Persians, who transported them to the customhouses on the Byzantine border. The sea route used was as follows: Chinese merchants transported their wares on vessels as far as the island of Taprobane (now Ceylon), south of the peninsula of Hindostan. There Chinese goods were reloaded, chiefly into Persian vessels, which carried their cargo by way of the Indian Ocean and the Persian Gulf to the mouths of the Tigris and Euphrates, whence they were forwarded along the Euphrates to the Byzantine customhouse situated on this river. Byzantine commerce with the East, therefore, depended very closely upon the relations between the Empire and Persia, and since wars with Persia were a regular occurrence in Byzantine life, trade relations with the East suffered constant interruptions and great harm. The main article of trade was Chinese silk, the production of which was guarded in deep secrecy by China. In view of the difficulties involved in its production, its prices and the prices of silk stuffs greatly in demand on Byzantine markets rose at times to unbelievable figures. Besides Chinese silk, China and India exported to the West perfumes, spices, cotton, precious stones, and other articles demanded primarily in the Byzantine Empire. Unreconciled to the economic dependence of the Byzantine Empire upon Persia, Justinian set himself the goal of finding a trade route to China and India which would lie outside of the realm of Persian influence.

Cosmas Indicopleustes.—During this period a remarkable literary work made its appearance, the *Christian Topography* or *Cosmography,* written by Cosmas Indicopleustes[99] in the middle of the sixth century. This work is ex-

[99] Indicopleustes means "sailor to India," or "sailor of the Indian Sea." This work was translated into English by J. MacCrindle, *The Christian Topography of Cosmas, an Egyptian Monk.* See C. Beazley, *The Dawn of Modern Geography,* I, 190–96, 273–303. The fullest and most illuminating sketch of Cosmas' work according to E. Winstedt, *The*

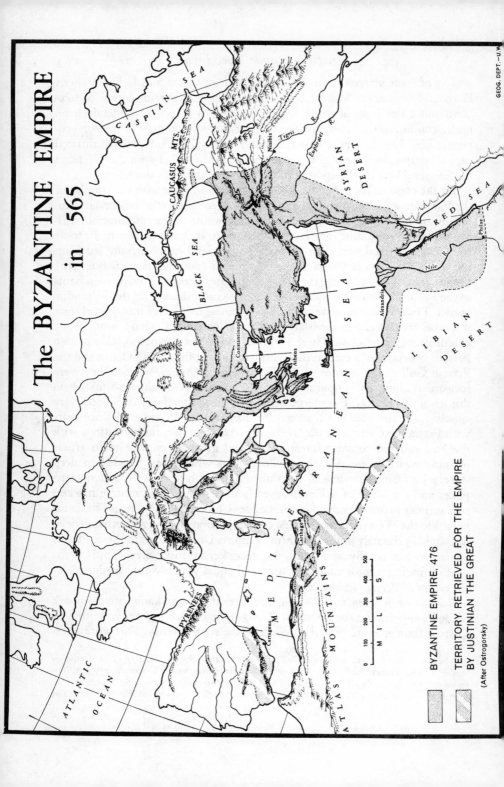

The BYZANTINE EMPIRE in 565

CASPIAN SEA

CAUCASUS MTS.

BLACK SEA

Danube R.

Constantinople

Athens

Danube R.

Save R.

ALPS

PYRENEES

ATLANTIC OCEAN

Cartagena

Carthage

ATLAS MOUNTAINS

MEDITERRANEAN SEA

Nisibis

Tigris

Euphrates R.

SYRIAN DESERT

RED SEA

Philae

Nile

Alexandria

LIBIAN DESERT

0   100   200   300   400   500

MILES

BYZANTINE EMPIRE, 476

TERRITORY RETRIEVED FOR THE EMPIRE
BY JUSTINIAN THE GREAT

(After Ostrogorsky)

GEOG. DEPT.—U.W.

tremely valuable for the information it contains about the geography of the basins of the Red Sea and the Indian Ocean as well as about the commercial relations with India and China.

Cosmas was born in Egypt, very likely in Alexandria. He engaged in commerce from his early youth, but, discontented with the trade conditions in his country, he undertook a number of distant journeys during which he visited the shores of the Red Sea, the Sinaitic peninsula, Ethiopia (Abyssinia), and perhaps reached as far as Ceylon. He was a Christian of the Nestorian faith, and in his later life became a monk. His Greek surname, Indicopleustes, is found even in very old versions of his work.

The fundamental aim of *The Christian Topography* is to prove to the Christians that, regardless of the system of Ptolemy, the earth does not have the shape of a globe, but rather that of an oblong rectangular box similar to the sanctuary in the tabernacle of Moses, while the entire universe is analogous in form to the general form of the tabernacle. But it is the great historical importance of this work, which lies in the information about geography and commerce, which is relevant here. The author conscientiously informed his reader about the sources used and evaluated each of them thoroughly. He discriminated between his own observations as an eyewitness and the information obtained from eyewitnesses, and facts learned by hearsay. From his own experience he described the palace of the Abyssinian king in the city of Axum (in the so-called Kingdom of Axum), and gave an accurate account of several interesting inscriptions in Nubia and on the shores of the Red Sea. He told also of Indian and African animals, and, most important of all, gave very valuable information about the island Taprobane (Ceylon), explaining its commercial importance during the early Middle Ages. It appears from this account that in the sixth century Ceylon was the center of world commerce between China on one hand and eastern Africa, Persia, and through Persia the Byzantine Empire, on the other hand. In Cosmas' words, "the island, being as it is in a central position, is much frequented by ships from all parts of India and from Persia and Ethiopia."[100] The Persian Christians who remained permanently on this island were of the Nestorian faith and had their own church and clergy.

It is interesting to note that in spite of an almost complete absence of direct trade relations between the Byzantine Empire and India, Byzantine coins from the epoch of Constantine the Great appear in Indian markets, carried there apparently, not by Byzantine merchants, but by the mediating Persians

Christian Topography of Cosmas Indicopleustes, vi. M. V. Anastos, "The Alexandrian Origin of the *Christian Topography of Cosmas Indicopleustes,*" *Dumbarton Oaks Papers,* III (1946), 75–80.

[100] Cosmas Indicopleustes, *Topographia christiana,* XI; ed. Migne, *Patrologia Graeca,* LXXXVIII, 445; ed. Winstedt, 322; ed. MacCrindle, 365.

and Abyssinians (Axumites). Coins with the names of the Byzantine emperors of the fourth, fifth, and sixth centuries—Arcadius, Theodosius, Marcian, Leo I, Zeno, Anastasius I, Justin I—have been found in southern and northern India.[101] In the international economic life of the sixth century the Byzantine Empire played a role so important that, according to Cosmas, "all the nations carry on their trade in Roman money (the Byzantine gold coin, *nomisma* or *solidus*), from one extremity of the earth to the other. This money is regarded with admiration by all men to whatever kingdom they belong, since there is no other country in which the like of it exists."[102]

Cosmas told a very interesting story which shows the profound respect commanded in India by the Byzantine gold coin (*nomisma*):

The King of Ceylon, having admitted a Byzantine merchant, Sopatrus, and some Persians to an audience and having received their salutations, requested them to be seated. He then asked them: "In what state are your countries, and how go things with them?" To this they replied: "They go well." Afterward, as the conversation proceeded, the King inquired: "Which of your kings is the greater and the more powerful?" The elderly Persian, snatching the word, answered: "Our king is both the more powerful and the greater and richer, and indeed is King of Kings, and whatsoever he desires, that he is able to do." Sopatrus, on the other hand, sat mute. So the King asked: "Have you, Roman, nothing to say?" "What have I to say," he rejoined, "when he there has said such things? But if you wish to learn the truth you have the two kings here present. Examine each and you will see which of them is the grander and the more powerful." The King, upon hearing this, was amazed at his words and asked: "How say you that I have both kings here?" "You have," replied Sopatrus, "the money of both—the *nomisma* of one, and the drachma, that is, the miliarision of the other. Examine the image of each and you will see the truth. . . ." After having examined them, the King said that the Romans were certainly a splendid, powerful, and sagacious people. So he ordered great honor to be paid to Sopatrus, causing him to be mounted on an elephant and conducted round the city with drums beating and high state. These circumstances were told us by Sopatrus himself and his companions, who had accompanied him to that island from Adule; and as they told the story, the Persian was deeply chagrined at what had occurred.[103]

[101] See R. Sewell, "Roman Coins in India," *Journal of the Royal Asiatic Society*, XXXVI (1904), 620–21. M. Khvostov, *History of Oriental Commerce in Greco-Roman Egypt*, 230. E. Warmington, *The Commerce Between the Roman Empire and India*, 140.

[102] *Topographia christiana*, II; ed. Migne, *Patrologia Graeca*, LXXXVIII, 116; ed. Win-

stedt, 81; ed. MacCrindle, 73.

[103] *Ibid.*, XXI; ed. Migne, 448–49; ed. MacCrindle, 368–70. This story appears to be traditional, as Pliny related a somewhat similar anecdote of the ambassadors from Ceylon in the reign of Claudius. Pliny, *Naturalis Historia*, VI, 85. See J. E. Tennent, *Ceylon* (5th ed., 1860), I, 566.

In addition to the historical-geographical value, the work of Cosmas is also of great artistic value because of the numerous pictures (miniatures) which adorn his text. It is likely that some of these pictures were the work of the author himself. The original manuscript of the sixth century has not survived, but the later manuscripts of *The Christian Topography* contain copies of the original miniatures and thus serve as a valuable source for the history of early Byzantine, especially Alexandrine, art. "The miniatures in the work of Cosmas," said N. P. Kondakov, "are more characteristic of Byzantine art of the period of Justinian, or rather of the brilliant part of his reign, than any other monument of that period, except some of the mosaics at Ravenna."[104]

The work of Cosmas was later translated into Slavonic and became widely spread among the Slavs. There exist numerous Russian versions of *The Christian Topography* supplemented with the portrait of Cosmas Indicopleustes and numerous pictures and miniatures which are of much interest in the history of old Russian art.[105]

Protection of Byzantine commerce.—Justinian made it his aim to free Byzantine commerce of its dependence on Persia. This involved establishing direct communication with India by way of the Red Sea. The northeastern corner of the Red Sea (in the Gulf of Akaba) was occupied by the Byzantine port, Ayla, whence Indian wares could be transported by a land route through Palestine and Syria to the Mediterranean Sea. Another port, Clysma (near present-day Suez), was situated on the northwestern shore of the Red Sea, and from it was directly connected with the Mediterranean Sea. On one of the islands at the entrance to the Gulf of Akaba, Iotabe (now Tiran), near the southern extremity of the Sinai peninsula, a customhouse for bygoing vessels was established during Justinian's reign.[106] But the number of Byzantine ships in the Red Sea was not sufficient for carrying on a regulated commerce. This fact forced Justinian to establish close relations with the Christian Abyssinians in the Kingdom of Axum, urging them to buy silk in India and then resell it to the Byzantine Empire. He apparently wanted them to play the part of trade mediators between the Byzantine Empire and India, as the Persians had done up to that time. But these attempts on the part of the Emperor were not successful, for the Abyssinian merchants could not compete with Persian influence in India and the monopoly of silk buying still remained in the hands of Persian merchants. In the end Justinian did not succeed in opening up new routes for direct trade with the East. In intervals of peace the

[104] *Histoire de l'art byzantin considéré principalement dans les miniatures,* I, 138; Russian ed. (1876), 88.
[105] See E. Redin, *The Christian Topography of Cosmas Indicopleustes, from Greek and Russian Versions,* ed. D. V. Aïnalov.
[106] See W. Heyd, *Histoire du commerce du Levant au moyen âge,* I, 10. Diehl, *Justinien,* 390. R. P. F.-M. Abel, "L'Isle de Jotabe," *Revue biblique,* XLVII (1938), 520–24.

Persians still remained the mediators in the most important trade, and continued to make large profits.

Chance came to the aid of Justinian and helped him solve the highly significant problem of the Empire's silk trade. Some person or persons[107] successfully evaded the watchfulness of the Chinese inspectors and smuggled into the Byzantine Empire some silkworm eggs from Serinda, which formed the basis of a new industry for the Greeks. They made rapid progress. Large plantations of mulberry trees sprang up and many factories for weaving silk stuffs were quickly established. The most important of these silk factories were situated in Constantinople; others were founded in the Syrian cities of Beirut, Tyre, and Antioch, and later in Greece, mainly at Thebes. One existed in Alexandria in Egypt, for Egyptian clothes were sold in Constantinople.[108] The silk industry became a state monopoly and yielded the government a large income, which was not sufficient, however, to ameliorate the critical financial situation of the empire. Byzantine silk stuffs were carried to all parts of western Europe and adorned the palaces of western kings and the residences of rich merchants. This caused some highly significant changes in the commerce of Justinian's period, and his successor, Justin II, could show to a Turkish ambassador visiting his court the industry in full swing.[109]

Justinian undertook the colossal task of defending the Empire from the attacks of enemies by constructing a number of fortresses and well-protected border lines. In a few years he erected on all the borders of the Empire an almost uninterrupted line of fortifications (*castella*) in northern Africa, on the shores of the Danube and Euphrates, in the mountains of Armenia, and on the distant Crimean peninsula, thus restoring and enlarging the remarkable defensive system created by Rome during an earlier period. By this constructive work Justinian, according to Procopius, "saved the empire."[110] "If we were to enumerate the fortresses," Procopius wrote in *On Buildings*, "which were erected here by the Emperor Justinian, to people living in distant foreign lands, deprived of the opportunity to verify personally our words, I am

[107] The sources differ on this point. Procopius (*De bello gothico*, IV, 17; ed. Haury, II, 576) ascribes the exploit to several monks. In *Excerpta e Theophanis Historia* (Bonn ed., 484; ed. L. Dindorf, *Historici Graeci minores*, I, 447) the person is given as one Persian. Complete confusion of facts and names exists in F. Richthofen, *China. Ergebnisse eigener Reisen und darauf gegründeter Studien*, I, 528–29, 550. The Serinda of Procopius is sometimes identified with Khotan. Richthofen, *China*, I, 550–51. Heyd, *Histoire du commerce du Levant*, I, 12. Bury, *Later Roman Empire*, II, 332 and n. 1. On the history of the silk industry in the Byzantine Empire in general see the very important article of R. E. Lopez, "Silk Industry in the Byzantine Empire," *Speculum*, XX (1945), 1–42 (with several illustrations).

[108] J. Ebersolt, *Les Arts somptuaires de Byzance*, 12–13. G. Rouillard, *L'Administration de l'Egypt* (2nd ed., 1928), 83.

[109] *Excerpta e Theophanis Historia*, Bonn ed., 484; *Fragmenta Historicorum Graecorum*, IV, 270.

[110] *De aedificiis*, II, 1, 3; Bonn ed., 209; ed. Haury, III, 2, 46.

convinced that the number of constructions would seem to them fabulous and completely incredible."[111] Even today the existing ruins of numerous fortresses along the borders of the former Byzantine Empire astonish the modern traveler. Nor did Justinian limit his construction to fortifications alone. As a Christian emperor he fostered the building of many temples, of which the incomparable St. Sophia of Constantinople stands out as an epoch-making mark in the history of Byzantine art. St. Sophia is described later. In all likelihood he carried his construction even to the mountains of the far-off Crimea, and erected there a great church (*basilica*), in Dory, the chief center of the Gothic settlement. A fragment of an inscription with his name has been excavated there.[112]

IMMEDIATE SUCCESSORS OF JUSTINIAN

When the powerful figure of Justinian disappeared from the stage of history, his entire artificial system of government, which had temporarily kept the empire in proper balance, fell to ruin. "At his death," said Bury, "the winds were loosed from prison; the disintegrating elements began to operate with full force; the artificial system collapsed; and the metamorphosis in the character of the empire, which had been surely progressing for a long time past, though one is apt to overlook it amid the striking events of Justinian's busy reign, now began to work rapidly and perceptibly."[113] The time between the years 565 and 610 belongs to one of the most cheerless periods in Byzantine history, when anarchy, poverty, and plagues raged throughout the Empire. The confusion of this period caused John of Ephesus, the historian of the time of Justin II, to speak of the approaching end of the world.[114] "There is perhaps no period of history," said Finlay, "in which society was so universally in a state of demoralization."[115] The events of this period, however, show that this deplorable picture is somewhat exaggerated and therefore is to be rectified.

The successors of Justinian were: Justin II the Younger (565–78), Tiberius II (578–82), Maurice (582–602), and Phocas (602–10). The most outstanding of these four rulers was the energetic soldier and able leader, Maurice. Sophia, the strong-willed wife of Justin II who greatly resembled Theodora, exerted much influence on government affairs. The most significant events in the external affairs of the Empire during this period were the Persian War, the struggle with the Slavs and Avars in the Balkan peninsula, and the Lom-

[111] *Ibid.*, IV, 4, 1; Bonn ed., 277; ed. Haury, III, 2, 116.

[112] Vasiliev, *Goths in the Crimea*, 71.

[113] *Later Roman Empire*, II, 67.

[114] *Ecclesiastical History*, I, 3; ed. Payne-Smith, 3; ed. Brooks, 1–2.

[115] *A History of Greece*, ed. H. F. Tozer, I, 298. K. Amantos thinks that this deplorable picture is somewhat exaggerated. Ἱστορία τοῦ Βυζαντινοῦ κράτους, I, 260.

bard conquest of Italy. In the internal life of the Empire the firmly orthodox policy of the emperors and the formation of two exarchates were significant.

The Persian wars

The fifty years' truce with Persia established by Justinian in 562 was broken by Justin II, who refused to continue the payment of the set annual sum. A common hostility to Persia developed interesting relations between the Byzantine Empire and the Turks, who had appeared shortly before this period in Western Asia and along the shores of the Caspian Sea. They occupied the territory between China and Persia; the latter they viewed as their main enemy. Turkish ambassadors crossed the Caucasian Mountains, and after a long journey reached Constantinople, where they were accorded an amiable reception. Tentative plans began to develop for an offensive and defensive Turco-Byzantine alliance against Persia. The Turkish embassy made a very interesting proposal to the Byzantine government to mediate in the silk trade with China, avoiding Persian interference—the very thing Justinian had striven to attain, the only difference being that Justinian had hoped to arrange this by a southern sea route with the aid of the Abyssinians while the Turks were considering the northern land route. Negotiations however did not culminate in the formation of a real alliance for combined action against Persia, because the Byzantine Empire at the end of the sixties was more concerned with western developments, particularly in Italy where the Lombards were attacking. Besides, Justin considered the Turkish military forces rather inadequate.

The result of the short-lived Roman-Turkish friendship was tension between Byzantium and Persia.[116] During the reigns of Justin, Tiberius, and Maurice an almost continuous war was conducted against the Persians. During the reign of Justin II this was very unsuccessful for Byzantium. The siege of Nisibis was abandoned, the Avars from beyond the Danube invaded the Byzantine provinces in the Balkans, and Daras, an important fortified border town, after a siege of six months passed into the hands of the Persians. This loss so deeply impressed the weak-minded Justin that he became insane, and it was the Empress Sophia who, by paying 45,000 pieces of gold, obtained the respite of a year's truce (574).[117] A Syrian chronicle of the twelfth century, based of course on an earlier source, remarked: "On learning that Daras had been captured . . . the emperor was in despair. He ordered shops to be closed and commerce to cease."[118]

[116] Bury, *Later Roman Empire*, 97. Kulakovsky, *Byzantium*, II, 359. Stein, *Justinus II und Tiberius*, 21. S. Vailhé, "Projet d'alliance turco-byzantine au VIᵉ siècle," *Échos d'Orient*, XII (1909), 206–14.

[117] On this war Bury, *Later Roman Empire*, II, 95–101. Kulakovsky, *Byzantium*, II, 360–69. Stein, *Justinus II und Tiberius*, 38–55.

[118] *Chronique de Michel le Syrien*, trans. J. B. Chabot, II, 312.

The Persian war under Tiberius and Maurice was more successful for the Byzantine Empire because Maurice's able leadership was aided by internal dispute in Persia for the throne.[119] Maurice's peace treaty was of great importance: Persarmenia and eastern Mesopotamia, with the city of Daras, were ceded to Byzantium; the humiliating condition of annual tribute was canceled; and finally, the Empire, free of the Persian menace, was able to concentrate its attention on western affairs, especially on the unceasing attacks of the Avars and Slavs in the Balkan peninsula.[120] Another war with Persia began under the reign of Phocas, but the discussion of this war is deferred because, while it was of exceedingly great importance to the Byzantine Empire it was not concluded until the reign of Heraclius.

Slavs and Avars

Very important events took place in the Balkan peninsula after the death of Justinian, although unfortunately present knowledge of them is limited by the fragmentary material that appears in the sources. During Justinian's reign the Slavs frequently attacked the provinces of the Balkan peninsula, penetrating far into the south and threatening at times even the city of Thessalonica. These irruptions continued after Justinian's death. There were then large numbers of Slavs remaining in the Byzantine provinces, and they gradually occupied the peninsula. They were aided in their aggression by the Avars, a people of Turkish origin living at that time in Pannonia. The Slavs and Avars menaced the capital and the shores of the Sea of Marmora and the Aegean, and penetrated into Greece as far as the Peloponnesus. The rumor of these invasions spread to Egypt, where John, bishop of Nikiu, wrote in the seventh century, during the reign of the Emperor Phocas: "It is recounted that the kings of this epoch had by means of the barbarians and the foreign nations and the Illyrians devastated Christian cities and carried off their inhabitants captive, and that no city escaped save Thessalonica only; for its walls were strong, and through the help of God the nations were unable to get possession of it."[121] A German scholar of the early nineteenth century held the

[119] On this war see Stein, *Justinus II und Tiberius*, 58–86 (under Tiberius as Caesar), 87–102 (under Tiberius as Augustus).

[120] On the Persian war under Tiberius and Maurice, Kulakovsky, *Byzantium*, II, 383–94, 426–46. M. J. Higgins, *The Persian War of the Emperor Maurice. I. The Chronology, with a Brief History of the Persian Calendar*. Higgins, "International Relations at the Close of the Sixth Century," *The Catholic Historical Review*, XXVII (1941), 279–315. Higgins' hero is Tiberius, "a towering figure not unworthy to stand beside the greatest personalities in the long annals of the Empire" (p. 315). V. Minorsky, "Roman and Byzantine Campaigns in Atropatene," *Bulletin of the School of Oriental and African Studies*, XI (1944), 244–48 (campaign of A.D. 591). P. Goubert, *By zance avant l'Istam*, 80–117.

[121] *Chronicle of John, bishop of Nikiu*, trans. M. Zotenberg, *Notices et extraits des manuscrits de la Bibliothèque Nationale*, XXIV (1883), ch. CIX, 430; trans. to English R. H. Charles, 175–76.

theory, discussed at length later, that at the end of the sixth century the Greeks were completely destroyed by the Slavs. Studies of the problem of Slavic settlement in the Balkan peninsula depend greatly upon the *Acts* of the martyr Demetrius, the protector of Thessalonica, one of the main Slavonic centers in the peninsula.[122]

At the end of the sixth and the beginning of the seventh century the persistent southward movement of the Slavs and Avars, which Byzantine troops were unable to stop, produced a profound ethnographic change in the peninsula, since it became occupied largely by Slavonic settlers. The writers of this period were, in general, poorly acquainted with the northern tribes and they confuse the Slavs and Avars because they attacked the Empire jointly.

After the death of Justinian, Italy was insufficiently protected against the attacks of enemies, which explains the ease and speed with which it was again conquered by a new German barbarian tribe, the Lombards, who appeared there only a few years after Justinian had destroyed the Ostrogothic kingdom. In the middle of the sixth century the Lombards, in alliance with the Avars, destroyed the kingdom of the barbarian tribe of the Gepids (Gepidae) on the Middle Danube. Later, perhaps in fear of their own allies, they advanced from Pannonia into Italy under the leadership of their king (*ḳonuṅg*), Alboin, moving with their wives and children. They included many different tribes, among whom the Saxons were particularly numerous. Popular tradition has accused Narses, a former general in Justinian's army and the aged ruler of Italy, of having invited the Lombards into his country, but this accusation must be considered unfounded. After the accession of Justin II he retired because of old age and died shortly after in Rome.

In the year 568 the Lombards entered northern Italy. A wild barbaric horde, Arian by faith, they laid waste all the localities through which they passed. They soon conquered northern Italy, which became known as Lombardy. The Byzantine ruler, lacking sufficient means for resisting them, remained within the walls of Ravenna, which the barbarians by-passed as they moved on to the south. Their large hordes dispersed over almost the entire peninsula, occupying the unprotected cities with great ease. They reached southern Italy and soon occupied Benevento (Beneventum). Though they did not capture Rome, they surrounded the Roman province on three sides: from the north. east, and south. They cut off all connections between Ravenna and Rome, so that Rome could hope for no help there and still less for help from the even more distant rulers of Constantinople, who were passing through one of the most difficult and troubled periods in the history of the East. The Lombards had soon founded in Italy a large Germanic kingdom. Tiberius, and even more earnestly Maurice, tried to establish an alliance with the Frankish king

[122] See, e.g., O. Tafrali, *Thessalonique des origines au XIVe siècle*, 101–8.

Childebert II (570–595) in the hope of inducing him to open hostilities against the Lombards in Italy, but the effort ended in failure. Several embassies were exchanged, and Childebert did several times send troops to Italy, but always with the aim of reconquering the ancient Frankish possessions for himself rather than with the intention of helping Maurice. More than a century and a half was to elapse before the Frankish kings, summoned by the pope not the Emperor, were able to destroy the Lombard domination in Italy.[123] Left to its own fate, Rome, which withstood more than one Lombard siege, found its protector in the person of the pope, who was forced not only to care for the spiritual life of his Roman flock but also to organize the defense of the city against the Lombards. It was at this time, at the end of the sixth century, that the Roman Church produced one of its most remarkable leaders, pope Gregory I, the Great. He had earlier been papal *apocrisiarius* or nuncio at Constantinople, where he resided some six years without succeeding in mastering even the rudiments of the Greek language.[124] But in spite of this linguistic deficiency he was very well acquainted with the life and policies of Constantinople.

The Lombard conquest of Italy demonstrated clearly the impotence of Justinian's external policy in the West, where the Empire did not possess sufficient forces for maintaining the conquered Ostrogothic kingdom. It also laid the foundation for the gradual alienation of Italy from the Byzantine Empire and for the weakening of the imperial political authority in Italy.

Religious problems

The successors of Justinian favored orthodoxy and the Monophysites were at times—as during the reign of Justin II—subjected to extremely severe persecution. Relations between the Byzantine Empire and the Roman Church during the reign of Maurice and Phocas are interesting to consider. Gregory protested against the assumption by the Bishop of Constantinople of the title "ecumenical" and, in a letter to Maurice, Gregory accused the patriarch, John the Faster, of haughtiness:

> I am compelled to cry aloud and say *O tempora! O mores!* When all of Europe is given over to the power of barbarians, when cities are destroyed, camps overthrown, provinces depopulated, when the husbandman no longer tills the soil, when idol-worshippers are raging and contending for the slaughter of the faithful —and then priests, who ought to lie weeping on the ground and in ashes, seek for themselves names of vanity and glory in new and profane titles. Do I, in this matter, most pious Lord, defend my own cause? Do I resent my own special

---

[123] See Bury, *Later Roman Empire,* II, 160–66. G. Reverdy, "Les Relations de Childebert II et de Byzance," *Revue historique,* CXIV (1913), 61–85.

[124] On Gregory's sojourn in Constantinople, see F. Dudden, *Gregory the Great: His Place in History and Thought,* I, 123–57. Probably Gregory was recalled to Rome in 586 (156–57).

wrong? Nay, I defend the cause of Almighty God and the cause of the Universal Church. He is to be coerced, who does wrong to the Holy Universal Church, who swells in heart, who covets in a name of singularity, who also puts himself above the dignity of your Empire through a title peculiar to himself.[125]

The pope did not attain the desired concession, and for a time even ceased to send his representative to Constantinople. When in the year 602 a revolution broke out in the capital against Maurice, Pope Gregory addressed a letter to the new emperor, Phocas, in terms quite unbefitting this foolish tyrant on the Byzantine throne:

Glory be to God in the highest. . . . Let the heaven rejoice, and let the earth be glad (Ps. 95:11). Let the whole people of the republic hitherto afflicted exceedingly, grow cheerful for your benignant deeds! . . . Let every single person's liberty be now at length restored to him under the yoke of the pious empire. For there is this difference between the kings of other nations and the emperors: that the kings are lords of slaves, but the emperors of the Roman state are lords of freemen.[126]

Phocas was apparently pleased, for later he forbade the patriarch of Constantinople to bear the ecumenical title, declaring that "the apostolic throne of the blessed apostle Peter was the head of all churches."[127]

Thus while Phocas suffered defeat in all his external and internal undertakings and inspired the deep wrath and irritation of his subjects, his relations with Rome, based on his concessions to the pope, were peaceful and friendly throughout his reign. In memory of these friendly relations the exarch of Ravenna erected in the Roman Forum a column with laudatory inscriptions to Phocas. This monument is still in existence.

Formation of the exarchates and the revolution of 610

In connection with the Lombard conquest an important change took place in the government of Italy, which, together with a similar contemporary innovation in the administration of North Africa, laid the foundation for the new provincial administration of the Empire: the so-called system of *themes*.

The Byzantine authorities in Italy had not been able to offer the proper resistance to the Lombards, who conquered two-thirds of the peninsula with great ease. Therefore in the face of great danger, the Byzantine government determined to strengthen its power in Italy by placing the civil administrative functions in the hands of the military rulers. Byzantine administration in Italy was to be headed by a military governor-general, the exarch, who was

---

[125] *Epistolae*, V, 20; ed. Migne, *Patrologia Latina*, LXXVII, 746–47; *Monumenta Germaniae Historica, Epistolarum*, I, 322 (V, 37); English trans. *Nicene and Post-Nicene Fathers*, XII, 170–71.

[126] *Epistolae*, XIII, 31; ed. Migne, *Patro-*

logia Latina, LXXVII, 1281–82; *Mon. Germ. Hist., Epistolarum*, II, 397 (XIII, 34); *Nicene and Post-Nicene Fathers*, XIII, 99.

[127] *Liber Pontificalis*, ed. L. Duchesne, I, 316.

to direct the activities of all civil officials from his residence at Ravenna. The formation of the Ravenna exarchate dates back to the end of the sixth century, to the period of Emperor Maurice. This combination of administrative and judicial functions with military authority did not involve the immediate abolition of civil officials. They continued to exist along with the military rulers, but acted under the guidance of the military exarch. Only later the civil officials seem to have been completely replaced by military authorities. The exarch, as a representative of imperial power, followed in his administration certain principles of Caesaropapism, so much favored by the emperors. This policy was expressed in such acts, for example, as the interference as a final authority in the religious affairs of the exarchate. Unlimited in his power, the exarch was given imperial honors. His palace at Ravenna was considered sacred and called *Sacrum palatium,* a name usually applied only to an imperial residence. Whenever he arrived at Rome, he was accorded an imperial reception: the senate, the clergy, and the populace met him outside the city walls in triumphant procession. All military affairs, the entire administration, judicial and financial matters—all were at the full disposal of the exarch.[128]

Just as the Ravennese exarchate arose because of the attacks of the Lombards in Italy, so the formation of the African exarchate in the place of the former Vandal kingdom was called forth by a similar menace on the part of the native African Moors, or, as they are sometimes called in sources, the Maurusii (Berbers), who frequently engaged in serious uprisings against the Byzantine troops who occupied that country. The beginning of the African, or Carthaginian, exarchate (often called so because the residence of the exarch was at Carthage) dates also from the end of the sixth century, the time of Emperor Maurice. The African exarchate was founded on the same principles as its predecessor at Ravenna, and was endowed with similar unlimited power.[129]

Naturally, it was only extreme necessity that could force the Emperor to create such an unlimited office as that of the exarch, who, granting the desire and the presence of certain conditions, could become a very dangerous rival of the Emperor himself. And in reality the African exarch was to raise the banner of sedition against Phocas, and the son of the exarch was to become emperor in the year 610. In Africa the exarchs were chosen very wisely by Maurice and demonstrated much skill and energy in governing the land, defending it successfully against the attacks of the natives. On the other hand, the exarchs of Ravenna were unable to overcome the Lombard menace.

According to the French scholar, Diehl,[130] the two exarchates must be

---

[128] On the formation of the Ravenna exarchate see Charles Diehl, *Études sur l'administration byzantine dans l'exarchat de Ravenne (568-751),* 3-31.

[129] Diehl, *L'Afrique byzantine,* 453-502.
[130] *Études byzantines,* 277 (L'Origine du régime des thèmes).

viewed as the beginning of the *theme* (province or district) organization, that provincial reform in the Byzantine Empire which started in the seventh century and spread gradually through the entire territory of the Empire. Its distinguishing feature was the gradual dominance of the military authority over the civil. While the attacks of the Lombards and Moors produced significant changes in the West and the South at the end of the sixth century, the attacks of the Persians and Arabs caused later the introduction of similar measures in the East, and the onslaught of the Slavs and Bulgars resulted in the same reforms in the Balkan peninsula.

The unsuccessful external policy of Phocas in regard to the Avars and the Persians, as well as the bloody terror which was his only means of maintaining his position, finally resulted in the revolt of the African exarch, Heraclius. Egypt soon joined in this revolt, and the African fleet under the direction of the exarch's son, also named Heraclius, sailed forth to the capital, which deserted Phocas and came over to the side of Heraclius. Phocas was captured and executed. Heraclius, the son, ascended the Byzantine throne and thus started a new dynasty.

The problem of the Slavs in Greece

As a result of the investigation of sources on the Slavonic invasions into the Balkan peninsula in the second half of the sixth century, a theory of the complete Slavonization of Greece arose in the early part of the nineteenth century and aroused heated disputes among scholars.

In the twenties of the last century, when all of Europe was seized with deep sympathy for the Greeks who had raised the banner of revolt against the Turkish yoke, when these champions of freedom, through their heroic resistance, succeeded in maintaining their independence and created, with the help of European powers, an independent Greek kingdom, when enthusiastic European society viewed these heroes as sons of ancient Hellas and recognized in them the traits of Leonidas, Epaminondas, and Philopoemen— then it was that from a small German town came a voice which astonished Europe by declaring that not one drop of real Hellenic blood runs through the veins of the inhabitants of the new Greek kingdom; that all the magnanimous impulse of Europe to aid the cause of the children of sacred Hellas was founded on a misunderstanding; and that the ancient Greek element had long ago disappeared and been replaced by new, entirely alien ethnographical elements, chiefly of Slavonic and Albanian origin. The man who ventured to advance openly and boldly this new theory, which shocked to the utmost the beliefs of contemporary Europe, was Fallmerayer, at that time professor of general history in one of the German lyceums.

In the first volume of his *History of the Peninsula of Morea in the Middle Ages,* which appeared in 1830, Fallmerayer wrote:

The Hellenic race in Europe is completely exterminated. The physical beauty, the sublimity of spirit, the simplicity of customs, the artistic creativeness, the races, cities, and villages, the splendor of columns and temples, even the name of the people itself, have disappeared from the Greek continent. A double layer of ruins and the mire of two new and different races cover the graves of the ancient Greeks. The immortal works of the spirit of Hellas and some ancient ruins on native Greek soil are now the only evidence of the fact that long ago there was such a people as the Hellenes. And were it not for these ruins, grave-hills and mausoleums, were it not for the site and the wretched fate of its inhabitants, upon whom the Europeans of our day in an outburst of human emotions have poured all their tenderness, their admiration, their tears, and their eloquence, we would have to say that it was only an empty vision, a lifeless image, a being outside the nature of things that has aroused the innermost depths of their souls. For not a single drop of real pure Hellenic blood flows in the veins of the Christian population of modern Greece. A terrific hurricane has dispersed throughout the space between the Ister and most distant corner of the Peloponnesus a new tribe akin to the great Slavonic race. The Scythian Slavs, the Illyrian Arnauts, children of Northern lands, the blood relations of the Serbs and Bulgars, the Dalmatians and Moscovites—those are the people whom we call Greeks at present and whose genealogy, to their own surprise, we have traced back to Pericles and Philopoemen. . . . A population with Slavonic facial features and with bow-shaped eyelashes and sharp features of Albanian mountain shepherds, of course, did not come from the blood of Narcissus, Alcibiades, and Antinous; and only a romantic eager imagination can still dream of a revival in our days of the ancient Hellenes with their Sophocleses and Platos.[131]

It was Fallmerayer's opinion that the Slavonic invasions of the sixth century created a situation in which the Byzantine Empire, without actually having lost a single province, could consider as its subjects only the population of the seacoast provinces and fortified cities. The appearance of the Avars in Europe was an epoch-making event in the history of Greece because they brought with them the Slavs and spurred them on to conquer the sacred soil of Hellas and the Peloponnesus.

Fallmerayer based his theory primarily on the data found in the writings of the church historian of the late sixth century, Evagrius, who wrote: "The Avars twice made an inroad as far as the Long Wall and captured Singidunum [Belgrade], Anchialus, and all of Greece, with other towns and fortresses, laying everything waste with fire and sword, while the greater part of the forces were engaged in the East."[132] It was this mention of all of Greece in Evagrius that gave Fallmerayer a basis for speaking of the extermination of the Greek nation in the Peloponnesus. The "Avars" of Evagrius did not confuse this German scholar, for at that period the Avars attacked the Byzantine

[131] *Geschichte der Halbinsel Morea während des Mittelalters,* I, iii–xiv.

[132] *Historia ecclesiastica,* VI, 10; ed. Bidez and Parmentier, 228.

Empire conjointly with the Slavs. This particular invasion which Fallmerayer referred to the year 589, did not exterminate the Greeks completely. The final blow to the Greek population came, as Fallmerayer believed, with the importation of the plague from Italy in the year 746. Reference to this is found in the famous quotation from the imperial writer of the tenth century, Constantine Porphyrogenitus, who remarked that after this terrible plague "the entire land was slavonized and became barbarian."[133] The year when Emperor Constantine Copronymus died (775) Fallmerayer estimated, may be considered the final date when the desolate land became once more, and at this time completely, filled with Slavs, who gradually covered Greece with their new cities, towns, and villages.[134]

In a later work Fallmerayer applied his conclusions to Attica without any real basis. In the second volume of his *History of the Peninsula of Morea* he advanced a new Albanian theory, according to which the Greek-Slavs who inhabited Greece were displaced and crushed by Albanian settlers during the second quarter of the fourteenth century, so that the Greek revolution of the nineteenth century was in reality the work of Albanian hands.

The first serious opponent of Fallmerayer was the German historian, Carl Hopf, who had studied thoroughly the problem of the Slavs in Greece and published a *History of Greece from the Beginning of the Middle Ages to Our Own Times,* in 1867. But Hopf fell into the other extreme because of his desire to reduce the significance of the Slavonic element in Greece at all costs. In his judgment, Slavonic settlements in Greece proper existed only from the year 750 until 807; previous to 750 there were none. Hopf showed that Fallmerayer's opinions on the Slavonization of Attica were based on a false document.[135]

The abundant literature on this subject, often contradictory and inconsistent in its nature, gives enough basis, however, for concluding that Slavonic settlements of very considerable size existed in Greece from the end of the sixth century, though they resulted neither in pan-Slavonization nor in the complete extermination of the Greeks. Moreover, various sources mention the presence of Slavs in Greece, primarily in the Peloponnesus, during all of the Middle Ages up to the fifteenth century.[136] The most important source on the

---

[133] *De Thematibus,* II, 53. Sometimes we find another translation: "The entire land was reduced into slavery and became barbarian," for Constantine Porphyrogenitus uses here an unusual verb, 'εσθλαβώθη, which is interpreted either "was slavonized" or "was reduced into slavery." I prefer the former.

[134] *Geschichte der Halbinsel Morea,* I, 208–10.

[135] *Geschichte Griechenlands vom Beginn des Mittelalters bis auf die neuere Zeit,* I, 103–19.

[136] A. A. Vasiliev, "The Slavs in Greece," *Vizantiysky Vremennik,* V (1898), 416–38. Since 1898, a vast literature on this debatable question has appeared; a detailed list of these publications can be found in the most recent book by A. Bon, *Le Péloponnèse Byzantin* (Paris, 1951), 30–31.

Slavonic penetration of the Balkan Peninsula is the *Acta* of St. Demetrius, mentioned above. This was properly used neither by Fallmerayer nor by Hopf; in fact, it has not been adequately investigated up to the present day.[137]

Scholars have frequently disputed the originality of Fallmerayer's theory. His opinion was nothing new. Slavonic influence in Greece had been spoken of before his time, though he was the first to express his judgments decisively and openly. In 1913 a Russian scholar stated on good grounds that the real originator of Fallmerayer's theory was Kopitar, a scholar of Slavonic studies in Vienna in the nineteenth century, who developed in his writings the idea of the significant part played by the Slavic element in the formation of the new Greek nation. He did not, it is true, develop this theory in detail; but neither did he create a sensation by an unscholarly paradox.[138] "The extremes of Fallmerayer's theory," Petrovsky said, "cannot at present be defended after a thorough study of the problems pertaining to it; but the theory itself, harmoniously and vividly expounded by the author, has a right to claim the attention even of those historians who disagree with it either entirely or partially."[139] Without question, this theory, in spite of some very obvious exaggerations, has played a very important part in the science of history by directing scholarly attention to a most interesting and at the same time most obscure question, the problem of the Slavs in Greece during the Middle Ages. The writings of Fallmerayer assume still wider general historical significance when viewed as the work of the first scholar who devoted his attention to the ethnographical transformations during the Middle Ages, not only in Greece, but in the Balkan Peninsula in general. At present in Soviet Russia the thesis of early penetration and settlement of the Slavs in the Balkan Peninsula is strongly supported. In contemporary Russian magazines, such as the *Historical Journal* and the *Messenger of Ancient History,* several articles on this subject have appeared. Fallmerayer is very popular with Russian historians, who proclaim that his work has not been adequately appreciated. The modern Slavophile movement in Soviet Russia seems even stronger than the similar movement of some hundred years ago, mentioned in the first chapter of this book.

LITERATURE, LEARNING, AND ART

Reflecting Justinian's multifarious activities, which amazed even his contemporaries, the epoch between 518 and 610 resulted in an abundant heritage

---

[137] See a very interesting chapter on the importance of the *Acta sancti Demetrii* in Gelzer, *Die Genesis der byzantinischen Themenverfassung,* 42–64. Also Tafrali, *Thessalonique,* 101.

[138] N. Petrovsky, "On the Problem of the Genesis of Fallmerayer's Theory," *Journal of the Ministry of Public Instruction* (1913), 143, 149.

[139] *Ibid.,* 104.

in various branches of learning and literature. The Emperor himself attempted literary creation in the fields of dogmatics and hymnology. Maurice also displayed a taste for letters; he not only patronized but also stimulated literature, and often spent a great part of the night discussing or meditating on questions of poetry or history.[140] This period produced several historians, whom Justinian's enterprises provided with a wealth of material.

The special historian of Justinian's period was Procopius of Caesarea, who has given a complete and well-rounded picture of the reign. Educated for the law, Procopius was appointed adviser and secretary to the famous general Belisarius, with whom he shared the campaigns against the Vandals, the Goths, and the Persians. He stands out both as historian and as writer. As a historian he was in a most advantageous position with regard to sources and firsthand information. His closeness to Belisarius gave him access to all official documents kept in the offices and archives, while his active participation in the campaigns and his excellent knowledge of the country gave him highly valuable living material based on personal observation and on information obtained from contemporaries.

In style and presentation Procopius frequently followed the classical historians, especially Herodotus and Thucydides. In spite of his dependence upon the Old Greek language of the ancient historians, and in spite of some artificiality of exposition, Procopius had a figurative, lucid, and vigorous style. He wrote three main works. The largest of these is *The History in Eight Books,* containing accounts of Justinian's wars with the Persians, Vandals, and Goths as well as accounts of many other sides of government life. The author spoke of the Emperor in a slightly laudatory tone, but in numerous instances he expresses the bitter truth. This work may be called a general history of Justinian's time. The second work of Procopius, *On Buildings,* is an unmitigated panegyric of the Emperor, probably written at his command, the main object of which is to give an account and description of the multitude of edifices erected by Justinian in all parts of his vast empire. In spite of rhetorical exaggerations and excessive praise, this work contains an abundance of geographical, topographical, and financial material, and serves therefore as a valuable source in the study of the social and economic history of the Empire. The third work of Procopius, *Anecdota,* or *The Secret History (Historia Arcana),* is distinctly different from the other two. It is a vicious libel upon the despotic rule of Justinian and his wife Theodora in which the author flings mud not only at the imperial couple but also at Belisarius and his wife, and in which Justinian is represented as the author of all the misfortunes which

---

[140] Menander, *Excerpta,* Bonn ed., 439; *Fragmenta Historicorum Graecorum,* IV, 202. Theophylact Simocatta, *Historia,* VIII, 13, 16; ed. de Boor, 311. Bury, *Later Roman Empire,* II, 182.

occurred in the Empire during this period. The contrast between this work and the other two is so striking that some scholars began to question the authenticity of *The Secret History,* for it seemed impossible that all three works had been composed by one and the same man. Only after a careful comparative study of *The Secret History* with all other sources pertaining to Justinian's epoch was it definitely decided that the work was really an authentic work of Procopius. When properly used, this work serves as an extremely valuable source on the internal history of the Byzantine Empire in the sixth century. Thus, all the works of Procopius, in spite of their exaggerations of the virtue or vice of Justinian's deeds, constitute a highly significant contemporary source for a closer acquaintance with the life of the period. But this is not all. Slavonic history and Slavonic antiquity find in Procopius invaluable information about the life and beliefs of the Slavs, while the Germanic peoples gather from him many facts about their early history.

A contemporary of Justinian and Procopius, the historian Peter the Patrician, a brilliant lawyer and diplomat, was repeatedly sent as ambassador to the Persian Empire and to the Ostrogothic court, where he was kept as prisoner for three years. His writings consisted of *Histories,* or *A History of the Roman Empire,* narrating, if one may judge by the extensive fragments in which alone it has survived, events from the second Triumvirate (from Augustus) to the time of Julian the Apostate, and a treatise *On the State Constitution* (*Katastasis* or *Book of Ceremonies*), part of which was included in the famous work of the time of Constantine Porphyrogenitus in the tenth century, *The Book of Court Ceremonies.*

From Procopius until the early part of the seventh century there was a continuous line of historical writings, and each historian carried on the work of those who preceded him.

Procopius was followed directly by the well-educated lawyer, Agathias, of Asia Minor, who left, in addition to some short poems and epigrams, the somewhat artificially written work, *On the Reign of Justinian,* which embraces the period from 552 to 558. Following Agathias, Menander the Protector wrote in the time of Maurice, his *History* which was a continuation of Agathias' work and related events from the year 558 until 582, i.e., up to the year of the accession of Maurice. Only fragments of this work are in existence today, but they give a sufficient basis for judging the importance of this source, particularly from the geographic and ethnographic point of view; they offer sufficient indication that he was a better historian than Agathias. The work of Menander was continued by Theophylact Simocatta, an Egyptian, who lived during the period of Heraclius and occupied the position of imperial secretary. Besides a small work on natural science and a collection of letters, he also wrote a history of the period of Maurice (582–602). The style of Theophylact is overcharged with allegories and artificial expressions to a much greater extent than that of his immediate predecessors. "In comparison with Procopius and Agathias," says Krumbacher, "he is the peak of a rapidly rising curve. The historian of Belisarius, in spite of bombast, is still simple and natural; more abounding in poetical flowery expressions is the poet Agathias; but both these writers seem quite unaffected in comparison with Theophylact, who surprises the reader at every turn with new, unexpected flashes of far-fetched images, allegories, aphorisms, and mythological and other subtleties."[141] But in spite of all this Theophylact is an excellent major source on the time of Maurice, and he also gives extremely valuable information about Persia and the Slavs in the Balkan peninsula at the end of the sixth century.

Justinian's ambassador to the Saracens and Abyssinians, Nonnosus, wrote a description of his distant journey. Time has preserved only one fragment, which is found in the works of the Patriarch Photius; but even this fragment gives excellent data on the nature and ethnography of the countries he visited. Photius also preserved a fragment of the history of Theophanes of Byzantium, who wrote at the end of the sixth century and probably covered in his work the period from the time of Justinian to the first years of the reign of Maurice. This fragment is important because it contains evidence bearing on the introduction of sericulture in the Byzantine Empire and includes also one of the earliest references to the Turks. Another source particularly valuable for church history of the fifth and sixth centuries is the work of Evagrius of Syria, who died at the end of the sixth century. His *Ecclesiastical History* in six books is a continuation of histories written by Socrates, Sozomen, and Theodoret. It contains an account of events from the Council of Ephesus, in the year 431, to the year 593. In addition to information on ecclesiastical events, it contains also interesting data on the general history of the period.

John the Lydian was distinguished for his excellent education, and Justinian thought so highly of him that he commissioned him to write an imperial panegyric. Besides other works, John left a treatise *On the Administration (magistrates) of the Roman State,* which has not yet been sufficiently studied and evaluated. It contains numerous interesting facts about the internal organization of the Empire and may serve as a valuable supplement to *The Secret History of Procopius.*[142]

The manifold significance of *The Christian Topography* of Cosmas Indicopleustes, the broad geographical scale of which so closely corresponded to Justinian's sweeping projects, has been discussed. To the field of geography also belongs the statistical survey of the Eastern Roman Empire of Justinian's

---

[141] K. Krumbacher, *Geschichte der byzantinischen Litteratur,* 249.

[142] Much information on John the Lydian's

work and its importance may be found in E. Stein, *Untersuchungen über das Officium der Prätorianenpräfektur seit Diokletian.*

period, which came from the pen of the grammarian Hierocles, and bears the title of *A Fellow-Traveler of Hierocles* (Συνέκδημος; *Synecdemus; Vademecum*). The author does not center his survey about the ecclesiastical, but rather about the political, geography of the Empire, with its sixty-four provinces and 912 cities. It is impossible to determine whether this survey was a product of Hierocles' own initiative or a result of a commission received from some high authority. In any event, in the dry survey of Hierocles exists an excellent source for determining the political position of the Empire at the beginning of Justinian's reign.[143] Hierocles was the principal source for geographical matters for Constantine Porphyrogenitus.

In addition to these historians and geographers, the sixth century also had its chroniclers. Justinian's epoch was still closely connected with classical literature, and the dry universal chronicles, which developed greatly in the later Byzantine period, appeared only as rare exceptions in this period.

A middle position between the historians and chroniclers was occupied by Hesychius of Miletus, who lived, in all likelihood, in the time of Justinian. His works survive only in fragments preserved in the writings of Photius and the lexicographer of the tenth century, Suidas. On the basis of these fragments it appears that Hesychius wrote a universal history in the form of a chronicle embracing the period from the time of ancient Assyria to the death of Anastasius (518). A large fragment of this work has survived, which is concerned with the early history of Byzantium even before the time of Constantine the Great. Hesychius was also the author of a history of the time of Justin I and the early reign of Justinian which differed greatly in style and conception from the first work, and contained a detailed narrative of events contemporary with the author. The third work of Hesychius was a dictionary of famous Greek writers in different branches of knowledge. Since he did not include the Christian writers, some scholars affirm that Hesychius was probably a pagan; this opinion, however, is not generally accepted.[144]

The true chronicler of the sixth century was the uneducated Syrian of Antioch, John Malalas, the author of a Greek chronicle of the history of the world, which, judging by the only surviving manuscript, relates events from the fabulous times of Egyptian history to the end of Justinian's reign. But it probably contained also accounts of a later period.[145] The chronicle is Christian and apologetic in its aims, exposing very clearly the monarchistic tend-

---

[143] The work of Hierocles was written before the year 535. Krumbacher, *Geschichte der byzantinischen Litteratur*, 417. G. Montelatici, *Storia della letteratura bizantina, 354–1453*, 76.

[144] Montelatici, *Storia della letteratura bizantina*, 63–64.

[145] Perhaps the chronicle of John Malalas came down to the first year of Justinian's reign, and in a new edition was added a continuation written either by the author himself or by another hand; see Bury, *Later Roman Empire*, II, 435.

encies of the author. Confused in content, mixing fables and facts, important events and minor incidents, it is clearly intended not for educated readers but for the masses, ecclesiastical and secular, for whom the author put down many varied and amusing facts. "This work represents a historical booklet for the people in the fullest sense of the term."[146] The style is particularly worthy of attention, for this work is the first considerable one written in the spoken Greek language, that vulgate Greek dialect, popular in the East, which mixed Greek elements with Latin and eastern expressions. Since it suited the taste and mentality of the masses, this chronicle exerted an enormous influence upon Byzantine, eastern, and Slavonic chronography. The large number of Slavonic selections and translations of the writings of Malalas are of great value in restoring the original Greek text of his chronicle.[147]

In addition to the large number of works written in Greek, to this epoch (518–610) belong also the Syrian writings of John of Ephesus, who died in the latter part of the sixth century (probably in the year 586).[148] Born in Upper Mesopotamia and a convinced Monophysite by faith, John spent many years of his life in Constantinople and in Asia Minor, where he occupied the see of Ephesus and made the personal acquaintance of Justinian and Theodora. He was the author of the *Lives of the Eastern Saints* or *Histories Concerning the Ways of Life of the Blessed Easterns* (*Commentarii de Beatis Orientalibus*), and the *Ecclesiastical History* (in Syriac), which embraced originally the period from Julius Caesar to the year 585. Of the latter only the most important and original part has survived, which deals with events from 521 to 585. It is an invaluable source for the period. Written from a Monophysitic point of view, this history of John of Ephesus reveals, not so much the dogmatic foundations of the Monophysitic disputes, as their national and cultural background. According to a scholar who has devoted himself to the special study of John's work, the *Ecclesiastical History* "throws much light upon the last phases of the struggle between Christianity and paganism by revealing also the cultural foundations of this struggle." It is also "of great value to the political and cultural history of the Byzantine Empire in the sixth century, especially with regard to determining the extent of eastern influences. In his narrative the author enters into all the details and minutiae of life, thus giving abundant material for a

---

[146] Krumbacher, *Geschichte der byzantinischen Litteratur*, 326.

[147] Books VIII–XVIII of Malalas' Slavonic version have been translated into English by M. Spinka in collaboration with G. Downey. In his review A. T. Olmstead wrote: "John Malalas was undoubtedly the world's worst chronicler. The historian may curse his chuck-leheadedness, but he must use him, for Malalas has preserved a great amount of the most important data which otherwise would have been lost." *The Chicago Theological Seminary Register,* XXXI, 4 (1942), 22.

[148] E. W. Brooks in *Patrologia Orientalis,* XVII (1923), vi.

close acquaintance with the manners and customs and the archeology of the period."[149]

The Monophysitic disputes, which continued throughout the sixth century, aroused much literary activity in the realm of dogmatics and polemics. Even Justinian did not abstain from participating in these literary disputes. The writings of the Monophysitic side in the Greek original have not been preserved. They can be judged either by citations found in the writers of the opposing camp or by the translations preserved in Syriac and Arabic literature. Among the writers of the orthodox side was a contemporary of Justin and Justinian, Leontius of Byzantium, who left several works against the Nestorians, Monophysites, and others. On the life of this dogmatist and polemic there is very scanty information.[150] He stands out as an example of an interesting phenomenon in the time of Justinian, namely, the fact that Plato's influence upon the church fathers was already beginning to give way to that of Aristotle.[151]

The development of monastic and eremitical life in the East during the sixth century left its traces in the works of ascetic, mystical, and hagiographic literature. John Climacus (ὁ τῆς κλίμακος) lived in solitude on Mount Sinai for a long period of years and wrote what is known as the *Climax*—"Spiritual ladder" (*Scala Paradisi*),[152] consisting of thirty chapters, or "rungs," in which he described the degrees of spiritual ascension to moral perfection. This work became favorite reading among the Byzantine monks, serving as a guide to the attainment of ascetic and spiritual perfection. But the remarkable popularity of the *Climax* was by no means confined to the East; there are many translations into Syriac, Modern Greek, Latin, Italian, Spanish, French, and Slavonic. Some of the manuscripts of the *Climax* contain many interesting illustrations (miniatures) of religious and monastic life.[153]

At the head of the hagiographic writers of the sixth century one must place Cyril of Scythopolis, a Palestinian, who spent the last years of his life in the famous Palestinian Laura of St. Sabas. Cyril wanted to compile a large collection of monastic "Lives," but did not succeed in completing this project, probably because of his premature death. Several of his works have survived. Among these are the lives of Euthymius and St. Sabas, and also several minor

---

[149] Dyakonov, *John of Ephesus*, 359.

[150] See F. Loofs, *Leontius von Byzanz*, 297–303; W. Rügamer, *Leontius von Byzanz*, 49–72.

[151] Rügamer, *Leontius von Byzanz*, 72.

[152] The reference here is to the biblical "heavenly ladder" seen by Jacob in his dream (Gen. 28:12). The Greek genitive ὁ τῆς

κλίμακος was latinized into "Climacus," so that Johannes Climacus is his traditional appellation in the west.

[153] For the reproduction of many miniatures of the *Climax*, see C. R. Morey, *East Christian Paintings in the Freer Collection*, 1–30. See also O. M. Dalton, *East Christian Art*, 316.

lives of saints. Because of the accuracy of narrative and the author's precise understanding of ascetic life, as well as the simplicity of his style, all the surviving works of Cyril serve as very valuable sources for the cultural history of the early Byzantine period.[154] John Moschus, also a Palestinian, who lived at the end of the sixth and early part of the seventh centuries, produced his famous work in Greek, *Pratum Spirituale* (Λειμών), "The spiritual meadow," on the basis of the experience gained during numerous journeys to the monasteries of Palestine, Egypt, Mount Sinai, Syria, Asia Minor, and the islands of the Mediterranean and Aegean Seas. The work contains the author's impressions of his journeys and much varied information about monasteries and monks. In some respects the contents of the *Pratum Spirituale* are of great interest for the history of civilization. It later became a favorite book, not only in the Byzantine Empire, but also in other lands, especially in Old Russia.

The poetical literature of this time also had several representatives during this period. It is quite certain that Romanus the Melode ("hymn-writer"), famous for his church songs, was at the height of his creative career in the time of Justinian. In the same period Paul the Silentiary composed his two poetical descriptions (in Greek verse) of St. Sophia and its beautiful pulpit (*ambo*). These works are of great interest in the history of art,[155] and were praised by his contemporary, the historian Agathias,[156] mentioned earlier. Finally, Corippus of North Africa, who later settled in Constantinople, a man of limited poetical ability, wrote two works in Latin verse. The first of these, *Johannis,* written in honor and praise of the Byzantine general, John (Johannes) Troglita, who quelled the revolt of the north African natives against the Empire, contains invaluable data about the geography and ethnography of North Africa as well as about the African War. The facts related by Corippus are at times more dependable than those given by Procopius. The second work of Corippus, the *Panegyric* or *Eulogy of Justin (in laudem Justini)*, describing in bombastic style the accession of Justin II the Younger and the first events of his reign, is inferior to the first poem, yet it contains many interesting facts about the ceremonial of the Byzantine court in the sixth century.

Papyri have revealed a certain Dioscorus, who lived in the sixth century in a small village of upper Egypt, the Aphrodito. A Copt by birth, he seems to have received a good general education with a thorough training in law; he also entertained literary ambitions. Though his large collection of deeds and

---

[154] See Eduard Schwartz, *Kyrillos von Skythopolis.*

[155] See the recent edition of both works by P. Friedländer, *Johannes von Gaza und Paulus Silentiarius,* 227–65; commentary, 267–305.

[156] *Historiae,* V, 9; Bonn ed., 296–97; ed. L. A. Dindorf, *Historici Graeci Minores,* II, 362.

other papyri furnish much precious information concerning the social and administrative history of the period, his poems contribute nothing to the glory of Hellenistic poetry; they represent the work of an amateur which is "full of the most glaring blunders, alike in grammar and prosody." According to H. Bell, he read at least a fair amount of Greek literature but wrote execrable verses.[157] J. Maspero calls Dioscorus the last Greek poet of Egypt, as well as one of the last representatives of Hellenism in the valley of the Nile.[158]

The closing of the Athenian pagan academy during Justinian's reign could result in no very serious harm to the literature and education of this period because the academy had already outlived its purpose. It was no longer of great import in a Christian empire. The treasures of classical literature penetrated gradually, often externally only, into the products of Christian literature. The university of Constantinople organized by Theodosius II continued to be active in Justinian's epoch. New works on jurisprudence show the importance of the study of law during this period. It was confined, however, to the formal mastery of literal translations of juridical texts and the writing of brief paraphrases and excerpts. We have no exact information as to how juridical instruction developed after the death of Justinian. While Emperor Maurice showed much interest in learning, his successor, Phocas, apparently halted the activities of the university.[159]

In the realm of art the epoch of Justinian bears the name of the First Golden Age. The architecture of his time created a monument unique in its kind— the Church of St. Sophia.[160]

St. Sophia or the Great Church, as it was called throughout the East, was constructed by the orders of Justinian on the site of the small basilica of St. Sophia ("divine wisdom") which was set on fire during the Nika revolt (532). In order to make this temple a building of unusual splendor, Justinian, according to late tradition, ordered the governors of the provinces to furnish the capital with the best pieces of ancient monuments. Enormous quantities of marble of various colors and shades were also transported to the capital from the richest mines. Silver, gold, ivory, and precious stones were brought in to add further magnificence to the new temple.

The Emperor chose for the execution of this grandiose project two gifted

[157] "Byzantine Servile State," *Journal of Egyptian Archaeology*, IV (1917), 104–5; Bell, "Greek Papyri in the British Museum," *Journal of Egyptian Archaeology*, V (1917), iii–iv. See also W. Schubart, *Einführung in die Papyruskunde*, 145–47, 495.

[158] "Un dernier poète grec d'Egypte: Dioscore, fils d'Apollôs," *Revue des études grecques*, XXIV (1911), 426, 456, 469.

[159] See F. Fuchs, *Die höheren Schulen von Konstantinopel*, 7–8.

[160] The most recent work on St. Sophia is E. H. Swift, *Hagia Sophia*. See also *Preliminary Reports on the Mosaics of St. Sophia at Istanbul* by Thomas Whittemore, beginning with the year 1933.

architects, Anthemius and Isidore. Both were natives of Asia Minor, Anthemius from the city of Tralles, and Isidore from Miletus. They attacked their great task with enthusiasm and skillfully guided the work of ten thousand laborers. The Emperor visited the construction personally, watching its progress with keen interest, offering advice, and arousing the zeal of the workers. In five years the construction was completed. On Christmas Day of the year 537 the triumphant dedication of St. Sophia took place in the presence of the Emperor. Later sources related that the Emperor, overwhelmed by his attainment, said upon entering the temple: "Glory be to God who deemed me worthy of this deed! I have conquered thee, Solomon!"[161] On this triumphant occasion the population was granted many favors and great celebrations were arranged in the capital.

Externally St. Sophia is very simple because its bare brick walls are void of any ornamentation. Even the famous dome seems somewhat heavy from the outside. At present St. Sophia is lost among the Turkish houses which surround it. In order to appreciate fully all the grandeur and splendor of the temple one must see it from the inside.

In former days the temple had a spacious court, the atrium, surrounded by porticoes in the center of which stood a beautiful marble fountain. The fourth side of the atrium adjoining the temple was a sort of outer porch or closed gallery (narthex) connected by five doors with the second inner porch. Nine bronze doors led from this porch into the temple; the central widest and highest royal door was intended for the emperor. The temple itself, approaching in its architecture the type of "domed basilicas," forms a very large rectangle with a magnificent central nave over which rises an enormous dome 31 meters in circumference, constructed with unusual difficulty at the height of 50 meters above the earth's surface. Forty large windows at the base of the dome let abundant light spread through the entire cathedral. Along both sides of the central nave were constructed two-storied arches richly decorated with columns. The floor and the columns are of many-colored marble, which was used also for parts of the walls. Marvelous mosaics, painted over in the Turkish period, formerly enchanted the eyes of the visitors. Particularly deep was the impression made upon pilgrims by the enormous cross at the top of the dome shining upon a mosaic-starred sky. And even today one can distinguish, under the Turkish painting in the lower part of the dome, the large figures of winged angels.

The most difficult task of the builders of St. Sophia, a feat yet unsurpassed even in modern architecture, was the erection of an enormous, and at the same time very light, dome. The task was accomplished, but the remarkable dome did not last very long; it caved in even during Justinian's period and had

---

[161] See *Scriptores originum Constantinopolitanarum*, ed. T. Preger, I, 105.

to be rebuilt on less daring lines at the end of his reign. Justinian's contemporaries spoke of St. Sophia with as much transport as did later generations, including the present. The Russian pilgrim of the fourteenth century, Stephen of Novgorod, wrote in his *Travels to Tsargrad* (Constantinople), "As for St. Sophia, Divine Wisdom, the human mind can neither tell it nor make description of it."[162] In spite of frequent and violent earthquakes, St. Sophia stands firm even today. It was transformed into a mosque in 1453. Strzygowski said: "In conception the church [St. Sophia] is purely Armenian."[163]

As time went on the true story of the erection of St. Sophia was transformed in literature into a sort of legend with a large number of miraculous details. From the Byzantine Empire these legends found their way into south-Slavic and Russian as well as into Muhammedan, Arabic, and Turkish literature. The Slavonic and Muhammedan versions present very interesting material for the history of international literary influences.[164]

The second famous church of the capital erected by Justinian was the Church of the Holy Apostles. This church had been built by Constantine the Great or by Constantius, but toward the sixth century it was in a state of complete dilapidation. Justinian pulled it down and rebuilt it on a larger and more magnificent scale. It was a cruciform church with four equal arms and a central dome between four other domes. Again the architects of the Church were Anthemius of Tralles and Isidore the Younger. When Constantinople was taken by the Turks in 1453 the church was destroyed to make room for the mosque of Muhammed II the Conqueror. A clearer conception of what the Church of the Holy Apostles was like can be obtained from St. Mark's at Venice, which was built on its model. It was copied also in St. John at Ephesus, and on French soil in St. Front at Perigueux. The beautiful lost mosaics of the Church of the Apostles have been described by Nicholas Mesarites, a bishop of Ephesus, at the beginning of the thirteenth century, and were thoroughly discussed by A. Heisenberg.[165] The Church of the Apostles is known to have been the burial place of the Byzantine emperors from Constantine the Great to the eleventh century.

The influence of Constantinopolitan construction was felt in the East, for instance, in Syria, and in the West in Parenzo, in Istria, and especially at Ravenna.

---

[162] "The Pilgrimage of Stephan of Novgorod," *Tales of the Russian People*, ed. T. Sakharov, II, 52. M. N. Speransky, *From the Ancient Novgorod Literature of the Fourteenth Century*, 50–76; the words quoted, 53.

[163] *Ursprung der christlichen Kirchenkunst*, trans. O. Dalton and H. Braunholtz, 46; see Dalton, *East Christian Art*, 93.

[164] See, e.g., M. N. Speransky, "The South-Slavic and Russian Texts of the Tale of the Construction of the Church of St. Sophia of Tzarigrad," *Memorial Volume in Honor of V. N. Zlatarsky*, 413–22. V. D. Smirnov, *Turkish Legends on Saint Sophia*.

[165] *Die Apostelkirche in Konstantinopel*, 10 ff.

St. Sophia may impress and charm now by its dome, by the sculptural orna-
ments of its columns, by the many-colored marble facing of its walls and
floor, and still more by the ingenuity of its architectural execution; but the
marvelous mosaics of this remarkable temple have heretofore been inaccessible, because they were painted over during the Turkish period. A new era
in the history of St. Sophia, however, started recently through the enlightened
policy of the modern Turkish republic under the leadership of Mustapha
Kemal Ataturk. The building was first of all thrown open to foreign archeologists and scholars. In 1931 an order of the Turkish government was issued
enabling the Byzantine Institute of America to lay bare and conserve the
mosaics of St. Sophia. Professor Thomas Whittemore, director of the Institute, secured permission to uncover and restore mosaics, and in 1933 work
began in the narthex. In December 1934, Mustapha Kemal announced that
the building had been closed as a mosque and would henceforth be preserved
as a museum and monument of Byzantine art. Owing to Whittemore's untiring and systematic work the marvelous mosaics of St. Sophia are gradually
reappearing in all their brilliance and beauty. Since Whittemore's death in
1950, his work has been continued by Professor Paul A. Underwood.

An excellent conception of Byzantine mosaics exists in the West in the
northern Italian city of Ravenna. Fifteen hundred years ago Ravenna was a
prosperous city on the Adriatic coast. During the fifth century it served as a
refuge of the last Western Roman emperors; in the sixth century it became
the capital of the Ostrogothic kingdom, and finally, from the middle of the
sixth century to the middle of the eighth century, it was the administrative
center of Byzantine Italy reconquered from the Ostrogoths by Justinian. It
was the home of the Byzantine viceroy or exarch. This last period was the
brilliant period of Ravenna, when political, economic, intellectual, and artistic activity poured forth in an abundant stream.

The artistic monuments of Ravenna are bound up with the memory of
three persons: first, Galla Placidia, the daughter of Theodosius the Great and
the mother of the western emperor, Valentinian III, second, Theodoric the
Great, and third, Justinian. Putting aside the earlier monuments of the time
of Galla Placidia and Theodoric, we shall speak briefly only about the
Ravenna monuments of Justinian's time.

Throughout his long reign Justinian was greatly interested in promoting
the construction of monuments of civil and religious architecture in various
places of his enormous empire. Upon conquering Ravenna he finished the
construction of those churches which had been begun under the Ostrogothic
sway. Among these churches two are of particularly great importance from
an artistic point of view. They are the Church of St. Vitale and the Church

of St. Apollinare in Classe (the Ravennan port, Classis). The main artistic value of these churches lies in their mosaics.

About three miles from the city of Ravenna, in the deserted marshy locality occupied in the Middle Ages by the prosperous trading port of the city, rises the simple outline of the Church of St. Apollinare in Classe, representing in shape a genuine ancient Christian basilica. On one side of this church stands the round campanile constructed later. The interior has three naves. The ancient sarcophagi, decorated by sculptural images and situated along the church walls, contain the remains of the most famous archbishops of Ravenna. The mosaic of the sixth century can be seen in the lower part of the apse. It represents St. Apollinare, the protector of Ravenna, standing with raised arms, surrounded by lambs, in the midst of a peaceful landscape; above him, on the blue starred sky of the large medallion, beams a jeweled cross. The other mosaics of this church date from a later period.[166]

For the study of the artistic achievements of Justinian's period the church of St. Vitale in Ravenna contains the most valuable material. Here the mosaics of the sixth century have been preserved almost intact. The domed church of St. Vitale is covered on the inside from top to bottom with marvelous sculptural and mosaic decorations. The apse of this church is particularly well known because the two most famous mosaics are found on its two side walls. One of them represents Justinian surrounded by the bishop, the priests, and his court; the other is a picture of his wife, Theodora, with her ladies. The garb of the figures in these pictures is very striking in its splendor and magnificence. Ravenna, sometimes referred to as an "Italian-Byzantine Pompeii," or "la Byzance occidentale,"[167] offers the most valuable material for the evaluation of early Byzantine art of the fifth and sixth centuries.

The building activities of Justinian were not limited to the erection of fortifications and churches. He constructed also many monasteries, palaces, bridges, cisterns, aqueducts, baths, and hospitals. In the distant provinces of the Empire the name of Justinian is connected with the construction of the monastery of St. Catherine on Mount Sinai. In the apse of its church is a famous mosaic of a transfiguration ascribed to the sixth century.[168]

Several very interesting miniatures and textiles of that epoch have survived.[169] And although under the influence of the church, sculpture in general was in a state of decline, there were a large number of exceedingly graceful and beautiful ivory carvings, particularly among the diptych-leaves and the

[166] Dalton, *East Christian Art*, 77–78.
[167] See, e.g., Charles Diehl, *Ravenne*, 8, 132.
[168] See the article on this subject by V. Beneševič, "Sur la date de la mosaïque de la Transfiguration au Mont Sinaï," *Byzantion*, I (1924), 145–72.
[169] See Diehl, *Manuel d'art byzantin*, I, 230–77.

special group of consular diptychs, the series beginning in the fifth century and ending with the abolition of the consulate in 541.

Almost all the writers of this period and the builders of St. Sophia and of the Apostles were natives of Asia or northern Africa. The Hellenistic civilized East still continued to fertilize the intellectual and artistic life of the Byzantine Empire.

A survey of the long, various, and complicated reign of Justinian shows that in the majority of his projects he did not attain the desired results. It is quite evident that the brilliant military undertakings in the West, a direct outcome of his ideology of a Roman Caesar obliged to reconquer the lost territories of the Empire, were not successful in the end. They were decidedly out of harmony with the true interests of the Empire, centering primarily in the East; hence they contributed much to the decline and ruin of the country. The lack of means followed by a reduction of the army made it impossible for Justinian to establish himself firmly in the newly conquered provinces, and the results became evident during the reign of his successors. The religious policy of the Emperor was also a failure, for it did not bring about religious unity and resulted only in additional disturbances in the eastern Monophysitic provinces. Justinian met with most complete failure in his administrative reforms, which were begun with pure and sincere intentions and which led to the impoverishment and depopulation of villages, particularly because of excessive taxation and extortions by local officials.

Two of Justinian's achievements, however, left a deep mark in the history of human civilization and completely justify the surname of "Great." These two achievements are his code of civil law and the cathedral of St. Sophia.

CHAPTER IV: THE HERACLIAN EPOCH

(610–717)

HERACLIUS and his immediate successors on the Byzantine throne form a dynasty which was probably of Armenian descent. At least this may be inferred from the Armenian historian of the seventh century, Sebeos, the invaluable source on the time of Heraclius, who writes that the family of Heraclius was related to the famous Armenian house of the Arsacids.[1] Somewhat contradictory to this assertion are references in several sources to the light golden hair of Heraclius.[2] He reigned from 610 to 641. By his first wife, Eudocia, he had a son Constantine, who reigned after the death of his father for a few months only and also died in the year 641. He is known in history as Constantine III (one of the sons of Constantine the Great being considered as Constantine II). After the death of Constantine III the throne was occupied for several months by Heraclonas (Heracleon), a son of Heraclius by his second wife, Martina. He was deposed in the autumn of 641, and the son of Constantine III, Constans II, was proclaimed emperor and ruled from 641 to 668. The Greek form of his name, Constas (Latin, Constans), is probably a diminutive of Constantine, his official name; on Byzantine coins, in the western official documents of the period, and even in some Byzantine sources he is called Constantine. The people apparently called him Constans. He was succeeded by his energetic son Constantine IV (668–85). Constantine IV is usually surnamed Pogonatus, meaning "the bearded," but modern scholarship attributes this surname to the father rather than to the son.[3] With the death of Constantine IV in the year 685 ended the best period of the Heraclian dynasty, although his son, the last ruler of this dynasty, Justinian II, surnamed Rhinotmetus ("with a cut-off nose"), ruled twice, from 685 to 695 and from 705 to 711. The period of Justinian II, distinguished by many atrocities, has not yet been sufficiently studied. It seems reasonable to suppose that the Emperor's cruel treatment of the representatives of the nobility was due not

[1] *The History of the Emperor Heraclius,* chap. xxxii; Russian ed. (1862), 129; French trans. F. Macler, 108.

[2] See A. Pernice, *L'Imperatore Eraclio,* 44. H. Grégoire, "An Armenian Dynasty on the Byzantine Throne," *Armenian Quarterly,* I

(1946), 4–21. He calls the whole period from 582 to 713 the first Armenian era in Byzantine history (p. 8).

[3] See E. W. Brooks, "Who was Constantine Pogonatus?" *Byzantinische Zeitschrift,* XVII (1908), 460–62.

only to mere arbitrariness, but also to the concealed dissatisfaction of those members of the aristocracy who were not willing to become reconciled to his strong will and extreme autocratic policy and who strove to dethrone him. Some sources reveal clearly a traditional hostile tendency toward Justinian II. He was dethroned in 685. His nose and tongue were cut off[4] and he was exiled to the Crimean city of Cherson; he fled to the Khagan (Khan) of the Khazars, whose sister he later married. Still later, with the aid of the Bulgarians, he succeeded in regaining the Byzantine throne, and upon his return to the capital took cruel revenge on all those who had participated in his downfall. This tyranny called forth a revolution in the year 711, during which Justinian and his family were massacred. The year 711 marks the end of the Heraclian dynasty. During the period between the two reigns of Justinian II there were two accidental emperors: the military leader from Isauria, Leontius (695–98), and Apsimar, who assumed the name of Tiberius upon his accession to the throne (Tiberius III, 698–705). Some scholars are inclined to consider Apsimar-Tiberius of Gotho-Greek origin.[5] After the cruel deposition of Justinian II in the year 711, for a period of six years (711–17) the Byzantine throne was occupied by three accidental rulers: the Armenian Vardan or Philippicus (711–13); Artemius, renamed Anastasius during the coronation ceremony (Anastasius II, 713–15); and Theodosius III (715–17). The state of anarchy which prevailed in the Byzantine Empire from the year 695 ended in 717 with the accession of the famous ruler Leo III, who initiated a new epoch in the history of the Byzantine Empire.

EXTERNAL PROBLEMS

The Persian wars and the campaigns of Avars and Slavs

Heraclius, a very gifted and active emperor, seemed practically a model ruler after the tyrannical Phocas. He proclaimed that "power must shine more in love than in terror," reported the poet George of Pisidia, a contemporary, who described in good verse the emperor's Persian campaigns and the invasion of the Avars.[6] "Heraclius was the creator of Mediaeval Byzantium," Ostrogorsky said, "whose state conception is Roman, whose language and culture are Greek, whose faith is Christian."[7] Heraclius' achievements are the more noteworthy because at the time of his accession the position of the Empire was extremely dangerous. The Persians were menacing it from

---

[4] Not so completely as to prevent him from speaking.

[5] J. B. Bury, *A History of the Later Roman Empire,* II, 354.

[6] *De expeditione persica,* vss. 90–91; ed. I.

Bekker, *Corpus Scriptorum Historiae Byzantinae,* 17. This collection is referred to hereafter as Bonn ed.

[7] *Geschichte des byzantinischen Staates,* 96.

the east, the Avars and Slavs from the north, and internal affairs, after the unfortunate reign of Phocas, were in a state of complete anarchy. The new Emperor had neither money nor sufficient military force, and profound disturbances shook the Empire during the early part of his reign.

In the year 611 the Persians undertook to conquer Syria and they occupied Antioch, the main city of the eastern Byzantine provinces. Soon after they seized Damascus. Upon completing the conquest of Syria, they moved on to Palestine, and in the year 614 began the siege of Jerusalem, which lasted for twenty days. Then the Persian towers and battering-rams broke through the city wall, and, as one source put it, "the evil enemies entered the city with a rage which resembled that of infuriated beasts and irritated dragons."[8] They pillaged the city and destroyed the Christian sanctuaries. The Church of the Holy Sepulcher, erected by Constantine the Great and Helen, was robbed of its treasures and set on fire. The Christians were exposed to merciless violence and slaughter. The Jews of Jerusalem sided with the Persians and took active part in the massacres, during which, according to some sources, 60,000 Christians perished. Many treasures from the sacred city were transported to Persia, and one of the dearest relics of Christendom, the Holy Cross, was taken to Ctesiphon. Numerous prisoners were sent to Persia, including the Patriarch of Jerusalem, Zacharias.[9]

This devastating Persian conquest of Palestine and the pillage of Jerusalem represent a turning point in the history of this province.

This was a disaster unheard of since the occupation of Jerusalem in the reign of Titus, but this time the calamity could not be remedied. Never again did this city have an era similar to the brilliant epoch under Constantine, and the magnificent buildings within its walls, such as the Mosque of Omar, never again created an epoch in history. From now on the city and its buildings constantly declined, step by step, and even the Crusades, so abounding in results and various spoils for Europe, caused only trouble, confusion, and degeneration in the life of Jerusalem. The Persian invasion immediately removed the effects of the imported artificial Graeco-Roman civilization in Palestine. It ruined agriculture, depopulated the cities, destroyed temporarily or permanently many monasteries and lauras, and stopped all trade development. This invasion freed the marauding Arabian tribes from the ties of association and the fear which had controlled them, and they began to form the unity which made possible their general attacks of a later period. From now on the cultural development of the country is ended. Palestine enters upon that troubled period which might very naturally be called the period of the Middle Ages, were it not for the fact that it has lasted to our own times.[10]

[8] Antiochus Strategus, *The Capture of Jerusalem by the Persians in the Year 614,* trans. N. Marr, 15; trans. F. C. Conybeare, *English Historical Review,* XXV (1910), 506. P. Peeters, "La Prise de Jerusalem par les Perses," *Mélanges de l'Université de Saint-Joseph,* IX (1923).

[9] See H. Vincent and F. M. Abel, *Jérusalem. Recherches de topographie, d'archéologie et d'histoire,* II, pt. 4, 926–28.

[10] N. P. Kondakov, *An Archeological Journey through Syria and Palestine,* 173–74.

The ease with which the Persians conquered Syria and Palestine may be explained partly by the religious conditions in these provinces. The majority of the population, particularly in Syria, did not adhere to the official orthodox faith supported by the central government. The Nestorians, and later the Monophysites, of these provinces were greatly oppressed by the Byzantine government; hence they quite naturally preferred the domination of the Persian fire-worshipers, in whose land the Nestorians enjoyed comparative religious freedom.

The Persian invasion was not limited to Syria and Palestine. Part of the Persian army, after crossing all of Asia Minor and conquering Chalcedon on the Sea of Marmora near the Bosphorus, encamped near Chrysopolis (present-day Scutari), opposite Constantinople, while another Persian army set out to conquer Egypt. Alexandria fell, probably in the year 618 or 619. In Egypt, just as in Syria and Palestine, the Monophysitic population heartily preferred Persian to Byzantine domination. The loss of Egypt was a heavy blow to the Byzantine Empire, for Egypt was the granary of Constantinople. Stoppage of the supply of Egyptian grain had heavy repercussions on economic conditions in the capital.

With the heavy losses in the south and east caused by the Persian wars, there appeared another great menace to the Byzantine Empire from the north. The Avaro-Slavonic hordes of the Balkan peninsula, headed by the Khagan of the Avars, moved southward, pillaging and destroying the northern provinces and reaching as far as Constantinople, where they broke through the city walls. This expedition was not a campaign, but rather a series of raids, which furnished the Khagan with numerous captives and rich spoils which he carried off to the north.[11] These invaders are mentioned in the writings of Heraclius' western contemporary, Isidore, bishop of Seville, who remarked in his chronicle that "Heraclius entered upon the sixteenth (fifth) year of his reign, at the beginning of which the Slavs took Greece from the Romans, and the Persians took Syria, Egypt, and many provinces."[12] At about this time (624) Byzantium was losing its last possessions in Spain, where the Visigoths' conquest was completed by King Suinthila (Swinthila). The Balearic Islands remained in the hands of Heraclius.[13]

---

[11] Probably this Avar invasion took place in 617. See N. Baynes, "The Date of the Avar Surprise," *Byzantinische Zeitschrift*, XXI (1912), 110–28.

[12] Isidore's chronology is not accurate. Isidori Hispalensis, *Chronica Majora*; ed. J. P. Migne, *Patrologia Latina*, LXXXIII, 1056 (the fifth year of the reign); ed. T. Mommsen,

Monumenta Germaniae Historica, Auctorum Antiquissimorum, XI, *Chronica Minora*, II, 479 (the sixteenth year of the reign).

[13] See F. Görres, "Die byzantinischen Besitzungen an den Küsten des spanisch-westgothischen Reiches (554–624)," *Byzantinische Zeitschrift*, XVI (1907), 530–32. E. Bouchier, *Spain Under the Roman Empire*, 59–60. P.

After some hesitation the Emperor decided to begin war with Persia. In view of the exhaustion of the treasury, Heraclius had recourse to the valuables of the churches in the capital and the provinces, and ordered a large amount of gold and silver coins to be made from them. As he had anticipated, he was able to remove the menace of the Khagan of the Avars in the north by sending him distinguished hostages and a large sum of money. In the spring of 622 Heraclius crossed to Asia Minor, where he recruited a large number of soldiers and trained them for several months. The Persian campaign, which incidentally aimed at recovering the Holy Cross and the sacred city of Jerusalem, assumed the form of a crusade.

Modern historians think it probable that Heraclius conducted three Persian campaigns between the years 622 and 628. All three were brilliantly successful. A contemporary poet, George of Pisidia, composed an *Epinikion* (Song of Victory) for the occasion, entitled the *Heraclias;* and in another poem, the *Hexaemeron* ("The Six Days"), on the creation of the world, he alluded to the six-year war in which Heraclius vanquished the Persians. A twentieth-century historian, Th. I. Uspensky, compared Heraclius' war with the glorious campaigns of Alexander the Great.[14] Heraclius secured the aid of the Caucasian tribes and formed an alliance with the Khazars. The northern Persian provinces bordering the Caucasus formed one of the main arenas of military action for this reign.

While the Emperor was absent leading the army in distant campaigns, the capital became exposed to very serious danger. The Khagan of the Avars broke the agreement with the Emperor and in the year 626 advanced toward Constantinople with huge hordes of Avars and Slavs. He also formed an agreement with the Persians, who immediately sent part of their army to Chalcedon. The Avaro-Slavonic hordes besieged Constantinople to the extreme apprehension of the population, but the garrison of Constantinople was successful in repelling the attack and putting the enemy to flight. As soon as the Persians heard of this repulse, they withdrew their army from Chalcedon and directed it to Syria. The Byzantine victory over the Avars before Constantinople in 626 was one of the main causes of the weakening of the wild Avar kingdom.[15]

Meanwhile, at the end of 627 Heraclius completely routed the Persians in a battle which took place near the ruins of ancient Nineveh (in the neighborhood of modern Mosul on the Tigris), and advanced into the central

Goubert, "Byzance et l'Espagne wisigothique (554–711)," *Études byzantines*, II (1945), 48–49, 76–77.
[14] *History of the Byzantine Empire*, I, 684.

[15] Pernice, *L'Imperatore Eraclio*, 141–48. J. Kulakovsky, *History of Byzantium*, III, 76–87.

Persian provinces, collecting rich spoils. He sent to Constantinople a long and triumphant manifesto, describing his successes against the Persians and announcing the end of the war and his brilliant victory.[16] "In 629 Heraclius' glory was complete; the sun of his genius had dissipated the darkness which hung over the Empire, and now to the eyes of all a glorious era of peace and grandeur seemed opening. The eternal and dreaded Persian enemy was prostrated forever; on the Danube the might of the Avars was rapidly declining. Who could then resist the Byzantine armies? Who could menace the Empire?"[17] At this time the Persian king Chosroes was dethroned and killed, and his successor, Kawad Sheroe, opened peace negotiations with Heraclius. According to their agreement the Persians returned to the Byzantine Empire the conquered provinces of Syria, Palestine, and Egypt, and the relic of the Holy Cross. Heraclius returned to the capital in great triumph, and in 630, with his wife Martina, he left for Jerusalem, where the Holy Cross was restored to its former place to the great joy of the entire Christian world. The contemporary Armenian historian Sebeos gave an account of this occasion:

There was much joy at their entrance to Jerusalem: sounds of weeping and sighs, abundant tears, burning flames in hearts, extreme exaltation of the emperor, of the princes, of all the soldiers and inhabitants of the city; and nobody could sing the hymns of our Lord on account of the great and poignant emotion of the emperor and of the whole multitude. The emperor restored [the Cross] to its place and returned all the church objects, each to its place; he distributed gifts to all the churches and to the inhabitants of the city and money for incense.[18]

It is interesting to note that Heraclius' victory over the Persians is mentioned in the Koran. "The Greeks have been overcome by the Persians in the nearest part of the land; but after their defeat, they shall overcome the others in their turn, within a few years."[19]

The significance of the Persian campaigns of Heraclius.—This Persian war marks a very significant epoch in the history of the Byzantine Empire. Of the two main world powers of the early Middle Ages, the Byzantine Empire and Persia, the second definitely lost its former significance and became a weak state soon to cease its political existence because of the attacks of the Arabs. The victorious Byzantine Empire dealt the death blow to its constant enemy, reclaimed all the lost eastern provinces of the Empire, restored the Holy Cross to the Christian world, and at the same time freed its capital

[16] This manifesto is preserved in *Chronicon Paschale,* 727–34; Italian trans. Pernice, *L'Imperatore Eraclio,* 167–71.

[17] Pernice, *ibid.,* 179. See V. Minorsky, "Roman and Byzantine Campaigns in Atropatene," *Bulletin of the School of Oriental and African Studies,* XI, 2 (1944), 248–51 (Heraclius' campaigns A.D. 626 and 628).

[18] *Emperor Heraclius,* trans. Patkanov, 111; trans. F. Macler, 91. In the last sentence both translators give "benediction" for "gifts." See Kulakovsky, III, *Byzantium,* 118, n. 1.

[19] Koran, XXX, 1; in the section entitled "The Greeks"; trans. G. Sale, 330–31.

of the formidable menace of the Avaro-Slavonic hordes. The Byzantine Empire seemed to be at the height of its glory and power. The sovereign of India sent his congratulations to Heraclius on his victory over the Persians, together with a great quantity of precious stones.[20] The king of the Franks, Dagobert, sent special ambassadors to make a perpetual peace with the Empire.[21] Finally in 630 the queen of the Persians, Borane, apparently also sent a special envoy to Heraclius and made formal peace.[22]

Heraclius officially assumed the name basileus for the first time after the successful outcome of the Persian war, in the year 629. This name had been in use for centuries in the East, particularly in Egypt, and with the fourth century it became current in the Greek-speaking parts of the empire, but it had not previously been accepted as an official title. Up to the seventh century the Greek equivalent of the Latin "emperor" (*imperator*) was the term "autocrator" (αὐτοκράτωρ), that is, an autocrat, which does not correspond etymologically to *imperator*. The only foreign ruler to whom the Byzantine emperor consented to give the title of basileus (with the exception of the distant king of Abyssinia) was the king of Persia. Bury wrote: "So long as there was a great independent Basileus outside the Roman Empire, the emperors refrained from adopting a title which would be shared by another monarch. But as soon as that monarch was reduced to the condition of a dependent vassal and there was no longer a concurrence, the Emperor signified the events by assuming officially the title which had for several centuries been applied to him unofficially."[23]

The Arabs

The reclaimed provinces of Syria, Palestine, and Egypt with their predominating Monophysitic population again brought to the fore the painful and highly significant question of the government's attitude toward the Monophysites. The lasting and persistent struggle of Heraclius with the Persians, in spite of the brilliant final outcome, was bound to weaken temporarily the military power of the Byzantine Empire because of the heavy losses in man power and the exceedingly heavy financial strain. But the Empire

[20] Theophanes, *Chronographia;* ed. C. de Boor, 335.

[21] *Chronicarum quae dicunter Fredegarii Scholastici*, IV, 62. *Mon. Germ. Hist. Scriptores rerum merovingicarum*, II, 151. Cf. also *Gesta Dagoberti I regis Francorum*, 24; *Mon. Germ. Hist.*, 409.

[22] *Chronica Minora*, I; trans. I. Guidi, *Corpus scriptorum christianorum orientalium, Scriptores Syri*, ser. III, iv. Agapius (Mahboub) de Menbidg, *Histoire universelle*, ed.

A. A. Vasiliev, *Patrologia Orientalis*, VIII (1912), II (2), 453 (193). *Chronique de Michel le Syrien*, trans. J. B. Chabot, II, 420. See T. Nöldeke, *Geschichte der Perser und Araber zur Zeit der Sasaniden*, 391–92. Nöldeke, *Aufsätze zur persischen Geschichte*, 129.

[23] *The Constitution of the Later Roman Empire*, 20. J. B. Bury, *Selected Essays*, ed. H. Temperley, 109. This point of view was challenged by E. Stein, *Byzantinische Zeitschrift*, XXIX (1930), 353.

did not get the much-needed period of rest because, soon after the end of the Persian war, there appeared a formidable menace, entirely unexpected and at first not fully appreciated: the Arabs. They opened up a new era in the world's history by their attacks upon the Byzantine Empire and Persia.

Gibbon spoke of their advance as follows: "While the Emperor triumphed at Constantinople or Jerusalem, an obscure town on the confines of Syria was pillaged by the Saracens, and they cut in pieces some troops who advanced to its relief; an ordinary and trifling occurrence, had it not been the prelude of a mighty revolution. These robbers were the apostles of Mahomet; their fanatic valor had emerged from the desert; and in the last eight years of his reign Heraclius lost to the Arabs the same provinces which he had rescued from the Persians."[24]

Muhammed and Islam.—Long before the Christian era the Arabs, a people of Semitic origin, occupied the Arabian peninsula and the Syrian desert which lies to the north of it and stretches as far as the Euphrates River. The peninsula of Arabia, embracing an area equal to approximately one-fourth of Europe, is surrounded by the Persian Gulf on the east, the Indian Ocean on the south, and the Red Sea on the west; in the north it runs gradually into the Syrian desert. Historically, the best-known provinces of the peninsula were (1) Nedjd, on the central plateau; (2) Yemen, or Fortunate Arabia, in the southwest of the peninsula; and (3) Hidjaz, the narrow strip along the coast of the Red Sea, extending from the north of the peninsula to Yemen. The arid land was not everywhere habitable, and the Arabs, who were a nomadic people, occupied chiefly central and northern Arabia. The Bedouins, who were nomads, considered themselves the pure and genuine representatives of the Arabian race and the true bearers of personal dignity and valor. They treated with arrogance and even with contempt the settled inhabitants of the few cities and hamlets.

The Roman Empire was inevitably bound to come into collision with the Arabian tribes on its eastern Syrian border, which it was forced to protect. For this purpose the Roman emperors erected a line of border fortifications, so-called Syrian *limes* which resembled, on a small scale, of course, the famous *limes romanus* on the Danubian border, erected for defense against Germanic attacks. Some ruins of the principal Roman fortifications along the Syrian border survive at present.[25]

As early as the second century B.C. independent states began to form among the Arabs of Syria. They were strongly influenced by the Aramean and Greek civilizations; hence they are sometimes referred to as the Arabo-Aramean Hellenistic kingdoms. Among the cities, Petra became particularly wealthy

---

[24] *The History of the Decline and Fall of the Roman Empire*, ed. J. B. Bury, ch. 46.

[25] On the Syrian *limes* see R. Dussaud, *Les arabes en Syrie avant l'islam*, 24–56.

and important because of its advantageous position at the crossing of great commercial routes. The magnificent ruins of this city attract the attention of historians and archeologists even today.

From a cultural and political point of view the most important of all Syrian-Arabic kingdoms in the epoch of the Roman Empire was Palmyra, whose valiant queen, the Hellenistically educated Zenobia, as the Roman and Greek writers call her, formed a large state in the second half of the third century A.D. by conquering Egypt and the major part of Asia Minor. According to B. A. Turaev,[26] this was the first manifestation of the reaction of the East and the first breaking up of the Empire into two parts, eastern and western. The Emperor Aurelian restored the unity of the Empire, and in the year 273 the conquered queen had to follow the triumphal chariot of the conquerer when he entered Rome. Rebellious Palmyra was destroyed. Its imposing ruins, however, like those of Petra, still attract scholars and tourists. The famous epigraphic monument of Palmyra, the tariff of Palmyra, engraved on a stone of enormous size and containing very valuable information about the trade and finance of the city, has been transferred to Russia and is now at the Hermitage in Leningrad.

Two Arabian dynasties stand out very distinctly during the Byzantine period. One, the dynasty of the Ghassanids in Syria, Monophysitic in its religious tendencies and dependent upon the Byzantine emperors, became particularly powerful in the sixth century under Justinian, when it aided the Byzantine Empire in its military undertakings in the East. This dynasty probably ceased to exist in the early seventh century, when the Persians conquered Syria and Palestine. The second Arabian dynasty, the Lakhmids, centered in the city of Hira on the Euphrates. Because of its vassal relations with the Persian Sassanids it was hostile to the Ghassanids. It also ceased at the beginning of the seventh century. In the city of Hira Christianity, in its Nestorian form, had a body of adherents, and even some members of the Lakhmid dynasty accepted it. Both dynasties had to defend the borders of their kingdom, the Ghassanids on the Byzantine side and the Lakhmids on the Persian. Apparently both vassal states disappeared at the beginning of the seventh century, so that at the time of Muhammed's advance there was not a single political organization within the confines of the Arabian peninsula and the Syrian desert which could be called a state. There had existed in Yemen since the end of the second century B.C. the kingdom of the Sabaeans-Himyarites (Homerites). But in about the year 570 Yemen was conquered by the Persians.[27]

[26] *History of the Ancient East* (2nd ed., 1914), II, 373.
[27] *Excerpta e Theophanis Historia*, Bonn ed., 485; see Nöldeke, *Geschichte der Perser und Araber*, 249–50. C. Conti Rossini, *Storia d'Etiopia*, 199.

Before the time of Muhammed the ancient Arabs lived in tribal organizations. Blood relationship was the only basis for common interests, which were confined almost exclusively to loyalty, protection, aid, and revenge upon enemies for insults suffered by the tribe. The least occasion sufficed for starting lasting and bloody struggle between tribes. References to these ancient times and customs have been preserved in old Arabic poetry, as well as in prose tradition. Animosity and arrogance were the two predominant elements in the mutual relations of different tribes of ancient Arabia.

The religious conceptions of the ancient Arabs were primitive. The tribes had their own gods and sacred objects, such as stones, trees, and springs, through which they aspired to divine the future. In some parts of Arabia the worship of stars prevailed. According to one expert in Arabic antiquity, the ancient Arabs in their religious experiences hardly rose above the feelings of a fetishist before the worshiped object.[28] They believed in the existence of friendly, and, more frequently, unfriendly, forces which they called *djinn* (demons). Among the Arabs the conception of the higher invisible power of Allah was vague. Prayer as a form of worship was apparently unknown to them, and when they turned to the deity, their invocation was usually an appeal for aid in revenging some injury or injustice suffered from an enemy. Goldziher asserted also that "the surviving pre-Islamic poems do not contain any allusions to a striving toward the divine even on the part of the more sublime souls, and give only slight indications about their attitude to the religious traditions of their people."[29]

The nomadic life of the Bedouins was naturally unfavorable to the development of distinct permanent places for the performance of religious worship, even of a very primitive form. But there were, besides the Bedouins, the settled inhabitants of cities and hamlets which sprang up and developed along the trade routes, mainly on the caravan road leading from the south to the north, from Yemen to Palestine, Syria, and the Sinaitic peninsula. The richest among the cities along this route was Mecca (Macoraba, in ancient writings), famous long before Muhammed's appearance. Second in importance was the city of Yathrib, the future Medina, situated farther north. These cities were convenient stopping points for the trade caravans traveling from the north and south. There were many Jews among the merchants of Mecca and Yathrib, as well as among the population of other portions of the peninsula, such as northern Hidjaz and Yemen. From the Romano-Byzantine provinces of Palestine and Syria in the north, and from Abyssinia through Yemen in the south, many Christians penetrated into the peninsula. Mecca became

---

[28] I. Goldziher, "Die Religion des Islams," in *Die Kultur der Gegenwart: Die Reli-* *gionen des Orients,* ed. P. Hinneberg, III, I, part 2, 102.
[29] *Ibid.,* 102.

the central gathering point for the mixed population of the peninsula. From remote times there existed in Mecca the sanctuary Kaaba (the Cube) which was originally distinctly non-Arabic. It was a cube-shaped stone building, about thirty-five feet high, concealing the main object of worship, the black stone. Tradition claimed that this stone had been sent down from heaven, and associated the erection of the sanctuary with the name of Abraham. Because of its advantageous commercial position, Mecca was visited by merchants from all Arabian tribes. Some legends affirm that, in order to attract more visitors to the city, idols of various tribes were placed within the Kaaba, so that representatives of each tribe could worship their favorite deity during their stay in Mecca. The number of pilgrims increased constantly, being particularly great during the sacred period of the "Peace of God," an observance which more or less guaranteed the territorial inviolability of the tribes who sent representatives to Mecca. The time of religious festivals coincided with the great fair at Mecca, where the Arabs and foreign merchants carried out trade transactions which gave Mecca enormous profits. The city was rapidly growing very wealthy. About the fifth century A.D. a distinguished tribe of Kuraish began to dominate in the city. The material interests of the money-loving Meccans were not neglected, and the sacred gatherings were often utilized by the citizens for the promotion of their own selfish interests. According to one scholar, "with the dominance of the nobility, charged with performing the traditional ceremonies, the city assumed a materialistic, arrogantly plutocratic character, and deep religious satisfaction could not be found there."[30]

Under the influence of Judaism and Christianity, with which the Arabs had ample opportunity to become acquainted in Mecca, there appeared even before Muhammed isolated individuals truly inspired by religious ideals distinctly different from the dry ritual of the old religious customs. An aspiration toward monotheism and the acceptance of the ascetic form of living were the distinguishing ideals of these modest apostles. They found gratification in their personal experiences but did not influence or convert the people about them. The man who unified the Arabs and founded a world religion was Muhammed, who, from a modest preacher of penitence, became at first a prophet, and later the chief of a political community.

Muhammed was born about 570. He was a member of the Hashimite clan, one of the poorest clans of the Kuraish tribe. His parents died while he was still very young, and he had to earn his own living by acting as a driver of camels in the trade caravans of the rich widow Khadidja. His material con-

[30] *Ibid.,* 103. See also P. H. Lammens, "La Mecque à la veille de l'hégire," *Mélanges de l'Université de Saint-Joseph,* IX (1924), 439; Lammens, "Les sanctuaires préislamiques dans l'Arabie Occidentale," *ibid.,* XI (1926), 173.

dition improved greatly when he married her. He was of a sensitive, sickly disposition from early childhood, and under the influence of his contact with the Jews and Christians began to meditate more and more upon the religious organization of Mecca. The doubts which frequently arose in his mind caused him many moments of despair and endless suffering, and he became subject to nervous attacks. During his solitary wanderings on the outskirts of Mecca he was troubled by visions, and within him strengthened the conviction that God had sent him to save His people who had followed the wrong path.

Muhammed was forty years old when he determined to express his views openly, at first as a modest preacher of morality in his own family. Later he began to preach to a small group of people from the lower classes, and shortly after to some distinguished citizens. The chiefs of Kuraish, however, were openly against Muhammed and made it impossible for him to remain in Mecca. He secretly departed with his followers from his native city in the year 622, and went northward to the city of Yathrib, whose population, including the Jews, had frequently urged him to come to their city, promising him more favorable living conditions. They received him and his followers very warmly and later changed the name of their city to Medina, meaning "the city of the prophet."

The year of the migration or, as it is more frequently but incorrectly called, the year of the flight (*hidjra* in Arabic, distorted by Europeans into *hegira*) of Muhammed from Mecca to Medina marks the Muhammedan era.[31] Beginning with the year 622, the Arabs and all other Muslim peoples count their chronology by using as a unit the lunar year, which is somewhat shorter than the solar year. The Muhammedans usually consider Friday, July 16, of the year 622 the beginning of the first year of the hegira. This chronology, however, was introduced only during the sixteenth year counting from 622.

The original sources bearing on Muhammedanism are unsatisfactory; there is almost no authentic information about the early Meccan period of Muhammed's life. At that time his teaching was of such a vague, almost chaotic, nature that it was not yet possible to call it a new religion.

In Medina Muhammed became the head of a large community and began to lay the foundations for a political state on a religious basis. Having developed the main principles of his religion, introduced certain religious ceremonies, and strengthened his political position, he set out to conquer Mecca in the year 630. Upon entering the city he immediately destroyed its idols and all survivals of polytheism. The cult of an only God—Allah—was the basis of the new religion. Muhammed granted a sort of amnesty to all his enemies,

---

[31] It is better not to translate the word "*hidjra*" by flight, because "to flee" is not implied in the Arabic root "*hadjara*," which means "to break off relations, abandon one's tribe, emigrate"; see *Encyclopédie de l'Islam*, II, 320-21.

and allowed no murder or robbery. From that time Muhammed and his followers freely made their pilgrimages to Mecca and practiced their new rites.
Muhammed died in the year 632.

He was not a logical thinker; hence his religious teaching can hardly be
presented in a systematic way. This teaching was not an original creation; it
had developed under the influence of other religions—Christianity, Judaism,
and to some extent Parsism (Zoroastrianism), the religion of the Persian
kingdom of the Sassanids of that time. Modern historians have reached the
conclusion that "the original Muhammedan community, contrary to earlier
opinion, was more closely related to Christianity than to Judaism."[32] Muhammed had become acquainted with other religions in his youth during
his travels with the caravans, and later in Mecca and Yathrib (Medina). The
distinctive feature of his teaching is a realization of the complete dependence
of man upon God and a blind resignation to His will. The faith is strictly
monotheistic, and God is considered unlimited in his power over His creatures.
The Muhammedan religion assumed the name of Islam, which means "resignation or submission to God," and the followers of Islam are called Muslims,
or Muhammedans. At the basis of this religion lies the distinct idea of a single
God, Allah. The statement "There is only one God and Muhammed is his
apostle" is one of the fundamental principles of Islam. Both Moses and Jesus
Christ were recognized as prophets, Christ being the penultimate prophet; but
the new teaching claimed that neither was as great as Muhammed. During
his sojourn in Medina Muhammed declared that his religious teaching represented a pure restoration of the religion of Abraham, corrupted by the Christians and Jews. One of Muhammed's first problems was to lead the Arabs out
of their state of barbarism (*Djahiliyya* in Arabic), and inculcate in them
higher moral principles. Instead of the widely spread cruel custom of revenge,
he preached to his people peace, love, and self-control. He was responsible
for putting an end to the custom which prevailed among certain Arabian
tribes of burying alive newly born girls. He also attempted to regulate marital
relations and limit polygamy by reducing the legally permissible number
of wives to four, allowing more freedom in this respect to himself alone. In
place of the old tribal conceptions, he advanced the idea of personal rights,
including the right of inheritance. Muhammed introduced some directions
regarding prayer and fasting; it was necessary to face in the direction of the
Kaaba during prayer, and the great fasting period was set in the ninth month,
called Ramadan. The weekly holiday was set on Friday. The new teaching
prohibited the use of blood, wine, pork, and the flesh of animals which died

---

[32] See V. Barthold, "The Orientation of the
First Muslim Mosques," *Annual Publications
of the Russian Institute of Art History*, I
(1922), 116. C. H. Becker, *Vom Werden und
Wesen der Islamischen Welt: Islamstudien*, I,
429.

a natural death or which had served as sacrifices for pagan idols. Gambling was also prohibited. Belief in angels and the devil was compulsory for all Muslims, and the conceptions of heaven and hell, of the Resurrection, and the Last Judgment were distinctly materialistic. The basic elements of these conceptions can be found in the Jewish-Christian apocryphal literature. Muhammed included in his teaching the mercy of God, the repentance of sinners, and the advocacy of good deeds. Modern religious rules and regulations developed gradually, some after the death of Muhammed. Thus, for example, prayer at a set time had not yet been strictly established, even in the time of the Umayyads (Omayyads, Ommiads).[33] The prescribed requirements can be reduced to five: (1) the profession of faith in an only God, Allah, and his prophet, Muhammed; (2) the performance of a definite prayer at a set time with the strict observance of prescribed rituals; (3) the contribution of a certain sum of money toward meeting the military and charitable expenses of the Muhammedan community; (4) fasting during the month of Ramadan; and (5) the pilgrimage to the Kaaba in Mecca (in Arabic such a pilgrimage is called *hadj*). All the basic principles and regulations of the Muhammedan faith are laid down in a sacred book of revelations of Muhammed, the Koran, which is subdivided into 114 chapters (*Sura* in Arabic). The tales of Muhammed's teachings and deeds, collected later in various books, bear the name of *Sunna*.

The history of early Islam in the time of Muhammed is obscure and debatable because of the present condition of sources bearing upon this period. And yet for the history of the Byzantine Empire during the seventh century this problem is of extreme significance, since its adequate solution may affect greatly the explanation of the unusual and rapid military success of the Arabs, who took from the Byzantine Empire its eastern and southern provinces: Syria, Palestine, Egypt, and North Africa.

The observations of three profound students illustrate the prevalence of contradictory opinions among scholars with regard to Islam. Goldziher wrote, "There is no doubt that Muhammed thought of spreading his religion beyond the borders of Arabia and of transforming his teaching, originally communicated only to his nearest relatives, into a force which would dominate the entire world."[34] Grimme stated that on the basis of the Koran one is led to believe that the final aim of Islam was "the complete possession of Arabia."[35] Caetani wrote that the prophet never dreamed of converting the entire land of Arabia and all the Arabs.[36]

[33] I. Goldziher, *Muhammedanische Studien,* II, 20.
[34] Goldziher, "Die Religion des Islams," in *Die Kultur der Gegenwart: Die Religionen des*

Orients, ed. P. Hinneberg, III, I, 106.
[35] *Mohammed,* I, 123. Charles Diehl and G. Marçais, *Le Monde oriental de 395 à 1018,* 176.
[36] *Studi di storia orientale,* III, 236, 257.

In Muhammed's lifetime not all of Arabia came under his sway. It may be said generally that Arabia, during all of its existence, never recognized a sole ruler for the entire land. In reality Muhammed dominated a territory which occupied perhaps less than a third of the peninsula. This area became strongly influenced by the new ideas of Islam, but the remaining part of Arabia persisted under a political and religious organization differing very little from that which had existed before the appearance of Muhammed. Christianity prevailed in the southwest of the peninsula, in Yemen. The tribes of northeastern Arabia also adopted the Christian faith, which soon became the predominating religion in Mesopotamia and in the Arabian provinces along the Euphrates River. Meanwhile, the official Persian religion was constantly and rapidly declining. Thus, at the time of his death Muhammed was neither the political ruler of all Arabia nor its religious leader.

It is interesting to note that at first the Byzantine Empire viewed Islam as a kind of Arianism and placed it on a level with other Christian sects. Byzantine apologetic and polemic literature argues against Islam in the same manner as it did against the Monophysites, the Monotheletes, and the adherents of other heretical teachings. Thus John Damascene, a member of a Saracen family, who lived at the Muhammedan court in the eighth century, did not regard Islam as a new religion, but considered it only an instance of secession from the true Christian faith similar in nature to other earlier heresies. The Byzantine historians also showed very little interest in the rise of Muhammed and the political movement which he initiated.[37] The first chronicler who records some facts about the life of Muhammed, "the ruler of the Saracens and the pseudo-prophet," was Theophanes, who wrote in the early part of the ninth century.[38] In the conception of medieval western Europe Islam was not a distinct religion, but a Christian sect, akin in its dogmas to Arianism; and even in the later part of the Middle Ages Dante, in his *Divine Comedy*, considered Muhammed a heretic and calls him a "sower of scandal and schism" (*Seminator di scandalo e di scisma* [*Inferno*, XXVIII, 31–36]).

Causes of the Arabian conquest in the seventh century.—It is customary to point out the religious enthusiasm of the Muslims, which frequently rose to a state of religious fanaticism and absolute intolerance, as one of the main causes for the striking military success of the Arabs in their combat with Persia and the Byzantine Empire in the seventh century. The Arabs are supposed to have rushed upon the Asiatic and African provinces with a determination to carry out the will of their prophet, who had prescribed the conversion of the entire world to the new faith. The victories of the Arabs are ordinarily

[37] See K. Güterbock, *Der Islam im Lichte der byzantinischen Polemik*, 6, 7, 11, 67–68.
[38] *Chronographia*, ed. de Boor, 333. See W. Eichner, "Die Nachrighten über den Islam bei den Byzantinern," *Der Islam*, XXIII (1936), 133–62, 197–244.

explained by the religious enthusiasm which prepared the fanatical Muslims to regard death with disdain and made them invincible.

This view should be recognized as unfounded. At the time of Muhammed's death there were few convinced Muslims, and even this small number remained in Medina until the end of the first great conquests. Very few of the followers of Muhammed fought in Syria and Persia. The great majority of the fighting Arabs consisted of Bedouins who knew of Islam only by hearsay. They were concerned with nothing but material, earthly benefits, and craved spoils and unrestrained license. Religious enthusiasm did not exist among them. Besides, early Islam was tolerant in nature. The Koran states directly that "God will not force anyone beyond his capacity" (II, 257). The indulgent attitude of early Islam toward Christianity and Judaism is well known. The Koran speaks of God's tolerance of other faiths: "If thy Lord wished, he would make the people as one religious community" (XI, 120). The religious fanaticism and intolerance of the Muslims are later phenomena, alien to the Arabic nation and explainable by the influence of the Muslim proselytes. The victorious conquests of the Arabs in the seventh century cannot be credited to religious enthusiasm and fanaticism.

According to some recent investigations, such as Caetani's, the real causes of the irrepressible onward rush of the Arabs were materialistic. Arabia, limited in natural resources, could no longer satisfy the physical needs of its population, and threatened by poverty and hunger, the Arabs were forced to make a desperate attempt to free themselves "from the hot prison of the desert." Unbearable living conditions were responsible for the crushing force with which the Arabs rushed upon the Byzantine Empire and Persia. There was no religious element in this movement.[39]

Though this view is correct to a certain extent, one cannot find a full explanation of the military success of the Arabs in material needs alone. Included also among the causes were internal conditions in the eastern and southern Byzantine provinces so easily occupied by the Arabs, Syria, Palestine, and Egypt. Their growing religious dissatisfaction has been repeatedly pointed out. Monophysitic and partly Nestorian in their adherence, they came into conflict continually with the inexorable central government, particularly after the death of Justinian the Great. It was the unyielding policy of the emperors that rendered the provinces of Syria, Palestine, and Egypt ready to secede from the Byzantine Empire and become subjects of the Arabs, who were known for religious tolerance and were interested only in obtaining regular taxes from the conquered provinces. The religious convictions of the conquered peoples concerned the Arabs little.

[39] Caetani, *Studi di storia orientale*, I, 368.

On the other hand, the orthodox portion of the eastern provinces was also dissatisfied with the policy of the central authorities because of some concessions to the Monophysites, especially in the seventh century. In connection with the Monothelete tendency of Heraclius, Eutychius, the Christian Arabian historian of the tenth century, said that the citizens of Emesa (Hims) called the Emperor a "Maronite (Monothelete) and an enemy of our faith,"[40] and Beladsori, another Arabian historian of the ninth century, said that they then turned to the Arabs, saying, "Your rule and your justice are more agreeable to us than that tyranny and those insults to which we have been subject."[41] Of course, this is Muhammedan testimony; but it accurately reflects the frame of mind of the orthodox population. The major part of the population of the Byzantine provinces of Syria and Palestine was of Semitic origin and largely of Arabic descent, and that the Arabian conquerors met in the subjected provinces a people of their own race who spoke their own tongue. According to one scholar, "It was, therefore, not a question of conquering a foreign land, whose taxes would constitute the only direct gain, but also of reclaiming part of their own fatherland which was declining under the foreign yoke."[42] In addition to the general religious dissatisfaction and the kinship to the Arabs, the Byzantine Empire and her army were weakened after the long-continued, though finally successful, campaigns against the Persians, and could not offer the proper resistance to the fresh Arabian forces.

In Egypt there were special causes for the weak resistance to the Arabs. The main reason must be sought in the general conditions prevailing in the Byzantine army. Numerically the troops were perhaps sufficiently strong; but the general organization of the army was poor. It was subdivided into many parts commanded by five different rulers or dukes (*duces*), entrusted with equal power. There was no unity of action among these governors. Their indifference to the general problems of the province, their personal rivalries, the lack of solidarity and coordination toward a common end, and their military incapacity paralyzed resistance. The soldiers were no better than their leaders. Numerous as the Egyptian army was, its poor leadership and poor training made it very unreliable and created a strong tendency toward defection. "There is no doubt that numerous causes explain the terrifying successes of the Arabs," Maspero said, "but the main cause of the Byzantine defeat in the

---

[40] *Annales*, ed. L. Cheikho, *Corpus Scriptorum Christianorum Orientalium, Scriptorum Arabici*, II, 5, 1.4. Latin trans. Migne, *Patrologia Graeca*, CIX, 1088.

[41] *Liber expugnationum regionum*, ed. M. J. De Goeje, 137; English trans. P. Hitti, *The Origins of the Islamic State*, I, 211. See

Barthold in the *Transactions of the Oriental College*, I (1925), 468.

[42] M. J. De Goeje, *Mémoire sur la conquête de la Syrie* (2nd ed., 1900), i. C. Becker, "The Expansion of the Saracens—the East," *Cambridge Medieval History*, II, 345.

valley of the Nile was the poor quality of the army which was intrusted, contrary to all expectations, with the task of defending Egypt."[43] On the basis of the study of papyri, Gelzer thought that the class of privileged large land- owners which arose in Egypt previous to the period of the Arabian conquests became practically independent of the central government and, though it did not create an actual local ruling body, was also one of the main causes for the fall of Byzantine domination.[44] Amélineau, also on the basis of a study of papyri, suggested as another important factor which facilitated the Arabian conquest the inadequate civil administration of Egypt.[45] The English papy- rologist H. I. Bell called the conquest of Egypt by the Arabs "no miracle, no example of divine vengeance on erring Christendom; it was merely the in- evitable collapse of a structure rotten at the core."[46] Thus the list of primary causes for Arabian success includes religious conditions in Syria, Palestine, and Egypt, the racial kinship of the population of the two first countries to the people of Arabia, the inadequacy of military forces, inefficient military or- ganization and poor civil administration, and class relations in Egypt.

Byzantine as well as the Arabic historical tradition exaggerates very greatly the numerical strength of the troops on both sides. In reality, the armies of the two contending sides were not very large. Some scholars set the number of Arabian soldiers who took part in the Syrian and Palestinian campaigns at 27,000 and even then fear that this figure is an exaggeration of the actual number.[47] The Byzantine army was probably even less numerous. Also, the military operations were carried on, not only by the Arabs of the peninsula, but also by the Arabs of the Syrian desert adjoining the Persian and Byzantine borders.

Closer study of early Islam clearly moves the religious element into the background for the political events of the period. "Islam changed into a po- litical force, because only as such could it triumph over its enemies. Had Islam remained forever a simple moral and religious teaching, its existence would have ceased quickly in skeptical, materialistic Arabia, particularly in the hostile atmosphere of Mecca."[48] "The champions of Islam had to deal not so much with the *conversion* of the infidels, as with their *subjection*."[49]

Arabian conquests up to the early eighth century. Constantine IV and the

---

[43] *Organisation militarire de l'Egypte By- zantine*, 119-32. A. E. R. Boak, "Byzantine Imperialism in Egypt," *American Historical Review*, XXXIV (1928), 8.

[44] *Studien zur byzantinischen Verwaltung Aegyptens*, 2.

[45] "La Conquête de l'Égypte par les Arabes," *Revue historique*, CXIX (1915), 282. G. Rouillard, *L'Administration civile de*

l'Egypte byzantine (2nd ed., 1928), 241-48.

[46] "The Byzantine Servile State in Egypt," *Journal of Egyptian Archaeology*, IV (1917), 106.

[47] Caetani, *Studi di storia orientale*, I, 370- 71.

[48] *Ibid.*, III, 3.

[49] I. Goldziher, *Vorlesungen über den Is- lam*, 25.

siege of Constantinople by the Arabs. Justinian II and the Arabs.—After the death of Muhammed (632), his relative, Abu-Bakr (Abu-Bekr) was elected as the leader of the Muslims with the title of Caliph (Khalifa), meaning "vicar." The three subsequent caliphs, Omar, Othman, and Ali, were also raised to their position by election, but did not form a dynasty. These four immediate successors of Muhammed are known as the "orthodox caliphs." The most significant conquests made by the Arabs on Byzantine territory fall in the time of Caliph Omar.

That Muhammed wrote to the rulers of other lands, including Heraclius, proposing that they accept Islam, and that Heraclius responded favorably, is now recognized as a later invention without historical foundation.[50] There are, however, even today scholars who accept this correspondence as a historical fact.[51]

In Muhammed's lifetime only separate detachments of Bedouins crossed the Byzantine border. But in the time of the second caliph, Omar, events developed rapidly. The chronology of the military events of the thirties and forties of the seventh century is obscure and confused, but probably events developed in the following order: In the year 634 the Arabs took possession of the Byzantine fortress Bothra (Bosra), beyond the Jordan; in 635 the Syrian city of Damascus fell; in 636 the battle on the River Yarmuk led to the Arabian conquest of the entire province of Syria; and in 637 or 638 Jerusalem surrendered after a siege which had lasted for two years. The two leading roles in this siege were played by Caliph Omar on one side and the famous defender of orthodoxy, Patriarch Sophronius of Jerusalem on the other. The text of the agreement upon which Sophronius surrendered Jerusalem to Omar and which established certain religious and social guaranties for the Christian population of the city has survived, with, unfortunately, some later alterations. The Christians had succeeded in removing the Holy Cross from Jerusalem before the Arabs entered the city, and in sending it to Constantinople. The conquest of Mesopotamia and Persia, which happened simultaneously with these Byzantine occupations, terminated the first period of the Arabian conquests in Asia. At the end of the thirties the Arabian chief Amr appeared at the eastern border of Egypt and began its conquest. After the death of Heraclius, in the year 641 or 642, the Arabs occupied Alexandria and the victorious Amr sent this message to Omar in Medina: "I have captured a city from the description of which I shall refrain. Suffice it to say that I

[50] See L. Caetani, *Annali dell' Islam*, I, 731–34. Huart regards the embassy of Muhammed to the "Caesar of Byzantium" as doubtful; cf. Huart, *Histoire des Arabes*, I, 145–55. J. Maspero calls the appeal of Muhammed "an Arabian legend which perhaps contains a histori-cal kernel"; *Histoire des patriarches d'Alexandrie*, 23. Diehl and Marçais, *Le Monde oriental*, 174.

[51] Bury, *Constitution of the Later Roman Empire*, II, 261. Butler, *The Arab Conquest of Egypt*, 139 ff.

have seized therein 4000 villas with 4000 baths, 40,000 poll-tax-paying Jews and four hundred places of entertainment for the royalty."[52] Toward the end of the forties the Byzantine Empire was forced to abandon Egypt forever. The conquest of Egypt was followed by further advances of the Arabs toward the western shores of North Africa. By the year 650 Syria, a part of Asia Minor and Upper Mesopotamia, Palestine, Egypt, and part of the Byzantine provinces in North Africa, were already under Arabian sway.

The conquests, by bringing the Arabs to the shores of the Mediterranean Sea, put before them new problems of a maritime nature. They had no fleet and were powerless against the numerous Byzantine vessels to which the new Arabian provinces along the seashore were easily accessible. The Arabs recognized the seriousness of the situation very quickly. The Syrian governor and the future caliph, Muawiya (Moawiya), actively began the construction of numerous vessels whose crews had to be gathered at first among the native Greco-Syrian population accustomed to seafaring. Recent studies of papyri reveal the fact that at the end of the seventh century the construction of ships and their equipment with experienced mariners was one of the great problems of the Egyptian administration.[53]

As early as the fifties of the seventh century, in the time of Constans II, the Arabian vessels of Muawiya began their attacks upon Byzantine districts and occupied the important maritime center, the island of Cyprus. Near the coast of Asia Minor they defeated the Byzantine fleet commanded by the Emperor himself, seized the island of Rhodes, destroying there the famous Colossus of Rhodes, and reached as far as Crete and Sicily, menacing the Aegean Sea and apparently heading for the capital of the Empire. The captives taken during these expeditions, particularly those of Sicily, were transported to the Arabian city of Damascus.

The Arabian conquests of the seventh century deprived the Byzantine Empire of its eastern and southern provinces and caused it to lose its important place as the most powerful state in the world. Territorially reduced, the Byzantine Empire became a state with a predominating Greek population, though not so completely as is believed by some scholars. The districts where the Greeks were in the great majority were Asia Minor with the neighboring islands of the Aegean Sea, and Constantinople with its adjoining province. By this time the Balkan peninsula in general, including the Peloponnesus, had changed considerably in its ethnographic composition because of the appearance of large Slavonic settlements. In the West the Byzantine Empire still possessed the separated parts of Italy which were not included in the Lombard

[52] P. K. Hitti, *History of the Arabs,* 164–65.
[53] See Becker, *Cambridge Medieval History,* II, 352. Becker, *Islamstudien,* I, 96. P. Kahle, "Zur Geschichte des mittelalterlichen Alexandria," *Der Islam,* XII (1922), 32–33, 35.

kingdom, namely, the southern portion of Italy with Sicily and several other neighboring islands of the Mediterranean Sea, Rome, and the exarchate of Ravenna. The Greek population, which centered primarily in the southern portion of these Byzantine possessions in Italy, increased very greatly in the seventh century, when Italy became the refuge for many inhabitants of Egypt and North Africa who did not wish to become subjects of the Arabian conquerors. It may be said that the Roman Empire was at this period transformed into a Byzantine Empire whose problems became narrower and lost their former sweeping nature. Some historians, for instance, Gelzer, think that the heavy territorial losses were indirectly even beneficial for the Byzantine Empire because they removed the foreign national elements, while "the population of Asia Minor and those parts of the Balkan peninsula which still recognized the authority of the Emperor, formed, by language and faith, a perfectly homogeneous and solidly loyal mass."[54] From the middle of the seventh century the attention of the Empire had to be directed chiefly to Constantinople, Asia Minor, and the Balkan peninsula. But even these diminished possessions were constantly threatened by the Lombards, Slavs, Bulgarians, and Arabs. L. Bréhier wrote that "this period initiated for Constantinople that historical rôle of perpetual defense which lasted until the fifteenth century with alternate periods of contraction and expansion."[55]

In connection with the repercussions of the Arabian conquests, it is extremely important to take into serious consideration the data of the Byzantine hagiographic texts, a source which has hitherto been overlooked or neglected. Byzantine hagiography gives a vivid and striking picture of the mass Byzantine migration from the borderland to the center of the Empire under pressure of Arabian invasions by land and sea. Hagiography confirms, enlarges, and illustrates well those extremely brief indications which historians and chroniclers supply. The paramount significance of the Arabian danger in causing congestion and condensation of the population in the central regions of the Empire may be henceforth considered fully proved.[56]

Further Arabian conquests in North Africa were stopped for a time by the energetic resistance of the Berbers. Military activity on the part of the Arabs was also halted because of the internal struggle which broke out between the last "orthodox caliph" Ali and the Syrian governor Muawiya. This bloody strife ended in the year 661 by the massacre of Ali and the triumph of Muawiya, who ascended the throne, inaugurating thus the new dynasty of the Umayyads (Omayyads). The new caliph made Damascus the capital of his kingdom.

[54] *Abriss der byzantinischen Kaisergeschichte*, 951.
[55] "La Transformation de l'empire byzantine sous les Héraclides," *Journal des Savants*, N.S. XV (1917), 402.
[56] See A. P. Rudakov, *Outlines in Byzantine Culture, based on Data from Greek Hagiography*, 65.

After his success in strengthening his power at home, Muawiya renewed the offensive war against the Byzantine Empire by sending his fleet against the Byzantine capital and by reviving the westward movement on North African territory.

The most trying period for the Byzantine Empire came during the reign of the energetic Constantine IV (668–85), when the Arabian fleet crossed the Aegean Sea and the Hellespont, entered the Propontis, and established itself in the city of Cyzicus. Using this harbor as their base, the Arabs repeatedly though unsuccessfully besieged Constantinople. They made their sieges annually, usually during the summer months. The Arabs did not take the capital, chiefly because the Emperor knew how to prepare the city for offering the necessary resistance. The successful defense carried on by the Byzantine army was due primarily to the use of "Greek fire," otherwise called "liquid" or "Marine" fire, invented by the architect Callinicus, a Syrian-Greek fugitive. The common name of this invention has led to some misapprehensions. "Greek fire" was a sort of explosive compound, thrust out by special tubes or siphons, which inflamed when it struck against the vessel of the enemy. The Byzantine fleet was equipped with special "siphonophore" vessels which caused terrific confusion among the Arabs. There were also other methods of hurling this "artificial fire" at the enemy. The peculiar quality of this fire was the fact that it burned even on water. For a very considerable period of time the secret of the composition of this fire was vigilantly guarded by the government, because this new weapon aided the success of the Byzantine fleet in numerous instances.[57]

All the attempts of the Arabian vessels to capture Constantinople failed. In the year 677 the hostile fleet departed, sailing toward the Syrian shores. On its way there, off the southern coast of Asia Minor, it was demolished by a severe storm. The military operations on land in Asia Minor were also unsuccessful for the Arabs. The aged Muawiya was forced to negotiate a peace

[57] The receipt for Greek fire is preserved in a treatise attributed to a certain Marcus Graecus, and was undoubtedly compiled in Greek as late as the ninth century; it was published in a Latin version under the title *Liber ignium a Marco Graeco descriptus*. The best edition is that of M. Berthelot, *La Chimie au moyen âge*, I, 100–35, with a French translation and accurate discussion on the treatise. A more recent edition: Henry W. L. Hime, *The Origin of Artillery*, 45–63. See Krumbacher, *Geschichte der byzantinischen Litteratur*, 636–37, par. 9, and Gibbon, *Decline and Fall of the Roman Empire*, ed. Bury, VI, 10 n. 22, 539–40. They do not know Berthelot's edition and cite the old edition of F. Höfer, *Histoire de la chimie*, I, 491–97. See also Max Jähns, *Handbuch einer Geschichte des Kriegswesens von der Urzeit bis zur Renaissance*, 512–14. C. Oman, *A History of the Art of War in the Middle Ages* (2nd ed., 1924), II, 206, 209–10. C. Zenghelis, "Le Feu gregeois," *Byzantion*, VII (1932), 265–86. Nicholas D. Cheronis, "Chemical Warfare in the Middle Ages. Kallinikos Prepared Fire," *Journal of Chemical Education*, XIV, 8 (1937), 360–65: Kallinikos discovered that the addition of saltpeter to the known incendiary mixtures increased their combustible powers (p. 364).

agreement with the Byzantine Emperor on the condition of paying him a definite annual tribute.[58]

By the successful repulse of the Arabs from Constantinople and by the advantageous peace treaty, Constantine performed a great service, not only for his own Empire, but also for western Europe, which was thus shielded from the serious Muslim menace. It is interesting to note that the success of Constantine made a strong impression in the West. According to one chronicler, when the news of Constantine's accomplishments reached the Khagan of the Avars and other western rulers, "they sent ambassadors with gifts to the Emperor and begged him to establish peaceful and loving relations with them . . . and there came a time of great peace in the East and in the West."[59]

During the first reign of Justinian II (685-95), the successor of Constantine IV, an event which was of considerable significance in the further development of Arabo-Byzantine relations occurred on the eastern Arabian border. The mountains of the Syrian Lebanon were inhabited for a long time by the so-called Mardaites, which may be translated "rebels," "apostates," or "bandits." They were organized as an army and served as the rampart of the Byzantine authorities in this district. After the Arabian conquest of Syria the Mardaites retreated northward to the Arabo-Byzantine border and caused the Arabs much trouble and anxiety by their constant raids upon the neighboring districts. According to a chronicle, the Mardaites formed "a brass wall"[60] which protected Asia Minor from Arabian irruptions. By the peace treaty negotiated under Justinian II the Emperor agreed to force the Mardaites to settle in the inner provinces of the Empire, and for this favor the caliph promised to pay a certain tribute. This step on the part of the Emperor "destroyed the brass wall." In later times the Mardaites are found as seafarers in Pamphylia (Southern Asia Minor), in the Peloponnesus, on the island of Cephalonia (Kephallenia) and in several other districts. Their removal from the Arabian border unquestionably strengthened the position of the Arabs in the newly conquered provinces and facilitated the subsequent Arabian offensive movement into the depth of Asia Minor. There is no sufficient ground for viewing this event, as does Professor Kulakovsky, as an act prompted by "the emperor's consideration for the Christians who were ruled by men of an alien faith."[61] The basis for this transmigration of the Mardaites was a purely political one.

In the sixties of the seventh century, simultaneously with the attempts to seize Constantinople in the East, the Arabian army began its westward movement in North Africa. At the close of the seventh century the Arabs took Car-

[58] See M. Canard, "Les Expéditions des Arabes contre Constantinople dans l'histoire et dans la légende," *Journal Asiatique*, CCVIII (1926), 63–80. Kahle, "Zur Geschichte der mittelalterlichen Alexandria," *Der Islam*, XII (1922), 33.

[59] Theophanes, *Chronographia*, ed. de Boor, 356.

[60] *Ibid.*, 364.

[61] Kulakovsky, *Byzantium*, III, 255.

thage, the capital of the African exarchate, and at the beginning of the eighth century they occupied Septem (now the Spanish fortress, Ceuta) near the Pillars of Hercules. About the same time the Arabs, under the leadership of their general, Tarik, crossed from Africa to Spain and rapidly conquered from the Visigoths the larger part of the peninsula. From the name of Tarik came the modern Arabic name of Gibraltar, meaning "the mountain of Tarik." Thus in the early part of the eighth century the Muhammedan menace to western Europe appeared from a different direction, namely, from the Pyrenean peninsula.

It is interesting to note how fast and how deep the Arab language and culture spread over Spain. A large number of urban Christians adopted Arabic culture though they did not adopt Islam; there were enough of them to constitute a social class, called by the epithet of Arab origin *Mozarabs,* that is, "arabicized." In the ninth century the bishop of Cordoba, Alvaro, complained in one of his sermons:

Many of my coreligionists read verses and fairy tales of the Arabs, study the works of Muhammedan philosophers and theologians not in order to refute them but to learn to express themselves properly in the Arab language more correctly and more elegantly. Who among them studies the Gospels, and Prophets and Apostles? Alas! All talented Christian young men know only the language and literature of the Arabs, read and assiduously study the Arab books. . . . If somebody speaks of Christian books they contemptuously answer that they deserve no attention whatever (*quasi vilissima contemnentes*). Woe! The Christians have forgotten their own language, and there is hardly one among a thousand to be found who can write to a friend a decent greeting letter in Latin. But there is a numberless multitude who express themselves most elegantly in Arabic and make poetry in this language with more beauty and more art than the Arabs themselves.[62]

A similar process may be noted in Egypt. The year 699, when the Arab language was rendered obligatory in public use, marks the final end of Greek and Egyptian literatures on Egyptian soil. After that date we have the era of translation of Coptic works into Arabic.[63]

The relations established between the Arabs and the population of Syria, Palestine, and Egypt differed greatly from those created in North Africa, in the territories of modern Tripoli, Tunis, Algeria, and Morocco. In Syria, Palestine, and Egypt the Arabs did not meet any strong resistance on the part of the population, but rather commanded the support and sympathy of the conquered people. In response the Arabs treated their new subjects with great

[62] *Alvari Cordubensis opera. Indiculus luminosus,* ed. F. H. Florez, *España Sagrada,* XI (1753), 274. See J. Kratchkovsky, *The Arab Culture in Spain,* 11-12.

[63] N. Baynes, *Journal of Egyptian Archae-* ology, XVIII (1932), 90. He refers to L. Lefort, "La Littérature égyptienne aux derniers siècles avant l'invasion arabe," *Chronique d'Egypte,* VI (1931), 315-23.

tolerance. With a few exceptions, they left the Christians their temples and the right to perform religious services, demanding in return only the regular payment of a definite tax and the assured political loyalty of the Christians to the Arabian rulers. Jerusalem, as one of the most revered places of Christendom, remained open to pilgrims who came to Palestine from distant points of western Europe to worship at the holy places. Jerusalem still kept its hostelries and hospitals for these pilgrims. It must also be remembered that in Syria, Palestine, and Egypt the Arabs came in contact with Byzantine civilization, and that influence soon became apparent among the conquerors. Briefly, in Syria and Palestine the conquerors and the conquered established peaceful relations which lasted for a considerable period of time. Somewhat less satisfactory was the state of affairs in Egypt; but even there the attitude to the Christians was quite tolerant, at least during the early years of the Arabian sway.

After the Arabian conquest the patriarchates of the occupied provinces fell into the hands of the Monophysites. In spite of this, the Muslim rulers granted certain privileges to the orthodox population of Syria, Palestine, and Egypt, and after some lapse of time the orthodox patriarchates of Antioch and Alexandria were also restored. These patriarchates still exist. The Arabian historian and geographer of the tenth century, Masudi, said that under the Arabian domination all four sacred mountains—Mount Sinai, Horeb, the Mount of Olives near Jerusalem, and "the Mount of Jordan" (Mount Thabor) —remained in the hands of the orthodox. Only gradually did the Monophysites and other "heretics," including the Muslims, borrow from the orthodox the cult of Jerusalem and the holy places. Along with Mecca and Medina, Jerusalem was later recognized as a sacred Muslim city. For the Muhammedans the sacred significance of the city was established by the fact that Muawiya assumed the rank of caliph in Jerusalem.[64]

Quite different was the state of affairs in North Africa. There the great majority of the Berber tribes, in spite of the official adoption of Christianity, still remained in their former state of barbarism and offered a very strong resistance to the Arabian armies, which repaid this opposition by terrible raids and devastation in the Berber districts. Thousands of captives were taken east and sold there into slavery. "In the dead cities of Tunis," said Diehl, "which are today in most cases in the same condition in which they were left by the Arabian invasion, one still finds at every turn some traces of these formidable raids."[65] When the Arabians finally succeeded in conquering the north African provinces, many of the natives migrated to Italy and Gaul. The African church, once so famous in the annals of Christian history, suffered a very heavy

[64] See J. Wellhausen, *Das Arabische Reich und sein Sturz*, 133; Barthold, *Transactions of* the Oriental College, I (1925), 468–69.
[65] *L'Afrique byzantine*, 590.

blow. Here is what Diehl says with regard to the events of this period: "For two centuries the Byzantine Empire had conserved in these districts the difficult heritage of Rome; for two centuries the empire made the great and steady progress of these provinces possible by the strong defence of their fortresses; for two centuries it upheld in this part of North Africa the traditions of classical civilization and converted the Berbers to a higher culture by means of religious propaganda. In fifty years the Arabian invasion undid all these achievements."[66] In spite of the rapid spread of Islam among the Berbers, however, Christianity still continued to exist among them, and even in the fourteenth century we hear of "some small Christian islands" in North Africa.[67]

The Slavonic advance in the Balkan Peninsula and in Asia Minor and the origin of the Bulgarian kingdom

From the second half of the sixth century the Slavs not only continually attacked and pillaged the Balkan possessions of the Byzantine Empire, but they reached as far as the Hellespont, Thessalonica, southern Greece, and the shores of the Adriatic Sea, and settled there in large numbers. The Avaro-Slavonic attack on the capital occurred in the year 626, during the reign of Heraclius; in the period of the Heraclian dynasty the Slavs persistently advanced into the peninsula and began to populate it very densely. Thessalonica became surrounded by Slavonic tribes and found it difficult to seek protection against their attacks even within its strong city walls.

In their vessels the Slavs descended to the Aegean Sea, attacking the Byzantine fleet and frequently cutting off the supply of provisions to the capital. The emperor Constans II was forced to undertake a campaign "against Sclavinia."[68] From this time dates the migration of large masses of Slavs to Asia Minor and Syria. Under Justinian II a horde of Slavs numbering no less than 80,000, according to V. I. Lamansky,[69] were transported to Opsikion, one of the themes of Asia Minor. One part of them (about 30,000) was mobilized by the Emperor and later took part in the struggle with the Arabs, during which they deserted the Emperor and sided with the Muhammedans. For this terrible offense the remaining Slavs of Opsikion were subjected to formidable massacres. A seal of the Slavonic military colony of Bithynia, a province in the theme of Opsikion, has survived from this period. It is a monument of great value, "a new fragment of Slavonic tribal history," which affords "a

[66] *Ibid.*, 592. E. Mercier, *Histoire de l'Afrique septentrionale*, I, 218.

[67] See H. Leclercq, *L'Afrique chrétienne*, II, 321–23. R. Basset says that the last native Christians among the Berbers disappeared in the twelfth century: *Encyclopédie de l'Islam*, I, 721.

[68] Theophanes, *Chronographia*, ed. de Boor, 347.

[69] *The Slavs in Asia Minor, Africa and Spain*, 3.

ray of light in the twilight of the great migrations," as B. A. Panchenko, who published and interpreted this seal, declared.[70] Beginning with the seventh century, the problem of Slavonic settlements in Asia Minor assumes a very profound significance.

The second half of the seventh century was marked also by the formation of the new Bulgarian kingdom on the northern border of the Byzantine Empire along the shore of the lower Danube, a state whose subsequent history was of extreme importance to the fate of the Empire. During this period the reference is to the old Bulgarians, a people of Hunnic (Turkish) origin, closely related to the tribe of Onogurs. Under Constans II a Bulgarian horde headed by Asparuch (Isperich), forced by the Khazars to move westward from the steppes bordering the Sea of Azov, settled at the mouth of the Danube, and later moved farther south, entering the part of Byzantine territory which is now known as Dobrudja. These Bulgarians, as V. N. Zlatarsky asserted, had previously formed an agreement with the Byzantine Empire by which, as allies of the Empire, they were supposed to protect the Danubian border against the attacks of other barbarians.[71] It is difficult to say whether this assertion is correct or not because very little is known about the early history of the Bulgarians. Even if such an agreement really existed, it did not last very long. The Bulgar horde greatly preoccupied the mind of the Emperor, and in the year 679 Constantine IV undertook a campaign against them. The expedition ended in the complete defeat of the Byzantine army, and the Emperor was forced to negotiate a treaty according to which he bound himself to pay the Bulgarians annual tribute and cede to them the land between the Danube and the Balkans, namely, the former provinces of Moesia and Smaller Scythia (now Dobrudja). The mouth of the Danube and part of the Black Sea coast remained in the hands of the Bulgarians. The newly formed kingdom, recognized perforce by the Byzantine Emperor, became a dangerous neighbor.

After becoming politically established, the Bulgarians gradually widened their territorial possessions and collided with the compact Slavonic population of the neighboring provinces. The Bulgarian newcomers introduced military organization and discipline among the Slavs. Acting as a unifying element among the Slavonic tribes of the peninsula who had lived up to this

[70] "The Slavonic Monument in Bithynia of the Seventh Century," *Transactions of the Russian Archeological Institute in Constantinople,* VIII, 1–2 (1902), 15.

[71] "Bulgarian Chronology," *Izvestia otdeleniya russkago yazyka i slovesnosti Akademii Nauk,* XVII, 2 (1912), 40. Zlatarsky, *A History of the State of Bulgaria in the Middle Ages,* I, 19–122, 135–36. Zlatarsky says that Isperich with his Bulgarians had settled in present day northern Dobrudja in the sixties of the seventh century, but before 668, when Constans II died (p. 138). J. Moravcsik, "Zur Geschichte der Onoguren," *Ungarische Jahrbücher,* X (1930), 72–73, 80, 84, 89.

time in separated groups, the Bulgarians gradually developed a powerful state which was, quite naturally, a great menace to the Byzantine Empire. In subsequent periods numerous military campaigns had to be organized by the Byzantine rulers against the Bulgarians and Slavs. Numerically weaker than the Slavs, the Bulgarian horde of Asparuch soon found itself under the great influence of the Slavonic atmosphere. Great racial changes took place among these Bulgarians; they gradually lost their original Hunnic (Turkish) nationality and became almost completely Slavonized by the middle of the ninth century, although even today they still bear their old name of Bulgarians.[72]

In 1899 and 1900 the Russian Archeological Institute at Constantinople undertook to excavate the supposed site of the older Bulgarian seat (aul) and discovered extremely valuable survivals. On the site of the old capital of the Bulgarian kingdom (Pliska, or Pliskova) near the modern village of Aboba in northeastern Bulgaria, somewhat northeast of the city of Shumla (Shumen), the excavators discovered the foundations of the palace of the early Khans of Bulgaria and part of its walls with towers and gates, the foundations of a large church, inscriptions, many artistic and ornamental objects, gold and bronze coins, and lead seals.[73] Unfortunately, these materials cannot be adequately evaluated and explained because the sources referring to this period are very scanty. One must confine himself at present to hypotheses and conjectures. Th. I. Uspensky, who directed the excavations, stated that the "discoveries made by the Institute on the site of the camp near Shumla have brought to light very important data which afford sufficient basis for the formation of a clear idea about the Bulgarian horde which settled in the Balkans, and about the gradual transformations caused by the influence of relations with the Byzantine Empire."[74] "As evidenced by the earliest monuments of Bulgarian customs and manners, found during the excavation of their old capital," the same scholar said, "the Bulgarians soon became subject to the cultural influence of Constantinople, and their Khans gradually assumed in their court the customs and ceremonies of the Byzantine court."[75] The major part of the monuments unearthed during the excavations belong to an epoch later than the time of Asparuch, chiefly to the eighth and ninth centuries. The excavations are far from being completed.

The proposal to move the capital of the Empire.—In the middle of the seventh century the position of Constantinople changed radically. The Arabian conquest of the eastern and southeastern Byzantine provinces, frequent

---

[72] See L. Niederle, *Manuel de l'antiqué slave*, I, 100–1.

[73] See "Materials of Bulgarian Antiquity. Aboba-Pliska," *Transactions of the Russian Archeological Institute in Constantinople*, X (1905).

[74] *Byzantine Empire*, I, 777.

[75] *Ibid.*, 729.

Arabian attacks on the provinces of Asia Minor, the successful expeditions of the Arabian fleet in the Mediterranean and Aegean Seas, and, on the other hand, the rise of the Bulgarian kingdom on the northern border and the gradual advance of the Balkan Slavs toward the capital, the Aegean coast, and into Greece created new and singular conditions in Constantinople, which now no longer felt secure. The capital had always drawn its power from the eastern provinces, and now a part of these had been taken away from the Empire, while the remaining part became exposed to danger and threats on many sides. Only with reference to these new conditions can we properly analyze the desire on the part of Constans II to leave Constantinople and move the capital back to old Rome, or some other point in Italy. The chroniclers explain the Emperor's departure from the capital by the fact that he was forced to flee by the hatred of the people, aroused by the Emperor's murder of his brother,[76] but this explanation can hardly be accepted from a historical point of view.

The true reason was that the Emperor no longer considered it safe to remain in Constantinople. Besides, it is very likely that he realized the inevitable approach of the Arabian menace from North Africa to Italy and Sicily, and decided to strengthen the power of the Empire in the western part of the Mediterranean Sea by his presence, which would enable him to take all measures for preventing the Arabs from spreading their conquest beyond the boundaries of Egypt. It is probable that the Emperor did not intend to leave Constantinople forever, but desired only to establish for the Empire a second central point in the West, as had been the case in the fourth century, hoping that it might aid in halting the further advance of the Arabs. In any event, in modern historical literature the westward yearning of Constans II, somewhat puzzling at first glance, is explained by no personal sensitivity of the Emperor, but by political conditions.

Meanwhile, the state of affairs in Italy did not promise peace. The exarchs of Ravenna, having ceased to feel the strong will of the Emperor because of the great distance which separated them from Constantinople and also because of the extreme complexity of conditions in the East, openly tended toward defection. The Lombards were in possession of a large part of Italy. The Emperor's authority, however, was still recognized in Rome, Naples, Sicily, and the southernmost part of Italy, where the population was predominantly Greek.

Upon leaving Constantinople, Constans II started out for Italy by way of Athens, and, after a sojourn in Rome, Naples, and the southern part of Italy, established himself in the Sicilian city of Syracuse. He spent the last five years of his reign in Italy without succeeding in accomplishing his original projects.

[76] George Cedrenus, *Historiarum compendium*, Bonn ed., I, 762.

His struggle with the Lombards was not successful. Sicily was still constantly menaced by the Arabs. A plot was formed against the Emperor and he was killed in a pitiful manner in one of the Syracusan bathhouses. After his death the idea of transferring the capital to the West was abandoned, and his son, Constantine IV, remained in Constantinople.

RELIGIOUS POLICY OF THE DYNASTY

Monotheletism and the "Exposition of Faith"

The Persian campaigns of Heraclius, by reclaiming for the Empire its Monophysitic provinces—Syria, Palestine, and Egypt—once more brought to the fore the problem of the government's attitude toward the Monophysites. Even during his campaigns Heraclius began negotiations with the Monophysitic bishops of the eastern provinces in order to bring about some sort of church unity by making certain concessions in the realm of dogma. It seemed that unity was possible if the Orthodox Church consented to recognize that Jesus Christ had two substances and one operation (energy, ἐνέργεια), or one will (θέλημα). From the last Greek word the teaching derived the name of Monotheletism, by which it is known in history.[77] Antioch and Alexandria, represented by their Monophysitic patriarchs appointed by Heraclius, were willing to work towards an agreement, as was Patriarch Sergius of Constantinople. But against the Monothelete doctrine rose the Palestinian monk, Sophronius, who lived in Alexandria, and his impressive arguments against the new teaching threatened to undermine the conciliatory policy of Heraclius. The Roman pope, Honorius, recognizing the danger of all disputes of dogmatical problems which had not been settled by the ecumenical councils, proclaimed that the teaching of one will was correct. Sophronius, raised to the rank of patriarch of Jerusalem, a position which afforded him ample opportunity for exerting still greater and wider influence, sent a synodical letter to the bishop of Constantinople in which he argued with great theological skill the unorthodoxy of the Monotheletic teaching. Anticipating the approach of great church disturbances, Heraclius issued the Ecthesis (ἔκθεσις) or Exposition of Faith, which recognized two natures and one will in Jesus Christ. The Christological part of this document was composed by Patriarch Sergius. The Emperor hoped that the Ecthesis would do much to reconcile the Monophysites with the orthodox, but his hopes were not realized. The new pope did not approve of the Ecthesis, and, attempting to defend the doctrine of the existence of two wills and two operations, proclaimed the Monotheletic teaching a heresy. This action introduced an unex-

---

[77] A very good article on Monotheletism   ed. Vacant and Amann, X, 2, cols. 2307-23.
is in *Le Dictionnaire de théologie catholique,*

pected animosity between the pope and the Emperor. Moreover, the Ecthesis was published when it could not have the great effect upon which Heraclius was counting. The Emperor's chief aim was to reconcile the eastern Monophysitic provinces with orthodoxy. But in the year 638, when the Ecthesis was published, Syria, Palestine, and the Byzantine portion of Mesopotamia no longer formed part of the Byzantine Empire, for they had been occupied by the Arabs. There was still the province of Egypt, but even its days were numbered. The Monophysitic question had lost its political importance, and the decree of Heraclius was of no consequence. For that matter, similar earlier attempts at religious compromise had never led to satisfactory results and never succeeded in solving the main problems, chiefly because of the constant obstinacy of the majority on each side.

"Type of Faith" of Constans II

After the death of Heraclius, in the reign of Constans II, religious policy developed as follows. The Emperor still remained an adherent of Monotheletism in spite of the fact that the movement had lost its political importance and stood in the way of friendly relations with the papal throne. After the loss of Egypt, conquered by the Arabs in the forties, the Emperor made a series of attempts at reconciliation with the pope, offering to make several changes in the doctrines of the Monothelete teaching. With this aim in view, Constans II issued in the year 648 the Typus (τύπος), or "Type of Faith," which forbade "all Orthodox subjects being in immaculate Christian faith and belonging to the Catholic and Apostolic Church, to contend and to quarrel with one another over one will or one operation [energy], or two operations [energies] and two wills."[78] Besides prohibiting disputes, the Type ordered the removal of the written discussions on this question, which meant the Ecthesis of Heraclius, posted in the narthex of St. Sophia. But this measure of Constans II did not effect the desired religious peace. In the presence of representatives of the Greek clergy, at the Lateran Synod, Pope Martin condemned "the most impious Ecthesis [*impiissima Ecthesis*]," and the "vicious Typus [*scelerosus Typus*]," and declared all those whose names were connected with the composition of the two decrees guilty of heresy.[79] The outstanding theologian of the seventh century, Maximus Confessor, resolutely opposed the Type as well as the Monothelete teaching in general. Great dissatisfaction with the Emperor's religious policy was also growing stronger in the eastern church.

Angered by the pope's action at the Lateran Synod, Constans II ordered the exarch of Ravenna to arrest Martin and send him to Constantinople. The

[78] J. D. Mansi, *Sacrorum conciliorum nova et amplissima collectio*, X, 1029–32; in English, K. J. von Hefele, *A History of the Coun-* *cils of the Church* (1896), V, 95–96.
[79] Mansi, *ibid.*, 1157–58; Hefele, *ibid.*, 112–13.

exarch carried out these orders, and Martin was convicted at Constantinople of an attempt to initiate an uprising against the Emperor in the western provinces. He was subjected to terrible humiliations and confined to prison. Somewhat later he was sent to the distant city of Cherson, on the southern coast of the Crimea, the usual place of exile for the disgraced in the Byzantine period. He died shortly after his arrival to the city. In his letters from Cherson the pope complained of bad living conditions and asked his friends to send him food, particularly bread, which "is talked of, but has never been seen."[80] Unfortunately Martin's letters give little interesting data concerning the cultural and economic conditions of Cherson in the seventh century.

The Emperor and the patriarch of Constantinople continued negotiations with the successors of Martin on the papal throne, and finally made peace with the second successor, Vitalian. The schism in the churches ceased. This religious reconciliation with Rome was politically important for the Byzantine Empire because it strengthened the position of the Emperor in Italy.

The famous opponent of Monotheletism, Maximus Confessor, was arrested by the Italian exarch and transferred to Constantinople, where he was convicted by a jury and cruelly mutilated. Maximus died as a martyr in distant exile.

The Sixth Ecumenical Council and religious peace

Although Monotheletism had lost its political significance, it still continued to sow discord among the people even after the prohibition of the Type. Then the successor of Constans II, Constantine IV, desirous of establishing complete religious peace in the Empire, convoked in the year 680 in Constantinople the Sixth Ecumenical Council, which condemned Monotheletism and recognized two natures in Jesus Christ displayed in his one hypostasis, and "two natural wills and operations [energies] going together harmoniously for the salvation of the human race."[81]

Peace with Rome was definitely re-established. The communication sent by the sixth council to the pope addressed him as "the head of the first see of the Universal Church, standing on the firm rock of faith," and declared that the pope's message to the Emperor expounded the true principles of religion.[82]

Thus, in the time of Constantine IV, the Byzantine government definitely expressed itself against Monophysitism and Monotheletism. The patriarchates of Alexandria, Jerusalem, and Antioch, torn from the Empire by the Arabian

[80] Martini Papae *Epistola*, XVI; ed. Migne, *Patrologia Latina*, LXXXVII, 202. See H. K. Mann, *The Lives of the Popes in the Early Middle Ages* (2nd ed., 1925), I, pt. 1, 400.

[81] Mansi, *Amplissima collectio conciliorum*, XI, 629–40; Hefele, *Councils of the Church*, V, 175.
[82] Mansi, *ibid.*, 683–88.

conquest, nevertheless took part in the Sixth Ecumenical Council by sending their representatives. The patriarch of Antioch, Macarius, who apparently lived in Constantinople and exercised jurisdiction only in Cilicia and Isauria,[83] argued the case of Monotheletism at the council, and for this stand was deposed and excommunicated. The decisions of the sixth council proved to Syria, Palestine, and Egypt that Constantinople had abandoned the desire to find a path for religious reconciliation with the provinces which no longer formed part of the Byzantine Empire. Religious peace with Rome was reached by way of resolute alienation from the Monophysitic and Monotheletic population of the eastern provinces, a fact which aided greatly the further strengthening of the Arabian power in these provinces. Syria, Palestine, and Egypt became definitely separated from the Byzantine Empire.

It cannot be said that the agreement reached with Rome on the Sixth Ecumenical Council lasted very long. Even in the reign of Justinian II, the successor of Constantine IV, relations between the Byzantine Empire and Rome became strained again. Desirous of completing the task of the Fifth and Sixth Ecumenical Councils, Justinian II summoned in 691 a synod in Constantinople, which was held in the Domed Hall. This council was called Trullan,[84] from the place of its meetings, or Quinisext (*Quinisextum*), because it completed the task of the two preceding ecumenical councils. This synod called itself ecumenical. Pope Sergius refused to sign the acts of the council by reason of certain clauses, such as the prohibition of fasting on Saturdays, and the permission to priests to marry. Following the example of Constans II, who had exiled Martin to the Crimea, Justinian ordered Sergius to be arrested and brought to Constantinople. But the army of Italy protected him against the imperial commissioner, who would have lost his life had it not been for the intercession of the pope.[85]

During the second reign of Justinian II (705–11), Pope Constantine came at the invitation of the Emperor to Constantinople, the last pope to be summoned to the capital of the Byzantine Empire. He was treated with highest honors by Justinian, who, the papal biographer claims, prostrated himself before the pope with the imperial crown upon his head, and kissed his feet.[86] Justinian and the pope reached a satisfactory compromise, but there is no exact information on it. Pope Constantine, as the German church historian, Hefele, pointed out, had by this time undoubtedly attained the fair middle path which Pope John VIII (872–882) subsequently followed by declaring that "he accepted all those canons which did not contradict the true faith,

[83] See E. W. Brooks, *English Historical Review,* XXXIV (1919), 117.

[84] In Greek ὁ τροῦλλος means a dome or cupola.

[85] See F. Görres, "Justinian II und das römische Papsttum," *Byzantinische Zeitschrift,* XVII (1908), 440–50.

[86] *Liber Pontificalis,* ed. L. Duchesne, I, 391.

good morals, and the decrees of Rome."[87] Pope Constantine returned safely to Rome and was welcomed by the people with great joy. Religious peace seemed finally established within the greatly reduced boundaries of the Empire.

ORIGIN AND DEVELOPMENT OF THEME ORGANIZATION

In Byzantine history the organization of the themes is usually connected with the epoch of the Heraclian dynasty. The organization of the themes means that peculiar provincial organization, prompted by the conditions of the times, whose distinguishing feature was the growth of the military power of the provincial governors, and finally their complete superiority over the civil authorities. This process was not sudden but gradual. For a long time the Greek word *theme* (τὸ θέμα) meant a military corps stationed in a province, and only later, probably in the eighth century, was it applied not only to the military detachment, but also to the province where it was stationed. Thus it began to be applied to the administrative divisions of the Empire.

The main Byzantine source on the problem of the themes is the work *On Themes,* written by Constantine Porphyrogenitus, the emperor of the tenth century, and hence dating from a period much later than the epoch of the Heraclian dynasty. This work has also the disadvantage of being based in some places on geographical works of the fifth and sixth centuries, used very superficially or copied verbatim. But although this work does not give much information on theme organization in the seventh century, it does connect the beginning of the system with the name of Heraclius. The Emperor said: "Since the reign of Heraclius the Libyan (i.e. African), the Roman Empire has become reduced in size and mutilated both from the east and from the west."[88] Very interesting, though not yet fully explained, material on this problem is found in the works of the Arabian geographers Ibn-Khurdadhbah (Khordadhbeh), of the first half of the ninth century, and Kudama, of the early tenth century, though these men, of course, were not contemporaries of the Heraclian epoch. For the study of the earlier period of the theme system, historians have made use of occasional remarks of chroniclers and especially of the Latin message of Justinian II to the pope, dating from the year 687, regarding the confirmation of the Sixth Ecumenical Council. This epistle contains a list of the military districts of that period, not yet referred to as themes, but denoted by the Latin word *exercitus* (army).[89] In historical sources of that time the Latin word *exercitus* and the Greek word στρατός or sometimes

---

[87] *Councils of the Church,* V, 240.
[88] *De thematibus,* 12.
[89] Mansi, *Amplissima collectio conciliorum,*

XI, 737–38. See also H. Gelzer, *Die Genesis der byzantinischen Themenverfassung,* 10–17.

στράτευμα were often used in the sense of a territory or province with military administration.

The true precursors of the theme organization were the exarchates of Ravenna and Carthage (Africa), established at the end of the sixth century. The attacks of the Lombards caused the drastic change in the administration of Italy, as those of the Berbers (Moors) caused in North Africa. The central government, with a view toward creating a more efficient defense against its enemies, attempted to form large territorial units with strong military authorities in its border provinces. The Persian, and later the Arabian, conquests of the seventh century, which deprived the Byzantine Empire of its eastern provinces, completely changed conditions in Asia Minor. From a land which practically never needed any serious defense it became transformed into a territory constantly and strongly menaced by its Muslim neighbors. The Byzantine government was forced to undertake decisive measures on its eastern border: military forces were regrouped and new administrative divisions were established, giving predominance to the military authorities, whose services at this time were of extreme importance. Equally great was the menace from the newly constructed Arabian fleet, which was almost master of the Mediterranean Sea as early as the seventh century, and threatened the shores of Asia Minor, the islands of the Archipelago, and even the shores of Italy and Sicily. In the northwest of the Empire the Slavs occupied a considerable part of the Balkan peninsula and penetrated far into Greece, including the Peloponnesus. On the northern border rose the Bulgarian kingdom (in the second half of the seventh century). These altered conditions forced the Empire to resort in the most insecure provinces to the establishment of extensive districts ruled by strong military power, similar to the exarchates. The Empire was militarized.[90]

The fact that the themes were not the result of one legislative act meant that each theme had its own history, sometimes a rather long one. The problem of the origin of themes can be solved only by special research on each individual theme. Kulakovsky's writings are of interest in this connection. The military measures taken by Heraclius after his victory over Persia were, he believed, the point of departure of the new administrative regime. Bréhier supported Kulakovsky in this view. Armenia may be an example of the militarization of the empire under pressure of the Persian danger, for when Heraclius reorganized Armenia, he appointed no civil administrator. The authority was purely military. The theme system, then, was merely the ap-

[90] See E. Stein, "Ein Kapitel vom persischen und vom byzantinischen Staate," *Byzantinisch-Neugriechische Jahrbücher,* I (1920), 76, 84. E. Darkó, "La militarizatione dell' Impero Bizantino," *Studi bizantini e neoellenici,* V (1939), 88–99.

plication to other provinces of the regime instituted in Armenia.[91] Th. Uspensky called attention to the Slavs. When they inundated the Balkan peninsula about the time of the theme formation, he said, they "contributed to the formation of the theme organization in Asia Minor by supplying a considerable number of volunteers for the colonization of Bithynia."[92] This statement is to be taken with caution, however, for there is no evidence of a mass Slav immigration into Asia Minor before the transporting of 80,000 Slavs to Opsikion under Justinian II at the end of the seventh century.

It is definitely known that for defense against the oncoming danger there were established in the East in the seventh century the following four large military districts, later called themes: 1) Armeniaci (Armeniakoi) in northeast Asia Minor bordering on Armenia; 2) Anatolici (Anatolikoi, from the Greek word Anatoli, ἀνατολή, "the east"); 3) "the imperial God-guarded Opsikion" (Greek ὀψίκιον, Latin, *obsequium*), in Asia Minor near the Sea of Marmora; and 4) the maritime *thema Caravisionorum,* called later, perhaps in the eighth century, Cibyrrhaeot (Cibyraiot), on the southern shore of Asia Minor and in the neighboring islands. The first two, occupying the entire middle portion of Asia Minor from the borders of Cilicia in the east to the shores of the Aegean Sea in the west were intended to serve as a protection against the Arabs. The third was to shield the capital from external enemies. The fourth, the maritime theme, was intended as a defense against the Arabian fleet.

A striking analogy exists between this theme organization and the militarization of the Persian Empire of the Sassanids, under the kings Kawadh and Chosroes Nushirvan, in the sixth century. In Persia also the whole territory of the empire was divided among four military commands. The analogy is so complete and so close that Stein explained it as a deliberate intention on the part of the Emperor to adopt the Persian reform. The sources, he said, give reason to believe that Heraclius studied the reforms of both Persian monarchs and perhaps even had access to some material from the Persian archives. "To learn from one's enemy has always been the desire of all true statesmen."[93]

In the Balkan peninsula the district of Thrace was created against the Slavs and Bulgarians, and later, perhaps at the end of the seventh century, the Greek military district of Hellas or Helladici (Helladikoi) was formed against Slavonic irruptions into Greece. About the same time, probably, the district of Sicily was organized against the maritime attacks of the Arabs, who were be-

[91] See Kulakovsky's articles on this problem, *Byzantium*, III, 287–431. See L. Bréhier, *Journal des Savants*, N.S. XV (1917), 412, 505.

[92] *Byzantine Empire,* I, 685–86. Kulakovsky, *Byzantium*, III, 395.
[93] Stein, *Byzantinisch-Neugriechische Jahrbücher,* I (1920), 84–85.

ginning to threaten the western part of the Mediterranean Sea. With very few exceptions these districts or themes were governed by strategi (*strategoi*). The ruler of the Cibyraiot (Cibyrrhaeot) theme was called the *drungarius* (vice-admiral), and the governor of Opsikion bore the title of *comes*.

The organization of the themes, then, may be traced back to Heraclius' attempt to militarize the Empire under pressure of the Persian danger. He succeeded in accomplishing, however, as far as is known, the reorganization only of Armenia. The brilliant victory over Persia which led to the recovery of Syria, Palestine, and Egypt, created an urgent need for reorganization in those provinces. Heraclius, however, had no time to accomplish this task because he speedily lost them again to the Arabs. The Persian danger had been eliminated, but a new, more menacing, Arab danger arose in its stead. Heraclius' successors, following his lead, created military districts (later called themes) against the Arabs. Simultaneously the emperors were led by the growing Slavonic and Bulgarian menace in the north of the Empire to extend these methods of defense and protection in the Balkan peninsula and in Greece.

In these military districts and in the exarchates the civil authorities did not immediately give way to military rulers. The civil administration, the civil provinces (eparchies), continued to exist under the new order in the majority of districts. The military authorities, however, invested with full powers in view of external dangers, steadily made themselves felt more and more strongly in civil administration. "Heraclius' seed," Stein remarked, "has marvelously grown."[94]

Heraclius has left some trace in Byzantine legislation. In the published collection of Novels his period is represented by four which deal with various questions referring to the clergy and are dated from 612 to 629. There are some indications of other laws of Heraclius which have not been preserved in their entirety but of which there are traces; and it is possible to prove that some of these laws were accepted and introduced into legislation in the West by the Germans and in the East by the Arabs. This can be proved at least for some laws dealing with forgery of coins, official seals, and public documents.[95]

PERIOD OF ANARCHY (711–17)

The three accidental rulers, Vardan or Philippicus, Anastasius II, and Theodosius III, who occupied the throne after Justinian II, were deposed in

[94] E. Stein, *Studien der Justinus II und Tiberius*, 140. G. Ostrogorsky, "Über die vermeintliche Reformtätigkeit der Issaurier," *Byzantinische Zeitschrift*, XXX (1929–30), 397–400.

[95] See R. Lopez, "Byzantine Law in the Seventh Century and its Reception by the Germans and the Arabs," *Byzantion*, XVI, 2 (1944), 445–61. The text of Heraclius' novels in K. E. Zachariä von Lingenthal, *Jus graecoromanum*, III, 38–48. J. and P. Zepos, *Jus graecoromanum*, I, 27–39.

rapid succession. Anarchy and mutiny prevailed throughout the Empire. By favoring Monotheletism, Vardan broke off peaceful relations with Rome. Anastasius, however, succeeded in restoring the former agreement with the pope. In external affairs the Empire was particularly unsuccessful. The Bulgarians, determined to take revenge for the murder of Justinian, who had been friendly towards them, moved southward as far as Constantinople. The Arabs, advancing persistently by land through Asia Minor and by water in the Aegean Sea and the Propontis, also menaced the capital. The Empire was going through a very critical period, similar to the one which had preceded the revolution of the year 610, and once more it was in need of an able, energetic man who could save it from inevitable ruin. Such a man appeared in the person of the strategus of the theme of Anatolici, Leo, a man with a very wide following. The weak Theodosius III, realizing his complete impotence against the approaching menace, renounced his imperial rank, and in the year 717 Leo entered Constantinople in triumphant procession and was crowned emperor by the patriarch in the temple of St. Sophia. He spared the life of Theodosius III. Leo thus rose from a military ruler entrusted with wide power in the theme organization to emperor.

LITERATURE, LEARNING, AND ART

With regard to letters and art, the period from 610 to 717 is the darkest epoch in the entire existence of the Empire. After the abundant activity of the preceding century, intellectual creativeness seemed to have died out completely. The main cause of the sterility of this period must be sought in the political conditions of the Empire, which was forced to direct all its energies toward defense against its external enemies. The Persian, and later the Arabian, conquest of the culturally advanced and intellectually productive eastern provinces of Syria, Palestine, Egypt, and North Africa, the Arabian menace to Asia Minor, the islands of the Mediterranean, and even the capital itself, the Avaro-Slavonic menace in the Balkan peninsula—all this created conditions practically prohibitive of any intellectual and artistic activity. Unfavorable conditions prevailed, not only in the provinces torn away from the Empire, but also in those which still formed part of it.

During this entire period the Byzantine Empire had not a single historian. Only the deacon of St. Sophia, George of Pisidia (a province in Asia Minor), who lived in the days of Heraclius, described in harmonious and correct verses the military campaigns of Heraclius against the Persians and the Avars. He left three historical works: (1) *On the Expedition of Emperor Heraclius against the Persians,* (2) *On the Attack of the Avars on Constantinople in the Year 626, and Their Defeat through the Intercession of the Holy Virgin,* and (3) *Heraclias,* a panegyric in honor of the Emperor on the occasion of his final victory over the Persians. Among other works of a polemic, elegiac, and theological nature we might point out the *Hexaemeron* (*Six Days*), a kind of philosophical-theological didactic poem on the creation of the universe with allusions to contemporary events. This work, dealing with the favorite subject of Christian writers, spread beyond the borders of the Byzantine Empire; for instance, a Slavo-Russian translation was made in the fourteenth century. The poetical genius of George of Pisidia was appreciated in later centuries, and in the eleventh century the famous Byzantine scholar and philosopher, Michael Psellus, was even asked to solve the problem: "Who was a better writer of verse, Euripides or George of Pisidia?" The modern scholarly world regards George as the best secular poet of the Byzantine period.[96]

Among the chroniclers were John of Antioch and the anonymous author of the *Chronicon Paschale* (*Easter Chronicle*). John of Antioch, who lived probably in the time of Heraclius, wrote a universal chronicle including the period from Adam to the death of the Emperor Phocas (610). In view of the fact that this work has survived only in fragments, there have been long disputes among scholars with regard to the identity of the author. Sometimes he has been even identified with John Malalas, also a native of Syrian Antioch. Insofar as the surviving fragments show, the work of John of Antioch should be recognized as much superior to the work of Malalas, for it does not consider world history from the narrow confines of a native of Antioch, and has, therefore, a much broader historical aim. It also exhibits a more skillful use of early sources. It was also in the time of Heraclius that some unknown clergyman composed the so-called *Chronicon Paschale* (*Easter Chronicle*) which, although it is nothing but a list of events from Adam until A.D. 629, contains several rather interesting historical remarks. The main value of this unoriginal work lies in the determination of the sources used and in that part which deals with events contemporary with the author.

In the field of theology the Monotheletic disputes of the seventh century, just as the Monophysitic disputes of earlier ages, gave rise to a fairly extensive literature which has not, however, been preserved, having been condemned by the councils of the seventh century and destined to perish early, in a manner similar to that of the Monophysitic writings. This literature must be judged, therefore, almost exclusively on the basis of the acts of the Sixth Ecumenical Council and the works of Maximus Confessor, which quote fragments of these extinguished works in the course of confuting them.

Maximus Confessor was one of the most remarkable Byzantine theologians. As a contemporary of Heraclius and Constans II, he was a convinced defender

[96] Krumbacher, *Geschichte der byzantinischen Litteratur,* 709.

of orthodoxy during the period of the Monothelete disputes of the seventh century. For his convictions he was sent to prison and, after numerous tortures, exiled to the distant Caucasian province of Lazica, where he remained until the end of his days. In his works dealing with polemics, the exegesis of the Scriptures, asceticism, mysticism, and liturgics he reflected chiefly the influence of the three famous church fathers—Athanasius the Great, Gregory of Nazianzus, and Gregory of Nyssa—as well as the mystical views of the so-called "Dionysius the Areopagite" (Pseudo-Areopagite), widely spread in the Middle Ages. The writings of Maximus were of particular importance in the development of Byzantine mystics. "By combining the dry speculative mysticism of Dionysius the Areopagite," wrote one of the modern students of Maximus, "with the living ethical problems of contemplative asceticism, the blessed Maximus created a living type of Byzantine mysticism which reappeared in the works of numerous later ascetics. He may thus be considered the creator of Byzantine mysticism in the full sense of the term."[97] Unfortunately Maximus did not leave a systematic account of his views, and they must be winnowed from his numerous writings. Besides his theological and mystical writings, Maximus left also a large number of interesting letters.

The influence and importance of the writings of Maximus were not confined to the East alone. They found their way into the West and were later reflected in the writings of the famous western thinker of the ninth century, John the Scot Eriugena (Johannes Scotus Eriugena), who was also greatly interested in the works of Dionysius the Areopagite, and later averred that he attained an understanding of the "obscurest" ideas of Dionysius only through the "marvelous manner" in which they were explained by Maximus, whom Eriugena calls "the divine philosopher," "the all-wise," "the most distinguished of teachers," etc. Maximus' work on Gregory the Theologian was translated by Eriugena into Latin.[98] A younger contemporary of Maximus, Anastasius Sinaita (of Mount Sinai), developed his own polemic and exegetic literary works in a manner similar to that of Maximus, exhibiting, however, much less genius.

In the field of hagiography one might point out the patriarch of Jerusalem, Sophronius, who lived through the Arabian siege of the sacred city and wrote an extensive narrative of the martyrdom and miracles of the Egyptian national saints, Cyrus and Johannes. This work contains much information on geography and on the history of manners and customs. Still greater in interest are the writings of Leontius, bishop of Neapolis in Cyprus, who also lived in the

[97] S. Epifanovich, *The Blessed Maximus Confessor and Byzantine Theology*, 137; Krumbacher, *Geschichte der byzantinischen Litteratur*, 63, 141.

[98] See A. Brilliantov, *The Influence of Eastern Theology upon Western as Evidenced by the Works of John the Scot Eriugena*, 50–52.

seventh century. He was the author of several "lives," among which the *Life of John the Merciful,* archbishop of Alexandria in the seventh century, is particularly valuable for the history of the social and economic life of the period. Leontius of Neapolis differs from the great majority of hagiographs in that he wrote his *Lives of Saints* for the mass of the population; hence his language reflects a strong influence of the popular spoken language.[99]

In the field of church hymn-writing the seventh century is represented by Andrew (Andreas) of Crete, a native of Damascus, who spent the major part of his life in Syria and Palestine after they had come under Arab sway. He was later appointed archbishop of Crete. As a writer of hymns he is famous chiefly because of his Great Canon, which is read even today in the orthodox church twice during Lent. Some parts of the Canon show the influence of Romanus the Hymn-writer (*Melode*). The Canon reviews the principal events of the Old Testament, beginning with the fall of Adam, and the words and deeds of the Saviour.

This brief survey of literary events during the dark and trying years of the Heraclian dynasty shows that most of the limited number of Byzantine writers of the period came from the eastern provinces, some already under the new rule of the Muslim conquerors.

In view of the external events of the Heraclian dynasty, it is not surprising that no monuments of art of that period exist today. However, the very small number of surviving monuments of the seventh century speak clearly of the solidity of the foundations laid for the artistic life of Byzantium in the Golden Age of Justinian the Great. And though, beginning with the second half of the sixth century, Byzantine art makes itself felt only very slightly within the Empire, its influence in the seventh century is very clearly marked beyond the borders of the Empire. A number of dated churches of Armenia represent splendid examples of Byzantine influence. Among these are the Cathedral of Edgmiatsin (Etschmiadzin), restored between 611 and 628, and the church of the citadel of Ani (622). The mosque of Omar at Jerusalem, built in 687–90, is a purely Byzantine work. Some frescoes of Santa Maria Antica at Rome belong to the seventh or the beginning of the eighth century.[100]

---

[99] See H. Gelzer, *Leontios' von Neapolis Leben des heiligen Johannes des Barmherzigen Erzbischofs von Alexandrien,* xli.

[100] See Charles Diehl, *Manuel d'art byzantine,* I, 329–59.

CHAPTER V: THE ICONOCLASTIC EPOCH

(717–867)

UNTIL recently the Emperor Leo III (717–741), the originator of the new dynasty, was called an Isaurian in historical writings, and his descendants were usually referred to às the Isaurian dynasty. However, at the close of the nineteenth century the opinion was advanced that Leo III was not an Isaurian by birth, but a Syrian.[1] This view is at present accepted by some scholars,[2] but is rejected by others.[3] The confusion on this point can be traced back to the early ninth century chronicler Theophanes, author of the main source on Leo's origin. He wrote: "Leo the Isaurian was a native of Germanicea, and was in reality from Isauria."[4] The papal librarian Anastasius, who translated Theophanes into Latin in the second half of the ninth century, made no mention of Isauria but stated that Leo came from the people of Germanicea and was a Syrian by birth (*genere Syrus*).[5] The *Life* of Stephen the Younger also calls Leo "a Syrian by birth" (ὁ συρογενής).[6] Germanicea was situated within the northern boundaries of Syria, east of Cilicia. An Arabian source referred to Leo as "a Christian citizen of Marash," i.e. Germanicea, who could speak fluently and correctly both the Arabic and Roman languages.[7] There is no reason to suppose that Theophanes confused the Syrian Germanicea with Germanicopolis, a city of the Isaurian province.[8] The Syrian origin of Leo is quite probable.

The son of Leo III, Constantine V Copronymus (741–75), married Irene, daughter of the Khagan of the Khazars (Chazars). He had by her a son, Leo IV, often called the Khazar (Chazar), who reigned from 775 to 780. Leo IV married a Greek girl from Athens, another Irene, who at his death became ruler of the Empire because her son, Constantine VI, proclaimed Em-

---

[1] See K. Schenk, "Kaiser Leons III Walten im Innern," *Byzantinische Zeitschrift,* V (1896), 296 ff.

[2] See N. Iorga, "Les origines de l'iconoclasme," *Bulletin de la section historique de l'Académie roumaine,* XI (1924), 147.

[3] J. A. Kulakovsky, *History of Byzantium,* III, 319.

[4] *Chronographia,* ed. C. de Boor, 391.

[5] *Chronographia tripertita,* ed. C. de Boor, 251.

[6] Ed. J. P. Migne, *Patrologia Graeca,* C, 1084.

[7] See E. W. Brooks, "The Campaign of 716–18 from Arabic Sources," *Journal of Hellenic Studies,* XIX (1899), 21–22.

[8] See Th. I. Uspensky, *History of the Byzantine Empire,* II (1), 5.

peror from 780 to 797, was a minor. Irene, a woman of great force and ambition, entered into a struggle for power with her son when he attained his
majority, and was victorious; she dethroned and blinded her son, and became
sole ruler of the Empire (797–802). She illustrates the problem of whether or
not in the Byzantine Empire women could exercise sovereign power on the
throne, i.e. be rulers of the Empire in the full meaning of the term. Since the
time of the founding of the Empire wives of emperors had borne the title
"Augusta," and in case of the minority of their sons, had fulfilled the functions
of imperial power, but always in the name of their sons. In the fifth century,
Pulcheria, sister of Theodosius, had been at the head of the regency during
the minority of her brother. Theodora, wife of Justinian the Great, had occupied an exceptional position of influence upon political affairs. But Theodora's political influence depended entirely upon the will of her husband, and
the other women had all ruled in the name of a son or a brother. Irene is the
first instance in Byzantine history of a woman ruling with full authority of supreme power. She was a true autocrat, ruling in her own right, and she
represented an innovation which contradicted the secular traditions of the
Empire. It is interesting to note that in official documents and decrees she
was not called "empress" but "Irene, the faithful emperor (*basileus*)."[9] Since
it was the conception of the period that only an emperor, a man, could be
the official lawgiver, it became necessary to adopt the fiction that Irene was
an emperor. She was dethroned by the revolution of the year 802, initiated
and led by one of the highest civil officials, Nicephorus, and she later died in
exile. Nicephorus ascended the throne, and thus, with Irene's deposition, ended
the Isaurian or Syrian dynasty. In the period from 717 to 802 the Byzantine
Empire was ruled by a dynasty of eastern origin from Asia Minor or northern
Syria, intermixed with Khazarian blood through the marriage of Constantine V.

The attitude toward Arabs, Bulgarians, and Slavs

At the time of Leo's accession to the throne the Byzantine Empire was
experiencing one of the most critical periods in its history. In addition to the
frightful internal anarchy caused by the Emperor's struggle with the representatives of the Byzantine aristocracy, which had become particularly aggressive since the time of the first deposition of Justinian II, there was the
Arabian menace in the East, which was coming closer to the capital. The
period resembled the seventies of the seventh century under Constantine IV,
and seemed even more critical in many respects.

[9] See K. E. Zachariä von Lingenthal, *Jus graeco-romanum,* III, 55. J. and P. Zepos, *Jus graecoromanum,* I, 45.

The Arabian forces on land passed through all of Asia Minor to the west, even during the reign of the two predecessors of Leo, and occupied Sardis and Pergamus, near the shores of the Aegean Sea. At the head of the Arabian troops stood a distinguished general, Maslamah. Only a few months after Leo's entry into Constantinople in 717, the Arabs moved on northward from Pergamus, reaching Abydos on the Hellespont, and upon crossing to the European shore, soon found themselves at the walls of the capital. At the same time a strong Arabian fleet consisting of 1,800 vessels of different types, according to the chronicle of Theophanes, sailed through the Hellespont and the Propontis and surrounded the capital by sea. A real siege of Constantinople ensued. Leo demonstrated his brilliant military ability, however, by preparing the capital for the siege in an excellent manner. Once more the skillful use of "Greek fire" caused severe damage in the Arabian fleet, while hunger and the extremely severe winter of 717–18 completed the final defeat of the Muslim army. By force of an agreement with Leo III, as well as in self-defense, the Bulgarians also were fighting against the Arabs on Thracian territory and caused heavy losses in their army. Slightly more than a year after the beginning of the siege, the Arabs departed from the capital, which was thus saved by the genius and energy of Leo III. The first mention of the chain which barred the way into the Golden Horn to the enemy ships was made in connection with this siege.

Historians attach very great significance to this failure of the Muslims to occupy Constantinople. It is justly claimed that by his successful resistance Leo saved, not only the Byzantine Empire and the eastern Christian world, but also all of western European civilization. The English scholar Bury calls the year 718 "an ecumenical date." The Greek historian Lampros compares these events to the Persian wars of ancient Greece and calls Leo the Miltiades of medieval Hellenism. If Constantine IV halted the Arabs under Constantinople, Leo III definitely forced them back. This was the last attack of the Arabs upon the "God-guarded" city. Viewed from this standpoint, Leo's victory assumes universal historical significance. The expedition of the Arabs against Constantinople, as well as the name of Maslamah, have left a considerable trace in the later Muhammedan legendary tradition; the name of the latter is also connected with a mosque, which, tradition says, he constructed at Constantinople.[10]

---

[10] J. B. Bury, *History of the Later Roman Empire*, II, 405; S. Lampros, Ἱστορία Ἑλλάδος, III, 729. For the most detailed and recent account of this siege and its legendary tradition, see M. Canard, "Les expéditions des Arabes contre Constantinople," *Journal Asiatique*, CCVIII (1926), 80–102. Constantine Porphyrogenitus also attributes the construction of a mosque in Constantinople to Maslamah. *De administrando imperio*, ed. J. J. Reiske and I. Bekker, *Corpus Scriptorum Historiae Byzantinae*, 101–2; ed. Moravcsik-Jenkins (1949), 92. P. Kahle, "Zur Geschichte der mittelalterlichen Alexandria," *Der Islam*, XII

And yet this was one of the most brilliant epochs in the history 'of the early caliphate. Powerful Calif Walid I (705-15), a contemporary of the period of anarchy in the Byzantine Empire, could vie with the emperors in his construction achievements. A mosque was erected in Damascus which, like St. Sophia for the Christians, remained for a long time the most magnificent structure of the Muslim world. Muhammed's grave at Medina was as splendid as the Holy Sepulcher at Jerusalem. It is interesting to note that among the Muslims these buildings were associated with legends relating not only to Muhammed but also to Christ. The first call of Jesus when he returns to earth, declares Muslim tradition, will come from one of the minarets of the mosque of Damascus, and the free space next to Muhammed's grave at Medina will serve for the grave of Jesus when he dies after his second advent.[11]

Gradually the struggle between the Empire and the caliphate assumed the character of a sacred war. The results were satisfactory to neither Greeks nor Arabs, for the Greeks did not gain Jerusalem and the Arabs did not gain Constantinople. "Under the influence of this outcome," said V. Barthold, "among the Christians as well as among the Muslims, the idea of the triumphant state changed to the idea of repentance, and both were expecting the end of the world. It seemed to both that only just before the end of the world could the final aims of their states be attained. In the Latin, as well as in the Greek, world a legend became current to the effect that before the end of the universe the Christian ruler (the Frankish king or the Byzantine emperor) would enter Jerusalem and hand over his earthly crown to the Saviour, while the Muslims expected the end of the world to be preceded by the fall of Constantinople.[12] It was not accidental that the reign of the 'sole pious' Umayyad calif, Omar II (717-20), came about the year 100 of the hegira (about the year 720), when the end of the Muslim state, and at the same time the end of the world, were expected after the unsuccessful siege of Constantinople in the time of the preceding calif, Suleiman."[13]

Fourteen years after the siege, in the year 732, the Arabian advance from Spain into western Europe was successfully arrested at Poitiers by Charles Martel, the all-powerful major-domo of the weak Frankish king.[14]

(1922), 34. X. A. Nomiku, "Τὸ πρῶτο τζαμὶ τῆς Κωνσταντινουπόλεως," Ἐπετηρὶς Ἑταιρείας Βυζαντινῶν Σπουδῶν, I (1924), 199-201.

[11] See Barthold, *Transactions of the Oriental College,* I (1925), 469-70.

[12] See H. Lammens, *Études sur le règne du calife Omaiyade Moawia I,* 444.

[13] Barthold, *Transactions of the Oriental College,* I (1925), 470-71. A. A. Vasiliev, "Medieval Ideas of the End of the World: West and East," *Byzantion,* XVI, 2 (1944), 472-73.

[14] In the Russian and first English editions of my *History of the Byzantine Empire* I have rather overestimated the significance of the battle of Poitiers: Russian ed. (1917), 222; 1st English ed. (1928), I, 290. See, e.g., A. Dopsch, *Wirtschaftliche und soziale Grundlagen der europäischen Kulturentwicklung* (2nd ed., 1924), II, 298.

After their defeat in the year 718 the Arabs did not undertake any more serious military actions against the Empire in the time of Leo III, especially since they were apparently menaced in the north by the Khazars. Leo III had arranged the marriage of his son and successor, Constantine, with the daughter of the Khagan of the Khazars, and he began to support his new kinsman. Thus, in his struggle with the Arabs Leo found two allies: first the Bulgarians, and later the Khazars. The Arabs did not remain quiet, however, but continued their attacks upon Asia Minor and penetrated frequently far into the west, reaching even Nicaea, i.e., almost touching the shores of the Propontis. At the end of his reign Leo succeeded in defeating the Arabs at Acroïnon in Phrygia (present-day Afiun-Qara-Hisar on the railroad to Konia). This defeat forced the Arabs to clear the western part of Asia Minor and retreat to the east. With the battle at Acroïnon the Muslims connected the legend of the Turkish national hero, Saiyid Battal Ghazi, the champion of Islam, whose grave is shown even today in one of the villages south of Eskishehr (medieval Dorylaeum). The historical figure personifying this hero was the champion of Muhammedanism, Abdallah al-Battal, who fell in the battle of Acroïnon.[15] The problem of the Arabian struggle, then, was brilliantly solved by Leo III.

In the middle of the eighth century serious internal troubles arose in the Arab caliphate in connection with the change of dynasties, when the Umayyads (Omayyads) were deposed by the Abbasids. The latter transferred the capital and the center of their government from Damascus to Bagdad on the Tigris, far removed from the Byzantine border. This made it possible for the successor of Leo III, Constantine V, to move the imperial border farther east along the entire boundary of Asia Minor by means of a number of successful expeditions.

But in the time of Irene, under the Caliph al-Mahdi, the Arabs again initiated a successful offensive movement into Asia Minor, and in the year 782–83 the Empress was forced to beg for peace. The resulting agreement, concluded for three years, was very humiliating for the Empire. The Empress assumed the obligation of paying the Arabs a yearly tribute of ninety or seventy thousand dinars (denarii) in semiannual instalments. It is very likely that the troops

[15] See J. Wellhausen, *Die Kämpfe der Araber mit den Romäern in der Zeit der Umaijiden,* 444–45; a special article on Battal in the *Encyclopédie de l'Islam,* I, 698. See also Barthold, *Transactions of the Oriental College,* I (1925), 470; D. B. Macdonald, "The Earlier History of the Arabian Nights," *Journal of the Royal Asiatic Society* (1924), 281; Canard, "Les expéditions des Arabes contre Constantinople," *Journal Asiatique,* CCVIII (1926), 116–18. W. M. Ramsay, "The Attempts of the Arabs to Conquer Asia Minor (641–964 A.D.) and the Causes of Its Failure," *Bulletin de la section historique de l'Académie roumaine,* XI (1924), 2. We shall resume the story of al-Battal later, in connection with the epic of Digenes Akrites.

sent by Irene to Macedonia, Greece, and the Peloponnesus in the same year (783) to quell the Slavonic revolt were taken from the eastern front, thus weakening the Byzantine position in Asia Minor. In the year 798, after the successful operations of the Arab army under the Caliph Harun-ar-Rashid, a new peace agreement was concluded with the Byzantine Empire, which was to pay a tribute, as in the time of al-Mahdi.

Very active relations existed between the emperors of the Isaurian dynasty and the Bulgarians. The latter, having recently gained a stronghold on the Lower Danube, were forced above all to defend their political existence against the Byzantine attempts to destroy the achievements of Asparuch. Internal conditions in the Bulgarian kingdom of the eighth century were very intricate. The Bulgarian chiefs competed with each other for the supreme rank of khan and initiated many dynastic disturbances, and, as new conquerors, the Bulgarians were forced to struggle with the conquered Slavs of the peninsula. The Bulgarian khans of the late seventh and early eighth centuries showed great ingenuity in handling relations with their most dangerous enemy, the Byzantine Empire. The Bulgarians had aided Justinian II in reclaiming the throne and rendered active assistance to Leo III in his drive to force the Arabs away from Constantinople. After this, for a period of over thirty years, the Byzantine writers say nothing about the Bulgarians. During the reign of Leo III the Bulgarian kingdom succeeded in maintaining peace with the Empire.

In the reign of Constantine V relations with the Byzantine Empire became strained. With the aid of the Syrians and Armenians, who had been transported from the eastern border and made to settle in Thrace, the Emperor constructed a number of fortifications along the Bulgarian border. Constantine treated with contempt the Bulgarian ambassador to Constantinople. Following this the Bulgarians began military operations. Constantine conducted eight or nine campaigns against the Bulgarians both on land and on sea, with the aim of annihilating the Bulgarian kingdom. These expeditions continued with varying results. In the end Constantine failed to attain his goal, but some historians call him "the first Bulgar-slayer" (*Bulgaroctonus*),"[16] because of his energetic struggle against the Bulgarians and because of the numerous fortresses he constructed against them.

Within Bulgaria dynastic troubles ceased at the end of the eighth century, and the sharp antagonism between the Bulgarians and the Slavs became less pronounced. In short, there came about the gradual formation of the Bulgaria of the ninth century, Slavonized and transformed into a powerful state with definite offensive projects as regards the Byzantine Empire. This offensive policy became evident in the late eighth century, in the time of Constantine

[16] A. Lombard, *Etudes d'histoire byzantine: Constantine V, empereur des Romains,* 59.

VI and his mother Irene, when the Byzantine Empire after its military failures was forced to agree to pay tribute to the Bulgarians.

In the military collisions between the Empire and the Bulgarians of the eighth century, the Bulgarian forces included also the Slavs, who formed part of their kingdom. The occupation of the Balkan peninsula by the Slavs also continued in the eighth century. One western pilgrim to the Holy Places, a contemporary of Leo III, visited the Peloponnesian city of Monembasia and wrote that it was situated in Slavonic (Slavinian) land (*in Slawinia terrae*).[17] There are references to the presence of Slavs in Dyrrachium and in Athens in the eighth century.[18] The following well-known lines (quoted also in an earlier part of this work) in the work of Constantine Porphyrogenitus, *On the Themes,* refer also to the days of Constantine V: "The whole of the Peloponnesus became slavonized and barbarian when the plague spread through the entire universe."[19] The reference here is to the formidable epidemic of 746–47, imported from Italy, which especially devastated the south of Greece and Constantinople. In an attempt to rehabilitate the capital after the epidemic, Constantine transported to Constantinople people from various provinces. Even in the opinion of the population, the Peloponnesus was Slavonized as early as the middle of the eighth century; to the same period must be referred the influx of new settlements in Greece established in place of those communities whose population was either extinguished by the epidemic or taken to the capital when the effort was being made to rehabilitate it. At the end of the eighth century the Empress Irene sent a special expedition "against the Slavonic tribes," to Greece, Thessalonica, and the Peloponnesus.[20] Later these Greek Slavs took an active part in the plot against Irene. This indicates clearly that in the eighth century the Slavs in the Balkan peninsula, including all of Greece, were not only definitely and strongly established, but even participated in the political life of the Empire. By the ninth century the Bulgarians and the Slavs became two very serious enemies of the Byzantine Empire.

The internal activities of the emperors of the Isaurian or Syrian dynasty

Legislation.—Leo III was not only a gifted leader and energetic defender of his Empire against external enemies, but also a wise and capable legislator. Even in the time of Justinian the Great, in the sixth century, the Latin text of his Code, Digest, and Institutes was little, or not at all, understood in the majority of provinces. In many districts, in the east particularly, old local customs were used in preference to official statutes, as was clearly evidenced

[17] Willibaldi, *Vita;* ed. G. H. Pertz, *Monumenta Germaniae Historica, Scriptorum,* XV, 93.

[18] A. A. Vasiliev, "The Slavs in Greece,"

Vizantiysky Vremennik, V (1898), 416–17.
[19] *De Thematibus,* 53–54.
[20] Theophanes, *Chronographia,* ed. de Boor, 456–57.

by the popularity of the Syrian Lawbook of the fifth century. The Novels (*Novellae*) issued in Greek dealt only with current legislation. Meanwhile, in the seventh century, as the Empire was gradually losing Syria, Palestine, and Egypt in the east, North Africa in the south, and the northern parts of the Balkan peninsula in the north, it was becoming more and more "Greek" by language. For wide and general use it became necessary to create a lawbook in Greek which would reflect all the changes in living conditions since the time of Justinian the Great.

Fully realizing the need for such a code, Leo III entrusted the task of compiling it to a commission whose members he chose personally. The efforts of this body resulted in the publication of a code entitled the Ecloga, issued in the name of the "wise and pious emperors, Leo and Constantine." There is some uncertainty as to the exact date of its publication. Some western scholars refer it to the end of Leo's reign (739-40),[21] although the Russian Byzantinist, V. G. Vasilievsky is inclined to ascribe it to a date nearer the beginning of Leo's reign (about the year 726).[22] Recently there has even been some doubt as to whether the Ecloga may be referred to the time of Leo III and Constantine V at all.[23] At present most modern students of the question set the date of publication as March, 726.[24]

The title of the Ecloga (meaning "selection" or "extract") is indicative of its sources. The title runs as follows: "An abridged selection of laws, arranged by Leo and Constantine, the wise and pious kings, from the Institutes, Digest, Code, Novels of the Great Justinian, and corrected with a view to greater humanity" (in Greek, εἰς τὸ φιλανθρωπότερον), or, as others translate this, "with a view to improvement."[25] The introduction states definitely that the decrees issued by the preceding emperors have been written in various books and that their meaning, difficult for some, is entirely incomprehensible for others, especially for those who do not live in the "God-guarded" imperial

[21] K. E. Zachariä von Lingenthal, *Geschichte des griechisch-römischen Rechts* (3rd ed., 1892), 16. P. Collinet, "Byzantine Legislation from Justinian (565) to 1453," *Cambridge Medieval History*, IV, 708 (March 740). V. Grumel, "La Date de la promulgation de l'Ecloge de Leon III," *Échos d'Orient*, XXXIV (1935), 331 (March 741).

[22] "Legislation of the Iconoclasts," *Journal of the Ministry of Public Instruction*, CXCIX (1878), 279-80; also in *Works of V. G. Vasilievsky*, IV, 163.

[23] See C. N. Uspensky, *Outlines of the History of Byzantium*, I, 216-18.

[24] D. Ginnis, "Das promulgationsjahr der Isaurischen Ecloge," *Byzantinische Zeitschrift*,

XXIV (1924), 356-57. *A Manual of Roman Law, the Ecloga published by the Emperors Leo III and Constantine V of Isauria at Constantinople* A.D. 726, ed. E. H. Freshfield, 2. C. A. Spulber, *L'Eclogue des Isauriens*, 83; detailed discussion of the date of the Ecloga, 81-86. G. Ostrogorsky, "Die Chronologie des Theophanes im 7. und 8. Jahrhundert," *Byzantinisch-Neugriechische Jahrbücher*, VII (1930), 6, n. See also E. H. Freshfield, *Roman Law in the Later Roman Empire. The Isaurian Period*.

[25] K. E. Zachariä von Lingenthal, ed., *Collectio librorum juris graeco-romani ineditorum. Ecloga Leonis et Constantini*. Zepos, *Jus graecoromanum*, II, 11.

city.[26] The "various books" refer to Greek translations and commentaries of Justinian's lawbooks which were used in actual practice, frequently replacing the Latin originals. Very few people could understand these Greek translations and commentaries. The profusion of books and the variations and contradictions found in them produced considerable confusion in the civil law of the Byzantine Empire. Leo III saw clearly the existing state of affairs and made it his aim to relieve these conditions. The principles of the Ecloga, laid down in its introduction, are imbued with ideas of justice and righteousness. They maintain that judges must "refrain from all human passions and make decisions of true justice, developed by clear reasoning; they must not scorn the needy, or leave unpunished the strong man guilty of offense. . . . They must justly refrain from accepting gifts." All the officials in judicial service must receive definite salaries from the imperial "pious treasury," so that "they take nothing from any person who might come under their jurisdiction, in order that the prediction of the Prophet, 'They sold the righteous for silver' (Amos, 2:6), should not come true and that we should not be visited by the wrath of God for becoming transgressors of his commandments."[27]

The contents of the Ecloga, subdivided into eighteen titles, deal mainly with civil law, and only to a slight extent with criminal law. They treat of marriage, betrothal, dowry, testaments, and intestacies, of wardship, enfranchisement of slaves, witnesses, various liabilities connected with sale, purchase, rent, etc. Only one title contains a chapter of criminal law on punishments.

The Ecloga differed in many respects from the Justinian Code, and even contradicted it at times by accepting the decisions of customary law and judicial practices which existed parallel with the official legislative works of Justinian. When compared with the latter, the Ecloga represents a considerable step forward in many respects. For instance, its marriage laws included the introduction of higher Christian conceptions. True, the chapter on penalties abounds in punishments which prescribe the maiming of the body, such as cutting off a hand, tongue, or nose, or blinding the convict. But this fact does not permit one to consider the Ecloga a barbarian law, because in most cases these punishments were intended to take the place of the penalty of death. In this sense the Isaurian emperors were right in claiming that their legal accomplishments were "greater in their humanity" than the work of the preceding emperors. Also the Ecloga prescribed equal punishment to the distinguished and the common, to the rich and the poor, while the Justinian

---

[26] Ecloga, par. 11. Zepos, Jus graecoromanum, II, 13.

[27] Ecloga, par. 11, 13; the Russian trans. Vasilievsky, "Legislation of the Iconoclasts," Journal of the Ministry of Public Instruction,

CXCIX (1878), 283–85 and Works, IV, 168–69. Spulber, L'Eclogue, 5–9. Freshfield, Roman Law, 68–70. Both give an English trans. Zepos, Jus graecoromanum, II, 14, 16–17.

law frequently prescribed different penalties without any real basis for the discrimination. The Ecloga is distinguished by an abundance of references to the Scriptures for confirmation of different juridical principles. "The spirit of Roman Law became transformed in the religious atmosphere of Christianity."[28] Throughout the eighth and ninth centuries, until the time of the accession of the Macedonian dynasty (867), the Ecloga served as a manual for the teaching of law, taking the place of Justinian's Institutes, and it was more than once subjected to revision; for instance, there was the Private Ecloga (*Ecloga privata*) and the Private Enlarged Ecloga (*Ecloga privata aucta*).[29] When, after the accession of Basil the Macedonian, a change took place in favor of Justinian law, the legislative deeds of the Isaurian emperors were officially declared to be nonsense (literally "silly talk"), which contradicted divine dogma and destroyed salutary laws.[30] Still, even the emperors of the Macedonian dynasty borrowed many chapters from the condemned lawbook for their own legislative works, and even in their times the Ecloga was again revised.

It is interesting to note that the Ecloga of Leo and Constantine later formed part of the juridical collections of the orthodox church, especially in Russia. It is found in the printed Russian *Kormchaia Kniga,* i.e., *The Book of Rules* or *Administrative Code,* under the title, "The chapters of the wisest Tsar Leo and Constantine, the two faithful emperors."[31] There are other traces of the influence of the Ecloga upon documents of ancient Slavonic legislation.

The Ecloga can hardly be considered "an extremely daring innovation," as was claimed by the Greek Byzantinist, Paparrigopoulo, an ardent admirer of the Isaurian emperors. "At present, when the principles advanced by the compilers of the Ecloga are accepted by the civil legislation of the most progressive nations," he declared, "the hour has finally come to accord esteem to the genius of the men who, a thousand years ago, fought for the inauguration of doctrines which have triumphed only in our own days."[32] These are the comments of an enthusiastic Hellenic patriot, but nevertheless the modern world should recognize the high significance of the Ecloga in initiating a new

---

[28] Bury, *Constitution of the Later Roman Empire,* II, 414.

[29] The date of these is debatable, but they probably should be assigned to some time prior to the accession of Basil I the Macedonian in 867. See Zachariä von Lingenthal, *Jus graeco-romanum,* IV, 4. E. H. Freshfield, *A Revised Manual of Roman Law. Ecloga privata aucta,* 2. Spulber, *L'Eclogue,* 94–95. But cf. Zachariä von Lingenthal, *Geschichte des griechisch-römischen Rechts* (3rd ed., 1892), 36 (on the *Ecloga privata aucta* in South Italy

under Norman domination).

[30] Zachariä von Lingenthal, *Collectio librorum,* 62. Zepos, *Jus graecoromanum,* II, 237.

[31] In this book, known in Russia soon after the adoption of Christianity in the tenth century A.D., were laid down the apostolic church rules and the rules of the ecumenical councils as well as the civil laws of the orthodox Byzantine emperors.

[32] *Histoire de la civilisation hellénique,* 205, 209.

period in the history of the Graeco-Roman or Byzantine law, a period which lasted until the accession of the Macedonian dynasty, when the Justinian law was restored to its former place but with many essential modifications. The Ecloga of Leo III was intended above all to meet the demands of the living realities of the period.

In connection with the Isaurian dynasty, and especially with the name of Leo III, scholars discuss three other legislative documents: the Rural Code or Farmer's Law (νόμος γεωργικός), the Military Code (νόμος στρατιωτικός), and the Rhodian Sea Law (νόμος ῥοδίων ναυτικός). Varying versions of these three documents usually appear in numerous surviving manuscripts after the Ecloga or after other juridical works, without indication of the names of the authors or of the time of first publication. Hence to attribute them to one time or another depends upon internal evidence, an evaluation of their contents and language, and comparison with other similar documents.

The Rural Code (νόμος γεωργικός) has attracted the greatest attention among the three works. The greatest authority on Byzantine law, the German scholar Zachariä von Lingenthal, changed his mind about this. He began by thinking it the work of a private hand and he assigned it to the eighth or ninth century. It was compiled, he thought, partly from the legislation of Justinian and partly from local custom.[33] Later he was inclined to believe that the Rural Code was a product of the legislative activity of the Emperors Leo and Constantine, and that it was published either simultaneously with the Ecloga or soon after its appearance.[34] He agreed with the Russian scholars V. G. Vasilievsky and Th. I. Uspensky who characterized this document as a collection of rural police regulations dealing with common offenses among people engaged in agriculture. It is concerned primarily with various kinds of thefts of lumber, field and orchard fruit, trespasses and oversights of herdsmen, harm done to animals, and harm done by cattle. The Russian scholar B. A. Pančenko, who made a special study of this document, called the Rural Code "a supplementary record to the customary law practiced among the peasants; it is dedicated to that law, so necessary for the peasants, which did not find its expression in legislation."[35]

The work is not dated. Some scholars refer it to the epoch of Leo III. But it must be admitted that the problem is far from being definitely solved. According to Pančenko, "the need for such a law might have been felt even in the seventh century; the nature of the lawbook, barbarian and naively empirical, is closer in spirit to the time of the greatest decline of civilization than

[33] *Historiae Juris Graeco-Romani Delineatio*, 32.

[34] Zachariä von Lingenthal, *Geschichte des Griechisch-römischen Rechts* (3rd ed., 1892), 250. This opinion has been shared by Vasiliev-

sky, "Legislation of the Iconoclasts," *Journal*, CXCIX (1878), 97; *Works*, IV, 199.

[35] *Peasant Property in the Byzantine Empire. The Rural Code and Monastic Documents*, 86.

to the period of the compilation of the Ecloga."[36] It has not yet been proved that the Rural Code was issued in the eighth century, and it is possible that its publication will be found to have taken place at an earlier period. Vernadsky and Ostrogorsky stated that the Rural Code was "elaborated" under Justinian II, at the end of the seventh century.[37] The last word on the subject was said by the Russian historian E. Lipshitz in 1945. After reconsidering all previous opinions, she was inclined to accept the second half of the eighth century as the most probable date of the Rural Code; in other words she confirmed the old opinion of Zachariä von Lingenthal and Vasilievsky.[38]

The Rural Code has also attracted the attention of scholars because it contains no reference to the colonate or serfdom which predominated in the later Roman Empire. It does contain, however, indications of various new phenomena: personal peasant property, communal landownership, the abolition of compulsory service, and the introduction of freedom of movement. These are usually connected by scholars with the extensive Slavonic settlements in the Empire, which presumably imported conditions peculiar to their own life, chiefly the commune. The proposition argued in Pančenko's book that the Rural Code does not refer to the commune is rightly denied in modern literature. Th. I. Uspensky, however, overestimated the importance of this law when he assigned to it the significance of a general measure for the whole Empire and claimed even that it "must serve as a point of departure in the history of the economic development of the East" with regard to the free peasant class and the class of small landowners.[39] This opinion might create the impression that serfdom was generally abolished in the seventh or eighth centuries, which was not really the case.[40] Diehl, who in his *History of the Byzantine Empire* considered the Rural Code the achievement of Leo III and his son, also went rather too far in stating that it "aimed to restrain the disquieting development of the great domains, to arrest the disappearance of the small free estates, and to insure to the peasants better living conditions."[41]

---

[36] *Ibid.*, 30.

[37] G. Vernadsky, "Sur les origines de la Loi agraire byzantine," *Byzantion*, II (1926), 173. G. Ostrogorsky, "Die wirtschaftlichen und sozialen Entwicklungs-grundlagen des byzantinischen Reiches," *Vierteljahrschrift für Sozial-und Wirtschaft Geschichte*, XXII (1929), 133. E. Stein is also inclined to accept this dating, *Byzantinische Zeitschrift*, XXIX (1930), 355. F. Dölger rejects this theory, *Historische Zeitschrift*, CXLI (1929), 112–13.

[38] E. Lipschitz, "The Byzantine Peasantry and Slavonic Colonization (Particularly upon the Data of the Rural Code)," *Vizantiysky Sbornik*, 1945, 104–5.

[39] *Byzantine Empire*, I, 28. See also A. Vogt, *Basile Ier empereur de Byzance (867–86) et la civilisation byzantine à la fin du IXe siècle*, 378.

[40] Runciman also asserted that the Isaurian emperors met these innovations with the very definite policy of abolishing serfdom. See Runciman, *The Emperor Romanus Lecapenus and His Reign*, 225.

[41] *Histoire de l'Empire Byzantin*, 69; trans. G. B. Ives, 56. See Diehl's brief remark on the importance of the Rural Code for the eighth century in Charles Diehl and G. Marçais, *Le Monde Oriental de 395 à 1018*, 256 and n. 23.

The English scholar W. Ashburner edited, translated, and thoroughly investigated the Rural Code, although he knew no Russian and was therefore unacquainted with the results of the Russian investigations. Ashburner was inclined to agree with Zachariä von Lingenthal that the Farmer's Law, as it stands, forms part of the legislation of the iconoclasts and that it is to a great extent a compilation of existing customs. But at the same time Ashburner differed from Zachariä von Lingenthal in three important particulars: (1) the origin of the law; (2) the legal position of the agricultural class under the law; and (3) the economic character of the two forms of tenancy to which it refers. The relationship of the Rural Code to the Ecloga, he maintained, is not as close as Zachariä von Lingenthal would make it, and he believed that in the state of society described by the Rural Code the farmer could migrate freely from place to place. He agreed with the German scholar, however, that the "style of command" of this law suggests that it was not a product of private hands but a work of legislative authority.[42]

The theory of the exceptional influence of the Slavs upon the internal customs of the Byzantine Empire, given weight by the authority of Zachariä von Lingenthal and supported by outstanding Russian scholars in the field of Byzantine history, has come to occupy a firm place in historical literature. In addition to the general accounts of Slavonic settlements in the Empire, these scholars used as the main basis for their theory the fact that the conception of small free peasantry and the commune were foreign to Roman law; hence they must have been introduced into Byzantine life by some new element, in this case the Slavonic. V. N. Zlatarsky recently supported the theory of Slavonic influence on the Rural Code, which he referred to Leo III, and explained it by Leo's Bulgarian policy. Leo saw that the Slavs under his power were very much tempted to pass over to the Bulgarians and conclude with them a Bulgaro-Slavonic alliance. Therefore he introduced into his law Slavonic manners and customs, hoping thereby to render conditions more attractive to the Slavs.[43] But a closer study of the codes of Theodosius and Justinian, of the Novels of the latter, and, in recent times, of the data of papyrology and the lives of saints, distinctly proves that there existed in the Roman Empire villages populated by free landholders, and that communal landownership was in existence in very early times. No general conclusion, therefore, can be made on the basis of the Rural Code; it may serve only as another evidence of the fact that in the Byzantine Empire the small free

[42] "The Farmer's Law," *Journal of Hellenic Studies*, XXX (1910), 84; XXXII (1912), 68–83. Text ed. C. Ferrini, *Byzantinische Zeit-schrift*, VII (1898), 558–71; reprinted in *Opera di Contardo Ferrini*, I, 375–95.

[43] V. N. Zlatarsky, *A History of the State of Bulgaria in the Middle Ages*, I, 197–200.

peasantry and the free rural commune existed parallel with serfdom. The theory of Slavonic influence must be discarded and attention should be turned to the study of the problem of small free peasantry and the village commune in the period of the early and later Roman Empire on the basis of both new and old materials which have not been sufficiently utilized.[44]

In recent times there have been several interesting attempts to compare the Rural Code with the texts of the Byzantine papyri,[45] but on the basis of the mere resemblance in phraseology, very striking at times, no definite conclusions should be made with regard to any borrowing. Such a resemblance, declared Mr. Ashburner, only proves what needs no proof: that lawyers of the same epoch use the same phrases.[46]

The Rural Code is of great interest from the point of view of Slavonic studies. An Old Russian translation of this code forms part of a compilation of the greatest value in contents and historical significance, bearing the title of *The Lawbook by Means of Which All Orthodox Princes Have to Regulate All Affairs*. The famous Russian canonist, A. S. Pavlov, produced a critical edition of this Russian version of the Rural Code. The latter is found also in the old Serbian juridical books.

In manuscripts of legal works the Sea Law and the Military Law are frequently appended to the Ecloga or other legal documents. Both laws are undated; but on the basis of certain deductions, which do not, however, finally solve the problem, they are referred by some scholars to the period of the Isaurian dynasty.

The Maritime Law (νόμος ναυτικός, *leges navales*), or, as it is sometimes called in manuscripts, the Rhodian Sea Law, is a statute regulating commercial navigation. Some scholars suppose that this law was extracted from the second chapter of the fourteenth book of the Digest, which contains an almost exact borrowing from Greek law of the so-called "Rhodian Law of Jettison," *lex Rhodia de jactu,* dealing with the division of losses between the owner of the ship and the owners of the cargo in cases where part of the cargo had to be thrown overboard in order to save the vessel. At present the dependence

---

[44] See the very interesting chapters on this subject in two Russian books which are practically unknown to European and American scholars: C. N. Uspensky, "The So-Called 'Rural Code,'" *Outlines in the History of Byzantium,* 162–82; and A. P. Rudakov, *Outlines in the Byzantine Culture Based on Data of Greek Hagiography,* 176–98. See also G. Vernadsky, "Notes on the Peasant Community in Byzantium," *Ucheniya Zapiski osnovanniya Russkoy Uchebnoy Kollegiey v Prage,*

I, 2 (1924), 81–97. Vernadsky was not acquainted with the two preceding works. See also N. A. Constantinescu, "Réforme sociale ou réforme fiscale?" *Bulletin de la section historique de l'Académie roumaine,* XI (1924), 95–96.

[45] Vernadsky, "Sur les origines de la Loi agraire byzantine," *Byzantion,* II (1926), 178–79.

[46] "The Farmer's Law," *Journal of Hellenic Studies,* XXXII (1912), 71.

of the Rhodian Law on the Digest, as well as its connection with the Ecloga, which has been emphasized by Zachariä von Lingenthal, is not accepted by scholars.[47]

The form in which this law has come down to us was compiled from materials of very different epochs and natures; most of it must have been derived from local customs. Ashburner said that Part III of the Sea Law was evidently intended to be a part of Book LIII of the Basilics,[48] and inferred that a second edition of the Sea Law was made either by or under the direction of the men who compiled the Basilics. The texts which exist today represent in substance the second edition.[49]

In style the Maritime Law is of a rather official character, while in contents it differs greatly from the Digest of Justinian because it apparently reflects some influence of later times. Thus, for example, this law fixes the liability on the part of the shipowner, the lessee merchant, and the passengers for the safety of the ship and the cargo. In case of storm or piracy they were all expected to make good the losses. This provision was intended to serve as a sort of insurance, and, together with other peculiar rulings, resulted from the fact that from the time of Heraclius in the seventh century maritime commerce and navigation in general were greatly endangered by the sea raids of Arabian and Slavic pirates. Piracy became such a habitual phenomenon that the shipowners and merchants could continue their commercial enterprises only by assuming a common risk.

The time of the compilation of the Sea Law can be determined only approximately. It was probably put together unofficially between 600 and 800 A.D. In any case, there is no reason for attributing a common origin to the three books, the Sea Law, the Rural Code, and the Soldier's Law.[50]

In spite of the return of the Macedonian dynasty to the standards of the Justinian law, the Sea Law persisted in actual practice and influenced some of the Byzantine jurists of the tenth, eleventh, and twelfth centuries. This survival indicates that Byzantine trade navigation did not recover after the seventh and eighth centuries. The Italians, who later monopolized the trade of the Mediterranean Sea, had their own sea statutes. With the decline of Byzantine sea commerce the Maritime Law became obsolete, so that there are no references to it in the juridical documents of the thirteenth and fourteenth centuries.[51]

The Military Law or Soldier's Law (νόμος στρατιωτικός, *leges militares*)

---

[47] See W. Ashburner, *The Rhodian Sea Law*, lxviii, lxxviii, cxiii.

[48] On this code of the Macedonian epoch, see pp. 342–43.

[49] *Rhodian Sea Law*, cxii, cxiii.

[50] *Ibid.*, cxii, cxiv.

[51] See a very accurate article on the Rhodian Law by H. Kreller, "Lex Rhodia. Untersuchungen zur Quellengeschichte des römischen Seerechtes," *Zeitschrift für das Gesamte Handelsrecht und Konkursrecht*, XXV (1921), 257–367.

is an extract from the Greek paraphrases of Justinian's Digest and Code, the Ecloga, and several other sources which were added to the law in later times. It consists mainly of an enumeration of penalties inflicted upon men in military service for such offenses as mutiny, disobedience, flight, adultery. The punishments provided are extremely harsh. If the opinion of scholars that it belongs to the time of the Isaurian dynasty[52] were correct, it would give an excellent indication of the strictness of the military discipline introduced by Leo III. But unfortunately the scanty information does not support a positive statement that the law belongs to this period. In fact, all that has been said on the Rural Code, the Sea Law, and the Military Law must be summed up by stating that not one of these three small codes can be regarded with certainty as the work of the Isaurian emperors.[53]

The themes.—The majority of scholars, beginning with Finlay, refer the reorganization and completion of the provincial theme system which originated in the seventh century, to the eighth century, sometimes to the time of Leo III in particular. Finlay wrote: "A new geographical arrangement into themes . . . was reorganized by Leo and endured as long as the Byzantine government."[54] Gelzer was particularly categorical in this regard. "Leo definitely removed the civil officials and transferred the civil power in the provinces into the hands of military representatives."[55] Th. I. Uspensky wrote: "Only in the time of Leo the Isaurian does an abrupt turn take place in the direction of strengthening the power of the theme *strategus* at the expense of the civil administration of the province."[56] But the fact still remains that no information exists on Leo's achievements in the field of provincial organization. There exists a list of themes with some references to their organization, which belongs to the Arabian geographer of the first half of the ninth century, Ibn-Khurdadhbah (Ibn-Khordadhbeh).[57] Upon comparing his data with the data on the themes of the seventh century, scholars have reached some con-

[52] See Zacharia von Lingenthal, *Geschichte des griechische-römischen Rechts* (3rd ed., 1892), 16-17; *idem*, "Wissenschaft und Recht für das Heer vom 6. bis zum Anfang des 10. Jahrhunderts," *Byzantinische Zeitschrift*, III (1894), 448-49.

[53] Diehl and Collinet took the view that the three laws were the work of the Isaurian dynasty, *Cambridge Medieval History*, IV, 4-5, 708-10. But in the introduction (xiii) Bury said that, in his opinion, after the investigations of Ashburner such a view is quite untenable, at least in regard to the first two codes.

[54] *History of the Byzantine Empire from DCXIV to MLVII* (2nd ed., 1856), 13-14; ed. H. F. Tozer, II, 29.

[55] *Die Genesis der byzantinischen Themenverfassung*, 75.

[56] *Byzantine Empire*, I, 812; II, 55-56.

[57] The Arabic text of Ibn-Khurdadhbah with a French trans. M. J. de Goeje, *Bibliotheca Geographorum Arabicorum*, VI, 77 ff. See Gelzer, *Die Genesis der byzantinischen Themenverfassung*, 82 ff.; E. W. Brooks, "Arabic Lists of Byzantine Themes," *Journal of Hellenic Studies*, XXI (1901), 67 ff. See also a list of Byzantine themes in a Persian geography of the end of the tenth century. *Hudud al-Alam. The Regions of the World. A Persian Geography 372 A.H.-982 A.D.*, trans. V. Minorsky, 156-58, 421-22.

clusions with regard to certain changes in the eighth century in the time of the Isaurian dynasty. It appears that in Asia Minor, in addition to the three themes of the seventh century, two new themes were created in the eighth century, probably in the time of Leo III: (1) the Thracesian theme in the western part of Asia Minor, formed from the western districts of the vast theme of the Anatolics and named after the European garrisons from Thrace stationed there, and (2) the theme of the Bucellarians in the eastern part of the vast Opsician theme (Opsikion), which derived its name from the Bucellarians, i.e., some Roman and foreign troops employed by the Empire or by private individuals. Constantine Porphyrogenitus said that the Bucellarians followed the army, supplying it with provisions.[58] Thus toward the beginning of the ninth century Asia Minor had five themes, to which the sources pertaining to this period refer as the "five eastern themes" (for instance, under the year 803).[59] On European territory there were apparently only four provinces by the end of the eighth century: Thrace, Macedonia, Hellas, and Sicily. But if the question of the number of themes in Asia Minor in the early part of the ninth century may be considered settled, the problems of the complete removal of civil authorities and the transfer of their functions to the military governors still remain uncertain. The decisive role of Leo III in the theme organization cannot be proved; it is merely a hypothesis.[60]

The completion and extension of the system of themes under the Isaurian dynasty was indissolubly connected with the external and internal dangers which threatened the Empire. The formation of the new themes by dividing the immense territories of the earlier themes was dictated by political considerations. By his own experience Leo knew very well how dangerous it was to leave too large a territory in the hands of an all-powerful military governor, who could revolt and lay claim to the imperial title. Thus the external danger required the strengthening of the centralized military power, especially in the provinces menaced by the enemies of the Empire—the Arabs, Slavs, and Bulgarians; and on the other hand, the internal danger from the too-powerful military governors (*strategi*), whose loose dependence on the central power often resembles vassal relations, made it imperative to reduce the extensive stretches of territory under their rule.

Desiring to increase and regulate the financial income of the Empire, indispensable for his varied undertakings, Leo III raised the poll tax in Sicily

[58] *De Thematibus*, 28.

[59] Theophanes Continuatus, *Historia*, Bonn ed., 6.

[60] See Kulakovsky, *Byzantium*, III, 391–92. E. Stein, "Ein Kapitel vom persischen und vom byzantinischen Staate," *Byzantinisch-Neugriechische Jahrbücher*, I (1920), 75–77.

G. Ostrogorsky, "Über die vermeintliche Reformtätigkeit der Isaurier," *Byzantinische Zeitschrift*, XXX (1929–30), 397. Ostrogorsky, *Geschichte des byzantinischen Staates*, 105 and n. 4. Diehl and Marçais, *Le Monde oriental*, 256.

and Calabria by one-third of its original amount; in order to carry out this measure effectively he ordered that a record be kept of the birth of all male children. The chronicler, who is hostile to the iconoclasts, compared this order with the treatment accorded by the Egyptian Pharaoh to the Jews.[61] Near the end of his reign Leo III levied upon all the subjects of the Empire a tax for the repair of the walls of Constantinople which had been destroyed by frequent and violent earthquakes. That this task was completed in his time is evidenced by the fact that many inscriptions on the towers of the inner walls of Constantinople bear the names of Leo and his son and coemperor, Constantine.[62]

Religious controversies and the first period of Iconoclasm

The history of the Iconoclastic[63] movement falls into two periods. The first lasted from 726 to 780 and ended officially with the Seventh Ecumenical Council; the second lasted from 813 to 843 and ended in the so-called "restoration of orthodoxy."

The study of the iconoclastic epoch affords great difficulties because of the present condition of sources. All the works of the iconoclasts, the imperial decrees, the acts of the iconoclastic councils of the year 753-54 and 815, the theological treatises of the iconbreakers, etc., were destroyed by the triumphant image-worshipers. Some survivals of iconoclastic literature are known to us only by fragments introduced into the works of the image-worshipers for the purpose of refuting them. Thus, the decree of the iconoclastic council of 753-54 has been preserved in the acts of the Seventh Ecumenical Council, though perhaps not in its complete original form. The decree of the council of 815 has been discovered in one of the treatises of Patriarch Nicephorus, while numerous fragments of iconoclastic literature are found in the polemic and theological treatises of the antagonists of the movement. Particularly interesting in this respect are the three famous *Treatises Against Those Who Depreciate the Holy Images* of the renowned theologian and hymn-writer, John Damascene (of Damascus), a contemporary of the first two iconoclastic emperors. In order to disseminate their ideas, the iconoclasts sometimes resorted to the writing of spurious works. The surviving sources on iconoclasm, then, are biased by hostility to the movement; hence in later times scholars have differed greatly in their estimate of the iconoclastic period.

Scholars have turned their attention first of all to the question of the causes for the movement against images, which lasted with some intervals for over

[61] Theophanes, *Chronographia*, ed. de Boor, 410. See F. Dölger, *Regesten der Kaiserurkunden des oströmischen Reiches*, I, no. 300, 36. E. Stein, *Byzantinische Zeitschrift*, XXIX (1930), 355.

[62] See A. van Millingen, *Byzantine Constantinople*, 98–99, and the illustrations between these pages.

[63] Iconoclast, the Greek word for "icon-breaker"; iconodule, "icon-worshiper."

one hundred years with very serious consequences to the Empire. Some students of this period have seen in the policy of the iconoclastic emperors religious causes, while others have believed that the causes were chiefly political. It was thought that Leo III determined to destroy images because he hoped that this measure would remove one of the chief obstacles to a closer relationship of the Christians with the Jews and Muhammedans, who disapproved of icons. He is credited with believing that a closer religious kinship with these two denominations would facilitate their subjugation to the Empire. A very thorough study of the iconoclastic period has been made by the well-known Greek historian, Paparrigopoulo, whose biased views with regard to the Ecloga have been pointed out. According to him it is incorrect to apply the term "iconoclastic" to this epoch because it does not fully define the period. His belief is that parallel with the religious reform which condemned images, prohibited relics, reduced the number of monasteries, and yet left the basic dogmas of the Christian faith intact, there was also a social and political reform. It was the intention of the iconoclastic emperors to take public education out of the hands of the clergy. These rulers acted, not from personal or dynastic whims, but on the basis of mature and extended deliberations, with a clear understanding of the needs of society and the demands of public opinion. They were supported by the most enlightened element of society, by the majority of the high clergy, and by the army. The final failure of the iconoclastic reforms should be attributed to the fact that there were still many people devotedly attached to the old faith, and hence extremely antagonistic to the new reforms. This group included chiefly the common people, women, and the enormous number of monks. Leo III was apparently unable to educate the people in the new spirit.[64] Such, in brief, are the views of Paparrigopoulo with regard to this epoch; but there is no doubt that he exaggerated when he regarded the reform activities of the emperors of the eighth century as a remarkable attempt at a social, political, and religious revolution. Still, he was the first scholar to point out the complexity and importance of the iconoclastic period, thus inducing others to pay closer attention to it. There were some who believed that the iconoclastic policy of the emperors was prompted by both religious and political considerations, with a decided predominance of the latter; they maintained that Leo III, desirous of being the sole autocratic ruler in all aspects of life, hoped, by prohibiting the worship of images, to liberate the people from the strong influence of the church, which used image-worship as one of its strongest tools in securing the allegiance of the laity. Leo's final ideal was to attain unlimited power over a religiously united people. The religious life of the Empire was to be regulated

---

[64] Paparrigopoulo, *Histoire de la civilisation héllenique*, 188–91. The same views were developed by the author earlier in his *History of the Greek People*, III.

by the iconoclastic policy of the emperors, which was intended to aid these rulers in the realization of their political ideals "surrounded by the halo of reformatory zeal."[65] In more recent times some scholars (the Frenchman Lombard, for instance) began to view iconoclasm as a purely religious reform which aimed to arrest "the progress of the revival of paganism" in the form of excessive image-worship, and "restore Christianity to its original purity." Lombard believed that this religious reform developed parallel with the political changes, but had a history of its own.[66] The French Byzantine scholar, Bréhier, called particular attention to the fact that iconoclasm involves two distinctly different questions: (1) the habitually discussed question of image-worship itself, and (2) the problem of the legality of religious art, i.e., the question as to whether or not it was permissible to resort to art as a means of depicting the supernatural world, and of representing the Saints, the Holy Virgin, and Jesus Christ. In other words, Bréhier brought to the fore the question of the influence of iconoclasm upon Byzantine art.[67] Finally, C. N. Uspensky shifted the emphasis from iconoclasm to the policy of the government against the rise and growth of monasterial landownership. He wrote:

Leo's administrative measures were basically and essentially directed from the very beginning against the monasteries, which toward the eighth century came to occupy a very unnatural position in the empire. In its fundamental aims the policy of Leo III was not based upon any religious considerations, but the persecuted monastic groups, the defenders of monastic feudalism, found it to their advantage to transfer the dispute to theological grounds in order to be able to claim that the activity of the emperors was atheistic and heretical, thus discrediting the movement and undermining the confidence of the masses in their emperor. The true nature of the movement was thus skillfully disguised and can be rediscovered only with very great effort.[68]

In view of these varied opinions, it is evident that the iconoclastic movement was an extremely complex phenomenon; and unfortunately the condition of the sources still prevents its clarification.[69]

---

[65] K. Schwarzlose, *Der Bilderstreit, ein Kampf der Griechischen Kirche um ihre Eigenart und ihre Freiheit,* 42, 46, 48, 50.

[66] *Constantine V,* 105, 124, 127, 128.

[67] *La Querelle des images,* 3–4.

[68] *Outlines in the History of Byzantium,* 213, 237. See Iorga, "Sur les origine de l'iconoclasme," *Bulletin de la section historique de l'Académie roumaine,* XII (1924), 147–48. G. Ostrogorsky vigorously rejects C. Uspensky's theory, *Byzantinische Zeitschrift,* XXX (1929–30), 399 and n. 2.

[69] Recent surveys of the iconoclastic movement have been made by H. Leclercq, "Images," *Dictionnaire d'archéologie chrétienne,* VII, 180–302; and by Th. I. Uspensky, *Byzantine Empire,* II, 22–53, 89–109, 157–74. See also E. J. Martin, *History of the Iconoclastic Controversy;* J. Marx, *Der Bilderstreit der byzantinischen Kaiser;* G. B. Ladner, "Origin and Significance of the Byzantine Iconoclastic Controversy," *Medieval Studies,* II (1940), 127–49. L. Bréhier, "Iconoclasme," *Histoire de l'Église,* ed. A. Fliche and V. Martin, V, 431–70 (until 754). Very important; an excellent bibliography.

In the first place, all the iconoclastic emperors were of eastern origin: Leo III and his dynasty were Isaurians, or perhaps Syrians; the restorers of iconoclasm in the ninth century were Leo V, an Armenian, and Michael II and his son Theophilus, born in the Phrygian province of central Asia Minor. The restorers of image-worship were both women, Irene and Theodora, Irene of Greek descent and Theodora from Paphlagonia in Asia Minor, a province on the coast of the Black Sea bordering Bithynia and at no great distance from the capital. Neither of them, that is, came from the central parts of the peninsula. The place of origin of the iconoclastic rulers cannot be viewed as accidental. The fact of their eastern birth may aid in reaching a clearer understanding of both their part in the movement and the meaning of the movement itself.

The opposition to image-worship in the eighth and ninth centuries was not an entirely new and unexpected movement. It had already gone through a long period of evolution. Christian art in representing the human figure in mosaics, fresco, sculpture, or carving had for a long time unsettled the minds of many deeply religious people by its resemblance to the practices of forsaken paganism. At the very beginning of the fourth century the Council of Elvira (in Spain) had ruled "that there must be no pictures (*picturas*) in the church, that the walls should have no images of that which is revered and worshipped" (*ne quod colitur et adoratur in parietibus depingatur*).[70]

In the fourth century, when Christianity received legal sanction and later became the state religion, the churches were beginning to be embellished with images. In the fourth and fifth centuries image-worship rose and developed in the Christian church. Confusion with regard to this practice persisted. The church historian of the fourth century, Eusebius of Caesarea, referred to the worship of images of Jesus Christ and the apostles Peter and Paul as "a habit of the Gentiles."[71] Also in the fourth century Epiphanius of Cyprus related in a letter that he had torn in pieces a church curtain (*velum*) with the image of Jesus Christ or one of the saints, because it "defiled the church."[72] In the

---

[70] J. D. Mansi, *Sacrorum conciliorum nova et amplissima collectio*, II, 11 (*Consilium Liberitanum*, par. XXXVI). On a different interpretation of this text see Leclercq, *Dictionnaire d'archéologie chrétienne*, VII, 215. But the text is clear. On the authenticity of the act of the Council of Elvira, see, e.g., A. Harnack, *Geschichte der altchristlichen Litteratur bis Eusebis*, II. *Die Chronologie*, II, 450: "ihre Echtheit . . . bedarf keiner Beweisfuhrung." The date of the Council, A. Piganiol, *L'Empereur Constantin le Grand*, 81–82.

[71] *Historia ecclesiastica*, VII, 18, 4.

[72] The Greek text in G. Ostrogorsky, *Stu-

dien zur Geschichte des byzantinischen Bilderstreites*, 74; cf. the Latin version, *ibid.*, 74, 86. P. Maas, "Die ikonoclastiche Episode in dem Briefe des Epiphanios an Johannes," *Byzantinische Zeitschrift*, XXX (1929–30), 282; also in Migne, *Patrologia Graeca*, XLIII, 390. Against the authenticity, D. Serruys, in *Comptes rendus de l'Académie des inscriptions et belles-lettres*, I (1904), 361–63; and Ostrogorsky, *Geschichte des byzantinischen Bilderstreites*, 83–88. But H. Grégoire, *Byzantian* IV (1909), 769–70; F. Dölger, in *Göttingische gelehrte Anzeigen* (1929), 357–58 (very interesting review of Ostrogorsky's

fifth century a Syrian bishop, before he was ordained to his high post, denounced icons. In the sixth century a serious upheaval in Antioch was directed
against the worship of pictures, and in Edessa the rioting soldiers flung stones
at the miraculous image of Christ. There were instances of attacks upon
images and of the destruction of some icons in the seventh century. In western
Europe the bishop of Massilia (Marseilles) at the end of the sixth century
ordered that all icons be removed from the churches and destroyed. Pope
Gregory I the Great wrote to him praising him for his zeal in advocating
that nothing created by human hands should serve as an object of adoration
(*nequid manufactum adorari posset*), but at the same time reprimanding him
for the destruction of the images since thereby he had taken away all chance
for historical education from people who are ignorant of letters but "could
at least read by looking at the walls what they cannot read in books."[73] In
another letter to the same bishop the pope wrote: "In that thou forbadest them
to be adored, we altogether praise thee; but we blame thee for having broken
them. . . . To adore a picture is one thing (*picturam adorare*), but to learn
through the story of the picture what is to be adored, is another."[74] In the
opinion of Gregory the Great and many others, then, images served as a
means of popular education.

The iconoclastic tendencies of the eastern provinces were somewhat influenced by the Jews, whose faith forbade image-worship, and who at times
attacked any form of such worship with great violence. A similar influence
began to be exerted from the second half of the seventh century by the Muslims, who, guided by the words of the Koran, "Images are an abomination
of the work of Satan" (V. 92), viewed icon-worship as a form of idolatry. It
is frequently stated by historians that the Arabian câliph Yazid II issued a
decree in his state three years before Leo's edict by which he prescribed the
destruction of images in the churches of his Christian subjects; the authenticity
of this story, without much basis for the doubt, is sometimes questioned.[75] In
any event, Muhammedan influence upon the eastern provinces should be taken
into consideration in any study of the anti-image movement. One chronicler refers to Emperor Leo as "the Saracen-minded" (σαρακηνόφρων),[76]

book). Maas, *Byzantinische Zeitschrift*, XXX
(1929–30), 279, 286; and Stein, *Byzantinische
Zeitschrift*, XXIX (1928), 356.

[73] *Epistolae*, IX, 105; ed. Migne, *Patrologia
Latina*, LXXVII, 105; ed. L. M. Hartmann,
Mon. Germ. Hist., Epistolarum, II, 195; Eng-
lish trans. *A Select Library of Nicene and
Post-Nicene Fathers of the Christian Church*,
ed. P. Schaff and others, 2nd ser., XIII, 23.

[74] *Epistolae*, XI, 13; ed. Migne, LXXVII,

1128; ed. Hartmann, VI, 10; *Nicene and Post-
Nicene Fathers*, XIII, 54.

[75] See, e.g., C. Becker, *Vom Werden und
Wesen der Islamischen Welt: Islamstudien*,
I, 446 (he asserted that the edict of Yazid was
issued).

[76] Theophanes, *Chronographia*, ed. de Boor,
405. Iorga called this epithet "un sobriquet et
une calomnie," *Bulletin de la section historique de l'Académie roumaine*, XI (1924),
143, n. 3.

although in reality there is very little basis for claiming that he was directly influenced by Islam. Finally, one of the widely known Eastern medieval sects, the Paulicians, who lived in the east-central part of Asia Minor, was also strongly opposed to image-worship. Briefly, in the eastern Byzantine provinces of Asia Minor there had grown up by the time of Leo III a strong iconoclastic movement. One of the Russian church historians, A. P. Lebedev, wrote: "It may be positively asserted that the number of iconoclasts before the iconoclastic period [in the eighth century] was large, and that they were a force of which the church itself had ample reason to be afraid."[77] One of the main centers of the iconoclastic movement was Phrygia, one of the central provinces in Asia Minor.

Meanwhile image-worship had spread very widely and grown very strong. Images of Jesus Christ, the Holy Virgin, and various saints, as well as pictures of scenes from the Old and New Testaments, were used in profusion for decorating Christian temples. The images placed in various churches of this period were either mosaics, frescoes, or carvings in ivory, wood, or bronze—in other words, they were both painted images and statue images, while many small pictures were reproduced in illuminated manuscripts (miniatures). Particularly great was the reverence for the so-called "icons not made by human hands," which, in the belief of the faithful, were supposed to possess miraculous powers. Images found their way into family life, for icons were sometimes chosen as godfathers for children, and embroidered images of saints decorated the parade dress of the Byzantine aristocracy. The toga of one of the senators bore embroidered pictures representing the history of the entire life of Jesus Christ.

The image-worshipers sometimes took the adoration of pictures too literally, adoring not the person or the idea represented by the image, but the image itself or the material of which it was made. This fact was a great temptation for many of the faithful, to whom this adoration of inanimate objects appealed because of its kinship with pagan practices. "In the capital," according to N. P. Kondakov, "there was at the same time a characteristic increase in the number of monasteries, monastic communes, and convents of all kinds which multiplied very rapidly and reached incredible proportions by the end of the eighth century (perhaps, more correctly, toward the eighth century)."[78] In the opinion of I. D. Andreev, the number of Byzantine monks in the iconoclastic period may be estimated without any exaggeration at 100,000. "Remembering," said this scholar, "that in Russia of today [this is written in 1907], with its 120,000,000 population spread over a vast territory, there are only about 40,000 monks and nuns, it is easy to imagine how dense must have

[77] *Ecumenical Councils of the Sixth, Seventh, and Eighth Centuries* (3rd ed., 1904), 142.   [78] *Iconography of the Holy Virgin*, II, 3.

been the net of monasteries covering the comparatively small territory of the Byzantine Empire."[79]

And while, on the one hand, the worship of ordinary and miraculous icons and relics confused many people who had grown up under the prevailing influences of the period, the excessive development of monachism and the rapid growth of monasteries, on the other hand, clashed with the secular interests of the Byzantine state. In view of the fact that large numbers of healthy young men embraced the spiritual life, the Empire was losing necessary forces from its army, agriculture, and industry. Monachism and the monasteries frequently served as a refuge for those who wished to escape governmental duties; hence many of the monks were not men who had been prompted to retire from worldly affairs by a sincere desire to follow higher ideals. Two aspects in the ecclesiastical life of the eighth century should be distinguished—the religious and the secular.

The iconoclastic emperors, born in the East, were well acquainted with the religious views prevalent in the eastern provinces; they grew up with these views and were closely identified with them. Upon ascending the Byzantine throne they brought their views to the capital and made them the basis of their church policy. These emperors were neither infidels nor rationalists, as used to be maintained. On the contrary, they were men of a sincere and convinced faith, and desired to purge religion of those errors which permeated it and diverted it from its true original course.[80] From their point of view, image-worship and the adoration of relics were both survivals of paganism which had to be abolished at all costs in order to restore the Christian faith to its original pure form. "I am emperor and priest," wrote Leo III to Pope Gregory II.[81] With this claim as a point of departure, Leo III considered it his legal right to make his own religious views compulsory for all his subjects. This attitude cannot be viewed as an innovation. It was the accepted caesaro-

---

[79] *Germanus and Tarasius, Patriarchs of Constantinople,* 79.

[80] On the interesting correspondence on doctrinal questions between the Calif Umar II and Leo III, which has been preserved by the Armenian historian Ghevond and may be spurious, see an accurate study by A. Jeffery, "Ghevond's Text of the Correspondence between Umar II and Leo III," *Harvard Theological Review,* XXXVII (1944), 269–332.

[81] Gregorii II, *Epistola,* XIII: *ad Leonem Isaurum imperatorem;* Migne, *Patrologia Latina,* LXXXIX, 521 (*imperator sum et sacerdos*). The problem of whether the letters of Gregory II to Leo III are spurious (see L. Guérard, "Les Lettres de Grégoire II à Léon

L'Isaurien," *Mélanges d'archéologie et d'histoire,* X [1890], 44–60) or genuine (see, e.g., H. Mann, *The Lives of the Popes* [2nd ed., 1925], I, 498–502), is not very important for our purpose. In any case the letter was written or fabricated on very good evidence. See J. B. Bury, Appendix 14 to the fifth volume of his edition of Gibbon; Hefele-Leclercq, *Histoires des conciles,* III (2), 659–64. Cabrol, *Dictionnaire d'archéologie chrétienne,* VII (1), 248. A new edition of the letters of Gregory II by E. Caspar, *Zeitschrift für Kirchengeschichte,* LII (1933), 29–89, esp. 76. More recent studies are rather in favor of the authenticity of the letters.

papistic view of the Byzantine emperors particularly prevalent in the time of Justinian the Great, who had also considered himself the sole authority in spiritual as well as in temporal matters. Leo III, too, was a convinced representative of the idea of Caesaropapism.

The first nine years of Leo's reign, devoted to repelling external enemies and to establishing the security of the throne, were not marked by any measures with regard to images. The ecclesiastical activity of the Emperor during this period was expressed only in his demand that the Jews and the eastern sect of Montanists be baptized.

Only in the tenth year of his rule, i.e., in the year 726, did the Emperor, according to the chronicler Theophanes, "begin to speak of the destruction of the holy and all-honoured icons."[82] The majority of contemporary scholars believe that the first edict against images was promulgated in 726 or perhaps 725. Unfortunately the text of this decree is unknown.[83] Soon after the proclamation of the edict Leo ordered the destruction of the venerated statue of Christ situated above one of the doors of the Chalke, as the magnificent entrance to the imperial palace was called. The destruction of this icon caused a riot, in which the main participants were women. The imperial officer delegated to destroy the image was killed, but his murder was avenged by the Emperor's severe punishment of the defenders of the statue. These victims were the first martyrs of icon worship.

Leo's hostility toward image worship aroused very strong opposition. The patriarch of Constantinople, Germanus, and Gregory II, the pope of Rome, were strongly opposed to the policy of the Emperor. In Greece and on the islands of the Aegean Sea a revolt broke out in defense of images. Although this was quickly suppressed by Leo's army, this strong reaction on the part of the population made it impossible for him to undertake further decisive measures.

Finally, in the year 730, the Emperor convoked a sort of council where another edict against sacred images was promulgated. It is highly probable that this council did not produce a new edict, but merely restored the decree of the year 725 or 726.[84] Germanus, who refused to sign this decree, was deposed and forced to retire to his estate, where he spent the last years of his life peacefully. The patriarchal chair was filled by Anastasius, who willingly signed the edict. Thus, the decree against images was now issued not only on behalf of the Emperor, but also in the name of the church, since it was

[82] *Chronographia,* ed. de Boor, 404.

[83] Of the recent publications see, e.g., Charles Diehl, "Leo III and the Isaurian Dynasty (717–802)," *Cambridge Medieval History,* IV, 9. Leclercq, in *Dictionnaire d'arché-* ologie chrétienne, VII (1), 240–41; Th. I. Uspensky, *Byzantine History,* II, 25 ff.

[84] See Leclercq, "Constantin," *Dictionnaire d'archéologie chrétienne,* III, 248 (he refers the second edict to the year 729).

sanctioned by the signature of the patriarch. This authority was of great value to Leo.

Concerning the period which followed the proclamation of this edict, namely, the last eleven years of Leo's reign, sources are silent with regard to the persecution of images. Apparently there were no instances of ill treatment. In any event, systematic persecution of images in the reign of Leo III is out of the question. At most, there were only a few isolated instances of open image destruction. According to one scholar, "In the time of Leo III there was rather a *preparation* to persecute images and their worshipers than actual persecution."[85]

The assertion that the image-breaking movement of the eighth century began, not by the destruction of images, but by hanging them higher up, so as to remove them from the adoration of the faithful, must be disregarded, for the majority of images in Byzantine churches were painted frescoes or mosaics which could not be removed or transferred from the church walls.

Leo's hostile policy against images has found some reflection in the three famous treatises "Against Those Who Depreciate the Icons," by John Damascene, who lived in the time of the first iconoclastic emperor within the boundaries of the Arabian caliphate. Two of these treatises were written, in all likelihood, in the time of Leo. The date of the third one cannot be determined with any degree of accuracy.

Pope Gregory II, who opposed Leo's policy of image-breaking, was succeeded by Pope Gregory III, who convoked a council in Rome and excluded the iconoclasts from the church. Following this step, middle Italy detached itself from the Byzantine Empire and became completely controlled by papal and western European interests. Southern Italy still remained under Byzantine sway.

Quite different was the picture in the reign of Constantine V Copronymus (741–75), the successor of Leo III. Educated by his father, Constantine followed a very determined iconoclastic policy and in the last years of his reign, initiated the persecution of monasteries and monks. No other iconoclastic ruler has been subjected to so much slander in the writings of the iconodules as this "many-headed dragon," "cruel persecutor of the monastic order," this "Ahab and Herod." It is very difficult, therefore, to form an unprejudiced opinion of Constantine. It is with some exaggeration that E. Stein called him the boldest and freest thinker of all eastern Roman history.[86]

The Council of 754 and its aftermath.—At the time of Constantine's accession the European provinces were still devoted to icon worship, while those

---

[85] Andreev, *Germanus and Tarasius*, 71.   [86] *Studien zur Geschichte des byzantinischen Reiches*, 140.

of Asia Minor had among their population a large number of iconoclasts. Constantine spent the first two years of his reign in constant struggle with his brother-in-law Artavasdus, who was leading a rebellion in defense of images. Artavasdus succeeded in forcing Constantine to leave the capital, and was proclaimed emperor. During his year of rule over the Empire he restored image worship. Constantine succeeded, however, in deposing Artavasdus and he reclaimed the throne and severely punished the instigators of the revolt. Yet the attempt of Artavasdus demonstrated to Constantine that icon worship might be restored without great difficulties, and it forced him to take more decisive steps to strengthen the validity of iconoclastic views in the conscience of the masses.

With this aim in view Constantine decided to convoke a council which would work out the foundations of an iconoclastic policy, sanction its validity, and thus create among the people the conviction that the Emperor's measures were just. This council, attended by more than three hundred bishops, convened in the palace of Hieria on the Asiatic shore of the Bosphorus facing Constantinople. It gathered in the year 754.[87] The members of the council did not include any patriarchs, for the see of Constantinople was vacant at that time, while Antioch, Jerusalem, and Alexandria refused to participate, and the papal legates also failed to appear at the sessions. In later times these facts were used as a sufficient basis by opponents of this council for claiming that its decisions were invalid. Several months after the opening of the sessions the council was transferred to Constantinople, where the election of a new patriarch had meanwhile taken place.

The decree of the council of 754, which has been preserved in the acts of the Seventh Ecumenical Council (perhaps in parts and in a somewhat modified form), definitely condemned image worship by proclaiming the following:

Supported by the Holy Scriptures and the Fathers, we declare unanimously in the name of the Holy Trinity, that there shall be rejected and removed and cursed out of the Christian Church every likeness which is made out of any material whatever by the evil art of painters. Whoever in the future dares to make such a thing or to venerate it, or set it up in a church or in a private house, or possesses it in secret, shall, if bishop, priest or deacon, be deposed, if monk or layman, anathematised and become liable to be tried by the secular laws as an adversary of God and an enemy of the doctrines handed down by the Fathers.

Besides the general significance of this proclamation for image-worship, this decree is notable also for prescribing that persons guilty of icon worship should

---

[87] On the date, Ostrogorsky, *Geschichte des byzantinischen Bilderstreites,* 14, n. 1. *Histoire de l'Église,* ed. Fliche and Martin, V, 468.   The year 753 has usually been accepted up to this time.

be tried by imperial laws, thus placing the iconodules under the jurisdiction of temporal power. This fact was later used by the members of the Seventh Ecumenical Council as an explanation of the extraordinary harshness manifested by some emperors with regard to the church and to the monks. Anathema was proclaimed for any person who "ventures to represent the divine image of the Logos after the incarnation with material colours . . . and the forms of the saints in lifeless pictures with material colours which are of no value, for this notion is erroneous and introduced by the devil." The decree ends with the following: "To New Constantine and the most pious, many years! . . . To the most pious and orthodox [empress] many years! . . . You have established the dogmas of the Holy Six Ecumenical Councils. You have destroyed all idolatry." . . . Anathema was proclaimed against the Patriarch Germanus, the "worshiper of wood," and Mansur, i.e., John Damascene, "inclined to Muhammedanism, the enemy of the Empire, the teacher of impiety, the perverter of the Scriptures."[88]

The unanimous decree of the council made a very strong impression upon the people. "Many who had been troubled by a vague impression of the error of the iconoclasts," said Professor Andreev, "could now grow calm; many who had formerly wavered between the two movements could now, on the basis of the convincing argument of the council decisions, form decisive iconoclastic views."[89] The mass of the people were required to give oath that they would forsake the worship of images.

The destruction of images, after the council, became ruthlessly severe. Images were broken, burned, painted over, and exposed to many insults. Particularly violent was the persecution of the cultus of the Blessed Virgin.[90] Many image-worshipers were executed, tortured, or imprisoned, and lost their property. Many were banished from the country and exiled to distant provinces. Pictures of trees, birds, animals, or scenes of hunting and racing replaced the sacred images in the churches. According to the *Life* of Stephen the Younger, the church of the Holy Virgin at Blachernae in Constantinople, deprived of its former magnificence and covered with new paintings, was transformed into a "fruit store and aviary."[91] In this destruction of painted icons (mosaics and frescoes) and statues many valuable monuments of art have perished. The number of illuminated manuscripts destroyed was also very large.

[88] Mansi, *Amplissima collectio conciliorum,* XIII, 323, 327, 346, 354, 355; Hefele, *History of the Councils of the Church,* V, 313–15. See an interesting discussion of the influence on the Acts of the Council of 754 of Constantine's works against icon-worship in Ostrogorsky, *Geschichte des byzantinischen Bilderstreites,* 7–29.

[89] *Germanus and Tarasius,* 96.

[90] See Ostrogorsky, *Geschichte des byzantinischen Bilderstreites,* 29–40.

[91] Migne, *Patrologia Graeca,* C, 1120. V. G. Vasilievsky, "The Life of Stephen the Younger," *Works,* II, 324.

The destruction of images was accompanied also by the destruction of relics. Time has preserved a satire of the iconoclastic period on the excessive adoration of relics in which the author speaks of ten hands of the martyr Procopius, of fifteen jaws of Theodore, of four heads of George, etc.[92]

Constantine V displayed extreme intolerance toward the monasteries and initiated a crusade against the monks, those "idolaters and lovers of darkness."[93] His struggle with monachism was so intense that some scholars find the question of a more accurate definition of the reforms of this period somewhat debatable, claiming that it is difficult to determine whether it was a struggle against images or a fight directed against the monks; C. N. Uspensky stated definitely that "historians and theologians have purposely distorted the reality of facts by advancing the 'iconomachia,' rather than the 'monachomachia,' of the period."[94] The persecutions of monks expressed itself in many severe measures. They were forced to put on secular dress, and some were compelled to marry by force or threats. In one instance they were forced to march in file through the hippodrome, each holding a woman by the hand, amid the sneers and insults of the crowd of spectators. The chronicler Theophanes relates that a governor in Asia Minor assembled the monks and nuns of his province at Ephesus and said to them, "Let each who wishes to obey the Emperor and us put on the white dress and take a wife immediately; those who do not do so shall be blinded and exiled to Cyprus," and he was congratulated by Constantine V, who wrote: "I have found in you a man after my own heart who carries out all my wishes."[95] Cyprus apparently was one of the emperor's places of exile for recalcitrant monks. It is recorded that five monks managed to escape from there, reached the territory of the caliphate, and were brought to Bagdad.[96] Monasteries were taken away from the monks and transformed into barracks and arsenals. Monasterial estates were confiscated. Laymen were forbidden to take refuge in the cowl. All these regulations led to a wide migration of monks to districts unaffected by the Emperor's iconoclastic persecutions. According to some scholars, in the time of Leo and Constantine Italy alone received about 50,000 of these refugees.[97] This

[92] Paparrigopoulo, *History of the Greek People*, ed. P. Karolides, III, 703–7. This satire belongs to the poet of the first half of the eleventh century, Christopher of Mytilene. See *Die Gedichte des Christophoros Mitylenaios*, ed. E. Kurtz, 76–80 (no. 114); Russian trans. D. Shestakov, "The Three Poets of the Byzantine Renaissance," *Transactions of the University of Kazan*, LXXIII, 11–14.
[93] Vasilievsky, "Life of Stephen," *Works*, II, 322.
[94] *History of Byzantium*, I, 228.
[95] Theophanes, *Chronographia*, ed. de Boor,

445, 446. Similar information is reported in the *Life of S. Romanus the Néomartyr*. P. Peeters, "S. Romain le Néomartyr († 1 mai 780) d'après un document géorgien," *Analecta Bollandiana*, XXX (1911), 413. S. Romanus, born in Galatia *circa* 730, left his country for the East, was captured by the Arabs, and suffered martyrdom on the shores of the Euphrates in 780.
[96] *The Life of S. Romanus the Néomartyr*, 419.
[97] Andreev, *Germanus and Tarasius*, 78.

event was of enormous significance for the fate of medieval southern Italy, for it upheld there the predominance of the Greek nationality and the Orthodox church. But even southern Italy was apparently not altogether free from icono-clastic troubles. At least there is a very interesting indication that in the ninth century A.D. St. Gregory the Decapolite fell into the hands of an iconoclastic bishop of the south-Italian city of Hydrus (now Otranto).[98] Many monks migrated also to the northern shores of the Euxine (the Black Sea), and to the coast of Syria and Palestine. Among the martyrs who suffered under Constantine V, Stephen the Younger is particularly famous.

During the reign of Leo IV the Khazar (775–80) the internal life of the Empire was calmer than under his father Constantine V. Although Leo, too, was an adherent of iconoclasm, he felt no acute enmity towards the monks, who once more regained a certain amount of influence. In his brief reign he did not manifest himself as a fanatical iconoclast. It is very likely that he was influenced to some extent by his young wife, Irene, an Athenian who was famous for her devotion to image-worship and to whom all image-worshipers of the empire turned hopeful faces. "His moderate attitude in the icon con-troversy," Ostrogorsky explained, "was an appropriate transition from the tactics of Constantine V to the restoration of the holy images under the Em-press Irene."[99] With Leo's death in 780 ended the first period of iconoclasm. Because his son, Constantine VI, was a minor, the rule of the Empire was entrusted to Irene, who was determined to restore image worship.

In spite of her definite leanings toward image-worship, Irene did not under-take any decisive measures in the direction of its official restoration during the first three years of her reign. This postponement was due to the fact that all the forces of the Empire had to be directed to the internal struggle with the pretender to the throne and to the external fight with the Slavs who lived in Greece. Furthermore, the restoration of icon-worship had to be approached with great caution, because the major part of the army was favorably inclined to iconoclasm, and the canons of the iconoclastic council of 754 declared by Constantine as imperial laws continued to exert a certain amount of influence upon many people in the Byzantine Empire. It is quite likely, however, that many members of the higher clergy accepted the decrees of the iconoclastic council by compulsion rather than by conviction; hence they constituted, according to Professor Andreev, "an element which yielded readily to the reformatory operations of the iconoclastic emperors, but which would not form any real opposition to the measures of an opposite tendency."[100]

In the fourth year of Irene's reign the see of Constantinople was given to Tarasius, who declared that it was necessary to convoke an ecumenical council

---

[98] See F. Dvornik, *La vie de saint Grégoire de Décapolite et les Slaves Macédoniens au IXe siècle*, 41, 58.

[99] *Geschichte des byzantinischen Bilder-streites*, 38.

[100] *Germanus and Tarasius*, 98.

for the purpose of restoring image-worship. Pope Hadrian I was invited to attend and to send his legates. The council gathered in the year 786 in the Temple of the Holy Apostles. But the troops of the capital, hostile to icon-worship, rushed into the temple with drawn swords and forced the assembly to disperse. It seemed that the iconoclastic party had triumphed once more, but it was only for a brief period. Irene skillfully replaced the disobedient troops by new soldiers, more loyal to her ideals.

In the following year (787) the council convened in the Bithynian city of Nicaea, where the First Ecumenical Council had been held. Seven meetings of the council, from which the Emperor and Empress were absent, took place in Nicaea. The eighth and last assembly was held in the imperial palace at Constantinople. The number of bishops who came to this council exceeded three hundred. This was the seventh and last ecumenical council in the history of the eastern church.

Image-worship was restored by the decree of this council. The adoration of holy images was confirmed, and those who disagreed with the ruling of the council were anathematized. Excommunication was also proclaimed for those "who called the holy images idols and who asserted that the Christians resort to icons as if the latter were Gods, or that the Catholic church had ever accepted idols." The bishops of the council acclaimed "a New Contantine and a New Helen."[101] It was ruled that relics had to be placed in all of the restored temples from which these necessary attributes of an orthodox church were absent. The transformation of monasteries into common dwellings was severely condemned, and orders were issued to restore all the monasteries abolished and secularized by the iconoclasts. The council devoted much of its attention to raising the morality of the clergy by condemning the buying of church offices for money (simony), etc. It also prohibited the existence of mixed monasteries (for both sexes).

The great importance of the Nicene Council does not lie only in the restoration of image-worship. This council created for the iconodules the organization which they had lacked in their early struggle with their opponents; it collected all theological arguments in favor of images, which could later be used by the iconodules in their disputes with the iconoclasts. In brief, the council provided for the iconodule party a weapon which facilitated all future struggles with their antagonists when the second period of the iconoclastic movement set in.

The so-called "iconoclastic" activities of the emperors of the eighth century were only one, and perhaps not the most important, aspect of that period. For most of the data on this period comes from the later one-sided literary tradition of the triumphant icon-worshiping party which destroyed practically all the

101 Mansi, *Amplissima collectio conciliorum*, XIII, 739–40.

iconoclastic documents. But owing to some occasional and scattered information which has survived one may conclude that the main energy of Leo III and Constantine V was directed toward the secularization of large monasterial landed property and the limitation of the enormous number of monks, that is to say, against the elements which, by escaping state control and by functioning with almost complete independence, were undermining the vital forces and unity of the Empire.

The coronation of Charles the Great and the significance of this event for the Byzantine Empire

"The coronation of Charles is not only the central event of the Middle Ages; it is also one of those very few events of which, taking them singly, it may be said that if they had not happened, the history of the world would have been different."[102] At present this event is important primarily because it concerned the Byzantine Empire.

In the conception of the medieval man the Roman Empire was a single empire, so that in previous centuries two or more emperors were viewed as two rulers governing one state. It is wrong to speak of the fall of the Western Roman Empire in the year 476. The idea of a single empire lay behind the militaristic policy of Justinian in the sixth century, and this idea was still alive in the year 800, when the famous imperial coronation of Charles the Great occurred in Rome.

While theoretically the conception of a single empire still prevailed in the ideology of the Middle Ages, in actual reality this conception was obsolete. The eastern or Byzantine Graeco-Slavic world of the late eighth century and the western Romano-Germanic world of the same period were, in language, in ethnographical composition, and in cultural problems, two distinctly different, separate worlds. The idea of a single empire was out of date and is a historical anachronism from the modern point of view, though not in the opinion of the Middle Ages.

Iconoclasm contributed its share toward preparing the event of 800. The papacy, which energetically protested against the iconoclastic measures of the Byzantine emperors and excommunicated the iconoclasts, turned to the West in the hope of finding friendship and defense in the Frankish kingdom among the rising major-domos (mayors of the palace), and later the kings of the Carolingian house. At the end of the eighth century the Frankish throne was occupied by the most famous representative of this house, Charles the Great or Charlemagne. Alcuin, a scholar and teacher at his court, wrote him a famous letter in June 799:

[102] J. Bryce, *The Holy Roman Empire*, 50.

Hitherto there have been three exalted persons in the world. (The first is) the Apostolic sublimity who rules in his stead the see of the blessed Peter, the chief of the Apostles. . . . Another is the imperial dignitary and secular possessor of the second Rome; but the report of how wickedly the ruler of that empire was dethroned, not through aliens but through his own citizens,[103] spreads everywhere. The third is (the possessor of) the royal dignity which the will of our Lord Jesus Christ has bestowed upon you as a ruler of the Christian people, more excellent in power than the other dignitaries, more famous in wisdom, more sublime in the dignity of the kingdom. You are the avenger of crimes, the guide of those who have gone astray, the consoler of those who are in distress; it is given to you to exalt the good.[104]

The mutual interests of the pope and the king of the Franks which eventually led to the coronation of the latter is a complex question, variously regarded in historical literature. The event itself is well known. On Christmas Day of the year 800, during the solemn service in the Church of St. Peter, Pope Leo III placed the imperial crown upon the head of the kneeling Charles. The people present in the church proclaimed "To Charles, the most pious Augustus crowned by God, to the Great and Peace-giving, many years and victory!"

Scholars have expressed differing opinions on the significance of Charles' acceptance of the imperial rank. Some have believed that the title of emperor gave him no new rights and that in reality he still remained, as before, only "a king of the Franks and Lombards, and a Roman patrician";[105] that is, that in receiving the crown Charles assumed only a new name. Others have thought that through the coronation of Charles in the year 800 a new western empire was created which was entirely independent of the existence of the Eastern or Byzantine Empire. To regard the event of 800 in either of these ways would mean to introduce into this analysis the opinions of later times. At the end of the eighth century there was not, and could not be, any question of a "titulary" emperor, or of the formation of a separate western empire. The coronation of Charles must be analyzed from a contemporary point of view, i.e. as it was looked upon by the participants of the event, by Charles the Great and Leo III.

Neither of these rulers intended to create a western empire which would counterbalance the Eastern Empire. Charles was undoubtedly convinced that upon receiving the title of emperor in the year 800 he became the sole ruler and the continuator of the single Roman Empire. The event meant only that Rome had reclaimed from Constantinople the right of imperial election.

---

[103] Alcuin refers here to the dethronement and blinding of the Emperor Constantine VI by his own mother, Irene.

[104] *Mon. Germ. Hist., Epistolarum,* IV; *Epistolae Carolini Aevi,* II, 288 (no. 173).

[105] W. Sickel, "Die Kaiserwahl Karls der Grossen. Eine rechtsgeschichtliche Erörterung," *Mitteilungen des Instituts für österreichische Geschichtsforschung,* XX (1899), 1–2, 3.

The mind of that time could not conceive of the simultaneous existence of two empires; in its very substance the Empire was single. "The imperial dogma of a sole empire rested upon the dogma of a sole God, since only in his capacity of God's temporary deputy could the emperor exercise divine authority on earth."[106] The prevailing conditions of this period facilitated the popular acceptance of this view of imperial power, and it was the only view possible at the time.

Relations between Charles and the Byzantine Emperor had begun long before 800. In 781 a marriage had been arranged between Rotrud, Charles' daughter, whom the Greeks called Eruthro, and Constantine, Emperor of Byzantium, at that time about twelve years old, whose mother Irene was the real ruler of the Empire.[107] A western historian of the period, Paul the Deacon, wrote to Charles: "I rejoice that your beautiful daughter may go across the seas and receive the sceptre in order that the strength of the kingdom, through her, be directed to Asia."[108]

The fact that in the Byzantine Empire in the year 797 Irene dethroned the legal emperor, her son Constantine, and became the autocratic ruler of the Empire, was in sharp contradiction to the traditions of the Roman Empire, where no woman had ever ruled with full imperial authority. From the point of view of Charles and Pope Leo, then, the imperial throne was vacant, and in accepting the imperial crown Charles ascended this vacant throne of the undivided Roman Empire and became the legal successor, not of Romulus Augustulus, but of Leo IV, Heraclius, Justinian, Theodosius, and Constantine the Great, the emperors of the eastern line. An interesting confirmation of this view is found in the fact that in western annals referring to the year 800 and to subsequent years, where events were recorded by the years of Byzantine emperors, the name of Charles follows immediately after the name of Constantine VI.

If such was the view of Charles with regard to his imperial rank, then what was the attitude of the Byzantine Empire to his coronation? The Eastern Empire, too, treated it in accordance with the prevailing views of the period. In upholding Irene's rights to the throne, the Byzantine Empire looked upon the event of 800 as one of the many attempts of revolt against the legal ruler, and feared, not without reason, that the newly proclaimed emperor, following the example of other insurgents, might decide to advance toward Constantinople in order to dethrone Irene and seize the imperial throne by force. In the eyes of the Byzantine government this event was only a revolt of some western provinces against the legal ruler of the empire.[109]

---

[106] A. Gasquet, *L'Empire byzantin et la monarchie franque,* 284–85.

[107] Dölger, *Regesten,* I, 41 (no. 339); sources and literature are indicated.

[108] "Versus Pauli Diaconi, XII," *Poetae latini aevi carolini,* I, 50.

[109] In 1893, J. B. Bury published a very interesting and daring paper on Charles the

Charles was of course fully aware of the precariousness of his position and of the fact that his coronation did not settle the question of his rule over the eastern part of the empire. The German historian P. Schramm, who called Charles' coronation "an act of violence which infringed on the rights of the Basileus," pointed out the fact that Charles did not name himself "Emperor of the Romans," the official title of the Byzantine emperors, but *"imperium Romanum gubernans."*[110] Charles realized that after Irene the Byzantine Empire would elect another emperor, whose right to the imperial title would be recognized as indisputable in the East. Anticipating complications, Charles opened negotiations with Irene by proposing marriage to her, hoping "thus to unite the Eastern and Western provinces."[111] In other words, Charles understood that his title meant very little unless recognized by the Byzantine Empire. Irene received the marriage proposal favorably, but shortly after she was dethroned and exiled (in the year 802) so that the project was never executed.

After Irene's fall the Byzantine sceptre came into the hands of Nicephorus, and between Charles and Nicephorus negotiations were carried on, probably in regard to the recognition of Charles' imperial title. But it was not until the year 812 that the legates of the Byzantine Emperor Michael I Rangabé saluted Charles at Aix-la-Chapelle (Aachen) as emperor. This finally legalized the imperial election of the year 800. It is also perhaps from the year 812 that as a counterpoise to the title yielded to Charlemagne, the title "Emperor of the Romans" (Βασιλεὺς τῶν Ῥωμαίων) began to be used officially in Byzantium, designating the legitimate sovereign of Constantinople, as the symbol of supreme power of the Byzantine emperors.[112] From the year 812 onward there were two Roman emperors, in spite of the fact that in theory there was still only one Roman Empire. "In other words," said Bury, "the

---

Great and Irene in which he attempted to suggest that the original conception of the imperial coronation of 800 came from Irene herself. Bury, "Charles the Great and Irene," *Hermathena,* VIII (1893), 17–37. This paper has remained practically unknown to scholars, and even Bury himself, though he did not expressly reject his own suggestion, omitted mention of it in his *History of the Eastern Roman Empire,* 317–21, when he discussed the negotiations between Charles and the Byzantine court. See N. Baynes, *A Bibliography of the Works of J. B. Bury,* 7–8, 136. Baynes remarked of Bury's silence: "This is a pity: one feels that it is a theory which *ought* to have been true!"

[110] *Kaiser, Rom und Renovatio,* I, 12–13.

[111] Theophanes, *Chronographia,* ed. de Boor, 475. Diehl rejects the existence of these negotiations, *Cambridge Medieval History,* IV, 24. In 800 Irene was fifty years old. See Bury, "Charles the Great and Irene," *Hermathena,* VIII (1893), 24; Irene was only forty-four in 794. Ostrogorsky is doubtful of the negotiations: *Geschichte des byzantinischen Staates,* 128, n. 2.

[112] See F. Dölger, "Bulgarisches Cartun und byzantinisches Kaisertum," *Actes du IVᵉ Congrès international des études byzantines,* September, 1934. *Bulletin de l'Institut archéologique Bulgare,* IX (1935), 61. G. Brătianu, *Études byzantines d'histoire économique et sociale,* 193.

act of 812 A.D. revived, in theory, the position of the fifth century. Michael I and Charles, Leo V and Lewis the Pious, stood to one another as Arcadius to Honorius, as Valentinian III to Theodosius II; the *imperium Romanum* stretched from the borders of Armenia to the shores of the Atlantic."[113] It is self-evident that this unity of the Empire was purely nominal and theoretical. Both empires led distinctly different lives. Furthermore, the very idea of unity was being forgotten in the West.

The imperial rank obtained by Charles for the West was not long lived. During the ensuing troubles, followed by the disintegration of Charles' monarchy, the title fell to casual holders. It disappeared completely in the first half of the tenth century, only to rise again in the second half, but this time in its unhistorical form of "The Holy Roman Empire of the German Nation."

Only after the year 800 is it possible to speak of an Eastern Roman Empire, and J. B. Bury did this by entitling the third volume of his *History of the Byzantine Empire,* which embraces events from 802 (the year of Irene's fall) to the beginning of the Macedonian dynasty, *A History of the Eastern Roman Empire,* while the first two volumes of his work bear the title of *A History of the Later Roman Empire.*

Summary of the activities of the Isaurian dynasty

Historians place much value upon the services of the first rulers of the Isaurian line, particularly upon the achievements of Leo III, and justly so, for the latter, having ascended the throne after a highly troubled period of anarchy, showed himself to be an eminent general, a gifted administrator, and a wise legislator who understood the problems of his time. The religious policy of the iconoclasts stands quite apart from their other activities. In most of the historical writings Leo III is praised very highly. For instance, the Greeks recognize him "as one of the greatest rulers of the Eastern Empire, and one of the benefactors of humanity,"[114] the Germans, "as one of the greatest men on the imperial throne," who clearly understood the need for "radical reform at the head and in the members,"[115] "a man who was destined to restore the empire by means of iron and blood, a person of great military

[113] *Eastern Roman Empire,* 325. See also L. Halphen, *Les barbares des grandes invasions aux conquêtes turques du XI⁰ siècle,* 243–50. The title "Emperor of the Romans" has been discovered on an imperial seal of the eighth century. In reference to this Dölger stated that the solemn title "Emperor of the Romans" occurs frequently in official documents after 812, but not before, but it might occasionally have been used before that date.

Dölger, *Byzantinische Zeitschrift,* XXXVII (1937), 579. Grégoire, *Byzantion,* XI (1936), 482. For a general discussion of this question, see Ostrogorsky, *Geschichte des byzantinischen Staates,* 137, n. 2.

[114] Paparrigopoulo, Ἱστορία τοῦ ἑλληνικοῦ ἔθνους, III, 467.

[115] K. Schenk, "Kaiser Leons III Walten im Innern," *Byzantinische Zeitschrift,* V (1896), 289, 296.

genius."[116] An English scholar referred to Leo's achievements as "the regeneration of the Roman Empire,"[117] while a French historian characterized the deeds of the Isaurian emperors as "one of the very greatest and most admirable efforts that has ever been made for raising the moral, material, and intellectual level of the people," and compared the importance of their "sweeping attempt at organization with the measures undertaken by Charles the Great."[118] In recent times Charles Diehl made the statement that "from the government of the Isaurian emperors a new principle of life sprung forth, which was to enrich the world forever."[119] In the somewhat casual estimates of Russian scholars, who, with the exception of the church historians, have not yet made any attempts at a detailed study of the general history of the Isaurian emperors, there is no excessive praise for these rulers. The three volumes of J. A. Kulakovsky deal only with events up to the epoch of the iconoclastic emperors. The first volume of *Lectures in Byzantine History,* by S. P. Shestakov, which covers this period, does not contain any estimate. A very interesting and fresh appraisal of the antimonasterial and antimonastic movement is found in the *Outlines* of C. N. Uspensky. Finally, Th. I. Uspensky remarked: "Leo the Isaurian is responsible for the rather rude manner with which the delicate problem of faith and worship of God was left by the government to the military and police authorities, who offended the religious feeling of the people and made of the local problem an event of state importance."[120]

While recognizing unusual energy and some administrative genius on the part of the first two iconoclastic emperors, and admitting that Leo III unquestionably saved the Empire, one must, on the basis of all the available historical materials, abstain from excessive praise of the Isaurian dynasty. For their policy, no matter how sincere on their part, introduced great internal troubles into the life of the Empire, which was seriously disturbed for more than a hundred years. Even in its first period in the eighth century the iconoclastic movement alienated Italy and brought about very strained relations with the pope, who excommunicated the iconoclasts and turned to the West for aid and protection. The resulting friendship with the Frankish rulers initiated a new and extremely significant period of medieval history. At the same time the foundation for the future final rupture between the churches was gradually being laid. During the Isaurian period the Byzantine Empire lost middle Italy, including the Ravenna exarchate, which was conquered in the middle of the eighth century by the Lombards and later handed over to the pope by Pippin the Short.

[116] H. Gelzer, *Abriss der byzantinischen Kaisergeschichte,* 960.
[117] Bury, *Later Roman Empire,* II, 410.
[118] Lombard, *Constantine V,* 169.
[119] *Cambridge Medieval History,* IV, 26.
[120] *Byzantine Empire,* II, 22.

However, no complete history of the Isaurian dynasty has yet been written, and many significant problems of this period still remain unsolved. For example, the question of the reduction of the number of monks and monasteries and of the apparently frequent secularization of monasterial lands calls for investigation. A more thorough study of the social aspect of the iconoclastic policy of the Isaurian emperors is at present one of the essential problems of Byzantine history. Careful research into this question may throw much new light upon the entire so-called "iconoclastic" epoch and disclose in it more profound meaning and still greater universal historical significance.

SUCCESSORS OF THE ISAURIANS AND THE AMORIAN OR PHRYGIAN DYNASTY (820–67)

The emperors from 802 to 867 and their origin

The time from the beginning of the ninth century until the accession of the Macedonian dynasty in the year 867 has been viewed by historians as a transitional period from the epoch of the revival of the Empire under the Isaurian emperors to the brilliant time of the Macedonian emperors. But the most recent studies show that this period is not a mere epilogue and is much more than a prologue. It appears to have an importance of its own and signifies a new phase in Byzantine culture.[121]

The revolution of the year 802 deposed Irene and raised Nicephorus I (802–11) to the Byzantine throne. According to oriental sources, Nicephorus was of Arabian origin.[122] One of his ancestors must have migrated into Pisidia, a province in Asia Minor, where Nicephorus was later born. The revolution of 802 was in its nature very rare in the annals of Byzantine history. An overwhelming majority of political uprisings in the Byzantine Empire were organized and led by military generals, leaders of the army. The case of Nicephorus was an exception to this general rule, for he was in no way connected with the army and held only the high post of minister of finance. This emperor fell in battle with the Bulgarians in the year 811, and the throne passed, for a few months, to his son Stauracius, who had also been severely wounded in the Bulgarian campaign. Stauracius died in the same year (811), but even before his death he was deposed in favor of the curopalates Michael I, a member of the Greek family of Rangabé, married to Procopia, a sister of the unfortunate Strauracius and a daughter of Nicephorus I. But Michael I also ruled only for a short period of time (811–13), for he was deposed, chiefly because

---

[121] Bury, *Eastern Roman Empire*, viii.
[122] See, e.g., Tabari, *Annales*, III (2), 695. *Chronique de Michel le Syrien*, trans. J. B. Chabot, III (1), 15. E. W. Brooks, "Byzantines and Arabs in the Time of the Early Abbasids," *English Historical Review* (1900), 743. Cf. Brătianu, *Études byzantines*, 187, 191–95 (on Nicephorus' general policy).

of his unsuccessful campaign against the Bulgarians, by the military commander Leo, an Armenian by birth, known in history as Leo V the Armenian (813–20). In the year 820 Leo V was killed and the throne passed to one of the commanders of the guards, Michael II (820–29), surnamed the "Stammerer." He came from the fortress of Amorion in Phrygia, a province of Asia Minor; hence his dynasty (820–67), represented by three rulers, is called the Amorian or Phrygian dynasty. He was a coarse and ignorant provincial who had spent his youth in Phrygia "among heretics, Hebrews, and half-hellenized Phrygians."[123] One late Syrian source asserts even that he was a Jew by birth.[124] When he died the throne passed to his son, Theophilus (829–42), who was married to the famous restorer of orthodoxy, Theodora, from Paphlagonia in Asia Minor. The last member of this dynasty was their son, the corrupt and incapable Michael III (842–67), who has come down through the ages with the despicable surname of "Drunkard."

No Byzantine emperor has been so badly treated, both in Byzantine tradition and in later literature, as this Michael III "the Drunkard," "a Byzantine Caligula." His incredible frivolity, his persistent drunkenness, his horrible impiety and abominable scurrility have been many times described. Recently, however, H. Grégoire opened an especially vigorous campaign to restore Michael's reputation. He pointed out many facts of Michael's epoch, particularly the energetic and successful fighting against the eastern Arabs, and he declared that this last sovereign of the Amorian dynasty possessed the temperament of a genius and truly inaugurated the triumphant phase of Byzantine history (843–1025).[125] One cannot go quite so far as Grégoire in characterizing Michael as a genius; indeed, since he was assassinated at the age of twenty-eight, perhaps he did not live long enough to show the extent of his powers. While he possessed some highly undesirable qualities, it should be asserted that he had energy and initiative, and in addition—and this is probably more important—he managed to choose and keep near him talented and able advisers and executives. Grégoire has justly emphasized the deep impression left in popular tradition and popular songs by Michael's successful military activities against the eastern Arabs. His victory in the north over the Russians in 860–61 left an equally deep trace.[126]

During the minority of Michael III his mother Theodora was the official ruler of the Empire for fourteen years; she entrusted all government affairs to her favorite, Theoctistus. When Michael came of age he ordered that Theoctistus be killed, compelled his mother to take holy orders, and assumed

[123] Bury, *Eastern Roman Empire*, III, 78.
[124] *Chronique de Michel le Syrien*, trans. Chabot, III (1), 72.
[125] See H. Grégoire, "Du nouveau sur le Patriarche Photius," *Bulletin de la classe des lettres de l'Académie royale de Belgique*, XX (1934), 38–39. In several other articles and studies Grégoire emphasizes the same idea.
[126] A. A. Vasiliev, *The First Russian Attack on Constantinople in 860–861*.

the rule of the Empire. This drastic change was instigated and led chiefly by Bardas, uncle of the Emperor and brother of Theodora, who soon rose to the highest ranks of curopalates and Caesar, and became very influential in all government affairs. An Arab ambassador who had an audience with Michael has left an interesting picture of his complete indifference in state affairs. The ambassador wrote: "I did not hear a single word from his lips from the time of my arrival till my departure. The interpreter alone spoke, and the Emperor listened and expressed his assent or dissent by motions of his head. His uncle managed all his affairs."[127] Highly gifted in many ways, Bardas successfully fought the enemies of the Empire and showed a clear understanding of the interests of the church. He honestly strove to spread more light and education among his people. But he, too, was treacherously killed through the intrigues of the new court favorite, Basil, the future founder of the Macedonian dynasty. After Bardas' death Michael adopted Basil and crowned him with the imperial crown. Their joint rule lasted only a little over a year, for Basil, suspecting that Michael was plotting against him, persuaded some friends to kill his benefactor after one of the court feasts. Basil then became the sole ruler of the Empire and the founder of the most famous dynasty in Byzantine history.

Thus during the period from 802 until 867 the throne was occupied by two Arabs or Semites; by one Greek, Michael I, married to the daughter of Nicephorus I, an Arabian; by one Armenian; and finally, by three Phrygians, or one might almost say, half-Greeks. It was the first time in Byzantine history that the Byzantine throne had fallen into the hands of the Semitic race. It is evident that during this period eastern elements played a very important part in the rule of the Empire.

External relations of the Byzantine Empire

Arabs and Slavs and the insurrection of Thomas the Slavonian.—In the ninth century hostile relations between the Byzantine Empire and the Arabs were almost incessant. On the eastern land borderline these relations assumed the aspect of reiterated collisions which occurred with almost annual regularity and were accompanied by frequent exchanges of prisoners. On the Muhammedan side of the border a line of fortifications, intended as a defense against the attacks of the Byzantine army, was erected from Syria to the confines of Armenia. Similar fortified cities were to be found on the Byzantine side. All the fortifications formed a sort of *limes* in Asia Minor. Only

---

[127] This story has been preserved by the Arab historian Tabari, *Annales,* ed. de Goeje, III, 1451; Russian trans. A. A. Vasiliev, *Byzantium and the Arabs,* I, 188; supplement, 58. V. R. Rosen, *The Emperor Basil Bulgaroc-* *tonus,* 147; French trans. A. A. Vasiliev, *Byzance et les Arabes,* I, 321–22. Diehl and Marçais, *Le Monde oriental,* I, 320, n. 135. In English, Bury, *Eastern Roman Empire,* 280–81.

in very few instances did the collisions along the eastern border in the ninth century assume the aspect of serious campaigns deep into the country. Parallel with the gradual political decline and weakening of the caliphate in the ninth century, which came as a result of serious internal disturbances and the predominance of Persians, and later of Turks, the continuous attacks of the Muslims upon the Byzantine Empire from the East ceased to threaten, as they did in the seventh and eighth centuries, the very existence of the Empire. These attacks continued, however, to bring great harm to the border provinces by injuring the prosperity of the population, by reducing their taxpaying ability, and by killing many of the inhabitants. The first thirty years of the ninth century were crowned by the reigns of the famous caliphs, Harun-ar-Rashid (786–809) and Mamun (813–33), under whom Persian influence enjoyed almost exclusive predominance and forced Arabian nationality into the background. In their political ideas the caliphs of the ninth century, particularly Mamun, resembled the Byzantine emperors in that they believed their authority to be unlimited in all phases of the life of their state.

Although the Arabo-Byzantine collisions in the East, with very few exceptions, did not result in any serious consequences for either side, the operations of the Muslim fleet in the Mediterranean Sea, which led to the occupation of Crete, the greater part of Sicily, and a number of important points in southern Italy, were of exceedingly great significance.

One of the interesting situations in the Arabo-Byzantine relations of the first half of the ninth century was the participation of the Arabs in the insurrection of Thomas during the reign of Michael II. This insurrection was organized in Asia Minor, by Thomas, a Slav by birth, and assumed the proportions of a grave civil war, which lasted for a period of over two years. It was the central event of the time of Michael II and is of much interest from the political and religious, as well as the social, point of view. Politically it was significant because Thomas succeeded in gaining over to his side all of Asia Minor excepting the troops of two themes. Under his standards, according to some sources, were gathered various nationalities of Asia Minor and the borderlands of the Caucasus. Besides his own kinsmen, the Slavs, who had formed some immense colonies in Asia Minor after their mass migrations from the European continent, the army of Thomas included Persians, Armenians, Iberians, and members of several other Caucasian tribes.[128] Thomas stood at the head of such a powerful force that Caliph Mamun did not hesitate to form a close alliance with him to aid him in deposing Michael, for which the Arabs were promised certain Byzantine border territories. With the consent of, or at the instance of, Mamun, Thomas was crowned at Antioch

---

[128] The letter of the Emperor Michael to the western emperor Louis the Pious, Baronii   *Annales ecclesiastici,* ed. Theiner, XIV, 63; Genesius, Bonn ed., 33.

as basileus of the Romans by Job, the patriarch of the city, and the Byzantine Emperor had to face a very dangerous and formidable rival. The eastern Arabs were apparently greatly interested in the development of this insurgent movement.

From the religious point of view the insurrection is very interesting because Thomas utilized the discontent of the large part of the population aroused by the renewed iconoclastic policy, and announced that he was an adherent of image-worship, claiming even to be Constantine, the son of Irene who had restored orthodoxy in an earlier period. This policy won over numerous supporters.

Some social strife resulted from this movement. Thus, in Asia Minor the tax collectors sided with Thomas, and there was, according to one source, an uprising of "slaves against masters."[129] The lower classes rose against their oppressors, the landowners, in a desire to build a better and brighter future for themselves. According to the same source, the ensuing civil war, "like some bursting cataracts of the Nile, flooded the earth, not with water, but with blood."[130]

Supported by the fleet in the Aegean Sea, Thomas directed his forces against Constantinople. On his way he easily overcame the resistance offered by Michael's troops, and he besieged the capital both on land and on sea. When he arrived at the European shores the Slavs of Thrace and Macedonia joined his forces. The siege of Constantinople lasted a full year. Michael was very hard pressed, but he triumphed as a result of two events. On the one hand, he succeeded in defeating Thomas' fleet; on the other, he was aided by the Bulgarians, who appeared unexpectedly in the north under the leadership of their king, Omurtag, and defeated the land forces of the insurgents. Thomas could not regain his former strength and was doomed to fail. He was forced to flee, and was later captured and executed; the remnants of his forces were easily destroyed. This complicated revolution, which lasted for more than two years, was completely extinguished in the year 823, and Michael could then feel fairly secure on his throne.[131]

For the Byzantine Empire the outcome of this insurrection was of considerable importance. Its failure was also a failure to restore image-worship. The defeat of Thomas meant also the defeat of Caliph Mamun in his offensive projects against the Byzantine Empire. Furthermore, this uprising in all probability created very serious social changes in Asia Minor. In the sixth

[129] Theophanes Continuatus, *Historia*, Bonn ed., 53.
[130] *Ibid*.
[131] For the most detailed critical account of the insurrection of Thomas, see Vasiliev, *Byzantium and the Arabs*, 21-43; French trans., 22-49. Bury, *Eastern Roman Empire*, 84-110. Th. I. Uspensky, *Byzantine Empire*, II (1), 279-92. The editors of the French version of my book say that I consider Thomas of Armenian origin (p. 26). This is not the case. I continue to regard him as a Slav.

century under Justinian the Great the system of large landed estates cultivated by peasants in a servile condition flourished widely in the Empire. In sources of subsequent centuries there are some references to small holdings and small peasant landowners. In the tenth century, however, the predominance of large landownership reappeared once more, particularly in Asia Minor. This may have been a result of Thomas' uprising, which undoubtedly caused the ruin of a large number of small landowners who were unable to meet the heavy government taxes and were thus forced to transfer their property to their wealthy neighbors. Whatever the cause, the reappearance of large estates in the tenth century began to threaten even the power of the Emperor. This was particularly true in Asia Minor.[132]

Until the end of the thirties of the ninth century the Byzantine clashes with the Arabs had no serious consequences. At this time the caliphate was undergoing great internal disturbances, which were furthered at times through the skillful interference of the Byzantine government. The son of Michael II, Theophilus, was defeated in Asia Minor in 830, but in the following year (831) gained a victory in Cilicia over an Arab army of frontier troops and for his success received a brilliant triumph in Constantinople.[133] The ensuing years were not very successful for Theophilus. An Arab historian even says that Mamun looked forward to the entire subjugation of the Empire.[134] Theophilus sent Mamun an envoy bearing proposals of peace. But in 833 Mamun died and was succeeded by his brother Mutasim. During the first years of his rule there was a suspension of hostilities. In 837 Theophilus reopened an offensive which was extremely successful. He captured and burned the fortress of Zapetra and invaded some other places. He received for this success a triumph which was a repetition of the pageants and ceremonial which had attended his return six years before.[135] In 838, however, Mutasim equipped a large army which penetrated deep into Asia Minor and after a long siege occupied the important fortified city of Amorion in Phrygia, the birthplace of the ruling dynasty, "the eye and foundation of Christianity," in the exaggerated words of the Arabian chronicle. Mutasim expected to march upon Constantinople after his successful occupation of Amorion, but he was forced to give up his plans and return to Syria when he received alarming news of a military conspiracy at home.[136]

[132] Finlay, *History of Greece*, ed. Tozer, II, 133; Bury, *Eastern Roman Empire*, II, 110.

[133] See Vasiliev, *Byzantium and the Arabs*, 82–92; in French, 103–14; Bury, *Eastern Roman Empire*, 254, 472–77. The triumph in Constantini Porphyrogenitus, *De cerimoniis aulae byzantinae*, 503–7.

[134] Yaqubi, *Historiae*, ed. M. Th. Houtsma,

II, 573; Vasiliev, *Byzantium and the Arabs*, appendix, 9; French ed., 274.

[135] Vasiliev, *ibid.*, 113–17; in French, 37–43. Bury, *Eastern Roman Empire*, 260–62. The triumph in *De cerimoniis*, 507–8.

[136] Tabari, *Annales*, III, 1236; in Russian, Vasiliev, *Byzantium and the Arabs*, appendix, 30; in French, 294–95. The most detailed ac-

In the annals of the Greek Church the siege of Amorion is connected with the miraculous story of forty-two distinguished prisoner martyrs who, on their refusal to embrace Islam, were led to the banks of the Tigris and beheaded. Their bodies were thrown into the river, but miraculously floated on top of the water; they were then rescued from the river by some Christians and given solemn burial.[137]

The disaster of Amorion made a very strong impression upon Theophilus. He lost all hope of effectively resisting the Arabian attacks with his own forces, and, fearing to lose the capital, he turned to the western states for help. His ambassadors appeared in Venice; in Ingelheim at the court of the Frankish king, Lewis the Pious; and even in the far west, in Spain, at the Court of the Umayyad emir. The western rulers all received the ambassadors in a friendly manner, yet they gave Theophilus no active assistance.

During the remaining period of the Amorian dynasty, in the later years of Theophilus' reign and the reign of Michael III, internal strife within the caliphate prevented the eastern Arabs from renewing serious campaigns against the Byzantine Empire. Indeed, on several occasions Byzantine troops succeeded in defeating the Arabs. In the year 863 Omar, the emir (governor) of Melitene, sacked the Byzantine city of Amisus (Samsun) on the shore of the Black Sea, and, infuriated by the fact that the sea put a bound to his further advance, he was said, like Xerxes, to have scourged the water. But in the same year, on his return, he was intercepted and surrounded by Byzantine troops under the command of Petronas. The battle of Poson took place (the location of this has not been identified with any exactness) and the Arab forces were almost annihilated and Omar himself was slain.[138] This brilliant victory of Byzantine arms resounded in the Hippodrome in Constantinople, and a special chant, which has been preserved in the sources, celebrated the death of the emir on the field of battle.[139]

The first Russian attack on Constantinople.—Amid these annual conflicts with the Arabs, the sources suddenly began to speak of the first attack of the

count of the Amorian campaign in the Arab chronicle of Tabari, *Annales*, III, 1236–56; in Russian, 30–46; in French, 295–310. For the campaign in general, in Russian, 119–40;. in French, 144–77. Bury, *Eastern Roman Empire*, 262–72. Bury, "Mutasim's March Through Cappadocia in A.D. 838," *Journal of Hellenic Studies*, XXIX (1909), 120–29.

[137] See *Acta 42 martyrum Amoriensium*, ed. V. G. Vasilievsky and P. Nikitin, *Transactions of the Imperial Academy of Sciences*, VIII Ser., VII, 2 (1905), 35. The Greek text and detailed commentary in Russian. The *Acta* gives some interesting historical material. See

Bury, *Eastern Roman Empire*, 271–72. Also *A Greek Text of the Life of 42 Martyrs of Amorion*, after the MSS of the Bibliothèque Nationale de Paris, No. 1534, ed. A. A. Vasiliev, *Transactions*, VIII ser., III, 3 (1898), 16.

[138] Vasiliev, *Byzantium and the Arabs*, I, 199–201; Bury, *Eastern Roman Empire*, III, 283–84.

[139] Constantini Porphyrogeniti *De ceremoniis aulae byzantinae*, I, 69; Bonn ed., 332–33. See J. B. Bury, "The Ceremonial Book of Constantine Porphyrogennetos," *English Historical Review*, XXII (1907), 434.

"Ros," or the Russians, upon Constantinople. Until comparatively recent times this event was referred by the great majority of historians to the year 865 or 866, and it was frequently connected with the campaign of the Russian princes, Ascold and Dir. But since 1894, when a short anonymous chronicle found in Brussels was published by the Belgian scholar, Franz Cumont, this opinion has been recognized as erroneous. This chronicle gives very exact information: the Russians approached Constantinople in two hundred vessels on the eighteenth of June of the year 860, but were heavily defeated and lost many of their ships.[140] Some scholars were doubtful about the earlier dating of this event long before the publication of the anonymous chronicle, and on the basis of various chronological calculations were inclined to believe that 860 was the correct date. Thus, the famous Italian scholar of the eighteenth century, Assemani, set the date of this first attack of the Russians at the end of 859 or early in 860, although later scholars completely forgot the result of his investigation.[141] Fourteen years before the appearance of the anonymous chronicle of Brussels, and entirely independent of Assemani, the Russian church historian, Golubinsky, also arrived at the conclusion that this attack took place either in 860 or at the very beginning of 861.[142]

In one of his sermons, Patriarch Photius, a contemporary of this event, referred to the Russians as the "Scythian, coarse and barbarian people," and to their attack as a "barbarous, obstinate, and formidable sea," a "terrible northern storm."[143]

Struggles with the western Arabs.—At the same time as the eastern military operations, the Empire was also struggling with the western Arabs. North Africa, conquered by the Arabs with so much difficulty in the seventh century, soon freed itself from the domination of the eastern caliphs, so that after the year 800 the Abbasid caliphs ceased to exercise any authority in the provinces west of Egypt, and an independent Aghlabid dynasty, which possessed a powerful fleet, rose in Tunis in the early part of the ninth century (in 800).

All the Byzantine possessions in the Mediterranean Sea were seriously menaced by the Arabs during this period. Even in the early part of the ninth century, in the time of Nicephorus I, the African Arabs aided the Peloponnesian Slavs in their uprising and the siege of the city of Patrae (Patras). During the reign of Michael II the Byzantine Empire lost the strategically and commercially important island of Crete, which was captured by Arabian emigrants from Spain, who had first sought shelter in Egypt and then ad-

[140] *Anecdota Bruxellensia,* I. *Chroniques byzantines du Manuscrit* 11376, ed. F. Cumont, 33.

[141] *Kalendaria Ecclesiae Universae,* I, 240–43; IV, 9.

[142] *A History of the Russian Church,* I (1), 21–22; (2nd ed., 1901), II (1), 40.

[143] *In Rossorum incursionem Homilae,* I–II. *Lexicon Vindobonense,* ed. A. Nauck, 201, 209, 221.

vanced to Crete. The leader of these Arabs founded a new city on this island and surrounded it by a deep moat, *handak* in Arabic, from which the new name of the island, Chandax, or Candia, originated.[144] From then on Crete became the nest of piratical bands which raided and devastated the islands of the Aegean Sea and the seacoast districts, causing thus great political and economic disturbances in the Byzantine Empire.

Still more serious for the Byzantine Empire was the loss of Sicily. As early as the seventh and eighth centuries this island had become subject to Arabian attacks, although these were not very serious. But in the time of the Amorian dynasty conditions changed. At the end of the reign of Michael II a man named Euphemius organized an uprising against the Emperor and was later proclaimed the ruler of the Empire. He soon realized that his own forces were not sufficient to resist the imperial troops, and appealed for aid to the African Arabs. The latter arrived in Sicily; but instead of aiding Euphemius, they began the conquest of the island, and Euphemius was killed by adherents of the Emperor.[145] In the opinion of an Italian historian, Gabotto, Euphemius was a dreamer, an idealist, a valiant fighter for the independence of his country, and a continuator of the traditional policy of creating in Italy an independent state, "the Roman Italian Empire" (*Impero romano italiano*). Gabotto's characterization of Euphemius, however, is not confirmed by the evidence.[146] The Arabs became established in Panormos (Palermo) and gradually occupied the greater part of Sicily, including Messina, so that by the end of the reign of the Amorian dynasty, of all the large Sicilian cities, only Syracuse remained in the hands of the Christians. From Sicily the most natural step for the Arabs was to advance into the Byzantine territories in southern Italy.

The Apennine peninsula has at its southern extremity two small peninsulas: the one in the southeast was known in antiquity as Calabria, and the other in the southwest as Bruttium. In the Byzantine period a change occurred in these names. From the middle of the seventh century Bruttium was used less and less frequently, and became gradually replaced by the name of Calabria,

[144] It is uncertain whether Crete was conquered by the Arabs in 823 or 825. See Vasiliev, *Byzantium and the Arabs*, 45–53; on the date, 49, n. 1; in French, 49–61. Bury, *Eastern Roman Empire*, 287–91. Brooks, in an article particularly important from the point of view of critical investigation of sources, attributed the conquest to 828. E. Brooks, "The Arab Occupation of Crete," *English Historical Review*, XXVIII (1913), 432.

[145] On the revolt of Euphemius, F. Gabotto,

Eufemio il movimento separatista nella Italia bizantina. See also Vasiliev, *Byzantium and the Arabs*, 56–75; in French, 61–88. Bury, *Eastern Roman Empire*, 294–302, 478–80. Amari's fundamental work is, of course, indispensable.

[146] Gabotto, *ibid.*, 6–7. Vasiliev, *ibid.*, 73–74; in French, 85. Cf. M. Amari, *Storia dei Musulmani di Sicilia*, I, 282; (2nd ed., 1933), 412.

which thus began to be applied to both small peninsulas; in other words, Calabria then signified all of the Byzantine possessions in southern Italy around the Gulf of Tarentum.[147]

The political position in Italy in the ninth century appears as follows: The Byzantine Empire retained Venice, the greater part of Campania, with the Duchy of Naples and two other duchies, as well as the two small southern peninsulas. Venice and Campania were only slightly politically dependent upon the Byzantine Empire, for they had an autonomous government of their own. The south of Italy was directly subject to the Empire. The greater part of Italy was in the hands of the Lombards. At the end of the seventh century the Lombard Duke of Beneventum won Tarentum from the Byzantine Empire; thus he reached as far as the shores of the Gulf itself and separated the two Byzantine districts from one another so that after this conquest the two smaller peninsulas could communicate only by sea. After the Italian conquests of Charles the Great and his imperial coronation in Rome the entire Apennine peninsula, except the Byzantine territories, was formally placed under the authority of the western Emperor; in reality, however, his power in the south did not reach any further than the borders of the papal state and the Duchy of Spoleto. The Duchy of Beneventum remained an independent state.

Contemporary with the gradual conquest of Sicily, the Arabian fleet also began to raid the Italian shores. The occupation of Tarentum in the time of Theophilus was a grave and direct menace to the Byzantine provinces in southern Italy. The Venetian fleet which came to the aid of the Emperor in the Gulf of Tarentum suffered a heavy defeat. Meanwhile the Arabs occupied the important fortified city of Bari on the eastern shore of the peninsula, and from there directed their conquests of the inner Italian districts. The western emperor, Lewis II, came there with his army, but was defeated and forced to retreat. At the same time, in the forties of the ninth century, Arabian pirates appeared at the mouth of the Tiber and threatened Rome, but upon capturing rich spoils, they departed from the old capital. The Roman basilicas of St. Peter and St. Paul, situated outside the city walls of Rome, were damaged greatly during this attack.

In summary, the Arabo-Byzantine contacts during the period of the Amorian dynasty resulted in failure in the West for the Byzantine Empire. Crete and Sicily were lost; the former only until 961, the latter forever. A number of important points in southern Italy also passed into the hands of the Arabs, although by the middle of the ninth century these did not form a large continuous territory. The results of the struggle with the Arabs along the eastern border were very different. Here the Empire succeeded in keeping its territories almost intact. The few insignificant changes along this border

---

[147] See J. Gay, *L'Italie Méridionale et l'Empire Byzantin*, 5–6.

had no bearing upon the general course of events. In this respect the efforts of the Amorian dynasty were of much importance to the Empire, because for a period of forty-seven years the emperors of this line were able to withstand the aggressive operations of the eastern Arabs and preserve, on the whole, the integrity of Byzantine territory in Asia Minor.

The Byzantine Empire and the Bulgarians in the epoch of the Amorian Dynasty.—At the beginning of the ninth century the Bulgarian throne was occupied by Krum, an able warrior and wise organizer, who proved to be extremely dangerous to the Byzantine Empire. Nicephorus, having sensed in him a powerful enemy capable of gaining over to his side the Slavonic population of Macedonia and Thessaly, transferred many colonists from other parts of the Empire to these two provinces. By this measure, which, according to one source, aroused much dissatisfaction among the emigrants, the Emperor hoped to avert the danger of an alliance between the Bulgarians and the Slavs of the before named provinces.[148]

In the year 811, after several clashes with the Bulgarians, Nicephorus undertook a large expedition against Krum, during which he was lured with his army into ambush and defeated very severely. Nicephorus himself fell in battle, his son Stauracius was seriously wounded, and the army was almost completely annihilated. Since the famous battle near Hadrianople in the year 378, during which Valens had been killed on the field of action against the Visigoths, there had been no other instance before Nicephorus of the death of an emperor in battle with the barbarians. Krum made a bowl out of the skull of the dead emperor and the "Bulgarian boliads" (nobles)[149] were forced to drink from it.

In 813 Krum also defeated Michael I, who advanced against him at the head of an army so powerful that even the Asiatic forces had been withdrawn from the eastern frontier to strengthen it. But the numerical superiority of the Byzantine troops was of no avail; they were decisively beaten and put to a flight that was arrested only when they reached the walls of Constantinople. In the same year, soon after the rise of Leo V the Armenian to the Byzantine throne, Krum carried the offensive to Constantinople, besieging the city in order "to fix his lance on the Golden Gate" (the walls of Constantinople), as one source put it.[150] Here, however, his successful progress was checked. He died suddenly, affording the Empire a temporary respite from the Bulgarian menace.[151]

One of the immediate successors of Krum, Omurtag, "one of the most

[148] Theophanes, *Chronographia,* ed. de Boor, 486.

[149] *Ibid.,* 491. Cedreni, *Historiarum compendium,* Bonn ed., II, 42.

[150] Theophanes, *Chronographia,* ed. de Boor, 503.

[151] See Bury, *Eastern Roman Empire,* 339–54. Th. I. Uspensky, *Byzantine Empire,* II (1), 250–63. S. Runciman, *A History of the First Bulgarian Empire,* 51–70.

eminent figures in the early history of Bulgaria,"[152] in the time of Leo V concluded with the Byzantine Empire a peace agreement to last for thirty years. The agreement dealt mainly with the problem of defining the border lines between the two states in the province of Thrace. Traces of these lines can be seen even today in the shape of some remains of earthen fences.[153] After peace was definitely concluded with the Bulgarians, Leo V reconstructed some of the ruined cities of Thrace and Macedonia. He also erected a stronger new wall around the capital for a surer defense against possible future Bulgarian attacks.

Later Bulgaro-Byzantine relations were not marked by any outstanding events until the early fifties of the ninth century, when the Bulgarian throne passed into the hands of Boris (Bogoris; 852–889), whose name is closely connected with the accounts of the conversion of the Bulgarians to Christianity.

The Christian faith had found its way into Bulgaria long before the time of Boris, primarily through the Byzantine captives taken by the Bulgarians during their battles with the imperial troops. The pagan Bulgarian khans severely persecuted "the perverted and the perverters." Th. I. Uspensky asserted that "there is no doubt that Christianity began to spread in Bulgaria very early. . . . Even as early as the eighth century there were a number of Christians in the palaces of the princes. The struggles between the Christian and pagan parties were responsible for many of the troubled events in Bulgarian history, as well as for the frequent change of khans."[154]

The conversion of Boris to Christianity was prompted by the political situation in Bulgaria, which forced him to seek closer relations with the Byzantine Empire. Greek clergy came to Bulgaria to spread Christianity among the natives. About the year 864 King Boris was baptized and assumed the name of Michael, and soon after, his people also adopted Christianity. The story that the two famous Slavonic missionaries, the brothers St. Cyril and St. Methodius, participated directly in the baptism of Boris is not confirmed by authentic evidence. The fact that Bulgarians received baptism from the hands of the Byzantine clergy did much to increase the prestige and influence of the Byzantine Empire in the Balkan peninsula. Boris, however, soon realized that the Empire was not willing to grant the Bulgarian church complete independence. He wished to keep the right of guiding the spiritual life of Bulgaria, and he feared also that his kingdom might become politically dependent upon the Byzantine Empire. Boris decided to form an ecclesiastical

[152] Uspensky, *Byzantine Empire,* II (1), 263.
[153] See J. B. Bury, "The Bulgarian Treaty of A.D. 814 and the Great Fence of Thrace," *English Historical Review,* XXV (1910), 276–87.
[154] "Materials for Bulgarian Antiquities, Aboba-Plisca," *Bulletin of the Russian Archeological Institute in Constantinople,* X (1905), 197. See also Uspensky, *Byzantine Empire,* II (1), 453.

alliance with Rome. He sent a delegation to Pope Nicholas I asking him to send Latin priests to Bulgaria. The pope was very glad to comply with this request. Latin bishops and priests soon came to Bulgaria, and the Greek clergy was driven out. The pope's triumph was short-lived, however, for Bulgaria soon turned again to the Greek church, but this event occurred later, in the time of the Macedonian dynasty.[155]

While the relations between Constantinople and Rome were very strained at the time of the religious waverings of Boris, still there was no open breach in the church. The requests sent by Boris to the Greek and Latin clergy did not signify a choice of either Orthodoxy or Catholicism. Officially the church of this period was still a single universal church.

The second period of iconoclasm and the restoration of orthodoxy. The separation of churches in the ninth century

The first emperors of the period 802–67 were not iconoclastic in their policies, and it seemed almost that image-worship, restored by Irene, might gradually grow stronger and not become subject to new trials. The policy of Nicephorus was one of religious tolerance combined with the idea of temporal domination over the church. Although he recognized the decisions of the Council of Nicaea and the victory of the image-worshipers, he was not an ardent follower of the latter movement. To the true zealots of image-worship the tolerant policy of Nicephorus seemed as bad as heresy. It is very probable that religious questions interested the Emperor very little. They mattered only in so far as they concerned the state. Yet monasticism experienced some anxious moments in the time of Nicephorus, especially when the highly respected Patriarch Tarasius, beloved by all his people, was replaced by the new Patriarch Nicephorus, who was raised to his high rank by the will of the Emperor directly from among laymen. This election was strongly opposed by the famous Theodore of Studion and his followers, the Studites, who were later sent into exile.

Michael I Rangabé ruled only for a short period (811–13) and was under the constant influence of the patriarch and the monks. He was an obedient son of the church and defender of its interests. During his reign Theodore and the Studites were recalled from exile.

A quarter of a century had elapsed since the time Irene had restored image-worship, but the iconoclastic movement was still alive in the eastern provinces

[155] For the most recent accounts of the conversion of Bulgaria, see F. Dvornik, *Les Slaves, Byzance et Rome au IXe siècle*, 184–95; V. Zlatarsky, *History of Bulgaria in the Middle Ages*, I (2), 31–152. S. Runciman, *First Bulgarian Empire*, 104 (in September 865; refers to Zlatarsky's work). A. Vaillant and M. Lascaris, "La Date de la conversion des Bulgares," *Revue des études slaves*, XIII (1933), 13 (in 864). Th. I. Uspensky, *Byzantine Empire*, II, 451–79; conversion in 865.

of Asia Minor and in the ranks of the army. In 813, Leo, a military chief of Armenian birth, assumed the imperial title. In the time of his predecessors Leo enjoyed great authority as a gifted general and was careful to conceal his iconoclastic views; but as soon as he deposed Michael Rangabé and strengthened his own position on the throne he began to advance openly an iconoclastic policy. One source credits the Emperor with these words: "You see that all emperors who had accepted images and worshiped them died either in exile or in battle. Only those who had not adored images died a natural death while they still bore their imperial rank. These emperors were all placed in imperial sepulchers with high honors and buried in the temple of the Apostles. I want to follow their example and destroy images, so that, after my long life and the life of my son are over, our rule shall continue until the fourth and fifth generation."[156]

The iconoclastic measures of Leo V were vehemently opposed by Patriarch Nicephorus, who was later deposed by the Emperor. The rank of archbishop of Constantinople was conferred upon Theodotus, who was in complete agreement with Leo's religious policy. In the year 815 a second iconoclastic council was gathered in the temple of St. Sophia in Constantinople. The acts of this council were destroyed after the restoration of icon worship, but its decree has been preserved in one of the apologetic works of Patriarch Nicephorus, and has been published.[157]

"Having established and confirmed the divinely accepted doctrine of the Holy Fathers and in accordance with the six Holy Ecumenical Councils," this council "condemned the unprofitable practice, unwarranted by tradition, of making and adoring images, preferring worship in spirit and truth." The decree further indicated that with the change of masculine rule to feminine (Irene), "female simplicity" restored the adoration of "dead figures" and "lifeless icons," the lighting of candles and burning of incense. The council prohibited "the unauthorized manufacture of pseudonymous icons of the catholic church," rejected the adoration of images as confirmed by Patriarch Tarasius, and condemned the lighting of candles and lamps, as well as the offering of incense before images. Essentially this decree was a repetition of the basic ideas of the iconoclastic council of 754, whose acts it confirmed. The council stated that it was prohibited to adore images and useless to produce them. Since this council "abstained from calling images idols, because there are degrees of evil,"[158] it has sometimes been regarded as more tolerant than the first iconoclastic council. But the opinion has recently been advanced that

[156] *Scriptor incertus de Leone Bardae filio,* Bonn ed., 349.
[157] On this council see Ostrogorsky, *Geschichte des byzantinischen Bilderstreites,* 46–60.
[158] M. D. Serruys, "Les actes du Concile Iconoclaste de l'an 815," *Mélanges d'archéologie et d'histoire,* XXIII (1903), 348–49. A later and better edition in Ostrogorsky, *Geschichte des byzantinischen Bilderstreites,* 48–51.

the second iconoclastic movement, particularly under Leo V and Theophilus, was neither more moderate nor more tolerant than that under Leo III and Constantine V, but "only spiritually poorer."[159]

The iconoclastic emperors of the second period, Leo V the Armenian, Michael II the Stammerer, and Theophilus, had to carry out their religious policy under conditions which differed greatly from those which had prevailed in the first period. The second period lasted only for about thirty years (815–43), and was thus much shorter than the first period which had lasted for more than fifty years. The iconoclasts of the first period took the iconodules, so to say, unawares. The latter were not sufficiently organized nor prepared for the struggle. The ruthless measures against images forced them to unite their ranks, strengthen their faith, develop methods of fighting, and collect all their dogmatic and polemic materials. The iconoclasts of the second period, therefore, met a much stronger resistance than had their predecessors. The struggle became more difficult for them. Especially strong was the opposition advanced by the abbot of the monastery of Studion, Theodore, and his followers, the Studites, convinced defenders of image-worship, who exerted a great influence upon the mass of the people. Furthermore, Theodore openly wrote and spoke against the intervention of imperial power in the affairs of the church and defended the principles of church independence and freedom of conscience. Angered by Theodore's attitude and activity, the Emperor sent him into distant exile and banished many of his followers.

According to the surviving sources, which are almost without exception hostile to the iconoclasts, the persecution of images and their worshipers was very severe in the time of Leo V. These sources name martyrs who suffered in this period. On the other hand, even the most vehement opponents of Leo V acknowledge that he was very efficient and skillful in defending the Empire and wise in his administrative measures. According to one historian, Patriarch Nicephorus, deposed by Leo, "said after Leo's death that the state of the Romans lost a very great, though impious, ruler."[160] Still other contemporaries called Leo "the creeping snake," and compared his time with "winter and a thick fog."[161]

Opinions vary regarding the religious views of Leo's successor, Michael II. While some historians consider him neutral and indifferent, and a man who "followed the path of tolerance and proclaimed the great principles of freedom of conscience,"[162] others call him a "convinced iconoclast, though not a fanatic," "determined to support Leo's iconoclastic reforms because they har-

[159] Ostrogorsky, *ibid.*, 56.

[160] Genesius, *Regna*, Bonn ed., 17–18; see also Theophanes Continuatus, *Historia*, Bonn ed., 30.

[161] See A. Dobroklonsky, *Blessed Theodore the Confessor and Abbot of Studion*, I, 850.

[162] Gelzer, *Abriss der byzantinischen Kaisergeschichte*, 967; Schwarzlose, *Der Bilderstreit*, 72; Ternovsky, *The Graeco-Eastern Church*, 487.

monized with his personal convictions, refusing at the same time to continue the further persecution of image-worship."[163] A recent investigator believed that Michael's "political program consisted of an attempt to pacify all religious disputes even though this involved an enforced silence on debatable questions and a tolerant attitude toward each of the dissenting elements."[164]

However, in spite of his iconoclastic tendencies, Michael did not initiate another period of persecution of image-worshipers, although when Methodius, who later became the patriarch of Constantinople, delivered the papal letter to the Emperor and called upon him to restore icon worship, he was subjected to a cruel scourging and was imprisoned in a tomb. In comparing the time of Leo V with the reign of Michael II contemporaries used such phrases as "the fire has gone out, but it is still smoking," "like a crawling snake the tail of heresy has not yet been killed and is still wriggling," "the winter is over, but real spring has not yet arrived," etc.[165] The death of the famous defender of images and church freedom, Theodore of Studion, took place in the time of Michael II.

Theophilus, the successor of Michael II and the last iconoclastic emperor, was a man well versed in theological matters, distinguished by his fervent adoration of the Virgin and the saints, and the author of several church songs. Historical opinions of Theophilus are extremely contradictory, ranging all the way from the most damnatory to the most eulogistic statements. With regard to iconoclasm, the reign of Theophilus was the harshest time of the second period of the movement. The Emperor's main adviser and leader in iconoclastic matters was John the Grammarian, later patriarch of Constantinople, the most enlightened man of that period, who was accused, as was frequently the case with learned men in the Middle Ages, of practicing sorcery and magic. The monks, many of whom were icon-painters, were subject to severe punishments. For example, the palms of the monk Lazarus, an image-painter, were burned with red-hot iron; for their zealous defense of images the two brothers Theophanes and Theodore were flogged and branded on their foreheads with certain insulting Greek verses composed by Theophilus himself for the purpose, and hence they were surnamed the "marked" (*graptoi*).

And yet a more critical examination of the surviving sources on Theophilus might force historians to forsake the claim that persecutions were excessively severe in his time. The facts giving evidence of cruel treatment of iconodules are few. Bury believed that the religious persecutions of Theophilus did not go beyond a certain geographical boundary, for the Emperor insisted upon

[163] N. Grossu, *The Blessed Theodore of Studion*, 151.

[164] Dobroklonsky, *Theodore the Confessor*, I, 849.

[165] *Ibid.*, 850.

the destruction of images only in the capital and its immediate environs. Bury was also of the opinion that during the entire second period of iconoclasm image-worship flourished in Greece and on the islands and coasts of Asia Minor. This fact has not been fully appreciated by historians. The English scholar believed also that only in a few exceptional cases did the Emperor resort to severe punishments.[166] Much still remains to be done for a correct historical estimate of the second period of the iconoclastic movement.

Theodora, the wife of Theophilus, was a zealous adherent of image-worship, and her religious tendencies were well known to her husband. When Theophilus died in 842, Theodora became the official ruler of the Empire because of the minority of her son Michael. Her first problem was to restore image-worship. Apparently the opposition of the iconoclasts was not as strong in 842 as it had been in the time of Irene, the first restorer of image-worship, for it took Theodora only a little more than one year to convoke a council to confirm her religious tendencies, while Irene had to spend seven years in the same task. John the Grammarian was deposed from the patriarchal throne and the see of Constantinople was given to Methodius, who had suffered much in the time of Michael. The acts of the council convoked by Theodora have not been preserved, but other sources show that they confirmed the canons of the Council of Nicaea and restored image-worship. When the council finished its work, solemn service was performed in the temple of St. Sophia on the first Sunday in Lent, on the eleventh day of March, 843 A.D. This day is still solemnized as the feast of orthodoxy in the Greek Orthodox church. Until very recent times the year 842 was generally recognized as the correct date of the restoration of images.[167]

In the Near East the second period of iconoclasm was marked by the publication of a joint letter to protect images under the names of the three eastern patriarchs of the ninth century, Christopher of Alexandria, Job of Antioch, and Basil of Jerusalem.

In summary: The iconoclastic party drew its forces mainly from the court party and the army, including its leading generals, among whom some succeeded in attaining the high imperial rank, as did Leo III, Leo V, and Michael II. The iconoclastic tendencies of the army are attributed by some scholars to the fact that the greatest number of soldiers was drafted from among the eastern nationalities, mainly the Armenians, who had been transferred by

[166] *Eastern Roman Empire*, III, 140–41.

[167] See C. de Boor, "Der Angriff der Rhos auf Byzanz," *Byzantinische Zeitschrift*, IV (1895), 449–53. Vasiliev, *Byzantium and the Arabs*, appendix, 142–46; in French, 418–21 (on the year of the restoration of Orthodoxy). On some good evidence, C. Loparev asserted that the restoration of orthodoxy took place not on the eleventh of March but on the eleventh of February, 843: "Hagiography of the Eighth and Ninth Centuries as a Source of Byzantine History," *Revue Byzantine*, II (1916), 172, n. 1.

the government in large numbers to the western provinces, mostly to Thrace. Hence the majority of the army was iconoclastic by conviction. According to one scholar, "the Orthodox cult impressed the eastern soldiers as an alien religion, and they felt justified in using any kind of violence against those whom they called idolaters."[168] As to the court party and the higher clergy, it may be said that the government officials and a number of bishops did not follow the dictates of their convictions, but professed views in accordance with their fears and ambitions. The population of Constantinople and the great majority of the clergy favored image-worship. The iconoclastic emperors were both gifted warriors and wise administrators, victorious over the Arabs and Bulgarians, and some of them may even be credited with having saved Christianity and the rising western civilization; but they did not persecute images in the name of their political aims and ambitions. Their religious measures were prompted rather by a sincere conviction that they were working toward improvement in the church and the purification of Christianity. The religious reforms of these emperors were at times even detrimental to the accomplishments of their wise political activities. The fight with the iconodules introduced great internal disturbances and weakened the political strength of the Empire. It also led to a rupture with the western church and the gradual separation of Italy from the Byzantine Empire. Only the policy pursued by the iconoclastic emperors toward the monks and monasteries is to be explained by political motives. It is very difficult to form a detailed judgment about the theological doctrine of the iconoclasts because almost all the literature pertaining to the problems of iconoclastic dogma was destroyed by the iconodules. Even among the iconoclasts there were men of moderate, as well as of extremely radical, tendencies. Image-painting was looked upon as a potential cause of two possible dangers: the return to paganism, or the return to one of the heresies condemned by the ecumenical councils. In connection with the second period of the iconoclastic movement it is important to emphasize that while in the eighth century the Isaurians were always supported by the eastern provinces of Asia Minor this was not true in the ninth century. During the second period of iconoclasm "enthusiasm for iconoclastic ideas absolutely weakens; the movement was already spiritually exhausted."[169]

The iconodule party was composed of the population of the western provinces, Italy and Greece, all the monks and the greater part of the clergy, majority of the inhabitants of Constantinople, although they were at times forced by circumstances to feign that they were supporting iconoclasm, and finally, the population of several other sections of the Empire, such as the islands of the Aegean and some of the coast provinces of Asia Minor. The

[168] Bréhier, La Querelle des images, 40.   358. Ostrogorsky, Geschichte des byzanti-
[169] Uspensky, Byzantine Empire, II (1),   nischen Staates, 53, 59.

theological doctrine of the image-worshipers, as developed by such leaders as John Damascene and Theodore of Studion, was based on the Holy Scriptures. They considered images not only a means of enlightening the people but believed also that by preserving the holiness and merits of their prototypes —Christ, the Virgin, and the saints—the icons possessed miraculous power.

The iconoclastic epoch has left deep traces in the artistic life of the period. Numerous beautiful monuments of art, mosaics, frescoes, statues, and miniatures were destroyed during the struggle waged upon images. The richly decorated walls of temples were either plastered over or newly ornamented. "Briefly," said N. P. Kondakov, "the church life of the capital became subject to that protestant desolation which was destined to displace, sooner or later, all the artistic life of Byzantium. . . . A large number of educated and wealthy people migrated with their families to Italy; thousands of monks founded numerous cave habitations and hermitages throughout the vast territory of southern Italy, Asia Minor and Cappadocia, which were painted by Greek artists. Hence Greek art and iconography of the eighth and ninth centuries must be sought outside of the Byzantine Empire: in Asia Minor or in southern and middle Italy."[170] But parallel with the destruction of artistic monuments bearing the images of Christ, the Virgin, and the saints, the iconoclasts began to create a new type of art by turning to new subjects. They introduced ornament and began to present *genre* scenes, such as pictures of the chase, the Hippodrome, trees, birds, and beasts. Some remarkable works of art in ivory, enamels, and a number of interesting miniatures have also come down from the time of the iconoclastic movement. In general the artistic tendencies of the iconoclasts are viewed by art historians as a return to the classical traditions of Alexandria and a very significant tendency toward realism and the study of nature.[171] One important outcome of the iconoclastic epoch was the disappearance of sculptural representations of holy persons or sacred scenes from the eastern church. Officially, neither the church nor the state prohibited these images; hence they apparently disappeared of their own accord. This is viewed by some historians as a partial victory for the iconoclasts over the extreme icon-worshipers.[172]

Iconoclastic influences were reflected also on Byzantine coins and seals. An entirely new coin and seal type developed under the sway of iconoclastic ideas in the eighth century. The new coins and seals sometimes bore only legends without any images of Christ, the Holy Virgin, or the saints; a cross or a cruciform monogram was sometimes used. On the whole, the type on the coins was confined almost exclusively to representations of the cross and the

[170] *Iconography of the Holy Virgin*, II, 5.
[171] See Charles Diehl, *Manuel d'art byzantin*, 340; (2nd ed., 1925), I, 366.
[172] See Bury, *Eastern Roman Empire*, III, 430.

imperial family. Human portraiture fares hardly better than the sacred images of the precedent times: it is conventional throughout.[173] Later, when image-worship was restored, images of Christ, the Virgin, and the saints again appeared on the coins and seals.

Iconoclasm alienated Italy and the papacy from the Empire and was one of the main causes for the final breach in the church in the ninth century. The coronation of Charles the Great in 800 brought about still greater estrangement between the pope and the Byzantine Empire. The final rupture took place in the second half of the ninth century in the reign of Michael III, during the rise of the famous case of Photius and Ignatius in Constantinople.

Ignatius, widely known in his time for his zeal in defending image-worship, was deposed from the patriarchal throne and his high rank was conferred upon Photius, a layman, the most learned man of the period. Two parties formed then in the Byzantine Empire; one sided with Photius, the other with Ignatius, who refused to give up his title voluntarily. They continually anathematized each other and their heated disputes finally forced Michael III to convoke a council. Pope Nicholas I, who sided with Ignatius, was also invited to attend, but he sent only his legates. The latter, under the influence of bribes and threats and against the wish of the pope, confirmed the deposition of Ignatius and the election of Photius as patriarch of Constantinople. In opposition to this decision Pope Nicholas convoked a council in Rome which anathematized Photius and reinstated Ignatius. Michael paid no attention to the proclamation of this Roman council, and in a sharp note to the Pope stated that the church of Constantinople repudiated his claims to the leadership of the universal church. This incident came at the time of the conversion of the Bulgarian king, Boris, to Christianity, in which the interests of Constantinople and Rome clashed seriously, as we have pointed out elsewhere. In the year 867 (the year of Michael's death) another council was convoked at Constantinople which condemned and anathematized the pope for his heretical doctrine in adding the *filioque* to the Christian creed, and also for his illegal intervention in the affairs of the church of Constantinople. The pope and the patriarch in their turn anathematized each other, and thus occurred the split in the church. With the death of Michael III the state of affairs changed. The new Emperor, Basil I, began his reign by deposing Photius and reinstating Ignatius.[173a]

[173] See W. Wroth, *Catalogue of the Imperial Byzantine Coins in the British Museum,* I, xciii. O. M. Dalton, *East Christian Art,* 224.

[173a] On Photius see the monumental work of Francis Dvornik, *The Photian Schism, History and Legend* (Cambridge, 1948).

A movement so profound, complex, and intense as iconoclasm was bound to arouse wide literary activity. Unfortunately, however, the literature of the iconoclasts was destroyed almost completely by the triumphant image-worshipers, and is known today only by scanty fragments preserved in the works of the opponents of iconoclasm, who cited them for the purpose of refutation. It may be said, then, that practically all the surviving literary works of the iconoclastic period represent only one point of view.

Like the preceding period of the Heraclian dynasty, the iconoclastic epoch had no historians, though the chroniclers of this period have left numerous works, helpful to a correct understanding of Byzantine chronography and its sources and also highly valuable for the study of the iconoclastic period itself. George Syncellus,[174] who died in the early part of the ninth century, left a *Chronography* from the creation of the universe to the reign of Diocletian (284 A.D.), which he wrote during his stay in a monastery. While this work does not throw any light on the iconoclastic period, for the author did not deal with contemporary events, it is of considerable value for the elucidation of some problems of earlier Greek chronography, whose works George used as sources.

At the instance of George Syncellus his chronicle was continued in the early part of the same century by his friend, Theophanes the Confessor, whose influence as a chronicler upon the literature of subsequent periods was very great. He was a vehement enemy of the iconoclasts in the second period of the movement. He was submitted by Leo V the Armenian to an inquest, and after being confined in jail for some time, was exiled to one of the islands of the Aegean Sea, where he died in the year 817. The chronicle of Theophanes deals with the period from the reign of Diocletian, where George Syncellus left off his record of events, up to the fall of Emperor Michael I Rangabé, in the year 813. In spite of the clearly expressed eastern-orthodox point of view, very apparent in his analysis of historical events and personalities, and in spite of the biased nature of the account, the work of Theophanes is very valuable, not only because of its rich material from earlier sources, some of which have not been preserved but also because, as a contemporary source on the iconoclastic movement, it devotes more space to it than was usual with other Byzantine chroniclers. The work of Theophanes was the favorite source of subsequent chroniclers. The Latin translation of his chronicle, made by the papal librarian, Anastasius, in the second half of the ninth century, was

---

[174] Syncellus: a high ecclesiastical honor (title) in the Byzantine Empire. Literally, it means "cell-mate."

of the same value to the medieval chronography of the West as the Greek original was for the East.[175]

Another significant writer of this period was Nicephorus, patriarch of Constantinople in the early part of the ninth century. For his bold opposition to iconoclasm in the time of Leo V the Armenian, he was deposed and exiled. In his theological works, of which some are still unpublished, Nicephorus defends with a remarkable power based on deep conviction the correctness of the iconodulist views. He refutes the arguments of the iconoclasts chiefly in his three "Refutations of the Ignorant and Godless Nonsense of the Impious Mammon [the name he applied to Constantine V] against the Salutary Incarnation of the Word of God."[176] From the historical point of view, his *Brief History,* which narrates events from the death of Emperor Maurice in the year 602 until the year 769, is of considerable value. In spite of the fact that in attempting to make this work a popular account suitable for a wider circle of readers, Nicephorus gave it a somewhat didactic character, it still remains a source of importance, since it contains many interesting facts regarding the political and church history of the period. The very striking similarity of this *History* and the work of Theophanes may be explained by the fact that both used one common source.[177]

Finally, George the Monk (Monachus) Hamartolus, also a convinced enemy of the iconoclasts, left a universal chronicle from Adam to the death of Emperor Theophilus in 842 A.D., in other words, until the final victory of image-worship. This work is of much value for the cultural history of the period because it contains many discussions of problems which preoccupied the Byzantine monastics of that period, namely, the nature of monasticism itself, the spread of iconoclastic heresy, and the spread of the Saracen faith. It also gives a vivid picture of the aspirations and tastes of the Byzantine monasteries of the ninth century. The chronicle of Hamartolus formed the basis for later Byzantine arrangements of universal history, and exerted enormous influence upon the early pages of Slavonic literatures, particularly the Russian. Suffice it to say that the beginning of Russian chronicles is very closely connected with the work of Hamartolus. A manuscript of the old Slavo-Russian translation of Hamartolus contains 127 miniatures, which have not yet been thoroughly studied and appreciated, but which are of greatest importance for the history of the Russian and Byzantine art of the thirteenth century. This manuscript is the only illustrated copy of the Chronicle of Hamartolus that has come down to us.[178] With the exception of one anony-

---

[175] On Theophanes, see G. Ostrogorsky, "Theophanes," *Real-Encyclopädie der Classischen Altertumswissenschaft,* ed. A. F. Pauly, G. Wissowa and others, II (1934), 2127–32.

[176] See Migne, *Patrologia Graeca,* C, 205 ff.

[177] R. Blake, "Note sur l'activité littéraire de Nicéphore Ier, patriarche de Constantinople," *Byzantion,* XIV (1939), 1–15.

[178] D. Aïnalov, "La Chronique de George Hamartolus," *Compte-rendu du deuxième*

mous writer on Emperor Leo V the Armenian,[179] Hamartolus is the only contemporary chronicler of the period from 813 to 842. He dealt with this period from a narrow monastic point of view, using mostly oral accounts of contemporaries and personal observations. The manuscript tradition of Hamartolus' work, which was changed and enlarged many times in later centuries, has survived in such a complicated and entangled form that the question of his authentic original text forms one of the most difficult problems of Byzantine philology. It was only in the early part of the twentieth century that a critical edition of the Greek text of Hamartolus was published.[180] Recently there appeared a critical edition of the old Slavo-Russian translation of the chronicle of Hamartolus, supplemented by the Greek text of the continuation of this chronicle which formed the basis of the Slavonic translation.[181]

Iconoclastic literature was almost completely destroyed by the triumphant image-worshipers; yet part of the detailed acts of the iconoclastic council of the year 754 have survived in the acts of the Seventh Ecumenical Council. Fragments of an extensive work against icon worship written by Constantine V Copronymus have been preserved in the three *Rufutations* of Patriarch Nicephorus. This emperor was also the author of some other literary works.[182] Leo V ordered the compilation of a general work favorable to iconoclasm and based on the Bible and the church fathers, and a similar project was proposed at the iconoclastic council of the year 754; neither of these works has survived. A number of iconoclastic poems have been preserved in the works of Theodore of Studion. The Seventh Ecumenical Council decreed that all iconoclastic literature should be destroyed, and its ninth canon reads as follows: "All the childish plays, the raging mockeries and false writings directed against the honored icons must be presented to the episcopate of Constantinople and there added to all other books of heretics. Anyone found guilty of hiding these works if bishop, or presbyter, or deacon, will be deposed; if monk or layman, will be excommunicated."[183]

An enormous amount of literary material dealing with the defense of image-worship and highly important in its influence upon writings of later periods has been left by a man who spent all his life in a province which no longer formed part of the Empire. His name is John Damascene, a native

Congrès international des études byzantines, 1927, 127–33.

[179] On this important contemporary source see H. Grégoire, "Un nouveau fragment du 'Scriptor incertus de Leone Armenio,'" *Byzantion,* XI (1936), 417–28. Grégoire, "Du nouveau sur la Chronographie byzantine: le 'Scriptor incertus de Leone Armenio' est le dernier continuateur le Malalas," *Bulletin de la classe des lettres de l'Académie Royale de* *Belgique,* XXII (1936), 420–36.

[180] Georgius Monachus, *Chronikon,* ed. C. de Boor.

[181] V. M. Istrin, *The Chronicle of George Hamartolus in Its Old Sloveno-Russian Version.*

[182] See Ostrogorsky, *Geschichte des byzantinischen Bilderstreites,* 7–14.

[183] Mansi, *Amplissima collectio conciliorum,* XIII, 430.

of Syria, which was then under Arabian domination. He was minister of the caliph in Damascus and died about 750 A.D. in the famous Palestinian Laura of St. Sabas. John has left many works in the fields of dogmatics, polemics, history, philosophy, oratory, and poetry. His principal work is *The Source of Knowledge,* the third part of which, entitled "An Exact Exposition of the Orthodox Faith," was an attempt at a systematic presentation of the main foundations of the Christian faith and Christian dogmatics. Through this exposition John placed in the hands of the image-worshipers a powerful weapon for their struggle with their opponents, a weapon they had lacked in the early part of the iconoclastic movement. Later, in the thirteenth century, this work was used by the famous father of the western church, Thomas Aquinas, as a model for his *Summa Theologiae.* Among the polemic works of John Damascene we must point out three treatises "against those who depreciate holy images," where the author firmly and boldly defends image-worship. In ecclesiastical literature John is particularly famous for his church hymns, which are somewhat more intricate in form than the church songs of Romanus the Hymnwriter (Melode), although in depth of poetical force and profound doctrine they are among the best of the hymns of the Christian church. John was also the author of many beautiful canons for festivals of the Lord, about the Holy Virgin, or in honor of prophets, apostles, and martyrs. Especially solemn is his Easter service, whose chants express the deep joy of believers because of Christ's victory over death and hell. Under John's pen, church hymns reached the highest point of their development and beauty. After him there were no remarkable writers in the field of Byzantine church poetry.[184]

The name of John Damascene is also closely connected with the romance *Barlaam and Josaphat,* which enjoyed the widest popularity in all languages throughout the Middle Ages. No doubt the plot of the tale was derived from the well-known legend of Buddha. It is highly probable that the story was simply a version of the life of Buddha adopted by the Christians of the East for their own use; the author himself said that the story was brought to him from India. Throughout the Middle Ages, down to recent times, the romance was almost universally attributed to John Damascene, but in 1886 the French orientalist, H. Zotenberg, advanced some proofs that John could not have been the author, and many writers have accepted his conclusions.[185] But in recent years writers on this subject are less decided, and lean more toward the older point of view. Thus, while the author of an article on John Damascene pub-

[184] M. Jugie, "La Vie de S. Jean Damascène," *Échos d'Orient,* XXIII (1924), 137-61. O. Bardenhewer, *Geschichte der altkirch-* *lichen Literatur,* V, 51-65.

[185] See K. Krumbacher, *Geschichte der byzantinischen Litteratur,* 886-90.

lished in the *Catholic Encyclopedia* in 1910 says that the romance *Barlaam and Josaphat* is dubiously attributed to John,[186] the most recent editors and translators of this romance think that the name of St. John of Damascus still has a right to appear on the title page of their edition.[187]

The second period of iconoclasm was marked by the activity of the well-known defender of image-worship, Theodore of Studion, the abbot of a famous monastery of Constantinople which had declined in the time of Constantine V, but was revived under the administration of Theodore. Under his administration a new rule was worked out for the monastery on the basis of community life *(cenoby)*; the intellectual needs of the monks were to be satisfied by a school established at the monastery. The monks were to be trained in reading, writing, and the copying of manuscripts, the study of the Holy Scriptures and the works of fathers of the church, and the art of composing hymns, which they sang during services.

As one of the great religious and social workers in the stormy period of iconoclasm, Theodore demonstrated his ability as an eminent writer in various branches of literature. His dogmatic polemical works aimed to develop the fundamental theses concerning images and image-worship. His numerous sermons, which form the so-called Small and Large Catechisms, proved to be the most popular of his writings. He also left a number of epigrams, acrostics, and hymns. The latter cannot be studied and analyzed to any great extent because some of them are still unpublished, while others have appeared in unscientific editions, such as the Russian service books. His large collection of letters of a religious-canonic and social nature is of very great value for the cultural history of his times.

The two last reigns of this period were marked by the creative activity of the interesting figure of Kasia, the only gifted poetess of the Byzantine period. When Theophilus decided to choose a wife, a bride show was arranged in the capital, for which the most beautiful maidens of all provinces were gathered in Constantinople. Kasia was one of them. The Emperor had to walk along the rows of maidens with a golden apple, and hand it to the one he desired to choose as his wife. He was about to hand it to Kasia, who pleased him more than any of the maidens, but her rather bold answer to his question caused him to change his intention and choose Theodora, the future restorer of orthodoxy. Kasia later founded a monastery where she spent the rest of her life. Kasia's surviving church poems and epigrams are distinguished by original thought and vivid style. According to Krumbacher, who made a

[186] J. B. O'Conner, "John Damascene," *Catholic Encyclopedia,* VIII, 459–61.

[187] St. John Damascene, *Barlaam and Joasaph;* with English trans. C. R. Woodward and H. Mattingly, xii.

special study of her poems, "she was also a wise but singular woman, who combined a fine sensitiveness and a deep religiousness with an energetic frankness and a slight tendency to feminine slander."[188]

The persecution of image-worshipers, glorified in later times by the triumphant iconodules, provided rich material for numerous lives of saints and gave rise to the brilliant period of Byzantine hagiography.

In the time of the Amorian dynasty some progress was made in the field of higher education in the Byzantine Empire and some advance in various branches of knowledge. Under Michael III, his uncle, Caesar Bardas, organized a higher school in Constantinople.[189] This higher school was located in the palace; its curriculum consisted of the seven main arts introduced in earlier pagan times and adopted later by Byzantine and western European schools. They are usually referred to as the "seven liberal arts" (*septem artes liberales*), divided into two groups: the *trivium,* grammar, rhetoric, and dialectics, and the *quadrivium,* arithmetic, geometry, astronomy, and music. Philosophy and ancient classical writers were also studied in this school. Striving to make education accessible to everybody, Bardas proclaimed that the school would be free of charge; the professors were well paid from the government treasury. The famous scholar of this period, Photius, was one of the teachers in the higher school of Bardas.

This school became the center about which gathered the best minds of the Empire during the subsequent reign of the Macedonian dynasty. Photius, whose first patriarchate fell in the time of Michael III, became the central force in the intellectual and literary movement of the second half of the ninth century. Exceptionally gifted, with a keen love of knowledge and an excellent education, he later devoted his entire attention and energy to educating others. His education had been many-sided, and his knowledge was extensive not only in theology but also in grammar, philosophy, natural science, law, and medicine. He gathered about himself a group of men who strove to enrich their knowledge. A man of inclusive scientific learning, Photius, as was customary in medieval times, was accused of having devoted himself to the study of the forbidden sciences of astrology and divination. Legendary tradition claims that in his youth he had sold his soul to a Jewish magician,[190] and in this, according to Bury, "the Patriarch appears as one of the forerunners

---

[188] Krumbacher, *Geschichte der byzantinischen Litteratur,* 716; see also Bury, *Eastern Roman Empire,* 81-83.

[189] Cf. F. Fuchs, *Die höheren Schulen von Konstantinopel im Mittelalter,* 18; Fuchs thought that Bardas' university was a new institution. The tale that Leo III burned the University of Constantinople, along with its library and professors, is merely a later legend. See L. Bréhier, "Notes sur l'histoire de l'enseignement supérieur à Constantinople," *Byzantion,* IV (1929), 13-28; III (1927), 74-75. Fuchs, *Die höheren Schulen,* 9-10 (bibliography).

[190] Symeon Magister, *De Mihaele et Theodora,* chap. xxxi, 670.

of Faustus."[191] As the most learned man of his time, he did not limit himself to teaching, but devoted much of his time to writing and has left a rich and varied literary heritage.

Among the works of Photius, his *Bibliotheca,* or, as it is frequently called, *Myriobiblon* (thousands of books), is especially important. The circumstances which suggested this work are very interesting. A kind of reading club seems to have existed at the house of Photius where a select circle of his friends assembled to read aloud literature of all kinds, secular and religious, pagan and Christian. The rich library of Photius was at the service of his friends. Yielding to their requests he began to write synopses of the books which had been read.[192] In the *Bibliotheca* Photius gave extracts from numerous works, sometimes brief, sometimes extensive, as well as his own essays based on these abstracts, or critical comments on them. Here are many facts about grammarians, orators, historians, natural scientists, doctors, councils, and the lives of saints. The greatest value of this work lies in the fact that it has preserved fragments of writings which have disappeared. The *Bibliotheca* deals only with writers of prose. His numerous other works belong to the field of theology and grammar, and he has left also many sermons and letters. In two of his sermons he refers to the first attack of the Russians on Constantinople in the year 860, of which he was an eyewitness.

In his striking universality of knowledge and in his insistence upon the study of ancient writers, Photius was representative of that intellectual movement in the Byzantine Empire which became very apparent, especially in the capital, from the middle of the ninth century, and was expressed in such events as the opening of Bardas' university, in which Photius himself devoted much time to teaching. In his lifetime and as a result of his influence, a closer and more friendly relation developed between secular science and theological teaching. So broad-minded was Photius in his relations to other people that even a Muhammedan ruler (Emir) of Crete could be his friend. One of his pupils, Nicolaus Mysticus, the Patriarch of Constantinople in the tenth century, wrote in his letter to the Emir's son and successor that Photius "knew well that, although difference in religion is a barrier, wisdom, kindness, and the other qualities which adorn and dignify human nature attract the affection of those who love fair things; and, therefore, notwithstanding the difference of creeds, he loved your father, who was endowed with these qualities."[193]

Patriarch John the Grammarian, an iconoclast, impressed his contemporaries by his profound and varied learning, and was even accused of being a magician. Another distinguished man was Leo, a remarkable mathematician

[191] Bury, *Eastern Roman Empire,* III, 445.
[192] *Ibid.,* 446.

[193] *Epistola II;* ed. Migne, *Patrologia Graeca,* CXI, 37; see Bury, *Eastern Roman Empire,* III, 439.

of the time of Theophilus. He became so famous abroad through his pupils that the Caliph Mamun, zealously interested in promoting education, begged him to come to his court. When Theophilus heard of this invitation he gave Leo a salary and appointed him as public teacher in one of the Constantinopolitan churches. Although Mamun had sent a personal letter to Theophilus begging him to send Leo to Bagdad for a short stay, saying that he would consider it as an act of friendship, and offering for this favor, as tradition has it, eternal peace and 2000 pounds of gold, the Emperor refused to grant this demand. In this case Theophilus treated science "as if it were a secret to be guarded, like the manufacture of Greek fire, deeming it bad policy to enlighten barbarians."[194] In later years Leo was elected archbishop of Thessalonica. When deposed in the time of Theodora for his iconoclastic views, Leo continued to teach at Constantinople and became the head of the higher school organized by Bardas. It is well to remember that the apostle of the Slavs, Constantine (Cyril), studied under the guidance of Photius and Leo, and previous to his Khazar mission occupied the chair of philosophy in the higher school of the capital.

This brief account will suffice to indicate that literary and intellectual life flourished in the time of the iconoclastic movement, and it would undoubtedly be seen to be more intensive and varied had the works of the iconoclasts survived through the ages.

In connection with the letters exchanged between Theophilus and Mamun regarding Leo the Mathematician, it is interesting to consider the question of mutual cultural relations between the caliphate and the Empire in the first half of the ninth century. At this time the caliphate, ruled by Harun-ar-Rashid and Mamun, was experiencing a brilliant development of learning and science. In his desire to outrival the glories of Bagdad, Theophilus built a palace in imitation of Arabian models. Certain evidence indicates that the influence of Bagdad upon the Byzantine Empire was very stimulating,[195] but this difficult problem extends beyond the limits of this book.

It has been argued frequently that in the field of art the iconoclastic epoch produced only negative results. And it is true that numerous valuable monuments of art were destroyed by the iconoclasts. "Their violence is to be deplored; their vandalism impoverished not only the centuries in which it was exercised, but those in which we ourselves are living."[196] But, on the other hand, the iconoclastic epoch brought a new stream of life into Byzantine art by reviving once more Hellenistic models, especially those of Alexandria,

---

[194] Theophanes Continuatus, *Historia*, Bonn ed., 190; Bury, *Eastern Roman Empire*, 436–38.

[195] *Ibid.*, 438; but cf. F. Fuchs, *Die höheren Schulen*, 18.

[196] O. M. Dalton, *Byzantine Art and Archaeology*, 14.

and by introducing oriental decoration borrowed from the Arabs, who in their turn had borrowed it from Persia. And though the iconoclasts categorically suppressed religious art with images of Christ, the Virgin, and saints, they were tolerant toward the presentation of the human figure in general, which became more realistic during this period under the influence of Hellenistic models. Genre scenes of everyday life became the favorite subject of artists, and on the whole there was a decided predominance of purely secular art. An example of this tendency is the fact that in place of the fresco representing the Sixth Ecumenical Council, Constantine V Copronymus ordered a portrait of his favorite charioteer.

The artistic monuments of the epoch, both religious and secular, have perished almost completely. Some mosaics in the churches of Thessalonica (Salonika) may fall within the limits of this period. A group of ivory carvings, especially ivory caskets, may also be attributed to the ninth century. The illuminated manuscripts of the iconoclastic epoch, the illustrations of which were the work of Byzantine monks, testify to the new spirit which had penetrated art. From the point of view of marginal illustrations the Chludoff (Chludov) Psalter is especially interesting. This oldest of illuminated psalters has been preserved at Moscow.[197] But it is greatly to be regretted that so few data exist for the study of art in the iconoclastic period. Many of the surviving materials are attributed to the iconoclastic epoch only on the basis of probable evidence, and not with full certainty.

Diehl thus appraised the significance of the iconoclastic epoch for the subsequent second Golden Age of Byzantine art under the Macedonian dynasty:

It was to the time of the iconoclasts that the Second Golden Age owed its essential characteristics. From the iconoclastic epoch proceed the two opposite tendencies which mark the Macedonian era. If at that time there flourished an imperial art inspired by classical tradition and marked by a growing interest in portraiture and real life which imposed its dominant ideas upon religious art, if in opposition to this official and secular art there existed a monastic art more severe, more theological, more wedded to tradition, if from the interaction of the two there issued a long series of masterpieces; it is in the period of iconoclasm that the seeds of this splendid harvest were sown. Not merely for its actual achievements, but for its influence upon the future, does this period deserve particular attention in the history of Byzantine art.[198]

[197] Diehl, *Manuel d'art byzantin* (2nd ed., 1925), 379–81; Dalton, *East Christian Art*, 309.
[198] *Manuel d'art byzantin* (2nd ed., 1925), I, 385–86; Dalton, *Byzantine Art and Archaeology*, 16; see also Bury, *Eastern Roman Empire*, 429–34.

CHAPTER VI: THE MACEDONIAN EPOCH

(867–1081)

THE history of the Macedonian dynasty falls into two periods, unequal in significance and duration. The first period extends from 867 to 1025, the year of the death of Emperor Basil II; the second, the brief period from 1025 to 1056, when Empress Theodora, the last member of this dynasty, died.

The first period was the most brilliant time of the political existence of the Empire. The struggle in the east and in the north with the Arabs, Bulgarians, and Russians, was crowned with brilliant success for Byzantine arms by the second half of the tenth and the beginning of the eleventh century. This was achieved in spite of some failures at the end of the ninth and in the early part of the tenth century. This triumph of the Byzantine Empire was especially great under Nicephorus Phocas and John Tzimisces, and reached its highest point in the reign of Basil II. In his time the separatist movements in Asia Minor were suppressed; Byzantine influence in Syria was strengthened; Armenia was in part annexed to the Empire and in part reduced to vassal dependence; Bulgaria was transformed into a Byzantine province; and Russia, upon adopting Christianity from Byzantium, entered into closer religious, political, commercial, and cultural relations with the Empire. This was the moment of the highest strength and glory ever attained by the Empire. The intensive legislative work, expressed in the publication of a gigantic code, the Basilics, and a number of famous novels directed against the pernicious growth of large landownership, and the intellectual advance associated with the names of Patriarch Photius and Constantine Porphyrogenitus add further glory and significance to the first period of the Macedonian dynasty.

After the year 1025, when the powerful figure of Basil II disappeared from the historical stage, the Empire entered a time of frequent court revolutions and anarchy which led to the troubled period of 1056–81. With the accession of the first of the Comneni, who seized the throne in 1081, the Empire regained its strength. Internal order was re-established, and for some time intellectual and artistic activity flourished once more.

THE ORIGIN OF THE DYNASTY

The question of the origin of the founder of the Macedonian dynasty has called forth many contradictory opinions, mainly because sources vary greatly on this point. While Greek sources speak of the Armenian or Macedonian extraction of Basil I, and Armenian sources assert that he was of pure Armenian blood, Arabic sources call him a Slav. On the one hand, the generally accepted name "Macedonian" is applied to this dynasty, but on the other hand, some scholars still consider Basil an Armenian, and still others, especially Russian historians prior to the seventies of the nineteenth century, speak of him as a Slav. The majority of scholars consider Basil an Armenian who had settled in Macedonia, and speak of his dynasty as the Armenian dynasty. But in view of the fact that there were many Armenians and Slavs among the population of Macedonia, it might be correct to assume that Basil was of mixed Armeno-Slavonic origin.[1] According to one historian who has made a special study of Basil's time, his family might have had an Armenian ancestry, which later intermarried with Slavs, who were very numerous in this part of Europe (Macedonia), and gradually became very much Slavonized.[2] A more exact definition of the Macedonian dynasty from the point of view of its ethnographic composition might be Armeno-Slavic. In recent years scholars have succeeded in determining that Basil was born in the Macedonian city of Charioupolis.[3]

Basil's life previous to his election to the throne was very unusual. As an unknown youth he came to Constantinople to seek his fortune, and there attracted the attention of courtiers by his tall stature, his enormous strength, and his ability to break in the wildest horses. Stories of young Basil reached Emperor Michael III. He took him to court and later became completely subject to his new favorite, who was soon proclaimed co-ruler and crowned with the imperial crown in the temple of St. Sophia. He repaid these favors received from the Emperor very brutally: When he noticed that Michael was becoming suspicious of him, he ordered his men to slay his benefactor, and then proclaimed himself emperor (867–86). After him the throne passed on to his sons, Leo VI the Philosopher or the Wise (886–912),[4] and Alexander

[1] See A. A. Vasiliev, "The Origin of Emperor Basil the Macedonian," *Vizantiysky Vremennik*, XII (1906), 148–65.

[2] A. Vogt, *Basile I, et la civilisation byzantine à la fin du IXe siècle*, 21, n. 3. See N. Adonz, "L'âge et l'origine de l'empereur Basile I (867–86)," *Byzantion*, IX (1934), 223–60 (Armenian origin). Sirarpie der Nersessian, *Armenia and the Byzantine Empire*, 20:

The Armenian origin of Basil I is now generally recognized.

[3] A. Papadopoulos-Kerameus, *Fontes historiae Imperii Trapezuntini*, 79. See N. A. Bees, "Eine unbeachtete Quelle über die Abstammung des Kaisers Basilios I., des Mazedoniers," *Byzantinisch-neugriechische Jahrbücher*, IV (1923), 76.

[4] A. Vogt, "La jeunesse de Leon VI le Sage," *Revue Historique*, CLXXIV (1934), 389–428.

(886–913). Leo's son, Constantine VII Porphyrogenitus (913–59), remained indifferent to affairs of state and devoted all his time to literary work in the midst of the most learned men of his time. The administrative power was in the hands of his father-in-law, the skillful and energetic admiral, Romanus Lecapenus (919–44).[5] In the year 944 the sons of Romanus Lecapenus forced their father to abdicate and retire to a monastery, and declared themselves emperors. They were deposed in 945 by Constantine Porphyrogenitus, who ruled independently from 945 until 959. His son, Romanus II, reigned only four years (959–63), leaving at his death his widow Theophano with two minor sons, Basil and Constantine. Theophano married the capable general, Nicephorus Phocas, who was proclaimed emperor (Nicephorus II Phocas, 963–69). His reign ceased when he was slain, and the throne passed to John Tzimisces (969–76), who claimed the imperial title because he had married Theodora, a sister of Romanus II and a daughter of Constantine VII Porphyrogenitus. Only after the death of John Tzimisces did the two sons of Romanus II, Basil II, surnamed Bulgaroctonus (the Bulgar-Slayer, 976–1025) and Constantine VIII (976–1028), become rulers of the Empire. Administrative power was concentrated mainly in the hands of Basil II, under whom the Empire rose to its highest power and glory. With his death began the period of decline for the Macedonian dynasty. After the death of Constantine VIII the aged senator, Romanus Argyrus, married to Constantine's daughter, Zoë, became emperor and ruled from 1028 until 1034. Zoë survived him, and at the age of about fifty-six married her lover, Michael the Paphlagonian, who was proclaimed emperor at his wife's entreaty, and ruled as Michael IV the Paphlagonian from 1034 to 1041. During his reign and in the brief reign of his nephew, Michael V Calaphates (1041–42), another accidental and insignificant figure, there was much disturbance and acute discontent in the Empire, which ended in the deposition and blinding of Michael V. For about two months the Byzantine Empire was ruled by the unusual combination of authority in the hands of Zoë, widowed for the second time, and of her younger sister, Theodora. In the same year (1042) Zoë married for the third time, and her new husband was proclaimed emperor. He ruled as Constantine IX Monomachus from 1042 until 1055. Zoë died before her third husband, but Theodora survived Constantine Monomachus and became the sole ruler of the Empire after his death (1055–56). After the reign of Irene, the famous restorer of image worship at the end of the eighth and early ninth centuries, the rule of Zoë and Theodora marks the second and last instance of feminine rule. Each of them occupied the throne as the autocratic and sovereign basilissa, i.e., Empress of the Romans. Shortly before her death Theodora yielded to the

---

[5] A very high opinion of Romanus Leca- penus' personality and activity in S. Runci- man, *The Emperor Romanus Lecapenus, and His Reign*, 238–45.

demands of the court party and elected the aged patrician, Michael Stratioticus, as her successor. He ascended the throne after Theodora's death in the
year 1056. Theodora was the last ruler of the Macedonian dynasty, which occupied the throne for a period of 189 years.

Byzantine relations with the Arabs and Armenia

The main problem in the external policy of Basil I, the founder of the
Macedonian dynasty, was the struggle with the Muslim world. Conditions
were unusually favorable for great achievements in this struggle, because in
his time the Empire maintained peaceful relations with Armenia in the east,
with Russia and Bulgaria in the north, and in the west with Venice and the
western emperor. Added to these advantages was the internal dissension
within the eastern caliphate aroused by the increasing influence of the Turks
at the Arabian court, the defection of Egypt, where the independent dynasty
of the Tulunids arose in the year 868, the civil wars among the North African
Arabs, and the difficult position of the Spanish Umayyads in the midst of the
local Christian population. Basil's position then was very advantageous for
a successful struggle with the eastern and western Arabs. But although the
Empire fought against the Arabs almost without interruption throughout the
reign of Basil I, it did not take full advantage of the favorable external conditions.

The successful military campaign which opened at the beginning of the
seventies in the eastern part of Asia Minor against the followers of the sect
of the Paulicans resulted in the Emperor's occupation of their main city of
Tephrice. This conquest not only widened the extent of Byzantine territory,
but also placed Basil face to face with the eastern Arabs. After several vigorously contested battles, the clashes between the two sides assumed the form
of regular annual collisions which were not of very great consequence. Victory
was sometimes on the side of the Greeks and sometimes on the side of the
Arabs, but in the end the Byzantine borderline in Asia Minor moved considerably to the east.

Far more serious were Basil's relations with the western Arabs, who at that
time possessed the greater part of Sicily and occupied some important points
in southern Italy. The troubled affairs of Italy caused the intervention of the
western Emperor, Louis II, who occupied the important city of Bari. It was
with this ruler that Basil I formed an alliance for a combined attempt to drive
the western Arabs out of Italy and Sicily. But this alliance did not succeed
and was soon dissolved. After the death of Louis the population of Bari handed
over their city to Byzantine officials.

Meanwhile the Arabs occupied the strategically important island of Malta, south of Sicily, and in the year 878 they took Syracuse by assault after a siege of nine months. An interesting description of the siege of Syracuse was written by an eyewitness, the monk Theodosius, who was living there at the time, and after the fall of the city was imprisoned by the Arabs in Palermo. He related that during the siege a famine raged in the city, and the inhabitants were forced to eat grass, skins of animals, ground bones mixed with water, and even corpses. This famine caused an epidemic which carried off an enormous part of the population.[6] After the loss of Syracuse, among important points in Sicily the Byzantine Empire retained only the city of Tauromemium or Taormina on the eastern coast of the island. This loss was a turning point in Basil's external policy. His plans for a general attack on the Arabs were not to be realized. The occupation of Tarentum in southern Italy by Basil's troops and their successful advance into the interior of this country under the leadership of their general, Nicephorus Phocas, during the last years of Basil's reign might be considered as some consolation after the failure at Syracuse, however.

Notwithstanding the negative outcome of the western alliance against the Arabs, Basil attempted another alliance with the Armenian King Ashot Bagratid (Bagratuni) for the purpose of defeating the eastern Arabs. But at the time of the formation of this union Basil died. In spite of the loss of Syracuse and the unsuccessful campaigns against the Arabs, Basil increased somewhat the extent of Byzantine possessions in Asia Minor, and restored the lost importance of Byzantine rule in southern Italy. "The aged Basil," said a recent student of his period, "could die in peace. He had fulfilled, both in the east and in the west, a very great military task, which was at the same time a civilizing task. The Empire left by Basil was stronger and more imposing than the one he had received."[7]

The peaceful relations maintained by Basil with all his neighbors, excepting the Arabs, were broken under his successor, Leo VI the Wise (886–912). A war broke out with the Bulgarians, which ended with their victory. It was during this war that the Magyars (Hungarians) appeared in Byzantine history for the first time. Toward the end of Leo's reign the Russians stood near Constantinople. Armenia, the ally of the Byzantine Empire, exposed to incessant Arabian invasions, did not receive the aid she expected from Byzantium. In addition to all this the question of the Emperor's fourth marriage aroused strong internal disturbances. As a result of these external and internal

---

[6] Θεοδοσίου Μοναχοῦ τοῦ καὶ γραμματικοῦ ἐπιστολὴ πρὸς Λέοντα Διάκονον περὶ τῆς ἁλώσεως Συρακούσης, ed. Hase, 180–81; ed. C. Zuretti, 167. See A. A. Vasiliev, *Byzantium and the Arabs*, II, 59–68.
[7] Vogt, *Basile Ier*, 337. Cf. *Cambridge Medieval History*, IV, 54.

complications the problem of the struggle with Islam became more complex and difficult for the Empire.

The campaigns against the Arabs were generally ineffective in the time of Leo VI. In the military clashes on the eastern borders the Arabs were at times as victorious as the Greeks. Neither side gained much from these collisions. In the west the Muslims occupied the city of Rhegium (Reggio) on the Italian shore of the Strait of Messina and after this the Strait was completely in the hands of the Arabs. In 902 they conquered Tauromenium or Taormina, the last important fortified point of Byzantine Sicily. With the fall of this city Sicily was, so to say, entirely in the hands of the Arabs, for the smaller cities which still belonged to the Greeks were of no importance in the later history of the Empire. The eastern policy of Leo VI during the second half of his reign in no way depended upon his relations with the Sicilian Arabs.

The beginning of the tenth century was marked by active operations of the Muslim fleet. Even at the end of the ninth century Cretan pirates had repeatedly raided the coasts of the Peloponnesus and the islands of the Aegean Sea. These sea raids of the Arabs became still more dangerous when their Syrian and Cretan fleets began to act together. The attack of Thessalonica by the Muslim fleet under the leadership of the Greek renegade, Leo of Tripolis, in 904 is the most famous deed of the Arabs in this period. The city was taken only after a long and difficult siege, but a few days after its fall the conquerors departed with a large number of prisoners and rich spoils, setting sail eastward to Syria. It was only after this disaster that the Byzantine government began the fortification of Thessalonica. A detailed account of the Arabian raid of the city came from the pen of John Cameniates, a priest who lived through all the hardships of the siege.[8]

The successful naval operations of the Arabs forced the Byzantine rulers to devote more attention to the improvement of their own fleet. The result was that in 906 the Byzantine admiral Himerius gained a brilliant victory over the Arabs in the Aegean. But in 911 the great sea expedition of Leo VI against the allied eastern and Cretan Arabs, also headed by Himerius, ended in complete failure for the empire. In his exact account of the composition of this expedition Constantine Porphyrogenitus spoke of the presence of 700 Russians.[9]

Thus the Byzantine struggle with the Arabs was highly unsuccessful in the time of Leo VI: in the west Sicily was definitely lost; in southern Italy

[8] *De excidio Thessalonicensi narratio*, ed. I. Bekker, *Corpus Scriptorum Historiae Byzantinae*, 487–600. See Vasiliev, *Byzantium and the Arabs*, II, 143–53. A. Struck, "Die Eroberung Thessalonikes durch die Sarszenen im Jahre 904," *Byzantinische Zeitschrift*, XIV (1905), 535–62. O. Tafrali, *Thessalonique des origines au XIVe siècle*, 143–56.

[9] *De Cerimoniis aulae byzantinae*, II, 44; Bonn ed., 651.

Byzantine troops failed to accomplish anything after the recall of Nicephorus Phocas; on the eastern border the Arabs were slowly but persistently
going forward; and on the sea the Byzantine fleet suffered several serious
defeats.

In spite of the religious animosity toward the Arabs and the military clashes
with them official documents at times referred to them in very friendly terms.
Thus the patriarch of Constantinople of this period, Nicholas Mysticus, wrote
to "the most illustrious, most honorable and beloved" Emir of the island of
Crete that "the two powers of the whole universe, the power of the Saracens
and that of the Romans, are excelling and shining as the two great luminaries
in the firmament. For this reason alone we must live in common as brothers
although we differ in customs, manners, and religion."[10]

In the long reign of Constantine VII Porphyrogenitus (913–59) and Romanus I Lecapenus (919–44) the Byzantine Empire could not struggle effectively with the Arabs until the end of the third decade of the tenth century,
because all its forces were thrown into the Bulgarian war. Luckily for the
Empire, the caliphate was at this time going through a period of disintegration and internal strife, and separate independent dynasties were being
formed. However, one successful operation of the Byzantine fleet may be
mentioned: in 917 the renegade pirate Leo of Tripoli, who in 904 had captured Thessalonica, was overwhelmingly defeated at Lemnos.[11]

After the Bulgarian campaign very capable generals appeared in the Greek
and Arab armies. The Greek domesticus John Curcuas was, in the words of
the chronicler, a "second Trajan or Belisarius" and a conquerer of "nearly
thousands of cities." A special work was even written about him, but it has
not been preserved.[12] His genius brought in a new "dawn on the eastern
border"; with him there seemed to come a "new spirit into the imperial eastern
policy, a spirit of confident aggression."[13] The Arabs, too, had an efficient
chief in the person of Saif-ad-Daulah, a member of the independent dynasty
of the Hamdanids, which ruled Aleppo. His court became a center of flourishing literary activity, and his period was called by contemporaries the "Golden
Age." Toward the middle of the tenth century Curcuas achieved numerous
victories in Arabian Armenia and occupied many cities in upper Mesopotamia.
In 933 Melitene was captured by Curcuas, and in 944 the city of Edessa was
forced to give up its precious relic, the miraculous image of the Savior (*man-
dilion*, τὸ μανδίλιον), which was transported to Constantinople with great
pomp. This was the last triumph of Curcuas. These successes made him "the

---

[10] *Epistola*, I; ed. J. P. Migne, *Patrologia
Graeca*, CXI, 28. See J. Hergenröther, *Photius,
Patriarch von Constantinopel*, II, 600; Vasiliev,
Byzantium and the Arabs, appendix, 197.

[11] Vasiliev, *ibid.*, 219.

[12] Theophanes Continuatus, *Historia*, Bonn
ed., 427–28.

[13] Runciman, *Romanus Lecapenus*, 69, 135,
241–49.

hero of the moment,"[14] but his popularity alarmed the government and he was removed from his post. At that time Romanus Lecapenus fell, and in the next month his sons also were dethroned. Constantine Porphyrogenitus became sole emperor. "It was the end of an era; new actors were strutting onto the stage."[15]

The epoch of Romanus Lecapenus was of very great importance for the Byzantine policy in the East. After three centuries of keeping to the defensive, the Empire under the guidance of Romanus and John Curcuas assumed the offensive and began to triumph. The frontier was in a very different condition from what it had been at the time of Romanus' accession. The border provinces were comparatively free from Arab raids. During the last twelve years of Romanus' reign Muhammedan raiders only twice crossed the frontier. Romanus appointed as commander-in-chief Curcuas, "the most brilliant soldier that the Empire had produced for generations. He infused a new spirit into the imperial armies, and led them victorious deep into the country of the infidels. . . . John Curcuas was the first of a line of great conquerors and as the first is worthy of high praise. And in the praise, a part should be given to Romanus Lecapenus to whose judgment the Empire owed his services and under whose rule were passed those twenty glorious years."[16]

The last years of Constantine Porphyrogenitus were marked by desperate battles with Saif-ad-Daulah, and although the Greeks had been beaten in several of these collisions, the outcome of the struggle was the defeat of the Arabs in northern Mesopotamia and the crossing of the Euphrates by the Byzantine army. During these years of struggle John Tzimisces, the future emperor, distinguished himself by his capable leadership. But the large sea expedition organized against the Cretan Arabs in 949 resulted in complete failure and the loss of numerous vessels. Six hundred and twenty-nine Russians were among the Byzantine warriors who participated in this campaign.[17] The constant clashes between the Greeks and the Muslims in the west, in Italy, and Sicily were of no importance for the general course of events.

The eastern conquests of John Curcuas and John Tzimisces, which extended the borders of the Empire beyond the Euphrates, inaugurated a brilliant period of Byzantine victories over the Muslims. In the words of the French historian, Rambaud, "All the failures of Basil I were revenged; the road was opened to Tarsus, Antioch, Cyprus, and Jerusalem. . . . Before his death Constantine could rejoice because during his reign so many great acts had been performed for the cause of Christ. He opened the era of Crusades for the East

---

[14] *Ibid.*, 145. A rich collection of Arab texts referring to Saif-ad-Daulah in M. Canard, *Sayf al Daula.*

[15] Runciman, *Romanus Lecapenus,* 146.

[16] *Ibid.*, 146–50.

[17] On this expedition, Vasiliev, *Byzantium and the Arabs,* II, 279–86.

as well as for the West, for the Hellenes as well as for the Franks [i.e., for the western European nations]."[18]

During the brief reign of Romanus II (959-63), his capable and energetic general, Nicephorus Phocas, the future emperor, occupied the island of Crete, thus destroying the nest of Arabian pirates who had terrorized the population of the islands and coasts of the Aegean Sea. By reconquering Crete the Empire regained an important strategic and commercial point in the Mediterranean Sea.[19] Nicephorus Phocas was equally successful in the ensuing war with Saif-ad-Daulah in the east. After a difficult siege he succeeded in temporarily occupying Aleppo, the seat of the Hamdanids.

The achievements of the next three emperors—Nicephorus Phocas, John Tzimisces, and Basil II Bulgaroctonus—form the most brilliant pages of the military history of the Empire in its struggle with Islam. During his six years' reign (963-69) Nicephorus Phocas concentrated his attention on the East, although occasionally he diverted it to the hostile acts of the Bulgarians, which became more serious due to the intervention of the Russian prince, Sviatoslav. Some of the Emperor's forces were also absorbed in the collisions with the German king, Otto the Great, in Italy. In the East the Byzantine troops followed the conquest of Tarsus by the occupation of Cilicia, while the fleet succeeded in taking from the Arabs the important island of Cyprus. In connection with the fall of Tarsus the Arab geographer of the thirteenth century, Yaqut, narrates an interesting story based on the accounts of refugees. Under the walls of Tarsus, he said, Nicephorus Phocas ordered that two banners be raised as emblems of "the land of the Romans" and "the land of Islam," and commanded the heralds to announce that around the first banner should gather all who desired justice, impartiality, safety of property, family life, children, good roads, just laws, and kind treatment; and around the second, all those who upheld adultery, oppressive legislation, violence, extortion, the seizure of landed estates, and the confiscation of property.[20]

The occupation of Cilicia and Cyprus opened for Nicephorus the road to Syria, and he began to work toward the realization of his cherished dream: the conquest of Antioch, the heart of Syria. After a preliminary irruption into Syria, Nicephorus besieged Antioch, and when it became evident that the siege would last a very long time, the Emperor left his army and returned to the capital. During his absence, in the last year of his reign (969), his soldiers took Antioch with enormous spoils, thus fulfilling his great ambition. "Thus did Christian arms reconquer the great city of Antioch, the glorious Theoupolis [the name applied to the city by Justinian the Great], that ancient

[18] *L'Empire grec au dixième siècle. Constantin Porphyrogénète*, 436.
[19] A. M. Shepard, *The Byzantine Reconquest of Crete* (A.D. 960), 1121-30.

[20] *Geographisches Wörterbuch*, ed. Wüstenfeld, III, 527. See V. Barthold, *Transactions of the Oriental College*, I (1925), 476.

rival of Byzantium in the east, the city of great patriarchs and great saints, councils and heresies."[21] Soon after the fall of Antioch the Byzantine troops took one more important Syrian center, the city of Aleppo, the residence of the Hamdanids. There is in existence the interesting text of the agreement between the Byzantine general and the master of Aleppo.[22] This treaty defined very carefully the boundaries and names of the Syrian districts ceded to the Byzantine Emperor and of those over which he was to become suzerain. Chief among the conquered points was Antioch. The city of Aleppo (Haleb, in Arabic) became a vassal state of the Empire. The Muslim population was taxed in favor of Byzantium, while the Christians of the vassal districts were freed from all taxation. The ruler of Aleppo (the emir) agreed to aid the Emperor in case of war with the non-Muhammedans of those provinces. He also bound himself to protect Byzantine trade caravans which might enter his territory. The reconstruction of the destroyed churches was guaranteed to the Christians. Freedom to change from Christianity to Muhammedanism or vice versa was also guaranteed.

The treaty was concluded after the death of Nicephorus Phocas, murdered at the end of the year 969. Never before had the Muslims been subjected to so much humiliation. Cilicia and a part of Syria with Antioch were taken from them, and a very large portion of their territory was placed under the suzerainty of the Empire.

The Arabian historian of the eleventh century, Yahya of Antioch, writes that the Muslim population was certain that Nicephorus Phocas would conquer all of Syria and other provinces, too. "The incursions of Nicephorus," wrote this chronicler, "became a pleasure for his soldiers, for nobody attacked them or opposed them; he marched wherever he pleased, and destroyed whatever he liked, without encountering any Muslim, or anyone else who would divert him and prevent him from doing that which he wished. . . . Nobody could resist him."[23] The Greek historian of the time, Leo the Deacon, wrote that had Nicephorus not been assassinated, he would have been able "to fix the boundaries of their [i.e. Greek] Empire in the east as far as India, and in the west as far as the confines of the world," in other words, the Atlantic Ocean.[24]

In the West the policy of Nicephorus Phocas was a failure. In his time the last points in Sicily which still belonged to the Empire were conquered by the Muslims, so that Sicily was completely in their hands. The main problem

[21] G. Schlumberger, *Un empereur byzantin au dixième siècle. Nicéphore Phocas,* 723.
[22] In the works of the Arabian historian of the thirteenth century, Kamal-ad-Din. See G. Freytag, *Regnum Saahd-Aldaulae in oppido Halebo,* 9–14. The Latin trans. Bonn ed. Leo the Deacon, *Historiae,* 391–94.
[23] *Histoire de Yahya-ibn-Said d'Antioche,* ed. and trans. J. Kratchkovsky and A. A. Vasiliev, *Patrologia Orientalis,* XVIII (1924), 825–26 (127–28); ed. L. Cheikho, 135.
[24] *Historiae,* V, 4; Bonn ed., 81.

of John Tzimisces (969–76), who succeeded Phocas, was to secure the conquests in Cilicia and Syria. During the first years of his reign he could not participate personally in the military activities on the eastern border, because the Russian and Bulgarian wars, and the insurrection of Bardas Phocas demanded his undivided attention. He was victorious in the northern wars, and he also succeeded in suppressing the rebellion of Bardas Phocas. The Italian complications were settled through the marriage of the Byzantine princess, Theophano, to the heir of the German throne, the future Emperor Otto II. Only then was it possible for John Tzimisces to turn to his eastern problems.

His campaigns against the eastern Muslims were highly successful. Regarding his last campaign an interesting source is the letter from John Tzimisces to his ally, Ashot III, king of Armenia, preserved in the works of the Armenian historian, Matthew of Edessa.[25] This letter shows that the Emperor, in aiming to achieve his final goal of freeing Jerusalem from the hands of the Muslims, undertook a real crusade. He departed with his army from Antioch, entered Damascus, and in his southward movement advanced into Palestine, where the cities of Nazareth and Caesarea voluntarily delivered themselves to the Emperor; even Jerusalem began to plead for mercy. "If the pagan Africans who lived there," wrote the Emperor in his letter to Ashot, "had not hidden out of fear of us in the seacoast castles, we would have entered, with God's help, the sacred city of Jerusalem and prayed to God in the Holy Places."[26] But before reaching Jerusalem John Tzimisces directed his forces northward along the seacoast, and conquered many cities on his way. In the same letter the Emperor said, "Today all Phoenicia, Palestine, and Syria are freed from the Muhammedan yoke and recognize the authority of the Byzantine Greeks."[27] This letter, of course, contains many exaggerations. When it is compared with the testimony of the authentic information given by the Christian Arabian historian, Yahya of Antioch, it is evident that the results of the Palestinian campaign were much less notable. In all probability the Byzantine army did not go far beyond the boundaries of Syria.[28]

When the Byzantine soldiers returned to Antioch, the Emperor left for Constantinople, where he died early in 976. One Byzantine chronicler wrote, "All nations were horror-stricken by the attacks of John Tzimisces; he enlarged the land of the Romans; the Saracens and Armenians fled, the Persians feared him; and people from all sides carried gifts to him, beseeching him to

[25] E. Dulaurier, "Chronique de Matthieu d'Edesse," *Bibliothèque historique arménienne*, 16–24. Chr. Kuchuk-Ioannesov, "The Letter of Emperor John Tzimisces to the Armenian King Ashot III," *Vizantiysky Vremennik*, X (1903), 93–101.
[26] Dulaurier, *ibid.*, 20; Kuchuk-Ioannesov, *ibid.*, 98.
[27] Dulaurier, *ibid.*, 22; Kuchuk-Ioannesov, *ibid.*, 100.
[28] See Barthold, *Transactions of the Oriental College*, I (1925), 466–67. He said that the entire account of the invasion of Palestine belongs to the realm of fantasy.

make peace with them; he marched as far as Edessa and the River Euphrates, and the earth became filled with Roman armies; Syria and Phoenicia were trampled by Roman horses, and he achieved great victories; the sword of the Christian cut down like a sickle."[29] However this last brilliant expedition of John Tzimisces did not accomplish the annexation of the conquered provinces, for his army returned to Antioch, which became the main base of the Byzantine military forces in the east during the latter part of the tenth century.

Under the successor of John Tzimisces, Basil II (976-1025), the general state of affairs was not favorable for an aggressive policy in the east. The menacing insurrections of Bardas Sclerus and Bardas Phocas in Asia Minor and the continuing Bulgarian war demanded Basil's undivided attention. Yet when the rebellions had been suppressed, the Emperor frequently participated in the struggle with the Muslims, even though the Bulgarian war had not ceased. The Syrian possessions of the Empire were greatly menaced by the caliph of Egypt, and the vassal city of Aleppo was occupied many times by the enemy's army. By his personal appearance in Syria, at times unexpected, Basil frequently succeeded in restoring Byzantine influence in this province, but failed to make any significant new conquests. At the very outset of the eleventh century a treaty of peace was reached by the Emperor and the Egyptian Caliph Hakim of the dynasty of the Fatimids. During the remaining part of Basil's reign there were no more serious collisions with the eastern Arabs. Meanwhile, Aleppo freed itself of its vassal dependence on the Byzantine Empire.

Although officially peaceful relations were established between Basil and the Caliph Hakim, the latter sometimes pursued a policy of cruel persecution of the Christians, which undoubtedly greatly chagrined Basil as a Christian emperor. In 1009 Hakim ordered the destruction of the Church of the Holy Sepulcher and Golgotha at Jerusalem. Church relics and riches were seized, monks were exiled, and pilgrims persecuted. The contemporary Arabian historian, Yahya of Antioch, said that the executor of the severe will of Hakim "endeavored to destroy the Holy Sepulcher itself and raze it to the ground; he broke to pieces the greater portion of it and destroyed it."[30] The terrified Christians and Jews thronged the Muslim offices, promising to deny their religion and accept Islam. Hakim's decree ordering the destruction of the temple was signed by his Christian minister.

Basil II did nothing, apparently, for the defense of the persecuted Christians and their sanctuaries. After Hakim's death (1021) a period of tolerance toward Christians again set in, and in 1023 the patriarch of Jerusalem, Niceph-

[29] George Hamartolus, *Continuator*, ed. E. Muralt, 865.

[30] V. Rosen, *The Emperor Basil Bulgaroctonus*, 46; in Russian, 48. *Annales Yahia Ibn Said Antiochensis*, ed. L. Cheikho, 196.

orus, was sent to Constantinople to announce that the churches and their property had been restored to the Christians, that the Church of the Holy Sepulcher and all the destroyed churches in Egypt and Syria had been rebuilt, and that, in general, the Christians were safe in the dominions of the caliph.[31] Of course, these tales of the rapid restoration of temples in such a brief period of time were exaggerated.

In the west the Sicilian Arabs continued their raids on southern Italy, and the Byzantine government, occupied in solving other problems, could do nothing against them. The intervention of the German Emperor Otto II (related to the Byzantine throne) in Italian affairs resulted after some successes in a severe defeat at the hands of the Arabs. By the end of his reign Basil II had begun to plan an extensive expedition for the reconquest of Sicily, but he died in the course of its preparation.

The anarchy which set in after Basil's death emboldened the Muslims to start a series of offensive movements, which were particularly successful in the districts of Aleppo. The situation was somewhat improved for the Empire by the young and gifted general, George Maniaces, who succeeded in occupying Edessa in the early thirties of the eleventh century, taking from it its second relic, the apocryphal letter of Jesus Christ to Abgar, king of Edessa.[32] After the fall of this city Emperor Romanus III proposed a treaty to the Muslims. Its first two conditions, concerning the city of Jerusalem, deserved special attention. First, the Christians should obtain the right to rebuild all the destroyed churches, and the Church of the Holy Sepulcher should be restored at the expense of the imperial treasury. Second, the Emperor should keep the right of appointing the patriarch of Jerusalem. As a result of disagreement regarding several conditions of the treaty, negotiations lasted for a long time. The caliph seems not to have opposed these two demands. When the final agreement was reached in 1036, the Emperor received the right of restoring the Church of the Holy Sepulcher at his expense,[33] and in 1046 the Persian traveler, Nasiri-Khusrau, who had visited the restored church, described it as a most spacious building with a capacity of eight thousand persons; the edifice, he said, was built with the utmost skill, of colored marbles, with ornamentation and sculptures; inside the church was adorned everywhere with pictures and Byzantine brocade worked in gold. The legend recorded by this Persian traveler noted that even the Emperor himself came to Jerusalem, but privily, so that no one should recognize him. The Persian related: "In the days when Hakim was ruler of Egypt, the Greek

---

[31] See Barthold, *Transactions of the Oriental College,* I (1925), 477. The best source here is Yahya.

[32] See p. 306 for discussion of the first relic of Edessa, the miraculous image of the Savior.

[33] Yahya, *Annales,* ed. Cheikho, 270–71; Ibn-al-Athir ed. Tornberg, IX, 313. See Barthold, *Transactions of the Oriental College,* I (1925), 477–78.

Caesar came in this manner to Jerusalem. When Hakim received news of this arrival, he sent for one of his cup-bearers and said to him, 'There is a man of such and such a countenance and condition whom thou wilt find seated in the mosque of the Holy City; go thou, therefore, and approach him, and say that Hakim hath sent thee to him, lest he should think that I, Hakim, knew not of his coming; but tell him to be of good cheer, for I have no evil intention against him.' "[34]

The Empire's attempts to reconquer Sicily did not bring about any definite results, in spite of the fact that George Maniaces was victorious in several battles. It is interesting to know that the Sicilian expedition of this period included the Varangian-Russian Druzhina (company) which served the Empire. The famous hero of Scandinavian sagas, Harald Haardraade, also participated in this campaign. In the middle of the eleventh century the Byzantine Empire was confronted by a new enemy, the Seljuq Turks, who were prominent in the subsequent period of Byzantine history.

Thus, in the time of the Macedonian dynasty, in spite of the troubled period which followed the death of Basil II, the efforts of John Curcuas, Nicephorus Phocas, John Tzimisces, and Basil II widened the eastern borders of the Empire as far as the Euphrates, and Syria, with Antioch, once more formed part of Byzantine territory. This was the most brilliant period in the history of Byzantine relations with the eastern Muslims.

At the same time very important and animated relations developed between the Empire and Armenia. For many centuries Armenia was the apple of discord between Rome and Persia. Their ancient struggle for this buffer state had finally led to the division of Armenia between them at the end of the fourth century. The smaller western part with the city of Theodosiopolis (now Erzerum) had been taken by the Roman Empire; the larger eastern part had fallen to the Persian Sassanids, and was known in the east as Persarmenia. According to one historian, the political division of Armenia "into two parts, eastern and western, led to a cultural break in the life of the Armenian people due to the difference between the Byzantine and Iranian rule."[35] Justinian the Great introduced important military and civil reforms in Armenia with the intention of destroying some of the surviving local customs and transforming Armenia into an ordinary imperial province.

In the seventh century, after the conquest of Syria and the defeat of Persia, the Arabs occupied Armenia. Armenian, Greek, and Arabic sources give contradictory accounts of this event. The Armenians later tried to take advantage of the troubled affairs of the caliphate, which frequently turned the attention

---

[34] Nasir-i-Khusrau, *A Diary of a Journey Through Syria and Palestine,* trans. Guy le Strange, 59–60.

[35] N. Adonz, *Armenia in the Epoch of Justinian,* 3–4.

of the Arabs away from Armenian problems, and made several attempts to throw off the new yoke. These attempts at revolt were repaid by terrible devastations on the part of the Arabs. N. Marr said that at the beginning of the eighth century Armenia was completely ruined by the Arabs; "the feudal lords were exterminated with much cruelty and the glorious achievements of Christian architecture were destroyed. In short, the fruit of all the cultural efforts of the preceding centuries was reduced to nothing."[36]

When the Arabian caliph found himself greatly in need of Armenian aid for his struggle with the Byzantine Empire in the middle of the ninth century, he conferred the title of "Prince of Princes" upon the Armenian ruler Ashot, of the family of Bagratids. The wise administration of this ruler received general recognition, and at the end of the ninth century the caliph conferred upon him the title of king. By this act a new Armenian kingdom, ruled by the dynasty of Bagratids, was definitely established. When news of this reached Basil I, shortly before his death, he hastened to bestow a similar honor upon the new king of Armenia by sending him a royal crown and signing with him a treaty of friendship and union. Basil, in a letter, called Ashot his beloved son, and assured him that of all states Armenia would always remain the closest ally of the Empire.[37] This shows clearly that both the Emperor and the caliph attempted to secure Ashot the Bagratid as an ally in their struggle against each other.[38]

The anarchy which set in after Ashot's death forced the Muslims to intervene in the internal affairs of Armenia, and it was only in the reign of Ashot II "the Iron" in the first half of the tenth century[39] that the Armenian territory was cleared to some extent of the Arabs, with the help of the Byzantine army and the assistance of the King of Iberia (Georgia, Gruzia). Ashot himself visited the court of Romanus Lecapenus at Constantinople and was accorded a triumphant reception. He was the first ruler to assume the title of Shahinshah, meaning "King of Kings," of Armenia. His successor, Ashot III, transferred the official capital of his kingdom to the fortress of Ani in the second half of the tenth century, where in a subsequent period many magnificent edifices were erected. The city which grew up there became a rich center of civilization. Up to World War I the ruins of Ani were within the boundaries of Russia, and to them the Russian scholar N. Marr devoted much time. His excavations resulted in brilliant discoveries, highly significant not

[36] "The Caucasian Cultural World and Armenia," *Journal of the Ministry of Public Instruction*, LVII (1915), 313–14; see Barthold, *Transactions of the Oriental College*, I (1925), 467.
[37] Jean Catholicos, *Histoire d'Arménie*, trans. A. J. Saint-Martin, 126.

[38] Vasiliev, *Byzantium and the Arabs*, 83–84. J. Laurent, *L'Arménie entre Byzance et l'Islam depuis la conquête arabe jusqu'en 886*, 282–83. Grousset, *Histoire de l'Arménie* (Paris, 1947), 394–97.
[39] On this period see Runciman, *Romanus Lecapenus*, 125–33, 151–74.

only for the history of Armenia and the civilization of the Caucasian peoples in general, but also for a clearer conception of Byzantine influence in the Christian East.

The new disturbances in Armenia in connection with the invasions of the Seljuq Turks forced Basil II to assume personal leadership as soon as the Bulgarian war was over. As a result, one part of Armenia was annexed to the Empire and the other part placed in vassal dependence. This new expansion of the Empire in the East, for which the capital accorded Basil a triumphant reception, was the last military victory in the active and glorious reign of the aged basileus.[40] In the forties of the eleventh century, under Constantine IX Monomachus, the new capital of Armenia, Ani, was taken over by the Empire. This put an end to the rule of the Bagratids (Bagratuni). The last member of the dynasty was induced to come to Constantinople, where he received in place of his lost kingdom lands in Cappadocia, a money pension, and a palace on the Bosphorus. The Byzantine Empire, however, was unable to maintain its power in Armenia because the people were greatly dissatisfied with the administrative as well as the religious policy of the central government. Most of the Byzantine troops who occupied Armenia, moreover, were removed and recalled to Europe to defend Constantine Monomachus, first against the insurrection of Leo Tornikios, and then against the Patzinaks (Pechenegs). The Turks, taking advantage of the existing state of affairs, made frequent irruptions into Armenia and gradually conquered it.

Relations of the Byzantine Empire with the Bulgarians and Magyars

The relations with Bulgaria in the time of the Macedonian emperors were extremely significant for the Empire. Although in the time of King Simeon Bulgaria became a formidable enemy of the Byzantine Empire, threatening even the capital and the Emperor's power, the rulers of the Macedonian dynasty completely subjected this kingdom and transformed it into a Byzantine province.

During the reign of Basil I peaceful relations were maintained with Bulgaria. Immediately after the death of Michael III the negotiations concerning the restoration of the union between the Bulgarian and Greek churches came to a happy ending. King Boris went so far as to send his son, Simeon, to be educated in Constantinople. These friendly relations were very advantageous for both sides. Relieved of all anxiety about his northern borders, Basil could pour all his forces into the struggle with the eastern Arabs in the heart of Asia

---

[40] J. Laurent, *Byzance et les Turcs Seldjoucides dans l'Asie occidentale jusqu'en 1081,* 16–18. On the details of this expedition into Armenia and on Basil's relations with Abasgia and Iberia see G. Schlumberger, *L'Épopée byzantine à la fin du dixième siècle,* II, 498–536. Grousset, 547–80.

Minor and the western Muslims in Italy. Boris, in his turn, needed peace for the internal upbuilding of his kingdom, which had only recently adopted Christianity.

After the accession of Leo VI (886), peace with Bulgaria was broken immediately because of some dispute regarding certain customs duties which were highly detrimental to Bulgarian trade. Bulgaria was ruled at this time by its very famous King Simeon, son of Boris. His "love of knowledge led him to reread the books of the ancients,"[41] and he rendered his kingdom great services in the realms of culture and education. His wide political schemes were to be realized at the expense of the Byzantine Empire. Leo VI, aware of the fact that he was unable to offer adequate resistance to Simeon because the Byzantine army was engaged in the Arabian campaigns, appealed for help to the wild Magyars. The latter agreed to make a sudden invasion of Bulgaria from the north in order to divert Simeon's attention from the Byzantine borders.

This was a very significant moment in the history of Europe. For the first time, at the end of the ninth century, a new people, the Magyars (Hungarians, Ugrians; Byzantine sources frequently call them Turks, and western sources sometimes refer to them as Avars),[42] became involved in the international relations of European states, or, as C. Grot put it, this was "the first appearance of the Magyars on the arena of European wars as an ally of one of the most civilized nations."[43] Simeon was defeated by the Magyars in several early battles, but he showed much skill in handling the difficult situation, by trying to gain time in negotiations with the Byzantine Empire, during which he succeeded in winning over the Patzinaks. With their aid he defeated the Magyars and forced them to move north to the place of their future state in the valley of the Middle Danube. After this victory Simeon turned his attention to the Byzantine Empire. A decisive victory over the Greek troops brought him to the very walls of Constantinople. The defeated Emperor succeeded in negotiating a peace treaty according to which he bound himself to refrain from any hostile action against the Bulgarians and to send rich gifts to Simeon every year.

After the Arabian siege and pillage of Thessalonica in the year 904, Simeon

[41] Nicolai Mystici *Epistola,* XX; ed. Migne, *Patrologia Graeca,* CXI, 133.

[42] The problem of the origin of the Magyars is very complicated. It is very difficult to determine whether they were of Finno-Ugrian or of Turkish origin. See J. B. Bury, *History of the Eastern Roman Empire,* III, 492; the *Cambridge Medieval History,* IV, 194–95. J. Moravcsik, "Zur Geschichte der Onoguren," *Ungarische Jahrbücher,* X (1930), 86, 89. C. A. Macartney, *The Magyars in the Ninth Century,* esp. 176–88. I have not seen a book by J. Szinnyei, *Die Herkunft der Ungarn, ihre Sprache und Urkultur.*

[43] *Moravia and Magyars from the Ninth Until the Beginning of the Tenth Centuries,* 291.

became very desirous of annexing this great city to his kingdom. Leo VI succeeded in preventing the realization of this scheme only by ceding to the Bulgarians other lands of the Empire. The boundary stone set up between Bulgaria and the Byzantine Empire in 904 still exists. It bears an interesting inscription concerning the agreement between the two powers,[44] about which the Bulgarian historian Zlatarsky commented: "According to this agreement all the Slavonic lands of contemporary southern Macedonia and southern Albania, which until this time belonged to the Byzantine Empire, now [in 904] became part of the Bulgarian Kingdom; in other words, by this treaty Simeon united under the Bulgarian sceptre all those Slavonic tribes of the Balkan peninsula which gave Bulgarian nationality its ultimate aspect."[45] From the time of this treaty until the end of Leo's rule no collisions occurred between Bulgaria and the Byzantine Empire.

During the period which elapsed between the death of Leo VI and the death of Simeon the Bulgarian in 927 there was almost continuous warfare between the Empire and Bulgaria, and Simeon very definitely strove to conquer Constantinople. In vain did Patriarch Nicholas Mysticus send him abject epistles, written "not with ink, but with tears."[46] At times the patriarch tried to abash Simeon and threatened that the Byzantine Empire would form an alliance with the Russians, the Patzinaks, the Alans, and the western Turks, i.e., the Magyars or Hungarians.[47] But Simeon was well aware that these projected alliances could not be realized, and hence the threats had no effect upon him. The Bulgarian army defeated the Greeks in several battles. Greek losses were especially severe in 917, when the Byzantine troops were annihilated at the river Achelous, close to Anchialus (in Thrace). The historian Leo the Deacon visited the site of the battle at the end of the tenth century and wrote: "Even now one can see heaps of bones close to Anchialus, where the Roman army, taking to flight, was ingloriously cut to pieces."[48] After the battle of Achelous the way to Constantinople lay open to Simeon. But in 918 the Bulgarian armies were occupied in Serbia.[49] In 919 the clever and energetic admiral Romanus Lecapenus became emperor. Meanwhile the Bulgarians forged their way as far south as the Dardanelles,[50] and in 922 took Hadrianople (Odrin).

[44] Th. I. Uspensky, "The Boundary Stone between Byzantium and Bulgaria under Simeon," *Transactions of the Russian Archeological Institute at Constantinople*, III (1898), 184–94.

[45] "Accounts of the Bulgarians in the Chronicle of Simeon Metaphrastes and Logothete," *Sbornik za narodni umotvoreniya, nauka i knizhnina*, XXIV (1908), 160. See also Zlatarsky, *A History of the State of Bulgaria in the Middle Ages*, I (2), 339–42.

[46] Nicolai Mystici, *Epistola*, V; ed. Migne, *Patrologia Graeca*, CXI, 45.

[47] *Ibid.*, XXIII; ed. Migne, *ibid.*, 149–52.

[48] *Historiae*, VII, 7; Bonn ed., 124.

[49] On Serbia and Byzantium in the first half of the tenth century see C. Jireček, *Geschichte der Serben*, I, 199–202. F. Šišić, *Geschichte der Kroaten*, I, 127–29, 140–43. S. Stanojević, *History of the Serbian People* (3rd ed., 1926), 52–53.

[50] Zlatarsky, *Bulgaria in the Middle Ages*,

Thence their troops penetrated into Middle Greece on the one hand and on the other to the walls of Constantinople, which they threatened to occupy at any moment. The suburban palaces of the Emperor were put to the torch. Meanwhile, Simeon attempted to form an alliance with the African Arabs for a joint siege of the capital. All of Thrace and Macedonia, excepting Constantinople and Thessalonica, were in the hands of the Bulgarian forces. Excavations made by the Russian Archaeological Institute of Constantinople near Aboba in northeastern Bulgaria have revealed several columns intended for the great church near the king's palace; their historical interest lies in their inscriptions, which list the names of the Byzantine cities Simeon occupied. It was partly on the possession of the larger part of Byzantine territory in the Balkan peninsula that Simeon based his right to call himself "emperor of the Bulgarians and Greeks."

In 923 or 924 the famous interview between Romanus Lecapenus and Simeon took place under the walls of Constantinople. The Emperor, who arrived first, came from his imperial yacht and Simeon from the land. The two monarchs greeted each other and conversed; Romanus' speech has been preserved.[51] Some sort of truce was arranged, with conditions comparatively not too harsh, though Romanus had to pay a yearly tribute to Simeon. Simeon, however, was now compelled to retreat from Constantinople because he anticipated great danger from the newly formed Serbian kingdom, which was carrying on negotiations with the Byzantine Empire, and also because he had not attained satisfactory results in his negotiations with the Arabs. He later began to organize a new campaign against Constantinople, but he died in the midst of his preparations (927).

In the time of Simeon Bulgarian territory expanded enormously. It extended from the shores of the Black Sea to the Adriatic coast, and from the lower Danube to central Thrace and Macedonia, as far as Thessalonica. For these achievements, Simeon's name is significant for the first attempt to replace Greek domination in the Balkan peninsula by Slavonic supremacy.

Simeon was succeeded by the meek Peter, who by his marriage became related to the Byzantine Emperor. The peace treaty that was signed by the Empire recognized his royal title, as well as the Bulgarian patriarchate established by Simeon. This peace lasted for some forty years. After the long succession of brilliant Bulgar victories, the terms of this peace, very satisfactory to Byzantium, "scarcely disguised the fact that actually Bulgaria had col-

I (2), 412 (in 920). Runciman, *Romanus Lecapenus,* 87 (in 919). Cf. Runciman, *A History of the First Bulgarian Empire,* 163 (the Dardanelles are not mentioned).

[51] Theophanes Continuatus, *Historia,* Bonn ed., 408–9. Symeon Magister, Bonn ed., 737–

38. See Zlatarsky, *Bulgaria in the Middle Ages,* I (2), 464–69, esp. 467, n. 1. Sources are indicated. Runciman, *First Bulgarian Empire,* 169–72. Runciman, *Romanus Lecapenus,* 90–93, 246–48 (in 924).

lapsed."[52] This treaty represented a real success of wise and energetic policy on the part of Romanus Lecapenus. "Great Bulgaria" of Simeon's time was torn asunder by internal strife under Peter. In connection with the collapse of the political might of Bulgaria, the Magyars and the Patzinaks invaded Thrace in 934 and penetrated as far as Constantinople. In 943 they reappeared in Thrace. Romanus Lecapenus concluded with them a five years' peace, which was renewed after his fall and lasted throughout the reign of Constantine Porphyrogenitus.[53] Later, in the second half of the tenth century, the Magyars invaded the Balkan peninsula several times. The decline of Bulgaria's strength was very advantageous for the Byzantine Empire. Nicephorus Phocas and John Tzimisces continued to struggle persistently with the Bulgarians, and were aided by the Russian Prince Sviatoslav at the invitation of Nicephorus Phocas. When the success of Russian arms in Bulgaria brought Sviatoslav to the very borders of the Empire, however, the Emperor became greatly disturbed, and with reason, because the Russian troops later advanced so far on Byzantine territory that an early Russian chronicler reports that Sviatoslav "had almost reached the walls of Tzargrad (Constantinople)."[54] John Tzimisces directed his forces against the Russians under the pretext of defending Bulgaria from the onslaught of the new conquerors. He defeated Sviatoslav, conquered all of Eastern Bulgaria, and captured the entire Bulgarian dynasty. The annexation of eastern Bulgaria was thus definitely completed in the time of John Tzimisces.

After his death the Bulgarians took advantage of the internal complications in the Empire and rebelled against Byzantine domination. The outstanding leader of this period was Samuel, the energetic ruler of western independent Bulgaria, and probably the founder of a new dynasty, "one of the most prominent rulers of the First Bulgarian Empire."[55] For a long time the struggle of Basil II with Samuel went against the Byzantine Empire, chiefly because its forces were engaged in eastern wars. Samuel conquered many new districts and proclaimed himself king of Bulgaria. Only at the beginning of the

[52] Runciman, *Romanus Lecapenus,* 100.

[53] See J. Marquart, *Osteuropäische und ostasiatische Streifzüge,* 60–74 (on the invasion of 934). Runciman, *Romanus Lecapenus,* 103–8.

[54] The *Laurentian Chronicle,* under 971.

[55] See enthusiastic appreciation of Samuel's activity in Zlatarsky, *Bulgaria in the Middle Ages,* I (2), 742–43. On Samuel, see also Runciman, *First Bulgarian Empire,* 241–43. The status of eastern and western Bulgaria at the time is debatable and presents a very complicated question. The hypothesis has recently been set forth that John Tzimisces conquered the whole of the Bulgarian Empire, both west and east, and that only after his death, during the internal troubles in Byzantium, did Samuel revolt in the west and succeed in establishing his Sloveno-Macedonian Empire. See D. Anastasijević, "A Hypothesis of Western Bulgaria," *Bulletin de la Société Scientifique de Skoplje,* III (1927), 1–12; in French, *Mélanges Uspensky.* See also J. Ivanov, "The Origin of the Family of the Tsar Samuel," *Volume in Honor of V. N. Zlatarsky,* 55.

eleventh century did fortune begin to smile upon Basil. So cruel was his fight with the Bulgarians that he was given the name of Bulgaroctonus ("Slayer of the Bulgarians"). When Samuel beheld 14,000 Bulgarians blinded by Basil II and sent back to their homeland, he died of shock received from this horrible sight. After his death in 1014, Bulgaria was too weak to resist the Greeks, and was soon conquered by the Byzantine Empire. In 1018 the first Bulgarian kingdom ceased to exist, for it was transformed into a Byzantine province ruled by an imperial governor. It preserved its internal autonomy to a certain extent, however.

The Bulgarian rebellion, which broke out against the Empire in about the middle of the eleventh century under the leadership of Peter Delyan, was suppressed and resulted in the nullification of Bulgarian autonomy. During the period of Byzantine domination the districts populated by Bulgarians gradually were penetrated by Hellenic culture. The Bulgarian people, however, maintained their nationality, which reached particular strength when the Second Bulgarian Kingdom was formed in the twelfth century.

According to an Austrian historian, "the downfall of the Bulgarian Kingdom in 1018 belongs among the most important and decisive events of the eleventh century, and of the Middle Ages in general. The Roman (Byzantine) Empire was again raised up and extended from the Adriatic to the Black Sea, from the Danube to the southern extremity of the Peloponnesus."[56]

The Byzantine Empire and Russia

In the time of the Macedonian dynasty very animated relations developed between Russia and Byzantium. According to the Russian chronicler, during the reign of Leo VI the Wise in the year 907 the Russian Prince Oleg appeared at the walls of Constantinople with numerous vessels. After pillaging the environs of the capital and killing a large number of people, Oleg forced the Emperor to initiate negotiations and reach a final agreement. Although no sources, Byzantine, western, or eastern, known up to recent times, refer to this expedition or to the name of Oleg, this account of the Russian chronicler, touched with legendary detail as it is, is based on actual historical events. It is very probable that this preliminary agreement of 907 was confirmed in 911 by a formal treaty which, also according to the old Russian chronicler, provided important trade privileges for the Russians.[57]

---

[56] K. R. von Höfler, *Abhandlungen aus dem Gebiete der slavischen Geschichte,* I, 229.
[57] See G. Ostrogorsky, "L'expédition du prince Oleg contre Constantinople," *Annales de l'Institut Kondakov,* XI (1940), 47-62. Ostrogorsky has fully proved once more that the expedition of Oleg was a real historical fact. I specifically emphasize my statement, because at present the study of early Russian history is again passing through a crucial period. A wave of hypercriticism has swept over the minds of several eminent western European scholars. They classify Oleg as a legendary figure, waging a "legendary" cam-

The famous history of Leo the Deacon, an invaluable source for the second half of the tenth century, has an interesting passage which does not usually receive due consideration, although at present it ought to be viewed as the sole hint at Oleg's treaties found in Greek sources. This hint is the threat to Sviatoslav which Leo the Deacon put into the mouth of John Tzimisces: "I hope you have not forgotten the defeat of your father Igor who, having *scorned the sworn agreements* (τὰς ἐνόρκους σπονδάς), came by sea to the imperial city with a great army and numerous vessels."[58] These "sworn agreements" made with the Byzantine Empire before Igor's time must have been the agreements of Oleg reported by the Russian chronicler. It might be interesting to compare the reference just given with the accounts found in Byzantine sources of the presence of Russian subsidiary troops in the Byzantine army from the early tenth century, and with the corresponding clause of the treaty of 911 (as given in the Russian chronicle), which permits the Russians, if they should so desire, to serve in the army of the Byzantine Emperor.[59]

In 1912 a Jewish scholar in America, Schechter, edited and translated into English the surviving fragments of an interesting Jewish medieval text on Khazaro-Russian-Byzantine relations in the tenth century. The value of this document is especially great because of the fact that it mentions the name of "Helgu [Oleg], the King of Russia" and contains some new evidence about him, such as the story of his unsuccessful expedition to Constantinople.[60] The chronological and topographical difficulties presented by this text are still in a stage of preliminary investigation; hence it is too early to pass any definite

paign against Constantinople. Authentic Russian history is supposed to have started only in the year 941 with the expedition of the Russian Prince Igor against Constantinople; everything before this date is classed as legend and tradition tinged with fable. See H. Grégoire, "La légende d'Oleg et l'expedition d'Igor," *Bulletin de la classe des lettres de l'Académie Royale de Belgique,* XXIII (1937), 80–94. It would be out of place to list here the names of the subscribers to this point of view. Vasiliev, "The Second Russian Attack on Constantinople," *Dumbarton Oaks Papers,* VI (1951), 161–225.

[58] *Historiae,* VI, 10; Bonn ed., 106. See Rambaud, *L'Empire grec au dixième siècle,* 374. A. Kunik, *On the Report of the Toparchus Gothicus,* 87. M. Suzumov, "On the Sources of Leo the Deacon and Scylitzes," *Vizantiyskoe Obozrenie,* II, 1 (1916), 165.

[59] Vasiliev, *Byzantium and the Arabs,* II, 166–67.

[60] S. Schechter, "An Unknown Khazar Doc-

ument," *Jewish Quarterly Review,* N.S. III (1912–13), 181–219; the name of Helgu, 217–18. See P. C. Kokovtzov, "A New Jewish Document on the Khazars and the Khazaro-Russo-Byzantine Relations in the Tenth Century," *Journal of the Ministry of Public Instruction,* XLVIII (1913), 150–72. Kokovtzov, "A Note on the Judeo-Khazar Manuscripts at Cambridge and Oxford," *Comptes-rendus de l'Académie des Sciences de l'Union des Républiques Soviétiques Socialistes* (1926), 121–24. A new interpretation of this letter is given by V. A. Moshin, "Again on the Newly Discovered Khazar Document," *Publications of the Russian Archaeological Society in the Kingdom of Serbs, Croats, and Slovenes,* I (1927), 41–60; the author denies the name of Oleg and refers the data of the documents to the later events of the years 943–45. A new Russian translation of this document by Kokovtzov, *A Hebrew-Khazar Correspondence of the Tenth Century,* xxvi–xxxvi, 113–23.

judgment about this unquestionably interesting document. In any event, the publication of this text has brought about a new attempt to re-examine the chronology of Oleg given by the old Russian chronicles.

In the time of Romanus Lecapenus the capital was twice attacked by the Russian Prince Igor. His name has been preserved not only in Russian chronicles, but in Greek and Latin sources as well. His first campaign in the year 941 was undertaken on numerous vessels which sailed to the Bithynian coast of the Black Sea and to the Bosphorus. Here the Russians pillaged the seacoast and advanced along the Asiatic shore of the Strait to Chrysopolis (now Scutari, facing Constantinople), but the expedition ended with complete failure for Igor. A large number of Russian vessels were destroyed by Greek fire, and the remnants of Igor's fleet returned to the north. The Russian prisoners captured by the Greeks were put to death.

Igor's forces for his second campaign in 944 were much greater than those of his earlier expedition. The Russian chronicler related that Igor organized a large army of "Varangians, Russians, Poliane, Slavs, Krivichi, Tivertsy, and Patzinaks."[61] The Byzantine Emperor, frightened by these preparations, sent his best noblemen (*boyars*) to Igor and to the Patzinaks, offering them costly gifts and promising to pay Igor a tribute similar to that received by Oleg. In spite of all this Igor started out for Constantinople, but when he reached the banks of the Danube he consulted his *druzhina* (company) and decided to accept the conditions proposed by the Empire and return to Kiev. In the following year the Greeks and Russians negotiated a treaty on conditions less favorable to the Russians than those of Oleg. This peace agreement was to last "as long as the sun shall shine and the world shall stand, in the present centuries, and in the centuries to come."[62]

The friendly relations established by this treaty were expressed more concretely under Constantine VII Porphyrogenitus in the year 957, when the Russian Grand Princess Olga (Elga) arrived at Constantinople and was magnificently received by the Emperor, the Empress, and the heir to the throne. Olga's reception has been described in detail in an official contemporary record, the famous work of the tenth century *Concerning the Ceremonies of the Byzantine Court*.[63] The relations of Nicephorus Phocas and John Tzimis-

[61] The Poliane, Krivichi, and Tivertsy were the tribes of the eastern branch of the eastern Slavs, who established themselves on the banks of the Dnieper and its tributaries as well as on the banks of the Dniester.

[62] The *Laurentian Chronicle*, under 945 (at the close of the treaty). A. Shakhmatov, *The Story of the Current Times*, I, 60; in English, S. H. Cross, *The Russian Primary Chronicle*, 160–63. A vast literature exists on treaties between Byzantium and Russia, especially in

Russian. See Vasiliev, *Byzantium and the Arabs*, II, 164–67, 246–49, 255–56. J. Kulischer, *Russische Wirtschaftsgeschichte*, I, 20–30. K. Bártová, "Igor's Expedition on Tsargrad in 941," *Byzantinoslavica*, VIII (1939–1946), 87–108.

[63] Constantini Porphyrogeniti, *De Cerimoniis aulae byzantinae*, II, 15; Bonn ed., 594–98. See also Cross, *Russian Primary Chronicle*, 168–69.

ces with the Russian prince Sviatoslav have been discussed in connection with the Bulgarian wars.

Still more important were the relations of Basil II Bulgaroctonus with the Russian Prince Vladimir, whose name is closely connected with the conversion of Russia to Christianity. In the ninth decade of the tenth century the position of the Emperor and his dynasty seemed very critical. Bardas Phocas, the leader of the rebellion against Basil, won over to his side almost all of Asia Minor and drew close to the capital; at the same time the northern provinces of the Empire were in danger of being invaded by the victorious Bulgarians. Basil appealed for help to the northern Prince Vladimir, and succeeded in forming an alliance with him on the condition that Vladimir should send 6000 soldiers to aid Basil, for which he was to receive the hand of the Emperor's sister, Anna, and promise to accept Christianity and convert his people. With the help of this subsidiary Russian regiment, the so-called "Varangian-Russian Druzhina" (Company), the insurrection of Bardas Phocas was suppressed and its leader killed. But Basil was apparently unwilling to live up to his promise of arranging the marriage of his sister, Anna, to Vladimir. Then the Russian prince besieged and took the important Byzantine city of Cherson (Chersonesus, or Korsun) in the Crimea and forced Basil to yield and fulfill his original promise. Vladimir was baptized and married the Byzantine princess, Anna. It is not known exactly whether Russia's conversion to Christianity took place in 988 or in 989. Some scholars accept the former date; others, the latter. Peaceful and friendly relations were established between Russia and the Byzantine Empire, and they lasted for a considerable length of time. Both countries engaged freely in extensive trade with one another.

According to one source, during the reign of Constantine Monomachus, in 1043, "the Scythian merchants" (i.e., Russians) in Constantinople and the Greeks had a quarrel, during which a Russian nobleman was killed.[64] It is very probable that this incident was used by Russia as a sufficient motive for a new campaign against the Byzantine Empire. The Russian Great Prince Iaroslav the Wise sent his older son, Vladimir, with a large army on numerous vessels to Byzantine shores. This Russian fleet was almost demolished by the imperial forces through the use of Greek fire. The remnants of the Russian army of Vladimir hastened to retreat.[65] This expedition was the last undertaken by the Russians against Constantinople in the Middle Ages. The ethnographic changes which occurred in the steppes of present-day southern Russia

---

[64] Georgii Cedreni *Historiarum compendium,* Bonn ed., II, 551.

[65] Our chief sources: Michael Psellus, *Chronographia,* ed. C. Sathas, *Bibliotheca Graeca Medii Aevi,* IV, 143–47; ed. E. Renauld, II, 8–13. Georgii Cedreni *Historiarum compendium,* Bonn ed., II, 551–55. See V. G. Vasilievsky, *Works,* I, 303–8. Schlumberger, *L'Épopée byzantine,* III, 462–76.

in the middle of the eleventh century because of the appearance of the Turkish tribe of the Polovtzi removed all possibilities of direct relations between Russia and the Byzantine Empire.

The Patzinak problem

In the eleventh century the Patzinaks of the Greek sources, or the Pechenegs of the Russian chronicles, exerted enormous influence upon the fate of the Empire for a considerable length of time. There was even a period, shortly before the First Crusade, when for the only time in their brief and barbarian historical existence the Patzinaks played a very significant part in world history.

The Byzantine Empire had known the Patzinaks for a long time. They had settled some time in the ninth century on the territory of modern Wallachia, north of the Lower Danube, and in the plains of what is now Southern Russia, so that their territory extended from the Lower Danube to the shores of the Dnieper, and sometimes even beyond this river. In the west the border line between their territory and the Bulgarian kingdom was definitely established, but in the east there was no district boundary because the Patzinaks were constantly forced to the west by other barbaric nomadic tribes, especially by the Uzes and the Cumans, or Polovtzi. The Patzinaks, the Uzes, and the Cumans were all tribes of Turkish origin, and therefore akin to the Seljuq Turks, who began to menace Byzantine possessions in Asia Minor in the eleventh century. The Cumanian dictionary or lexicon, which survives today, proves convincingly that the language of the Cumans or the Polovtzi is so closely related to other Turkish tongues that the difference between them is only that of dialects. For future historical developments this kinship between the Patzinaks and the Seljuq Turks was of very great importance.

The Byzantine rulers considered the Patzinaks as their most significant northern neighbors because they were the basic element in maintaining the equilibrium of the Empire's relations with the Russians, Magyars, and Bulgarians. Constantine Porphyrogenitus devoted much space to the Patzinaks in his work *On the Administration of the Empire,* written in the tenth century and dedicated to his son Romanus, who was to succeed him on the Byzantine throne. The royal writer advises his son first of all to maintain peaceful and friendly relations with the Patzinaks for the benefit of the Empire; for so long as the Patzinaks remain friendly to the Empire, neither the Russians, nor the Magyars, nor the Bulgarians will be able to attack Byzantine territory. From many things recorded by Constantine in this work it is also evident that the Patzinaks served as mediators in the trade relations of the Byzantine districts in the Crimea (the theme of Cherson) with Russia, Khazaria, and other neighboring countries.[66] Hence the Patzinaks of the tenth century were of great importance to the Byzantine Empire, both politically and economically.

In the second half of the tenth and early part of the eleventh centuries conditions changed. Eastern Bulgaria was conquered by John Tzimisces, and Basil II continued the conquest until all of Bulgaria was under Byzantine sway. The Patzinaks, who had formerly been separated from the Byzantine Empire by the Bulgarian kingdom, now became direct neighbors of the Empire. These new neighbors were so strong and numerous and aggressive that the Empire was unable to offer adequate resistance to their onslaught, caused by the pressure of the Polovtzi from behind. Theophylact of Bulgaria, the church writer of the eleventh century, spoke of the irruptions of the Patzinaks, whom he called Scythians: "Their invasion is a flash of lightning; their retreat is both heavy and light at the same time: heavy with spoils and light in the speed of their flight. . . . The most terrible thing about them is that they exceed in number the bees of the springtime, and no one knows yet how many thousands, or tens of thousands they count; their number is incalculable."[67] Until the middle of the eleventh century, however, the Empire, apparently, had no cause to fear the Patzinaks. They became dangerous only when, in the middle of that century, they crossed the Danube.

V. G. Vasilievsky, who was the first among historians to make clear the historical significance of the Patzinaks, wrote in 1872 concerning their advance into Byzantine territory: "This event, which has escaped the attention of all modern historical works, had enormous significance for the history of humanity. In its consequences it was almost as important as the crossing of the Danube by the western Goths, which initiated the so-called migration of nations."[68]

Constantine Monomachus (1042–55) assigned the Patzinaks certain Bulgarian districts for settlement and gave them three fortresses on the shore of the Danube. It became the duty of the Patzinak settlers to defend the borders of the Empire from the attacks of their kinsmen who remained on the other side of the river, as well as against the campaigns of the Russian princes.

But the Patzinaks on the northern shores of the Danube were persistently advancing to the south. In the early period of their irruptions they had crossed the Danube in large numbers (some sources speak of 800,000 people)[69] and

[66] Constantini Porphyrogeniti *De administrando imperio*, 67–74; ed. Moravcsik-Jenkins, 48–56.

[67] *Oratio in Imperatorem Alexium Comnenum;* ed. Migne, *Patrologia Graeca*, CXXVI, 292–93.

[68] "Byzantium and the Patzinaks," *Works*, I, 7–8.

[69] Georgii Cedreni *Historiarum compendium*, Bonn ed., 585.

had descended as far as Hadrianople, while some of their smaller detachments had reached the capital. Still, the troops of Constantine Monomachus were able to resist these hordes and deal them very painful blows. But toward the end of Constantine's reign it became more difficult to oppose the advance of the Patzinaks. The expedition organized by the Emperor toward the end of his reign resulted in a complete annihilation of the Byzantine army. "In a terrible night of slaughter the crushed Byzantine regiments were destroyed by the barbarians almost without any resistance; only a small number of them escaped somehow and reached Hadrianople. All the gains of former victories were lost."[70]

This complete defeat made it impossible for the Empire to begin a new struggle with the Patzinaks, and the Emperor was forced to buy peace at a very heavy price. His generous gifts induced them to promise to live peacefully in their provinces north of the Balkans. The Empire also bestowed Byzantine court titles upon the Patzinak princes. Thus, in the later years of the Macedonian dynasty, especially in the time of Constantine Monomachus, the Patzinaks were the most dangerous enemy of the Empire in the north.

Relations with Italy and western Europe

The Italian developments of this period consisted primarily of the successful Arabian campaigns in Sicily and southern Italy. By the middle of the ninth century the republic of St. Mark (Venice) freed itself completely of Byzantine power and became an independent state. The Empire and this new state treated each other like independent governments in all the negotiations which arose later, for example, in the time of Basil I. In the ninth century their interests coincided in many points in so far as the aggressive movement of the western Arabs and the Adriatic Slavs were concerned.

From the time of Basil I an interesting correspondence with Louis II exists. It appears from the letters exchanged by these two rulers that they were engaged in a heated dispute regarding the illegal adoption of the imperial title by Louis II. Thus, even in the second half of the ninth century the results of the coronation of 800 were still in evidence. Although some historians have asserted that the letter of Louis II to Basil is spurious,[71] recent historians do not support this opinion.[72] Basil's attempt to form an alliance with Louis II failed. The Byzantine occupation of Bari and Tarentum and the successful operations of Nicephorus Phocas against the Arabs in southern Italy raised

[70] Vasilievsky, "Byzantium and the Patzinaks," *Works*, I, 24.

[71] See, e.g., M. Amari, *Storia dei Musulmani di Sicilia*, I, 381; (2nd ed., 1933), I, 522–23. A. Kleinclausz, *L'Empire Carolingien: ses origines et ses transformations*, 443 ff.

[72] J. Gay, *L'Italie Méridionale et l'Empire Byzantin*, 84, 87, 88. L. M. Hartmann, *Geschichte Italiens im Mittelalter*, III (1), 306–7. F. Dvornik, *Les Slaves, Byzance et Rome au IXᵉ siècle*, 220–21.

Byzantine influence in Italy toward the end of Basil's reign. The smaller Italian possessions, such as the duchies of Naples, Beneventum, Spoleto, the principality of Salerno, and others, frequently changed their attitude toward the Byzantine Empire in correspondence with the course of the Byzantine campaign against the Arabs. Disregarding the recent break with the eastern church, Pope John VIII began active negotiations with Basil I, for he fully appreciated the extent of the Arabian menace to Rome. In striving to form a political alliance with the Eastern Empire the pope showed his readiness to make many concessions. Some scholars go so far as to attribute the absence of an emperor in the West for three and a half years after the death of Charles the Bold (877) to the fact that John VIII purposely delayed the coronation of a western ruler in order to avoid hurting the feelings of the Byzantine Emperor, whose aid was so much needed by Rome.[73]

In the time of Leo VI, Byzantine possessions in Italy were divided into two themes: Calabria and Longobardia. The Calabrian theme was all that was left of the vast Sicilian theme because, through the fall of Syracuse and Taormina, Sicily was entirely in the hands of the Arabs. As a result of the success of Byzantine arms in Italy Leo VI definitely separated Longobardia from the theme of Kephallenia, or the Ionian Islands, and made it an independent theme with its own strategus. Because of the incessant warfare, during which Byzantine forces were not always victorious, the borders of Calabria and Longobardia changed frequently. With the increase of Byzantine influence in southern Italy in the tenth century there was also a noticeable growth in the number of Greek monasteries and churches, some of which later became important cultural centers.

In the same century the Byzantine Empire and Italy witnessed the rise of a strong rival in the person of the German ruler, Otto I, crowned with the imperial crown in Rome by Pope John XII in 962. He is known in history as the founder of "The Holy Roman Empire of the German Nation." Upon assuming the imperial title, Otto strove to become master of all Italy. This was, of course, a direct infringement upon Byzantine interests, especially in Longobardia. Negotiations between Otto and the eastern Emperor, Nicephorus Phocas, who was at this time probably dreaming of an offensive alliance with the German ruler against the Muslims, progressed very slowly, and Otto suddenly made an unsuccessful inroad into the Byzantine provinces of southern Italy.

For new negotiations with the eastern Emperor the German ruler sent to Constantinople his legate, Liudprand, the bishop of Cremona, who had been once before ambassador to the Byzantine court in the time of Constantine Porphyrogenitus. The population on the shores of the Bosphorus did not

---

[73] A. Gasquet, *L'Empire byzantin et la monarchie franque,* 459-60.

greet him with due respect, and he was exposed to great humiliation and many insults. He later wrote an account of his second sojourn at the Constantinopolitan court in the form of a malicious libel, which was in sharp contrast to his reverent description of his first visit to the eastern capital. From this second account, usually known as the *Relation on the Constantinopolitan Legation* (*Relatio de legatione constantinopolitana*), it appears that the Byzantine Empire continued the old disputes about the title of basileus assumed by the western ruler. Liudprand accused the Byzantines of being weak and inactive, and justified the claims of his sovereign. In one part of this work he wrote, "Whom does Rome serve, about whose liberation you make so much noise? To whom does the city pay taxes? And did not this ancient city formerly serve courtesans? And then, in a time when all men were asleep and even in a state of impotence, my sovereign, the most august emperor, freed Rome of that shameful servitude."[74] When Liudprand became aware of the fact that the Greeks were prolonging the negotiations intentionally in order to gain time for the organization of an Italian campaign, forbidding him meanwhile to hold any communications with his Emperor, he made every effort to depart from Constantinople, succeeding only after much trouble and prolonged delay.

The break between the two empires was accomplished, and Otto I invaded the province of Apulia. However, the new Byzantine Emperor, John Tzimisces, completely altered the Byzantine policy toward Italy. Not only did he conclude a treaty of peace with the German ruler, but he strengthened his relations with him by arranging the marriage of Otto's son and heir, Otto II, to the Byzantine Princess Theophano. Thus an alliance was finally formed between the two empires. The Arabian attacks on southern Italy, against which the successor of John Tzimisces, Basil II, could do nothing because his attention was claimed by the internal disturbances in the Byzantine Empire, forced the young Emperor Otto II (973–983) to organize a campaign against the Arabs. In one of the battles he was defeated, and died soon after. From this time on German advance into the Byzantine themes of Italy ceased for a long period of time.

At the end of the tenth century an administrative reform took place in Byzantine Italy. The former strategus of Longobardia was replaced by the catapan of Italy, who resided in Bari. As long as the various Italian kingdoms were engaged in mutual strife, the Byzantine catapan was able to handle the difficult problem of defending the southern coast of Italy against the Saracens.

The son of the Princess Theophano, Otto III (983–1002), educated in profound reverence for the Byzantine Empire and classical culture, was a contemporary and a relative of Basil II and a pupil of the famous scholar,

[74] *Legatio,* chap. XVII.

Gerbert, who later became Pope Sylvester II. Otto III made no secret of his hatred for German coarseness, and dreamed of the restoration of the ancient Empire with Old Rome as the capital. According to James Bryce, "None save he desired to make the seven-hilled city again the city of dominion, reducing Germany and Lombardy and Greece to their rightful place of subject provinces. No one else so forgot the present to live in the light of the ancient order; no other soul was so possessed by that fervid mysticism and that reverence for the glories of the past whereon rested the idea of the Medieval Empire."[75] Although the prestige of ancient Rome was extremely high in Otto's imagination, still he was attracted chiefly to eastern Rome, to that court of fairy-like magnificence where his mother had been born and bred. Only in following the footsteps of the Byzantine rulers did Otto III hope to restore the imperial throne in Rome. He called himself *imperator romanorum,* and referred to the future world-monarchy as *Orbis romanus.* This young enthusiast, whose illusory schemes promised to introduce disturbance and difficulty into the life of the Byzantine Empire, died suddenly at the very beginning of the eleventh century, at the age of twenty-two (1002).

While in the early eleventh century Byzantine provinces in southern Italy were made safe from Arabian attacks through the interference of the Venetian fleet, they soon became exposed to danger from a new and formidable enemy, the Normans, who later began to threaten the Eastern Empire. The first large detachment of Normans arrived in Italy at the beginning of the eleventh century at the invitation of Meles, who rose in rebellion against Byzantine domination. The allied forces of Meles and the Normans were defeated, however, near Cannae, so famous in history since the victory of Hannibal during the Second Punic War. Basil II owed part of his success in this battle with the Normans to the Russian soldiers, who served in the ranks of the Byzantine army. The victory at Cannae strengthened the position of Byzantium in southern Italy to such an extent that in the fourth decade of the eleventh century Emperor Michael IV the Paphlagonian equipped an expedition for the reconquest of Sicily from the Arabs. This expedition was led by George Maniaces. In his army were the Scandinavian hero, Harald Haardraade, and the Varangian-Russian Druzhina (Company). Although this campaign was successful, and achieved, among other things, the occupation of Messina, the reconquest of Sicily was not accomplished, mainly because George Maniaces was recalled when he was suspected of having ambitious schemes.[76]

---

[75] *The Holy Roman Empire,* 148.
[76] On Harald in the army of George Maniaces, see V. G. Vasilievsky, "The Varangian-Russian and Varangian-English Company (druzina) in Constantinople," *Works,* I, 289–90. R. M. Dawkins, "Greeks and Northmen," *Custom Is King: Essays presented to Dr. R. R. Marett,* 45–46.

During the period of strife between Byzantium and Rome which ended in the division of churches in 1054, the Normans sided with Rome and began to advance, slowly but steadily, in Byzantine Italy. By the end of this period, i.e., about the middle of the eleventh century, there arose among the Normans in Italy a very capable and energetic leader, Robert Guiscard, whose major activities developed in the period subsequent to the Macedonian dynasty.

SOCIAL AND POLITICAL DEVELOPMENTS

Church affairs

The major event in the church life of the Byzantine Empire in the time of the Macedonian dynasty was the final separation of the Christian church into the eastern Orthodox and the western Catholic, which took place in the middle of the eleventh century after long disputes which lasted for almost two centuries.

The first act of Basil I in the realm of church affairs was the deposition of Patriarch Photius and the reinstatement of Ignatius, who had been deposed in the time of Michael III. By this measure Basil hoped to strengthen his position on a throne which did not rightfully belong to him. He felt that by raising Ignatius he was accomplishing the double purpose of maintaining peaceful relations with the pope and gaining the support of the Byzantine people, many of whom, as he knew very well, were partisans of the deposed Ignatius. In their letters to the pope both Basil and Ignatius acknowledged his authority and influence in the affairs of the eastern church. The Emperor, for example, wrote, "Spiritual Father and divinely reverend Pontiff! Hasten the improvement of our church and through your interference with injustice give us an abundance of goods, namely, pure unity and spiritual joining free from any contention and schism, a church one in Christ, and a flock obedient to one shepherd." Ignatius sent the pope a letter full of humility, requesting that the Roman patriarch send vicars to Constantinople. In the concluding statement he wrote, "With them [the vicars] we should well and suitably arrange our church, which we have received by the providence of God manifested in the intercession of the sublime Peter and at your instance and intervention."[77] These letters indicate a moment of apparent triumph for the papacy in the East, but Pope Nicholas I did not live to witness this victory, because the letters sent to him from Byzantium came after his death and were received by his successor, Hadrian II.

At the Roman councils, and later in Constantinople in the year 869, in the

---

[77] J. Mansi, *Sacrorum Conciliorum Nova et Amplissima Collectio*, XVI, 47, 49. See A. Lebedev, *A History of the Separation of the* *Churches in the Ninth, Tenth and Eleventh Centuries* (2nd ed., 1905), 117, 120. Dvornik, 136 ff.

presence of papal legates, Photius was deposed and anathematized with his partisans. The Constantinopolitan council of 869 was recognized as an ecumenical council by the western church and is still considered as such.

In its own church life, then, the Empire yielded to the pope in all points. Quite different was the Emperor's attitude toward the problem of religious affairs in Bulgaria, where the Latin clergy had triumphed at the end of the reign of Michael III. In spite of the pope's displeasure and the opposition of the papal legates, Basil I succeeded in achieving the removal of Latin priests from Bulgaria, and Bulgarian King Boris again formed a union with the eastern church. This event exerted much influence upon the later historical fate of the Bulgarian people.

During his confinement, in which he was subjected to great privations, the deposed and excommunicated Photius continued to enjoy the admiration of his followers, who remained true to him throughout Ignatius' patriarchate. Basil himself soon recognized that his attitude toward Photius had been wrong, and he tried to correct it. He began by recalling Photius from confinement and bringing him to the Byzantine court, where he was entrusted with the education of the Emperor's children. Later, when Ignatius died at a very advanced age, Basil offered Photius the patriarchal throne. This reinstatement of Photius marked the beginning of a new policy toward the pope.

In the year 879 a council was convoked in Constantinople. In the number of participating hierarchs and in the general magnificence of the setting it surpassed even some of the ecumenical councils. According to one historian, this council "was, on the whole, a truly majestic event, such as had not been seen since the time of the Council of Chalcedon."[78] The legates of Pope John VIII also came to this council, and not only were they forced to consent to the absolution of Photius and the restoration of his communion with the Roman church, but they also had to listen without any contradiction to the reading of the Nicaeo-Constantinopolitan Creed, which did not include the *filioque* so widely used in the West. At the last session of the council the legates exclaimed, "If any man refuse to recognize Photius as the Holy Patriarch and decline to be in communion with him, his lot shall be with Judas, and he shall not be included among the Christians!" The Catholic historian of Photius wrote that "praises to Photius were the opening statements of the council, and its sessions were closed also with the glorification of the patriarch."[79] This council also argued that the pope was a patriarch like all other patriarchs, that he possessed no authority over the entire church, and hence that it was not necessary for the patriarch of Constantinople to receive the confirmation of the Roman pontiff. Greatly angered, the pope sent a legate

[78] Hergenröther, *Photius,* II, 462.   [79] *Ibid.,* II, 524. See Dvornik, 187.

to Constantinople to insist upon the annulment of any measure passed at the council which was disagreeable to the pope. The legate was also to obtain certain concessions regarding the Bulgarian church. Basil and Photius refused to yield in any of these points and even went so far as to arrest the legate. It was formerly believed that when news of this act of defiance reached John VIII he anathematized Photius in a solemn ceremony in the Church of St. Peter in the presence of a large number of his flock, holding the Gospel in his hands. This was the so-called second schism of Photius. Recent investigations by Amann, Dvornik, and Grumel, however, have shown that the second schism of Photius never existed, and that neither John VIII or any of his successors anathematized Photius.[80] Relations between the Empire and Rome did not cease completely, however, but they became casual and indefinite. Photius did not remain in the patriarchal chair until the end of his life, for he was forced to leave it in 886, when his pupil, Leo VI, succeeded Basil I. Five years later Photius died. Throughout his long lifetime he played a very significant part in the religious as well as in the intellectual life of the Byzantine Empire.

The reign of Basil I was marked also by a number of attempts to spread Christianity among pagan and heterodox peoples. Probably in his time the Empire endeavored to convert the Russians to Christianity, but very little light has been thrown on this subject. A source asserts that Basil persuaded the Russians "to take part in salutary baptism"[81] and accept the archbishop ordained by Ignatius. As yet it is difficult to determine which Russians the writer of this source had in mind. The conversion of the greater part of the Slavonic tribes settled in the Peloponnesus took place in the time of Basil I; the pagan Slavs remained in the mountains of Taygetus. It is also known that Basil forced the Jews of the Empire to accept Christianity.

The deposition of Photius by Leo VI can be explained by Leo's fear of the growing political influence of the patriarch and his party, as well as by Leo's desire to raise his brother Stephen to the patriarchal throne. Through this latter measure he hoped to acquire unlimited authority in the church affairs of the Empire; Photius' strong will would have opposed the Emperor's tendency to rule over ecclesiastical matters. Under Leo's successors there was a noticeable tendency toward a reconciliation with the Roman church through mutual concessions.

The church problems of the Byzantine Empire became especially compli-

[80] See a very fine survey of this question by H. Grégoire, "Du nouveau sur le Patriarche Photius," *Bulletin de la classe des lettres de l'Académie Royale de Belgique*, XX (1934), 36–53. Dvornik, *The Photian Schism*, 202–236.
[81] Theophanes Continuatus, *Historia*, Bonn ed., 342–43.

cated at the beginning of the tenth century during the patriarchate of Nicholas Mysticus, a relative and pupil of Photius and the most remarkable of his successors. According to one historian, "the most noble traits of Photius were reincarnated in his pupil, Nicholas Mysticus, who, more than any one else, strove to follow the ideal example of a patriarch symbolized by Photius."[82] This patriarch left a very interesting collection of letters invaluable from the historical and ecclesiastical points of view.

Strong disagreements arose between Leo and Nicholas Mysticus on account of the Emperor's fourth marriage, vehemently opposed by the patriarch on the basis that it was against all church laws.[83] In spite of this, the Emperor forced a presbyter to perform the marriage ceremony between him and Zoë, who thus became his fourth wife (his first three wives had died in rapid succession). After the wedding had been performed, in the absence of a patriarch, Leo himself placed the imperial crown upon Zoë's head; this later gave Nicholas Mysticus occasion to say that the Emperor was to Zoë "both groom and bishop."[84] The eastern patriarchs, when questioned with regard to this problem, expressed themselves in favor of allowing Leo to marry for the fourth time.[85] This marriage excited great confusion among the population of the Empire. The recalcitrant Nicholas Mysticus was deposed and exiled. At the Constantinopolitan council it was determined to grant a dispensation to the Emperor without dissolving his fourth marriage. After long deliberations the rank of patriarch was conferred upon Euthymius.

The council did not bring harmony to the Empire. Two parties were formed among the Byzantine clergy. The first, which sided with Nicholas Mysticus, was against the confirmation of the Emperor's fourth marriage and denounced the new patriarch, Euthymius. The other, a minority party, was in agreement with the decision of the council concerning Leo's marriage, and recognized Euthymius as the chosen leader of the church. The dissension between these two parties spread from the capital into the provinces, and an obstinate struggle developed everywhere between the Nicholaites and the Euthymites. Some scholars view this struggle as a continuation of the former animosity between the Photinians (or Photians) and the Ignatians, which had subsided only for a short while.[86] In the end the Emperor saw that only the energetic and experienced Nicholas Mysticus could remedy the situation,

[82] Hergenröther, *Photius,* III, 655.
[83] See an interesting article on the four marriages of Leo the Wise in Charles Diehl, *Figures byzantines* (4th ed., 1909), I, 181–215; English trans. H. Bell, *Byzantine Portraits,* 172–205.
[84] *Epistola,* XXXII; ed. Migne, *Patrologia Graeca,* CXI, 197.
[85] Eutychii Alexandrini patriarchae, *Annales;* ed. L. Cheikho, B. Carra de Vaux, H. Zayyat, II, 74; ed. Migne, *Patrologia Graeca,* CXI, 1145.
[86] N. Popov, *The Emperor Leo VI the Wise,* 160.

and shortly before his death (912) Leo VI recalled Nicholas from confinement, deposed Euthymius, and reinstated the former on the patriarchal throne.[87]

In the interests of religious peace in the Empire Nicholas Mysticus strove to restore the friendly relations with Rome which had been severed because of the pope's approval of Leo's fourth marriage. During the regency of Zoë, who ruled during the minority of her son, Constantine VII Porphyrogenitus, Nicholas Mysticus was deprived of influence. But in the year 919, when the government was transferred to Constantine's father-in-law, Romanus I Lecapenus, and Zoë was forced to embrace monastic life, Nicholas Mysticus again rose to his former influential position. The main event in the last years of his patriarchate was the convocation in 920 of a council in Constantinople, which consisted of Nicholaites and Euthymites. They composed the *Tome of Union* (ὁ τόμος τῆς ἐνώσεως), approved by the general assembly. This act proclaimed that marriage for the fourth time was "unquestionably illicit and void, because it was prohibited by the church and intolerable in a Christian land."[88] No direct reference was made in the *Tome* to the fourth marriage of Leo the Wise. Both parties remained satisfied by the decision of the council. It is probable, as Drinov supposed, that the reconciliation between the Nicholaites and the Euthymites was prompted also by "the terror aroused in the Byzantine population by the success of Bulgarian arms."[89] After the council several letters were exchanged with the pope, and he agreed to send to the capital two bishops, who were to condemn the conflicts aroused by Leo's fourth marriage. Direct communications were thus re-established between the churches of Rome and Constantinople. The Russian church historian, A. P. Lebedev, summed up the outcome of this period: "Patriarch Nicholas emerged as full victor in this new clash between the churches of Constantinople and Rome. The Roman church has to yield to the church of Constantinople and condemn its own acts."[90] After the death of Nicholas Mysticus in 925, Romanus Lecapenus gained complete control over the church, and, as Runciman said, "Caesaropapism once more emerged victorious."[91]

Emperor Nicephorus Phocas was a very interesting personality from the ecclesiastical point of view. This most capable warrior, whose name is closely bound up with the brilliant pages of Byzantine military history, had devoted

---

[87] A very valuable source for Leo's fourth marriage and for the general history of the period is *Vita Euthymii: Ein Anecdoton zur Geschichte Leo's des Weisen A.D. 886–912*, ed. C. de Boor; in addition to the Greek text, de Boor gives a very valuable study on the *Vita* from the historical point of view.

[88] Popov, *Leo VI*, 184. Cf. Mansi, *Amplissima collectio conciliorum*, XVIII, 337–38.

[89] *The Southern Slavs and Byzantium in the Tenth Century*, 21; reprinted in *Works of M. S. Drinov*, ed. V. N. Zlatarsky, I, 365–520.

[90] *Separation of the Churches* (2nd ed., 1905), 325.

[91] Runciman, *Romanus Lecapenus*, 70, 243.

much of his time and attention, especially before he ascended the throne, to monastic ideals. He had even worn the hair shirt, and he kept up intimate relations with St. Athanasius of Athos, the famous founder of the large monastery on Mount Athos. The *Life* of Saint Athanasius even relates that once in a transport of religious zeal Nicephorus supposedly confided to Athanasius his sacred dream of forsaking all worldly vanity in order to devote himself to the service of God.[92] The Byzantine historian, Leo the Deacon, wrote that Nicephorus was "indomitably firm in his prayers to God and his nocturnal devotions; he maintained a very high spirit in his church hymns, and had no leanings toward anything vain."[93] Nicephorus Phocas was semi soldier, semi recluse.[94] Many Byzantine people were greatly exercised when the ascetically inclined Emperor married the young and beautiful Theophano, the widow of Emperor Romanus II, who had a very dubious reputation. Traces of this feeling are found in the inscription on the sarcophagus of Nicephorus, which says that this emperor "vanquished all but woman."[95]

The most important ecclesiastic measure of Nicephorus was his famous Novel of the year 964 with regard to monasteries and the philanthropic institutions connected with them. In the time of the Macedonian dynasty monastic landownership had assumed unusual proportions and frequently expanded at the expense of the free peasant holdings defended by several emperors of this dynasty. Even before the iconoclastic period, i.e., at the end of the seventh and the beginning of the eighth centuries, the eastern church had already been in possession of enormous landed estates. This led some scholars to compare the possessions of the eastern church with the similar landed wealth of the western church in the time of the Frankish kings, who complained of the emptiness of their treasury caused by the transfer of their lands into the hands of the clergy. The iconoclastic emperors of the eighth century waged a campaign against monasteries. Some were closed and their possessions confiscated by the treasury. This reform was simultaneous with the analogous secularization of church property in the western Frankish kingdom under the famous major-domo, Charles Martel. With the failure of iconoclasm and the rise of the Macedonian dynasty, the number of monasteries and the extent of their landed property began to increase very rapidly. Already the Novel of Romanus I Lecapenus had expressed the intention of limiting somewhat the growth of monasterial landed estates. A more decisive step in this direction was taken by Nicephorus Phocas in 964, when he published his Novel.

92 *Vie de Saint Athanase l'Athonite,* ed. L. Petit, *Analecta Bollandiana,* XXV (1906), 21.
93 *Historiae,* V, 8; Bonn ed., 89.
94 Schlumberger, *Nicéphore Phocas,* 366.
95 An epitaph of John, the bishop of Meli-

tene, on Nicephorus Phocas. It is published in the Bonn ed. of Leo the Deacon, *Historiae,* 453, and in the edition of Cedrenus, *Historiarum compendium,* II, 378. See K. Krumbacher, *Geschichte des byzantinischen Litteratur,* 368.

This Novel states that, since the "obvious disease" of excessive cupidity has become widely spread in the monasteries and "other sacred institutions," and since "the acquisition of many-acred enormous estates and the numerous cares of fruit trees" cannot be regarded as a commandment of the Apostles or as a tradition of the Fathers, the Emperor desires to "root out the God-hated evil of ambition," and, in order to attain this end, forbids the founding of new monasteries, as well as the contribution of endowments and donations toward the upkeep of old monasteries, hospitals, and hostelries, or any gifts for the benefit of metropolitans and bishops.[96]

This harsh decree, which must have aroused great discontent among the religious-minded population, could not very long remain in force, even imperfectly. Basil II abrogated the Novel of Nicephorus Phocas "as a law outrageous and offensive not only to the churches and hospitals but also to God himself."[97] He restored the monasterial laws of the time of Basil I and Leo VI the Wise, i.e., the Basilics and the Novel of Constantine Porphyrogenitus. One of the reasons for Basil's abolition of the Novel of Nicephorus Phocas was his conviction that this law had brought upon the Empire the anger of God when, toward the end of the tenth century, both internal and external complications brought the Empire to the verge of ruin.

Nicephorus Phocas made an important step in the direction of strengthening Byzantine ecclesiastical organization in the southern Italian provinces of Apulia and Calabria, where papal and western influence was becoming very prominent in the second half of the tenth century, especially after the coronation of the German King Otto I and the growth of Longobardian power in the southern parts of Italy. Through his patriarch, Nicephorus Phocas prohibited the Latin ritual in Apulia and Calabria, and prescribed the observance of the Greek church ceremonial. This measure served as one of the many causes for the further alienation of the papacy from the Byzantine Empire. During the last years of Nicephorus' reign the pope began to address him as the "Emperor of the Greeks," while the title of "Emperor of the Romans," an official title of the Byzantine rulers, he transferred to Otto of Germany. It is also interesting to note the attempt of Nicephorus Phocas to venerate as martyrs all soldiers who had fallen in the struggle with the infidels. This attempt was vehemently opposed by the patriarch and the bishops, and the Emperor was forced to give up his scheme.

The names of Nicephorus Phocas and John Tzimisces are connected with

[96] K. E. Zachariä von Lingenthal, *Jus graeco-romanum*, III, 292–96. V. G. Vasilievsky, "Materials for the Internal History of Byzantium; Measures in Favor of Peasant Landownership," *Journal of the Ministry of Public Instruction*, CCII (1879), 224 ff. J. and P. Zepos, *Jus graecoromanum*, I, 249–52.

[97] Zachariä von Lingenthal, *Jus graecoromanum*, III, 303. Vasilievsky, *Journal*, CCII (1879), 220. Zepos, *Jus Graecoromanum*, I, 259.

the beginning of a new era in the life of Mount Athos, famous for its monasteries. Individual hermits had lived on this mountain since the very beginning of monasticism in the fourth century, and several small and poor monasteries grew up there about the seventh century. During the period of the iconoclastic troubles of the eighth century the inaccessible districts of Mount Athos were sought as a refuge by many persecuted image-worshipers, who brought with them numerous church utensils, relics, and manuscripts. But life on Mount Athos was not safe because of the repeated maritime raids of the Arabs, during which many monks were killed or carried off as prisoners. Previous to the middle of the tenth century Mount Athos had gone through several periods of desolation. In the time of Nicephorus Phocas, the Athonian monastic organizations became much stronger, especially when St. Athanasius founded the first large monastery with its cenobitic organization and new set of rules (*typikon,* in Greek, the usual name for monastic rules in the Byzantine Empire) which determined the further life of the monastery. The hermits (anchorites) of Mount Athos, opposed to the introduction of cenobitic monasticism, sent a complaint against Athanasius to John Tzimisces, the successor of Nicephorus Phocas, accusing Athanasius of breaking the ancient customs of the Holy Mountain (as Athos was called in the *typikon* of Athanasius). Tzimisces investigated this complaint and confirmed the ancient Athonian rule, which tolerated the existence of both anchorites and cenobites. Following the lead of St. Athanasius, many new monasteries, Greek and others, were founded. In the time of Basil II there was already one Iberian or Georgian monastery; emigrants from Italy founded two, a Roman and an Amalfitan. Bishop Porphyrius Uspensky, a profound Russian student of the Christian East, asserted that when the aged Athanasius died (about 1000 A.D.) there were three thousand "various monks" on Mount Athos.[98] As early as the eleventh century there was a Russian Laura on this mountain. The name of Holy Mountain for Mount Athos, as an official term, appears for the first time in the second set of rules (*typikon*) given by Emperor Constantine IX Monomachus about the middle of the eleventh century.[99] The administration of the monasteries was entrusted to a council of Abbots (Igumens) headed by the *first one* among them, the *protos* (from the Greek πρῶτος, "the first"). The council was known as the *protaton.* Thus, in the time of the Macedonian dynasty Mount Athos became a very important cultural center, not only for the Byzantine Empire, but for the world at large.

The problem of the division of churches which became so acute in the ninth century was brought to a final solution in the middle of the eleventh century. And while the main causes of this break were doctrinal, the final

[98] *History of Athos,* III (1), 154.
[99] *Ibid.,* 93, 170–71. P. Meyer, *Die Hauptur-* *kunden für die Geschichte der Athosklosters,* 153.

break was undoubtedly accelerated by the changed conditions in Italy in the middle of the eleventh century. In spite of the prohibitions of Nicephorus Phocas, Latin church influence continued to penetrate into the church organization of Apulia and Calabria. In the middle of the eleventh century the papal throne was occupied by Leo IX, whose interests were not limited by ecclesiastical affairs, but extended also into the field of political interests. The Cluniac movement, which embraced wide circles of western European clergy, developed under the direct protection of the pope. The aim of this movement was to reform the church, raise its low morals, give firmness to its loose discipline, and destroy the worldly manners and customs which had permeated the life of the church (such as simony, wedlock of the clergy, secular investiture, etc.). Whenever the advocates of this movement penetrated into a province, they placed its spiritual life in direct dependence upon the pope. The remarkable progress made by the Cluniac movement in southern Italy greatly displeased the Eastern church. Leo IX was convinced that he had also a sound political basis for intervening in the affairs of southern Italy. For instance, during the exchange of messages between the pope and the patriarch of Constantinople (Michael Cerularius) the pope referred to the famous *Donation of Constantine* (*Donatio Constantini*), which had presumably placed in the hands of the bishop of Rome not only spiritual but also temporal power. Yet, in spite of the various complications which arose between the East and the West, a break between the churches was not to be expected in the near future, especially since the Byzantine Emperor Constantine IX Monomachus was inclined to seek a peaceful solution to the problem.

Papal legates were sent to Constantinople, among them the very haughty Cardinal Humbert. All of them, especially Humbert, acted insolently and arrogantly toward the patriarch, forcing him to refuse to carry on further negotiations with them. The patriarch also refused to make any concessions to Rome. Then, in the summer of the year 1054, the legates deposited upon the altar of St. Sophia a bull of excommunication, which proclaimed anathema for Patriarch "Michael and his followers, guilty of the above-mentioned errors and insolences . . . along with all heretics, together with the devil and his angels."[100] In response to this action Michael Cerularius convoked a council at which he excommunicated the Roman legates and all people connected with them who had come to "the God-guarded city like a thunder, or a tempest, or a famine, or, better still, like wild boars, in order to overthrow truth."[101]

Thus did the final separation of the western and eastern churches occur in the year 1054. The attitude of the three eastern patriarchs toward this break

[100] Migne, *Patrologia Latina*, CXLIII, 1004.   [101] Lebedev, *Separation of the Churches,*
347.

was exceedingly important for Michael Cerularius. Through the patriarch of Antioch he notified the patriarchs of Jerusalem and Alexandria of the separation of the churches, accompanying the news with fitting explanations. In spite of the scantiness of sources on this point, it may be stated with certainty that the three eastern patriarchates remained loyal to orthodoxy and supported the patriarch of Constantinople.[102]

For the patriarch of Constantinople the break of 1054 could be considered a great victory, which made him completely independent of the papal pretensions of the West. His authority became much greater in the Slavonic world and in the three eastern patriarchates. But for the political life of the Empire this break was fatal, because it definitely destroyed all possibilities of any lasting future political understanding between the Empire and the West, which remained under the strong influence of the papacy. And this was fatal because the Byzantine Empire was at times greatly in need of western help, especially when the eastern Turkish menace arose. Bréhier's appraisal of the consequences of this break was: "It was this schism, which, by rendering fruitless all efforts at conciliation between the Empire of Constantinople and the West, paved the way for the fall of the Empire."[103]

The final break of 1054 was felt immediately only in official circles by the clergy and the government. The great mass of the population reacted very calmly to this separation, and for some time even remained unaware of the distinction between the teachings of Constantinople and of Rome. The attitude of Russia to this phenomenon was interesting. The Russian metropolitans of the eleventh century, appointed or confirmed by Constantinople, quite naturally accepted the Byzantine point of view, but the mass of Russian people had no grievances whatever against the Latin church and could find no errors in its teachings. For example, the Russian prince of the eleventh century appealed to the pope for help against the usurper, and this appeal did not arouse any surprise or protest.[104]

Legislation of the Macedonian emperors and social and economic relations within the Empire

Prochiron and Epanagoge.—The time of the Macedonian dynasty was a period of stirring legislative activity. Basil I desired to create a general code of Graeco-Roman or Byzantine law containing a chronological arrangement of legislative acts, both old and new. In other words, he planned to revive the legislative work of Justinian by adapting it to changed conditions, and to

---

[102] See L. Bréhier, *Le Schisme oriental du XIe siècle*, 232–41.
[103] "The Greek Church," *Cambridge Medieval History*, IV, 273. See also J. Gay, *Les papes du XIe siècle et la chrétienté*, 166–67. M.

Jugie, "Le Schisme de Michel Cérulaire," *Échos d'Orient*, XXXVI (1937), 440–73.
[104] On this subject there are many interesting data in the book by B. Leib, *Rome, Kiev, et Byzance à la fin du XIe siècle*, 18–19, 51, 70.

add to it the laws which had appeared in later times. The four parts of the Justinian code, written mostly in Latin and very bulky, were usually studied only in their Greek abridged versions, or in expositions, abstracts, and commentaries based on the Latin original. Many of these, though widely used, were very inaccurate and frequently mutilated the original texts. Basil I intended to exclude the old laws annulled by later Novels, and to introduce a number of new laws. The Latin terms and expressions retained in the new code were to be explained in Greek, for Greek was to be the language of Basil's legislative work. The Emperor himself characterized his attempted reform in the field of law as "a purging of ancient laws" (ἀνακάθαρσις τῶν παλαιῶν νόμων).[105]

Knowing that the completion of the projected code would take much time, Basil issued meanwhile a smaller work entitled the Prochiron (ὁ πρόχειρος νόμος), i.e., a manual of the science of law. This was to supply people interested in legal works with a brief account of the laws by which the Empire was to be ruled. The preface to the Prochiron refers to these laws as laws establishing in the Empire righteousness, "by which alone, according to Solomon, a nation is exalted" (Proverbs 14:34).[106] The Prochiron was subdivided into forty titles (*tituli*) and contained the principal norms of civil law and a complete list of penalties for various offenses and crimes. Its main source, especially for the first twenty-one sections, were the Institutes of Justinian. Other parts of the Justinian code were used to a much lesser degree. So usual was the recourse to the Greek revised and abridged versions of this older code that even the compilers of the Prochiron resorted to them rather than to the Latin originals. The Prochiron refers to the Ecloga of Leo and Constantine as a "subversion of the good laws which was useless for the empire," and states that "it would be unwise to keep it in force."[107] Yet in spite of this harsh judgment, the Ecloga of the Isaurian emperors was apparently so practical and popular that the Prochiron used much of its contents, especially in the titles following the twenty-first. According to the introduction to the Prochiron, all persons interested in a more detailed study of active law were supposed to use the larger code of sixty books, also compiled in Basil's time.[108]

[105] *Imperatorem Basilii Constantini et Leonis Prochiron,* ed. K. E. Zachariä von Lingenthal, par. 3, 10. E. Freshfield, *A Manual of Eastern Roman Law,* 51. Zepos, *Jus graecoromanum,* II, 117.

[106] Zachariä von Lingenthal, *ibid.,* par. 4.

[107] *Ibid.,* par. 9. Freshfield, *Manual of Eastern Roman Law,* 51; Zepos, *Jus graecoromanum,* II, 116.

[108] In the twelfth century appeared the *Ecloga ad Prochiron mutata,* applied to the Greek-speaking subjects of the Norman Kingdom of Sicily. See K. E. Zachariä von Lingenthal, *Geschichte der griechisch-römischen Rechts* (3rd ed., 1892), 36. E. Freshfield, *A Manual of Later Roman Law—the Ecloga ad Prochiron mutata,* 1. Zachariä von Lingenthal, *Jus graeco-romanum,* IV, 53. The author of the code lived between the tenth and the twelfth centuries.

By the end of Basil's reign a new volume of laws was compiled and published under the title of the Epanagoge (ἡ ἐπαναγωγή, "introduction"). Several scholars have somewhat incorrectly considered this legislative work as merely a revised and enlarged Prochiron.[109] According to its preface, the Epanagoge was an introduction to the forty volumes of "purified" older laws[110] collected also in Basil's time; it, too, was divided into forty titles. Just what these two collections—one in sixty books mentioned in the Prochiron, the other in forty books mentioned in the Epanagoge—represented, is not certain. They were probably not finished for publication in Basil's time but formed the foundation of the Basilics published by his successor, Leo VI. Some scholars believe that the Epanagoge was never really published, and remained only in the form of a draft,[111] while others hold that this work was an officially published law.[112]

The Epanagoge differs very greatly from the Prochiron. In the first place, its first part contains entirely new and very interesting chapters on imperial authority, on the power of the patriarch, and other civil and ecclesiastic officials, which gives a very clear picture of the foundations of the public and social structure of the Empire and of the relations of the church to the state.[113] In the second place, the materials borrowed for the Epanagoge from the Prochiron are arranged in a new manner. It is almost certain that Patriarch Photius took part in the compilation of the Epanagoge, and his influence is especially evident in the definition of the relation of imperial power to the power of the patriarch, and in the treatment of the position to be occupied by the ecumenical patriarch of New Rome with regard to all the other patriarchs, who were to be considered only as local hierarchs. Following in the footsteps of the Prochiron, the introduction to the Epanagoge refers to the Ecloga of the iconoclastic emperors as "the gossip of the Isaurians, intended to oppose the divine doctrine and to destroy the salutary laws."[114] This part of the Epanagoge speaks also of the complete abrogation of the Ecloga, and yet uses some of its materials.

It may be mentioned here that the Epanagoge, together with a number of other Byzantine legal collections, has been translated into Slavonic, and many extracts from it are to be found in Slavonic codes and in the Russian *Book of*

---

[109] Vogt, *Basile Ier*, 134; *Cambridge Medieval History*, IV, 712.

[110] *Collectio librorum juris graeco-romani ineditorum*, ed. Zachariä von Lingenthal, 62. Zepos, *Jus graecoromanum*, II, 237.

[111] Zachariä von Lingenthal, *Geschichte des griechisch-römischen Rechts*, 22.

[112] V. Sokolsky, "Concerning the Nature and Meaning of the Epanagoge," *Vizantiysky Vremennik*, I (1894), 26–27. See also G. Ver-

nadsky, "The Tactics of Leo the Wise and the Epanagoge," *Byzantion*, VI (1931), 333–35.

[113] See G. Vernadsky, "Die kirchlich-politische Lehre der Epanagoge und ihr Einfluss auf das russische Leben im XVII. Jahrhundert," *Byzantinisch-neugriechische Jahrbücher*, VI (1928), 121–25.

[114] Zachariä von Lingenthal, ed., *Collectio librorum juris*, 62. Zepos, *Jus graecoromanum*, II, 237.

Rules (the so-called *Kormchaia Kniga*), or the Administrative Code, mentioned as early as the tenth century. The ideas expressed in the Epanagoge exerted great influence upon the later history of Russia. For instance, the documents concerning the cause of Patriarch Nikon in the time of Tsar Aleksei Mikhailovich (seventeenth century) contain direct quotations from the rulings of the Epanagoge with reference to the authority of the Emperor.[115]

The Prochiron and the Epanagoge, together with the work on the "purification of ancient law," represent the successful achievements of the time of Basil I. Going back, so to speak, to the elements of the somewhat neglected Roman law, Basil revived Justinian law and brought it closer to the life of his time by adding later laws called forth by changed social and economic conditions.

The Basilics and the Tipucitus.—Basil's accomplishments in the field of law made it possible for his son and successor, Leo VI the Wise, to publish the Basilics (τὰ βασιλικά), which represented the most complete monument of Graeco-Roman or Byzantine law. In it all parts of Justinian's code are reshaped and combined into one code written in Greek. For this purpose a commission of qualified jurisconsults was appointed. The name of the Basilics originated not, as was formerly incorrectly supposed, from the name of Basil I, in whose time much material had been prepared for them, but from the Greek word *basileus,* meaning tsar, emperor; hence the proper translation for the title would be "Imperial Laws."

The compilation of Leo VI, subdivided into sixty books, followed the aim set out by Basil I: it strove to revive the legislative work of Justinian by omitting laws which had lost their significance or were not applicable to the changed conditions of Byzantine life. The Basilics do not, therefore, represent a complete, literal translation of the Justinian code, but an adaptation of it to the new conditions of life. Some Novels and other legal documents published after Justinian, including even several Novels of Basil I and Leo VI, were also used as sources for the Basilics.[116] No one manuscript has preserved the whole of the Basilics, but various manuscripts have preserved parts, so that more than two-thirds of the whole exists.

[115] G. Vernadsky, "Die kirchlich-politische Lehre der Epanagoge," *Byzantinisch-neugriechische Jahrbücher,* VI (1928), 127-42. He speaks of the influence of the ideas of the Epanagoge on the epoch of the Patriarchs Filaret (1619-31) and Nikon (1652-58).

[116] See the edict (*proemium*) found in the beginning of the Basilics, in *Basilicorum Libri LX,* ed. G. Heimbach, I, xxi-xxii; ed. I. D. Zepos, I (1896), 3. The exact date of the Basilics has not been definitely determined

(between 886 and 892, in 888, 889, or 890). See G. Heimbach, "Ueber die angebliche neueste Redaction der Basiliken durch Constantinus Porphyrogeneta," *Zeitschrift für Rechtsgeschichte,* VIII (1869), 417. Heimbach, *Basilicorum Libri LX,* VI. *Prolegomena et Manuale Basilicorum continens,* 111. P. Collinet "Byzantine Legislation From the Death of Justinian (565) to 1453," *Cambridge Medieval History,* IV, 713.

From the point of view of the reconstruction of the lost books of the Basilics a work of the eleventh or twelfth century is very important, the *Tipucitus* (Τιπούκειτος),[117] attributed to a Byzantine jurisconsult, Patzes.[118] The book is a table of contents of the Basilics, giving the rubrics and most important chapters under each title and indicating analogous passages in all of them. The *Tipucitus* has not yet been published in its entirety.[119]

The revived classical code of the Basilics, however, carefully adapted to existing conditions, still remained artificial and inadequate. That is why many parts of the Ecloga remained in force even after the appearance of the Basilics and were later revised and enlarged many times. The Basilics, however, is a colossal achievement in the domain of Byzantine jurisprudence and culture, ranking after the *Corpus Iuris Civilis*. It is still a book almost under seven seals, and a scientific and exhaustive study of it will undoubtedly reveal new horizons and wide perspectives.[120]

The Book of the Eparch.—To the time of Leo VI may perhaps be referred a most interesting document, "an invaluable treasure for the internal history of Constantinople,"[121] the so-called *Book of the Eparch* or *Book of the Prefect,* discovered in Geneva by the Swiss scholar, Nicole, at the end of the nineteenth century.[122] The date of this document has not been definitely established. It may have been compiled during the reign of Leo VI or later in the tenth century, perhaps even under Nicephorus Phocas (after 963).[123]

[117] The title is derived from the Greek words Τί ποῦ κεῖται, in Latin, *quid ubi invenitur?*

[118] On the author of the *Tipucitus*, see Τιπούκειτος *sive Librorum LX Basilicorum Summarium praefatio*, in *Studi e testi*, XXV. G. Ferrari, in *Byzantinische Zeitschrift*, XXVII (1927), 165–66. P. Collinet said that the *Tipucitus* is the work of an unknown author (*Cambridge Medieval History*, IV, 722). See also P. Noailles, "Tipucitus," *Mélanges de Droit Romain dédiés à George Cornil*, II, 175–96. A. Berger, "Tipoukeitos: The Origin of a Name," *Traditio*, III (1945), 394–402. Berger wrote: "If we recall the modern reference books known as *Who's Who* we can translate the title of Patzes' work as "What is Where" (p. 400). Very useful study.

[119] A summary of books I–XII, ed. C. Ferrini and J. Mercati; a summary of Books XIII–XXIII, in *Librorum LX Basilicorum Summarium;* Books XIII–XXIII, ed. F. Dölger, in *Studi e testi*, 51. Some articles by Ferrini on the manuscripts and reconstruction of the Basilics in *Opere di Contardo Ferrini*, I,

349–63.

[120] See Lawson's opening lines in his study on the Basilica: The Basilica occupies the central place in Byzantine law, and yet to all but experts it is practically unknown. F. H. Lawson, "The Basilica," *The Law Quarterly Review*, XLVI (1930), 486. A. A. Vasiliev, "Justinian's Digest," *Studi bizantini e neoellenici*, V (1939), 734. Very useful information on the Basilics is to be found in A. Albertoni, *Per una esposizione del diritto bizantino*, 43, 55–57.

[121] Th. I. Uspensky, "The Eparch of Constantinople," *Transactions of the Russian Archeological Institute at Constantinople*, IV, 2 (1890), 90.

[122] *Le Livre du préfet ou l'édit de l'empereur Léon le Sage sur les corporations de Constantinople*, ed. J. Nicole. For other editions, see the bibliography.

[123] In 1935 a Greek historian, A. P. Christophilopoulos, apparently fixed the exact date: between the first of September, 911 and the eleventh of May, 912. Τὸ ἐπαρχικὸν βιβλίον Λέοντος Τοῦ Σοφοῦ καὶ αἱ συντεχνίαι ἐν Βυζαντίῳ, 13. In his review of the book,

The rank of eparch or prefect of Constantinople was applied in the Byzantine Empire to the governor of the capital; he was entrusted with almost unlimited authority, and stood, so to speak, on the highest rank of the Byzantine bureaucratic ladder. It was his duty first of all to maintain public order and safety in the capital, and for this purpose he had at his disposal a large body of employees known as the *secretum* of the eparch. Besides these duties, he also had jurisdiction over the corporations and guilds of craftsmen and traders in the capital. The *Book of the Eparch* throws much light on this side of Constantinopolitan life, scarcely touched upon by earlier sources. It lists the various ranks of craftsmen and traders, and gives an account of the internal organization of their guilds, of the government's attitude to them, and so forth. The list of corporations in this document is headed by an organization which in the modern conception would not fall into the general class of craft or trade associations, namely by the corporation of notaries (οἱ ταβουλλάριοι, *tabularii*), who, among other things, were required to be familiar with the sixty books of the Basilics. Then follow the guilds of jewelers, silk-producers, silk-weavers, linen-makers, makers of wax, soap, and leather, and the bakers. The list of traders found in the *Book of the Eparch* speaks of money-changers, traders in silk goods and dresses, dealers in raw silk, sellers of perfumes, wax, and soap; grocers, butchers, sellers of pigs, fish, horses, and bread, and tavern keepers. Each corporation enjoyed a monopoly, and severe penalty was provided for anyone who attempted to pursue two trades, even if they were very similar. The internal life of the guilds, their organization and work, the grant of markets, the regulation of prices and profit, export and import from and to the capital, and many other problems were regulated under very strict government supervision. Free trade and free production were unknown in the Byzantine Empire. The eparch of Constantinople was the only high official who had the right to intervene personally, or through his representatives, in the life of the guilds and regulate their production or trade.[124] The account

---

G. Mickwitz declared that the Greek author had solved the controversy. *Byzantinisch-neugriechische Jahrbücher,* XII (1936), 369. See also Mickwitz, *Die Kartellfunktionen der Zünfte,* 205. But Christophilopoulos based his conclusion on the erroneous description by Papadopoulos-Kerameus of a Greek manuscript preserved in Constantinople. According to Papadopoulos-Kerameus, this manuscript contained the *Book of the Prefect,* but we know now that that is not the case. It contains instead some ordinances of the Palestinian architect, Julian Ascalonites. Christophilopoulos' "discovery" then is to be discarded. See D.

Ghines, "Τὸ ἐπαρχικὸν βιβλίον καὶ οἱ νόμοι Ἰουλιανοῦ τοῦ Ἀσκαλωνίτου," Ἐπετηρὶς Ἑταιρείας Βυζαντινῶν Σπουδῶν, XIII (1937), 183–91; esp. 183–85. The relevant Greek text of the manuscript, 187–91.

[124] A vast literature exists on the *Book of the Prefect;* it is indicated by Ostrogorsky, *Geschichte des byzantinischen Staates,* 177, n. 3. The best study is by A. Stöckle, *Spätromische und byzantinische Zünfte,* 147–48 (on the dating). In Russian, P. V. Bezobrazov, *Vizantiysky Vremennik,* XVIII (1911), 33–36; also his addition to his Russian translation of G. F. Hertzberg, *Geschichte der Byzantiner.*

of the Byzantine guilds found in this source provides data for an interesting comparison with the medieval guilds of western Europe.

Over a hundred novels from the period of Leon VI exist, which supply rich material for the internal history of the Byzantine Empire at the end of the ninth and the beginning of the tenth century, and which have not yet been adequately studied and utilized.[125]

The "powerful" and the "poor."—The legislative works of Basil I and Leo VI in the ninth and tenth centuries brought about a temporary revival in the field of juridical literature which expressed itself, on the one hand, in the appearance of numerous commentaries and interpretations of the Basilics (such commentaries were usually known as *scholia*), and, on the other hand, in the publication of various abridged collections and manuals. The tenth century was marked also by an exceedingly interesting tendency in the legislative work of the Byzantine emperors, who were compelled to express through a number of Novels their reaction to one of the most acute questions in the social and economic life of that period, namely, the problem of the excessive development of large landownership, highly detrimental to small peasant landholding and the free peasant community.

In the time of the Macedonian dynasty the class of the "powerful" (δυνατοί), or magnates, had again grown very prominent. At the other extreme stood the class of the "poor" people (πένητες), who may be compared with the poor people (*pauperes*) of medieval western Europe, and the orphans (*siroti*) of the Moscow period in Russian history. The poor people of the Byzantine Empire of the tenth century were those small peasant owners and members of organized communes whom heavy taxes and various duties forced to appeal for protection to the powerful magnates and pay for that protection the price of their freedom and independence.

The rise of the powerful in the tenth century, seemingly sudden at first glance, may be partly explained by the aftereffects of the insurrection of Thomas in the third decade of the ninth century. This was especially true of Asia Minor, where the number of large landowners grew to enormous proportions in the tenth century. The severe and lasting nature of this insurrection caused the ruin of a vast number of small landholders, forcing them to transfer their property to their wealthy neighbors. But this was only one of the many causes of the development of large estates. On the whole, the problem of the growth of large landownership in the Byzantine Empire during the ninth and tenth centuries has not yet been sufficiently elucidated.

[125] Zachariä von Lingenthal, *Jus graeco-romanum*, III, 65-226. Zepos, *Jus graecoromanum*, I, 54-191. See H. Monnier, *Les nouvelles de Léon le Sage*. C. A. Spulber, *Les nouvelles de Léon le Sage*. See also Ostrogorsky's remarks in *Geschichte des byzantinischen Staates*, 172.

The rulers of the Macedonian dynasty, at least those from Romanus Lecapenus (919–44) to Basil II, who died in 1025, energetically defended the cause of the small landowners and the peasant communes against the infringements of the powerful. The reasons must be sought in the excessive growth of the large landholdings. The powerful, who controlled a vast number of serfs and immense landed estates, could easily organize and subsidize armies composed of their dependents, and were thus enabled to conspire against the central government. The emperors, by their efforts to crush the strength of the powerful and uphold the interests of the small peasantry and the peasant commune, were at the same time defending their own power and throne, seriously threatened in the tenth century, especially by Asia Minor.

The emperors were also compelled to defend the so-called "military holdings." Even in the time of the Roman Empire it had been customary to assign land to soldiers on the border lines of the Empire, and sometimes even within the Empire, on the condition that they should continue to serve in the army. These allotments survived until the tenth century, although they were in a state of decline. They, too, were threatened in the ninth and tenth centuries by the powerful, who strove to buy up these military estates just as they did the small peasant holdings. The emperors of this period also made attempts to defend these military fiefs.

The measures taken by the rulers of the Macedonian dynasty in defense of peasant and military landholding were in reality very simple. They prohibited the powerful from buying their way into peasant communities or from acquiring peasant and military allotments. The government's campaign in this direction was initiated by the publication of a Novel in the year 922 by Romanus I Lecapenus, the co-regent of Constantine Porphyrogenitus. This Novel proposed three regulations: (1) in any sale and temporary or hereditary lease of real estate, i.e., land, houses, vineyards, etc., the preferential right would belong to the peasants and their free commune; (2) the powerful would be forbidden to acquire the property of the poor in any manner, whether it be by donation, will, patronage, purchase, rent, or exchange; (3) the military allotments alienated in any manner during the last thirty years, and also those which were about to be alienated, would be returned to their original owners without any compensation to the holders.

The terrible disasters which occurred in the Empire soon after the publication of this Novel put these measures of Romanus to a difficult trial. The untimely frosts, terrible famine, and pestilence made the lot of the peasants very hard. The powerful took advantage of the desperate position of the peasants and bought up their holdings at very low prices, or for mere trifling amounts of bread. This shocking open practice of the powerful forced Romanus to publish in 934 a second Novel in which he harshly reproved the cruel avidity of the wealthy class, stating that they were "to the unhappy villages like a plague or gangrene, which had eaten its way into the body of the village, bringing it closer to final peril."[126] This Novel provided that the peasants from whom the powerful had bought land against the law during or after the year of famine could redeem their holdings at the price at which they had sold it; the new owners were to be removed immediately after payment was made by the peasant. After a brief remark about the successful operations of the Byzantine army, the Novel contained the following concluding statement: "If we have attained such success in our struggle with our external enemies, then how can we fail to crush our domestic and internal enemies of nature, men, and good order, through our rightful desire of freedom and the sharpness of the present law?"[127]

But this decree of Romanus failed to halt the development of large land-ownership and the dissolution of small peasant households and communities. In a subsequent Novel of Constantine Porphyrogenitus it was officially stated that the older laws were not observed. The restrictions placed upon the rich in Constantine's reign surpassed those of Romanus. Nicephorus Phocas, who rose to the throne through his marriage to the widow of Romanus II, was a member of the powerful class, and, quite naturally, understood and favored the interests of that class more than any of his predecessors. In the words of V. G. Vasilievsky, the Novel of Nicephorus Phocas "unquestionably indicates a certain reaction in the field of legislation in favor of the powerful class, even though it speaks only of an equally just treatment of both sides."[128] This Novel stated that "ancient legislators considered all rulers as champions of justice, calling them a general and equal benefit to all," and indicates that the predecessors of Nicephorus Phocas have deviated from this original ideal. "They completely neglected to care for the prosperity of the powerful, and did not even permit them to remain in possession of what they had already acquired."[129] By the abrogation of previous rulings, Nicephorus Phocas gave new freedom to the lawlessness and growth of the powerful class.

The sternest foe of the powerful class was Basil II Bulgaroctonus. Two leaders of the powerful families of Asia Minor, Bardas Phocas and Bardas Sclerus, rebelled against the Emperor and nearly deprived him of the throne. Only the intervention of the Russian auxiliary corps sent by Prince Vladimir prevented the fall of the Emperor. It is not surprising, therefore, that Basil II

[126] Zachariä von Lingenthal, *Jus graeco-romanum,* III, 247. Zepos, *Jus graecoromanum,* I, 210.

[127] Zachariä von Lingenthal, *Jus graeco-romanum,* III, 252. V. G. Vasilievsky, "Materials for the Internal History of Byzantium," *Journal of the Ministry of Public Instruction,* CCII (1879), 188; *Works,* IV, 281. Zepos, *Jus graecoromanum,* I, 214.

[128] Vasilievsky, *ibid.,* 206; *Works,* IV, 302.

[129] Zachariä von Lingenthal, *Jus graeco-romanum,* III, 297. Zepos, *Jus graecoromanum,* I, 253–54.

viewed the large landowners as his most dangerous enemies, and was very harsh and unscrupulous in his treatment of them. Once, in passing through Cappadocia, Basil and his entire army were lavishly entertained in the enormous estate of Eustathius Maleinus. Suspecting that his host might be a possible rival, and fearing that he might attempt to follow in the footsteps of Phocas and Sclerus, the Emperor took him to the capital and forced him to remain there to the end of his days. After the death of Maleinus, his vast estates were confiscated. A similar incident was related in the Novel itself. The story stated that the Emperor heard that a certain Philocales of Asia Minor, a poor peasant by birth, had become famous and wealthy, attained high rank in service, and had seized the village in which he lived and transformed it into his own estate, changing even its name. Basil ordered that all the magnificent buildings which belonged to Philocales should be completely destroyed and razed to the ground and the land returned to the poor. By the orders of the Emperor Philocales himself was again reduced to the state of a simple peasant.[130] There is no doubt that the families of Phocas, Sclerus, and Maleinus, and such individuals as Philocales, were only a few of the large landowning class of Asia Minor.

The famous Novel of 996 abolished the forty years' prescription which protected the rights of the powerful who had illegally seized peasant estates and who tried "to extend this term either by means of gifts, or by means of power, in order to acquire final ownership of that which they had acquired from the poor by wicked means."[131] The estates acquired by the powerful from village communities previous to the issue of Romanus' first law were to remain in the hands of the powerful only if the latter could prove their rights of ownership by written evidence or by a sufficient number of witnesses. The Novel stated that the demands of the treasury could not consider any prescription; hence the state "may claim its rights by going back to the time of Caesar Augustus."[132] The problem of military fiefs also compelled the Macedonian rulers to issue several novels.

In addition to the Novel of 996, Basil II issued a decree concerning the tax called *allelengyon,* meaning mutual warrant (ἀλληλέγγυον). As far back as the early part of the ninth century (in so far as the brief statement on this point in one of the sources shows)[133] Emperor Nicephorus I issued orders which placed upon their richer neighbors the responsibility for the full payment of taxes of the poor. The *allelengyon* as a tax was nothing new. It represented a

[130] Zachariä von Lingenthal, *ibid.,* 310; Vasilievsky, "Materials," *Journal of Public Instruction,* CCII (1879), 217; *Works,* IV, 314–15; Zepos, *ibid.,* 265.

[131] Zachariä von Lingenthal, 308; Vasilievsky, 215–16, *Works,* IV, 312–13; Zepos, I, 263.

[132] Zachariä von Lingenthal, III, 315; Vasilievsky, 220, *Works,* IV, 317; Zepos, 269.

[133] Theophanes, *Chronographia,* ed. de Boor, 486. Bury, *Eastern Roman Empire,* III, 214.

continuation, and at the same time a variation, of the late Roman system of the *epibole* (see in discussion of Anastasius): "The *allelengyon* system of payment imposed excessively heavy charges on the peasantry, and this sufficiently explains why membership of a village community was considered burdensome, and why a peasant usually preferred to own a detached property."[134] The orders of Nicephorus I aroused so much hatred toward the Emperor that his successors were apparently compelled to forsake this tax. When the need of money for the upkeep of the Bulgarian war became very great and the desire to deal the powerful a heavy blow had grown very strong in Basil II, he revived the law which made the wealthy landowners responsible for the taxes of the poor, if the latter were unable to pay them. If this measure, so strongly defended by Basil II, had remained in force for a long time, it might have gone far to ruin the powerful owners of both ecclesiastical and temporal estates. But the *allelengyon* was enforced only for a brief period of time. In the first half of the eleventh century Romanus III Argyrus, who acquired the throne through his marriage to Zoë, the daughter of Constantine VIII, urged by his interest in the welfare of the powerful and by his desire to find a way for reconciliation with the higher clergy and landed nobility, repealed the hated *allelengyon*.

On the whole, the decrees of the Macedonian emperors of the tenth century, though limiting to some extent the encroachments of the powerful, accomplished very few definite results. In the eleventh century the famous Novels were gradually forgotten and abandoned. The same century witnessed a material change in the internal policy of the Byzantine emperors, who began to favor and openly protect large landownership, hastening the wide development of serfdom. Still, the free peasant commune and the free small landowners did not disappear entirely from the Empire. These institutions continued to exist and will be discussed in connection with later periods.

Provincial administration

The provincial administration of the Empire in the ninth century and in the time of the Macedonian dynasty continued to develop along the path of theme organization, discussed in an earlier chapter. This development expressed itself, on the one hand, in the further breaking up of the older themes and consequently in the increase in the number of themes, and, on the other hand, in elevating to the position of themes districts which previously had borne some other name, such as *clisurae*.

---

[134] G. Ostrogorsky, "Agrarian Conditions in the Byzantine Empire in the Middle Ages," *Cambridge Economic History*, I, 202–3. The question of the connection between the *epibole* and *allelengyon* still remains debata- ble. See F. Dölger, *Beiträge zur Geschichte der byzantinischen Finanzverwaltung besonders des 10. und 11. Jahrhunderts*, 129–30. See also G. Brătianu, *Études byzantines d'histoire économique et sociale*, 197–201.

Both exarchates, which are considered by historians as the true precursors of themes, had become alienated from the Empire: the Carthagenian or African exarchate was conquered by the Arabs in the middle of the seventh century, while the Ravenna exarchate was occupied in the first half of the eighth century by the Longobards, who were soon forced to cede the conquered territories of this exarchate to the Frankish king, Pippin the Brief. He, in his turn, handed them over to the pope in 754, thereby laying the foundations for the famous medieval papal state. In the seventh century the Byzantine Empire had, in addition to the exarchates, five military governments which did not yet bear the name of themes. At the beginning of the ninth century there were ten themes: five Asiatic, four European, and one maritime. On the basis of data found in the works of the Arabian geographer of the ninth century, Ibn-Khurdadhbah, and in other sources, historians claim that there were twenty-five military districts in the ninth century, but that not all of these were themes. Among them were included two *clisurarchiae,* one *ducatus,* and two *archontatus.* The ceremonial treatise of precedence at court, written by the court marshal (*atriclines*), Philotheus, in 899 and usually included as part of the so-called book on *Ceremonies of the Byzantine Court* of the time of Constantine Porphyrogenitus, lists twenty-five themes.[135] In his work *Concerning Themes* (tenth century), Constantine Porphyrogenitus gives a list of twenty-nine themes: seventeen Asiatic, including the four sea themes, and twelve European, including the Sicilian theme, part of which formed the theme of Calabria in the tenth century after the Arabian conquest of Sicily proper. The twelve European themes included also the theme of Cherson (Korsun) in the Crimea, founded probably as far back as the ninth century, and frequently referred to as "the Klimata" or "Gothic Klimata." The list published by V. Beneševič and attributed to the reign of Romanus Lecapenus before 921–927 gives thirty themes.[136] In the eleventh century the number rose to thirty-eight.[137] Most of them were governed by a military governor, the *strategus.* Because of the frequent changes in the number of themes, and because of the lack of sources on the historical development of the theme organization, knowledge of this important side of Byzantine life is still very limited and inexact.

Something should be said of the *clisurae* and the *clisurarchs.* The name *clisura,* which even today means a "mountain pass" in Greek, was applied in the Byzantine period to a "frontier fortress" with limited neighboring terri-

---

[135] J. B. Bury, *The Imperial Administrative System in the Ninth Century, with a revised text of the Kletorologion of Philotheos,* 146–47.

[136] V. Beneševič, "Die byzantinischen Ranglisten nach dem 'Kletorologion Philothei,'" *Byzantinisch-neugriechische Jahrbücher,* V (1926), 118–22; on the dating, 164–65.

[137] See N. Skabalanovich, *The Byzantine State and Church in the Eleventh Century,* 193–230.

tory, or, more generally, to "a small province" ruled by a *clisurarch,* whose authority was not as great as that of the strategus, and did not, in all probability, combine both military and civil responsibilities. Some of the *clisurae,* as, for instance, those of Seleucia, Sebastea in Asia Minor, and a few others, eventually rose in importance by being transformed into themes.

The strategi who stood at the head of the themes had a large body of subordinates. At least in the time of Leo VI the Wise the strategi of the eastern themes, including the sea themes, were receiving definite maintenance from the government treasury, while the strategi of the western themes were supported by the revenues of their respective districts and not by the treasury.

The theme organization had reached the highest stage of its development in the time of the Macedonian dynasty. After this period the system began to decline gradually, partly because of the conquests of the Seljuq Turks in Asia Minor, and partly because of the changes which took place in Byzantine life during the period of crusades.

THE TIME OF TROUBLES (1056–81)

The emperors

As early as 1025, after the death of Basil II Bulgaroctonus, the Empire entered upon a period of troubles, frequent changes of accidental rulers, and the beginning of a general decline. Empress Zoë succeeded in raising each of her three husbands to the throne. In the year 1056, with the death of Empress Theodora, Zoë's sister, the Macedonian dynasty was definitely extinguished. A period of troubles set in and lasted for twenty-five years (1056–81). It ended only with the accession of Alexius Comnenus, the founder of the famous dynasty of the Comneni.

This period, characterized externally by frequent changes on the throne, which was occupied for the most part by incapable emperors, was a very significant period in the history of the Byzantine Empire; for during these twenty-five years those conditions developed in the Empire which later called forth the crusade movements in the West.

During this period the external enemies of the Byzantine Empire exerted pressure on all sides: the Normans were active in the west, the Patzinaks and Uzes in the north, and the Seljuq Turks in the east. In the end the territory of the Byzantine Empire was considerably reduced.

Another distinguishing feature of this period was the struggle waged by the military element and the large landowning nobility (especially that of Asia Minor) against the central bureaucratic government. This struggle between the provinces and the capital ended, after a number of fluctuations, in the victory of the army and the landowners, which was a victory of the provinces over the capital. Alexius Comnenus was at the head of the victorious side.

All the Emperors of the period of troubles of the eleventh century were of Greek origin. In the year 1056 the aged Empress Theodora was compelled by the court party to select as her successor the aged patrician, Michael Stratioticus. Theodora died soon after her choice had been made, and Michael VI Stratioticus, the candidate of the court party, remained on the throne for about a year (1056–57). Against him an opposition formed, headed by the army of Asia Minor, which proclaimed as emperor their general, Isaac Comnenus, a representative of a large landowning family famous for his struggle with the Turks. This was the first victory of the military party over the central government during the period of troubles. Michael Stratioticus was forced to abdicate and spend the remainder of his days as a private individual.

This victory of the military party was short-lived. Isaac Comnenus ruled only from 1057 to 1059, and then renounced the throne and took holy orders. The reasons for his abdication are still not very clear. It may be that Isaac Comnenus was a victim of skillful plotting on the part of those who were dissatisfied with his independent active rule. It is known that he considered the interests of the treasury of primary importance, and in order to increase its income he laid his hands upon lands illegally acquired by large landowners, secular as well as ecclesiastic, and reduced the salaries of high officials. It seems probable that the famous scholar and statesman, Michael Psellus, had something to do with this conspiracy against Isaac Comnenus.

Isaac was succeeded by Constantine X Ducas (1059–67). This gifted financier and defender of true justice devoted all his attention to the affairs of civil government. The army and military affairs in general interested him very little. His reign may be characterized as a reaction of the civil administration against the military element which had triumphed in the time of Isaac Comnenus, or as the reaction of the capital against the provinces. It was "the unhappy time of the domination of bureaucrats, rhetoricians, and scholars."[138] And yet the threatening advances of the Patzinaks and Uzes from the north and the Seljuq Turks from the east did not justify the antimilitary nature of Constantine's administration. The Empire was urgently in need of a ruler who could organize the necessary resistance to the enemy. Even such an antimilitarist of the eleventh century as Michael Psellus wrote: "The army is the backbone of the Roman state."[139] In view of this a strong opposition was formed against the Emperor. When he died in 1067 imperial authority passed for a few months to his wife, Eudocia Macrembolitissa. The military party

---

[138] Gelzer, *Abriss der byzantinischen Kaisergeschichte,* 1006.

[139] K. Sathas, *Bibliotheca graeca medii aevi,* IV, 58.

compelled her to marry the capable general Romanus Diogenes, born in Cappadocia. He ascended the throne as Romanus IV Diogenes and ruled from 1067 to 1071.

His accession marks the second victory of the military party. The four years' rule of this soldier-emperor ended very tragically for him when he was captured and became a prisoner of the Turkish sultan. Great tumult arose in the capital when it received the news of the Emperor's captivity. After some hesitation a new emperor was proclaimed, the son of Eudocia Macrembolitissa by Constantine Ducas, her first husband, and a pupil of Michael Psellus. He is known in history as Michael VII Ducas, surnamed Parapinakes.[140] Eudocia found protection by assuming the veil. When Romanus had been set free by the Sultan and had returned to the capital, he found the throne occupied by a new ruler, and in spite of the fact that he was given the assurance of personal safety upon his return, he was barbarously blinded and died shortly after.

Michael VII Ducas Parapinakes (1071–78) was fond of learning, scholarly disputes, and verse-writing, and was not at all inclined toward military activity. He restored the bureaucratic regime of his father, Constantine Ducas, which was unsuitable to the external position of the Empire. The new successes of the Turks and Patzinaks were persistently demanding that the Empire be guided by a soldier-emperor supported by the army, which alone could save it from ruin. In this respect "the spokesman of popular needs, who gave hopes of fulfilling them"[141] was the strategus of one of the themes in Asia Minor, Nicephorus Botaniates. He was proclaimed emperor in Asia Minor and forced Parapinakes to assume the cowl and retire to a monastery. He then entered the capital and was crowned by the patriarch. He remained on the throne from 1078 until 1081, but as a result of old age and physical weakness he was unable to deal with either internal or external difficulties. At the same time the large landowning aristocracy in the provinces did not recognize his rights to the throne, and many pretenders who disputed these rights appeared in various parts of the Empire. One of them, Alexius Comnenus, a nephew of the former Emperor, Isaac Comnenus, who was also related to the ruling family of Ducas, showed much skill in utilizing the existing conditions for reaching his goal, the throne. Botaniates had abdicated and retired to a monastery, where he later took holy orders. In the year 1081 Alexius Comnenus was crowned emperor and put an end to the period of troubles. The accession of this first ruler of the dynasty of the Comneni in the

---

[140] The surname Parapinakes originated from the fact that, during the bad harvest which occurred in the time of this ruler, a *nomisma* (Byzantine gold coin) was demanded, not for a whole *medimnus* (measure) of bread, but for a *pinakion,* as a quarter of *medimnus* was called.

[141] Skabalanovich, *Byzantine State and Church,* 115.

eleventh century marked still another victory of the military party and large provincial landowners.

It was very natural that during such frequent changes of rulers and unceasing hidden and open strife for the throne the external policy of the Empire should have suffered greatly and caused Byzantium to descend from the high position it had occupied in the medieval world. This decline was furthered by the complicated and dangerous external conditions brought about by the successful operations of the main enemies of the Empire: the Seljuq Turks in the east, the Patzinaks and Uzes in the north, and the Normans in the west.

The Seljuq Turks

The Byzantine Empire had known the Turks for a long time. A project of a Turko-Byzantine alliance existed in the second half of the sixth century. The Turks also served in Byzantium as mercenaries as well as the imperial bodyguard.[142] They were numerous in the ranks of the Arabian army on the eastern borders of the Empire, and they took an active part in the taking as well as the plundering of Amorion in 838. But these relations and conflicts with the Turks were of little or no consequence to the Empire until the eleventh century. With the appearance of the Seljuq Turks on the eastern border in the first half of the eleventh century conditions changed.[143]

The Seljuqs, or Seljucids, were the descendants of the Turkish prince Seljuq, who was in the service of a Turkestan khan about the year 1000. From the Kirghiz steppes Seljuq had migrated with his tribe to Transoxiana, near Bukhara, where he and his people embraced Islam. In a short period of time the strength of the Seljuqs had increased to such an extent that the two grandsons of Seljuq were able to lead the savage Turkish hordes into attacks on Khorasan (Khurasan).

The aggressive movement of the Seljuqs in western Asia created a new epoch in Muslim, as well as in Byzantine, history. In the eleventh century the caliphate was no longer a united whole. Spain, Africa, and Egypt had long since led a political life independent of the caliph of Bagdad. Syria, Mesopotamia, and Persia were also divided among various independent dynasties

---

[142] See Constantini Porphyrogeniti, *De cerimoniis aulae byzantinae,* Bonn ed., 661. Harun-ibn-Yahya (in the ninth century) in M. de Goeje, *Bibliotheca geographorum arabicorum,* VII, 121, 124. Harun-ibn Yahya's description of Constantinople is inserted in the Arab geographical work of Ibn-Rustah (of the tenth century). A. A. Vasiliev, "Harun-ibn-Yahya and his Description of Constantinople," *Annales de l'Institut Kondakov,* V (1932), 156, 158. Marquart, *Osteuropäische und ostasiatische Streifzüge,* 216, 219, 227.

[143] See P. Wittek, "Von der byzantinischen zur türkischen Toponymie," *Byzantion,* I (1935), 12–53. Wittek, "Deux chapitres de l'histoire des Turcs de Roum," *ibid.,* XI (1936), 285–302.

and separate rulers. After their conquest of Persia in the middle of the eleventh century the Seljuqs penetrated into Mesopotamia and entered Bagdad. From now on the caliph of Bagdad was under the protection of the Seljucids, whose sultans did not reside at Bagdad, but exercised their authority in this important city through a general. Shortly after this, when the strength of the Seljuq Turks increased still more because of the arrival of new Turkish tribes, they conquered all of western Asia, from Afghanistan to the borders of the Byzantine Empire in Asia Minor, and the Egyptian caliphate of the Fatimids.

From the middle of the eleventh century the Seljuqs became a very prominent factor in the history of the Byzantine Empire, for they began to menace its border provinces in Asia Minor and in the Caucasus. In the fourth decade of the eleventh century Constantine IX Monomachus annexed to the Empire Armenia with its new capital, Ani. Armenia was therefore no longer a buffer state between the Empire and the Turks; when it was attacked, Byzantine territory was attacked. Moreover in this attack the Turks were very successful. Turkish troops were also advancing into Asia Minor.

During the very active, though very brief, rule of Isaac Comnenus, the eastern border was well defended against the attacks of the Seljuqs. But after his fall the antimilitary policy of Constantine Ducas weakened the military power of Asia Minor and facilitated the advance of the Turks into Byzantine districts. It is not unlikely, according to one historian, that the government viewed "the misfortunes of these stubborn and arrogant provinces" with some pleasure. "The East, like Italy, paid a heavy price for the mistakes of the central government."[144] Under Constantine X Ducas, and during the subsequent seven months' rule of his wife, Eudocia Macrembolitissa, the second of the Seljuq sultans, Alp Arslan, conquered Armenia and devastated part of Syria, Cilicia, and Cappadocia. In Caesarea, the capital of Cappadocia, the Turks pillaged the main sanctuary of the city, the Church of Basil the Great, where the relics of the saint were kept.[145] A Byzantine chronicler wrote of the time of Michael Parapinakes (1071–1078): "Under this emperor almost the whole world, on land and sea, occupied by the impious barbarians, has been destroyed and has become empty of population, for all Christians have been slain by them and all houses and settlements with their churches have been devastated by them in the whole East, completely crushed and reduced to nothing."[146]

The military party found a husband for Eudocia in the person of Romanus

[144] C. Neumann, *Die Weltstellung des byzantinischen Reiches vor den Kreuzzügen,* 107; in French, 104.

[145] Michaelis Attaliotae *Historia,* 94; Joannis Scylitzae *Historia,* 661.

[146] 'Ανωνύμου Σύνοψις Χρονική; Sathas, *Bibliotheca Graeca Medii Aevi,* VII, 169. On the Turkish devastations in the eleventh century before 1071 see also the *Chronique de Michael le Syrien,* trans. Chabot, III, 158–65.

Diogenes. The new Emperor conducted several campaigns against the Turks and achieved some success in the early battles. His army, made up of various tribes—Macedonian Slavs, Bulgarians, Uzes, Patzinaks, Varangians, and Franks (a name applied in this period to all western European nationalities)—lacked good training and solid organization and was not able to offer strong resistance to the rapid movement of the Turkish cavalry and their quick and bold nomadic attacks. The most untrustworthy part of the Byzantine army was the Uze and Patzinak light cavalry, which, in the course of their conflicts with the Turks, immediately felt a tribal kinship with the latter.

The last campaign of Romanus Diogenes ended with the fatal battle of 1071 near Manzikert (Manazkert, now Melazgherd), in Armenia, north of Lake Van. Shortly before the combat the detachment of Uzes with their leader went over to the side of the Turks. This caused great unrest in the army of Romanus Diogenes. At the crisis of the battle one of the Byzantine generals began to spread the rumor of the defeat of the imperial army. The soldiers became panic-stricken and turned to flight. Romanus, who fought heroically throughout the battle, was captured by the Turks, and upon his arrival in the enemy's camp was greeted with great honor by Alp Arslan.

The victor and the vanquished negotiated an "eternal" peace and a treaty of friendship whose main points, as indicated in Arabian sources, were: (1) Romanus Diogenes obtained his freedom by the payment of a definite sum of money; (2) Byzantium was to pay a large annual tribute to Alp Arslan; (3) Byzantium was to return all Turkish captives.[147] Romanus upon his return to Constantinople found the throne occupied by Michael VII Ducas; Romanus was blinded by his foes, and died shortly after.

The battle of Manzikert had marked consequences for the Empire. Although according to the treaty the Byzantine Empire probably ceded no territory to Alp Arslan,[148] its losses were very great, for the army which defended the borders of Asia Minor was so completely destroyed that the Empire was unable to resist the later advance of the Turks there. The woeful condition of the Empire was further aggravated by the weak antimilitary administration of Michael VII Ducas. The defeat at Manzikert was a death blow to Byzantine domination in Asia Minor, that most essential part of the Byzantine Empire. After the year 1071 there was no longer a Byzantine

[147] See G. Weil, *Geschichte der Chalifen*, III, 115–16. J. Laurent, "Byzance et les Turcs Seldjoucides en Asie Mineure, leurs traités antérieurs à Alexis Comnène," Βυζαντίς, II (1911–12), 106–26. An excellent article by C. Cahen, "La campagne de Mantzikert d'après les sources musulmanes," *Byzantion*, IX (1934), 613–42.

[148] J. Laurent, *Byzance et les Turcs Seldjoucides dans l'Asie occidentale jusqu'en 1081*, 95: this treaty "perhaps required a cessation of territory"; but we do not know the detailed clauses of this treaty (p. 95, n. 1). See also Cahen, "La campagne de Mantzikert," *Byzantion*, IX (1934), 637–38.

army to resist the Turks. One scholar goes so far as to say that after this battle all of the Byzantine state was in the hands of the Turks.[149] Another historian calls the battle "the death hour of the great Byzantine Empire," and continues that "although its consequences, in all their horrible aspects, were not felt at once, the East of Asia Minor, Armenia, and Cappadocia—the provinces which were the homes of so many famous emperors and warriors and which constituted the main strength of the Empire—were lost forever, and the Turk set up his nomadic tents on the ruins of ancient Roman glory. The cradle of civilization fell prey to Islamic barbarism and to complete brutalization."[150]

During the years which elapsed from the catastrophe of 1071 to the accession of Alexius Comnenus in 1081, the Turks took advantage of the unprotected position of the Empire and the internal strife of its parties, who frequently appealed for aid, and penetrated still deeper into the life of Byzantium. Separate detachments of Turks reached as far as the western provinces of Asia Minor. The Turkish troops which aided Nicephorus Botaniates in his seizure of the throne accompanied him as far as Nicaea and Chrysopolis (now Scutari).

In addition, after the death of Romanus Diogenes and Alp Arslan, neither Turks nor Empire considered themselves bound by the treaty negotiated by these rulers. The Turks utilized every occasion for pillaging Byzantine provinces in Asia Minor, and, according to a contemporary Byzantine chronicler, entered these provinces not as momentary bandits but as permanent masters.[151] This statement, however, is exaggerated, at least for the period prior to 1081. As J. Laurent asserted, "In 1080, seven years after their first appearance on the shores of the Bosphorus, the Turks had yet been established nowhere; they had founded no state; they had been always merely errant and disorderly pillagers."[152] The successor of Alp Arslan entrusted military leadership in Asia Minor to Suleiman-ibn-Qutalmish, who occupied the central part of Asia Minor and later founded there the sultanate of Rum, or Asia Minor.[153] Since its capital was the richest and most beautiful Byzantine city in Asia Minor, Iconium (now Konia), this state of the Seljuqs is often called the sultanate of Iconium.[154] From its central position in Asia Minor the new sultanate spread out as far as the Black Sea in the north and the Mediterranean

[149] A. Gfrörer, *Byzantinische Geschichten,* III, 791.

[150] Gelzer, *Abriss der byzantinischen Kaisergeschichte,* 1010.

[151] Joannis Scylitzae *Historia,* Bonn ed., 708.

[152] Laurent, *Byzance et les Turcs,* 13-26, 97 (esp. n. 3), 110-11.

[153] The word *Rum,* which is merely the word Romans, was used by Muslim writers to denote the medieval Byzantine Greeks and their possessions; *Rum* was also used as a name for Asia Minor.

[154] For this early period, Iconium is indicated as the capital in oriental sources; Greek sources call Nicaea Suleiman's residence. Laurent, *Byzance et les Turcs,* 8 and n. 1, 11 and n. 1. Laurent, "Byzance et l'origine du sultanat de Roum," *Mélanges Charles Diehl,* I, 177-82.

coast in the south, and became a dangerous rival of the Empire. The Turkish troops continued to move farther to the west, and the forces of the Byzantine Empire were not strong enough to oppose them.

The onward movement of the Seljuqs and perhaps the menacing advances of the northern Uzes and Patzinaks toward the capital compelled Michael VII Ducas Parapinakes, in the early part of his reign, to appeal for western aid by sending a message to Pope Gregory VII, promising to repay the pope's assistance by bringing about a union of the churches. Gregory VII reacted favorably and sent a number of messages to the princes of western Europe and to "all Christians (*ad omnes christianos*), in which he stated that "the pagans were exerting great pressure upon the Christian Empire and had devastated with unheard-of cruelty everything almost as far as the walls of Constantinople."[155] But Gregory's appeals brought about no material results, and no aid was sent from the West. Meanwhile, the pope became involved in the long and severe struggle for investiture with the German king Henry IV. At the time of the accession of Alexius Comnenus it became very evident that the westward movement of the Seljuqs was the deadliest menace to the Empire.

The Patzinaks

Toward the end of the Macedonian period the Patzinaks were the most dangerous northern enemies of the Byzantine Empire. The imperial government gave them permission to settle in the districts north of the Balkans, and bestowed Byzantine court ranks upon several Patzinak princes. But these measures provided no real solution to the Patzinak problem, first because the Patzinaks were unable to accustom themselves to a settled life, and also because new hordes of Patzinaks and their kinsmen, the Uzes, were continually arriving from beyond the Danube, directing their entire attention to the south, where they could raid Byzantine territory. Isaac Comnenus was very successful in opposing the advances of the Patzinaks, "who had crawled out of their caves."[156] He restored Byzantine authority on the Danube, and was also able to offer strong opposition to the attacks of the Turks.

In the time of Constantine Ducas the Uzes appeared on the Danube. "This was an actual migration; an entire tribe, numbering 600,000, with all its goods and chattels, was crowded on the left bank of the river. All efforts to prevent their crossing were in vain."[157] The districts of Thessalonica, Macedonia, Thrace, and even Hellas became subject to terrible devastation. One contemporary Byzantine historian remarks even that "the entire population of

[155] Migne, *Patrologia Latina*, CXLVIII, 329.
645.
[156] Joannis Scylitzae *Historia*, Bonn ed.,
[157] Vasilievsky, "Byzantium and the Patzinaks," *Works*, I, 26.

Europe was considering (at that time) the question of emigration."[158] When this terrible menace was removed the mass of people ascribed their relief to miraculous aid from above. Some of the Uzes even entered the Emperor's service and received certain government lands in Macedonia. The Patzinaks and Uzes who served in the Byzantine army played an important part in the fatal battle at Manzikert.

The new financial policy of Michael VII Ducas Parapinakes, who on the advice of his prime minister reduced the money gifts usually sent to the cities of the Danube, aroused unrest among the Patzinaks and Uzes of the Danubian districts. They formed an alliance with the nomads on the other side of the Danube, reached an agreement with one of the Byzantine generals who rebelled against the Emperor, and, together with other tribes, including perhaps the Slavs, moved on to the south, pillaged the province of Hadrianople, and besieged Constantinople, which suffered greatly from lack of provisions. At this critical moment Michael Parapinakes, under pressure of the Seljuq and Patzinak attacks, sent the appeal for aid to Pope Gregory VII.

The skillful plotting of Byzantine diplomacy succeeded, apparently, in sowing discord among the allied forces which surrounded the capital. They raised the siege and returned to the banks of the Danube with rich spoils. By the end of this period the Patzinaks were active participants in the struggle between Nicephorus Botaniates and Alexius Comnenus for the Byzantine throne.

The Uze and Patzinak problem was not settled in the time of troubles, which preceded the time of the Comneni dynasty. This northern Turkish menace, which at times threatened the capital itself, was handed down to the dynasty of the Comneni.

The Normans

Toward the end of the period of the Macedonian dynasty the Normans appeared in Italy, and, taking advantage of the internal difficulties in the Byzantine Empire and its breach with Rome, began to advance successfully into the southern Italian possessions of the Empire. The eastern government could do nothing against this menace because its entire forces were thrown into the struggle with the Seljuq Turks, who, together with the Patzinaks and Uzes in the north, seemed to be the natural allies of the Normans. To use the words of Neumann, "the Empire defended itself in Italy only with its left arm."[159] A strong weapon of the Normans in their struggle with the Byzantine Empire was their fleet, which in a later period was a great aid to the Norman land forces. In the middle of the eleventh century the Normans

[158] Michaelis Attaliotae *Historia*, 84.   [159] Neumann, *Die Weltstellung des byzantinischen Reiches*, 103; in French, 100.

had also a very capable leader in the person of Robert Guiscard, "who, from a chief of brigands, rose to the rank of a founder of an Empire."[160]

The main object of Robert Guiscard was the conquest of Byzantine southern Italy. Although the Byzantine Empire was confronted with many grave difficulties, the struggle in Italy in the fifties and sixties of the eleventh century progressed with alternating success. Robert conquered Brindisi, Tarentum, and Reggio (Rhegium); yet a few years later the first two cities were conquered by Byzantine troops sent to Bari, which numbered Varangians among their soldiers. In a later period of this struggle success was on the side of the Normans.

Robert Guiscard besieged Bari, which was at that time the main center of Byzantine domination in southern Italy, and one of the most strongly fortified cities of the peninsula. It was only through cunning methods that, in the ninth century, the Muslims had succeeded in occupying Bari for a brief period of time. In the same century the city offered very stubborn resistance to the western Emperor Lewis II. Robert's siege of Bari was a difficult military undertaking, greatly aided by the Norman fleet, which blockaded the port. The siege lasted about three years and ended in the spring of 1071, when Bari was compelled to yield to Robert.[161]

The fall of Bari signified the end of Byzantine domination in southern Italy. From this very important point in Apulia Robert could quickly achieve the final conquest of the small remnants of Byzantine dominions in the inner parts of Italy. This conquest of southern Italy also set Robert's forces free for the reconquest of Sicily from the Muslims.

The subjection of southern Italy by the Normans did not destroy all of Byzantine influence. The admiration for the Eastern Empire, its traditions, and its splendor was still felt very strongly throughout the West. The Western Empire of Charlemagne, or that of Otto of Germany, represented in many ways a reflection of the eastern customs, ideas, and external living conditions sanctified by many centuries. The Norman conquerors of southern Italy, as represented by Robert Guiscard, must have felt a still greater fascination in the Byzantine Empire.

Robert, the duke of Apulia, who considered himself the legal successor of the Byzantine emperors, preserved the Byzantine administrative organization in the conquered districts. Thus we find that Norman documents speak of the theme of Calabria, and indicate that cities were governed by strategi or exarchs and that the Normans were striving to attain Byzantine titles. The Greek language was preserved in the church services of Calabria, while in some districts Greek was used as the official language in the time of the

---

[160] *Ibid.*, 102; in French, 99.   [161] On the sources, Gay, *L'Italie Méridionale*, 536, n. 3.

Normans. Generally speaking, the conquerors and the conquered lived side by side, without merging, maintaining their own language, customs, and habits.

The ambitious plans of Robert Guiscard went beyond the limited territories of southern Italy. Well aware of the internal weakness of the Byzantine Empire and her grave external difficulties, the Norman conqueror began to dream of seizing the imperial crown of the basileus.

The fall of Bari in the spring of 1071 and the fatal battle of Manzikert in August of the same year make it evident that the year 1071 was one of the most important dates in the course of the whole Byzantine history. Southern Italy was definitely lost in the West, and in the East the domination of the Empire in Asia Minor was doomed. Territorially reduced and deprived of her main vital source, Asia Minor, the Eastern Empire considerably declined from the second half of the eleventh century. Notwithstanding some revival under the Comneni, the Empire was gradually yielding its political as well as its economic importance to the states of Western Europe.

Emperor Michael VII Ducas Parapinakes fully understood the extent of Robert's menace to the Empire and wanted to avert it by means of inter-marriage between the two royal houses. The Emperor's son became engaged to Robert's daughter. But this did not seem to relieve the existing situation, and after Michael's deposition the Normans resumed their hostilities against the Empire. At the time of the accession of the Comneni they were already preparing to transfer their military attacks from Italy to the eastern coast of the Adriatic Sea. The period of troubles which resulted in the retreat of imperial power on all borders of the Empire, both in Asia and in Europe, and which was characterized by almost incessant internal strife, left for the new dynasty of the Comneni a very difficult political heritage.

EDUCATION, LEARNING, LITERATURE, AND ART

The time of the Macedonian dynasty, marked by stirring activity in the field of external and internal affairs, was also a period of intense development in the sphere of learning, literature, education, and art. This epoch witnessed the clearest exhibition of the characteristic traits of Byzantine learning, expressed in the progress of a closer union between secular and theological elements or the reconciliation of the ancient pagan wisdom with the new ideas of Christianity in the development of universal and encyclopedic knowledge, and finally, in the lack of original and creative genius. During this period the higher school of Constantinople was once more the center of education, learning, and literature, about which the best cultural forces of the Empire were gathered.

Emperor Leo VI the Wise, a pupil of Photius, though not endowed with great literary genius, wrote several sermons, church hymns, and other works. His greatest service was expressed in his efforts to uphold the intellectual atmosphere created by Photius, so that, in the words of one historian, he "made for himself a place of honor in the history of Byzantine education in general, and of its ecclesiastical education in particular."[162] Leo favored and protected all men of learning and letters; in his time "the imperial palace was sometimes transformed into a new academy and lyceum."[163]

The outstanding figure in the cultural movement of the tenth century was Emperor Constantine VII Porphyrogenitus, who did much for the intellectual progress of Byzantium, not only by protecting education, but also by contributing many original writings. Constantine left all government affairs to Romanus Lecapenus, and devoted the greater part of his time to the field which interested him. He succeeded in becoming the heart of an intense literary and scholarly movement to which he contributed greatly by active participation. He wrote much, induced others to write, and attempted to raise the education of his people to a higher level. His name is closely connected with the erection of many magnificent buildings; he was passionately interested in art and music, and spent large sums of money on the compilation of anthologies from ancient writers.

A large number of writings of the time of Constantine VII in the tenth century are preserved. Some of them were written by Constantine himself, others with his personal aid, while still others, in the form of anthologies of ancient texts and encyclopedias with extracts on various questions, were compiled at his suggestion. Among his works are his eulogistic biography of his grandfather, Basil I. Another work, *On the Administration of the Empire,* dedicated to his son and successor, contains interesting and valuable information about the geography of foreign countries, the relations of the Byzantine Empire with neighboring nations, and Byzantine diplomacy. This work opens with chapters on the northern peoples, the Patzinaks, Russians, Uzes, Khazars, Magyars (Turks), who, especially the first two, played a dominating part in the political and economic life of the tenth century. It also deals with Arabs, Armenians, Bulgarians, Dalmatians, Franks, southern Italians, Venetians, and some other peoples. The work contains also the names of the rapids of the Dnieper, given in two languages, "Slavonic" and "Russian," that is, Scandinavian. It is one of the most important bases on which rests the theory of the Scandinavian origin of the first "Russian" princes. It was composed between 948 and 952 (or 951) and written in an order different from that of the modern published text. Bury, who wrote a special study on the treatise, called it a patchwork.[164] It gives, however, an impressive idea of the

---

[162] Popov, *Leo VI,* 232.
[163] *Ibid.*

[164] J. B. Bury, "The Treatise *De administrando Imperio,*" *Byzantinische Zeitschrift,*

political, diplomatic, and economic power of the Empire in the tenth century.[165] Much geographical material is found also in his third work, *On Themes,* based partly on geographical works of the fifth and sixth centuries. It was also in his time that the large work *On the Ceremonies of the Byzantine Court* was compiled. This was primarily a detailed description of the complicated code of life at the imperial court, and might almost be considered as a book of "court regulations." It was compiled chiefly on the basis of official court records of various periods, and the data found in it on baptism, marriage, coronation, burial of emperors, on various church solemnities, on the reception of foreign ambassadors, on the equipment of military expeditions, on offices and titles, and many other aspects of life form an invaluable source for the study, not only of the life at court, but also of the social life of the whole Empire. The Byzantine court ceremonial which sprang up and developed out of the court ceremonies of the late Roman Empire of the time of Diocletian and Constantine the Great later penetrated the court life of western Europe and the Slavonic states, including Russia. Even some of the court ceremonies of Turkey of the twentieth century bear traces of Byzantine influence. Constantine is also responsible for the lengthy account of the triumphant removal of the miraculous image of the Saviour from Edessa to Constantinople in the year 944. Popular tradition claimed that this image had been originally sent by Christ to the Prince of Edessa.

From the circle of literary and scholarly men gathered about Constantine came the historian Joseph Genesius, the author of a history from the time of Leo V to that of Leo VI (813–86), and Theodore Daphnopates, who wrote a historical work which has not survived, some diplomatic letters, several sermons for Christian holidays, and a number of biographies. At the instance of the Emperor, Constantine the Rhodian wrote a poetic description of the Church of the Apostles, which is especially valuable because it gives us a picture of this famous church which was later destroyed by the Turks.

Among the encyclopedias which appeared under Constantine was the famous collection of *Lives of Saints,* compiled by Simeon Metaphrastes. To the early tenth century belongs also the *Anthologia Palatina,* compiled by Constantine Kephalas. It derives its name from the only manuscript, the Codex Palatinus, which is now at Heidelberg, Germany. The claim of some scholars that Constantine Kephalas was no other than Constantine the

XV (1906), 517–77. G. Manojlović of Zagreb, published in Serbo-Croatian four interesting memoirs on this treatise, *Publications of the Academy of Zagreb,* CLXXXII, CLXXXVI–VII (1910–11). The author summarized his four memoirs in French at the International Congress of Byzantine Studies in Belgrade in 1927; see *Compte-rendu du Congrès* (1929), 45–47.

[165] Now we have a new critical edition of the *De administrando imperio* by G. Moravcsik with an English translation by R. Jenkins (1949).

Rhodian should be considered improbable. The *Anthologia Palatina* is a large collection of short poems of both Christian and pagan times, and stands out as an example of the fine literary taste of the tenth century.[166]

The time of Constantine Porphyrogenitus witnessed also the compilation of the famous *Lexicon* of Suidas. There is no information whatever on the life and personality of the author of this lexicon, which is the richest source for the explanation of words, proper names, and articles of general use. The literary and historical articles concerning works which have not come down to the present are of especially great value. In spite of many shortcomings, "the *Lexicon* of Suidas is a lofty monument of the compilatory diligence of Byzantine scholars at the time when the learned activity of the rest of Europe had completely declined. This was a new evidence of the wide extent to which the Byzantine Empire, in spite of all the internal and external upheavals, preserved and developed the remnants of ancient culture."[167]

Another eminent figure of the period of the Macedonian dynasty was Arethas, archbishop of Caesarea, in the early part of the tenth century. His broad education and profound interest in literary works, both ecclesiastic and secular, were reflected in his own writings. His Greek commentary on the Apocalypse, the first as far as is known, his notes on Plato, Lucian, and Eusebius, and finally his valuable collection of letters, preserved in one of the Moscow manuscripts and still unpublished, indicate that Arethas of Caesarea was an outstanding figure in the cultural movement of the tenth century.[168]

Patriarch Nicholas Mysticus, well known for his active part in the ecclesiastical life of this period, left a valuable collection of over 150 letters. It contains messages written to the Arabian Emir of Crete, to Simeon of Bulgaria, to the popes, to Emperor Romanus Lecapenus, to bishops, monks, and various officials of civil administration. From them come materials on the internal and political history of the tenth century.

Leo the Deacon, a contemporary of Basil II and an eyewitness of the events of the Bulgarian war, left a history in ten books which covers the time from 959-975 and contains accounts of the Arabian, Bulgarian, and Russian campaigns of the Empire. This history is all the more valuable because it is the only contemporary Greek source dealing with the brilliant period of Nicephorus Phocas and John Tzimisces. The work of Leo the Deacon is also invaluable for the first pages of Russian history because of the extensive data on Sviatoslav and his war with the Greeks.

The monograph of John Cameniates, a priest of Thessalonica, on the

---

[166] See Krumbacher, *Geschichte der byzantinischen Litteratur*, 727. Montelatici, *Storia della letteratura bizantina*, 120, 125.

[167] Krumbacher, *ibid.*, 568. On recent studies see bibliography.

[168] On Arethas and his environment see some interesting data in M. A. Shanguin, "Byzantine Political Personalities of the First Half of the Tenth Century," *Vizantiysky Sbornik* (1945), 228-36.

Arabian conquest of Thessalonica in 904, of which Cameniates was an eye-witness, has already been mentioned.

Among the chroniclers of this period was the anonymous continuator of Theophanes (Theophanes Continuatus), who described events from 813 to 961 on the basis of the works of Genesius, of Constantine Porphyrogenitus, and of the continuator of George Hamartolus. The question of the identity of the author of this compilation is still unsolved.[169]

The group of chroniclers of the tenth century are usually represented by four men: Leo the Grammarian, Theodosius of Melitene, the anonymous Continuator of George Hamartolus, and Symeon Magister and Logothete, the so-called Pseudo-Symeon Magister. But these are not original writers; all of them were copyists, abbreviators, or revisers of the Chronicle of Symeon Logothete, whose complete Greek text has not yet been published. There is, however, a published Old Slavonic version of it so that a fairly good idea can be formed of the unpublished Greek text.[170]

To the tenth century belongs also a very interesting figure in the history of Byzantine literature, John Kyriotes, generally known by his surname, Geometres. The height of his literary activity falls in the time of Nicephorus Phocas, John Tzimisces, and Basil II. The first of these was his favorite hero. He left a collection of epigrams and occasional poems, a work in verse on asceticism (Paradise), and some hymns in honor of the Holy Virgin. His epigrams and occasional poems are closely related to the important political events of his time, such as the deaths of Nicephorus Phocas and John Tzimisces, the insurrection of Bardas Sclerus and Bardas Phocas in his poem *The Rebellion,* the Bulgarian war, etc. All these are of special interest to the student of this period. One poem on his journey from Constantinople to Selybria, through districts which had seen military action, gives a strikingly forceful and pathetic picture of the sufferings and ruin of the local peasantry.[171] Krumbacher was undoubtedly right when he said that John Geometres belongs to the best aspect of Byzantine literature.[172] Many of his poems deserve trans-

[169] S. P. Shestakov of Kazan believes that the author of the Continuation of Theophanes was Theodore Daphnopates. See, e.g., his "The Question of the Author of the *Continuation of Theophanes,*" *Compte-rendu du deuxième congrès international des études byzantines* (1929), 35–45. See H. G. Nickles, "The Continuatio Theophanis," *Transactions of the American Philological Association,* LXVIII (1937), 221–27.

[170] This complicated problem was first elucidated in 1895 by Vasilievsky and was recently discussed in greater detail and clearly explained by Ostrogorsky. Vasilievsky, "The Chronicle of Logothe in Slavonic and Greek," *Vizantiysky Vremennik,* II (1895), 78–151. Ostrogorsky, "A Slavonic Version of the Chronicle of Symeon Logothete," *Annales de l'Institut Kondakov,* V (1932), 17–36. See also a brief but very clear summary of this question by Ostrogorsky in French, "L'Expédition du Prince Oleg contre Constantinople en 907," *Annales de l'Institut Kondakov,* XI (1939), 50.

[171] See Migne, *Patrologia Graeca,* CVI, 956–59; in Russian, Vasilievsky, *Works,* II, 121–22.

[172] Krumbacher, *Geschichte der byzantinischen Litteratur,* 734. The late Polish

lation into modern tongues. His prose works, of a rhetorical, exegetical, and oratorical character, are less interesting than his poems.

During the reign of Nicephorus Phocas also the pseudo-Lucianic Dialogue, *Philopatris* was compiled. This, it has been said, represents "a Byzantine form of humanism," and for the tenth century reveals "a renaissance of Greek spirit and classical tastes."[173]

One of the best of Byzantine poets, Christopher of Mytilene, who has only recently become well known, flourished in the first half of the eleventh century. His short works, written mainly in iambic trimeter in the form of epigrams or addresses to various persons, including a number of contemporary emperors, are distinguished by graceful style and fine wit.[174]

In the tenth century, when Byzantine civilization was experiencing a period of brilliant development, representatives of the barbarian West came to the Bosphorus for their education. But at the end of the tenth and beginning of the eleventh centuries, when the entire attention of the Empire was concentrated upon campaigns which raised the Empire to the pinnacle of its military fame, intellectual and creative activity declined somewhat. Basil II treated scholars with disdain. Anna Comnena, a writer of the twelfth century, remarks that "from the reign of Basil Porphyrogenitus (i.e., Basil II Bulgaroctonus) until that of (Constantine) Monomachus, learning was neglected by the majority of the people, but did not go down entirely, and later rose again."[175] Separate individuals continued to work diligently and spend long nights over books by the light of lamps.[176] But higher education with government support on a wide scale was revived only in the middle of the eleventh century under Constantine Monomachus, when a group of scholars, headed by the young Constantine Psellus, aroused the Emperor's interest in their projects and exerted much influence at court. Heated disputes began concerning the nature of the reforms of the higher school. While one party wanted a law school, the other demanded a philosophical school, i.e., a school for general education. The agitation constantly increased, and even assumed the aspect of street

philologist, J. Saidak, worked on the writings of John Geometres, particularly on his hymns in honor of the Holy Virgin. Saidak, "Que signifie Κυριώτης Γεωμέτρης?" *Byzantion*, VI (1931), 343–53. See Saidak's short item on John Geometres in his *Literatura Bizantyńska*, 725–26.

[173] S. Reinach, "Le Christianisme à Byzance et la question du Philopatris," in his *Cultes, mythes et religions* (3rd ed., 1922), I, 368, 391.

[174] See Krumbacher, *Geschichte der byzantinischen Litteratur*, 737–38. Montelatici,

Storia della letteratura bizantina, 128–30. *Die Gedichte des Christophoros Mytilenaios*, ed. E. Kurtz.

[175] Anna Comnena, *Alexias*, V, 8; ed. A. Reifferscheid, I, 177–78; trans. E. A. S. Dawes, 132. See G. Buckler, *Anna Comnena. A Study*, 262. See also Michael Psellus, *Chronography*, ed. Sathas, *Bibliotheca Graeca Medii Aevi*, IV, 19; ed. E. Renauld, I, 19.

[176] See F. Fuchs, *Die höheren Schulen von Konstantinopel im Mittelalter*, 24–25.

demonstrations. The Emperor found a good way out of the situation by organizing both a philosophical faculty and a school of law. The founding of the university followed in 1045. The Novel dealing with the founding of the law school has been preserved. The philosophical department, headed by the famous scholar and writer, Psellus, taught philosophy and aimed at giving its student a broad general education. The law school was a sort of juridical lyceum or academy.

A strong need was felt by the Byzantine government for educated and experienced officials, especially jurists. In the absence of special legal schools, young men gained their knowledge of law from practicing jurists, notaries, and lawyers, who very seldom possessed deep and extensive knowledge in this field. The juridical lyceum founded in the time of Constantine Monomachus was to aid in meeting this urgent need. The lyceum was directed by John Xiphilin, a famous contemporary and friend of Psellus. As before, education was free of charge. The professors received from the government good salaries, silk garments, living provisions, and Easter gifts. Admission was free for all those who desired to enter, regardless of social or financial status, providing they had sufficient preparation. The Novel on the founding of the juridical academy gives an insight into the government's views on education and juridical knowledge. The law school of the eleventh century had distinctly practical aims, for it was expected to prepare skillful officials acquainted with the laws of the Empire.[177]

The head of the philosophy school, Constantine Psellus, usually known by his monastic name of Michael, was born in the first half of the eleventh century. Through his excellent education, wide knowledge, and brilliant ability he rose very high in the esteem of his contemporaries and became one of the most influential personalities in the Empire. He was invited to the court, and there he was given important offices and high titles. At the same time he taught philosophy and rhetoric to a large number of students. In one of his letters Psellus wrote: "We have enthralled the Celts [i.e., the peoples of western Europe] and Arabs; and they have resorted to our glory even from the two continents; the Nile irrigates the land among the Egyptians, and my tongue [irrigates] their spirit. . . . One of the peoples calls me a light of wisdom, another, a luminary, and the third has honored me with the most beautiful names."[178] Following the example of his friend John Xiphilin, the head of the law academy, he took the monastic habit under the name of Michael and spent some time in a monastery. But solitary monastic life did not appeal to Psellus' nature. He left the monastery and returned to the

---

[177] *Ibid.* Contains detailed information on these two higher schools.

[178] Sathas, *Bibliotheca Graeca Medii Aevi,* V, 508.

capital, resuming his important place at court. Toward the end of his life
he rose to the high post of prime minister. He died near the end of the eleventh
century, probably in the year 1078.[179]

Living as he did in the time of unrest and decline of the Empire, accompanied by frequent changes on the throne which often meant changes in
policy, Psellus showed great ability in adjusting himself to the changing conditions of life. During his service under nine emperors he continued to rise
in rank and grow in influence. Psellus did not hesitate to use flattery, sub-
serviency, or bribes in order to build up his own well-being. It cannot therefore
be said that he possessed very high moral qualities, although in this regard
he was not different from a large number of men of that troubled and difficult
period.

He possessed many qualities however which placed him far above his
contemporaries. He was a highly educated man who knew much, read ex-
tensively, and worked assiduously. He achieved much in his lifetime and left
many works on theology, philosophy (in which he followed Plato), natural
sciences, philology, history, and law, and he wrote some poetry, a number
of orations, and many letters. The *History* of Psellus, describing events from
the death of John Tzimisces until the last years of the author's life (976–1077),
is a very valuable source for the history of the eleventh century, in spite of
certain prejudices in the account. In all his literary activity Psellus was a
representative of secular knowledge imbued with Hellenism. It is very apparent that he was not modest in his opinions of himself. In his chronography
he wrote, "I was certified that my tongue has been adorned with flowers even
in simple utterances; and without any effort natural sweetness falls in drops
from it."[180] Elsewhere Psellus said that Constantine IX "admired his eloquence exceedingly, and his ears were always attracted to his tongue"; that
Michael VI "admired him profoundly and tasted, as it behooves, the honey
which flowed from his lips"; that Constantine X "filled himself with his
words as with nectar"; that Eudocia "regarded him as a God."[181] Historians
still disagree in their appraisal of the personality and activity of Psellus. And
yet there seems to be little doubt that he must have occupied as high a place
in the Byzantine cultural life of the eleventh century as Photius did in the
ninth century, and Constantine Porphyrogenitus in the tenth.[182]

[179] Renauld, *Michel Psellos: Chronographie
ou Histoire d'un siècle de Byzance, 976–1077,*
I, ix.

[180] *Ibid.,* 139. Sathas, *Bibliotheca Graeca
Medii Aevi,* IV, 123–24.

[181] E. Renauld, *Étude de la langue et du style
de Michel Psellos,* 432–33; Renauld, *Psellos:
Chronographie,* I, xiv–xv.

[182] J. Hussey, "Michael Psellus," *Speculum,*
X (1935), 81–90. Hussey, *Church and Learning
in the Byzantine Empire, 867–1185,* 73–88. M.
Jugie, "Michael Psellus," *Dictionnaire de théologie catholique,* XIII (1936), 1149–58. V.
Valdenberg, "The Philosophical Ideas of Michael Psellus," *Vizantiysky Sbornik* (1945),
249–55.

The time of the Macedonian dynasty, especially the tenth century, is viewed as the period of the development of Byzantine epic poetry and Byzantine popular songs, whose chief hero was Basil Digenes Akrites. The intense life on the eastern border with its almost incessant warfare offered a wide field for brave deeds and dangerous adventures. The deepest and most durable impression was left in the memory of the people by the hero of these border provinces, Basil Digenes Akrites. The true name of this epic hero was, apparently, Basil; Digenes and Akrites were only surnames. The name "Digenes" may be translated as "born of two peoples," and originated because his father was a Muhammedan Arab and his mother a Christian Greek. Digenes was usually applied to children born of parents of different races. Akrites (plural *Akritai*) was a name applied during the Byzantine period to the defenders of the outermost borders of the Empire, from the Greek word *akra* (ἄκρα), meaning "border." The *Akritai* sometimes enjoyed a certain amount of independence from the central government, and are compared with the western European markgraves (meaning rulers of the borderlands, marches) and with the cossacks of the *ukraina* (meaning border, also) in the history of Russia.

The epic hero Digenes Akrites devoted all of his life to the struggle with the Muslims and Apelatai. The latter name, which originally meant "those who drive away the cattle," and later simply "robbers," was applied on the eastern border of the Byzantine Empire to mountain robbers, "those bold fellows, strong in spirit and body, half robbers and half heroes,"[183] who scorned the authority of the Emperor and the caliph, and devastated the lands of both. In times of peace these robbers were fought by the joint efforts of Christians and Muslims, while in times of war each side strove to gain the support of these daring men. Rambaud said that in the border districts "one felt far removed from the Byzantine Empire, and it might have seemed that one was not in the provinces of an enlightened monarchy, but in the midst of the feudal anarchy of the West."[184]

On the basis of various hints found throughout the epic of Digenes Akrites it may be asserted that the real event on which it is based took place in the middle of the tenth century in Cappadocia and in the district of the Euphrates. In the epic Digenes accomplishes great deeds and fights for the Christians and the Empire; in his conception orthodoxy and Romania (the Byzantine empire) are inseparable. The description of Digenes' palace gives a closer view of the magnificence and wealth found in the midst of the large landowners of Asia Minor so strongly resented by Basil II Bulgaroctonus. The original prototype of Digenes Akrites, however, has been said to be not Christian but

[183] A. N. Veselovsky, "The Poem of Digenes," *Vestnik Evropy* (1875), 753.

[184] *Etudes sur l'histoire byzantine,* 73.

the half-legendary champion of Islam, Saiyid Battal Ghazi, whose name is connected with the battle at Acroïnon in 740. The name of Digenes remained popular even in the later years of the Byzantine Empire. Theodore Prodromus, the poet of the twelfth century, when attempting to give due praise to Emperor Manuel Comnenus, could not find a better title for him than "the new Akrites."[185]

According to Bury, "As Homer reflects all sides of a certain stage of early Greek civilization, as the *Nibelungenlied* mirrors the civilization of the Germans during the period of the migrations, so the Digenes cycle presents a comprehensive picture of the Byzantine world in Asia Minor and of the frontier life."[186] This epic has survived the Byzantine Empire. Even today the people of Cyprus and Asia Minor sing of the famous Byzantine hero.[187] Near Trebizond travelers are still shown his grave, which, according to popular tradition, is supposed to protect the newly born against evil spells. In its contents the epic resembles very closely well-known western European epic legends, such as the *Song of Roland* of the time of Charlemagne, or *The Cid*, both of which also grew out of the struggle between Christianity and Muhammedanism.

The epic of Digenes Akrites is preserved in several manuscripts, the oldest of which belongs to the fourteenth century.[188] The study of it has recently entered a new phase in the illuminating researches initiated by H. Grégoire and brilliantly carried out by his collaborators, M. Canard and R. Goossens. It is almost certain that the historical prototype of Digenes was Diogenes, the *turmarchus* of the theme of Anatolici, in Asia Minor, who fell in 788 fighting against the Arabs. Many elements of the poem date from the events of the tenth century, when the Byzantine troops established themselves on the Euphrates and the tomb of Digenes, near Samosata, was identified about 940. Extremely interesting connections have been discovered between the Byzantine epic and Arabian and Turkish epics, and even with the *Tales of the Thousand-and-One Nights*. This epic, with its historical background and ramifications in the field of Oriental epics, presents one of the most fascinating problems of Byzantine literature.[189]

---

[185] *Bibliotheque grecque vulgaire*, ed. E. Legrand, I, 83 (v. 180), 96 (v. 546). Cf. *Poèmes Prodromiques en grec vulgaire*, ed. D. C. Hesseling and H. Pernot, 55 (v. 164). E. Jeanselme and L. Oeconomos, "La Satire contre les Higoumènes," *Byzantion*, I (1924), 328.

[186] J. B. Bury, *Romances of Chivalry on Greek Soil*, 18–19.

[187] Some "Acritic" songs have been published by S. Kyriakides, Ὁ Διγένης Ἀκρίτας

(1926), 119–50.

[188] See D. C. Hesseling, *La plus ancienne rédaction du poème épique sur Digenis Akritas*, 1–22.

[189] In 1942 H. Grégoire published an excellent summary of the studies of the epic in Modern Greek in *Digenis Akritas. The Byzantine Epic in History and Poetry*. Since this indispensable book is written in Modern Greek and hence accessible to a restricted number of readers, an English or French trans-

Byzantine epics in the form of popular ballads have been reflected in Russian epic monuments, and the epic of Digenes Akritas has its place there. In ancient Russian literature *The Deeds and Life of Digenes Akrites* appears; this was known even to the Russian historian, Karamzin (early nineteenth century), who at first viewed it as a Russian fairy tale. It was of no little importance in the development of old Russian literature, for old Russian life and letters were profoundly affected by Byzantine influence, both ecclesiastical and secular. It is interesting to note that in the Russian version of the poem on Digenes there are sometimes episodes which have not yet been discovered in its Greek texts.[190]

The intellectual and artistic life of the Empire in the difficult and troubled times continued to develop along the lines of the Macedonian period. The activity of Michael Psellus, for instance, was not interrupted. This alone may serve as an indication of the fact that the cultural life of the country did not cease to exist. Psellus was favored by the accidental rulers of the period as much as he was by the representatives of the Macedonian house.

Among the notable writers of this period was Michael Attaliates. He was born in Asia Minor, but later migrated to Constantinople and there chose a legal and juristic career. His surviving works belong to the field of history and jurisprudence. His history, embracing the period from 1034 to 1079, based on personal experience, gives a true picture of the time of the last Macedonian rulers and the years of the troubled period. The style of Michael Attaliates already showed evidences of the artificial renaissance of classicism which became so widespread under the Comneni. The law treatise of Michael, derived entirely from the Basilics, enjoyed very great popularity. His aim was to edit a very brief manual of law accessible to all. Highly valuable data on the cultural life of the Byzantine Empire in the eleventh century are found in the statute compiled by Michael for the poorhouse and monastery he founded. This statute contains an inventory of the property of the poorhouse and monastery which included, among other things, a list of books donated to the monasterial library.

The time of the Macedonian dynasty is of great importance for the history of Byzantine art. The period from the middle of the ninth century until the twelfth century, i.e., including the period of the subsequent dynasty of the Comneni, is characterized by scholars as the second Golden Age of Byzantine

lation would be highly desirable. Among Grégoire's numerous studies on the subject, I wish to indicate two which may be particularly useful as an introduction: "Le tombeau et la date de Digenis Akritas," and "Autour de Digenis Akritas," both in *Byzantion* VI (1931), 481–508; VII (1932), 287–320.

[190] See a very important work on this subject by M. Speransky, "Digenis' Deeds," *Sbornik Otdeleniya Russkago Yazika i Slovesnosti*, XCIX, 7 (1922); in French, P. Pascal, "Le 'Digenis' slave ou la 'Geste de Devgenij,' " *Byzantion*, X (1935), 301–34.

Art, the first Golden Age being the time of Justinian the Great. The icono-clastic crisis liberated Byzantine art from stifling ecclesiastic and monastic influences and indicated new paths outside of religious subjects. These paths led to the return to the traditions of early Alexandrian models, to the develop-ment of ornament borrowed from the Arabs and therefore closely related to the ornament of Islam, and to the substitution for ecclesiastical subjects of historical and profane motives, which were treated with greater realism. But the artistic creations of the epoch of the Macedonian dynasty did not limit themselves to merely borrowing or copying these subjects; it introduced some-thing of its own, something original.

The revived Greek style of the Macedonian and Comnenian periods was able to contribute something more than the physical grace of the fourth-century Hellen-istic manner; it had gathered to itself much of the gravity and strength of an earlier age. These qualities imposed themselves upon Middle Byzantine expression. Their influence excluded the clumsy forms of the sixth century, which continued only in religious centers in remote provinces where the power of the capital was not felt. They lent a dignity and graciousness, a restraint and balance, an undis-turbed refinement which became characteristics of Byzantine design in its maturer period. They grew into harmony with religious emotion; they had a seriousness which the work of Hellenistic times had not possessed. Though there may be exaggeration in saying that in its later centuries Byzantine art was systematically and progressively hellenized, it is certain that a thorough and complete orientaliza-tion was no longer possible.[191]

The famous Austrian art historian, J. Strzygowski, attempted to prove a theory which is closely connected with the epoch of the Macedonian dynasty. In his opinion the accession of the first ruler of this dynasty, an Armenian by birth, marked a new stage in the history of Byzantine art, namely, the period of the direct influence of Armenian art upon the artistic efforts of Byzantium. In other words, in place of the older notion that Armenia was under the strong influence of Byzantine art, Strzygowski attempted to prove the very opposite. It is true that Armenian influence was strongly felt in the time of the Mace-donian dynasty, and that many Armenian artists and architects worked in Byzantium. The New Church, built by Basil I, may have reproduced an Armenian plan; when in the tenth century the dome of St. Sophia was damaged by an earthquake, it was to an Armenian architect, builder of the cathedral of Ani in Armenia, that the work of restoration was entrusted. But though in Strzygowski's theories, as Ch. Diehl said, there are "many in-genious and seductive things," they cannot be accepted in full.[192]

Basil I was a great builder. He erected the New Church, the Nea, which was

[191] O. M. Dalton, *East Christian Art*, 17–18.   *uel d'art byzantin*, I, 476–78. Dalton, *East*
[192] J. Strzygowski, *Die Baukunst der Ar-*   *Christian Art*, 34–35.
menier und Europa. See Charles Diehl, *Man-*

as important an event in Basil's constructive policy as the erection of St. Sophia in that of Justinian. He constructed a new palace, the Kenourgion, and decorated it with brilliant mosaics. Basil I also restored and adorned St. Sophia and the Church of the Holy Apostles. St. Sophia, damaged by the earthquake of 989, was also the object of the care of the emperors of the tenth and eleventh centuries.

Under the Macedonian emperors there appeared for the first time the imperial ikon-painting schools, which not only produced large numbers of ikons and decorated the walls of churches, but also engaged in illustrating manuscripts. In the time of Basil II appeared the famous *Vatican Menologium,* or Menology, with beautiful miniatures—illustrations carried out by eight illuminators whose names are inscribed on the margins.[193] To this epoch belong also many other interesting, original, and finely executed miniatures.

The main center of artistic developments was the city of Constantinople, but the Byzantine provinces of that period have also preserved important monuments of art, such as the dated "Church of Skripu" (A.D. 874), in Boeotia; a group of churches on Mount Athos, dating from the tenth or early eleventh century; St. Luke of Stiris in Phocis (the early eleventh century); Nea Moni on Chios (the middle of the eleventh century), the monastery church of Daphni in Attica (the end of the eleventh century). In Asia Minor the numerous rock-cut churches of Cappadocia have preserved a large number of extremely interesting frescoes, many of which belong to the ninth, tenth, and eleventh centuries. The discovery and study of these Cappadocian frescoes, which "revealed an astonishing wealth of mural painting,"[194] are closely connected with the name of the G. de Jerphanion, S.I., who devoted most of his life to the minute investigation of Cappadocia, "a new province of Byzantine art."[195]

The influence of Byzantine art of the Macedonian period extended beyond the boundaries of the Empire. The most recent painting in the famous Santa Maria Antica at Rome, assigned to the ninth or tenth centuries, may take a place with the best products of the Macedonian Renaissance.[196] St. Sophia of Kiev (A.D. 1037), in Russia, as well as many other Russian churches, belong also to the "Byzantine" tradition of the epoch of the Macedonian emperors.

The most brilliant period of the Macedonian dynasty (867–1025) was also the best time in the history of Byzantine art from the point of view of artistic

---

[193] See Sirarpie der Nersessian, "Remarks on the Date of the Menologium and the Psalter Written for Basil II," *Byzantion,* XV (1940–41), 104–125.

[194] Dalton, *East Christian Art,* 250.

[195] Diehl, *Manuel d'art byzantin,* II, 567–79. See G. de Jerphanion, *Une nouvelle province de l'art byzantin. Les églises rupestres de Cappadoce,* I, part 1, with an album of excellent plates. Diehl (*Manuel d'art byzantin* [2nd ed., 1925–26], II, 908–9) could not yet use this work.

[196] Diehl, *ibid.,* II, 585.

vitality and originality. The subsequent period of troubles and the time of the Comneni, beginning with the year 1081, witnessed the rise of an entirely different, drier, and more rigid art.

"The Byzantine standards, which had been carried (in the time of Basil II) into Armenia, were by degrees withdrawn; those of the Seljuq Turks advanced. At home there reigned the spirit of immobility which finds its expression in ceremonies and displays, the spirit of an Alexius Comnenus and his court. All this was reflected in the art of the century preceding the invasion of the Crusaders from the West. The springs of progress dried up; there was no longer any power of organic growth; the only change now possible was a passive acceptance of external forces. Religious fervor was absorbed in formal preoccupations. The liturgical system, by controlling design, led to the production of manuals, or painter's guides, in which the path to be followed was exactly traced; the composition was stereotyped; the very colors were prescribed." [197]

[197] Dalton, *East Christian Art*, 18–19.